VOLVO
240/740/760/780/940/960
1990-93 REPAIR MANUAL

CHILTON'S

President, Chilton Enterprises	David S. Loewith
Senior Vice President	Ronald A. Hoxter
Publisher & Editor-In-Chief	Kerry A. Freeman, S.A.E.
Managing Editors	Peter M. Conti, Jr., W. Calvin Settle, Jr., S.A.E.
Assistant Managing Editor	Nick D'Andrea
Senior Editors	Debra Gaffney, Ken Grabowski, A.S.E., S.A.E.
	Michael L. Grady, Richard J. Rivele, S.A.E.
	Richard T. Smith, Jim Taylor
	Ron Webb
Project Managers	Martin J. Gunther, Jeffrey M. Hoffman
Director of Manufacturing	Mike D'Imperio
Editor	Neil Leonard, A.S.E.

CHILTON BOOK COMPANY

ONE OF THE **DIVERSIFIED PUBLISHING COMPANIES,**
A PART OF **CAPITAL CITIES/ABC, INC.**

Manufactured in USA
© 1994 Chilton Book Company
Chilton Way, Radnor, PA 19089
ISBN 0-8019-8428-9
Library of Congress Catalog Card No. 92-054908
1234567890 3210987654

Contents

Contents

SAFETY NOTICE

PART NUMBERS

SPECIAL TOOLS

ACKNOWLEDGMENTS

The Chilton Book Company expresses appreciation to Volvo North America for their generous assistance.

1

ROUTINE MAINTENANCE

HOW TO USE THIS BOOK

Chilton's Total Car Care Manual for the 1990-93 Volvo 200, 700 and 900 series, are intended to teach you more about the inner workings of your vehicle and save you money in its upkeep. The first two Sections will be the most used, since they contain maintenance and tune-up information and procedures. The following Sections deal with the more complex systems of the vehicle. Operating systems from engine through brakes are covered to the extent that we feel the average do-it-yourselfer should get involved.

Complicated repairs, such as internal transmission repairs, will not be covered. The knowledge, skills, and special tools required for such repairs are not readily available and/or affordable to the average vehicle owner.

In-depth repairs on the air conditioning system, will not be covered, due to certain environmental hazards. Section 609 of the Clean Air Act Amendments of 1990, requires that a person performing any repairs or service on a vehicle air conditioning system be properly trained and certified and no such person may perform such service without properly using approved refrigerant recycling equipment.

We will give you the detailed instructions to help you change your own brake pads and shoes, tune-up your engine, replace spark plugs and filters, and do many more jobs that will save you money, give you personal satisfaction and help you avoid problems. Section 10 is devoted to body and trim items. It will assist you with removal, installation and alignment on items such as doors, latches, windows, antennas, locks and seats.

Another purpose of this book is a reference guide for owners who want to understand their vehicle and/or their mechanics better. In this case, no tools at all are required. Knowing just what a particular repair job requires in parts and labor time will allow you to evaluate whether or not you are getting a fair price quote and help decipher itemized bills from a repair shop.

Before attempting any repairs or service on the vehicle, read through the entire procedure outlined in the appropriate section. This will give you the overall view of what tools and supplies will be required. Read ahead and plan ahead. Each operation should be approached logically and all procedures thoroughly understood before attempting any work. Some special tools that may be required can often be rented from local automotive jobbers or places specializing in renting tools and equipment. Check the yellow pages of your phone book.

All sections contain adjustments, maintenance, removal and installation, and overhaul procedures. When overhaul is not consider practical, we will tell you how to remove the part and then how to install the new or rebuilt replacement. In this way, you at least save the labor costs. Overhaul on some components (such as alternators or water pumps) are just not practical for do-it-yourselfers, but most removal and installation procedures are offer simple and well within the capabilities of the average owner.

Two basic mechanic's rules should be mentioned here. First, whenever the LEFT side of the vehicle is referred to, it is meant to specify the DRIVER'S side. Conversely, the RIGHT side of the vehicle means the PASSENGER'S side. Second, all screws and bolts are removed by turning counterclockwise, and tightened by turning clockwise, unless otherwise stated.

Safety is always the most important rule. Constantly be aware of the dangers involved in working on or around an automobile and take proper precautions to avoid the risk of personal injury or damage to the vehicle. Refer to section "Servicing Your Vehicle Safely and the SAFETY NOTICE on the acknowledgment page before attempting any service procedures and pay attention to the instructions provided. There are 3 common mistakes in mechanical work:

1. Incorrect order of assembly, disassembly or adjustment: When taking something apart or putting it together, doing things in the wrong order usually just costs you extra time; beside, damage can occur to the individual component or the vehicle. Read the entire procedure before beginning disassembly. Do everything in the order in which the instructions say you should do it, even if you can't immediately see a reason for it. When you're taking apart something that is very intricate (for example a carburetor), you might want to draw a picture of how it looks when assembled at one point in order to make sure you get everything back in its proper position. We will supply exploded views whenever possible, but sometimes the job requires more attention to detail than an illustration provides. When making adjustments (especially tune-up adjustments), do them in order. One adjustment often affects another and you cannot expect satisfactory results unless each adjustment is made only when it cannot be changed b y any other.

2. Overtorquing (or undertorquing) nuts and bolts. While it is more common for overtorquing to cause damage, undertorquing can cause a fastener to vibrate loose and cause serious damage, especially when dealing with aluminum parts. Pay attention to torque specifications and utilize a torque wrench in assembly. If a torque figure is not available remember that, if you are using the right tool to do the job, you will probably not have to strain yourself to get a fastener tight enough. The pitch of most threads is so slight that the tension you put on the wrench will be multiplied many times in actual force on what you are tightening. A good example of how critical torque is can be seen in the case of spark plug installation, especially where you are putting the plug into an aluminum cylinder head. Too little torque can fail to crush the gasket, causing leakage of combustion gases and consequent overheating of the plug and engine parts. Too much torque can damage the threads or distort the plug, which changes the spark gap at the electrode. Since more and more manufacturers are using aluminum in their engine and chassis parts to save weight, a torque wrench should be in any serious do-it-yourselfer's tool box.

There are many commercial chemical products available for ensuring that fasteners won't come loose, even if they are not torqued just right (a very common brand is Loctite®). If you're worried about getting something together tight enough to hold, but loose enough to avoid mechanical damage during assembly, one of these products might offer substantial insurance. Read the label on the package and make sure the product is compatible with the materials, fluids, etc. involved before choosing one.

3. Crossthreading. This occurs when a part such as a bolt is screwed into a nut or casting at the wrong angle and forced, causing the threads to become damaged.

Crossthreading is more likely to occur if access is difficult. It helps to clean and lubricate fasteners, and to start threading with the part to be installed going straight in, using your fingers. If you encounter resistance, unscrew the part and start over again at a different angle until it can be inserted and turned several times without much effort. Keep in mind that many parts, especially spark plugs, use tapered threads so that gentle turning will automatically bring the part you're threading to the proper angle if you don't force it or resist a change in angle. Don't put a wrench on the part until it's been turned in a couple of times by hand. If you suddenly encounter resistance and the part has not seated fully, don't force it. Pull it back out and make sure it's clean and threading properly.

Always take your time and be patient; once you have some experience, working on your vehicle will become an enjoyable hobby.

TOOLS AND EQUIPMENT

▶ **See Figure 1**

Naturally, without the proper tools and equipment it is impossible to properly service your vehicle. It would be impossible to catalog each tool that you would need to perform each or every operation in this book. It would also be unwise for the amateur to rush out and buy an expensive set of tools an the theory that he may need one or more of them at sometime.

The best approach is to proceed slowly, gathering together a good quality set of those tools that are used most frequently. Don't be misled by the low cost of bargain tools. It is far better to spend a little more for better quality. Forged wrenches, 6- or 12-point sockets and fine tooth ratchets are by far preferable to their less expensive counterparts. As any good mechanic can tell you, there are few worse experiences than trying to work on any vehicle with bad tools. Your monetary savings will be far outweighed by frustration and mangled knuckles.

Certain tools, plus a basic ability to handle them, are required to get started. A basic mechanics tool set, a torque wrench and a Torx® bits set. Torx® bits are hexlobular drivers which fit both inside and outside on special Torx® head fasteners used in various places on modern vehicles. Begin accumulating those tools that are used most frequently; those associated with routine maintenance and tune-up.

In addition to the normal assortment of screwdrivers and pliers you should have the following tools for routine maintenance jobs (your vehicle is equipped metric fasteners):

1. SAE/Metric wrenches, sockets and combination open end/box end wrenches in sizes from $\frac{1}{8}$ in. (3mm) to $\frac{3}{4}$ in. (19mm) and a spark plug socket ($\frac{13}{16}$ in. or $\frac{5}{8}$ in.). If possible, buy various length socket drive extensions. One break in this department is that the metric sockets available in the U.S. will all fit the ratchet handles and extensions you may already have ($\frac{1}{4}$ in., $\frac{3}{8}$ in., and $\frac{1}{2}$ in. drive).
2. Jackstands for support.
3. Oil filter wrench.
4. Oil filter spout for pouring oil.
5. Grease gun for chassis lubrication.
6. Hydrometer for checking the battery.
7. A container for draining oil.
8. Many rags (paper or cloth) for wiping up the inevitable mess.

In addition to the above items there are several others that are not absolutely necessary, but handy to have around. These include a hydraulic floor jack, oil-dry, a transmission funnel and the usual supply of lubricants, antifreeze and fluids, although these can be purchased as needed. This is a basic list for routine maintenance, but only your personal needs and desires can accurately determine your list of necessary tools.

The second list of tools is for tune-ups. While the tools involved here are slightly more sophisticated, they need not be outrageously expensive. There are several inexpensive tach/dwell meters on the market that are every bit as good for the average mechanic as an expensive professional model. Just be sure that it works on 4-, 6- and 8-cylinder engines. A basic list of tune-up equipment could include:

9. Tach/dwell meter.
10. Spark plug wrench.
11. Timing light (a DC light that works from the vehicle's battery is best, although an AC light that plugs into 110V house current will suffice at some sacrifice in brightness).
12. Wire spark plug gauge/adjusting tools.

Here again, be guided by your own needs. While not absolutely necessary, an ohmmeter can be useful in determining whether or not a spark plug wire is any good by measuring its resistance. In addition to these basic tools, there are several other tools and gauges you may find useful. These include:

13. A compression gauge. The screw-in type is slower to use, but eliminates the possibility of a faulty reading due to escaping pressure.
14. A manifold vacuum gauge.
15. A test light.
16. An induction meter. This is used for determining whether or not there is current in a wire. These are handy for use if a wire is broken somewhere in a wiring harness.

As a final note, you will probably find a torque wrench necessary for all but the most basic work. The beam type models are perfectly adequate, although the newer click (breakaway) type are more precise, and you don't have to crane your neck to see a torque reading in awkward situations. The breakaway torque wrenches are more expensive and should be recalibrated periodically.

Torque specification for each fastener will be given in the procedure in any case that a specific torque value is required. If no torque specifications are given, use the following values as a guide, based upon fastener size:

Bolts marked 6T
6mm bolt/nut — 5-7 ft. lbs.
8mm bolt/nut — 12-17 ft. lbs.
10mm bolt/nut — 23-34 ft. lbs.
12mm bolt/nut — 41-59 ft. lbs.
14mm bolt/nut — 56-76 ft. lbs.

Bolts marked 8T
6mm bolt/nut — 6-9 ft. lbs.
8mm bolt/nut — 13-20 ft. lbs.
10mm bolt/nut — 27-40 ft. lbs.
12mm bolt/nut — 46-69 ft. lbs.
14mm bolt/nut — 75-101 ft. lbs.

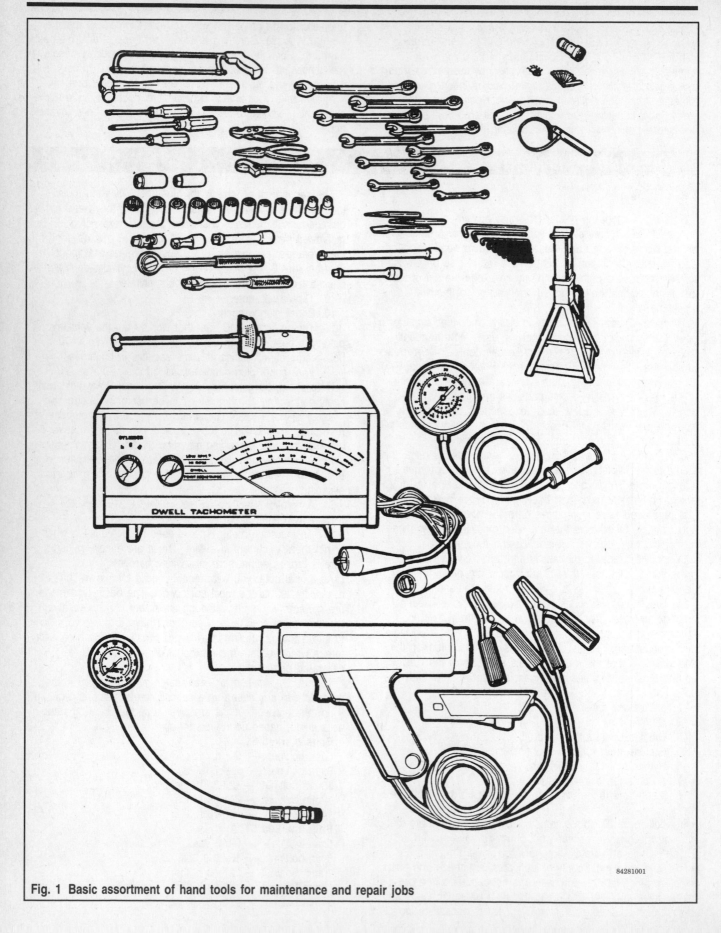

Fig. 1 Basic assortment of hand tools for maintenance and repair jobs

84281001

Special Tools

Normally, the use of special factory tools is avoided for repair procedures, since these are not readily available for the average vehicle owner. When it is possible to perform the job with more commonly available tool, it will be pointed out, but occasionally a special tool was designed to perform a specific function and should be used. When a special tool is indicated, it will be referred to by manufacturer's part number, and, where possible, an illustration of the tool will be provided so that an equivalent tool may be used. Before substituting another tool, you must be fully satisfied that neither your safety nor the performance of the vehicle will be compromised.

Some special tools are available commercially from major tool manufacturer. Others can be purchased through your Volvo dealer or local parts supplier.

SERVICING YOUR VEHICLE SAFELY

▶ **See Figure 2**

It is virtually impossible to anticipate all of the hazards involved with automotive maintenance and service but care and common sense will prevent most accidents.

The rules of safety for mechanics range from "don't smoke around gasoline," to 'use the proper tool for the job." The trick to avoid injuries is to develop safe work habits and take every possible precaution.

Do's

• Do keep a fire extinguisher and first aid kit within easy reach.

• Do wear safety glasses or goggles when cutting, drilling, grinding or prying. If you wear glasses for the sake of vision, then they should be made of hardened glass that can serve also as safety glasses, or wear safety goggles over your regular glasses.

• Do shield your eyes whenever you work around the battery. Batteries contain sulfuric acid. In case of contact with the eyes or skin, flush the area with water or a mixture of water and baking soda and get medical attention immediately.

• Do use safety stands for any under-car service. Jacks are for raising vehicles; safety stands are for making sure the vehicle stays raised until you want it to come down. Whenever the vehicle is raised, block the wheels remaining on the ground and set the parking brake.

• Do use adequate ventilation when working with any chemicals. Asbestos dust resulting from brake lining wear can cause cancer.

• Do disconnect the negative battery cable when working on the electrical system. The primary ignition system can contain up to 40,000 volts.

• Do follow manufacturer's directions whenever working with potentially hazardous materials. Both brake fluid and antifreeze are poisonous if taken internally.

• Do properly maintain your tools. Loose hammerheads, mushroomed punches and chisels, frayed or poorly grounded electrical cords, excessively worn screwdriver, spread wrenches (open end), cracked sockets can cause accidents.

• Do use the proper size and type of tool for the job being done.

• Do when possible, pull on a wrench handle rather than push on it, and adjust your stance to prevent a fall.

• Do be sure that adjustable wrenches are tightly adjusted on the nut or bolt and pulled so that the face is on the side of the fixed jaw.

• Do select a wrench or socket that fits the nut or bolt. The wrench or socket should sit straight, not cocked.

• Do strike squarely with a hammer to avoid glancing blows.

• Do set the parking brake and block the drive wheels if the work requires that the engine is running.

Don'ts

• Don't run an engine in a garage or anywhere else without proper ventilation — EVER! Carbon monoxide is poisonous. It is absorbed by the body 400 times faster than oxygen. It takes a long time to leave the human body and you can build up a deadly supply of it in you system by simply breathing in a little every day. You may not realize you are slowly poisoning yourself. Always use power vents, windows, fans or open the garage doors.

• Don't work around moving parts while wearing a necktie or other loose clothing. Short sleeves are much safer than long, loose sleeves. Hard-toed shoes with neoprene soles protect your toes and give a better grip on slippery surfaces. Jewelry such as watches, fancy belt buckles, beads or body adornment of any kind is not safe working around a car. Long hair should be hidden under a hat or cap.

• Don't use pockets for toolboxes. A fall or bump can drive a screwdriver deep into you body. Even a wiping cloth hanging from the back pocket can wrap around a spinning shaft or fan.

• Don't smoke when working around gasoline, cleaning solvent or other flammable material.

• Don't smoke when working around the battery. When the battery is being charged, it gives off explosive hydrogen gas.

• Don't use gasoline to wash your hands. There are excellent soaps available. Gasoline may contain lead, and lead can enter the body through a cut, accumulating in the body until you are very ill. Gasoline also removes all the natural oils from the skin so that bone dry hands will suck up oil and grease.

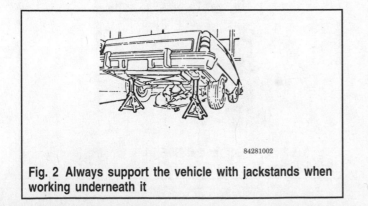

84281002

Fig. 2 Always support the vehicle with jackstands when working underneath it

• Don't service the air conditioning system unless you are equipped with the necessary tools and training. The refrigerant, R-12, is extremely cold and when exposed to the air, will instantly freeze any surface it comes in contact with, including your eyes. Although the refrigerant is normally nontoxic, R-12 becomes a deadly poisonous gas in the presence of an open flame. One good whiff of the vapors from burning refrigerant can be fatal.

MODEL IDENTIFICATION

The forth digit of the Vehicle Identification Number (VIN) designates the model (series) and is as follows:

A = 240
F = 740
G = 760
H = 780
J = 940
K = 960

SERIAL NUMBER IDENTIFICATION

In all correspondence with your Volvo dealer or when ordering parts, the vehicle type designation, chassis number and if applicable, the engine, transmission and rear axle (final drive) numbers should be quoted for proper identification.

Vehicle

The Vehicle Identification Number (VIN) is located on a plate visible through the windshield on the driver's side of the dash. This 17 digit character contains such information as manufacturer code, vehicle series, engine type and model year code. The 6th and 7th digits indicate the engine code. The tenth digit indicates the model year and are as follows:

L — 1990
M — 1991
N — 1992
P — 1993

The VIN can also be found on the Service Designation Number plate.

Engine

▶ **See Figures 3, 4 and 5**

The sixth and seventh digits of the VIN are the engine code and indicates the engine installed in the vehicle. The engine coding is as follows:

69 = B280F
82 = B230F (LH 3.1)
87 = B230F Turbocharged
88 = B230F (LH 2.4)
89 = B234F
95 = B6304F w/catalytic converter
98 = B6304G w/o catalytic converter

Found on each engine is an identification tag or stamping that indicates the engine type, serial number and part number. The tag or stamping is located in different places depending on the type of engine, the list below reveals the location of the tag or stamping.

B230F, B230FT and **B234F** — stamped into the left side of the block just below the head. An information tag is also affixed to the timing cover.

B280F — stamped on the cylinder block. On early models it can be found between the cylinder banks, toward the rear of the engine. On late models it can be found on the right front, between the inlet manifold and water pump.

B6304F — punched in the left-hand side of the cylinder block. An identification label is also affixed to the timing cover.

Transmission Number

The transmission type designation, serial number and part number appear on a metal plate affix to the left-hand side of the transmission, just above the transmission pan. Transmission identification is as follows:

M46 = 4-speed manual transmission, with controlled fifth gear (overdrive)

M47 = 5-speed manual transmission

AW70 = 4-speed automatic transmission, without lock-up clutch (controlled forth gear 'overdrive')

AW70L = 4-speed automatic transmission, with lock-up clutch (controlled forth gear 'overdrive')

AW71 = 4-speed automatic transmission, without lock-up clutch (controlled forth gear 'overdrive')

84281003

Fig. 3 B234F, B230F and B230F-Turbo engine identification location

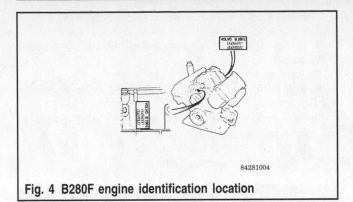

Fig. 4 B280F engine identification location

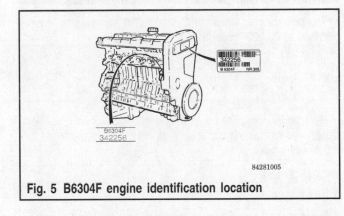

Fig. 5 B6304F engine identification location

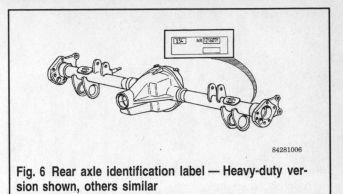

Fig. 6 Rear axle identification label — Heavy-duty version shown, others similar

AW72L = Basically the same transmission as the AW70L, but designed for heavier applications.

AW30-40 = 4-speed automatic transmission, with torque converter lock-up function (Electronically Controlled)

Rear Axles

▶ See Figure 6

The rear axle ratio and identification number (Part Number) is found on a label, located on the left-hand side of the axle housing and is as follows:

Volvo 1030 = Standard rear axle
Volvo 1031, 1035 and 1041 = Heavy-duty version
Volvo 1035 = Multi-link rear axle
Volvo 1045 = Multi-link rear axle, with automatic differential lock

ROUTINE MAINTENANCE

Your vehicle was inspected and service twice before it was delivered to you the customer. The first check was performed at the Volvo factory and the second at the Volvo dealer, prior to delivery.

After the vehicle is driven 600-1200 miles (1,000-2,000 km), it should be service according to the procedures specified in this manual. It is recommended that your vehicles be inspected and serviced every 5000 mile intervals. During every 5,000 mile (8,000 km) service, the following should be performed:

• Check brake fluid level
• Replace oil filter
• Replace engine oil and reset service indicator
• Check rear axle for leakage and oil level
• Check tires and tire pressure
• Check fluid level for automatic transmission
• Check condition of Automatic Transmission Fluid (ATF)
• Check manual transmission for leakage and oil level
• Check oil level of power steering reservoir
• Fill washer fluid reservoir
• Clean and oil power antenna
• (B2334F only): First 5,000 mile service: adjust the camshaft timing belt

Air Cleaner

The air cleaner element should be replaced every 30,000 miles (48,000 km) intervals. More frequent changes will be necessary if the vehicle is operated in dusty conditions.

REMOVAL & INSTALLATION

▶ See Figures 7, 8 and 9

The air cleaner assembly, on non-turbocharged engines, is located on the left-hand side of the vehicle, near the radiator. On turbocharged engine, the air cleaner assembly is located on the right-hand side of the vehicle, near the radiator. To remove, unsnap the clips retaining the air cleaner housing halves and remove the air cleaner cartridge.

Fuel Filter

The fuel filter is located underneath the vehicle, under the left rear seat. It is recommended that the fuel filter be replaced every 60,000 miles (96,000 km). The fuel filter should be replaced, immediately, upon evidence of dirt in the fuel system.

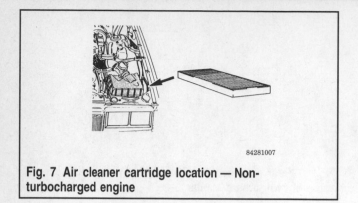

Fig. 7 Air cleaner cartridge location — Non-turbocharged engine

Fig. 8 Air cleaner cartridge replacement — Turbocharged engine

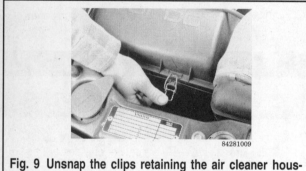

Fig. 9 Unsnap the clips retaining the air cleaner housing halves — Turbocharged engine shown

REMOVAL & INSTALLATION

▶ See Figure 10

✷✷CAUTION

Never smoke when working around gasoline! Avoid all sources of sparks or ignition. Gasoline vapors are EXTREMELY volatile!

1. Disconnect the negative battery cable.
2. Remove the fuel filler cap.

➡Have a container ready when loosening the fuel lines. Residual fuel in the lines will come out. Always use flared wrenches (special hex wrench) to gripped fuel lines or filter connections, when loosening.

3. Place a suitable container in position. Loosen the fuel filter connections.
4. Remove the clamp retaining the fuel filter to the bracket.
To install:
5. Transfer the bracket to the new filter.
6. Note the direction on the fuel filter and install the filter to the bracket.
7. Connect the fuel lines to the fuel filter. Check to ensure the copper seals are correctly installed.
8. Install the fuel filler cap.
9. Reconnect the negative battery cable.

Crankcase Ventilation

The positive crankcase ventilation (PCV) system should be serviced at 20,000 miles (32,000 km) intervals.

B230F Engine
▶ See Figure 11

Replace the flame guard at stated intervals. Check the hoses and nipples for condition and clogging. Failure to do so can result in loss of oil.

B6304F Engine
▶ See Figure 12

Replace the flame guard at stated intervals. Turn the flame guard cover approximately $\frac{19}{32}$ (15mm) to the left to remove.

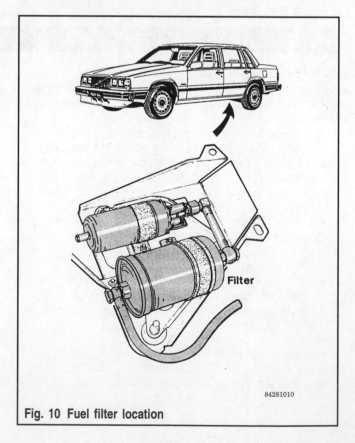

Filter

Fig. 10 Fuel filter location

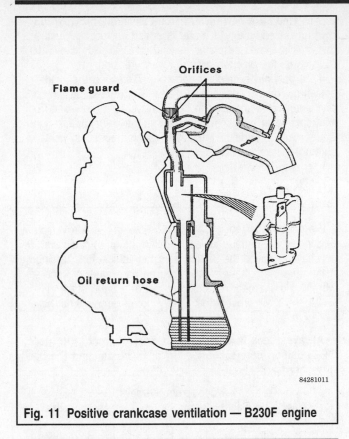

84281011

Fig. 11 Positive crankcase ventilation — B230F engine

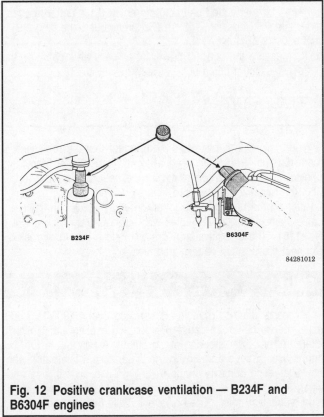

84281012

Fig. 12 Positive crankcase ventilation — B234F and B6304F engines

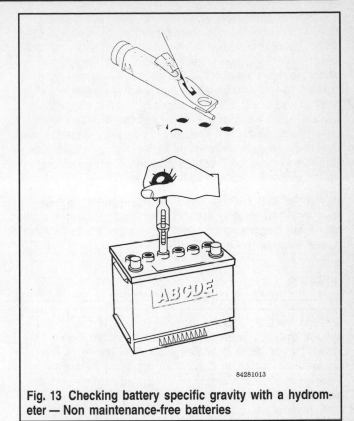

84281013

Fig. 13 Checking battery specific gravity with a hydrometer — Non maintenance-free batteries

Battery

SAFETY PRECAUTIONS

• When working around a battery, always shield your face and protect your eyes.
• Batteries normally produce explosive gases which can cause personal injury. Therefore, do not allow flames or sparks to came near the battery.
• Never check the level of the electrolyte in the presence of flame or when smoking.
• Never charge a battery in an unventilated area.
• Never smoke around a battery being charged.

GENERAL MAINTENANCE

It is recommended the battery be serviced every 20,000 miles (32,000 Km) intervals.
Keeping the battery top clean and dry reduces service problems and extends the battery life.

FLUID LEVEL

Unless you have a 'maintenance-free" battery, check the electrolyte (fluid) level frequently. Be sure that the vent holes in each cell cap are not blocked by grease or dirt. The vent holes allow hydrogen gas, formed by the chemical reaction in the battery, to escape safely.

Check the battery electrolyte level at least once a month, more often in hot weather or during periods of extended operation. The level should be maintained between the upper and lower levels marked on the battery case, or to the split ring within the well in each cell. If the electrolyte level is low, distilled water should be added until the proper level is reached. Tap water is to be avoided if possible; the minerals it contains can shorten battery life by reacting with the metal plates inside the battery. Each cell is completely separate from the others, so each cell must be filled individually. It's a good idea to add the distilled water with a squeeze bulb to avoid having electrolyte (sulfuric acid) splash out.

➡Vehicles that are regularly driven at highway speeds over moderate to long distances may require battery service more frequently. Constant charging of the battery will cause some water to evaporate.

CABLES

Check the battery cables for signs of wear or chafing and replace any cable or terminal that looks marginal. Battery terminals can be easily cleaned; inexpensive cleaning tools are an excellent investment that will pay for themselves many times over. They can usually be purchased from any well-equipped auto store or parts department. The accumulated white powder and corrosion can be cleaned from the top of the battery with an old toothbrush and a solution of baking soda and water. Before installing the battery cables, smear the cable clamps and battery poles with acid-resistant grease (Part No. 1161150-6 or equivalent); this will help to retard corrosion.

TESTING

▶ **See Figure 13**

Check the battery electrolyte level periodically, especially in hot weather or during periods of extended operation. The level should be maintained between the upper and lower levels marked on the battery case, or to the split ring within the well in each cell. If the electrolyte level is low, distilled water should be added until the proper level is reached. Tap water is to be avoided if possible; the minerals it contains can shorten battery life by reacting with the metal plates inside the battery. Each cell is completely separate from the others, so each cell must be filled individually. It's a good idea to add the distilled water with a squeeze bulb to avoid having electrolyte (sulfuric acid) splash out.

➡Vehicles that are regularly driven at highway speeds over moderate to long distances may require battery service more frequently. Constant charging of the battery will cause some water to evaporate.

At least once a year check the specific gravity of the battery electrolyte. It should be between 1.22 and 1.28 at room temperature. A reading of 1.00 or slightly above indicates nothing but water within the battery. The electrical process has stopped

and its time for a new battery. You cannot successfully add acid to a used battery. If water is added in freezing weather, the vehicle should be driven several miles to allow the water to mix with the electrolyte and prevent freezing.

If the battery becomes corroded, or if electrolyte should splash out during additions of water, a mixture of baking soda and water will neutralize the acid. This should be washed off with cold water after making sure that the cell caps are tight. Battery fluid is particularly nasty to painted surfaces; work carefully to avoid spillage.

CHARGING

If a charging is required while the battery is in the vehicle, disconnect the battery cables, negative (ground) cable first. If you have removed the battery from the vehicle for charging, make sure the battery is not sitting on bare earth or concrete while being charged. A block of wood or a small stack of newspapers will prevent the battery from losing internal heat while charging.

➡Always check to ensure the battery charger is in the OFF position before connecting or disconnecting the battery charger.

1. Remove the filler caps from the cells.
2. Check the electrolyte and top-up if necessary with distilled water.
3. Charge the battery for 10 hours at the recommended current. Recommended charging current = 0,1 x battery capacity. Example: Capacity = 55 Ah. Recommended charging current = 0.1 x 55 = 5.5A.
4. Measure the specific gravity of all cells after charging the battery. Maximum difference between cells = 0.03.

REPLACEMENT

When replacing a battery, it is important that the replacement have an output rating equal to or when greater than original equipment. When removing the battery, always disconnect the negative battery lead first, to prevent sparking. After positioning the replacement battery in your vehicle, smear the cable clamps and battery poles with acid-resistant grease (Part No. 1161150-6 or equivalent); this will help to retard corrosion. Connect the positive battery lead first.

Belts

Accessory drive-belt tension is checked every 6,000 to 7,500 miles. Loose belts can cause poor engine cooling and diminish alternator or power steering pump output. A belt that is too tight places a severe strain on the water pump, alternator, and power steering pump bearings. A belt will loosen with age and wear. A belt loose enough to slip on its pulleys will make a loud, squealing noise. The noise is usually heard under acceleration or during a sharp turn.

INSPECTION

Inspect all drive belts for cracks, glazed condition and frayed or broken cords. Replace any drive belts showing the above conditions.

➡️**If a drive belt continually gets cut, the crankshaft or accessory pulley might have a sharp projection on it. Have the pulley replaced if this condition exists.**

ADJUSTING

▶ **See Figure 14**

To check drive belt tension, push lightly on the belt midway between the pulleys. It should be possible to depress the drive belts 3/16 to 3/8 (5-10mm) halfway between pulleys. Remember that too tight is as damaging as too loose. Adjust if necessary.

Incorrect belt tension is corrected by moving the driven accessory (alternator, power steering pump, etc.) away from or toward the driving pulley. Loosen the mounting and adjusting bolts on the accessory and move it to loosen or tighten the belt. Once the belt tension is correct, retighten the mounting bolts and recheck the tension.

➡️**Never position a metal pry bar on the rear end of the alternator housing or against the power steering pump reservoir; they can be deformed easily.**

REMOVAL & INSTALLATION

1. Loosen the mounting and adjusting bolts on the accessory and move it to its extreme loosest position, generally by moving it toward the center of the motor.
2. Removing the old belt. Some belts run around a third or idler pulley, which acts as an additional pivot in the belt's path. It may be possible to loosen the idler pulley as well as the main component, making your job much easier. Depending on which belt(s) you are changing, it may be necessary to loosen or remove other interfering belts to get at the one(s) you want.
3. Check the pulleys for dirt or built-up material which could affect belt contact.
4. Carefully install the new belt. Gentle pressure in the direction of rotation is helpful. Adjust the belt tension.
5. Retighten the mounting bolts and recheck the tension.

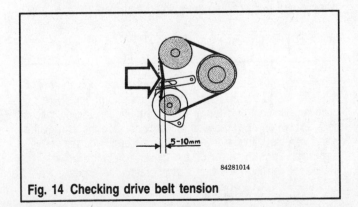

84281014

Fig. 14 Checking drive belt tension

Hoses

It is a good practice to inspect hoses during every oil change. Inspect for cracks, swelling and softness. When inspecting hoses, be sure to check the bottom radiator hose, as this one can be easily overlooked. Since the hoses are generally the weakest link in the cooling system, always inspect them before going on a long trip and at the onset of cold or hot weather. The hoses to and from the radiator are the most visible, but there are also other water hoses under the hood, notably the heater hoses running to the firewall. Check these hoses at the same time you check the radiator hoses.

REMOVAL & INSTALLATION

1. If necessary, allow the engine to cool.
2. Place a suitable drain pan into position. Remove the radiator cap and drain the cooling system.
3. Loosen the clamp on the hose and slide it back so it's out of the way. Gently break the grip of the hose on its fitting by twisting or prying with a suitable tool. Do not exert too much force or you will damage the radiator fitting.
4. Remove the hose.

To install:

➡️**Radiator hoses should be routed with no kinks and, when installed, should be in the same position as the original. If other than specified hose is used, make sure it does not rub against either the engine or the frame while the engine is running, as this may wear a hole in the hose.**

5. Slide the hose clamps back into position and retighten. When tightening the clamps, tighten them enough to seal in the coolant but not so much that the clamp cuts into the hose or causes it internal damage.
6. After replacing the hose, fill the system with coolant. Volvo strongly recommends the coolant mixture be a 50-50 mix of antifreeze and water. This mixture gives best combination of anti-freeze and anti-boil characteristics for year-round driving.
7. Replace and tighten the radiator cap. Start the engine and check visually for leaks. Allow the engine to warm up fully and continue to check your for signs of leakage.

Air Conditioning System

❄❄WARNING

R-12 refrigerant is a chlorofluorocarbon which, when released into the atmosphere, contributes to the depletion of the ozone layer in the upper atmosphere. Ozone filters out harmful radiation from the sun.

Consult the laws in your area before servicing the air conditioning system. In some states it is illegal to perform repairs involving refrigerant unless work is done by a certified technician.

The purpose of the air conditioning unit is to reduce the temperature in the passenger compartment to an acceptable level when ambient temperatures are high. The unit operates on the principle that heat is always transferred from a hot medium to a cold one. In practice, warm air from the passenger compartment is circulated passed an evaporator which contains a cold liquid. Heat is therefore transferred from the air to the liquid and the cooler air is blown into the passenger compartment.

A direct relationship exists between the pressure, temperature and volume of the refrigerant. By allowing the refrigerant to circulate in a closed system and altering the pressure and volume conditions, it is possible to get the refrigerant to boil (evaporate). For this purpose the warm air in the passenger compartment is directed through an evaporator, in which the refrigerant circulates. Heat is absorbed by the refrigerant and in doing so the warm air is cooled down and the refrigerant boils. It is this cold air which is blown into the passenger compartment by the fan. The heat which is absorbed by the refrigerant in the evaporator is transferred to the condenser in the engine compartment, where it is cooled by air flow with the aid of the engine and the electric fans. A compressor is used to circulate the refrigerant within the system.

➡**All 1993 Volvos used a totally CFC-free air conditioning system. The new refrigerant, R134A, is a freon-free material which has virtually no ozone-depleting potential. R134A is not for sale to the general public. Evacuating and charging air conditioning system, equipped with R134A, must be performed by a certified technician.**

SERVICE VALVE LOCATION

York Compressor System

The service valve location for high pressure side is at compressor's **DISCH** valve. The service valve location for the low pressure side is at compressor's **SUCTION** valve.

Except York Compressor System

The high pressure service valve is located on the compressor. The low pressure service valve is located on the receiver/drier assembly.

SYSTEM DISCHARGING

In order to protect the ozone layer, an approved R-12 Recovery/Recycling machine that meets SAE standard J1991 should be employed when discharging the system. Follow the operating instructions provided with the approved equipment exactly to properly discharge the system.

SYSTEM EVACUATING

If the air conditioning system has been opened to the atmosphere, it should be air and moisture free before being recharged with refrigerant. Moisture and air mixed with refrigerant will raise the compressor head pressure, possibly damage the system's components and will reduce the performance of

the system. To evacuate the system, perform the following procedure:

1. Leak test the system and repair any leaks found.
2. Connect an approved charging station, Recovery/Recycling machine or manifold gauge set and vacuum pump to the discharge and suction ports. The red hose is normally connected to the discharge (high pressure) line and the blue hose is connected to the suction (low pressure) line.
3. Open the discharge and suction ports and start the vacuum pump. If the pump is not able to pull at least 26 in. Hg of vacuum, there is a leak that must be repaired before evacuation can occur.
4. Once the system has reached at least 26 in. Hg of vacuum, allow the system to evacuate for at least 30 minutes. The longer the system is evacuated, the more contaminants will be removed.
5. Close all valves and turn the pump off. If the system loses more than 2 in. Hg of vacuum after 15 minutes, there is a leak that should be repaired.

SYSTEM CHARGING

1. Connect an approved charging station, Recovery/Recycling machine or manifold gauge set to the discharge and suction ports. The red hose is normally connected to the discharge (high pressure) line and the blue hose is connected to the suction (low pressure) line.
2. Follow the instructions provided with the equipment and charge the system with the specified amount of refrigerant.
3. Perform a leak test.

Windshield Wipers

Intense heat and ultra-violet rays from the sun, snow, ice and frost, road oils, acid rain, and industrial pollution all combine quickly to deteriorate the rubber wiper refills. One pass on a frosty windshield can reduce a new set of refills to an unusable condition. The refills should be replaced about twice a year or whenever they begin to streak or chatter on wet glass.

Blade life can be prolonged by frequent cleanings of the glass with a rag and a commercial glass cleaner. The use of a ammonia based cleaner will ease the removal of built-up road oils and grease from the glass. Ammonia based cleaners are harmful to painted surfaces. Be careful when applying them and don't fill the washer jug with an ammonia based solvent; when used it will run onto the painted bodywork.

WIPER REFILL REPLACEMENTS

If the wipers are not cleaning the windshield properly, only the refill has to be replaced. The blade and arm usually require replacement only in the event of damage. It is not necessary (except on new Tridon® refills) to remove the arm or the blade to replace the refill (rubber part), though you may have to position the arm higher on the glass. You can do this by turning the ignition switch on and operating the wipers. When they are positioned where they are accessible, turn the ignition switch off.

There are several types of refills and your vehicle could have any kind, since aftermarket blades and arms may not use exactly the same type refill as the original equipment.

Most Anco® styles use a release button that is pushed down to allow the refill to slide out of the yoke jaws. The new refill slides in and locks in place. Some Anco® refills are removed by noting where the metal backing strips or the refill is wider. Insert a small screwdriver blade between the frame and metal backing strip. Press down to release the refill from the retaining tab.

The Trico® style is unlocked at one end by squeezing 2 metal tabs, and the refill is slid out of the frame jaws. When the new refill is installed, the tabs will click into place, locking the refill.

The polycarbonate type is held in place by a locking lever that is pushed downward (out of the groove in the arm) to free the refill. When the new refill is installed, it will lock in place automatically.

The Tridon® refill has a plastic backing strip with a notch about an inch from the end. Hold the blade (frame) on a hard surface so that the frame is tightly bowed. Grip the tip of the backing strip and pull up while twisting counterclockwise. The backing strip will snap out of the retaining tab. Do this for the remaining tabs until the refill is free of the arm. The length of these refills is molded into the end and they should be replaced with identical types.

No matter which type of refill you use, be sure that all of the frame claws engage the refill. Before operating the wipers, be sure that no part of the metal frame is contacting the windshield.

Tires and Wheels

▶ **See Figure 15**

It is good practice to perform regular wheel and tire inspection, as follows:
- Check your tires whenever you stop for fuel. Look for low or underinflated tires.
- At least once a month, check all tires pressure. Check the tire pressure when cold, not after a long drive.
- At least twice a year, check for worn tires and loose wheel lug nuts. Also, check the pressure in the spare tire.
- Check the tire wear pattern. It may indicate unbalance, incorrect camber, toe-in or incorrect tire pressure.
- Check that the tires mounted on both front and both rear wheels are the same (Size, radial, cross-ply, thread and studded).
- Check the tread depth. Minimum allowable depth is 1/32 in. (1mm).

TIRE ROTATION

➡ **Mark the wheel position or direction of rotation on radial tires or studded snow tires before removal.**

So that the tires wear more uniformly, it is recommended that the tires be rotated every 6,000 miles. This can be done when all four tires are of the same size and load rating capacity. Any abnormal wear should be investigated and the cause corrected.

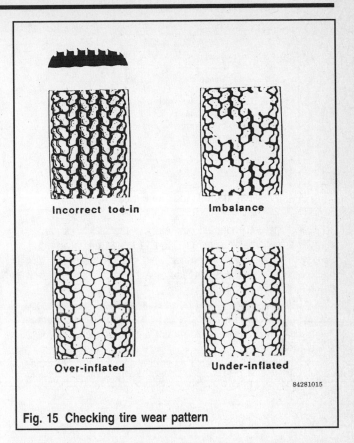

Incorrect toe-in   **Imbalance**

Over-inflated   **Under-inflated**

84281015

Fig. 15 Checking tire wear pattern

Radical tires should not be cross-switched; they'll last longer if their direction of rotation is not changed. They will wear very rapidly if reversed. Studded snow tires will lose their studs if their direction of rotation is reversed.

✳✳CAUTION

Avoid overtightening the lug nuts or the brake disc or drum may become permanently distorted. Alloy wheels can be cracked by overtightening. Generally, nut torque should not exceed 60 ft.lbs. Always tighten the nuts in a criss-cross pattern.

TIRE DESIGN

▶ **See Figure 16**

When buying new tires, you should keep the following points in mind, especially if you are switching to larger tires or a different profile series:

1. All four tires should be of the same construction type. Radial, bias, or bias-belted tires should not be mixed. Radial tires are highly recommended for their excellent handling and fuel mileage characteristics. Most new vehicles from 1980 on were delivered with radial tires as standard equipment.

2. The wheels must be the correct width for the tire. Tire dealers have charts of tire and wheel compatibility. A mismatch can cause sloppy handling and rapid tread wear. The tread width should match the rim width (inside bead to inside bead) within an inch. For radial tires the rim width should be 80% or less of the tire (not tread) width. The chart below gives an example of a tire size designation number.

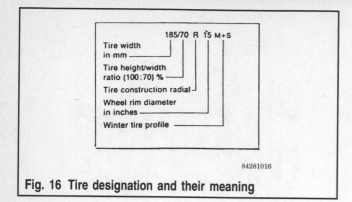

Fig. 16 Tire designation and their meaning

3. The height (mounted diameter) of the new tires can change speedometer accuracy, engine speed per given road speed, fuel mileage, acceleration, and ground clearance. Tire manufacturers furnish full measurement specifications to their dealers.

4. The spare tire should be usable, at least for low speed operation, with the new tires. This wheel and tire is for emergency use only. Never try to mount a regular tire on a special spare wheel.

5. No interference should exist between the tire and wheel assembly when the vehicle is loaded, on bumps or in turning through maximum range.

TIRE INFLATION

The importance of proper tire inflation cannot be overemphasized. A tire employs air under pressure as part of its structure. It is designed around the supporting strength of air at a specified pressure. For this reason, improper inflation drastically reduces the tire's ability to perform as it was intended.

Tire pressures should be checked regularly with a reliable pressure gauge. Inflate the tires to the recommended psi given in the 'Vehicle Capacity Label" located on the right front door post. Tire pressure should only be corrected when the tire is cold. Tire temperature rises after driving just a short distance.Generally: **Economy** and max 5 persons in vehicle: use 36 psi front and rear. **Comfort** and max 3 persons in vehicle: use 26-28 psi front and 27-30 psi rear.

CARE OF SPECIAL WHEELS

If you have invested money in magnesium, aluminum alloy or sport wheels, special precautions should be taken to make sure your investment is not wasted and that your special wheels look good for the lifetime of the car.

Special wheels are easily scratched and/or damaged. Occasionally check the rims for cracking, impact damage or air leaks. If any of these are found, replace the wheel. In order to prevent this type of damage, and the costly replacement of a special wheel, observe the following precautions:

• Use extra care not to damage the wheels during removal, installation, balancing, etc. After removal of the wheels from the car, place them on a mat or other protective surface.

• While driving, watch for sharp obstacles.

• When washing, use a mild detergent and water. Avoid cleansers with abrasives or the use of hard brushes. There are many cleaners and polishes for special wheels. Use them.

• If possible, remove your special wheels from the car during the winter months. Salt and sand used for snow removal can severely damage the finish.

• Make sure that the recommended lug nut torque is never exceeded or the wheel may crack. Never use snow chains on special wheels; severe scratching will occur.

FLUIDS AND LUBRICANTS

Fluid Disposal

Used fluids such as engine oil, transmission fluid, antifreeze and brake fluid are hazardous wastes and must be disposed of properly. Before draining any fluids, consult with the local authorities. In many areas, waste oil is being accepted as a part of recycling programs. A number of service stations and auto parts stores are also accepting waste fluids for recycling.

Be sure of the recycling center's policies before draining any fluids, as many will not accept different fluids that have been mixed together, such as oil and antifreeze.

Fuel and Engine Oil Recommendations

FUEL

The fuel you use plays a major role on how your engine will function. In order to maximize the efficiency and operation of your vehicle, it is important to use the recommended fuel. Only UNLEADED gasoline is to be used. The recommended octane is 95 = Research Octane Number (RON), 91 = (R+M)/2. The minimum octane rating is 91 = RON, 87 = (R+M)/2.

Some unleaded gasolines are a blend of ethanol (ethyl alcohol, grain alcohol), commonly referred to as "gasohol". If you use gasohol, it must contain no more than 10% ethanol and have a rating of at least 87 octane (R+M)/2. If you experience driveability, starting, or fuel economy problems, you should discontinue using gasohol.

✳✳WARNING

DO NOT use gasolines containing methanol (methyl alcohol). Vehicle performance may be affected through deterioration and damage to critical parts of the fuel system.

Always use detergent blend fuels to reduce the risk of intake valve carbon deposit build-up and clogged fuel injectors. Gasoline without deposit control additives could form deposits on injectors and may lead to lean run condition causing rough idle and poor driveability.

➡The use of fuel additives is NOT recommended, as they can adversely affect engine performance.

ENGINE OIL

♦ **See Figure 17**

Engine oil bearing the American Petroleum Institute (API) label, is recommended for all vehicles. This label certifies that the oil conforms to the applicable standards and specifications of the API.

The use of fuel economy improving oil is recommended, provided oil change intervals are followed. The addition of oil additives are not recommended, as they can adversely affect the engine.

SAE 15W/40 is recommended for use in extreme driving conditions that involve high oil temperature and consumption (Ex: mountain driving with frequent decelerations or fast motorway driving). DO NOT use this oil at low temperature, see viscosity chart.

➡**A service reminder light will come on for approximately 2 minutes after each start, after the vehicle has accumulated 5,000 miles (8,000 km) after the previous oil change and accompanying resetting.**

Engine

OIL LEVEL CHECK

♦ **See Figures 18 and 19**

It is a good idea to check the engine oil each time or at least every other time you fill your gas tank. Check the engine oil level with the vehicle on level ground in **P** position. When checking fluid level, use a clean rag that will not leave lint.

1. Be sure the vehicle is on level surface.
2. Shut OFF the engine and wait a few minutes to allow the oil to drain back into the oil pan.
3. Remove the engine oil dipstick and wipe clean with a link-free rag.
4. Re-install the dipstick and push it down until it is fully seated in the tube.
5. Once again, remove the dipstick and note the level on the indicator. If necessary, fill to the normal level.

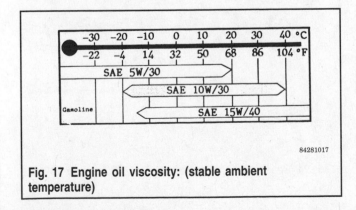

Fig. 17 Engine oil viscosity: (stable ambient temperature)

Fig. 18 Removing engine oil indicator — B230FT shown

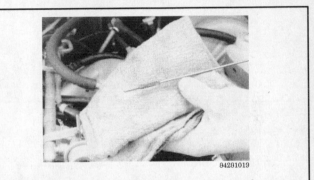

Fig. 19 Checking oil indicator, use a clean lint-free rag

OIL AND FILTER CHANGE

♦ **See Figures 20, 21, 22 and 23**

The engine oil and filter should be replace every 5,000 miles (8,000 km).

1. Operate the engine for a few minutes. This increases the engine oil temperature and allows the oil to flow more rapidly.

✳✳CAUTION

Engine oil can be scalding hot, if the vehicle was recently driven.

2. Apply the parking brake and block the wheels.
3. Raise and support the vehicle safely.
4. Position a suitable drain pan under the engine oil pan drain plug.
5. Using the proper size wrench, remove the oil pan drain plug. Allow the oil to drain completely. Re-install and tighten the drain plug. DO NOT OVERTIGHTEN.
6. Position the drain pan under the engine oil filter. Clean around the oil filter mounting surface with a shop rag. Using the special oil filter wrench (2903 or equivalent), remove the oil filter.
7. Lubricate the rubber oil seal of the new filter. Screw on by hand; retorque is necessary.
8. Lower the vehicle. Refill the crankcase to the normal oil level. Replace the filler cap.
9. Start the engine and check for leaks.
10. Shut OFF the engine. Wait a few minutes and check the oil level. Add oil if necessary.

Fig. 20 Engine oil pan drain plug — B230FT shown

Fig. 21 Engine oil filter location — 940 w/B230FT

2903

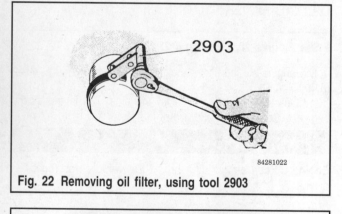
Fig. 22 Removing oil filter, using tool 2903

Fig. 23 Re-filling engine crankcase — B230FT

11. Reset the service indicator. See "Resetting Service Indicator" in this section.

RESETTING SERVICE INDICATOR

240/780 and 1990 740
▶ **See Figure 24**

The service reminder zeroing knob is located at the rear of the instrument panel. The indicator light illuminates after approximately 5,000 miles (8,000 km). It goes on for 2 minutes each time the engine is started until oil and filter have been changed and the counter reset.
Using a small screwdriver, depress the knob to reset.

Except 240/780 and 1990 740
▶ **See Figure 25**

The service reminder zeroing knob is located on the front of the instrument cluster, underneath a rubber grommet. Remove the rubber grommet; then using a small screwdriver, depress the knob to reset.

Manual Transmission

FLUID RECOMMENDATIONS

Automatic Transmission Fluid (ATF) type F or G is recommended for both the M46 and the M47 manual transmissions. On the M46, engine oil SAE 10W/40 is recommended for use in areas where temperature seldom drops below 14°F (10°C).

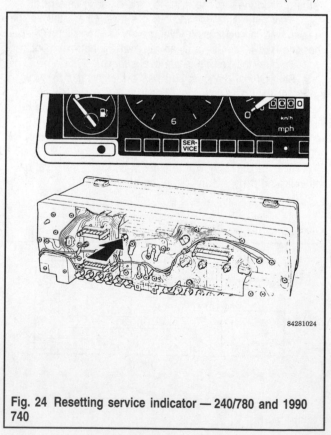
Fig. 24 Resetting service indicator — 240/780 and 1990 740

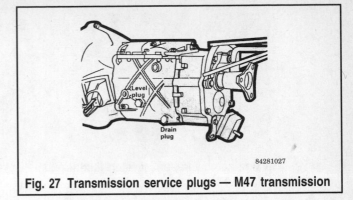

Fig. 25 Resetting service indicator — Except 240/780 and 1990 740

LEVEL CHECK

The fluid level should be checked at every 10,000 mile intervals.
1. Raise and support the vehicle safely.
2. Remove the transmission filler plug.
3. Check that the oil level is up to the filer plug hole. Top up, if necessary.
4. Install the transmission filler plug and lower the vehicle.

DRAIN AND REFILL

M46 Transmission
♦ See Figure 26

1. Raise and support the vehicle safely.
2. Placc a suitable container into position. Drain the oil by removing the transmission drain plug and overdrive cover.
3. After the oil is completely drained, reinstall the drain plug. Clean the strainer before reinstalling the overdrive cover.
4. Fill the transmission with the recommended lubricant, through the filler hole. The oil level should be up to the filer plug hole.
5. Install the filler plug. Lower the vehicle.

M47 Transmission
♦ See Figure 27

1. Raise and support the vehicle safely.
2. Place a suitable container into position. Drain the oil by removing the transmission drain plug. After the oil is completely drained, reinstall the drain plug.

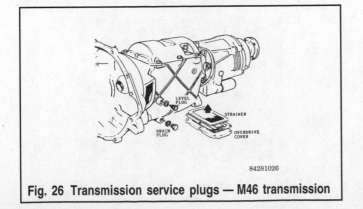

Fig. 26 Transmission service plugs — M46 transmission

Fig. 27 Transmission service plugs — M47 transmission

3. Fill the transmission with the recommended lubricant, through the filler hole. The oil level should be up to the filer plug hole.
4. Install the filler plug. Lower the vehicle.
5. Road test the vehicle and check for leaks.

Automatic Transmission

FLUID RECOMMENDATIONS

Automatic Transmission Fluid (ATF) type Dexron II® is recommended for all automatic transmissions.

LEVEL CHECK

♦ See Figures 28 and 29

The fluid level should be checked at every 10,000 mile intervals.
1. Check the transmission fluid level with the vehicle on level ground in **P** position, with the engine idling.
2. Remove the dipstick and wipe it clean, using a lint-free rag.

➡The dipstick has graduations for hot and cold transmission fluid levels.

3. Reinstall the dipstick. Remove it and check the dipstick markings.
    a. Cold fluid: At fluid temperatures below 105°F (40°C), the level may be below MIN mark.

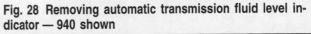

Fig. 28 Removing automatic transmission fluid level indicator — 940 shown

Fig. 29 Checking automatic transmission fluid level indicator, use a clean lint-free rag

b. Operating temperature: At fluid temperatures 195°F (90°C), the level may be above MAX mark.

4. Check the condition of the ATF. Discoloration and smell can be caused by heavy engine loads, such as towing. In this case, remove and clean oil pan, oil strainer and magnet. See 'Pan and Filter Service" in this section.

5. If topping up is necessary, fill through the dipstick tube.

DRAIN AND REFILL

❈❈CAUTION

Do not immediately drain the transmission fluid, if the vehicle was recently driven. Oil can be scalding hot.

1. Disconnect the negative battery cable.
2. Raise and support the vehicle safely.
3. Place a suitable drain pan beneath the transmission.
4. Remove the drain plug and drain the fluid.
5. Reinstall the drain plug. Lower the vehicle.
6. Fill the transmission with the proper fluid.
7. Connect the negative battery cable.
8. Firmly apply the parking brake and block the drive wheel. Start the engine and allow it to reach operating temperature. Check for leaks.
9. Move the gear selector lever through all ranges.
10. Wait approximately 2 minutes and check the fluid level in **P** position. Adjust as required.

PAN AND FILTER SERVICE

▶ See Figure 30

❈❈CAUTION

Do not immediately drain the transmission fluid, if the vehicle was recently driven. Oil can be scalding hot.

1. Disconnect the negative battery cable.
2. Raise and support the vehicle safely.
3. Place a suitable drain pan beneath the transmission.
4. Remove the drain plug and drain the fluid.
5. Remove the oil pan retaining bolts and remove the pan.
6. Clean the oil pan, strainer and particle magnet.
7. Apply oil to the pan gasket prior to installation. Use a new gasket.

Fig. 30 Automatic transmission pan drain plug

Rear Axle

FLUID RECOMMENDATIONS

The rear axle should be service with API GL-5, MIL-L-2105 B or C or equivalent, with a viscosity rating of SAE 90. When temperatures are below 15°F (-10°C), use SAE 80.

Use oils with the proper additives for vehicles equipped with limited slip differential.

LEVEL CHECK

▶ See Figure 31

The fluid level should be checked at every 10,000 mile intervals.

1. Raise and support the vehicle safely.
2. Remove the rear axle level plug.
3. Check that the oil level is up to the level plug hole. Top up, if necessary.
4. Reinstall the rear axle level plug and lower the vehicle.

Cooling System

FLUID RECOMMENDATIONS

Volvo's all-weather antifreeze Type C (blue-green) or equivalent, should be used on a year round basis. The cooling system should always contain 50% antifreeze solution and

Fig. 31 Removing rear axle level plug — 1041 shown

50% water. Studies have shown that extremely weak antifreeze solutions (10-20%) provide poor rust protection.

LEVEL CHECK

▶ **See Figure 32**

The coolant level should be checked at every 5,000 mile (8,000 km) intervals. The level should appear between the maximum and minimum marks of the translucent expansion tank. Do not remove the expansion tank filler cap except to top up the system, as air might become trapped in the system and reduce cooling efficiency. Top up the system with a mixture of 50% anti-freeze and 50% water; use this mixture all year round. If the engine is warm when you top up the cooling system, remove the filler cap slowly in order to allow any excess pressure to escape.

❋❋CAUTION

Always check or add fluid at the expansion tank. NEVER remove the radiator cap on a hot motor. You can be badly scalded by steam and hot liquid.

DRAINING AND REFILLING

It is recommended that the coolant be replaced at 30,000 mile (48,000 km) intervals. Perform this operation with the engine cold.

1. Raise the vehicle and support it safely.

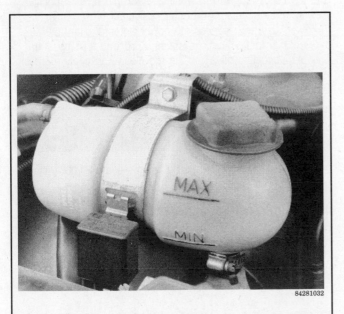

84281032

Fig. 32 Check the coolant level without removing the radiator cap. The level should appear between the maximum and minimum marks of the translucent expansion tank.

2. Remove the gravel shield, if equipped. Remove the expansion tank cap and set the heater controls to **Hot**.

3. Open the petcock on the side of the engine block. If the coolant is to be reused, collect it in a clean container.

4. Disconnect the lower radiator hose and allow the coolant to drain into a suitable container. On models with an expansion tank, either use a syphon or unfasten the tank and hold it up so that all of the coolant in it flows into the radiator.

5. Close the petcock(s), re-connect the lower radiator hose and add coolant to the expansion tank until coolant is level with the MAX mark on the tank.

6. Run the engine to normal operating temperature and check for leaks. Check the coolant level and refill if necessary.

FLUSHING AND CLEANING THE SYSTEM

Proceed with draining the system as outlined above. When the system has drained, reconnect hoses and secure as necessary. Move the temperature control for the heater to its hottest position; this allows the heater core to be flushed as well. Using a garden hose, fill the radiator and allow the water to run out the engine drain cocks. Continue until the water runs clear. Be sure to clean the expansion tank as well.

If the system is badly contaminated with rust or scale, you can use a commercial flushing solution to clean it out. Follow the manufacturer's instructions. Some causes of rust are air in the system, failure to change the coolant regularly, use of excessively hard or soft water, and/or failure to use the correct mix of antifreeze and water.

After the system has been flushed, continue with the refill procedures outlined above. Check the condition of the radiator cap and its gasket, replacing the cap if anything looks improper.

Brake Master Cylinder

▶ **See Figure 33**

FLUID RECOMMENDATIONS

It is recommended that only brake fluid meeting the specification DOT 4+ (DOT 4) be used in the brake system. AVOID mixing different makes of brake fluid.

LEVEL CHECK

The fluid level should be checked at every 5,000 mile (8,000 km) intervals. It is recommended that the fluid be replaced at 30,000 mile (48,000 km) intervals. If the vehicle is subjected to particularly hard wear, such as driving in mountainous regions, it should be changed at least once a year or every 15,000 miles (24,000 km).

1. Position the vehicle on a level surface.

2. Locate the brake fluid reservoir in the engine compartment. Check the fluid reservoir and brake lines for leaks.

3. Check the brake fluid without removing the cap. Adjust, if necessary. Use the recommended fluid. When filling the

Fig. 33 Check the brake fluid without removing the cap. Observing whether or not the fluid is up to the maximum mark on the translucent reservoir.

master cylinder, the greatest cleaniness should be observed to prevent dirt entering the system.

➡**Low fluid level may indicate worn brake pads.**

Power Steering Pump

FLUID RECOMMENDATIONS

Automatic Transmission Fluid (ATF) type F is recommended for the power steering system.

LEVEL CHECK

▶ **See Figures 34 and 35**

The fluid level should be checked at every 5,000 mile (8,000 km) intervals.

1. Operate the vehicle until normal operating temperature is reached.

2. Check the fluid level, with the engine idling, while fluid is still hot.

3. Wipe the reservoir housing clean.

4. Check that the fluid level is within the markings (MIN./MAX.) on the dipstick which is attach to the cover. Top up if necessary.

Chassis Greasing

Check the suspension and driveline every 10,000 miles (16,000 km) intervals. Use regular chassis lube on applicable joints if binding is noticed.

Fig. 34 Power steering fluid reservoir — 940 shown

Fig. 35 Checking power steering fluid level. Check that the fluid level is within the markings (MIN./MAX.) on the dipstick.

The upper and lower control arm ball joints as well as the tie rod and steering rod ball joints are lined with plastic (Teflon®) and do not require lubrication. However, check the rubber seals of these ball joints for cracking or damage. Replace any damaged seal with a new one, making sure to pack the new seal with multipurpose chassis grease.

Body Lubrication and Maintenance

Hood hinges: lubricate every 10,000 miles (16,000 km), use heavy oil.

Hood latch mechanism: lubricate every 10,000 miles (16,000 km), use general purpose grease.

Door hinges, stop and striker plates: lubricate every 10,000 miles (16,000 km). Lubricate the door hinges with heavy oil. Use door wax to lubricate the striker plates. Check that the latches lock in both outer and inner positions. Check that the door stops are in working order and provide positive locking in intermediate and outer positions.

Power Antenna: service the power antenna every 5,000 miles (8,000 km). Clean the antenna rod with ATF or other suitable lubricating oil. Wipe the rod clean and apply more oil on the antenna; then run the antenna up/down a few times. Repeat as necessary, until the antenna is clean and functions properly.

Wheel Bearings

The wheel bearings should be service every 30,000 miles (48,000 km) intervals.

A maintenance free type of front wheel hub is used on all 740/940/960 models. Hub and brake disc are separate components while the hub functions as the outer bearing race. The hub is mounted on a double row, grooved ball bearing.

The stub axle has a locknut which must not be reused. It is first torqued to 74 ft. lbs. (100 Nm) and then through an additional 45°.

REMOVAL, PACKING AND INSTALLATION

1. Remove the hub cap, and loosen the lug nuts a few turns.

2. Firmly apply the parking brake and block the rear wheels. Raise and support the vehicle safely. Remove the front wheels.

3. Remove the front caliper as outlined in Section 9 under, Front Caliper Removal and Installation.

4. Pry off the grease cap from the hub. Remove the cotter pin and castle nut. Use a hub puller to pull off the hub. On the 760 GLE, remove the brake disc. If the inner bearing remains lodged on the stub axle, remove it with a puller.

5. Using a drift, remove the inner and outer bearing rings.

6. Thoroughly clean the hub, brake disc, and grease cap.

To install:

7. Press in the new inner and outer bearing rings with a drift or bearing installation tool.

8. Press grease onto both bearings with a bearing packer. If one is not available, pack the bearings with as much wheel bearing grease as possible by hand. Also coat the outside of the bearings and the outer rings pressed into the hub. Fill the recess in the hub with grease up to the smallest diameter on the outer ring for the outer bearing. Place the inner bearing in position in the hub and press its seal in with a drift. The felt ring should be thoroughly coated with light engine oil.

9. Place the hub onto the stub axle. Install the outer bearing, washer, and castle nut.

10. Adjust the front wheel bearings by tightening the castle nut to 45 ft. lbs. to seat the bearings. Then, back off the nut 1/3 of a turn counterclockwise. Torque the nut to 12 in. lbs. If the nut slot does not align with the hole in the stub axle, tighten the nut until the cotter pin may be installed. Make sure that the wheel spins freely without any side play.

11. Fill the grease cap halfway with wheel bearing grease, and install it on the hub.

12. Install the front caliper.

13. Install the wheels. Remove the jackstand and lower the vehicle. Tighten the lug nuts to 60-70 ft. lbs. and install the hub cap.

TRAILER TOWING

General Recommendations

Trailer weight is the first and most important factor in determining whether or not your vehicle is suitable for towing the trailer you have in mind. The horsepower-to-weight ratio should be calculated. The basic standard is a ratio of 35:1. That is, 35 pounds of GVW for every horsepower.

To calculate this ratio, multiply your engine's rated horsepower by 35, then subtract the weight of the vehicle, including passengers and luggage. The resulting figure is the ideal maximum trailer weight that you can tow. One point to consider: a numerically higher axle ratio can offset what appears to be a low trailer weight. If the weight of the trailer that you have in mind is somewhat higher than the weight you just calculated, you might consider changing your rear axle ratio to compensate.

A general rule is that the tongue weight of the trailer should never exceed ten percent of the total weight of the trailer.

Vehicles with overdrive transmissions must not use the overdrive when towing. Volvo recommends that an optional Volvo automatic transmission oil cooler, P/N 1188253-7 or equivalent, be installed when trailer weight exceeds 2,000 lbs. (908 kg). When towing, remember that the engine and transmission are subjected to heavier than normal load; engine temperature should be watched closely for overheating and fluids should be checked regularly.

Necessary Equipment

There are three kinds of hitches: bumper mounted, frame mounted, and load equalizing.

Bumper mounted hitches are those which attach solely to the vehicle's bumper. Many states prohibit towing with this type of hitch when it attaches to the vehicle's stock bumper, since it subjects the bumper to stresses for which it was not designed. Aftermarket rear step bumpers, designed for trailer towing, are acceptable for use with bumper mounted hitches.

Frame mounted hitches can be of the type which bolts to two or more points on the frame, plus the bumper, or just to several points on the frame. Frame mounted hitches can also be of the tongue type, for Class I towing, or of the receiver type, for classes II and III.

Load equalizing hitches are usually used for large trailers. Most equalizing hitches are welded in place and use equalizing bars and chains to level the vehicle after the trailer is hooked up.

The bolt-on hitches are the most common, since they are relatively easy to install.

Check the gross weight rating of your trailer. Tongue weight is usually figured as 10% of gross trailer weight. Therefore, a trailer with a maximum gross weight of 2,000 lb. will have a maximum tongue weight of 200 lb. Class I trailers fall into this category. Class II trailers are those with a gross weight rating of 2,000-3,500 lb., while Class III trailers fall into the 3,500-6,000 lb. category. Class IV trailers are those over 6,000 lb. and are for use with fifth wheel trucks, only.

When you've determined the hitch that you'll need, follow the manufacturer's installation instructions exactly, especially when it comes to fastener torques. The hitch will subjected to a lot of stress and good hitches come with hardened bolts. Never substitute an inferior bolt for a hardened bolt.

Wiring

Wiring the car for towing is fairly easy. There are a number of good wiring kits available and these should be used, rather than trying to design your own. All trailers will need brake lights and turn signals as well as tail lights and side marker lights. Most states require extra marker lights for overwide trailers. Also, most states have recently required back-up lights for trailers, and most trailer manufacturers have been building trailers with back-up lights for several years.

Additionally, some Class I, most Class II and just about all Class III trailers will have electric brakes.

Add to this number an accessories wire, to operate trailer internal equipment or to charge the trailer's battery, and you can have as many as seven wires in the harness.

Determine the equipment on your trailer and buy the wiring kit necessary. The kit will contain all the wires needed, plus a plug adapter set which included the female plug, mounted on the bumper or hitch, and the male plug, wired into, or plugged into the trailer harness.

When installing the kit, follow the manufacturer's instructions. The color coding of the wires is standard throughout the industry.

One point to note: some domestic vehicles, and most imported vehicles, have separate turn signals. On most domestic vehicles, the brake lights and rear turn signals operate with the same bulb. For those vehicles with separate turn signals, you can purchase an isolation unit so that the brake lights won't blink whenever the turn signals are operated, or, you can go to your local electronics supply house and buy four diodes to wire in series with the brake and turn signal bulbs. Diodes will isolate the brake and turn signals. The choice is yours. The isolation units are simple and quick to install, but far more expensive than the diodes. The diodes, however, require more work to install properly, since they require the cutting of each bulb's wire and soldering in place of the diode.

One, final point, the best kits are those with a spring loaded cover on the vehicle mounted socket. This cover prevent dirt and moisture from corroding the terminals. Never let the vehicle socket hang loosely; always mount it securely to the bumper or hitch.

PUSHING and TOWING

Pushing is not recommended for your Volvo as possible mismatching of bumper heights, especially over undulating road surfaces, may result in rear-end body damage.

Any Volvo may be towed, however, by attaching a tow line to the towing loop located beneath the vehicle on the front axle member. Note that the front tow loop may be hidden behind a swing down panel in the front spoiler (below the bumper) on some models. The panel is easily opened with a small screwdriver. Never attach a tow line to the bumper.

✳✳WARNING

When towing the vehicle, the steering must be unlocked. Remember that the power assists for steering and brakes are inoperative when the engine is off. The brake and steering systems will still operate, but will require 3-4 times the normal effort.

If the vehicle is equipped with an automatic transmission, special precautions must be taken. The vehicle must be towed with the selector lever in the neutral (N) position. If the fluid level is correct in the transmission, the vehicle may be towed a maximum distance of 20 miles at maximum towing speed of 20 mph. If the transmission is faulty, or if it is necessary to tow the vehicle for a distance greater than 20 miles, the driveshaft must be disconnected, or the vehicle must be towed with the rear wheels raised. Failure to observe these precautions may result in damage to the automatic transmission.

If your vehicle is equipped with a manual transmission and fails to start, it may be push-started. Switch the ignition "on" and depress the clutch. Place the transmission in third gear and gradually release the clutch as the vehicle picks up speed. Once the engine fires, depress the clutch pedal and feather the gas.

Vehicles with automatic transmission MAY NOT be started by towing. If the battery is dead, the vehicle may be started with the use of jumper cables. See the following section on "Jump Starting".

Tow Trucks

If it becomes necessary to tow your Volvo, it is recommended that the vehicle ONLY be towed by wheel-lift equipment or transported on a flatbed.

JACKING

When raising the vehicle with a floor jack, position the jack under the crossmember at the front of the vehicle or under the differential case of the rear axle at the rear. When jacking at the front of the vehicle, do not position the jack under the gravel shield or the engine oil pan or you will damage these components.

NEVER crawl under a car supported only by a floor jack: use support stands. Do not position the support stands under lower control arms or other slanted surfaces as they might slip and allow the vehicle to fall. The support stands can be placed beneath the rear axle tubes at the rear of the vehicle and beneath the reinforced areas of the rocker panels or front frame members. The vehicle's weight should push vertically (downward) on the stands; the stands should be on a level and solid base.

✳✳CAUTION

Never use the tire changing jack to support the vehicle when working under it.

MAINTENANCE SERVICE SCHEDULE

	10	20	30	40	50	60	70	80	90	100	Op nr.	
miles x 1000												
km x 1000	16	32	48	64	80	96	112	128	144	160		
Months	12	24	36	48	60	72	84	96	108	120		Comments
Shift control, automatic transmission – check/adjust	X	X	X	X	X	X	X	X	X	X		Check when driving into shop.
Parking brake – check/adjust	X	X	X	X	X	X	X	X	X	X		Check when driving into shop.
Lighting, controls – check	X	X	X	X	X	X	X	X	X	X		
Windshield wiper/washer – check/adjust	X	X	X	X	X	X	X	X	X	X		
Kickdown cable – check/adjust	X	X	X	X	X	X	X	X	X	X		Not AW30-40 (960).
PCV – replace flame guard, clean nipple and hoses						X		X		X		
Engine – check for leaks	X	X	X	X	X	X	X	X	X	X		From above.
Lift vehicle to permit inspection from below.												
Engine/transmission – check for leaks	X	X	X	X	X	X	X	X	X	X		From below. In case of leak, check fluid level.
Drain engine oil (fill: D4), **replace oil filter**	X	X	X	X	X	X	X	X	X	X		

IMPORTANT!

Turbo models: Oil and oil filter to be replaced every 5,000 miles = 8,000 km.
960, engine B6304F: Extra oil and oil filter replacement at first 5,000 miles = 8,000 km

	10	20	30	40	50	60	70	80	90	100	Op nr.	Comments
Automatic transmission – drain fluid (fill: D5)		X		X		X		X		X		Not AW30-40 (960) (no oil change required).
Clutch negative play – check/adjust	X	X	X	X	X	X	X	X	X	X		240 only.
Tires – check	X	X	X	X	X	X	X	X	X	X		Check for damage and wear.
Brake pads – check	X	X	X	X	X	X	X	X	X	X		Minimum lining thickness, front 0.12"= 3 mm, rear 0.08"=2 mm. Check brake disc thickness when replacing brake pads.
Brake, hoses and pipes – check for damage/leaks	X	X	X	X	X	X	X	X	X	X		
Fuel, hoses and pipes – check for damage/leaks	X	X	X	X	X	X	X	X	X	X		
Fuel filter – replace						X						
Rear axle – check for leaks/fluid level	X	X	X	X	X	X	X	X	X	X		Check level in case of leakage.
Exhaust system – check condition/leaks/ suspension	X	X	X	X	X	X	X	X	X	X		

84281036

MAINTENANCE SERVICE SCHEDULE

	miles x 1000	10	20	30	40	50	60	70	80	90	100	Op nr.	Comments
	km x 1000	16	32	48	64	80	96	112	128	144	160		
	Months	12	24	36	48	60	72	84	96	108	120		
Lift front end so wheels and suspension hang free													
Front suspension, – retorque		X											
– check			X	X	X	X	X	X	X	X			
Wheel bearing play *240:* – check			X	X	X	X	X	X	X	X			
Steering gear, steering gear play and effort, front shock absorbers, control arm bushings, struts, ball joints, steering rod ends (tie-rod ends), stabilizer bar, links *240:* – check		X	X	X	X	X	X	X	X	X	X		
Steering gear *740/940/960:* – check			X		X		X		X		X		
Wheel bearing play, steering gear play and effort, steering rod ends (tie-rod ends), stabilizer bar and links, ball joints *740/940/960:* – check			X			X			X				
Control arm bushings, front shock absorbers *740/940/960:* – retorque			X										
– check					X		X		X		X		
Propeller shaft: support bearings – check for wear			X			X			X				
Propeller shaft: u-joints – check for wear		X	X	X	X	X	X	X	X	X	X		
Rear suspension – retorque		X											
– check			X	X	X	X	X	X	X	X			
Rear shock absorbers *240:* – check		X	X	X	X	X	X	X	X	X	X		
740/940/960: – check			X		X		X		X		X		
Corrosion protection, paint work – check			X		X		X		X		X		Limited check, does not substitute Corrosion Inspection of 18-24 and 48-54 months.

84281037

MAINTENANCE SERVICE SCHEDULE

miles x 1000	10	20	30	40	50	60	70	80	90	100	Comments
km x 1000	16	32	48	64	80	96	112	128	144	160	
Months	12	24	36	48	60	72	84	96	108	120	
Lower vehicle to ground											
Air filter cartridge – replace			X			X			X		
Spark plugs – replace			X			X			X		
Valve clearance – check/adjust			X			X			X		Not engines with 4 valves per cylinder. First service at 30,000 miles = 48,000 km, thereafter every 40,000 miles = 64,000 km.
Fill engine oil	X	X	X	X	X	X	X	X	X	X	See "Specifications" in this manual.
Automatic transmission fluid – fill		X		X		X		X		X	Except 960 models.
Fluid levels – check/adjust	X	X	X	X	X	X	X	X	X	X	Check levels of coolant, brake fluid, power steering fluid, washer fluid.
– cooling system pressure test	X	X	X	X	X	X	X	X	X	X	
Battery – check fluid level and clamping, state of charge	X	X	X	X	X	X	X	X	X	X	
Drive belts, except B6304F – check/adjust tension			X			X			X		
Timing gear belt, B230F, B230F-Turbo – replace				X						X	Adjust timing gear belt at first 5,000 miles = 8,000 km for B230F-Turbo engines and at 50,000 miles = 80,000 intervals thereafter.
– readjust	X					X					
Timing gear belt, B234F – replace				X						X	
Timing gear belt, B6304F – replace			X			X			X		Replacing at first 30,000 miles = 48,000 km is recommended by Volvo and free of charge for customer.
Auxiliary drive belts B6304F – replace						X					
EGR system – check/clean						X		X		X	First check at 60,000 miles = 96,000 km, thereafter every 20,000 miles = 32,000 km.
Doors, engine hood – lubricate hinges and hood latch	X	X	X	X	X	X	X	X	X	X	Also lubricate door stops, striker plates and locks.
Power antenna – clean	X	X	X	X	X	X	X	X	X	X	Recommended procedure at each service.
Brake fluid – replace			X			X			X		Minimum time intervals: every second year.
Reset service indicator	X	X	X	X	X	X	X	X	X	X	

84281038

CAPACITIES

Year	Model	Engine ID/VIN	Engine Displacement Liters (cc)	Engine Crankcase with Filter (qts.)	Transmission (pts.)			Transfer case (pts.)	Drive Axle (pts.)	Fuel Tank (gal.)	Cooling System (qts.)
					4-Spd	5-Spd	Auto.				
1990	240	B-230F	2.3 (2316)	4.0	—	3.2	15.6③	—	②	15.8	10.0
	240DL	B-230F	2.3 (2316)	4.0	—	3.2	15.6③	—	②	15.8	10.0
	740	B-230F	2.3 (2316)	4.0	—	3.2	15.6③	—	②	15.8	10.0
	740GL	B-230F	2.3 (2316)	4.0	—	3.2	15.6③	—	②	15.8	10.0
	740GLE	B-234F	2.3 (2316)	4.0	4.8	—	15.6③	—	②	15.8	10.0
	740 Turbo	B-230FT	2.3 (2316)	4.0④	4.8	—	15.6③	—	②	15.8	10.0
	760GLE	B-280F	2.8 (2849)	6.0	—	—	15.6③	—	②	21.0	10.5
	760 Turbo	B-230FT	2.3 (2316)	4.0④	—	—	15.6③	—	②	①	10.0
	780	B-280F	2.8 (2849)	6.0	—	—	15.6③	—	②	21.0	10.5
	780 Turbo	B-230FT	2.3 (2316)	4.0④	—	—	15.6③	—	②	21.0	10.5
1991	240	B-230F	2.3 (2316)	4.0	—	3.2	15.6③	—	②	15.8	10.0
	740	B-230F	2.3 (2316)	4.0	—	3.2	15.6③	—	②	15.8	10.0
	740 Turbo	B-230FT	2.3 (2316)	4.0④	4.8	—	15.6③	—	②	15.8	10.0
	940GLE	B-230	2.3 (2316)	4.0	—	—	15.6③	—	②	15.8	10.0
	940SE	B-230FT	2.3 (2316)	4.0④	—	—	15.6③	—	②	①	10.0
	940 Turbo	B-230FT	2.3 (2316)	4.0④	—	—	15.6③	—	②	15.8	10.0
	Coupe	B-230FT	2.3 (2316)	4.0④	—	—	15.6③	—	②	21.0	10.5
1992	240	B-230F	2.3 (2316)	4.0	—	3.2	15.6③	—	②	15.8	10.0
	240GL	B-230F	2.3 (2316)	4.0	—	3.2	15.6③	—	②	15.8	10.0
	740	B-230F	2.3 (2316)	4.0	—	—	15.6③	—	②	15.8	10.0
	740 Turbo	B-230FT	2.3 (2316)	4.0④	—	—	15.6③	—	②	15.8	10.0
	940GL	B-230	2.3 (2316)	4.0	—	—	15.6③	—	②	15.8	10.0
	940 Turbo	B-230FT	2.3 (2316)	4.0④	—	—	15.6③	—	②	15.8	10.0
	960	B-6304F	2.9 (2922)	6.0	—	—	15.6③	—	②	①	11.3
1993	240	B-230F	2.3 (2316)	4.0	—	3.2	15.6③	—	②	15.8	10.0
	940	B-230	2.3 (2316)	4.0	—	—	15.6③	—	②	19.8	10.0
	940 Turbo	B-230FT	2.3 (2316)	4.0④	—	—	15.6③	—	②	19.8	10.0
	960	B-6304F	2.9 (2922)	6.0	—	—	15.6③	—	②	①	11.3

NA—Not available

① 4-door—21.0
   5-door—15.8

② 1030 axle—2.8
   1031 axle—3.4

③ Total fluid capacity cannot be drained. Approx. 3.6 qt = 3.4 liter can be drained, the rest being stored in torque converter and control systems.

   When checking fluid level, vehicle should be on level ground in PARK position with engine idling. If topping up is necessary, fill through dipstick tube.

   Dipstick has graduations for hot and cold transmission fluid. When checking fluid level use a clean rag that will not leave lint.

④ On turbocharged engines, add 0.7 US qts. if cooler is drained.

84281039

VEHICLE IDENTIFICATION CHART

It is important for servicing and ordering parts to be certain of the vehicle and engine identification. The VIN (vehicle identification number) is a 17 digit number visible through the windshield on the driver's side of the dash and contains the vehicle and engine identification codes. The tenth digit indicates model year and the sixth and seventh digits indicate engine code. It can be interpreted as follows:

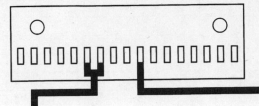

Engine Code							Model Year	
Code	Liters	Cu. In. (cc)	Cyl.	Fuel Sys.	Eng. Mfg.		Code	Year
69	2.8	175 (2849)	6	LH2.2	Volvo		L	1990
82	2.3	144 (2316)	4	LH3.1	Volvo		M	1991
87	2.3	144 (2316)	4	LH2.4	Volvo		N	1992
88	2.3	144 (2316)	4	LH2.4	Volvo		P	1993
89	2.3	144 (2316)	4	LH2.4	Volvo			
95	2.9	181 (2922)	6	Motronic 1.8	Volvo			

69 = B280F
82 = B230F (LH3.1)
87 = B230F—Turbocharged
88 = B230F (LH2.4)
89 = B234F
95 = B6304F with catalytic converter
LH—Bosch LH Fuel Injection

84281040

ENGINE IDENTIFICATION

Year	Model	Engine Displacement Liters (cc)	Engine Series (ID/VIN)	Fuel System	No. of Cylinders	Engine Type
1990	240	2.3 (2316)	B-230F	LH2.4	4	SOHC
	240DL	2.3 (2316)	B-230F	⑧	4	SOHC
	740	2.3 (2316)	B-230F	⑨	4	SOHC
	740GL	2.3 (2316)	B-230F	⑨	4	SOHC
	740GLE	2.3 (2316)	B-234F	LH2.4	4	DOHC①
	740 Turbo	2.3 (2316)	B-230FT②	LH2.4	4	SOHC
	760GLE	2.8 (2849)	B-280F	LH2.2	6	SOHC
	760 Turbo	2.3 (2316)	B-230FT②	LH2.4	4	SOHC
	780	2.8 (2849)	B-280F	LH2.2	6	SOHC
	780 Turbo	2.3 (2316)	B-230FT②	LH2.4	4	SOHC
1991	240	2.3 (2316)	B-230F	⑧	4	SOHC
	740	2.3 (2316)	B-230F	Regina	4	SOHC
	740GL	2.3 (2316)	B-230F	Regina	4	SOHC
	740 Turbo	2.3 (2316)	B-230FT②	LH2.4	4	SOHC
	940GLE	2.3 (2316)	B-234F	LH2.4	4	DOHC①
	940SE	2.3 (2316)	B-230FT②	LH2.4	4	SOHC
	940 Turbo	2.3 (2316)	B-230FT②	LH2.4	4	SOHC
	Coupe	2.3 (2316)	B-230FT②	LH2.4	4	SOHC
1992	240	2.3 (2316)	B-230F	⑤	4	SOHC
	240GL	2.3 (2316)	B-230F	⑥	4	SOHC
	740	2.3 (2316)	B-230F	⑦	4	SOHC
	740 Turbo	2.3 (2316)	B-230FT②	LH2.4	4	SOHC
	940GL	2.3 (2316)	B-230F	Regina	4	SOHC
	940 Turbo	2.3 (2316)	B-230FT②	LH2.4	4	SOHC
	960	2.9 (2922)	B-6304F④	Motronic 1.8	6	DOHC③
1993	240	2.3 (2316)	B-230F	⑤	4	SOHC
	940	2.3 (2316)	B-230F	Regina	4	SOHC
	940 Turbo	2.3 (2316)	B-230FT②	LH2.4	4	SOHC
	960	2.9 (2922)	B-6304F④	Motronic 1.8	6	DOHC③

LH—Bosch LH Fuel Injection
DOHC—Double Overhead Camshaft
SOHC—Single Overhead Camshaft
① 16 valve
② Turbocharged engine
③ 24 valve
④ B6304F—Fuel Injected w/Catalytic Converter
  B6304G—Fuel Injected w/o Catalytic Converter
⑤ Vehicle Identification Code (VIC)
    244-8201-131 LH 3.1
    244-8801-171 LH 2.4
⑥ Vehicle Identification Code (VIC)
    244-8202-231 LH 3.1
    244-8802-271 LH 2.4
⑦ With EGR—LH 2.4
  W/o EGR—Regina
⑧ USA Federal and Canada, without EGR, fuel
  system LH2.4:
    Manual transmission—1289368
    Automatic transmission—1289369
  USA Federal, without EGR, fuel system LH3.1:
    Manual transmission—1289338
⑨ California—LH2.4
  Except California—Regina

84281041

2

ENGINE PERFORMANCE AND TUNE-UP

TUNE-UP PROCEDURES

Neither tune-up nor troubleshooting can be considered independently, since each has a direct bearing on the other. An engine tune-up is a service designed to restore the maximum power, performance, economy and reliability in an engine and, at the same time, assure the owner of efficiency and trouble-free performance. Engine tune-up becomes increasingly important each year, to insure that pollutant levels are in compliance with federal emissions standards.

It is advisable to follow a definite and thorough tune-up procedure. Tune-up consists of 3 separate steps:

• Analysis — the process of determining whether normal wear is responsible for performance loss, and whether the parts require replacement or service.

• Parts Replacement — the removal of worn or failed mechanical parts.

• Service/Adjustment — during which parts may be cleaned, reset, or tightened and factory specifications are maintained or adjusted.

The extent of an engine tune-up is usually determined by the length of time since the previous service, although the type of driving and the general mechanical condition of the engine must be considered. Specific maintenance should also be performed at regular intervals, depending on operating conditions.

Troubleshooting is a logical sequence of procedures designed to lead you to the particular cause of trouble. Service usually comprises 2 areas, diagnosis and repair. While the apparent cause of trouble, in many cases, is worn or damaged parts, performance problems are less obvious. The first job is to locate the problem and cause. Once the problem has been isolated, refer to the appropriate section for repair, removal or adjustment procedures.

It is advisable to read the entire Section before beginning a tune-up, although those who are more familiar with tune-up procedures may wish to go directly to the instructions.

Spark Plugs

▶ See Figures 1, 2 and 3

Spark plugs are used to ignite the air and fuel mixture in the cylinders as the piston approaches Top Dead Center (TDC) on its compression stroke. The controlled explosion that results forces the piston down, turning the crankshaft and the rest of the drive train.

Volvo recommends that spark plugs be changed every 30,000 miles (48,000 km). Under severe driving conditions, those intervals should be more frequent. Severe driving conditions are:

1. Extended periods of idling or low speed operation, such as off-road or door-to-door delivery.

2. Driving short distances — less than 10 miles (16 km) — when the average temperature is below 10°F (-12°C) for 60 days or more.

3. Vehicle frequently operated in excessive dusty conditions.

Although Volvo recommends replacing the plugs at 30,000 miles intervals, it should be noted that this is a maximum interval. For some owners, 30,000 miles represents more than

three years of driving. A prudent owner will remove and check or replace the plugs more frequently. Even if they are not heavily worn, a new set will improve performance.

When you remove the spark plugs, check their condition. They are a good indicator of the engine's operating conditions.

A small deposit of light tan or gray material on a spark plug that has been used for any period of time is considered normal. Any other color, or abnormal amounts of deposit, indicate that there is something amiss in the engine. There are several reasons why a spark plug would foul and you can determine the fault just by observing the plug.

SPARK PLUG HEAT RANGE

Spark plug heat range is the ability of the plug to dissipate heat. The longer the insulator (or the farther it extends into the engine), the hotter the plug will operate; the shorter the insulator the cooler it will operate. A plug that absorbs little heat and remains too cool will quickly accumulate deposits of oil and carbon since it is not hot enough to burn them off. This leads to plug fouling and consequently to misfiring. A plug that absorbs too much heat will have no deposits, but, due to the excessive heat, the electrodes will burn away quickly and in some instances, preignition may result. Preignition takes place when plug tips get so hot that they glow sufficiently to ignite the fuel/air mixture before the actual spark occurs. This early ignition will usually cause a pinging during low speeds and heavy loads.

The general rule of thumb of choosing the correct heat range when picking a spark plug is as follow:

Cooler plug — if most of your driving is long distance, high speed travel

Hotter plug — if most of your driving involves short distances or heavy stop and go traffic.

Original equipment plugs can be termed 'Compromise Plugs', but most driver's never have the need for changing their plugs from the factory recommended heat range.

REMOVAL & INSTALLATION

▶ See Figures 4 and 5

✳✳WARNING

Remove and install spark plugs only when the engine is cold. This is particularly important on engines with aluminum heads.

1. Remove each spark plug wire by grasping its rubber boot at the end and twisting slightly to free the wire from the plug.

2. Using a spark plug socket, turn the plugs counterclockwise to remove them. Do not allow any foreign matter to enter the cylinders through the spark plugs holes.

3. Before installing the plugs, check the plug gap with a wire type gauge. With the ground electrode positioned parallel to the center electrode, the specified wire gauge must pass

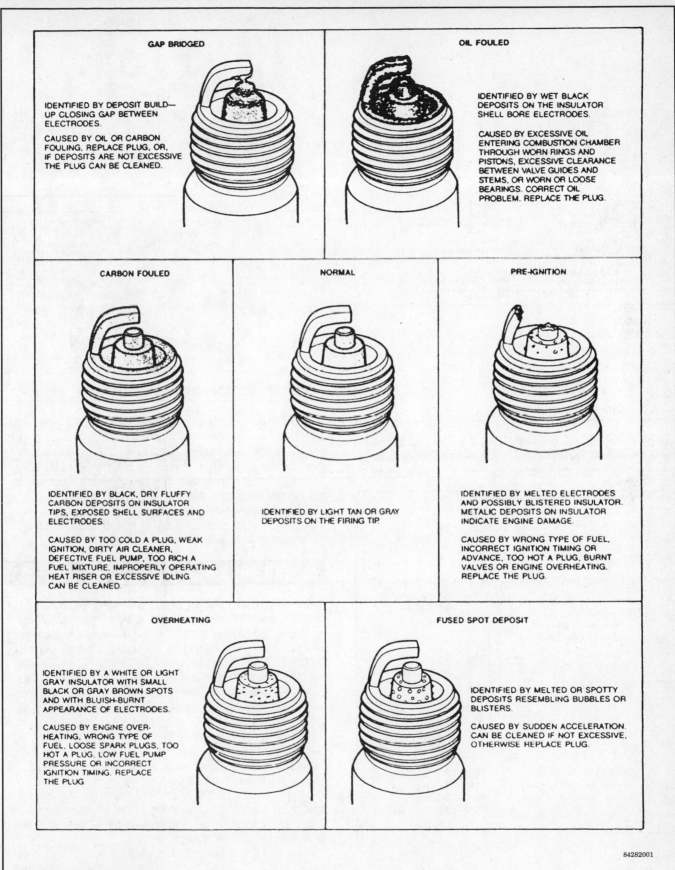

GAP BRIDGED

IDENTIFIED BY DEPOSIT BUILD—UP CLOSING GAP BETWEEN ELECTRODES.

CAUSED BY OIL OR CARBON FOULING, REPLACE PLUG, OR, IF DEPOSITS ARE NOT EXCESSIVE THE PLUG CAN BE CLEANED.

OIL FOULED

IDENTIFIED BY WET BLACK DEPOSITS ON THE INSULATOR SHELL BORE ELECTRODES.

CAUSED BY EXCESSIVE OIL ENTERING COMBUSTION CHAMBER THROUGH WORN RINGS AND PISTONS, EXCESSIVE CLEARANCE BETWEEN VALVE GUIDES AND STEMS, OR WORN OR LOOSE BEARINGS. CORRECT OIL PROBLEM. REPLACE THE PLUG.

CARBON FOULED

IDENTIFIED BY BLACK, DRY FLUFFY CARBON DEPOSITS ON INSULATOR TIPS, EXPOSED SHELL SURFACES AND ELECTRODES.

CAUSED BY TOO COLD A PLUG, WEAK IGNITION, DIRTY AIR CLEANER, DEFECTIVE FUEL PUMP, TOO RICH A FUEL MIXTURE, IMPROPERLY OPERATING HEAT RISER OR EXCESSIVE IDLING. CAN BE CLEANED.

NORMAL

IDENTIFIED BY LIGHT TAN OR GRAY DEPOSITS ON THE FIRING TIP.

PRE-IGNITION

IDENTIFIED BY MELTED ELECTRODES AND POSSIBLY BLISTERED INSULATOR. METALIC DEPOSITS ON INSULATOR INDICATE ENGINE DAMAGE.

CAUSED BY WRONG TYPE OF FUEL, INCORRECT IGNITION TIMING OR ADVANCE, TOO HOT A PLUG, BURNT VALVES OR ENGINE OVERHEATING. REPLACE THE PLUG.

OVERHEATING

IDENTIFIED BY A WHITE OR LIGHT GRAY INSULATOR WITH SMALL BLACK OR GRAY BROWN SPOTS AND WITH BLUISH-BURNT APPEARANCE OF ELECTRODES.

CAUSED BY ENGINE OVER-HEATING, WRONG TYPE OF FUEL, LOOSE SPARK PLUGS, TOO HOT A PLUG, LOW FUEL PUMP PRESSURE OR INCORRECT IGNITION TIMING. REPLACE THE PLUG

FUSED SPOT DEPOSIT

IDENTIFIED BY MELTED OR SPOTTY DEPOSITS RESEMBLING BUBBLES OR BLISTERS.

CAUSED BY SUDDEN ACCELERATION. CAN BE CLEANED IF NOT EXCESSIVE, OTHERWISE REPLACE PLUG.

84282001

Fig. 1 Spark plug diagnosis

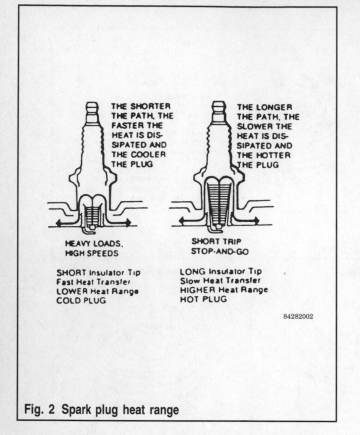

THE SHORTER THE PATH, THE FASTER THE HEAT IS DISSIPATED AND THE COOLER THE PLUG

THE LONGER THE PATH, THE SLOWER THE HEAT IS DISSIPATED AND THE HOTTER THE PLUG

HEAVY LOADS, HIGH SPEEDS

SHORT Insulator Tip
Fast Heat Transfer
LOWER Heat Range
COLD PLUG

SHORT TRIP STOP-AND-GO

LONG Insulator Tip
Slow Heat Transfer
HIGHER Heat Range
HOT PLUG

84282002

Fig. 2 Spark plug heat range

through the opening with a slight drag. If the air gap between the two electrodes is not correct, the ground electrode must be bent to bring it to specifications.

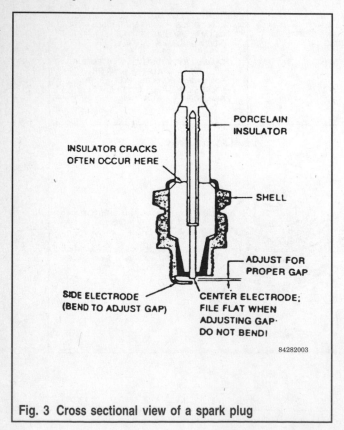

PORCELAIN INSULATOR

INSULATOR CRACKS OFTEN OCCUR HERE

SHELL

ADJUST FOR PROPER GAP

SIDE ELECTRODE (BEND TO ADJUST GAP)

CENTER ELECTRODE: FILE FLAT WHEN ADJUSTING GAP DO NOT BEND!

84282003

Fig. 3 Cross sectional view of a spark plug

84282004

Fig. 4 Removing spark plug wires

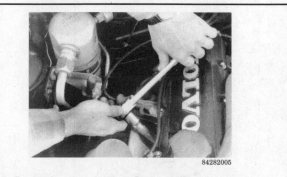

84282005

Fig. 5 Removing spark plug from engine

4. After the plugs are correctly gapped, inserted them into their holes, being careful not to crossthread. After each plug is hand threaded several turns, it may be tightened and torque to specifications: DO NOT OVER TIGHTEN SPARK PLUGS. Over Tightening a spark plug can be very costly. Damage to the cylinder head may result.

5. Install each spark plug wire on its respective plug, making sure that each spark plug end is making good metal-to-metal contact in its wire socket.

Spark Plug Wires

Visually inspect the spark plug cables for burns, cuts, or breaks in the insulation. Check the spark plug boots and the nipples on the distributor cap and coil. Replace any damaged wiring. If no physical damage is obvious, the wires can be checked with an ohmmeter for excessive resistance. Remove the distributor cap and leave the wires connected to the cap. Connect one lead of the ohmmeter to the corresponding electrode inside the cap and the other lead to the spark plug terminal. Replace any wire which shows over 35,000.

Test the coil wire by connecting the ohmmeter between the center contact in the cap and the other on the opposite end of the coil wire. If the resistance is higher than 15,000 ohms, replace the cable. It should be remembered that wire resistance is a function of length, and that the longer the cable, the greater the resistance. Thus, if the cables on your vehicle are longer than the factory originals, resistance will be higher and quite possibly outside of these limits.

When installing a new set of spark plug cables, replace the cables one at a time so there will be no mixup. Start by replacing the longest cable first. Install the boot firmly over the spark plug. Route the wire exactly the same as the original.

Insert the nipple firmly into the tower on the distributor cap. Repeat the process for each cable.

GASOLINE ENGINE TUNE-UP SPECIFICATIONS

Year	Engine ID/VIN	Engine Displacement Liters (cc)	Spark Plugs Gap (in.)	Ignition Timing (deg.) MT	Ignition Timing (deg.) AT	Fuel Pump (psi)	Idle Speed (rpm) MT	Idle Speed (rpm) AT	Valve Clearance In.	Valve Clearance Ex.
1990	B-230F	2.3 (2316)	0.028	12B②	12B②	43	775	775	0.016①	0.016①
	B-230FT	2.3 (2316)	0.028–0.032	12B	12B	43	750	750	0.016–0.018	0.016–0.018
	B-234F	2.3 (2316)	0.028	15B	15B	42	850	850	—	—
	B-280F	2.8 (2849)	0.024–0.028	—	16B	36	—	750	0.006–0.008	0.012–0.014
1991	B-230F	2.3 (2316)	0.028	12B②	12B②	43	775	775	0.016①	0.016①
	B-230FT	2.3 (2316)	0.028–0.032	12B	12B	43	750	750	0.016–0.018	0.016–0.018
	B-234F	2.3 (2316)	0.028	15B	15B	42	—	850	—	—
1992	B-230F	2.3 (2316)	0.028	—	12B②	43	750③	775	0.014–0.018	0.014–0.018
	B-230FT	2.3 (2316)	0.028–0.032	—	12B	43	—	775	0.014–0.018	0.014–0.018
	B-6304F	2.9 (2922)	0.024–0.028	—	5±2	43	—	700–800	Hyd.	Hyd.
1993	B-230F	2.3 (2316)	0.028	—	12B②	43	750③	775	0.014–0.018	0.014–0.018
	B-230FT	2.3 (2316)	0.028–0.032	—	12B	43	—	775	0.014–0.018	0.014–0.018
	B-6304F	2.9 (2922)	0.024–0.028	—	5±2	43	—	700–800	Hyd.	Hyd.

NOTE: The lowest cylinder pressure should be within 75% of the highest cylinder pressure reading. For example, if the highest cylinder is 134 psi, the lowest should be 101. Engine should be at normal operating temperature with throttle valve in the wide open position.
The underhood specifications sticker often reflects tune-up specification changes in production. Sticker figures must be used if they disagree with those in this chart.
Hyd.—Hydraulic
B—Before Top Dead Center
① Engine warm
② Rex 1: 10°/775
③ Volvo 240

84282061

FIRING ORDERS

▶ See Figures 6, 7 and 8

➡ To avoid confusion, remove and tag the wires one at a time, during replacement.

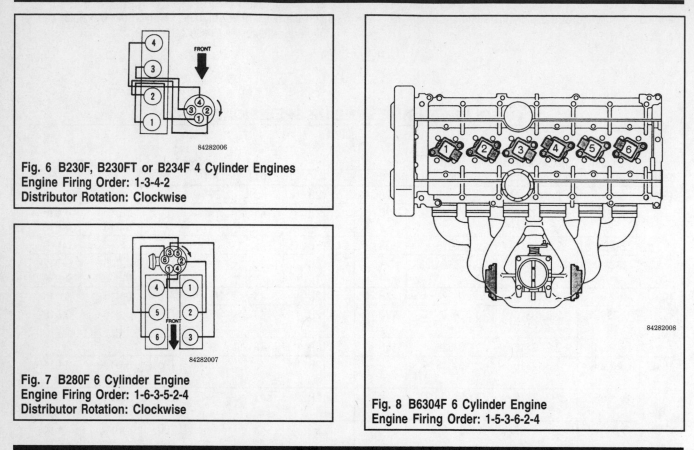

Fig. 6 B230F, B230FT or B234F 4 Cylinder Engines
Engine Firing Order: 1-3-4-2
Distributor Rotation: Clockwise

Fig. 7 B280F 6 Cylinder Engine
Engine Firing Order: 1-6-3-5-2-4
Distributor Rotation: Clockwise

Fig. 8 B6304F 6 Cylinder Engine
Engine Firing Order: 1-5-3-6-2-4

VOLVO EZK AND REX 1 IGNITION SYSTEMS

Description and Operation

▶ See Figures 9 and 10

Volvo uses several different ignition systems. The designation for these ignition systems are: EZ115K and EZ116K. In addition, a few models use the Bendix Regina engine management system and this ignition system is designated REX-1. The 960 model is equipped with the Bosch Motronic 1.8 engine management and ignition system.

The EZ115K, EZ116K and REX 1 ignition systems, used on 240, 700 and 940 models are like most engine management systems currently in use. The ignition and fuel control functions are closely integrated. Sensors feed information to an on-board computer which makes necessary adjustments. Some self-diagnostic capabilities are built into the computer to help troubleshooting.

Impulse Sensor

▶ See Figure 11

The Impulse Sensor, sometimes called an RPM and Crankshaft Position Sensor, is used to determine engine speed and Top Dead Center (TDC). This ensures precise ignition timing. The sensor is located at the rear of the engine block, above the flywheel. Engine speed is transmitted to the fuel control unit. The engine will not start without this signal.

EZ116K

On the flywheel, there are 60 markings for the impulse sensor, 58 which are drilled holes to provide information to the ignition control unit. There are no holes at 2 of the markings. These are 90 degrees Before Top Dead Center (BTDC), for cylinders No. 1 and No. 4. Ignition timing is based on these markings and other information such as engine load and temperature. This means that ignition timing can be controlled and that there is no need for ignition setting to be adjusted.

REX 1

On the flywheel, there are 44 markings for the impulse sensor, 40 which are drilled holes to provide information to the ignition control unit. There are no holes at 2 of the markings. These are 90 degrees Before Top Dead Center (BTDC), for cylinders No. 1 and No. 4. Ignition timing is based on these markings and other information such as engine load and temperature. This means that ignition timing can be controlled and that there is no need for ignition setting to be adjusted.

Knock Sensor

▶ See Figure 12

EZ116K

If knocking occurs, the knock sensor corrects ignition timing for each individual cylinder by gradually retarding the ignition for each cylinder that is knocking. If retarding is insufficient, a signal goes to the fuel system control unit, which enriches the

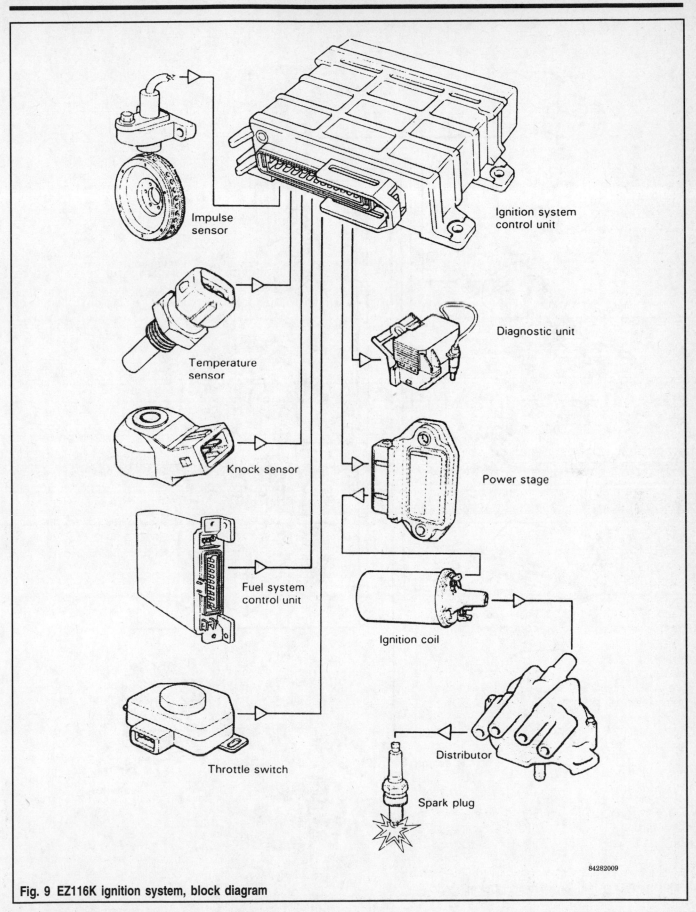

Impulse sensor

Ignition system control unit

Temperature sensor

Diagnostic unit

Knock sensor

Power stage

Fuel system control unit

Ignition coil

Throttle switch

Distributor

Spark plug

84282009

Fig. 9 EZ116K ignition system, block diagram

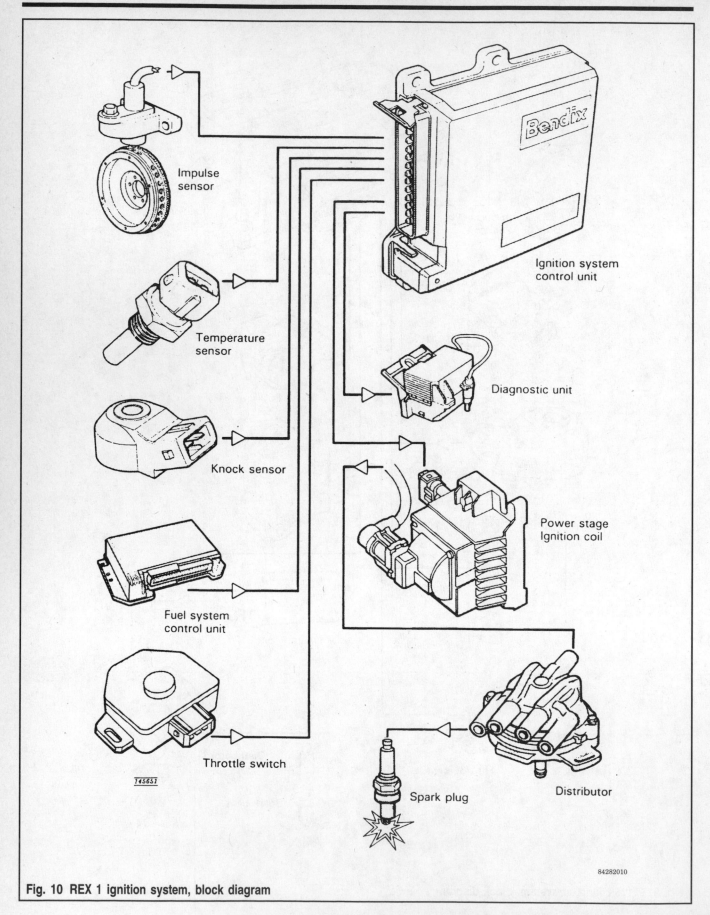

Impulse sensor

Temperature sensor

Knock sensor

Fuel system control unit

Throttle switch

Ignition system control unit

Diagnostic unit

Power stage Ignition coil

Spark plug

Distributor

145651

84282010

Fig. 10 REX 1 ignition system, block diagram

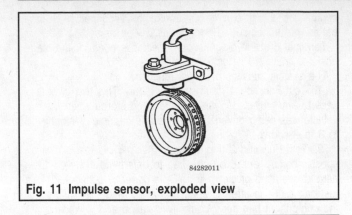

Fig. 11 Impulse sensor, exploded view

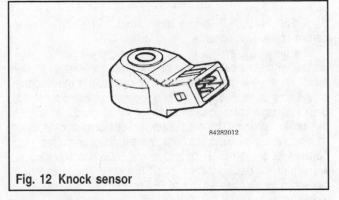

Fig. 12 Knock sensor

air/fuel mixture. This lowers the temperature and stops the knocking.

REX 1

If knocking occurs, the knock sensor corrects ignition timing for each individual cylinder by gradually retarding the ignition for each cylinder that is knocking. The REX 1 incorporates adaptive knock control. Which measures the background noise (due to bearing clearance etc.) in the engine just before firing and adjusts the reference level for knock sensing.

Power Stage

♦ **See Figure 13**

EZ116K

The power stage, also known as an ignition amplifier, receives firing signals from the control unit and acts as an electronic switch. It keeps current through the ignition coil constant regardless of battery voltage and engine speed, so that ignition

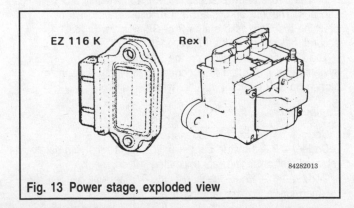

EZ 116 K   Rex I

Fig. 13 Power stage, exploded view

spark is effective. A current cut-off circuit prevents the ignition coil from overheating if the ignition switch is left in the **ON** position with the engine not running.

REX 1

The power stage on the REX 1 system is combined with the ignition coil into 1 unit.

Ignition Coil

♦ **See Figures 14 and 15**

EZ116K

The ignition coil used with this system is a special type of coil, with a low resistance primary winding, enabling it to generate very high ignition voltage even if the battery voltage is low.

REX 1

The power stage on the REX 1 system is combined with the ignition coil into a single unit (Power Stage/Ignition Coil). The power stage contains the electronic circuits that regulate the primary current of the ignition coil. When the power stage receives voltage (high control signal) from the control unit, it sends current through the primary windings of the ignition coil. When the control unit reduces this current (low control signal), the power stage cuts off the primary current of the ignition coil, creating a high voltage in the secondary windings.

The control unit compensates for any changes in the battery voltage by adjusting the dwell angle. This ensures that the ignition coil always receives a constant charge. When the engine is **OFF**, there are no signals from the impulse sensor. Under these conditions, the control unit sends a low control signal to the power stage, cutting off the current through the primary coil. This prevents the ignition coil from overheating when the ignition switch is left **ON** and the engine is not running.

Distributor

The only function of the distributor is to distribute voltage to the spark plugs. There are no advance functions built into the distributor. It is no longer possible to adjust ignition timing through the distributor.

Diagnosis and Testing

SERVICE PRECAUTIONS

- The ignition system operates with a very high output and there are hazardous voltages in the low and high voltage circuits.
- Always turn the ignition **OFF**, before separating connectors.
- Before disconnecting the control unit connector, remove fuse 1 (740), fuse 31 (760) to deactivate the ignition system.
- Never disconnect the battery while the engine is running.
- Always disconnect the battery when quick charging the battery.
- Never use a boost charger or voltage higher than 16 volts to start the engine.

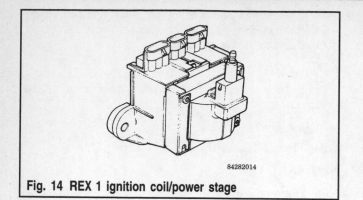

Fig. 14 REX 1 ignition coil/power stage

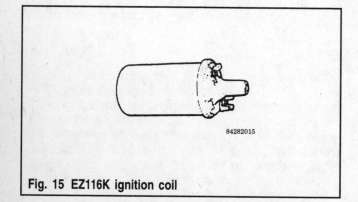

Fig. 15 EZ116K ignition coil

• When performing compression test, always disconnect terminal 1 on the ignition coil. Also disconnect the connectors from the injectors to prevent the engine from flooding.

• Always remove the control unit if the vehicle is to be stove or if welding is to be carried out. The control unit must not be exposed to temperatures above 176°F (80°C).

• Do not replace a control unit without first correcting the original fault, or the same fault may damage the new control unit.

• Do not be hasty in condemning the ECU. This system uses voltages and resistances that are very small. Examine the sensors, wiring and connectors carefully. The sensors operate in more harsh conditions than the ECU which is generally in a more protected location.

• Check all ground connections before condemning the ECU.

• Use care when working around vehicles equipped with Supplementary Restraint System (SRS), often known as 'air bags.' Vehicles equipped with SRS are generally recognized by the letters **SRS** molded into the steering wheel cover. Follow all precautions to avoid personal injury.

• A spare location in the fuse panel is used as a test terminal for SRS diagnostics. Never install a fuse in this position or connect accessories to this terminal.

SYSTEM DIAGNOSTICS

The EZ115K and EZ116K (called EZ-K) and REX 1 ignition systems, used on 240, 700 and 940 models incorporate a diagnostic feature which is built into the system control unit. The system is capable of diagnosing a certain number of faults, but not every possible fault. If power supply to the control unit is lost, control unit connector disconnected or the battery disconnected, all fault codes will be erased.

Terminal 6 of the diagnostic connector is used for the diagnosis of faults in the ignition system.

The system consists of 3 test functions:

1. Test Function 1 (fault code readout): This test gives access to any fault codes which have been stored when the vehicle was being driven. The system is capable of storing up to 3 fault codes.

2. Test Function 2 (input signal check): This test allows a specific component to be checked to determine if the component is operating properly and if it is correctly connected. This test can be used after a repair has been made, to ensure that the component has been correctly installed and is working properly.

3. Test Function 3 (output signal check): This test activates certain control components.

The diagnostic system is controlled by the diagnostic socket, which is located in the engine compartment, on the left shock tower. The diagnostic socket is common to the diagnostic systems of the fuel system and ignition system. Socket No. 6 on the diagnostic socket is used for the diagnosis of faults in the ignition system. The diagnostic socket incorporates a diode light and a button. Test functions are activated by pressing the button 1, 2 or 3 times. Fault codes are determined by the flashing of the diode light, in 3 digit numbers. The fault code digits can range between 1 and 9. The number of flashes indicates the value of the digit, which are separated by 3 second intervals.

When all the fault codes have been read and necessary repairs made, the fault codes must be erased. The fault codes must always be read with the ignition switch in the **ON** position, if not, the codes cannot be erased.

The EZ115K, EZ116K and REX 1 ignition systems incorporate active anti-knock control and ignition setting control. These 2 controls never need checking or adjustment.

READING CODES

Before any fault codes can be read from the diagnostic socket, the following conditions must be met:

1. The ignition switch must be in the **ON** position.
2. The selector cable must be installed into socket No. 6
3. The diagnostic socket button must be pressed 1 time, for at least 1 second, but not more than 3 seconds.

Every flash and pause between flashes is about half a second. The pauses between flashes is approximately 2.5-3 seconds. The ignition system test function is obtained by pressing the diagnostic button 2 or 3 times, for at least 1 second, but not more than 3 seconds.

The diagnostic unit used on the EZ116K and REX 1 ignition systems has 7 different fault codes. Its memory is capable of storing up to 3 different ignition system faults.

Engine Codes

Code 1-1-1 — No fault codes in memory.

Code 1-4-2 — Fault in control unit. Engine runs with safety-retarded ignition timing (approximately 10 degrees).

Code 1-4-3 — Knock sensor faulty. Engine runs with safety-retarded ignition timing (approximately 10 degrees).

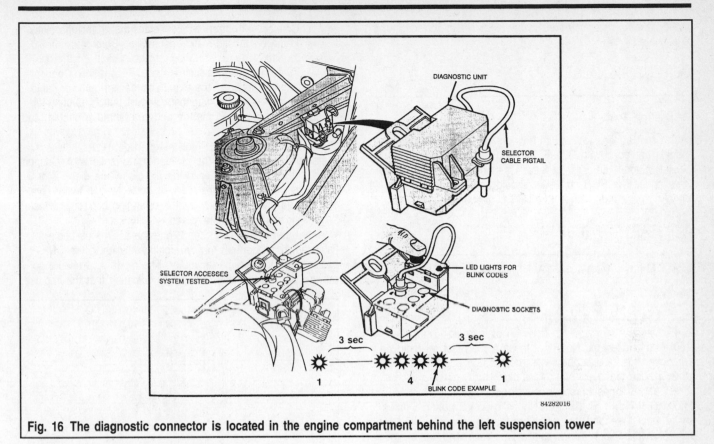

Fig. 16 The diagnostic connector is located in the engine compartment behind the left suspension tower

Code 1-4-4 — Load signal missing (from fuel system control unit). Control unit selects full-load ignition.

Code 2-1-4 — Engine speed sensor faulty.

Code 2-2-4 — Coolant temperature sensor inoperative.

Code 2-3-4 — Throttle switch for idling faulty. Engine runs with safety-retarded ignition timing (does not apply to REX 1 ignition system).

Code 3-3-4 — Throttle switch in idle position — okay (REX 1 ignition only).

Before a fault code can be read, the ignition switch must be in the **ON** position and selector cable installed into socket No. 6. Press the diagnostic socket button 1 time, for at least 1 second, but not more than 3 seconds. If fault Code 1-1-1 is flashed, it indicates that there are no fault codes in the memory. Press the button again to see if there are any more codes in the memory. If there are and a new code is flashed, the button must be pressed again.

CLEARING CODES

Erasing Fault Memory

When all fault codes have been read and the necessary repairs made, the memory must be erased. Erase the memory as follows:

1. Press the diagnostic socket button and hold for approximately 5 seconds.

2. After about 3-4 seconds, the diode light should light. When the diode light lights, press the button again and hold for approximately 5 seconds. Release the button. The diode light should go out.

3. Check that there are no codes in the memory by starting the engine and bring to normal operating temperature.

4. With the engine running, press the diagnostic socket button again. If there are no fault codes in its memory, fault Code 1-1-1 should flash.

INPUT SIGNALS

Functional Test

This test checks the throttle switch and the engine speed sensor as follows:

1. Turn the ignition switch to the **ON** position and install selector cable into socket No. 6.

2. Press the diagnostic socket button 2 times, for at least 1 second, but not more than 3 seconds. The diode light should start to flash.

3. Check the throttle switch by turning the throttle switch slightly from inside the engine compartment. The diode lamp should go out and then flash fault Code 3-3-4 which indicates proper operation of the idle switch. If no code is flashed and the diode lamp continues to flash, throttle switch is faulty.

4. After each test, the flashes of the diode lamp should return.

5. Operate the starter motor. The diode lamp should go out, then flash fault Code 1-4-1 for the engine speed sensor. If no code is flashed and the diode lamp continues to flash, the engine speed sensor is faulty.

If no fault codes are obtained and the diode lamp continues to flash, the switch or the wire are faulty since the control unit did not receive an activation signal. For this test, it does not matter whether a switch contact opens or closes, as long as it is activated.

OUTPUT SIGNALS

Regulation Test

This test applies to the EZ116K ignition system on California models equipped with B230F engine. Press the diagnostic socket button 1 time, for at least 1 second, but not more than 3 seconds. The EGR converter should operate for approximately 10 seconds. If not, the EGR converter is faulty.

NO START — NO SPARK

▶ See Figures 16, 17, 18, 19, 20, 21, 22 and 23

Testing

1. Attempt to start engine.
2. Check fuse No. 1 (model 740) or fuse No. 31 (model 760) in the fuse box. Note that these fuses must be removed whenever the ECU connector is removed or installed.
3. If fuse No. 1 (or No. 31) is okay, turn ignition switch to **ON**. Open diagnostic socket cover and install selector cable into socket No. 6. Press the diagnostic socket button 2 times, for at least 1 second, but not more than 3 seconds. The LED light should begin to flash rapidly. This command has the computer start a check of the basic system components. If the LED flashes rapidly, go on to Step 4.

  a. If the LED does not blink rapidly, there is a connection problem at the multi-pin connector at the ECU, which requires separate troubleshooting.

  b. To troubleshoot suspected ECU connector problems, turn the ignition **OFF** and locate the ECU so the ECU multi-pin connector can be accessed for inspection.

  c. On 700 models, if the diode light does not flash, remove panel from under left side of instrument panel, then disconnect connector from control unit. On 240 models, remove panels under instrument panel right side and firewall right side, then disconnect connector from control unit.

  d. Remove protective cover from control unit connector.

  e. Check to ensure that no terminal contacts have been pushed down in the connector.

  f. Connect a voltmeter between ground and terminal 5 on the control unit. Voltmeter should read approximately 12 volts. If no reading is obtained, check wire from control unit connector to terminal 30 of fuse box.

  g. Install selector cable into the underhood diagnostic box socket No. 6. Connect a voltmeter between ground terminal 1 on the control unit. Voltmeter should read approximately 12 volts. Press the diagnostic button. Voltmeter should read 0 volts.

  h. If there is no voltage at the control unit, check diagnostic socket connector. If voltmeter reads 12 volts when button is pressed, check the test connector.

  i. Test the diagnostic socket connector by connecting a voltmeter between ground and the blue wire on the diagnostic socket connector. Voltmeter should read approximately 12 volts.

  j. Connect an ohmmeter between ground and the black wire on the diagnostic socket connector. Ohmmeter should read 0 ohms.

  k. Turn the ignition switch to the **OFF** position. Connect an ohmmeter between the diagnostic socket selector cable and the pin under the diagnostic socket button. Ohmmeter should read infinity. Press the button, ohmmeter should read 0 ohms.

  l. Connect a suitable Multimeter/Diode Tester between the selector cable and the pin under the diode light. Connect the red lead of the tester to the pin below the diode light and the black lead to the selector cable lead. If tester gives a reading, then the diode light is operating correctly. If tester gives no reading, replace diagnostic socket.

4. If, after performing Step 2 and the LED does begin to flash rapidly as normal, turn the ignition switch to the **ON** position and run the starter motor. The diode light should go out and then flash test Code 1-4-1, indicating that the impulse

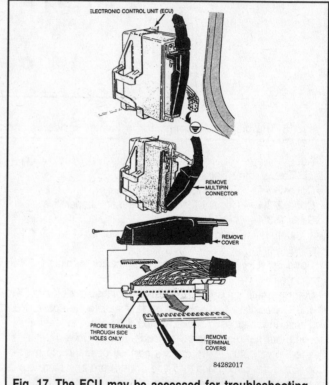

Fig. 17 The ECU may be accessed for troubleshooting. Probe cable connections from the side openings only

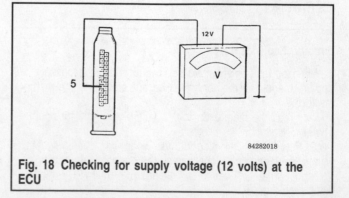

Fig. 18 Checking for supply voltage (12 volts) at the ECU

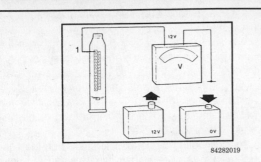

Fig. 19 Checking for supply voltage (12 volts) at the diagnostic circuit. Note pushbutton positions

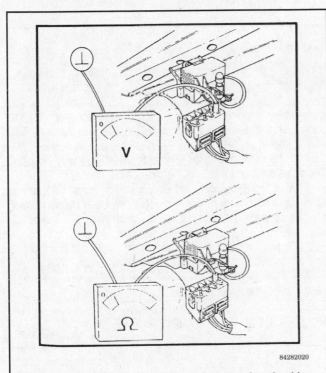

Fig. 20 Top: Testing diagnostic connector by checking for 12 volts at blue wire. Bottom: Checking for ground at black wire

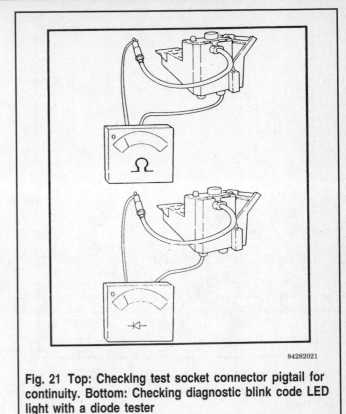

Fig. 21 Top: Checking test socket connector pigtail for continuity. Bottom: Checking diagnostic blink code LED light with a diode tester

blink rapidly, the throttle switch resistance should be checked. Use the following procedure:

a. Turn ignition **OFF**, access the ECU and disconnect the multipin connector.

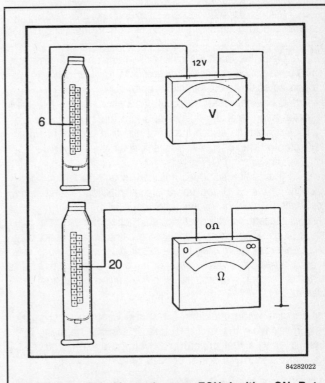

Fig. 22 Top: Checking voltage to ECU, ignition ON. Bottom: Checking ECU ground connection

sensor (crank sensor) is operating correctly. The engine will not start without a crank signal. If diagnostic unit does not respond with Code 1-4-1 and the LED continues to flash rapidly, check the impulse sensor as follows:

a. Turn ignition switch **OFF**.

b. Connect an ohmmeter between terminal 10 (red) and terminal 23 (blue) on the ECU control unit connector. Ohmmeter should read between approximately 215-265 ohms.

c. Check that electrical screen/shield is connected to terminal No. 11 on the control unit connector.

5. If Code 1-4-1 blinks, the crank signal should be okay. Turn the throttle in the engine compartment. The LED should go out, then blink out Code 3-3-4 as the computer tests the throttle switch idle position. If this Code blinks, it indicates the throttle switch is working properly; go to Step 5. If the diagnostic code does not respond with normal Code and continues to

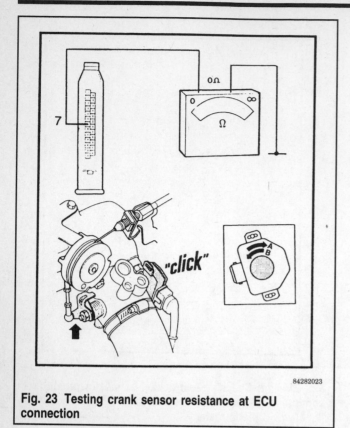

84282023

Fig. 23 Testing crank sensor resistance at ECU connection

b. Connect a Digital Volt/Ohm Meter (DVOM) between terminal 7 (Orange) and ground.

c. Reading should be 0 ohms.

d. Press accelerator slightly to open the throttle switch. Resistance should now become infinite.

e. If there appears to be a problem, take this reading at the switch to determine if the problem is in the switch or the wiring.

f. Open the throttle slightly while listening for the switch to operate. A click should be heard as the idle contacts open as soon as the throttle is opened.

g. If it is necessary to adjust the switch, loosen the 3MM socket head retaining screws and turn the switch clockwise slightly. Turn the switch back again until a click is heard. Tighten retaining screws. Recheck setting.

h. Turn ignition OFF.

6. If the engine still does not start, check the ground connections of the ECU and power stage amplifier. This ground connection should be securely tightened at the intake manifold.

7. If the engine still does not start, check for spark at the spark plugs. Disconnect a spark plug cable from 1 spark plug and connect a spare plug to the spark plug wire. Ground the spark plug and operate the starter motor. If a strong blue/white spark is present, the problem is in the engine or the fuel system.

➡Use care when checking for spark. Keep the test spark plug away from the fuel injectors. If a spark happens to flash over to a fuel injector, the voltage spike could feed back and destroy the fuel control unit.

8. If there is a weak spark or no spark, connect a spark plug onto the ignition coil terminal. Ground spark plug and operate starter motor. If a strong blue/white spark is present,

check the rotor, distributor housing and spark plug cables and replace if necessary.

9. If there is still a weak spark or no spark, fault is in the ignition coil or low tension section of the ignition system.

If the engine still does not start and tests indicate no spark or a weak spark, it indicates a problem in the coil, the coil control or ignition primary. It could also be a basic problem in the diagnostic system itself which is giving a false problem indication, which should be checked.

Continue troubleshooting by performing checks on the coil and the ignition primary system. Start by checking ECU power supply to see if power is getting to the ECU.

ECU POWER SUPPLY

Testing

Use care when testing around the ECU multi-pin connector. Never test the terminals from the front. This could result in damage to the terminals and make any faults worse. Note that the multi-pin connector has a shaped protective cover over the connector end. Remove the protective cover when testing. Terminals should be tested through holes in the side connector. Do not use excessive force. These terminals are very delicate. Terminals are numbered on the side of the connector.

1. After removing the multi-pin connector, inspect it carefully. Make sure no terminal contacts have been pushed down into the connector. Poor contact may result if any of the contact sleeves have been pushed down.

2. Connect a voltmeter between terminal 5 of the control unit connector and ground. Voltmeter should read 12 volts.

3. If there is no reading, check wire from control unit connector to 30-supply of fusebox.

POWER STAGE (AMPLIFIER) CHECK

Testing

▶ **See Figures 24, 25, 26 and 27**

EXCEPT REX 1 SYSTEM

1. Make sure ignition switch is OFF. Remove fuse No. 1 (model 740/940) or fuse No. 31 (model 760) from the fusebox. Note that these fuses must be removed whenever any connector to or from the ECU is removed or installed.

2. Remove the air filter to gain access to the power stage.

3. Remove the connector from the power stage.

4. Remove the rubber cover from the connector to expose the terminals. Never test the terminals from the front. This could result in damage to the terminals and make any faults worse.

5. Turn the ignition to ON.

6. Check the voltage to the power stage and ignition coil by connecting a voltmeter between ground and power stage connector terminal 4. Also test between ground and terminal 15 of the ignition coil. In both cases, voltage should be approximately 12 volts.

7. Crank the starter and check again. Voltage should still be at least 10.5 volts. If voltage is too low, check for a problem in the battery or charging system. If there is no voltage,

8. Test that the power stage is receiving signals from the ECU. Connect a voltmeter between terminal 5 and ground. Note voltmeter reading while operating starter motor. Voltmeter should show a pulsating reading between 0-2 volts. If voltmeter shows correct reading, check with a new power stage.

9. To check the power stage ground connection, connect an ohmmeter between connector terminal 2 and ground. Resistance should be 0 ohm.

10. Check that the wire from the ECU to the power stage is properly screened. The screen (shield) should be connected to terminal 3.

11. After testing, turn ignition key **OFF**. Connect power stage connector, air filter, air mass meter and hoses. Check all clips and retainers. Erase fault codes.

REX 1 SYSTEM

1. To check the ignition coil/power stage unit on REX 1 systems, make sure ignition switch is **OFF**. Unplug connector from coil/power stage unit.

2. Remove the ignition coil from the power stage by removing the 2 Torx head screws and lifting off the ignition coil.

3. Measure the resistance between the terminals of the ignition coil by connecting an ohmmeter between the low voltage terminals (+) and (—). Resistance should be 0.5 ohms.

4. Connect an ohmmeter between the high tension terminal and a low voltage terminal. Resistance should be approximately 5000 ohms.

5. Check that voltage is present at the ignition coil/power stage unit by first turning the ignition **ON**. Connect a voltmeter between ground and terminal A in the 3-way connector. There should be 12 volts. If the voltage is low, or none at all, check the point where the feed wire branches to the ECU and ignition coil/power stage unit.

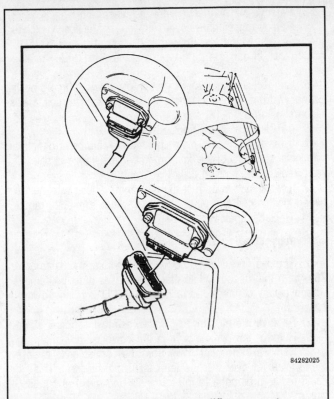

Fig. 24 Accessing power stage amplifier connector

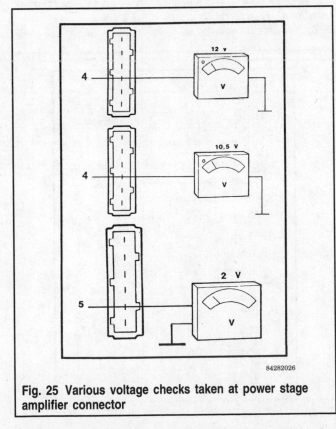

Fig. 25 Various voltage checks taken at power stage amplifier connector

check the blue wire from the central electrical unit to the ignition coil and power stage. Repair/replace as required.

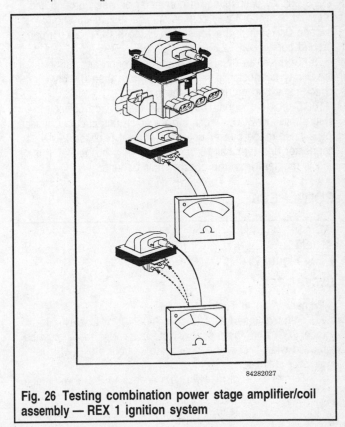

Fig. 26 Testing combination power stage amplifier/coil assembly — REX 1 ignition system

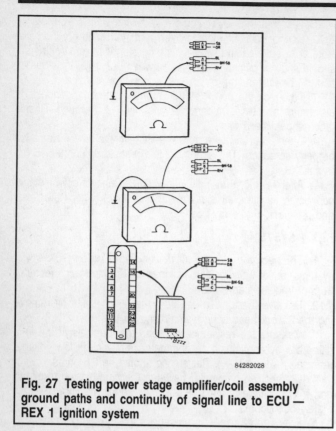

Fig. 27 Testing power stage amplifier/coil assembly ground paths and continuity of signal line to ECU — REX 1 ignition system

6. Check that the voltage does not fall below 10.5 volts when the starter motor is operated.

7. Turn ignition key **OFF**.

8. Check the ground connections of the ignition coil/power stage unit by connecting an ohmmeter between ground and terminal B of the 3-way connector. The resistance should not exceed 0.1 ohm. If the resistance is too high, check for bad ground connection.

9. Connect an ohmmeter between ground and terminal A of the 2-way connector. If resistance is more than 0.1 ohm, check for a bad ground connection.

10. Check the signal line between the ignition coil/power stage unit and ECU. Check for power on this circuit. Connecting a shop-made buzzer between terminal B of the 2-way connector and terminal 16 of the ECU may be helpful. If the line is problem free, the buzzer should sound.

COIL CHECK

Testing

▶ **See Figure 28**

EXCEPT REX 1

Primary Winding Test

1. Remove fuse No. 1 (model 740/940) or fuse No. 31 (model 760) from the fusebox. Note that these fuses must be removed whenever any connector to or from the ECU is removed or installed.

2. Remove the air filter to gain access to the power stage.

3. Remove the connector from the power stage.

4. Remove the rubber cover from the connector to expose the terminals. Never test the terminals from the front. This could result in damage to the terminals and make any faults worse.

5. Connect an ohmmeter between the power stage amplifier connector terminal 1 and terminal 15 of the ignition coil. Resistance should be 0.6-1.0 ohms.

6. If resistance is low, replace ignition coil.

7. If resistance is too high, connect an ohmmeter directly to terminals 1 and 15 of the ignition coil. If resistance is still to high, replace the ignition coil.

8. If resistance is correct (0.6-1.0 ohm), check wire between ignition coil and power stage amplifier connector terminal 1. Replace/repair wire as needed.

Secondary Winding Test

1. Remove fuse No. 1 (model 740) or fuse No. 31 (model 760) from the fusebox. Note that these fuses must be removed whenever any connector to or from the ECU is removed or installed.

2. Remove the air filter to gain access to the power stage.

3. Remove the connector from the power stage.

4. Remove the rubber cover from the connector to expose the terminals. Never test the terminals from the front. This could result in damage to the terminals and make any faults worse.

5. Connect an ohmmeter between the power stage amplifier connector terminal 1 and the ignition coil high tension terminal (coil tower). Resistance should be 6.5-9.0 ohms.

6. If resistance is higher or lower, replace the ignition coil.

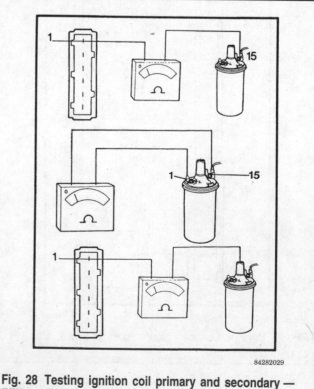

Fig. 28 Testing ignition coil primary and secondary — EZK ignition system

REX 1

Since the REX 1 system combines the ignition coil with power stage, testing for the REX 1 coil is contained in the power stage testing procedures.

DIAGNOSTIC SYSTEM CHECK

Testing

These tests are to make sure the diagnostic system is working properly.

1. Make sure ignition switch is **OFF**. Access the ECU. On 700 models, remove panel from under left side of instrument panel, disconnect connector from control unit. On 240 models, remove the panel in front of the right door pillar (passenger side), then disconnect connector from control unit.

2. Remove protective cover from control unit connector.

3. Check to ensure that no terminal contacts have been pushed down in the connector.

4. Insert the free end of the underhood diagnostic connector pigtail into socket No. 6.

5. Connect a voltmeter between ground and terminal 1 of the ECU multipin connector cable. Voltmeter should read 12 volts. Press down the diagnostic button. Voltmeter should now read 0 volts.

6. If there is no voltage at the ECU, measure at the test socket connector. If voltmeter shows 12 volt when the button is pushed, check the test connector.

7. To check the test connector, connect a voltmeter between the connector blue wire and ground. The voltmeter should read 12 volts. Connect an ohmmeter between the connector black wire and ground. The ohmmeter should read 0 ohm. Turn ignition **OFF**.

8. Connect an ohmmeter between the underhood diagnostic connector pigtail and pin 8 which is below the button on the diagnostic unit. The ohmmeter should read infinity. Press the button and the ohmmeter should read 0 ohms.

9. If a diode tester is available, connect it between the test socket LED and the diagnostic connector pigtail. Connect the red probe of the tester to the pin below the LED and the black probe to the diagnostic connector pigtail. If the tester gives a reading, it indicates the LED is okay. If the tester gives no reading, replace the test socket.

ECU GROUND CONNECTION

Testing

1. Make sure ignition switch is **OFF**. Access the ECU. On 700 models, remove panel from under left side of instrument panel, disconnect connector from control unit. On 240 models, remove the panel in front of the right door pillar (passenger side), then disconnect connector from control unit.

2. Remove protective cover from control unit connector.

3. Check to ensure that no terminal contacts have been pushed down in the connector.

4. Check control unit ground connection by connecting an ohmmeter between ground and terminal 20 on the control unit connector. Ohmmeter should read 0 ohms.

5. Also check terminal 14. Ohmmeter should read 0 ohms.

ENGINE TEMPERATURE SENSOR

▶ See Figure 29

Testing

1. Make sure ignition switch is **OFF**. Access the ECU. On 700 models, remove panel from under left side of instrument panel, disconnect connector from control unit. On 240 models, remove the panel in front of the right door pillar (passenger side), then disconnect connector from control unit.

2. Remove protective cover from control unit connector.

3. Check to ensure that no terminal contacts have been pushed down in the connector.

4. Check temperature sensor by connecting an ohmmeter between ground and terminal 2 on the control unit connector. At room temperature, the reading should be approximately 3000 ohms. The range is approximately 100 ohms at 250°F, to 5500 ohms at 32°F.

5. If reading obtained is incorrect, take reading at sensor to determine if fault is in the sensor or wire. Replace sensor or wire if necessary.

THROTTLE SWITCH

Testing

1. Make sure ignition switch is **OFF**. Access the ECU. On 700 models, remove panel from under left side of instrument panel, disconnect connector from control unit. On 240 models, remove the panel in front of the right door pillar (passenger side), then disconnect connector from control unit.

2. Remove protective cover from control unit connector.

3. Check to ensure that no terminal contacts have been pushed down in the connector.

4. Check the throttle switch by connecting an ohmmeter between ground and terminal 7 on the control unit connector. Ohmmeter should read 0 ohms.

5. Depress gas pedal slightly to open the throttle switch. Ohmmeter should read infinity.

6. If specifications are not as specified, take reading at throttle switch to determine if fault is in wiring or the switch.

7. Check the throttle switch setting by opening the throttle slightly and listening for the switch to operate. A click should be heard (switch opening) as soon as the throttle is opened. If not, adjust the throttle switch by loosening the mounting screws, then turn switch slightly clockwise, then counterclock-

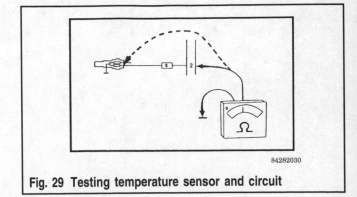

84282030

Fig. 29 Testing temperature sensor and circuit

wise until click is heard. Tighten mounting screws and check setting.

CRANK SENSOR (IMPULSE SENSOR)

Testing

1. Make sure ignition switch is **OFF**. Access the ECU. On 700 models, remove panel from under left side of instrument panel, disconnect connector from control unit. On 240 models, remove the panel in front of the right door pillar (passenger side), then disconnect connector from control unit.

2. Remove protective cover from control unit connector.

3. Check to ensure that no terminal contacts have been pushed down in the connector.

4. Check the engine speed sensor by connecting an ohmmeter between terminal 10 and terminal 23 on the control unit connector. Ohmmeter should read 215-265 ohms at room temperature.

5. If the engine is hot, allowable resistance can reach 280-300 ohms. Ensure that screen shield is connected to terminal 11 on the control unit connector.

KNOCK SENSORS

Testing

▶ See Figures 30, 31, 32, 33 and 34

1. Make sure ignition switch is **OFF**. Access the ECU. On 700 and on 940 models, remove panel from under left side of instrument panel, disconnect connector from control unit. On 240 models, remove the panel in front of the right door pillar (passenger side), then disconnect connector from control unit.

2. Remove protective cover from control unit connector.

3. Check to ensure that no terminal contacts have been pushed down in the connector.

4. Disconnect electrical connector from knock sensor, then install a jumper wire between terminal 1 and terminal 2.

5. Connect an ohmmeter between terminal 12 and terminal 13 on the control unit connector. Ohmmeter should read 0

ohms. If ohmmeter reads infinity, 1 or both wires are damaged (open circuit).

6. Remove the jumper wire, then check both wires. If wires are not damaged, install new knock sensor. Reconnect connectors and connect the control unit connector.

Component Replacement

▶ See Figure 35

Ignition system components are interrelated with the fuel system components. For most components the removal is straight forward, just remove the retaining screws and remove the part(s). For additional testing or replacement, check Section 5 'FUEL SYSTEM' of this manual.

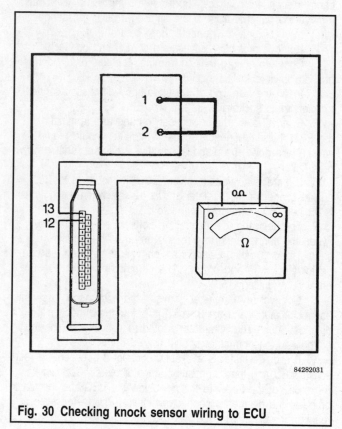

84282031

Fig. 30 Checking knock sensor wiring to ECU

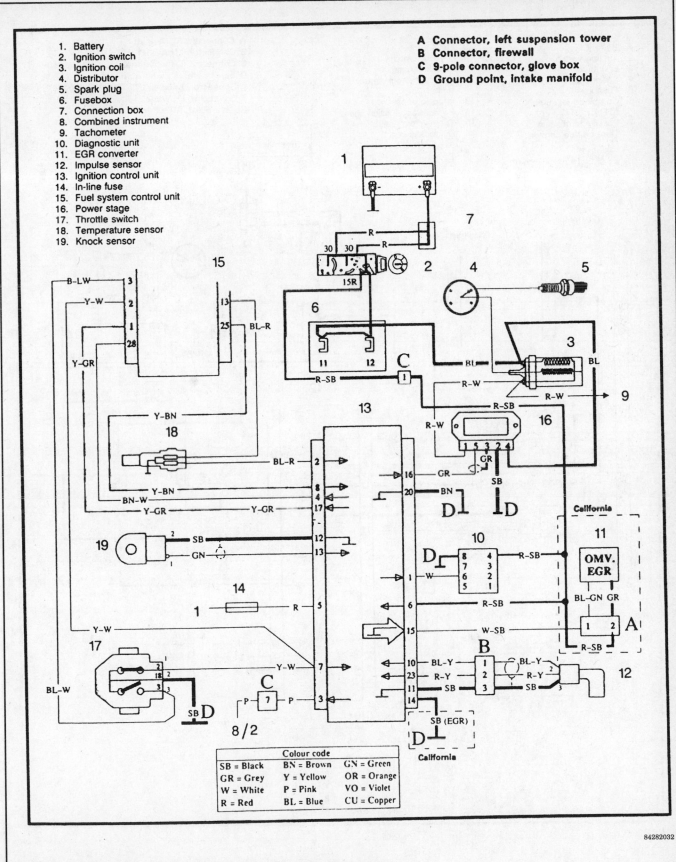

1. Battery
2. Ignition switch
3. Ignition coil
4. Distributor
5. Spark plug
6. Fusebox
7. Connection box
8. Combined instrument
9. Tachometer
10. Diagnostic unit
11. EGR converter
12. Impulse sensor
13. Ignition control unit
14. In-line fuse
15. Fuel system control unit
16. Power stage
17. Throttle switch
18. Temperature sensor
19. Knock sensor

A Connector, left suspension tower
B Connector, firewall
C 9-pole connector, glove box
D Ground point, intake manifold

Colour code

SB = Black	BN = Brown	GN = Green
GR = Grey	Y = Yellow	OR = Orange
W = White	P = Pink	VO = Violet
R = Red	BL = Blue	CU = Copper

84282032

Fig. 31 EZ116K ignition system wiring — 240 series with B230F engine

1. Battery
2. Ignition switch
3. Distributor
4. Spark plug
5. Fusebox
6. Combined instrument (CEL)
7. Positive terminal strip
8. Temperature sensor
9. Rev counter
10. Throttle switch
11. Knock sensor
12. Ignition system control unit
13. Impulse sensor
14. Power stage/ignition coil
15. Fuel system control unit
16. Diagnostic unit

A Connector, RH A-post
B Connector, LH A-post
C Connector, LH wheel housing, single-pole
D Earth terminal, inlet manifold
E Connector, bulkhead
F Connector, LH wheel housing
G Connector, RH wheel housing

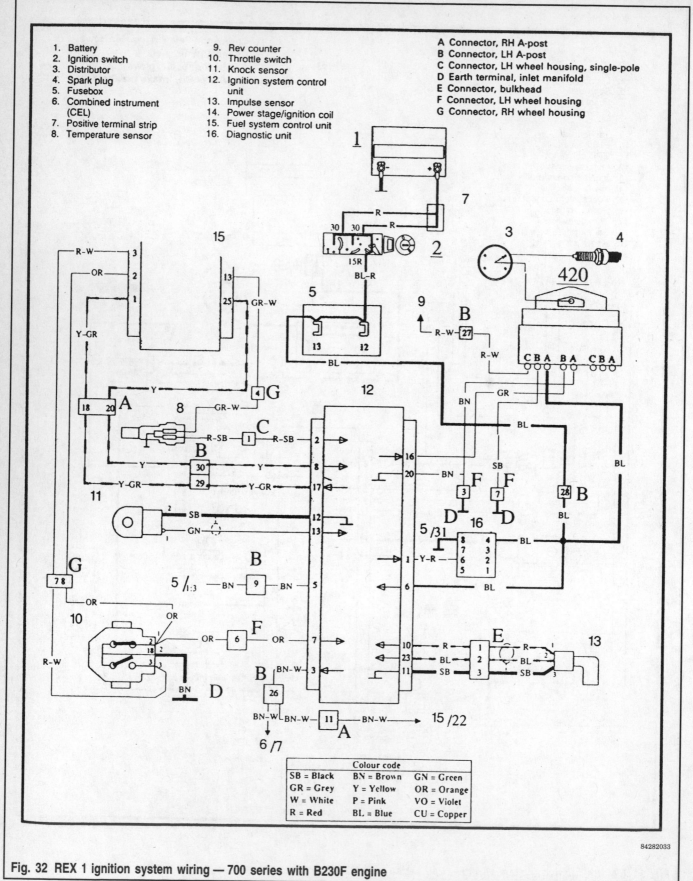

Colour code

SB = Black	BN = Brown	GN = Green
GR = Grey	Y = Yellow	OR = Orange
W = White	P = Pink	VO = Violet
R = Red	BL = Blue	CU = Copper

84282033

Fig. 32 REX 1 ignition system wiring — 700 series with B230F engine

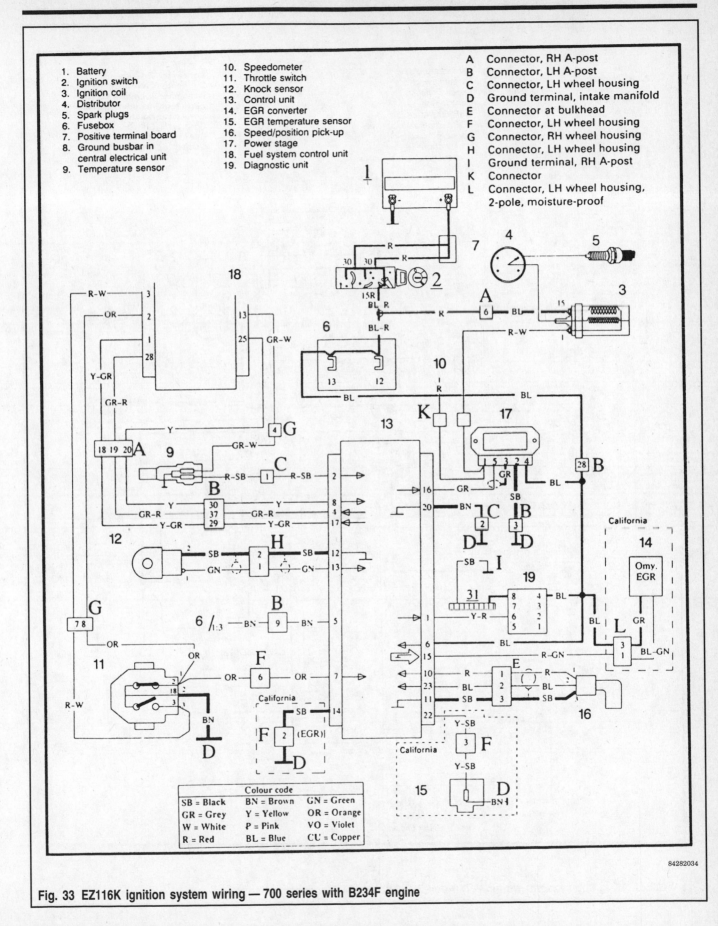

1. Battery
2. Ignition switch
3. Ignition coil
4. Distributor
5. Spark plugs
6. Fusebox
7. Positive terminal board
8. Ground busbar in central electrical unit
9. Temperature sensor
10. Speedometer
11. Throttle switch
12. Knock sensor
13. Control unit
14. EGR converter
15. EGR temperature sensor
16. Speed/position pick-up
17. Power stage
18. Fuel system control unit
19. Diagnostic unit

A Connector, RH A-post
B Connector, LH A-post
C Connector, LH wheel housing
D Ground terminal, intake manifold
E Connector at bulkhead
F Connector, LH wheel housing
G Connector, RH wheel housing
H Connector, LH wheel housing
I Ground terminal, RH A-post
K Connector
L Connector, LH wheel housing, 2-pole, moisture-proof

Colour code
SB = Black	BN = Brown	GN = Green
GR = Grey	Y = Yellow	OR = Orange
W = White	P = Pink	VO = Violet
R = Red	BL = Blue	CU = Copper

84282034

Fig. 33 EZ116K ignition system wiring — 700 series with B234F engine

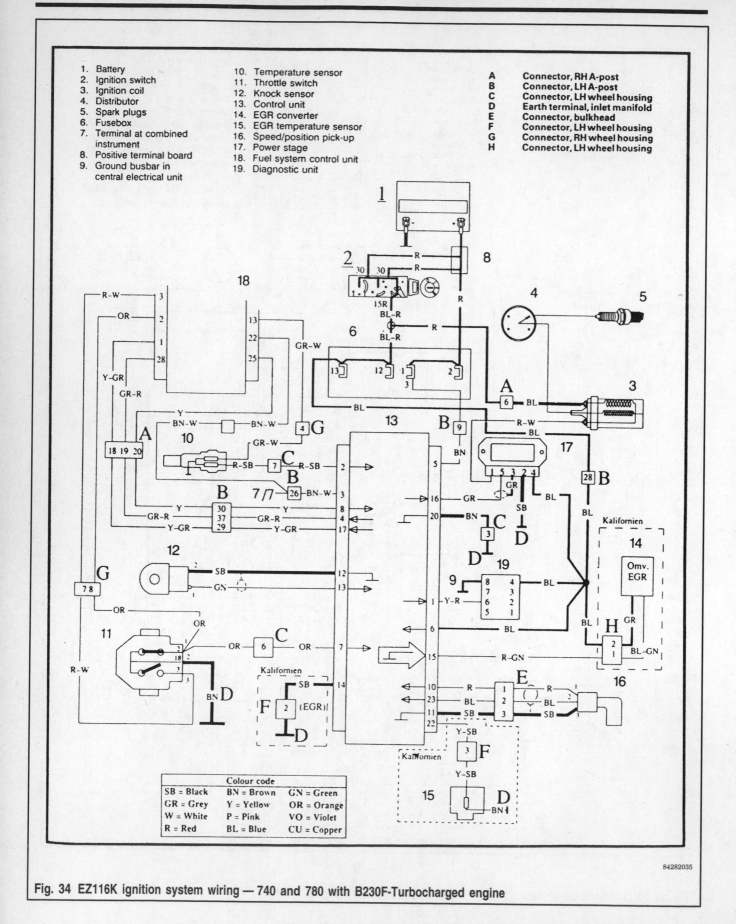

1. Battery
2. Ignition switch
3. Ignition coil
4. Distributor
5. Spark plugs
6. Fusebox
7. Terminal at combined instrument
8. Positive terminal board
9. Ground busbar in central electrical unit
10. Temperature sensor
11. Throttle switch
12. Knock sensor
13. Control unit
14. EGR converter
15. EGR temperature sensor
16. Speed/position pick-up
17. Power stage
18. Fuel system control unit
19. Diagnostic unit

A   Connector, RH A-post
B   Connector, LH A-post
C   Connector, LH wheel housing
D   Earth terminal, inlet manifold
E   Connector, bulkhead
F   Connector, LH wheel housing
G   Connector, RH wheel housing
H   Connector, LH wheel housing

Colour code		
SB = Black	BN = Brown	GN = Green
GR = Grey	Y = Yellow	OR = Orange
W = White	P = Pink	VO = Violet
R = Red	BL = Blue	CU = Copper

84282035

Fig. 34 EZ116K ignition system wiring — 740 and 780 with B230F-Turbocharged engine

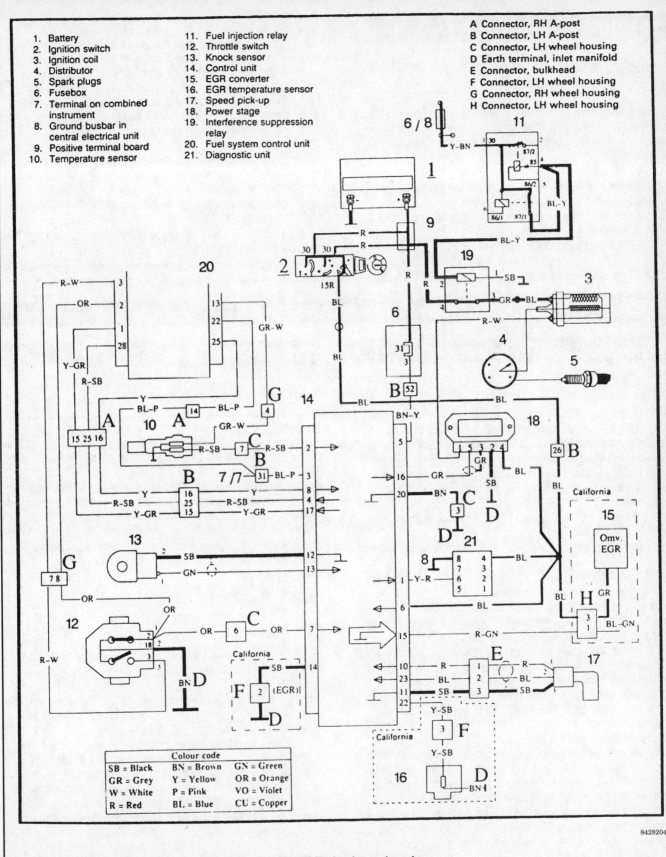

1. Battery
2. Ignition switch
3. Ignition coil
4. Distributor
5. Spark plugs
6. Fusebox
7. Terminal on combined instrument
8. Ground busbar in central electrical unit
9. Positive terminal board
10. Temperature sensor
11. Fuel injection relay
12. Throttle switch
13. Knock sensor
14. Control unit
15. EGR converter
16. EGR temperature sensor
17. Speed pick-up
18. Power stage
19. Interference suppression relay
20. Fuel system control unit
21. Diagnostic unit

A Connector, RH A-post
B Connector, LH A-post
C Connector, LH wheel housing
D Earth terminal, inlet manifold
E Connector, bulkhead
F Connector, LH wheel housing
G Connector, RH wheel housing
H Connector, LH wheel housing

Colour code

SB = Black	BN = Brown	GN = Green
GR = Grey	Y = Yellow	OR = Orange
W = White	P = Pink	VO = Violet
R = Red	BL = Blue	CU = Copper

84282040

Fig. 35 EZ116K ignition wiring — 760 series with B230F-Turbocharged engine

Ignition Timing

INSPECTION AND ADJUSTMENT

The ignition timing on these vehicles may be checked with a conventional timing light. The timing, however, cannot be adjusted. If the ignition setting is wrong, use the following procedure:

1. Check the throttle switch.
2. Check that the wiring to the crank sensor is correctly connected at the connector in the firewall.
3. Open the cover of the test connector and connect the cable to terminal 6.
4. Turn the ignition **ON**. Select Test Function 1 by pushing button once for more than 1 second and count the number of blinks. Note the number and press again in case there are more fault codes (up to 3). Note the fault codes to begin troubleshooting.

Code 1-1-1 — No fault codes in memory.

Code 1-4-2 — Fault in control unit. Engine runs with safety-retarded ignition timing (approximately 10 degrees).

Code 1-4-3 — Knock sensor faulty. Engine runs with safety-retarded ignition timing (approximately 10 degrees).

Code 1-4-4 — Load signal missing (from fuel system control unit). Control unit selects full-load ignition.

Code 2-1-4 — Engine speed sensor faulty.

Code 2-2-4 — Coolant temperature sensor inoperative.

Code 2-3-4 — Throttle switch for idling faulty. Engine runs with safety-retarded ignition timing (does not apply to REX 1 ignition system).

Code 3-3-4 — Throttle switch in idle position — okay (REX 1 ignition only).

5. If fault Code 1-1-1 (no fault in memory) appears, check the fuel system.
6. If the LED does not light when the button is pressed, or no code is blinked out check the connection at the ECU.

VOLVO MOTRONIC IGNITION SYSTEM

Description and Operation

▶ **See Figures 36 and 37**

Bosch Motronic 1.8 system is used on the Volvo 960 (2.9L B-6304F engine). This is a totally integrated engine management system. The fuel and ignition functions are controlled by the same on board computer in the Electronic Control Unit (ECU). This particular system uses a Distributorless Ignition System (DIS) where individual coil assemblies are mounted right on the spark plugs eliminating the distributor and associated wiring.

In addition to controlling the ignition and fuel injection functions, Motronic also:

• Determines whether the A/C compressor may be switched on

• Reduces the engine torque in response to a signal from the automatic transmission control unit, to insure smooth engagement of the different gears and also supplies the transmission control unit with information on engine running conditions for computing gear changes

• Controls the operation of the radiator fan

The control unit is provided with signals from the oxygen sensor, idling control functions and will retard the ignition timing to eliminate knock. The service requirement is minimal since neither the carbon monoxide level nor the idling speed require adjustment.

In the Motronic 1.8 system, each cylinder is equipped with an individual ignition coil to assure high voltage and accurate control of ignition. There is no distributor or spark plug cables.

The Electronic Control Unit (ECU) computes the instant at which each ignition coil must deliver its pulse. There are 6 coils controlled by two power units. The front unit is connected to cylinders 1, 3 and 5. The rear power unit serves cylinders 2, 4 and 6. Each unit incorporates 3 power stages (each connected to an individual coil). The ECU uses information from many sensors to compute the timing.

System Components

IGNITION COILS

▶ **See Figure 38**

The ignition coils are mounted directly on the spark plugs. The 2 power units which control the coils are mounted on the intake manifold, 1 on the front, 1 on the rear, for cooling. The front power unit is connected to cylinders 1, 3 and 5 while the rear unit serves cylinders 2, 4 and 6. Each power unit has 3 stages, each connected to an individual coil. The ignition voltage is extremely high, upwards of 40,000 volts to aid cold starts and to fire the lean mixtures required by emission laws.

CAMSHAFT SENSOR

▶ **See Figure 39**

The camshaft sensor is mounted at the rear of the cylinder head on the exhaust side. Its signals are used by the control unit to identify which pair of pistons (1-6, 5-2 or 3-4) are simultaneously approaching top dead center. Together with the timing pick-up signals, this enables the unit to identify the stroke being performed by the pistons.

The main components of the camshaft sensor are a Hall generator, trigger rotor and cover. As the rotor turns with the camshaft, it alternately shields and exposes the Hall element, generating high 5 volt and low 0 volt signals in turn. Since the vane and opening on the rotor are of the same width, and since the camshaft rotates at only half the crankshaft speed, the output signal changes only after a full crankshaft revolution. After 2 crankshaft revolutions, the signal from the Hall generator has reached 1 maximum and 1 minimum.

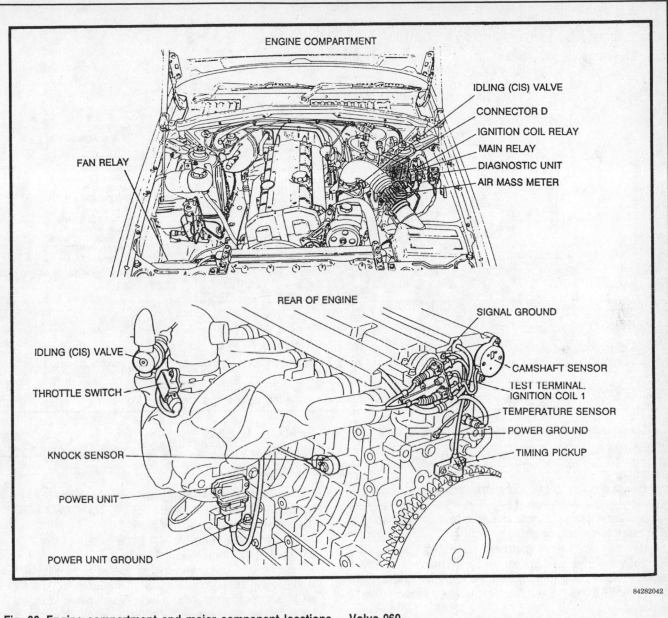

Fig. 36 Engine compartment and major component locations — Volvo 960

Diagnosis and Testing

SERVICE PRECAUTIONS

▶ **See Figure 40**

• Use caution when working around ignition system components. The ignition system operates at high power with dangerous voltages in both the low-tension and high-tension circuits, including connectors and similar fittings.

• Do not operate the fuel pump when the fuel lines are empty.

• Do not arc weld on the vehicle unless all the control units have been removed.

• The control unit must not be exposed to temperatures above 175°F (80°C), such as in a paint booth.

• Do not test the compression on the 960 until the ignition coils are removed, the ignition coil relay is disconnected and fuse No. 31 (to disarm fuel pumps) is removed.

• Do not disconnect the control unit harness connector before fuse No. 24 has been removed.

• Make sure all control unit connectors are fastened securely. A poor connection can cause an extremely high surge voltage, resulting in damage to integrated circuits.

• Keep any control unit harness at least 4 in. away from nearby harnesses to prevent a system malfunction due to external electronic interference.

• Keep all parts and harnesses dry during service.

• Before attempting to remove any parts, turn off the ignition switch and disconnect the battery ground cable.

• Always use a 12 volt battery as a power source.

• Do not attempt to disconnect the battery cables with the engine running.

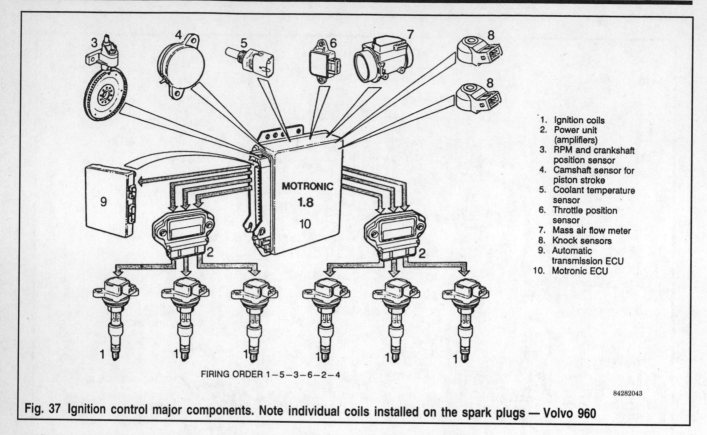

1. Ignition coils
2. Power unit (amplifiers)
3. RPM and crankshaft position sensor
4. Camshaft sensor for piston stroke
5. Coolant temperature sensor
6. Throttle position sensor
7. Mass air flow meter
8. Knock sensors
9. Automatic transmission ECU
10. Motronic ECU

FIRING ORDER 1—5—3—6—2—4

84282043

Fig. 37 Ignition control major components. Note individual coils installed on the spark plugs — Volvo 960

- Do not attempt to disassemble a control unit under any circumstances.
- If a battery cable is disconnected, the memory will be erased.
- Before connecting or disconnecting control unit ECU harness connectors, make sure the ignition switch is **OFF** and the negative battery cable is disconnected to avoid the possibility of damage to the control unit.
- Use care when working around vehicles equipped with Supplementary Restraint System (SRS), often known as 'air bags.' Vehicles equipped with SRS are easily recognized by the letters **SRS** molded into the steering wheel cover. Follow all precautions.
- When working around the instrument panel or steering column areas, take care to make sure that wiring is not pinched, abraded or penetrated by screws when working on soundproofing panels, knee cushion, ignition switch or column covers.
- The SRS crash sensor is located underneath the driver's seat. Never disconnect the sensor connector. Never install accessories near the sensor.
- Never undo the steering gear without first locking the contact reel and removing the steering wheel.
- A spare location in the fuse panel is used as a test terminal for air bag diagnostics on the Volvo 960. Never install a fuse in this position or connect accessories to this terminal.

READING CODES

▶ See Figure 41

To help with troubleshooting, the Motronic control unit is equipped with some diagnostic functions. There are 3 modes:
Self-Diagnosis, which is Test Mode 1
Function Testing, which is Test Mode 2
Control Testing, which is Test Mode 3
The diagnostic unit (switchbox) is located at the left rear side of the engine compartment. It has a pushbutton, several sockets to access different parts of the system and an LED light which flashes the codes. Access to the diagnostic system is provided by plugging in the diagnostic unit's selector plug, or 'pigtail' into socket 2 on the diagnostic unit when the ignition is switched **ON**.

Self-Diagnostics

TEST MODE 1

The control unit can record and store 18 different fault codes. Fault codes stored in the memory can be displayed by operating the test button. The control unit memory, which stores both the diagnostic codes and adaptive programs, can retain information for periods ranging from 10 minutes to 24 hours after interruption of the power supply.

All self-diagnostic system faults with the exception of a faulty knock sensor, are reversible. This means the ECU will again begin to use a faulty or missing signal immediately after is has been corrected, rather than remaining in the 'limp home' mode. However, the fault code will remain in the memory.

A warning lamp on the instrument cluster indicates emission-related faults which are detectable by the system. All fault

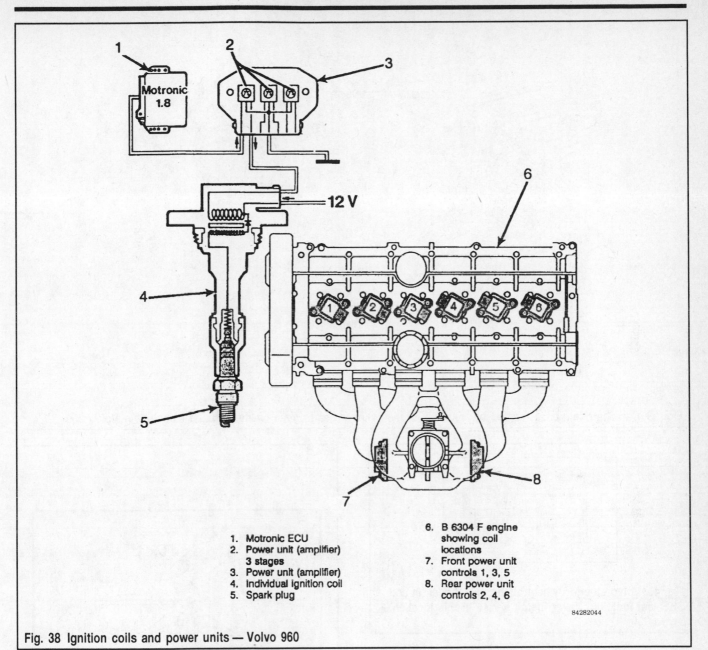

1. Motronic ECU
2. Power unit (amplifier) 3 stages
3. Power unit (amplifier)
4. Individual ignition coil
5. Spark plug
6. B 6304 F engine showing coil locations
7. Front power unit controls 1, 3, 5
8. Rear power unit controls 2, 4, 6

84282044

Fig. 38 Ignition coils and power units — Volvo 960

codes have 3 digits, each capable of ranging from 1 through 9. The fault codes are read from the series of flashes delivered by the LED. Each code requires 3 series of uninterrupted flashes, with a 3 second interval between each series of flashes to make the codes easy to read.

Flash codes used in the Volvo 960 Motronic system are:

Code 1-1-1 — No fault detected by diagnostic system
Code 1-1-2 — Control unit problem
Code 1-1-3 — Faulty injector
Code 1-2-1 — Air mass meter signal absent or faulty
Code 1-2-3 — Engine temperature signal absent or faulty
Code 1-3-1 — No signal from timing pickup
Code 1-3-2 — Battery voltage too high or too low
Code 1-4-3 — Front knock sensor signal absent or faulty
Code 2-1-2 — Oxygen sensor signal absent or faulty
Code 2-1-4 — Timing pickup signal absent intermittently
Code 2-2-3 — Idling valve signal absent of faulty
Code 2-3-1 — Oxygen sensor lean or rich in part-load range
Code 2-3-2 — Oxygen sensor control lean or rich at idling
Code 2-3-3 — Adaptive idling control outside control range
Code 2-4-3 — Signal from throttle switch absent or faulty
Code 3-1-1 — Speedometer signal absent
Code 3-1-4 — Camshaft sensor signal absent
Code 3-2-2 — Air mass meter burn-off signal absent
Code 4-3-3 — Rear knock sensor signal absent or faulty

The following procedure is for retrieving fault codes.

1. Open the diagnostic socket cover at the left side rear of the engine compartment. Install the selector plug into socket No. 2 for ignition or fuel system codes, or into socket No. 6 for EGR system codes on California vehicles.

2. Turn ignition to the **ON** position.

3. Enter Control Function 1 by pressing the button once. Hold the button for at least 1 second, but not more than 3 seconds.

4. Watch the LED and count the number of flashes in each of the 3 flash series, which will indicate a fault code. The flash

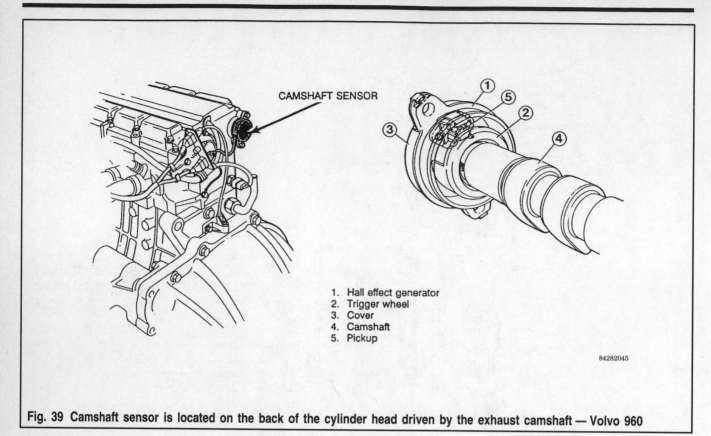

CAMSHAFT SENSOR

1. Hall effect generator
2. Trigger wheel
3. Cover
4. Camshaft
5. Pickup

84282045

Fig. 39 Camshaft sensor is located on the back of the cylinder head driven by the exhaust camshaft — Volvo 960

84282046

Fig. 40 Volvo steering wheel air bag identification and SRS test location. Never install a fuse in this location — Volvo 960

series are separated by 3 second intervals. Note the fault codes.

➡ If there are no fault codes in the diagnostic unit, the LED will flash 1-1-1 indicating the fuel system is operating correctly.

5. Depress the button again. If the same code is repeated, there are no additional codes stored. If the code is different, depress the button a third time and record the code, if different.

➡ The diagnostic memory is full when it contains 3 fault codes. Until those 3 are rectified and the memory erased, the system cannot give information on any other problems.

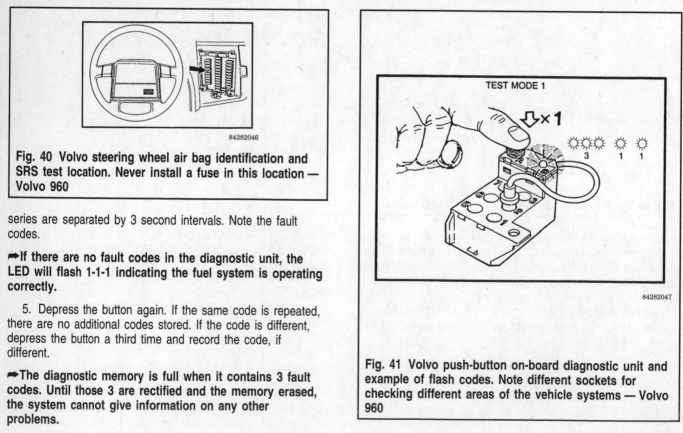

TEST MODE 1

×1

3 1 1

84282047

Fig. 41 Volvo push-button on-board diagnostic unit and example of flash codes. Note different sockets for checking different areas of the vehicle systems — Volvo 960

TEST MODE 2

This is function testing, a check to see that various systems are operating and send/receiving signals as required. Function testing is activated by pressing the button twice, holding the button for at least 1 second each time, but not more than 3 seconds each time and also allowing 1-3 seconds between operations, causing the LED to flash. The control unit delivers a diagnostic code (not a fault code) acknowledging the receipt of a signal from each of the following items:

Function Test Code 3-3-2: Throttle switch, when the throttle is moved from the idling position

Function Test Code 3-3-3: Throttle switch, when the throttle is moved from the full-load position

Function Test Code 1-2-4: Start inhibitor switch, via the transmission control unit, when the gear selector lever is moved from 1 of the drive positions to the **N** or **P** position

Function Test Code 1-4-1: Timing pick-up, when the starter motor is running

Function Test Code 1-1-4: Electronic Climate Control (ECC) control panel, when the A/C button is depressed or released

Function Test Code 1-3-4: Relay in ECC power unit and, as a result, A/C compressor electromagnetic clutch, when A/C is switched **ON**

TEST MODE 3

Control Testing, which is Test Mode 3, is activated by pressing the button 3 times, holding the button for at least 1 second each time, but not more than 3 seconds each time and also allowing 1-3 seconds between operations. The control unit then responds by activating, in order:

1. Radiator fan at half speed for 3 seconds
2. Radiator fan at full speed for 3 seconds
3. Injectors at 13 Hz
4. Idling (CIS) valve at 1 Hz
5. Relay in ECC power unit and, as a result, A/C compressor electromagnetic clutch, at 1 Hz.

This activation is repeated twice.

CLEARING CODES

When all the fault codes have been read and corrected, the diagnostic system memory can be erased as follows:

1. Turn ignition switch to the **ON** position.
2. Read fault codes again.
3. Press and hold diagnostic socket button for approximately 5 seconds, then release the button. After 3 seconds, the LED should light.
4. While the LED is lit, press button again for approximately 5 seconds. Release the button. The LED should go out. Memory is cleared.

➡**To ensure that the memory has been erased, press button again for 1 second but not more than 3 seconds. The LED should flash 1-1-1, indicating that the fuel system is operating properly.**

NO START — NO SPARK

◗ **See Figure 42**

It is recommended that a breakout box be used when troubleshooting the system. With the breakout box, voltage and resistance tests can be performed with all connections made and system sensors operating without endangering the ECU or delicate pin connections. All of the following tests and checks are based on using this piece of equipment. If such equipment is available, make sure the ignition switch is **OFF** when connecting or disconnecting the ECU. Remove fuse No. 24 when connecting or disconnecting the ECU.

Ground Connections Check

1. Using a breakout box, with the ignition key **OFF**, connect an ohmmeter between ground and terminals 19, 24, 26, 30 and 48 of the control unit. The meter should indicate approximately 0 ohms in all cases.
2. Check the power unit ground connections under each unit. These 2 components are mounted on the intake manifold. Connect an ohmmeter between ground and terminal 4 on front power unit connector, then between ground and terminal 4 on rear power unit connector. The meter should indicate approximately 0 ohms in both cases.
3. If high resistance is indicated, check the connectors and the wiring.

Voltage Check

1. With the ignition switch **OFF**, check for voltage supply to terminal 18 across fuse No. 24 and to terminal 36 across the main relay.
2. Connect a voltmeter across terminals 18 and 19, then across terminals 36 and 19 of the control unit. The voltmeter should indicate battery voltage in both cases. Check the fuse, wiring and the relay if no reading is obtained.
3. Turn the ignition switch **ON** and check that the voltage falls from battery voltage to approximately 0.1 volt at terminal 36.

Ignition Coil Voltage Supply
◗ **See Figure 43**

Fault Code 1-3-1 is reported if no signal is received from the camshaft sensor pick-up for 10 engine revolutions. The engine will not start as a result of this.

Fault Code 2-1-4 is reported only if a fault occurs when the engine is running. The code is set if what the control unit computes and what it actually sees are different. A slight roughness may be a symptom felt in this event.

1. Turn the ignition switch **ON**.
2. Connect a voltmeter between ground and the test terminal at the rear of the engine. The reading should be battery voltage.
3. If the reading is not battery voltage, check the coil relay, wiring and the connectors up to the ignition coils.
4. Attempt to start the engine.
5. If the engine still does not start, remove the ignition coil cover and remove one coil.
6. Fit a spare spark plug in the ignition coil and crank the engine.

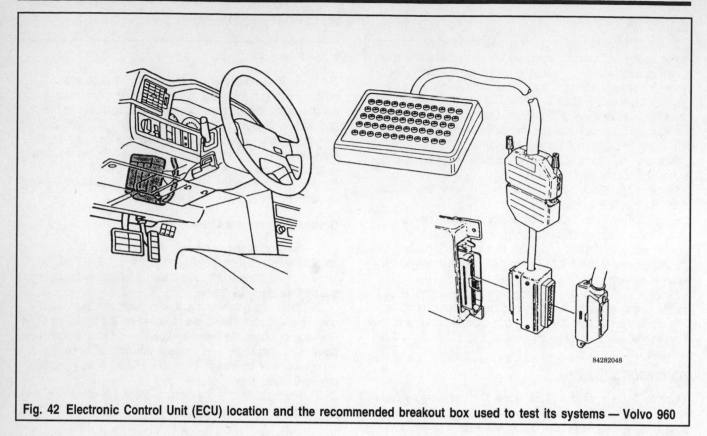

84282048

Fig. 42 Electronic Control Unit (ECU) location and the recommended breakout box used to test its systems — Volvo 960

7. If no spark is obtained, check the timing pick-up.

Ignition or Fuel System Identification

1. Use a voltmeter to check the injectors.
2. The voltage should be approximately 250-400 millivolts when the engine is hot.
3. If the voltage is correct, either the fault is in the ignition system or the injector is blocked. Check the fuel system for fault codes.

COIL CHECK

Firing Pulse at Coil Test

1. Use test diode 999-5280 or equivalent. Make an adaptor to fit between the ignition coil connector and the test diode.
2. Connect the test diode.
3. Start the engine. The LED should flash when a signal is present.
   a. If there is no signal, check the signal output from the control unit.
   b. If there is a signal present, replace the ignition coil or spark plug.

ECU-TO-COIL SIGNAL

Signal Output Check

1. Connect a voltmeter between ground and the control unit terminal that is connected to the ignition coil.

2. Start the engine.
3. The meter should indicate between 60-100 millivolts if the signal is correct.
4. If the reading is approximately 3.5 volts, there is an open circuit present between the control unit and the ignition coil.
5. If the signal is present, check the power unit and wiring. Stop the engine.

POWER UNIT AND WIRING

Testing

1. With the ignition switch **OFF**, connect the diode tester with the positive side connected to the control unit terminal for cylinder to be checked and to terminal 1 on corresponding ignition coil connector. Also check in reverse direction.
2. Connect the diode tester with the positive side connected to ground and to terminal 1 on the ignition coil connector. Also check in the reverse direction.
3. Check the wiring if a faulty diode is found.

VOLTAGE SIGNAL AND WIRING

Testing

1. Connect a voltmeter across terminals 42 and 19 of the control unit.
2. Turn the ignition switch **ON**.
3. Check the meter reading. It should be approximately 5.5 volts in **P** or **N**.

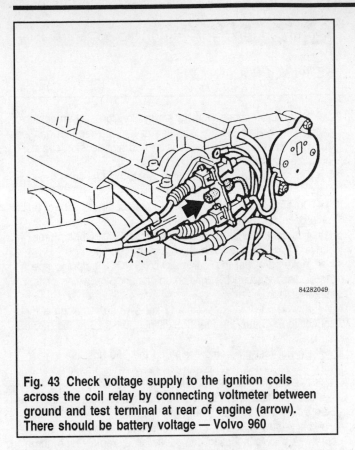

84282049

Fig. 43 Check voltage supply to the ignition coils across the coil relay by connecting voltmeter between ground and test terminal at rear of engine (arrow). There should be battery voltage — Volvo 960

4. Check the meter reading. It should be approximately 0.5 volts in **D** or **R**.

5. If there is no signal, check the lead between the control unit and the transmission control unit.

6. If the lead is intact, check the signal from the gear selector mechanism to the transmission control unit.

TIMING PICK-UP

Fault Code 1-3-1 is reported if no signal is received from the camshaft sensor pick-up for 10 engine revolutions. The engine will not start as a result of this.

Fault Code 2-1-4 is reported only if a fault occurs when the engine is running. The code is set if what the control unit computes and what it actually sees are different. A slight roughness may be a symptom felt in this event.

Testing In Control Function 2

1. Enter Control Function 2 and operate the starter motor.
2. Diagnostic Code 1-4-1 should be displayed, indicating a timing pick-up signal.

Timing Pick-up Signal Check

1. Connect a voltmeter across terminals 47 and 48, and set on the AC millivolt scale.
2. Operate the starter motor and check that the voltmeter displays 300-400 millivolts.

Absent or Faulty Signal Check

1. With the ignition switch **OFF**, remove fuse No. 24 and disconnect the control unit.
2. Connect an ohmmeter between terminals 47 and 48.
3. Check that the ohmmeter reads 200-400 ohms, depending on the temperature.
4. Reconnect the control unit.
5. Measure the resistance between terminals 48 and 19. The resistance should be 0 ohms.
6. Measure the resistance between terminals 48 and 30. The resistance should be 0 ohms.
7. On vehicles with automatic transmissions, check in Control Function 1 if speed signal fault is displayed.

BATTERY VOLTAGE

Fault Code 1-3-2 will set if the battery voltage falls below 8 volts or exceeds 16 volts for 5 seconds after the engine has started.

Voltage Check

1. Connect a voltmeter across terminals 18 and 19 of the control unit.
2. Start the engine and read the battery voltage.
3. Check the battery and charging system if the voltage is in abnormal range.

KNOCK SENSORS

Fault Codes 1-4-3 and 4-3-3 indicate that the front and rear knock sensor signals, respectively, are absent or faulty. The fault codes will be reported if the following 2 conditions are fulfilled:

1. The engine speed is at least 2970 rpm and a certain engine load has been exceeded.
2. The signal from either of the knock sensors to the control unit falls below 255 millivolts during 96 successive ignitions.

The control unit will then safety-retard the timing.

Wiring Check

The knock sensors themselves cannot be checked, only the wiring.

1. Disconnect the knock sensor connector and connect a jumper wire between the connector terminals.
2. Remove fuse No. 24 and disconnect the control unit.
3. Connect an ohmmeter between terminal 2 and terminal 11 or 29, depending on which knock sensor is affected. The reading should be 0 ohms.
4. Replace the knock sensor if the reading is correct. Do not replace it if the reading is incorrect. Torque the sensor to 15 ft. lbs. (20 Nm).
5. Reconnect the control unit.

CAMSHAFT SENSOR

The camshaft sensor is mounted at the end of the camshaft and enables the control unit to determine which cylinder requires fuel and ignition. As the camshaft performs a revolution every 2 crankshaft revolutions, the sensor signal goes high on 1 crankshaft revolution and low on the next. Fault Code 3-1-4 is reported if the signal remains constantly high or low for more than 30 seconds. Under these conditions, the control unit supplies double injection and double ignition while safety-retarding the timing.

Camshaft Sensor Signal Check

1. Remove fuse No. 31 to prevent the engine from starting.
2. Connect a voltmeter across terminals 8 and 19 of the control unit.
3. Operate the starter motor.
4. Check that the reading oscillates between 0.1-0.5 volts.

Absent or Faulty Signal Check

1. Check that the voltage across terminals 10 and 30 of the control unit is approximately 11 volts.
2. Check that terminal 30 is grounded.
3. Connect an ohmmeter between terminals 30 and 19 of the control unit. It should read 0 ohms.

Diagnostic Unit Testing

1. Turn the ignition switch **ON**.
2. Connect the test lead to socket 2 on the diagnostic unit.
3. Connect a voltmeter across terminals 55 and 19 on the control unit connector. The instrument should indicate 12 volts.
4. Press the button on the control unit. The instrument should indicate 0 volt.
5. If there is no voltage at the control unit, measure instead at the diagnostic unit connector.
6. If the voltmeter indicates 12 volts when the button is depressed, check the diagnostic unit.
7. Connect a voltmeter between ground and the blue lead in the diagnostic unit connector. It should read approximately 12 volts.
8. Turn the ignition switch **OFF**.
9. Connect an ohmmeter between ground and the black lead in the diagnostic unit connector. It should indicate approximately 0 ohms.
10. Connect an ohmmeter between the diagnostic unit test plug and the pin that is directly underneath the function selector button. The instrument should indicate infinity.
11. Depress the selector button. The ohmmeter should indicate 0 ohms.
12. Connect the red probe of a diode tester to the pin directly underneath the diagnostic unit LED and the black probe to the test plug, then switch the leads.
13. The LED is operating correctly if the tester shows an indication in one direction only. If it is defective, replace the diagnostic unit.

Component Replacement

SERVICE PRECAUTIONS

• Use caution when working around ignition system components. The ignition system operates at high power with dangerous voltages in both the low-tension and high-tension circuits, including connectors and similar fittings.
• Do not operate the fuel pump when the fuel lines are empty.
• Do not arc weld on the vehicle unless all the control units have been removed.
• The control units must not be exposed to temperatures above 175°F (80°C), such as in a paint booth.
• Make sure that the ignition switch is **OFF** before connecting or disconnecting the ignition coil, spark plug wiring or test instruments.
• Always use new gaskets and seals when remaking a fuel connection. Torque the fuel filter fittings to 15-26 ft. lbs. (20-35 Nm).
• Do not test the compression on the 960 until the ignition coils are removed, the ignition coil relay is disconnected and fuse No. 31 (to disarm fuel pumps) is removed.
• Do not disconnect the control unit harness connector before fuse No. 24 has been removed.
• Make sure all control unit connectors are fastened securely. A poor connection can cause an extremely high surge voltage, resulting in damage to integrated circuits.
• Keep any control unit harness at least 4 in. away from adjacent harnesses to prevent a system malfunction due to external electronic interference.
• Keep all parts and harnesses dry during service.
• Before attempting to remove any parts, turn off the ignition switch and disconnect the battery ground cable.
• Always use a 12 volt battery as a power source.
• Do not attempt to disconnect the battery cables with the engine running.
• Do not attempt to disassemble a control unit under any circumstances.
• If a battery cable is disconnected, the fault code memory will be erased.
• Before connecting or disconnecting control unit ECU harness connectors, make sure the ignition switch is **OFF** and the negative battery cable is disconnected to avoid the possibility of damage to the control unit.
• A spare location in the fuse box is used as a test terminal for air bag diagnostics on the 960. Never install a fuse in this position or connect accessories to this terminal.

CAMSHAFT SENSOR

Removal & Installation

1. The camshaft sensor is mounted at the rear of the cylinder head on the exhaust side. Disconnect the negative battery cable.
2. Remove any ducting or hoses that may be in the way, matchmarking for assembly.

3. Disconnect the electrical connector taking care not to damage the connector or pins. Ground connections are secured with electrical eyelets and small screws. Use care when disconnecting these pieces.

4. Remove the hold-down bolts for the sensor body.

5. Pull the camshaft sensor away from the cylinder head, noting the drive slots in the camshaft for reassembly.

To install:

6. Installation is the reverse of the removal procedure. Make sure the drive slots in the camshaft properly mesh with the camshaft sensor drive.

7. Install the hold-down bolts and make sure the electrical connection is secure.

IGNITION COILS

Removal & Installation

This system uses 6 individual coils, 1 on each spark plug.

1. Disconnect the negative battery cable.

2. Remove the large coil cover on the top of the engine that is secured to the cam cover. Use care not to drop any of the small retaining screws.

3. Remove any ducting or hoses that may be in the way, matchmarking for assembly.

4. Remove the hold-down capscrews from the coil top.

5. Disconnect the electrical connector from the coil top assembly.

6. Carefully pull the coil from the spark plug, pulling straight up while turning slightly to disengage from the top of the spark plug.

To install:

7. Installation is the reverse of the removal procedure. Press the coil straight down onto the spark plug. There should a slight 'click' as the coil seats on the spark plug top.

8. Install the hold-down capscrews, and make sure the electrical connection is secure.

9. Install the coil cover and make sure any hose connections that were removed are now secure.

IGNITION AMPLIFIERS

Removal & Installation

There are 2 ignition amplifiers. They are mounted on the intake manifold. One feeds odd number cylinder coils, the other, even numbers.

1. Remove any ducting or hoses that may be in the way, matchmarking for assembly.

2. Remove the hold-down capscrews from the amplifier being serviced.

3. Carefully disengage the electrical connector and lift the amplifier from the vehicle.

To install:

4. Installation is the reverse of the removal procedure. Use care make sure the hold-down capscrews are firmly in place, but use caution not to over-torque when working around light alloy parts.

5. Make sure the electrical connection is secure.

IGNITION TIMING

Motronic Ignition System

Although the timing may be checked, it is not adjustable. All timing functions are carried out by the ECU. The ignition timing may be checked with a conventional inductive timing light. Specification is 12 degrees BTDC @ 750 rpm.

VALVE LASH

ADJUSTMENT

The recommended maintenance interval for valve clearance adjustment is 30,000 miles (48,000 km). The clearance may be checked with the engine hot or cold.

B230F and B230FT Engines

▶ **See Figures 44, 45, 46, 47, 48, 49 and 50**

Valve clearance adjustment requires the following special tools:

1. Valve tappet depressor tool (Volvo tool 5022) — used to push down the tappet sufficiently to remove the adjusting disc.

2. A special designed pair of pliers (Volvo tool 5026) — to actually remove and install the valve adjusting disc.

3. A set of varying-thickness valve adjusting discs(sometimes called shims) to make the necessary corrections.

4. Feeler gauge — to check valve clearance.

❊❊WARNING

The use of the correct special tools or their equivalent is required for this procedure.

5. Disconnect the negative battery cable. Remove the valve cover. Rotate the engine, using the crankshaft center bolt, until No. 1 cylinder is at Top Dead Center (TDC). Both cam lobes for No. 1 cylinder should point up at equally large angles and the pulley timing mark should be at '0″ degrees.

6. Insert the correct size feeler gauge, as indicated, and check No. 1 cylinder valve clearance.

➡**Always check valve clearance with cylinder at TDC. Always turn 1/4 turn after TDC to set.**

7. If the clearance is incorrect, line up valve depressors. Turn the valve depressors so that the notches are at right angle to the engine center line.

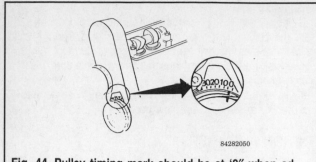

84282050

Fig. 44 Pulley timing mark should be at '0" when adjusting valves — B230F and B230FT engines

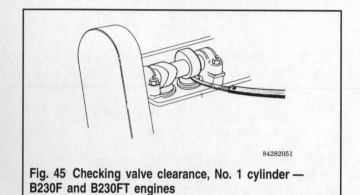

84282051

Fig. 45 Checking valve clearance, No. 1 cylinder — B230F and B230FT engines

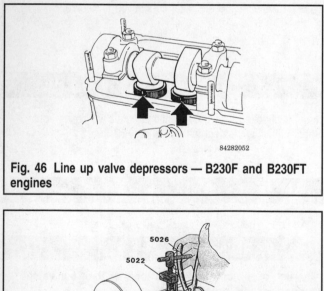

84282052

Fig. 46 Line up valve depressors — B230F and B230FT engines

84282053

Fig. 47 Attaching tool 5022 and removing disc — B230F and B230FT engines

8. Attach tool 5022 or equivalent and depress the valve depressors. Screw down the tool spindle until the depressor

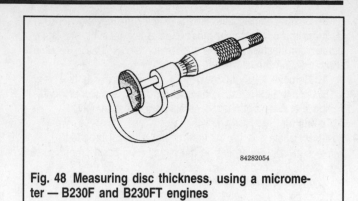

84282054

Fig. 48 Measuring disc thickness, using a micrometer — B230F and B230FT engines

84282055

Fig. 49 Disc, exploded view — B230F and B230FT engines

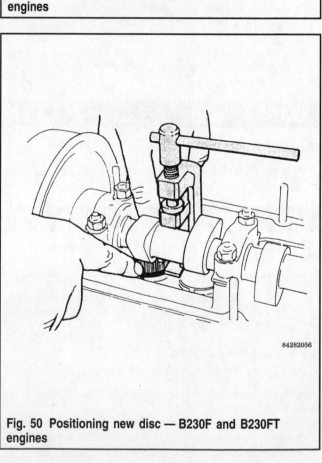

84282056

Fig. 50 Positioning new disc — B230F and B230FT engines

groove is just above the edge and accessible with the pliers. Use tool 5026 or equivalent to remove the disc.

9. Using a micrometer, measure the disc thickness. Calculate the thickness of disc to be used. Discs are available from 0.130-0.180 inch (3.30-4.50mm) in increments of 0.001 inch (0.05mm). Use the following example:

   a. Measure the clearance 0.50mm. Correct clearance 0.016 inch (0.40mm). Difference 0.004 inch (0.10mm).

   b. Measured thickness on existing disc: 0.150 inch (3.80mm). Correct thickness on new disc will thus be 0.150 + 0.004 inch = 0.154 inch (3.80 + 0.10mm = 3.90mm).

➡**It is advisable to use metric measurement to simplify calculations.**

10. Lubricate the new disc with clean engine oil and place into position. Remove tool 5022 or equivalent.

➡**Install the discs with marks DOWN.**

11. Rotate the engine crankshaft until No. 3 cylinder is at the correct position. Both cam lobes for No. 3 cylinder should point up at equally large angles. Check and adjust the clearance as described previously.

12. Repeat Step 7 for cylinder No. 4 and then cylinder No. 2.

13. Rotate the engine a few turns, then recheck all cylinders.

14. Install the valve cover, using a new valve cover gasket.

15. Connect the negative battery cable. Check engine operation.

B234F Engine

The B234F 16-valve engine has self adjusting valves and hydraulic tappets. They cannot be adjusted during routine maintenance.

B280F Engine

♦ See Figures 51, 52, 53 and 54

1. Disconnect the negative battery cable.
2. On right side of engine:
   a. Remove the oil filler cap with hoses.
   b. Remove the air conditioning compressor with bracket, and position aside.
   c. Remove the oil dipstick.
   d. Disconnect the wire bundle from the clamps on the valve cover.
3. On left side of engine:
   a. Disconnect the air inlet hose.
   b. Disconnect the main wiring harness clamp from the valve cover.
   c. Remove the spark plug wires and fuel lines from the valve cover.
4. Remove the valve covers.
5. Using a 36mm hex socket on the crankshaft pulley bolt, rotate the crankshaft until the mark on the pulley is opposite the '0" mark on the engine shoulder. Both rocker arms for No. 1 cylinder should have clearance.
6. Insert the proper size feeler gauge between the valve and adjusting screw. Check and if necessary, adjust the following valves: Intake 1, 2 and 4 and Exhaust: 1, 3 and 6.

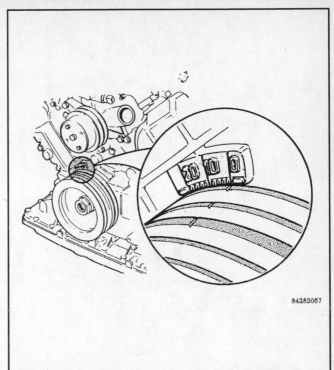

84282057

Fig. 51 Pulley timing mark should be at '0" mark on engine shoulder, when adjusting valves — B280F engine

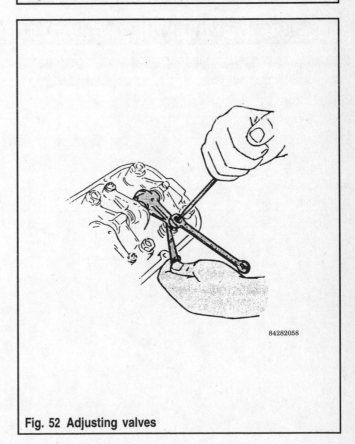

84282058

Fig. 52 Adjusting valves

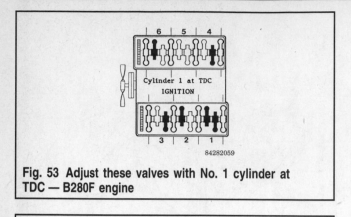

Fig. 53 Adjust these valves with No. 1 cylinder at TDC — B280F engine

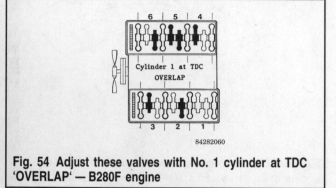

Fig. 54 Adjust these valves with No. 1 cylinder at TDC 'OVERLAP' — B280F engine

7. Rotate the crankshaft 1 complete turn (valve overlapping No. 1 cylinder), so that the mark on the pulley is again opposite '0' mark on the engine shoulder.

8. Check and if necessary, adjust the following valves: Intake 3, 5 and 6 and Exhaust: 2, 4 and 5.

9. Install the valve covers, using a new valve cover gaskets.

10. Reinstall all removed components.

11. Connect the negative battery cable. Check engine operation.

B6304F Engine

The B6304F engine is equipped with 24 hydraulic tappets. The oil-filled tappets are self-adjusting.

IDLE SPEED AND MIXTURE ADJUSTMENTS

Although the idle speed may be checked, it is not adjustable. All idle speed functions are carried out by the ECU.

3

ENGINE AND ENGINE REBUILDING

ENGINE ELECTRICAL

➡ Disconnecting the negative battery cable may interfere with the functions of the on board computer systems and may require the computer to undergo a relearning process, once the negative battery cable is reconnected.

Understanding the Engine Electrical System

The engine electrical system can be broken down into three separate and distinct systems:
1. The starting system
2. The charging system
3. The ignition system.

BATTERY AND STARTING SYSTEM

♦ See Figure 1

Basic Operating Principles

The battery is the first link in the chain of electrical components which work together to provide cranking of the automobile engine. In most modern vehicles, the battery is a lead/acid electrochemical device consisting of 6 2-volt (2 V) subsections connected in series so the unit is capable of producing approximately 12 V of electrical pressure. Each subsection, or cell, consists of a series of positive and negative plates held a short distance apart in a solution of sulfuric acid and water. The 2 types of plates are of dissimilar metals. This causes a chemical reaction to be set up, and it is this reaction which produces current flow from the battery when its positive and negative terminals are connected to an electrical appliance such as a lamp or motor. The continued transfer of electrons would eventually convert the sulfuric acid in the electrolyte to water, and make the 2 plates identical in chemical composition. As electrical energy is removed from the battery, its voltage output tends to d rop. Thus, measuring battery voltage and battery electrolyte composition are 2 ways of checking the ability of the unit to supply power. During the starting of the engine, electrical energy is removed from the battery. However, if the charging circuit is in good condition and the operating conditions are normal, the power removed from the battery will be replaced by the generator (or alternator) which will force electrons back through the battery, reversing the normal flow, and restoring the battery to its original chemical state.

The battery and starting motor are linked by very heavy electrical cables designed to minimize resistance to the flow of current. Generally, the major power supply cable that leaves the battery goes directly to the starter, while other electrical system needs are supplied by a smaller cable. During starter operation, power flows from the battery to the starter and is grounded through the car's frame and the battery's negative ground strap.

The starting motor is a specially designed, direct current electric motor capable of producing a very great amount of power for its size. One thing that allows the motor to produce a great deal of power is its tremendous rotating speed. It

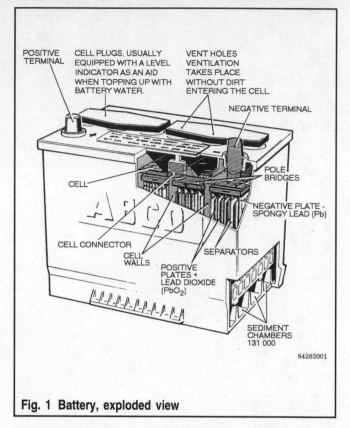

Fig. 1 Battery, exploded view

drives the engine through a tiny pinion gear (attached to the starter's armature), which drives the very large flywheel ring gear at a greatly reduced speed. Another factor allowing it to produce so much power is that only intermittent operation is required of it. This, little allowance for air circulation is required, and the windings can be built into a very small space.

The starter solenoid is a magnetic device which employs the small current supplied by the starting switch circuit of the ignition switch. This magnetic action moves a plunger which mechanically engages the starter and electrically closes the heavy switch which connects it to the battery. The starting switch circuit consists of the starting switch contained within the ignition switch, a transmission neutral safety switch or clutch pedal switch, and the wiring necessary to connect these in series with the starter solenoid or relay.

A pinion, which is a small gear, is mounted to a one-way drive clutch. This clutch is splined to the starter armature shaft. When the ignition switch is moved to the START position, the solenoid plunger slides the pinion toward the flywheel ring gear via a collar and spring. If the teeth on the pinion and flywheel match properly, the pinion will engage the flywheel immediately. If the gear teeth butt one another, the spring will be compressed and will force the gears to mesh as soon as the starter turns far enough to allow them to do so. As the solenoid plunger reaches the end of its travel, it closes the contacts that connect the battery and starter and then the engine is cranked.

As soon as the engine starts, the flywheel ring gear begins turning fast enough to drive the pinion at an extremely high rate of speed. At this point, the one-way clutch begins allowing the pinion to spin faster than the starter shaft so that the starter will not operate at excessive speed. When the ignition switch is released from the starter position, the solenoid is de-energized, and a spring contained within the solenoid assembly pulls the gear out of mesh and interrupts the current flow to the starter.

CHARGING SYSTEM

Basic Operating Principles

The automobile charging system provides electrical power for operation of the vehicle's ignition and starting systems and all the electrical accessories. The battery services as an electrical surge or storage tank, storing (in chemical form) the energy originally produced by the engine driven generator. The system also provides a means of regulating generator output to protect the battery from being overcharged and to avoid excessive voltage to the accessories.

The storage battery is a chemical device incorporating parallel lead plates in a tank containing a sulfuric acid/water solution. Adjacent plates are slightly dissimilar, and the chemical reaction of the 2 dissimilar plates produces electrical energy when the battery is connected to a load such as the starter motor. The chemical reaction is reversible, so that when the generator is producing a voltage (electrical pressure) greater than that produced by the battery, electricity is forced into the battery, and the battery is returned to its fully charged state.

The vehicle's alternator is driven mechanically, through V-belts, by the engine crankshaft. In an alternator, the field rotates while all the current produced passes only through the stator winding. The brushes bear against continuous slip rings rather than a commutator. This causes the current produced to periodically reverse the direction of its flow. Diodes (electrical one-way switches) block the flow of current from traveling in the wrong direction. A series of diodes is wired together to permit the alternating flow of the stator to be converted to a pulsating, but unidirectional flow at the alternator output. The alternator's field is wired in series with the voltage regulator.

The regulator consists of several circuits. Each circuit has a core, or magnetic coil of wire, which operates a switch. Each switch is connected to ground through 1 or more resistors. The coil of wire responds directly to system voltage. When the voltage reaches the required level, the magnetic field created by the winding of wire closes the switch and inserts a resistance into the generator field circuit, thus reducing the output. The contacts of the switch cycle open and close many times each second to precisely control voltage.

Ignition Coil

EZK Ignition System

The ignition coil used with this system is a special type of coil, with a low resistance primary winding, enabling it to generate very high ignition voltage even if the battery voltage is low.

REX 1 Ignition System

The ignition coil used on the REX 1 ignition system is combined with the power stage into a single unit (Power Stage/Ignition Coil). The power stage contains the electronic circuits that regulate the primary current of the ignition coil.

Bosch Motronic 1.8 Ignition System

In the Motronic 1.8 system, each cylinder is equipped with an individual ignition coil to assure high voltage and accurate control of ignition. There are 6 coils controlled by a power unit. There is no distributor or spark plug cables.

TESTING

EZK Ignition System
▶ See Figure 2

PRIMARY WINDING TEST

1. Remove fuse No. 1 (model 740/940) or fuse No. 31 (model 760) from the fusebox. Note that these fuses must be removed whenever any connector to or from the ECU is removed or installed.
2. Remove the air filter to gain access to the power stage.
3. Remove the connector from the power stage.
4. Remove the rubber cover from the connector to expose the terminals. Never test the terminals from the front. This could result in damage to the terminals and make any faults worse.
5. Connect an ohmmeter between the power stage amplifier connector terminal 1 and terminal 15 of the ignition coil. Resistance should be 0.6-1.0 ohms.
6. If resistance is low, replace ignition coil.
7. If resistance is too high, connect an ohmmeter directly to terminals 1 and 15 of the ignition coil. If resistance is still to high, replace the ignition coil.
8. If resistance is correct (0.6-1.0 ohm), check wire between ignition coil and power stage amplifier connector terminal 1. Replace/repair wire as needed.

SECONDARY WINDING TEST

1. Remove fuse No. 1 (model 740) or fuse No. 31 (model 760) from the fusebox. Note that these fuses must be removed whenever any connector to or from the ECU is removed or installed.
2. Remove the air filter to gain access to the power stage.
3. Remove the connector from the power stage.
4. Remove the rubber cover from the connector to expose the terminals. Never test the terminals from the front. This could result in damage to the terminals and make any faults worse.
5. Connect an ohmmeter between the power stage amplifier connector terminal 1 and the ignition coil high tension terminal (coil tower). Resistance should be 6.5-9.0 ohms.
6. If resistance is higher or lower, replace the ignition coil.

REX 1 Ignition System

Since the REX 1 system combines the ignition coil with power stage, testing procedures for the REX 1 coil is con-

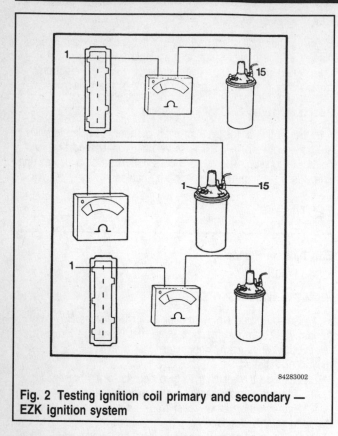

Fig. 2 Testing ignition coil primary and secondary — EZK ignition system

tained in Section 2 under 'VOLVO EZK AND REX 1 IGNITION SYSTEMS' — Power Stage (Amplifier) Check.

Bosch Motronic 1.8 Ignition System

In the Motronic 1.8 system, each cylinder is equipped with an individual ignition coil to assure high voltage and accurate control of ignition. There is no distributor or spark plug cables. Testing procedures for the Motronic 1.8 system is contained in Section 2 under 'MOTRONIC IGNITION SYSTEM' — No Start Check.

REMOVAL & INSTALLATION

Except Motronic Ignition System

1. Disconnect the negative battery cable.
2. Disconnect and tag the coil primary leads. Carefully remove the HT lead from the coil tower.
3. Remove the mounting bolt(s) from the ignition coil retaining bracket and remove the ignition coil.
4. Installation is the reverse of the removal procedure.

➡**The ignition coil used on the REX 1 ignition system is combined with the power stage into a single unit (Power Stage/Ignition Coil). The unit is service as an assembly.**

Bosch Motronic 1.8 Ignition System

This system uses 6 individual coils, 1 on each spark plug.
1. Disconnect the negative battery cable.
2. Remove the large coil cover on the top of the engine that is secured to the cam cover. Use care not to drop any of the small retaining screws.

3. Remove any ducting or hoses that may be in the way, matchmarking for assembly.
4. Remove the hold-down capscrews from the coil top.
5. Disconnect the electrical connector from the coil top assembly.
6. Carefully pull the coil from the spark plug, pulling straight up while turning slightly to disengage from the top of the spark plug.

To install:
7. Installation is the reverse of the removal procedure. Press the coil straight down onto the spark plug. There should a slight 'click' as the coil seats on the spark plug top.
8. Install the hold-down capscrews, and make sure the electrical connection is secure.
9. Install the coil cover and make sure any hose connections that were removed are now secure.

Ignition Module

REMOVAL & INSTALLATION

▶ **See Figure 3**

The Electronic Control Unit (ECU) is located behind the left side instrument panel. In order to gain access to the ECU the driver's side panel must be lowered. Release the catch and unplug the connector from the control unit.

➡**Never replace a control unit without first correcting the original fault. The fault may damage the new control unit.**

Distributor

The only function of the distributor is to distribute voltage to the spark plugs. There are no advance functions built into the distributor. It is no 'longer possible to adjust ignition timing through the distributor.

REMOVAL & INSTALLATION

▶ **See Figure 4**

1. Disconnect the negative battery cable.
2. Remove the protective cover and distributor cap.
3. Remove the rotor, dust cover and O-ring.

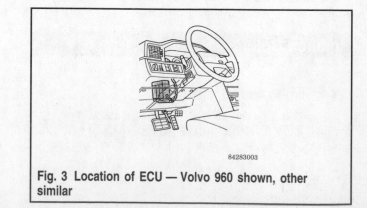

Fig. 3 Location of ECU — Volvo 960 shown, other similar

4. Remove the camshaft center bolt and rotor holder. Pull the distributor housing forward until its base rests against the rotor holder. Tap the distributor housing lightly, with a hammer, to release the rotor holder from the shaft.

5. To install, reverse the removal procedure. Tighten the rotor holder 52-66 ft. lbs. (70-90 Nm).

Alternator

ALTERNATOR PRECAUTIONS

Several precautions must be observed when performing work on alternator equipment.

• If the battery is removed for any reason, make sure that it is reconnected with the correct polarity. Reversing the battery connections may result in damage to the one-way rectifiers.

• Never operate the alternator with the main circuit broken. Make sure that the battery, alternator, and regulator leads are not disconnected while the engine is running.

• Never attempt to polarize an alternator.

• When charging a battery that is installed in the vehicle, disconnect the negative battery cable.

• When utilizing a booster battery as a starting aid, always connect it in parallel; negative to negative, and positive to positive.

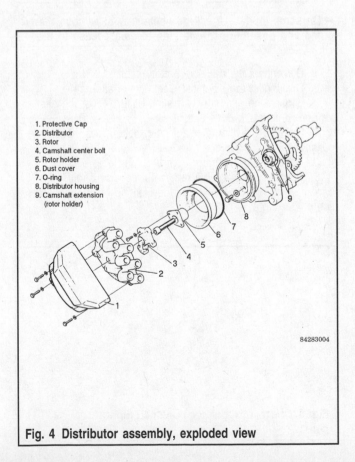

1. Protective Cap
2. Distributor
3. Rotor
4. Camshaft center bolt
5. Rotor holder
6. Dust cover
7. O-ring
8. Distributor housing
9. Camshaft extension
   (rotor holder)

84283004

Fig. 4 Distributor assembly, exploded view

• When arc (electric) welding is to be performed on any part of the vehicle, disconnect the negative battery cable and alternator leads.

• Never unplug the ECU while the engine is running or with the ignition in the **ON** position. Severe and expensive damage may result within the solid state equipment.

TESTING

Before an alternator can be determined faulty, first check for the following:
• defective battery
• damaged or loose cables
• loose alternator belt
• faulty voltage regulator

Measuring Unloaded Charging Voltage

1. Connect a voltmeter across the battery terminals.
2. Turn all accessories OFF. Run the engine at 2,000 rpm and note the voltage reading. Voltage should be 13.5-14.5 volts at 68°F (20°C).
   a. If the voltage is higher than 14.5 volts, the system is overcharging. Replace the voltage regulator and recheck.
   b. If the voltage is less than 13.5 volts, the charging voltage is too low. Check for a voltage drop.

Measuring Charging Voltage Under Load

1. Connect a voltmeter across the battery terminals.
2. Run the engine at 2,000 rpm and note the voltage reading.
3. Load the alternator, by switching on the vehicle accessories (low beam and parking lamps, rear window defogger, A/C-Heater fan on HI,...etc). Compare the reading with the previous Unloaded reading. Maximum voltage drop = 0.4 volt.
   a. If the difference is less that 0.4 volt, the charging is okay.
   b. if the difference is greater that 0.4 volt, check for voltage drop.

Checking Voltage Drop

POSITIVE CIRCUIT

1. Connect a voltmeter (range 0-4 volts) across the alternator B+ and battery positive pole.
2. Run the engine at 2,000 rpm and load the alternator, by switching on the vehicle accessories.
3. If the voltage drop is less than 0.2 volt, check the circuit from the alternator B+ to the starter motor and then to the battery +. Check to ensure the connections are not loose or corroded. If necessary, scrape and clean the terminals. Tighten all connectors and recheck.

NEGATIVE CIRCUIT

1. Connect a voltmeter (range 0-4 volts) across the alternator housing and battery negative pole.
2. Run the engine at 2,000 rpm and load the alternator, by switching on the vehicle accessories.
3. If the voltage drop is more than 0.2 volt, check the circuit between the battery negative pole and the vehicle's ground and engine. Check to ensure the connections are not

loose or corroded. If necessary, scrape and clean the terminals. Tighten all connectors and recheck.

Separating Alternator Faults From Voltage Regulator Faults

1. Disconnect the connector from the regulator and connect a bridge wire between D+ and DF (RED/GREEN wire and BROWN/WHITE wire).

2. Connect a voltmeter between the alternator B+ and ground. An inductive ammeter will also be helpful.

3. Load the alternator, by switching on the vehicle accessories (low beam and parking lamps, rear window defogger, A/C-Heater fan on HI,...etc). The ammeter should indicate at least 30-45 amperes.

4. Run the engine at 2,000 rpm and note the voltmeter reading.

5. If the voltmeter shows more than 15 volts, the alternator is okay. Replace the voltage regulator.

6. If the voltmeter shows less than 15 volts, the alternator or regulator harness is defective.

Checking Regulator Harness(Non-sealed Type)

Remove the regulator harness from the vehicle and check with an ohmmeter. If okay, replace the alternator.

Checking Regulator Harness(Sealed Type)

1. Disconnect the connector from the regulator. Connect an ohmmeter and check that D+ is connected to the alternator ground.

2. Run the engine at 1,500 rpm.

3. Check the armature resistance between DF and D-. Correct resistance = 4 ohms (4-10 ohms, depending on condition of brushes).

    a. If the resistance is less than 4 ohms, the alternator is defective.

    b. If the resistance is higher than 10 ohms, check for defective brushes, wiring or break in armature circuit.

Testing Alternator-Mounted Voltage Regulator

▶ **See Figures 5 and 6**

1. Check if the vehicle's charging system lamp is ON with the engine operating.

2. If the lamp is ON, check for a loose belt.

3. Connect a jumper wire between alternator D+ and B+, while the engine is operating.

    a. If the lamp still lights, check for an open circuit in the lead between the regulator (short, red) cable and alternator B+. Replace, if defective.

    b. If the cable is okay, then either the regulator or the alternator is defective. Replace the regulator and recheck. If the fault remains, replace the alternator.

4. If the vehicle's charging system lamp is OFF, check the bulb. Replace, if blown.

5. Check the brushes in the regulator. Replace the regulator if the brushes are worn (less that 0.2 in. (5mm) above the holder).

6. Check the alternator coil for an open circuit.

7. Connect an ohmmeter to the slip rings. If the resistance is more that 10 ohms (indicating an open circuit), replace the alternator and check the regulator. Otherwise, replace the regulator.

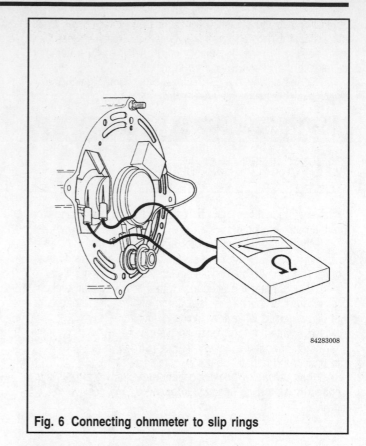

Fig. 6 Connecting ohmmeter to slip rings

REMOVAL & INSTALLATION

➡**On some models, it will be necessary to remove the air pump and position it to one side to gain access to the alternator.**

1. Disconnect the negative battery cable.

2. Disconnect the electrical leads to the alternator.

3. Loosen the alternator adjusting bolt(s). Pivot the alternator and remove the drive belt.

4. Remove the alternator adjusting bolt(s) and mounting bolts.

5. Remove the alternator from the vehicle.

6. To install, reverse the removal procedure. Adjust the drive belt tension as outlined in the Routine Maintenance section of Section 1.

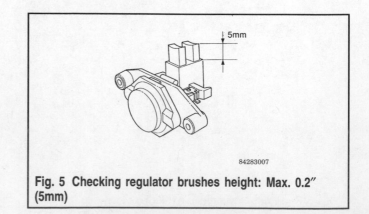

Fig. 5 Checking regulator brushes height: Max. 0.2″ (5mm)

Battery

REMOVAL & INSTALLATION

1. Remove the positive and negative cables from their terminals on the top of the battery. If the cables remain stuck to the terminals after loosening the cable clamps, use a puller to free them. Do not try to pry the cables off the terminals; damage to the battery case and/or the terminals may result.

2. Remove the battery hold-down bar and lift out the battery. Keep the battery upright to avoid spilling acidic electrolyte.

3. Clean the battery case and support shelf with a brush and rinse with clean, lukewarm water. Remove any deposits from the terminals and cable ends with a wire brush or battery terminal tool.

4. Replace the battery on its support shelf and install the hold-down bar.

5. Install the cables in their proper terminals and tighten the clamps. Coat the exposed metal of the cables and terminals with petroleum jelly to prevent corrosion.

Starter

TESTING

Before the starter motor can be determined faulty, first check for the following:
- defective battery
- damaged or loose cables
- ground straps between battery, vehicle's body and engine.
- starter motor cables are correctly connected

Checking Battery

1. Turn ON the high beams.

2. Operate the ignition switch and check the headlights.

3. If the lights dim considerable, the battery is poorly charged. Charge the battery or test with a new battery.

4. If the lights do not dim, test the starter with a separate battery.

Checking the Starter Control Circuit

1. Connect a separate lead between the battery B+ and terminal 50 on the starter motor.

2. If the starter motor operates, check for a faulty ignition switch or cables between the starter motor and switch.

3. If the starter motor does not operate, the starter motor is defective.

REMOVAL & INSTALLATION

1. Disconnect the negative battery cable at the battery.

2. Remove the starter motor retaining bolts.

3. Lower the starter and disconnect the leads from the starter motor.

4. Remove the starter motor from the vehicle.

5. To reinstall, position the starter motor to the flywheel housing. Apply locking compound to the bolt threads and install the retaining bolts finger-tight. Torque the bolts to approximately 25 ft. lbs.

6. Connect the starter motor leads and the negative battery cable.

SOLENOID REPLACEMENT

▶ See Figure 7

1. Disconnect the negative battery cable.

2. Remove the starter motor from the vehicle.

3. Remove the nut securing the cable to the field coil.

4. Remove the solenoid mounting bolts from the front of the starting motor. Remove the solenoid assembly.

5. Installation is the reverse of the removal procedure.

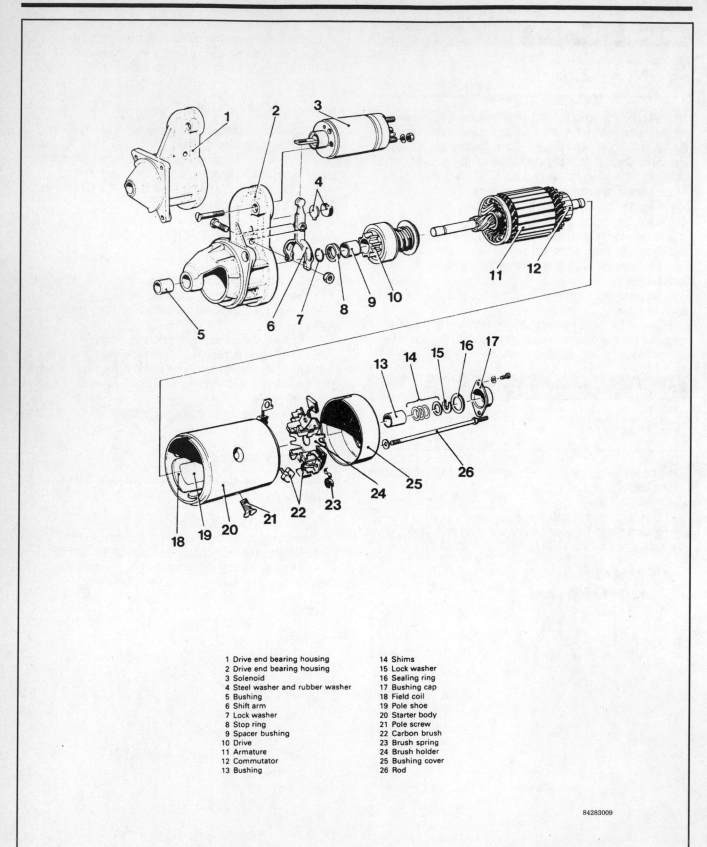

1 Drive end bearing housing	14 Shims
2 Drive end bearing housing	15 Lock washer
3 Solenoid	16 Sealing ring
4 Steel washer and rubber washer	17 Bushing cap
5 Bushing	18 Field coil
6 Shift arm	19 Pole shoe
7 Lock washer	20 Starter body
8 Stop ring	21 Pole screw
9 Spacer bushing	22 Carbon brush
10 Drive	23 Brush spring
11 Armature	24 Brush holder
12 Commutator	25 Bushing cover
13 Bushing	26 Rod

84283009

Fig. 7 Bosch starter motor, exploded view

ENGINE MECHANICAL

➡**Before performing any of the repairs listed in this portion of Section 3, refer to 'VOLVO SERVICE TIPS' in this Section for information that may apply to your specific situation or repair.**

Engine Overhaul Tips

Most engine overhaul procedures are fairly standard. In addition to specific parts replacement procedures and complete specifications for each individual engine, this Section is also a guide to acceptable rebuilding procedures. Examples of standard rebuilding practice are shown and should be used along with specific details concerning your particular engine.

Competent and accurate machine shop services will insure maximum performance, reliability and engine life. In most instances, it is more profitable for the do-it-yourself mechanic to remove, clean and inspect the component, buy the necessary parts and deliver these to a shop for actual machine work.

On the other hand, much of the rebuilding work (crankshaft, block, bearings, piston rods, and other components) is well within the scope of the do-it-yourself mechanic.

TOOLS

The tools required for an engine overhaul or parts replacement will depend on the depth of your involvement. With few exceptions, they will be the tools found in any mechanic's tool kit (see Section 1). More in-depth work will require some or all of the following:
a dial indicator (reading in thousandths) mounted on a universal base
micrometers and telescope gauges
jaw and screw-type pullers
scraper
valve spring compressor
ring groove cleaner
piston ring expander and compressor
ridge reamer
cylinder hone or glaze breaker
Plastigage®
engine stand
The use of most of these tools is illustrated in this Section. Many can be rented for a one-time use from a local parts jobber or tool supply house specializing in automotive work. Occasionally, the use of special tools is called for. See the information on Special Tools and Safety Notice in the front of this book before substituting another tool.

INSPECTION TECHNIQUES

Procedures and specifications are given in this Section for inspecting, cleaning and assessing the wear limits of most major components. Other procedures such as Magnaflux® and Zyglo® can be used to locate material flaws and stress cracks. Magnaflux® is a magnetic process applicable only to ferrous materials. The Zyglo® process coats the material with a fluorescent dye penetrate and can be used on any material Check for suspected surface cracks can be more readily made using spot check dye. The dye is sprayed onto the suspected area, wiped off and the area sprayed with a developer. Cracks will show up brightly.

OVERHAUL NOTES

Aluminum has become extremely popular for use in engines, due to its low weight. Observe the following precautions when handling aluminum parts:
Never hot tank aluminum parts; the caustic hot-tank solution will eat the aluminum.
Remove all aluminum parts (identification tag, etc.) from engine parts prior to the tanking.
Always coat threads lightly with engine oil or anti-seize compounds before installation, to prevent seizure.
Never overtorque bolts or spark plugs, especially in aluminum threads.
When assembling the engine, any parts that will be in frictional contact must be prelubed to provide lubrication at initial start-up. Any product specifically formulated for this purpose can be used, but engine oil is not recommended as a prelube.
When semi-permanent (locked, but removable) installation of bolts or nuts is desired, threads should be cleaned and coated with Loctite® or other similar, commercial non-hardening sealant.

REPAIRING DAMAGED THREADS

▶ **See Figures 8, 9, 10, 11 and 12**

Damage threads can usually be repaired with thread inserts. However, some threads cannot, or must not be repaired with threads inserts. Threads inserts and installation tools are available from Volvo.

Repairing Spark Plug Threads

1. Do not drill the hole. Use a combination tap (Volvo 9985823-5 or equivalent). Use thread insert (948756-2 or equivalent).
2. Measure the length and thread of the old hole.
3. Measure the depth of the hole. Drill out the hole to this depth. Cut the screw thread to such a depth that the thread insert makes contact with fully cut screw thread along its entire length. Clean the hole.
4. Assemble the installation tool:
   a. M6-M14 threads: Install the correct mandrel and crank in the installation tool (998 5820-0 or equivalent).
   b. M16 and coarser threads: Use the appropriate installation tool.
5. Fit the thread insert in the tool with the tang facing downwards.
6. Turn the crank clockwise until the tang of the thread insert engages the slot in the crank.

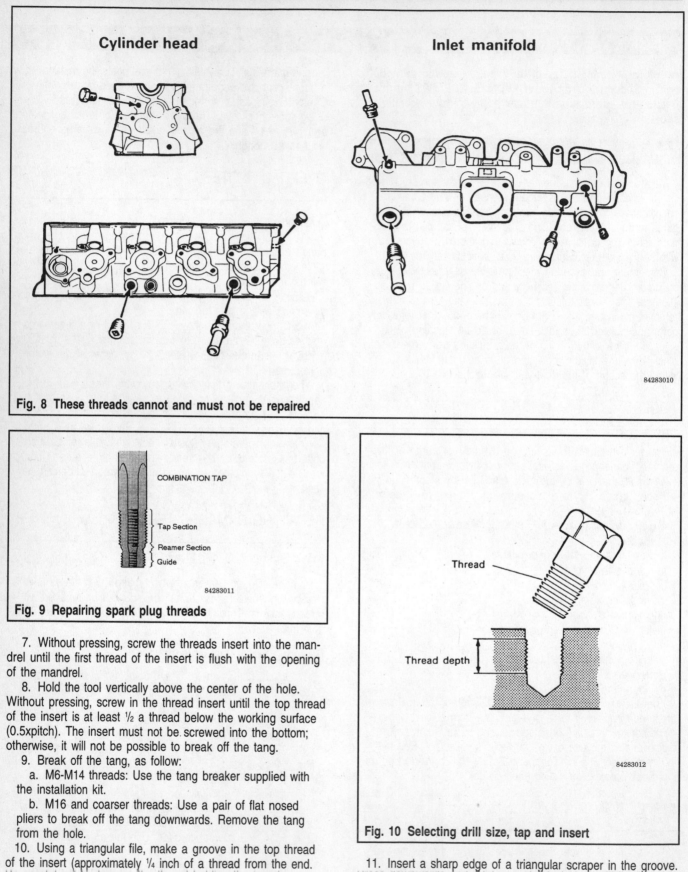

Fig. 8 These threads cannot and must not be repaired

Fig. 9 Repairing spark plug threads

Fig. 10 Selecting drill size, tap and insert

7. Without pressing, screw the threads insert into the mandrel until the first thread of the insert is flush with the opening of the mandrel.

8. Hold the tool vertically above the center of the hole. Without pressing, screw in the thread insert until the top thread of the insert is at least ½ a thread below the working surface (0.5xpitch). The insert must not be screwed into the bottom; otherwise, it will not be possible to break off the tang.

9. Break off the tang, as follow:

a. M6-M14 threads: Use the tang breaker supplied with the installation kit.

b. M16 and coarser threads: Use a pair of flat nosed pliers to break off the tang downwards. Remove the tang from the hole.

10. Using a triangular file, make a groove in the top thread of the insert (approximately ¼ inch of a thread from the end. Be careful not to damage the thread holding the insert.

11. Insert a sharp edge of a triangular scraper in the groove. Press downwards and rotate counterclockwise until the insert is removed.

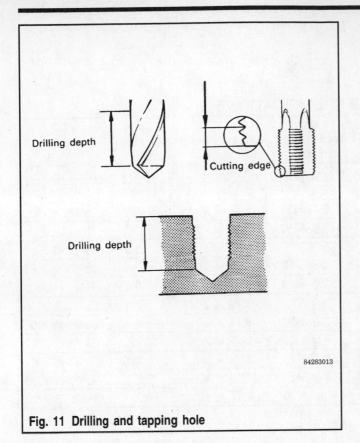

Fig. 11 Drilling and tapping hole

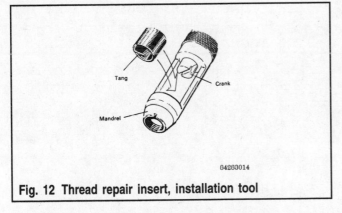

Fig. 12 Thread repair insert, installation tool

12. Clean the hole with a tap and fit a new insert.

COMPRESSION TESTING

A noticeable lack of engine power, excessive oil consumption and/or poor fuel mileage measured over an extended period are all indicators of internal engine war. Worn piston rings, scored or worn cylinder bores, blown head gaskets, sticking or burnt valves and worn valve seats are all possible culprits here. A check of each cylinder's compression will help you locate the problems.

As mentioned in the Tools and Equipment section of Section 1, a screw-in type compression gauge is more accurate that the type you simply hold against the spark plug hole, although it takes slightly longer to use. It's worth it to obtain a more accurate reading. Follow the procedures below.

1. Warm up the engine to normal operating temperature.

2. On B6304F engine, disconnect and remove the timing pick-up connector, ignition coil relay connector, and throttle pulley cover. Remove all ignition coils and spark plugs.

3. On all engine, remove all the spark plugs.

4. Disconnect the lead from terminal 1 and the high tension lead from the ignition coil.

5. Disconnect the injector connectors to avoid flooding the engine and diluting the engine oil. On B6304 engine, remove fuse No. 31 to disarm the fuel pump.

6. Block the throttle in fully open position or by having an assistant floor the accelerator pedal.

7. Screw the compression gauge into the no.1 spark plug hole until the fitting is snug.

❄❄WARNING

Be careful not to crossthread the plug hole. On aluminum cylinder heads use extra care, as the threads in these heads are easily ruined.

8. Operate the engine through five crankshaft revolutions, using a remote starter switch or ask your assistant to operate the ignition switch.

9. Read the compression gauge at the end of each series of cranks, and record the highest of these readings. Repeat this procedure for each of the engine's cylinders. The lowest cylinder pressure should be within 75% of the highest cylinder pressure reading. For example, if the highest cylinder is 134 psi, the lowest should be 101 psi.

A cylinder's compression pressure is usually acceptable if it is not less than 80% of the specified value. The difference between any two cylinders should be no more than 12-14 psi.

10. If a cylinder is unusually low, pour a tablespoon of clean engine oil into the cylinder through the spark plug hole and repeat the compression test. If the compression comes up after adding the oil, it appears that the cylinder's piston rings or bore are damaged or worn. If the pressure remains low, the valves may not be seating properly (a valve job is needed), or the head gasket may be blown near that cylinder. If compression in any two adjacent cylinders is low, and if the addition of oil doesn't help the compression, there is leakage past the head gasket. Oil and coolant in the combustion chamber can result from this problem. There may be evidence of water droplets on the engine dipstick when a head gasket has blown.

GENERAL ENGINE SPECIFICATIONS

Year	Engine ID/VIN	Engine Displacement Liters (cc)	Fuel System Type	Net Horsepower @ rpm	Net Torque @ rpm (ft. lbs.)	Bore × Stroke (in.)	Compression Ratio	Oil Pressure @ rpm
1990	B-230F	2.3 (2316)	④	114 @ 5400	136 @ 2750	3.78 × 3.15	9.8:1	35–85 @ 2000
	B-230FT	2.3 (2316)	④	①	②	3.78 × 3.15	8.7:1	35–85 @ 2000
	B-234F	2.3 (2316)	LH2.4	153 @ 5700	150 @ 4450	3.78 × 3.15	10.0:1	35–85 @ 2000
	B-280F	2.8 (2849)	LH2.2	144 @ 5100	173 @ 3750	3.58 × 2.87	9.5:1	⑤
1991	B-230F	2.3 (2316)	④	114 @ 5400	136 @ 2750	3.78 × 3.15	9.8:1	35–85 @ 2000
	B-230FT	2.3 (2316)	④	162 @ 4800	195 @ 3450	3.78 × 3.15	8.7:1	35–85 @ 2000
	B-234F	2.3 (2316)	LH2.4	153 @ 5700	150 @ 4450	3.78 × 3.15	10.0:1	35–85 @ 2000
1992	B-230F	2.3 (2316)	③	114 @ 5400	136 @ 2750	3.78 × 3.15	9.8:1	35–85 @ 2000
	B-230FT	2.3 (2316)	LH2.4	162 @ 4800	195 @ 3450	3.78 × 3.15	8.7:1	35–85 @ 2000
	B-6304F	2.9 (2922)	Motronic	204 @ 6000	197 @ 4300	3.27 × 3.54	10.7:1	36 @ 2000
1993	B-230F	2.3 (2316)	③	114 @ 5400	136 @ 2750	3.78 × 3.15	9.8:1	35–85 @ 2000
	B-230FT	2.3 (2316)	LH2.4	162 @ 4800	195 @ 3450	3.78 × 3.15	8.7:1	35–85 @ 2000
	B-6304F	2.9 (2922)	Motronic	204 @ 6000	197 @ 4300	3.27 × 3.54	10.7:1	36 @ 2000

NOTE: Horsepower and torque are SAE net figures. They are measured at the rear of the transmission with all accessories installed and operating. Since the figures vary when a given engine is installed in different models, some are representative rather than exact.

LH—Bosch LH Fuel Injection
① 740 Turbo—162 @ 4800
  760 Turbo—162 @ 4000
  780 Turbo—188 @ 5100
② 740 Turbo and 760 Turbo—195 @ 3450
  780 turbo—206 @ 3900
③ 240—LH
  740 and 940GL—Regina
④ Refer to "Engine Identification Chart"
⑤ Engine warm:
    14.2 psi @ 900 rpm
    56.8 psi @ 3000 rpm

84283087

CAMSHAFT SPECIFICATIONS

All measurements given in inches.

Year	Engine ID/VIN	Engine Displacement Liters (cc)	Journal Diameter					Elevation		Bearing Clearance	Camshaft End Play
			1	2	3	4	5	In.	Ex.		
1990	B-230F	2.3 (2316)	1.179–1.180	1.179–1.180	1.179–1.180	1.179–1.180	—	0.374	0.414	0.0012–0.0028	0.004–0.016
	B-230FT	2.3 (2316)	1.179–1.180	1.179–1.180	1.179–1.180	1.179–1.180	—	0.374	0.414	0.0012–0.0028	0.004–0.016
	B-234F	2.3 (2316)	NA	NA	NA	NA	—	0.370	0.370	0.0012–0.0028	0.004–0.016
	B-280F	2.8 (2849)	1.592–1.593	1.616–1.617	1.639–1.640	0.664–1.665	—	0.235	0.214	0.0014–0.0034	NA
1991	B-230F	2.3 (2316)	1.179–1.180	1.179–1.180	1.179–1.180	1.179–1.180	—	0.374	0.414	0.0012–0.0028	0.004–0.016
	B-230FT	2.3 (2316)	1.179–1.180	1.179–1.180	1.179–1.180	1.179–1.180	—	0.374	0.414	0.0012–0.0028	0.004–0.016
	B-234F	2.3 (2316)	NA	NA	NA	NA	—	0.370	0.370	0.0012–0.0028	0.004–0.016
1992	B-230F	2.3 (2316)	1.179–1.180	1.179–1.180	1.179–1.180	1.179–1.180	—	0.374	0.414	0.0012–0.0028	0.004–0.016
	B-230FT	2.3 (2316)	1.179–1.180	1.179–1.180	1.179–1.180	1.179–1.180	—	0.374	0.414	0.0012–0.0028	0.004–0.016
	B-6304F	2.9 (2922)	NA	NA	NA	NA	—	0.354	0.354	NA	0.002–0.008
1993	B-230F	2.3 (2316)	1.179–1.180	1.179–1.180	1.179–1.180	1.179–1.180	—	0.374	0.414	0.0012–0.0028	0.004–0.016
	B-230FT	2.3 (2316)	1.179–1.180	1.179–1.180	1.179–1.180	1.179–1.180	—	0.374	0.414	0.0012–0.0028	0.004–0.016
	B-6304F	2.9 (2922)	NA	NA	NA	NA	—	0.354	0.354	NA	0.002–0.008

NA—Not available

84283088

CRANKSHAFT AND CONNECTING ROD SPECIFICATIONS

All measurements are given in inches.

Year	Engine ID/VIN	Engine Displacement Liters (cc)	Crankshaft				Connecting Rod		
			Main Brg. Journal Dia.	Main Brg. Oil Clearance	Shaft End-play	Thrust on No.	Journal Diameter	Oil Clearance	Side Clearance
1990	B-230F	2.3 (2316)	2.4981–2.4986	0.0011–0.0033	0.0015–0.0058	5	2.1255–2.1260	0.0009–0.0028	0.006–0.014
	B-230FT	2.3 (2316)	2.4981–2.4986	0.0011–0.0033	0.0015–0.0058	5	2.1255–2.1260	0.0009–0.0028	0.006–0.014
	B-234F	2.3 (2316)	1.9640–1.9648	0.0011–0.0033	0.0015–0.0058	5	2.0472–2.0476	0.0009–0.0028	0.006–0.018
	B-280F	2.8 (2849)	2.7576–2.7583	0.0035	0.0028–0.0106	4	2.3611–2.3618	0.0079–0.0150	0.0079–0.0150
1991	B-230F	2.3 (2316)	2.4981–2.4986	0.0011–0.0033	0.0015–0.0058	5	2.1255–2.1260	0.0009–0.0028	0.006–0.014
	B-230FT	2.3 (2316)	2.4981–2.4986	0.0011–0.0033	0.0015–0.0058	5	2.1255–2.1260	0.0009–0.0028	0.006–0.014
	B-234F	2.3 (2316)	1.9640–1.9648	0.0011–0.0033	0.0015–0.0058	5	2.0472–2.0476	0.0009–0.0028	0.006–0.018
1992	B-230F	2.3 (2316)	2.4981–2.4986	0.0011–0.0033	0.0015–0.0058	5	2.1255–2.1260	0.0009–0.0028	0.006–0.014
	B-230FT	2.3 (2316)	2.4981–2.4986	0.0011–0.0033	0.0015–0.0058	5	2.1255–2.1260	0.0009–0.0028	0.006–0.014
	B-6304F	2.9 (2922)	2.5590	0.0009–0.0019	NA	NA	1.9690	NA	0.005–0.017
1993	B-230F	2.3 (2316)	2.4981–2.4986	0.0011–0.0033	0.0015–0.0058	5	2.1255–2.1260	0.0009–0.0028	0.006–0.014
	B-230FT	2.3 (2316)	2.4981–2.4986	0.0011–0.0033	0.0015–0.0058	5	2.1255–2.1260	0.0009–0.0028	0.006–0.014
	B-6304F	2.9 (2922)	2.5590	0.0009–0.0019	NA	NA	1.9690	NA	0.005–0.017

NA—Not available

84283089

VALVE SPECIFICATIONS

Year	Engine ID/VIN	Engine Displacement Liters (cc)	Seat Angle (deg.)	Face Angle (deg.)	Spring Test Pressure (lbs. @ in.)	Spring Installed Height (in.)	Stem-to-Guide Clearance (in.)		Stem Diameter (in.)	
							Intake	Exhaust	Intake	Exhaust
1990	B-230F	2.3 (2316)	45	44.5	158 @ 1.08	1.79	0.0012–0.0024	0.0024–0.0036	0.3132–0.3138	0.3128–0.3134
	B-230FT	2.3 (2316)	45	44.5	158 @ 1.08	1.79	0.0012–0.0024	0.0024–0.0036	0.3132–0.3138	0.3128–0.3134
	B-234F	2.3 (2316)	45	44.5	144 @ 1.04	1.69	0.0012–0.0024	0.0016–0.0028	NA	NA
	B-280F	2.8 (2849)	45	44.5	143 @ 1.18	1.85	①	①	②	②
1991	B-230F	2.3 (2316)	45	44.5	158 @ 1.08	1.79	0.0012–0.0024	0.0024–0.0036	0.3132–0.3138	0.3128–0.3134
	B-230FT	2.3 (2316)	45	44.5	158 @ 1.08	1.79	0.0012–0.0024	0.0024–0.0036	0.3132–0.3138	0.3128–0.3134
	B-234F	2.3 (2316)	45	44.5	144 @ 1.04	1.69	0.0012–0.0024	0.0016–0.0028	NA	NA
1992	B-230F	2.3 (2316)	45	44.5	158 @ 1.08	1.79	0.0012–0.0024	0.0024–0.0036	0.3132–0.3138	0.3128–0.3134
	B-230FT	2.3 (2316)	45	44.5	158 @ 1.08	1.79	0.0012–0.0024	0.0024–0.0036	0.3132–0.3138	0.3128–0.3134
	B-6304F	2.9 (2922)	45.25	45.5	270 @ 1.34	NA	0.0012–0.0024	0.0012–0.0024	NA	NA
1993	B-230F	2.3 (2316)	45	44.5	158 @ 1.08	1.79	0.0012–0.0024	0.0024–0.0036	0.3132–0.3138	0.3128–0.3134
	B-230FT	2.3 (2316)	45	44.5	158 @ 1.08	1.79	0.0012–0.0024	0.0024–0.0036	0.3132–0.3138	0.3128–0.3134
	B-6304F	2.9 (2922)	45.25	45.5	270 @ 1.34	NA	0.0012–0.0024	0.0012–0.0024	NA	NA

NOTE: Exhaust valves for turbo engines are stellite coated and must not be machined. They may be ground against the valve seat.

NA—Not available

① Tapered valve guide ID—0.3150–0.3158

② Tapered valve stem
  Intake
   Base—0.3135–0.3141
   Top—0.3139–0.3145
  Exhaust
   Base—0.3127–0.3133
   Top—0.3136–0.3141

84283090

PISTON AND RING SPECIFICATIONS

All measurements are given in inches.

Year	Engine ID/VIN	Engine Displacement Liters (cc)	Piston Clearance	Ring Gap			Ring Side Clearance		
				Top Compression	Bottom Compression	Oil Control	Top Compression	Bottom Compression	Oil Control
1990	B-230F	2.3 (2316)	0.0004–0.0012	0.0118–0.0217	0.0118–0.0217	0.0118–0.0256	0.0024–0.0036	0.0016–0.0028	0.0012–0.0026
	B-230FT	2.3 (2316)	0.0004–0.0012	0.0118–0.0217	0.0118–0.0217	0.0118–0.0256	0.0024–0.0036	0.0016–0.0028	0.0012–0.0026
	B-234F	2.3 (2316)	0.0004–0.0012	0.0118–0.0217	0.0118–0.0217	0.0118–0.0256	0.0024–0.0036	0.0016–0.0028	0.0012–0.0026
	B-280F	2.8 (2849)	0.0007–0.0015	0.0158–0.0236	0.0158–0.0236	0.0158–0.0571	0.0021–0.0029	0.0010–0.0021	0.0004–0.0092
1991	B-230F	2.3 (2316)	0.0004–0.0012	0.0118–0.0217	0.0118–0.0217	0.0118–0.0256	0.0024–0.0036	0.0016–0.0028	0.0012–0.0026
	B-230FT	2.3 (2316)	0.0004–0.0012	0.0118–0.0217	0.0118–0.0217	0.0118–0.0256	0.0024–0.0036	0.0016–0.0028	0.0012–0.0026
	B-234F	2.3 (2316)	0.0004–0.0012	0.0118–0.0217	0.0118–0.0217	0.0118–0.0256	0.0024–0.0036	0.0016–0.0028	0.0012–0.0026
1992	B-230F	2.3 (2316)	0.0004–0.0012	0.0118–0.0217	0.0118–0.0217	0.0118–0.0256	0.0024–0.0036	0.0016–0.0028	0.0012–0.0026
	B-230FT	2.3 (2316)	0.0004–0.0012	0.0118–0.0217	0.0118–0.0217	0.0118–0.0256	0.0024–0.0036	0.0016–0.0028	0.0012–0.0026
	B-6304F	2.9 (2922)	NA	0.0080–0.0160	0.0080–0.0160	0.0090–0.0200	0.0020–0.0033	0.0012–0.0026	0.0008–0.0022
1993	B-230F	2.3 (2316)	0.0004–0.0012	0.0118–0.0217	0.0118–0.0217	0.0118–0.0256	0.0024–0.0036	0.0016–0.0028	0.0012–0.0026
	B-230FT	2.3 (2316)	0.0004–0.0012	0.0118–0.0217	0.0118–0.0217	0.0118–0.0256	0.0024–0.0036	0.0016–0.0028	0.0012–0.0026
	B-6304F	2.9 (2922)	NA	0.0080–0.0160	0.0080–0.0160	0.0090–0.0200	0.0020–0.0033	0.0012–0.0026	0.0008–0.0022

NA—Not available

84283091

TORQUE SPECIFICATIONS
All readings in ft. lbs.

Year	Engine ID/VIN	Engine Displacement Liters (cc)	Cylinder Head Bolts	Main Bearing Bolts	Rod Bearing Bolts	Crankshaft Damper Bolts	Flywheel Bolts	Manifold Intake	Manifold Exhaust	Spark Plugs	Lug Nut
1990	B-230F	2.3 (2316)	④	80	②	③	51	12	12	18	①
	B-230FT	2.3 (2316)	④	80	②	③	51	12	12	18	①
	B-234	2.3 (2316)	⑤	80	②	③	51	12	12	18	①
	B-280F	2.8 (2849)	⑥	⑦	⑧	177–206	33–37	7–11	7–11	8–10	①
1991	B-230F	2.3 (2316)	④	80	②	③	51	12	12	18	①
	B-230FT	2.3 (2316)	④	80	②	③	51	12	12	18	①
	B-234F	2.3 (2316)	⑤	80	②	③	51	12	12	18	①
1992	B-230F	2.3 (2316)	④	80	②	③	51	12	12	18	①
	B-230FT	2.3 (2316)	④	80	②	③	51	12	12	18	①
	B-6304F	2.9 (2922)	⑨	NA	⑩	221	①	15	18	19	①
1993	B-230F	2.3 (2316)	④	80	②	③	51	12	12	18	①
	B-230FT	2.3 (2316)	④	80	②	③	51	12	12	18	①
	B-6304F	2.9 (2922)	⑨	NA	⑩	221	①	15	18	19	①

NA—Not available

① Torque lugs in a diagonal pattern:
P20—85 ft. lbs. (115 Nm)
P70/90—63 ft. lbs. (85 Nm)
② Torque in stages:
1st step—14 ft. lbs.
2nd step—angle-tighten 90°
③ Torque in stages:
1st step—43 ft. lbs.
2nd step—angle-tighten 90°
④ Torque in stages:
1st step—14 ft. lbs.
2nd step—43 ft. lbs.
3rd step—angle-tighten 90°
⑤ Torque in stages:
1st step—15 ft. lbs.
2nd step—30 ft. lbs.
3rd step—angle-tighten 115°
⑥ Tighten all bolts in stages:
1. Tighten bolts to 60 Nm (43 ft. lbs.)
2. a. Loosen bolt 1, tighten it to 20 Nm (15 ft. lbs.)
   b. Angle-tighten to 106 degrees using special tool 5098.
   c. Repeat this for remaining bolts using sequence shown in text.
   d. Loosen and tighten each bolt in turn.
On 1990 models using fixed washer bolts:
Tighten all bolts in stages:
1. Tighten bolts to 60 Nm (44 ft. lbs.)
2. a. Loosen bolts
   b. Tighten bolts to 40 Nm (30 ft. lbs.)
   c. Angle-tighten bolts 160°–180°
3. Adjust valves

⑦ Tighten all nuts in stages:
1. 30 Nm (22 ft. lbs.)
2. Slacken nut 1
3. Tighten nut 1 30–35 Nm (22–26 ft. lbs.)
4. Angle-tighten nut 1 73°–77°
5. Slacken and retighten the other nuts in the order specified in stages 2–4.
The 4 fasteners which hold No. 2 and 3 main bearings to engine block should be tightened to 20–25 Nm (15–18 ft.) after the main bearing nuts have been tightened to the specified torque.
⑧ 1. Oil threads
2. Tighten No. 1 bolt to 25 Nm (18 ft. lbs.)
3. Tighten No. 2 bolt to 25 Nm (18 ft. lbs.) + angle-tighten 75°
4. Angle-tighten No. 1 bolt 75°
5. Check/tighten both bolts to 50 Nm (37 ft. lbs.)
⑨ Cylinder head: stage 1—15 ft. lbs.
stage 2—44 ft. lbs.
stage 3 angle tightening—150°
Bolts should be tightened in sequence from center towards ends.
⑩ Tighten in stages:
1st step—15 ft. lbs.
2nd step—angle-tighten 90°

84283092

Engine

The following is an example of engine designations: **B230FT**
• B = gasoline (petrol)
• 230 = cylinder capacity
• F = fuel injection engine — with catalytic converter
• T = turbocharged

REMOVAL & INSTALLATION

B230F Engine

1. If equipped with manual transmission, remove the 4 retaining clips and lift up the shifter boot. Then, remove the snapring from the shifter.
2. Remove the battery.

3. Disconnect the windshield washer hose and engine compartment light wire. Scribe marks around the hood mount brackets on the under-side of the hood for later alignment. Remove the hood.
4. Remove the overflow tank cap. Drain the cooling system.
5. Remove the upper and lower radiator hoses. Disconnect the overflow hoses at the radiator. Disconnect the PCV hose at the cylinder head.
6. If equipped with automatic transmission disconnect the oil cooler lines at the radiator.
7. Remove the radiator and fan shroud.
8. Remove the air cleaner assembly and hoses.
9. Disconnect the hoses at the air pump. Remove the air pump and drive belt, if equipped.
10. Disconnect the vacuum pump hoses and remove the vacuum pump. disconnect the power brake booster vacuum hose.

11. Remove the power steering pump, drive belt and bracket. Position aside.

12. If equipped with air conditioning, remove the crankshaft pulley and compressor drive belt. Then, install the pulley again for reference. Remove the air conditioning wire connector and the compressor from its bracket and position aside. Remove the bracket.

13. Disconnect the vacuum hoses from the engine. Disconnect the carbon canister hoses.

14. Disconnect the distributor wire connector, high tension lead, starter cables and the clutch cable clamp.

15. Disconnect the wiring harness at the voltage regulator. Disconnect the throttle cable at the pulley and the wire for the air conditioning at the manifold solenoid.

16. Remove the gas cap. Disconnect the fuel lines at the filter and return pipe.

17. At the firewall, disconnect the electrical connectors for the ballast resistor and relays. Disconnect the heater hoses.

18. Disconnect the micro-switch connectors at the intake manifold and all remaining harness connectors to the engine.

19. Drain the crankcase.

20. Remove the exhaust manifold flange retaining nuts. Loosen the exhaust pipe clamp bolts and remove the bracket for the front exhaust pipe mount.

21. From underneath, remove the front motor mount bolts.

22. If equipped with automatic transmission, place the gear selector lever in **P** and disconnect the gear shift control rod from the transmission.

23. On manual transmission vehicles, disconnect the clutch cable. Then, loosen the set screw, drive out the pivot pin and remove the shifter from the control rod.

24. Disconnect the speedometer and the driveshaft from the transmission.

25. On overdrive equipped vehicles, disconnect the control wire from the shifter.

26. Raise and support the vehicle safely. Then, using a floor jack and a wooden block, support the weight of the engine beneath the transmission.

27. Remove the bolts for the rear transmission mount. Remove the transmission support crossmember.

28. Lift out the engine using the proper lifting equipment.

To install:

29. If detached, join the engine and transmission. Install the engine assembly in the vehicle and tighten all engine mounting bolts. Install the transmission crossmember and remove the floor-jack.

30. Install the driveshaft, speedometer cable, clutch cable (manual transmission) and gear selector mechanism.

31. Install the exhaust system. On turbocharger equipped vehicles, install the turbocharger and related exhaust pipes.

32. Install the air conditioner compressor and related accessory drive units. Install all accessory drive belts and tighten to the proper tension. Install the vacuum pump.

33. Install the radiator and shroud. Install all vacuum, coolant and fuel lines and hoses. Connect all electrical connectors previously disconnected.

34. Install the hood, windshield wipers, battery and any other component previously removed.

35. Fill the engine with oil, the radiator with coolant and the transmission with fluid.

36. Adjust the reversing lock clamp and the gear selector. Adjust the throttle valve/pulley, automatic transmission kickdown cable and link rod.

37. Start the engine and allow it to reach operating temperature. Check the ignition timing and adjust the engine idle. Check for leaks.

B234F Engine

♦ **See Figures 13, 14 and 15**

1. Disconnect the battery, negative cable first.

2. Disconnect the ground connection at the top of the side frame rail.

3. Release the bolted joint at the exhaust manifold front bracket.

4. Attach the sling or lifting equipment to the rear of the motor and support the motor from above. Release any wiring

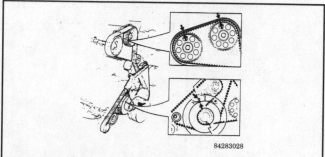

84283028

Fig. 13 Make certain all the marks align and engine is on TDC, cylinder No. 1 — B234F engine

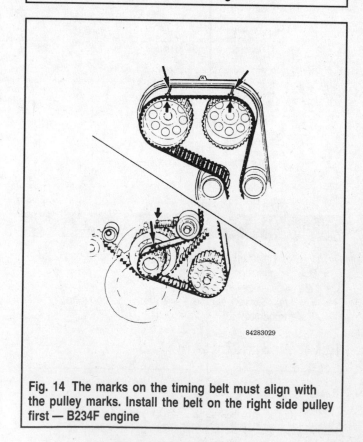

84283029

Fig. 14 The marks on the timing belt must align with the pulley marks. Install the belt on the right side pulley first — B234F engine

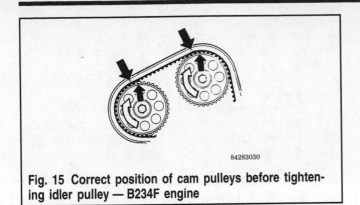

84283030

Fig. 15 Correct position of cam pulleys before tightening idler pulley — B234F engine

harnesses from their clips and place the wiring aside of the lifting gear.

5. Remove the splash guard under the engine, drain the engine oil and remove the air intake duct.

6. Undo the wiring clips on the front crossmember and right frame rail. Release the battery from the clips and work the wiring free of the roll bar.

7. If equipped with air conditioning, remove the compressor from its mount and position it aside. Do not disconnect any lines or hoses from the compressor.

8. Remove the bottom nut on the left engine mount.

9. On manual transmission vehicles, remove the clutch slave cylinder and position aside. Be careful of the rubber boot; it retains the piston within the cylinder.

10. Separate the front and rear universal joints. Unbolt the center support bearing and withdraw the driveshaft toward the rear of the vehicle.

11. Cut the rear cable tie holding the transmission wiring and separate the connectors.

12. For vehicles with manual transmission, the gear lever is removed by removing the locking bolt, removing the pivot pin between the lever and the selector rod and removing the circlip from the lever sleeve. Push the shift lever up and remove the bushings. For vehicles with automatic transmissions, the selector lever is disconnected by removing the clips from the joints between the lever and the selector rod. Withdraw the arm from the mounting.

13. Release the bolted joint at the front of the catalytic converter and release the oxygen sensor wire from the rear clip.

14. Remove the front exhaust pipe by removing the bolts at its joint to the exhaust manifold.

15. If equipped with automatic transmission, disconnect the oil lines at the transmission and plug the lines.

16. Remove the transmission crossmember. As soon as it is removed, position a floor jack below the transmission to support it.

➡ **The following steps are in the upper engine area. It may be helpful to temporarily remove the hoist equipment for access. The hoist will need to be reinstalled later in the removal.**

17. Remove the upper heat shield from the exhaust manifold. Remove the air hose from the lower heat shield.

18. Remove the top nut from the right motor mount.

19. Open the draincock on the right side of the engine block and drain the coolant into a container.

20. Label and remove the wiring from the distributor cap. Remove the cap and rotor and disconnect the braided engine ground wire.

21. Disconnect the wire to terminal 1 on the coil. Separate the wiring connectors on the right shock tower and release the cable clips on the firewall. Free the wiring from the clips.

22. Disconnect the heater hoses on the left firewall.

23. Release the fuel line connection at the left firewall and attend to any fuel spillage immediately. Plug the fuel lines.

24. Disconnect the wiring connector on the left side of the firewall and free the wires from the clips.

25. Disconnect the air mass meter, its wiring and the hoses connected to the air intake.

26. Release the throttle cable from the pulley.

27. Remove the vacuum hose to the brake booster from the intake manifold. Remove the evaporation hose from the intake manifold and the return line from the fuel distributor.

28. At the left shock tower, release the engine wiring harness from its clips and disconnect the wiring connectors. Remove the power steering reservoir from its clips.

29. Disconnect the coolant hoses at the thermostat housing and at the water pump.

30. Remove the drive belts.

31. Remove the radiator fan, the fan shroud and the drive pulley.

32. Remove the power steering pump from its mount. Place the pump on paper or rags atop the left shock tower. Do not disconnect any hoses from the pump.

33. If the lifting equipment was removed earlier, reconnect it.

34. Check the surroundings of the engine and transmission unit. With the exception of the jack and the motor mounts, there should be nothing connecting the engine/transmission assembly to the body of the vehicle. Take slight tension on the hoist and check that the engine is balanced. Reposition the lift points if the engine is not balanced.

35. Lift out the engine and the gearbox, being very careful of the radiator and surrounding components. Support the engine on appropriate stand.

To install:

36. When reinstalling, check the position and security of the hoist equipment. Lift the engine and gearbox into place in the vehicle.

37. Guide the engine mounts into place and support the transmission on the floor jack.

38. Replace the transmission crossmember and make sure the wiring for the oxygen sensor runs above the crossmember. Remove the floor jack when the crossmember is secure. The engine hoisting equipment may also be removed.

39. Use a new gasket and attach the exhaust pipe to the manifold. Attach the wire to the oxygen sensor.

40. Reconnect the shifting mechanism to the transmission.

41. Reconnect the transmission wiring and secure the harness with new wire ties.

42. Install the driveshaft. Tighten the front and rear universal joints and attach the center support bearing.

43. On manual transmission vehicle, connect the clutch slave cylinder. On automatic transmissions, connect the oil cooler lines.

44. Install the lower nut for the left motor mount. On vehicles with air conditioning, remount the compressor on its brackets.

45. Track the wiring between the anti-roll bar and the front crossmember. Install the cable clips on the crossmember and right side frame rail. Install the splash guard under the vehicle. Reconnect the wiring to the ground connection on the right frame rail.

46. Install the nut on the top of the right engine mount. Install the upper heat shield on the manifold and the air tube to the lower heat shield.

47. Reconnect the coolant hoses. The bottom hose connects to the water pump and the upper hose to the thermostat housing.

➡ **Note the marking on the upper hose. The hose must run at least 1 in. away from the alternator belt.**

48. Remount the power steering pump. Install its belt and the air conditioning belt, if equipped, and adjust to the correct tension.

49. Install the fan, pulley and shroud. Secure the wiring below the fan with new wire ties. Install the drive belt and adjust to the correct tension.

50. Reconnect the rear wiring harnesses on the firewall. Plug all connectors carefully and secure harnesses within the clips. Don't forget the wire to terminal 1 on the coil.

51. Reinstall the distributor rotor, cap and wires. Connect the braided engine ground cable.

52. Reconnect the wiring at the left shock tower. Make sure the wiring is secure in its clips. Install the power steering reservoir.

53. At the intake manifold, connect the vacuum line to the brake booster, the evaporation line and the return line for the fuel distributor.

54. At the left side of the firewall, attach the heater hoses and connect the fuel line.

55. Reattach the throttle cable to the pulley.

56. Install the air mass meter with its hoses and connections.

57. Fill the engine with proper coolant, set the heater to its hottest setting and check the system for leaks.

58. Install the engine oil.

59. Reconnect the battery leads (positive first) and the protective cap on the terminals.

60. Double check all installation items, paying particular attention to loose hoses or hanging wires, untightened nuts, poor routing of hoses and wires (too tight or rubbing) and tools left in the engine area.

61. Start the engine and check for leaks. This engine may be somewhat noisy when started; the noise will disappear as the tappets fill with oil.

B280F Engine

1. If equipped with manual transmission, remove the shifter assembly. From underneath, loosen the set screw and drive out the pivot pin. Then, pull up the boot, remove the reverse pawl bracket, snapring for the shifter and lift out the shifter.

2. Remove the battery.

3. Disconnect the windshield washer hose and engine compartment light wire. Scribe marks around the hood mount brackets on the underside of the hood for later hood alignment. Remove the hood.

4. Remove the air cleaner assembly.

5. Remove the splash guard under the engine.

6. Drain the cooling system.

7. Remove the overflow tank cap. Remove the upper and lower radiator hoses and disconnect the overflow hoses at the radiator.

8. If equipped with automatic transmission, disconnect the transmission cooler lines at the radiator.

9. Remove the radiator and fan shroud.

10. Disconnect the heater hoses, power brake hose at the intake manifold and the vacuum pump hose at the pump. Remove the vacuum pump and O-ring in the valve cover. Remove the gas cap.

11. At the firewall disconnect the fuel lines at the filter and return pipe, disconnect the relay connectors and all other wire connectors. Disconnect the distributor wires.

✳✳CAUTION

Use caution when disconnecting the fuel lines. The fuel lines may be under high pressure.

12. Disconnect the evaporative control carbon canister hoses and the vacuum hose at the EGR valve.

13. Disconnect the voltage regulator wire connector.

14. Disconnect the throttle cable and kickdown cable, on automatic transmission vehicles, the vacuum amplifier hose at the T-pipe and the hoses at the thermostat.

15. Disconnect the air pump hose at the backfire valve, the solenoid valve wire and the micro-switch wire.

16. Remove the exhaust manifold flange retaining nuts (both sides).

17. If equipped with air conditioning, remove the compressor and drive belt and place it aside. Do not disconnect the refrigerant hoses.

18. Drain the crankcase.

19. Remove the power steering pump, drive belt and bracket. Position aside.

20. From underneath, remove the retaining nuts for the front motor mounts.

21. Remove, as required, the front exhaust pipe.

22. On 49 states vehicles, remove the front exhaust pipe hangers and clamps and allow the system to hang.

23. If equipped with automatic transmission, place the shift lever in **P**. Disconnect the shift control lever at the transmission.

24. On manual transmission vehicles, disconnect the clutch cylinder from the bell housing. Leave the cylinder connected; secure it to the vehicle.

25. Disconnect the speedometer cable and driveshaft at the transmission.

26. Raise and safely support the vehicle. Place jackstands under the reinforced box member area to the rear of each front jacking attachment. Then, using a floor jack and a thick, wide wooden block, support the weight of the engine under the oil pan.

27. Remove the bolts for the rear transmission mount. Remove the transmission support crossmember.

28. Lift out the engine and transmission as a unit.

To install:

29. If separated, join the engine and transmission. Install the engine assembly in the vehicle and tighten all mounting bolts to specification. Install the transmission crossmember.

30. Install the driveshaft and speedometer cable. On manual transmission vehicles, install the clutch assembly and gear shift assembly. On automatic transmission vehicles install the gear selector assembly.

31. Install the exhaust system. Install all air conditioning compressor, power steering pump, air pump and alternator. Install and tighten all accessory drive belts to specification.

32. Connect the throttle and kick-down cables. Connect the charcoal canister and evaporative emissions control hoses.

33. Install the fuel lines and filter. Install the heater hoses and vacuum pump hoses.

34. Install the radiator, shroud and radiator hoses. Connect all other hoses or lines previously disconnected. Connect all electrical connections.

35. Install the hood, battery and gear selector.

36. Fill the cooling system with coolant, the engine with oil and the transmission with fluid. Start the engine and bring it to operating temperature. Adjust the timing and idle speed, as necessary, and check for leaks.

B6304F Engine

1. Disconnect the negative battery cable.

2. Disconnect the wiring connected to the positive terminal, battery positive lead, ground lead connection to the body at top of side member and clip on the side member.

3. Remove the battery.

4. Remove the auxiliary drive belt.

5. Remove the cooling fan.

6. Release the upper bolts and disconnect the connector at the relay in front of the battery. Disconnect the ground lead at the right-hand ground terminal.

7. Drain the cooling system.

8. Remove the upper and lower radiator hoses from the engine. Remove the radiator overflow hose.

9. Remove the transmission cooler lines from the radiator.

10. Remove the top nut on both left and right side engine mountings.

11. Disconnect and remove the large and small crankcase ventilation hoses, idling hose and idling valve lead.

12. Disconnect and remove the EVAP valve hoses(2) at the intake manifold. Disconnect the air mass meter connector, air preheater hose and throttle pulley cover.

13. Remove the servo pump mounting bolts (3 bolts at front and 2 at rear).

14. Disconnect and remove the fuel return line at the regulator and fuel line at bulkhead. Remove the throttle cable, cruise control vacuum hose and fuel line snap catches.

15. Remove the engine wiring harness cover and disconnect the harness connector. Disconnect the relay connector. Remove the harness duct retaining nuts.

16. Disconnect the heater hoses at bulkhead, ECC hoses at intake manifold and brake servo vacuum hose. Disconnect the timing pick-up and camshaft sensor connectors.

17. Support the engine at rear, using the engine removal tool assembly (5033, 5006, 5115, 5428 and 5429 or equivalent).

18. Remove the splashguard and air baffle under the engine.

19. Remove the radiator mounting bolts.

20. Drain the engine oil.

21. Disconnect the hose at the oil thermostat in cylinder block.

22. Disconnect the air conditioning compressor lead. Remove the air conditioning compressor mounting bolts. Support the compressor aside.

23. Remove the exhaust pipe flanges at the manifold. Remove the lower section of the air preheater pipe and remove the exhaust pipe shield.

24. Remove the oil pipe connections at gearbox. Plug the openings.

25. Remove the clips between the gear selector lever and control rod/reaction arm. Withdraw the rods from mounting.

26. Disconnect and remove the oxygen sensor wiring.

➡**Before separating the driveshaft, mark the coupling halves for reassembly.**

27. Disconnect the driveshaft and remove the transmission support member.

28. Place a jack under the transmission. Remove the lifting tools.

29. Remove the radiator upper attachments and lift out the radiator assembly.

30. Install the engine lifting tool (2810 or equivalent) and adjust the lifting yoke to ensure the engine is balanced.

➡**Position the wiring harnesses so as to avoid damage when lifting.**

31. Remove the jack from under the transmission.

32. Remove the engine and transmission assembly from the vehicle.

33. Mount the engine in the stand and fixture (Tool 2520 and 5297 or equivalent).

To install:

34. Install the lifting tools to the engine assembly.

35. Install the engine into the vehicle, guiding the engine mounting into position.

36. Install the mounting nuts. Torque to 37 ft. lbs. (50 Nm).

37. Position a jack to support the transmission. Remove the lifting tool.

38. Support the rear of the engine, using the 2 support rails and lifting beam assembly. Remove the jack from beneath the transmission.

39. Using the transmission lifting tool (5972 or equivalent), raise the transmission. Tighten the bolted joints between the support member and side members. Tighten the transmission bump stop nut 37 ft. lbs. (50 Nm).

40. Attach the control rod and reaction arm to the gear selector lever mounting. Install the locking clip.

41. Connect the oxygen sensor lead.

42. Install the driveshaft. Tighten the front and rear couplings noting the marks made during removal.

43. Inspect the preheater pipe O-ring, Connect the preheater pipe to the exhaust pipe. Tighten the sump bolts.

44. Install the air conditioning compressor.

45. Reconnect the hoses to the oil cooler. Torque to 22 ft. lbs. (30 Nm).

46. Remove the lifting tools from rear of engine.

47. Install the heater hoses.

48. Install the timing pick-up and camshaft position sensor connectors.

49. Connect the engine connector to the wiring harness connector at left side wheel housing. Connect the relay and install the wiring duct retaining nuts.

50. Connect the fuel hoses, vacuum hoses and electrical connectors.

51. Install the throttle cable and throttle pulley cover.

52. Install the servo pump. Install the auxiliaries drive belt.

53. Connect the radiator hoses and transmission oil pipes.

54. Install the cooling fan. Connect the cooling fan lead.

55. Connect the battery leads in holders. Install the battery. Connect the lead at the right side wheel housing and battery positive leads.

56. Raise the vehicle and support it safely.

57. Install the transmission lines. Install the exhaust pipe and heat shield.

➡**Loosen the catalytic convertor bolts; then re-tighten. This will prevent stress in the system.**

58. Install the radiator mounting bolts, air baffle and splashguard.

59. Fill the cooling system.

60. Connect the negative battery cable. Start the engine and check for leaks.

Engine Mounts

REMOVAL & INSTALLATION

B230F Engine

1. Disconnect the negative battery lead.

2. Assemble the engine lifting tools and raise the engine slightly.

3. Remove the engine mount retaining nuts.

4. When replacing the left-side engine mount, cut the strap for the power steering hose.

To install:

5. Place the engine mounts into position. On left-side engine mount, attach the bracket at the intake manifold and engine mount. Install the strap for the power steering.

6. Install the lower engine mounts on the front axle member. Lower the engine and remove the lifting tools.

7. Connect the negative battery lead.

B234F Engine

LEFT-SIDE

1. Disconnect the negative battery lead.

2. Remove the air mass meter and air inlet hose.

3. Remove the engine mounting bottom nut. If necessary, remove the front splashguard.

4. Assemble the engine lifting tools and raise the engine slightly.

➡**Be careful not to damage the fan blades by contact with the shroud.**

5. Remove the 3 bolts securing the mounting to the cylinder block. Remove the engine mount.

To install:

6. Place the engine mount into position with the cable clip and support at the top bolt.

7. Lower the engine, while guiding the bottom bolt of the mounting into the bracket. Install the retaining nut.

8. If removed, install the front splashguard.

9. Install the air mass meter and air inlet hose.

10. Connect the negative battery lead.

RIGHT-SIDE

1. Disconnect the negative battery lead.

2. Remove the air preheating hose from the bottom heat shield.

3. Remove the 4 nuts securing the bottom mounting plate.

4. Disconnect the air inlet hose from the throttle housing.

5. Assemble the engine lifting tools and raise the engine slightly.

➡**Be careful not to damage the fan blades by contact with the shroud.**

6. Remove the engine mounting and bottom mounting plate.

To install:

7. Place the engine mounting and bottom mounting plate into position.

8. Lower the engine, while guiding the mounting plate and mounting into position. Remove the lifting tools.

9. Install the 4 nuts securing the engine mounting and bottom mounting plate.

10. Install the air preheating hose and air inlet hose.

11. Connect the negative battery lead.

B280F Engine

FRONT MOUNT

1. Disconnect the negative battery lead.

2. Assemble the engine lifting tools and raise the engine slightly.

➡**Be careful not to damage the fan blades by contact with the shroud.**

3. Raise and support the vehicle safely. Remove the engine splashguard.

4. Remove the nuts and bolts securing the engine mounts, remove the engine mounts.

To install:

5. Place the engine mounts into position and install the mounting nuts and bolts.

➡**When installing the bolts, make certain the battery negative lead is fastened under 1 of them.**

6. Lower the engine and remove the lifting tools.

7. Connect the negative battery lead.

REAR MOUNT

1. Disconnect the negative battery lead.

2. Raise and support the vehicle safely.

3. Position a service jack beneath the transmission and raise the engine slightly.

4. Remove the engine mounting bushings, using a mandrel (5225 or equivalent).

To install:

5. Install the bushings, using the mandrel.

➡**When installing the bushings, note the position of the arrows on the bushings. The arrows must point to mark on the bracket.**

6. Remove the service jack and lower the vehicle.

7. Connect the negative battery lead.

B6304F Engine

1. Disconnect the negative battery cable.

2. Remove the engine mounting top nut.

3. Assemble the engine lifting tools and raise the engine slightly.

➡ **Be careful not to damage the fan blades by contact with the shroud.**

4. Raise the vehicle and support it safely. Remove the splashguard under the engine.

5. Remove the mounting nuts and bolts.

6. On left-side engine mount, remove the mount and bracket towards the front.

7. On right-side engine mount, remove the mount and bracket towards the rear.

To install:

8. Assemble the new mounting on the bracket. Install the mounting and bracket.

9. Install the splashguard. Lower the vehicle and remove the lifting tools.

10. Connect the negative battery lead.

Rocker Shafts

REMOVAL & INSTALLATION

B280F Engine

▶ **See Figures 16 and 17**

1. Disconnect the negative battery cable.

2. Remove the air cleaner assembly.

3. Disconnect the air pump bracket.

4. Remove the left valve cover, if necessary.

5. Tie the upper radiator hose aside and remove the oil filler cap and carbon canister hose.

6. On air conditioned vehicles, remove the air conditioning compressor from it bracket. Do not disconnect the hoses.

7. Remove the EGR valve.

8. Remove the air conditioning compressor rear bracket.

9. Remove the control pressure regulator.

10. Disconnect any hoses or wires in the way. Remove the right valve cover, if necessary.

➡ **Do not jar the head while the rocker and bolts are loose, as the cylinder liner O-ring seals may break, requiring engine disassemble.**

11. The rocker arm bolts double as cylinder head bolts. Loosen the head bolts by reversing the torque sequence. If removing both rocker shafts, mark them left and right.

To install:

12. Install the rocker shafts. Follow cylinder head installation procedure for proper torque specification and sequence. Adjust the valve lash.

13. Install the valve covers, EGR valve, control pressure regulator, air conditioning compressor and bracket and air pump.

14. Connect all fuel, coolant and vacuum lines previously disconnected. Connect all electrical connections previously disconnected. Connect the battery.

15. Start the engine and allow it to reach operating temperature. Adjust the timing and check for leaks.

Thermostat

To operate at peak efficiency, an engine must maintain its internal temperatures within certain upper and lower limits. The cooling system circulates fluid around the combustion cylinders and conducts this heated fluid to the radiator, where the heat is exchanged into the airflow created by the fan and the motion of the car.

While most people realize that an engine running too hot (overheated) is a sign of trouble, few know that an engine can run too cool as well. If the proper internal temperatures are not achieved, fuel is not burned efficiently, and the lubricating oil does not reach its best working temperature. While a too cold condition is rarely disabling, it can cause a variety of problems which can be mistaken for tune-up or electrical causes.

The thermostat controls the flow of coolant within the system. It reacts to the heat of the coolant and allows more fluid (or less) to circulate. Depending on the amount of fluid being circulated, more or less heat is drawn away from the inside of the engine. While we are beyond the days of having to install different thermostats for summer and winter driving, it is wise to check the function of the thermostat periodically. Special use of the vehicle such as trailer towing or carrying heavy loads may require the installation of a thermostat with different temperature characteristics.

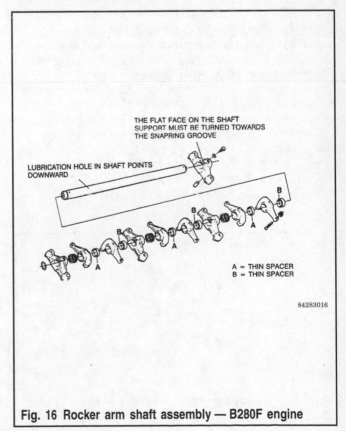

THE FLAT FACE ON THE SHAFT SUPPORT MUST BE TURNED TOWARDS THE SNAPRING GROOVE

LUBRICATION HOLE IN SHAFT POINTS DOWNWARD

A = THIN SPACER
B = THIN SPACER

84283016

Fig. 16 Rocker arm shaft assembly — B280F engine

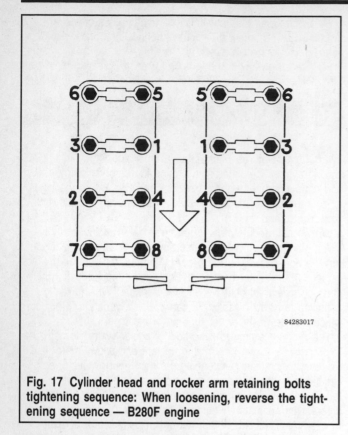

Fig. 17 Cylinder head and rocker arm retaining bolts tightening sequence: When loosening, reverse the tightening sequence — B280F engine

REMOVAL & INSTALLATION

▶ **See Figure 18**

1. Disconnect the negative battery cable.
2. Place a suitable drain pan into position and drain the cooling system, by opening the drain cock on the right-hand side of the engine block. Re-install the drain cock.
3. Remove the thermostat housing retaining bolts. Remove the thermostat housing, thermostat and gasket.
To install:
4. Before installing the thermostat, thoroughly clean the mating surfaces.
5. Fit a new gasket and place the thermostat into position.
6. Install the thermostat housing.
7. Fill the cooling system through the expansion tank.

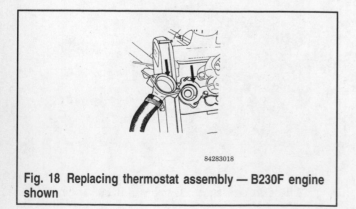

Fig. 18 Replacing thermostat assembly — B230F engine shown

8. Connect the negative battery lead. Start the engine and allow to reach normal operating temperature. Top up with coolant and check for leaks.

Intake Manifold

REMOVAL & INSTALLATION

B230F Engine

1. Disconnect the negative battery cable. Remove the air cleaner and all necessary hoses.
2. Remove the PCV valve.
3. Remove the connector at the cold start injector.
4. Remove the fuel hose from the cold start injector.
5. Remove the cold start injector.
6. Remove the connector on the auxiliary valve.
7. Disconnect the hoses at the auxiliary valve.
8. Remove the auxiliary valve.
9. On turbocharged vehicles, disconnect the turbocharger inlet hose, between turbo unit and intake manifold. Plug the hose immediately.
10. Remove the intake manifold brace.
11. Disconnect the distributor vacuum hose at the intake manifold.
12. Loosen the clamp for the rubber connecting pipe on the air-fuel control unit.
13. Remove the manifold bolts and remove the manifold.
To install:
14. Clean the gasket mating surfaces thoroughly. Install the intake manifold, using new gaskets, and tighten the bolts to 15 ft. lbs. (20 Nm).
15. Install the intake manifold brace, air-fuel control unit connecting pipe, turbocharger inlet hose (if equipped), auxiliary valve, cold start injector, fuel hose and PCV valve.
16. Connect all vacuum, fuel and coolant hoses previously disconnected. Connect all electrical connectors previously disconnected.
17. Connect the negative battery cable, start the engine and bring it to operating temperature. Adjust the timing and check for leaks.

B234F Engine

1. Remove the air mass meter and the air intake hose.
2. Detach the throttle pulley from the intake manifold and remove the link rod from the throttle lever.
3. Separate the throttle housing from the intake manifold and cut the cable tie holding the wiring to the vacuum hose connections.
4. Disconnect the lines and hoses from the manifold, including the brake booster vacuum hose, the evaporation line, the oil trap, the fuel pressure regulator line and the air control valve line. If equipped with a vacuum tank, disconnect its line at the manifold.
5. Disconnect the fuel return line at the distribution pipe. Disconnect the wiring to the injectors and remove the distribution pipe and injectors. Immediately protect these components from the entry of any dirt.
6. Unbolt and remove the intake manifold from the engine.

To install:

7. If installing a new manifold, it is necessary to transfer the various hose nipples and plugs to the new part. Install the manifold with a new gasket. Starting with the center bolts and working outward, tighten the bolts to 15 ft. lbs. (20 Nm).

8. Reconnect the hoses to their proper ports.

9. Position the injector wiring between cylinders 2 and 3 and reinstall the fuel distributor rail and the injectors. Tighten the pipe and the ground wires to the block. Connect the fuel pressure regulator line to the intake manifold.

10. Install the throttle pulley and connect the link rod.

11. Install the throttle housing with a new gasket. Check the operation of the throttle stops and switches.

12. Install the air mass meter and air inlet hose.

B280F Engine

▶ **See Figure 19**

1. Disconnect the negative battery cable. Remove the air cleaner and all necessary hoses.

2. Drain the radiator coolant.

3. Remove the throttle cable from the pulley and bracket.

4. On automatic transmission vehicles, remove the throttle cable that is connected to the transmission.

5. Remove the EGR pipe from the EGR valve to the manifold.

6. Disconnect the EGR vacuum line.

7. Remove the oil filler cap and PCV valve.

➡ **Cover the oil cap opening with a rag to keep dirt out.**

8. Remove the front manifold bolts and remove the front section of the manifold.

9. Disconnect the cold start connector, fuel line and injector.

10. Disconnect the pressure control regulator vacuum lines, fuel lines and the connector.

11. Remove the auxiliary valve and its necessary piping.

12. Disconnect the electrical connections at the air fuel control unit.

13. Remove all 6 spark plug wires.

14. Remove all 6 injectors.

15. Move the wiring harness to the outside of the manifold.

16. Disconnect the vacuum hose at the distributor and the intake manifold.

17. Disconnect the heater hose at the intake manifold.

18. Disconnect the hose to the diverter valve.

19. Disconnect the vacuum hose to the power brake booster.

20. Disconnect the throttle cable link.

21. Disconnect the wires to the micro-switch.

22. Pull the wires away from the intake manifold.

23. Remove the fuel filter line and the return line.

24. Remove the air control unit.

25. Disconnect the vacuum hose from the throttle valve housing.

26. Remove the pipe and cold start injector assembly.

27. Remove the intake manifold from the vehicle.

To install:

28. Clean all gasket mating surfaces thoroughly. Install the intake manifold using new gaskets and tighten the bolts to 7-11 ft. lbs. (10-15 Nm).

29. Install the cold start injector assembly, air control unit, fuel filter and return line, throttle cable, EGR valve, diverter valve, heater hose, injectors and spark plug wires.

30. Install all vacuum, fuel and coolant hoses previously removed. Connect all electrical connections previously disconnected.

31. Fill the radiator with coolant and check the engine and transmission oil. Connect the negative battery cable. Start the engine and bring to operating temperature. Check for leaks.

B6304F Engine

1. Disconnect the negative battery lead.

2. Disconnect the connector at the air mass meter.

3. Disconnect the idling valve lead and air hose. Remove the flame trap holder and remove the intake hose.

4. Remove the throttle pulley cover.

5. Disconnect and remove the throttle switch lead, throttle cable and bracket, cruise control vacuum servo and vacuum hoses at throttle housing.

6. Remove the injector cover plate and distribution manifold retaining bolts (3).

7. Disconnect the pressure regulator vacuum hose and fuel line bracket.

8. Carefully lift out the injector and distribution manifold assembly.

9. Remove the air preheater hose. Remove left and right side power stage connectors on the bottom of the manifold. Remove the manifold bottom mounting.

10. Disconnect the brake servo hose and vacuum hoses under the manifold.

11. Cut away the clamps securing the rubber sleeves between the manifold sections and lift out the outer manifold section.

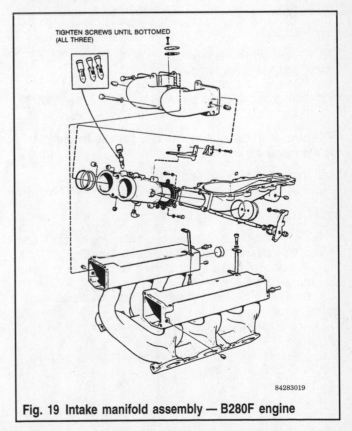

84283019

Fig. 19 Intake manifold assembly — B280F engine

12. Remove the upper bolts and loosen the lower bolts. Remove the inner section of the manifold.

To install:

13. Install the inner section of the manifold, using a new gasket. Install the rubber sleeves on the inner section and lubricate the free ends with vaseline. Install the mounting bolts and torque to 15 ft. lbs. (20 Nm).

14. Route the wiring between the second and third branches of the outer manifold section. Place the manifold against the lower section and connect the crankcase ventilation hoses.

15. Insert the manifold branches in the rubber sleeves. Secure with new Oetiker clamps.

16. Tighten the manifold lower mounting. Reconnect the vacuum hoses, brake servo hose, power stage connectors and air preheater hose.

17. Inspect the injector O-rings. Lubricate with vaseline.

18. Reconnect the fuel pressure regulator vacuum hose.

19. Press the fuel distribution manifold into position. Tighten the manifold.

20. Reconnect the injector connectors, EGR vacuum hoses. Install the injector cover.

21. Install the throttle cable, throttle pulley cover and vacuum hoses (cruise control and throttle housing).

22. Install the cable bracket at the throttle pulley. Reconnect the PCV, idling valve lead, air hose, air mass meter and throttle housing connector.

23. Connect the negative battery lead. Start the engine and check operation.

Exhaust Manifold

REMOVAL & INSTALLATION

B230F Engine

1. Disconnect the negative battery cable. Remove the air cleaner and all necessary hoses.
2. Remove the EGR valve pipe from the manifold.
3. Remove the exhaust pipe from the exhaust manifold.
4. Remove the manifold bolts and remove the manifold.

➡️**Remember to install new manifold gaskets before installing the manifold.**

5. Installation is the reverse of removal.
6. Torque the manifold bolts to 10-20 ft. lbs. (14-27 Nm).

B234F Engine

1. Disconnect the front exhaust pipe from the manifold. Disconnect the catalytic converter from the front muffler.
2. Remove the heat shields (top and bottom) from the manifold and remove the air preheat hose.
3. Disconnect the front exhaust pipe from the bracket on the bell housing.
4. Unbolt the exhaust manifold and remove it from the vehicle.
5. Install the manifold with a new gasket and tighten the bolts to 15 ft. lbs. (20 Nm).

6. Install the front exhaust pipe with a new gasket; tighten the joint to the manifold to 20 ft. lbs. (27 Nm). Reattach the catalytic converter to the front muffler.
7. Install the heat shields and the preheat hose.

B280F Engine

▶ See Figure 20

1. Raise and support the vehicle safely.
2. Unbolt the crossover pipe from the left and right side of the exhaust manifolds, if equipped.

➡️**If the vehicle has the Y-type exhaust pipe disconnect this pipe at the left and right manifolds.**

3. Remove any other necessary hardware.
4. Remove the left and right side manifolds.
5. Installation is the reverse of removal.

➡️**Always use new gaskets when reinstalling the manifolds.**

6. Torque the manifold bolts to 7-11 ft. lbs. (10-15 Nm).

B6304F Engine

1. Disconnect the negative battery lead.
2. Remove the exhaust pipe mounting nuts at the manifold joints.
3. Remove the heat shield retaining bolts and remove the heat shield.
4. Remove the exhaust manifold mounting nuts. Remove the exhaust manifold and gasket.

To install:

5. Before installation, clean the manifold and cylinder head mating surfaces.
6. Fit a new gasket and place the exhaust manifold into position. Install the mount lifting lug on studs between 3rd and 4th exhaust branches. Torque the studs to 15 ft. lbs. (20 Nm) and mounting nuts to 18 ft. lbs. (25 Nm).
7. Install the heat shield to rear manifold. Torque to 11 ft. lbs. (15 Nm).
8. Install the front exhaust pipe to manifold. Using thread locking compound, torque to 44 ft. lbs. (60 Nm).

➡️**Loosen the joint at the catalytic convertor and re-tighten to 18 ft. lbs. (25 Nm). This is necessary to prevent stresses in the system.**

9. Connect the negative battery lead. Start the engine and check for leaks.

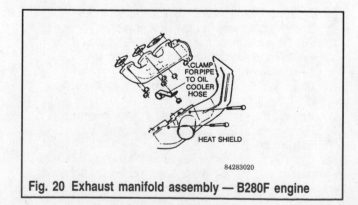

84283020

Fig. 20 Exhaust manifold assembly — B280F engine

Turbocharger

REMOVAL & INSTALLATION

▶ **See Figures 21, 22 and 23**

B230F-Turbocharged Engine

1. Disconnect the battery ground cable.
2. Disconnect expansion tank from retainer. Remove expansion tank retainer.
3. Remove preheater hose to the air cleaner. Remove the pipe and rubber bellows between the air/fuel control unit and the turbocharger unit. Pull out the crankcase ventilation hose from the pipe.
4. Remove the pipe and pipe connector between the turbocharger unit and the intake manifold.

➡**Cover the turbocharger intake and outlet ports to keep dirt out of the system.**

5. Disconnect the exhaust pipe and secure it aside.
6. Disconnect the spark plug wires at the plugs.
7. Remove the upper heat shield. Remove the brace between the turbocharger unit and the manifold.
8. Remove the lower heat shield by removing the 1 retaining screw under the manifold.
9. Remove the oil pipe clamp, retaining screws on the turbo unit and the pipe connection screw in the cylinder block under the manifold. Do not allow any dirt to enter the oil passages.
10. Remove the manifold retaining screws and washers. Let 1 nut remain in position to keep the manifold in position.

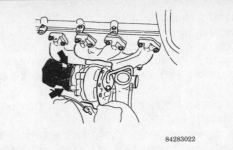

Fig. 22 Disconnect the turbocharger unit from the exhaust manifold — B230F Turbocharged engine

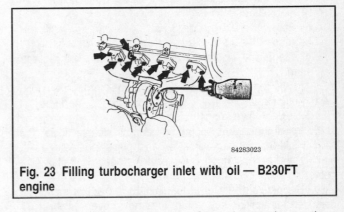

Fig. 23 Filling turbocharger inlet with oil — B230FT engine

11. Remove the oil delivery pipe. Cover the opening on the turbo unit.
12. Disconnect the air/fuel control unit by loosening the clamps. Move the unit with the lower section of the air cleaner

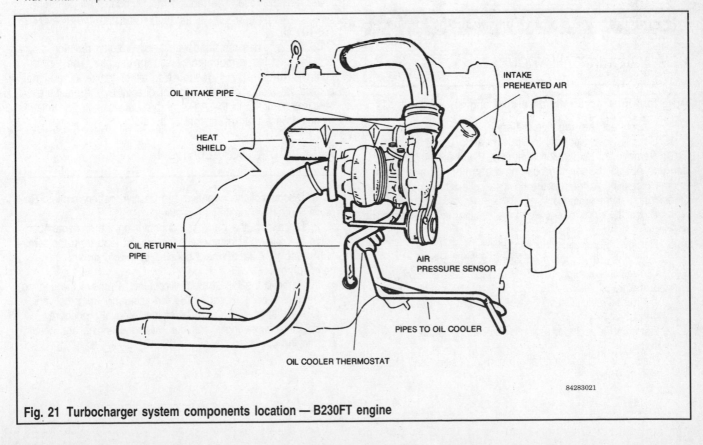

Fig. 21 Turbocharger system components location — B230FT engine

up to the right side wheel housing. Place a cover over the wheel housing as protection.

13. Remove the air cleaner filter.

14. Remove the remaining nut and washer on the manifold. Lift the assembly forward and up. Remove the manifold gaskets. Disconnect the return oil pipe O-ring from the cylinder block.

15. Disconnect the turbocharger unit from the manifold.

To install:

16. Be sure to use a new gasket for the exhaust manifold and a new O-ring to the return oil pipe. Keep everything clean during assembly and use extreme care in keeping dirt out of the various turbo inlet and outlet pipes and hoses.

17. Install the turbocharger on the exhaust manifold and tighten the bolts as follows:

   a. Stage 1 — 0.7 ft. lbs. (3 Nm)

   b. Stage 2 — 30 ft. lbs. (133 Nm)

   c. Stage 3 — Tighten all bolts an additional 120 degrees (1/3 turn).

18. Install the exhaust manifold and turbocharger assembly on the engine. Connect all oil pipes from and to the turbocharger using new O-rings.

19. Install the air/fuel control unit and air cleaner. Install the heat shields, spark plug wires, exhaust pipes, preheater assembly and expansion tank. Connect the negative battery cable.

20. Disconnect the wire at terminal 15 (brown) of the ignition coil. Use the ignition key to turn the engine over for about 30 seconds. This circulated the oil within the turbocharger, providing proper start-up lubrication.

21. Turn the ignition **OFF**, reconnect the coil wire, start the engine and allow it to idle for a few minutes prior to test driving.

Radiator

REMOVAL & INSTALLATION

➡**Perform this work only on a cold engine.**

1. Disconnect the negative battery cable.

2. Set the heater control to MAX. heat.

3. Remove the expansion tank cap. Place a suitable drain pan into position. Open the cock on the right-hand side of the engine block. Fit a hose to the cock to collect the coolant. Open the radiator drain cock.

4. Close the drain cocks when the coolant is completely drained.

5. Remove the cooling fan shroud.

6. Disconnect the upper and lower radiator hoses

7. On vehicles equipped with automatic transmissions, disconnect the transmission oil cooler lines at the radiator. Plug the lines immediately. Catch the spillage from the radiator in a separate pan.

8. Remove the radiator assembly from the vehicle.

To install:

9. Place the radiator and fan shroud in position and install the retaining bolts.

10. On automatic transmission vehicles, connect the oil cooler lines.

11. Install the lower and upper radiator hoses.

12. Connect the expansion tank hose. Make sure that the overflow hose is clear of the fan and is free of any sharp bends.

13. Fill the cooling system through the expansion tank, with a 50 percent antifreeze, 50 percent water solution.

14. Connect the negative battery cable. Run the engine until normal operating temperature is reached. Check for leaks. Top up the cooling system, as required. Replace the cap.

15. Check and top up the automatic transmission fluid level.

Engine Fan

REMOVAL & INSTALLATION

Belt Driven Type

1. Disconnect the negative battery cable.

2. Remove the top section of the fan shroud.

3. Slacken the drive blet(s), as required. Remove the fan assembly.

4. Installation is the reverse of the removal procedure. Adjust the drive belt(s) to the specified tension.

Electrical Cooling Fan

Some models are equipped with electrical cooling fans. The fan function is controlled by a thermocontact placed in the upper right corner of the radiator. Some vehicles may be equipped with a thermal switch in the radiator end tank or lower radiator hose. The fan, on most models, will generally switch ON when coolant temperatures are between 190-212°F (88-100°C).

B6304F engines are fitted with a fully electric radiator fan. The 2-speed fan is mounted behind the radiator. The fan is controlled by a relay, in response to either temperature signal sent to the Motronic control unit or directly by the pressure switches mounted in the A/C high-pressure circuit. The relay is mounted on a bracket in front of the battery.

REMOVAL & INSTALLATION

1. Disconnect the negative and positive battery cables. Remove the battery holder, as required.

2. Disconnect the harness connector on the crossmember. Undo the relay and disconnect the ground lead from the terminal on the right-hand wheel housing in the engine compartment.

3. Remove the fan shroud, if required. Remove the cooling fan mounting bolts. Remove the fan assembly from the vehicle.

4. Installation is the reverse of the removal procedure.

5. After completing installation, start the engine and check cooling fan operation.

Water Pump

REMOVAL & INSTALLATION

B230F and B234F Engines
▶ See Figure 24

1. Disconnect the negative battery cable.
2. Set the heater control to MAX. heat.
3. Remove the expansion tank cap. Place a suitable drain pan into position. Open the cock on the right-hand side of the engine block. Fit a hose to the cock to collect the coolant. Open the radiator drain cock.
4. Close the drain cocks when the coolant is completely drained.
5. Remove the radiator fan shroud. Remove the fan assembly.
6. Remove the lower radiator hose at the water pump. If required, remove the retaining bolt for the coolant pipe, beneath exhaust manifold, and pull the pipe rearward.
7. Remove the drive belts and water pump pulleys.
8. Remove the water pump bolts, washers and nuts. Remove the water pump assembly.
   To install:
9. Clean the gasket contact surfaces thoroughly and use a new gasket and O-rings, especially between the cylinder head and top of water pump.
10. Install the water pump and tighten the bolts to 11-15 ft. lbs. Install the coolant pipe, lower radiator hose, accessory drive belts and water pump pulley.
11. Install the fan and fan shroud. Fill the coolant system with coolant. Start the engine and allow it to reach operating temperature. Check for leaks. Add coolant as necessary.

B280F Engine
▶ See Figure 25

1. Disconnect the negative battery cable. On some variants of this engine it may be necessary to remove the front and main sections of the intake manifold.
2. Remove the overflow tank cap and drain the cooling system.
3. Disconnect both radiator hoses. On automatic transmission vehicles, disconnect the transmission cooler lines at the radiator. Disconnect the fan shroud. Remove the radiator and fan shroud.

4. Remove the fan.
5. Remove the hoses from the water pump to each cylinder head.
6. Remove the fan belts. Remove the water pump pulley.
7. Loosen the hose clamps at the rear of the water pump.
8. Remove the water pump from the block (3 bolts).
   To install:
9. Transfer the thermal time lender and temperature sensor to the new water pump.
10. Transfer the thermostat cover, thermostat and rear pump cover to the new pump.
11. Install the new pump and tighten the bolts to 11-15 ft. lbs. Install the clamps, water pump pulley and fan belts.
12. Install the hoses that reach to each cylinder head. Install the fan, shroud and radiator. If equipped with an automatic transmission, connect the transmission cooler lines. Install the intake manifold, as necessary.
13. Connect the negative battery cable and fill the radiator with coolant. Start the engine and allow it to reach operating temperature. Check for leaks.

B6304F Engine

1. Disconnect the negative battery cable.
2. Drain the cooling system, by opening the drain cock on the right side of the cylinder block. Re-install the drain cock.
3. Remove the timing belt.
4. Remove the water pump retaining bolts (7) and remove the water pump.
   To install:
5. Before installing the water pump, clean the mating surfaces.
6. Install the water pump, using a new gasket. Tighten and torque the mounting bolts 15 ft. lbs. (20 Nm).

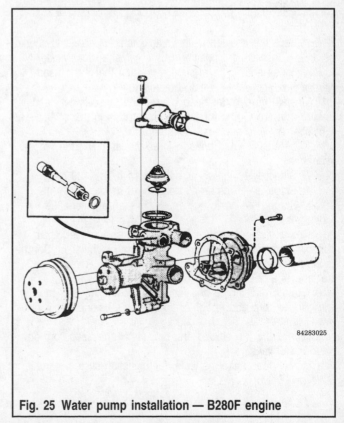

Fig. 25 Water pump installation — B280F engine

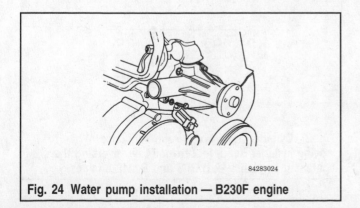

Fig. 24 Water pump installation — B230F engine

7. Install the timing belt.

8. Fill the cooling system.

9. Start the engine and check for leaks.

Cylinder Head

REMOVAL & INSTALLATION

B230F Engine

▶ See Figures 26 and 27

1. Disconnect the battery.

2. Remove the overflow tank cap and drain the coolant. Disconnect the upper radiator hose.

3. Remove the distributor cap and wires.

4. Remove the PCV hoses.

5. Remove the EGR valve and vacuum pump.

6. Remove the air pump, if equipped, and air injection manifold. Disconnect and remove all hoses to the turbocharger, if equipped. Plug all open hoses and holes immediately.

7. Remove the exhaust manifold and header pipe bracket.

8. Remove the intake manifold. Disconnect the manifold brace and the hose clamp to the bellows for the fuel injection air/flow unit. Disconnect the throttle cable and all vacuum hoses and electrical connectors to the fuel injection unit.

9. Remove the fuel injectors.

10. Remove the valve cover.

11. Loosen the fan shroud and remove the fan. Remove the shroud. Remove the upper belts and pulleys.

12. Remove the timing belt cover. Remove the timing belt.

13. Remove the camshaft, if necessary.

14. Loosen the cylinder head bolts by reversing the torque sequence. Remove the cylinder head.

To install:

15. Check the position of the crankshaft. No. 1 piston should be at TDC. Check the position of the camshaft for cylinder No. 1. Both lobes should be in such a position that if the head were install, the valves would be closed.

16. Install the cylinder head gasket and the cylinder head. Ensure that the O-ring for the water pump is in place. Apply a light coat of oil to the head bolts and install.

17. Tighten the head bolts in three stages using the proper sequence.

    a. Stage 1 — Tighten all bolts to 14 ft. lbs. (20 Nm).

    b. Stage 2 — Tighten all bolts to 43 ft. lbs. (60 Nm).

    c. Stage 3 — Angle tighten all bolts an additional 90 degrees.

18. Install the camshaft, camshaft gear and spacer, as required. Do not allow the cam to turn during installation. Set the timing belt tensioner and install the timing belt. Remove the tool from the belt tensioner to tension the belt.

19. Rotate the engine one full turn. Loosen the tensioner bolt one full turn and re-tighten to set the tensioner. Adjust the valve lash.

20. Install the fan shroud and fan. Install the accessory drive belts and pulleys.

21. Install the intake manifold, fuel injection system, throttle cable and valve covers.

22. Install the exhaust manifold and header pipe. Install the air pump assembly. If equipped with a turbocharger, install the turbocharger and related parts.

23. Install the EGR valve, vacuum pump, PCV hoses, distributor cap and wires, overflow tank and battery.

24. Fill the radiator with coolant, check the engine oil and transmission fluid. Start the engine and allow it to reach operating temperature. Check the timing.

B234F Engine

➡ **The use of the correct special tools or their equivalent, is required for this procedure.**

1. Disconnect the negative battery cable.

2. Remove the heat shield over the exhaust manifold.

3. Remove the cap from the expansion tank and open the draincock on the right side of the motor. Collect the drained coolant in a suitable container.

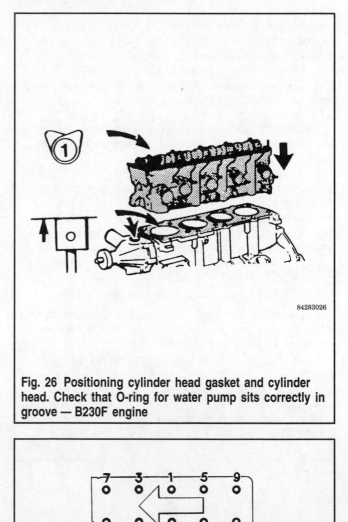

84283026

Fig. 26 Positioning cylinder head gasket and cylinder head. Check that O-ring for water pump sits correctly in groove — B230F engine

84283027

Fig. 27 Cylinder head bolt torque sequence. When removing cylinder head, loosen bolts by reversing the tightening sequence — B230F and B234F engines

4. Unbolt the exhaust pipe from the bracket, remove the manifold nuts and remove the manifold from the head.

5. On the left side of the motor, remove the support under the intake manifold and remove the bottom bolt in the cylinder block.

6. Remove the manifold intact and tie it or support it safely.

7. Disconnect the temperature sensor connectors, the heating hose under cylinders No. 3 and 4 and the upper radiator hose at the thermostat.

8. Remove the upper and lower timing belt covers.

9. Align the camshaft and crankshaft marks. Turn the engine to TDC, of the compression stroke, on cylinder No. 1 and make sure the pulley marks and the crank marks align.

10. Remove the protective cap over the timing belt tensioner locknut. Loosen the locknut, compress the tensioner, to release tension on the belts, and re-tighten the locknut, holding the tensioner in place.

11. Remove the timing belt from the camshafts. Do not crease or fold the belt.

➡**The camshafts and the crankshaft must not be moved when the belt is removed.**

12. Remove the timing belt idler pulleys.

13. Remove the camshaft drive pulleys. Use a counterhold wrench to prevent the cam from turning.

14. Remove the plate or panel behind the pulleys. Remove the cover plate for the ignition wires. Label and disconnect the ignition wiring from the spark plugs and the distributor cap; remove the coil wire from the distributor cap.

15. Remove the valve cover and gasket. Clean the surfaces of any gasket remains.

16. Remove the distributor housing from the camshaft carrier. Remove the ignition wire clip next to the left bolt.

17. Plug the spark plug holes with crumpled paper. Remove the center bearing cap for each camshaft. Remove the third nut in the center. Mark the cam bearing caps for proper reinstallation.

18. Install a camshaft press tool 5021 or similar, on the exhaust side cam in place of the removed bearing cap. When it is securely in place, remove the remaining bearing caps and nuts. Remove the tool and remove the exhaust camshaft.

19. Remove the intake camshaft in identical fashion.

➡**Label or identify each cam and its bearing caps. All removed components should be kept in order.**

20. Using a magnet or a small suction cup, remove the tappets. Store them upside down, to prevent oil drainage, and keep them in order; they are not interchangeable.

21. Remove the remaining 4 nuts in the center of the cam carrier and detach the carrier from the head. If it is stuck, tap it very gently with a plastic mallet. Remove the O-rings around the spark plug holes.

22. Wipe the remaining oil off the cylinder head and remove the bolts in order. When all the bolts are removed, the cylinder head may be lifted free of the vehicle.

➡**The head is aluminum. Support it on clean wood blocks or similar to avoid scoring the face.**

23. Clean the camshaft carrier and the head assembly of all gasket material and sealer. Carefully scrape the joint surfaces with a plastic scraper. Do not use metal tools to scrape or

clean. Wash the surfaces with a degreasing compound and blow the surfaces completely dry. Inspect the head bolts for any sign of stretching or elongation in the midsection. If this is observed or suspected, discard the bolt. Bolts may not be used more than 5 times.

To install:

24. Install the new head gasket and a new O-ring for the water pump. Carefully place the cylinder head into position; do not damage the gasket.

25. Clean the head bolts and apply a light coat of oil. Install them and tighten, in sequence, in 3 steps: to 15 ft. lbs. (20 Nm), then all to 30 ft. lbs. (41 Nm). Third Step is to tighten each bolt through 115 degree of arc in 1 continuous motion. The use of protractor fitting tool 5098 is strongly recommended for this task.

26. Install the exhaust manifold with a new gasket. Attach the front exhaust pipe to its bracket and install the heat shields.

27. On the left side of the motor, connect the temperature sensors, the heating hose under cylinders 3 and 4 and the upper coolant hose to the thermostat.

28. Fill the cooling system and check carefully for leaks, particularly around the head to block joint.

29. Install the intake manifold with a new gasket. Tighten the bottom bolts a few turns and place the manifold in position. Tighten all the bolts from the center outwards.

30. Reattach the support under the intake manifold and the cable clip. Double check all connections on and around the intake manifold.

31. Apply liquid sealing compound to the camshaft carrier. Use a small paint roller and coat the surfaces which match to the head and the bearing cap joint faces.

32. Install the cam carrier on the head and secure it with 4 of the 5 center nuts tightened to 15 ft. lbs. (20 Nm); do not install the middle nut.

33. Oil all matching surfaces on the cam carrier, bearing caps and tappets.

34. Insert the tappets; they must be inserted in their original order and place.

35. Install the exhaust side camshaft by placing it in the carrier with the pulley guide pin facing up. Using the rear bearing cap as a guide, press the cam into place with the press tool. Install the bearing caps in the original order.

36. Install the bearing cap nuts and tighten them in stages to 15 ft. lbs. (20 Nm). Remove the press tool and install the center bearing cap; tighten it in stages to 15 ft. lbs. (20 Nm).

37. Install the intake camshaft in the carrier with the pulley guide pin facing upwards.

38. Turn the distributor shaft to align the driver with the markings on the distributor housing. Install new O-rings on the housing and rotor shaft.

39. Using the rear bearing cap as a guide, press the cam into place with the press tool. Install the bearing caps in the original order.

40. Install the bearing cap nuts and tighten them in stages to 15 ft. lbs. (20 Nm). Remove the press tool and install the center bearing cap; tighten it in stages to 15 ft. lbs. (20 Nm).

41. Install the center nut in the cam carrier and tighten it to 15 ft. lbs. (20 Nm).

42. Double check the tightness of all the camshaft carrier nuts and the bearing cap nuts. All should be 15 ft. lbs.; do not overtighten.

43. Reinstall the distributor, connect the coil wire and install the ignition wire clip at the left bolt. Remove the paper plugs from the spark plug holes.

44. Use a silicone sealer and apply to the front and rear camshaft bearing caps. Install new gaskets for the valve cover and the spark plug wells. Install the spark plug gasket with the arrow pointing towards the front of the vehicle and the word 'UP' facing up. Make sure the valve cover gasket is correctly positioned and install the valve cover.

45. Reconnect the ground wire at the distributor.

46. Install the ignition wires and the cover plate.

47. Using a compression seal driver tool 5025 or similar, install the oil seals for the front of each camshaft. Camshafts must not be allowed to turn during this operation.

48. Install the upper backing plate over the ends of the camshafts and adjust the plate so the cams are centered in the holes.

49. Replace the idler pulleys and tighten their mounts to 18.5 ft. lbs. (25 Nm).

50. Install the camshaft drive pulleys, using a counterhold to prevent the cams from turning.

51. Making sure the camshaft pulleys are properly aligned with the marks on the backing plate, position the timing belt so the double mark on the belt coincides exactly with the top mark on the belt guide plate, at the top of the crankshaft. Place the belt onto the cam pulleys and make sure the single marks on the belt line up exactly with the marks on the pulleys. Fit the belt over the idler pulleys; right side idler first, then the left.

52. Double check that the engine is on TDC, of the compression stroke, for cylinder No. 1 and that all the belt markings line up as they should.

53. Loosen the tensioner locknut. Rotate the crankshaft clockwise 1 full turn until the belt markings again coincide with the pulley markings.

➡ **The engine must not be rotated counterclockwise while the tensioner is loose.**

54. Turn the crankshaft smoothly clockwise until the pulley marks are 1½ teeth beyond the marks on the backing plate.

55. Tighten the tensioner locknut. Install the lower timing belt cover.

56. Install the radiator fan and pulley, the alternator drive belt and the negative battery cable.

57. Double check all installation items, paying particular attention to loose hoses or hanging wires, untightened nuts, poor routing of hoses and wires (too tight or rubbing) and tools left in the engine area.

58. Start the engine and allow it to run until the thermostat opens. Use extreme caution; the timing belt is exposed.

➡ **This engine may be somewhat noisy when started. The noise will subside as oil reaches the tappets. Do not exceed 2500 rpm while the tappets are noisy.**

59. Shut the engine off, rotate the crankshaft to bring the engine to TDC, of the compression stroke, of cylinder No. 1 and use tool 998 8500 or equivalent, to check the belt tension. Correct deflection is 5.5 ± 0.2 units when measured between the exhaust camshaft pulley and the idler. If the tension is not correct, repeat Steps 51-54.

60. Install the upper timing belt cover. Start the engine and final check all functions.

B280F Engine

▶ **See Figures 28, 29, 30 and 31**

1. Disconnect the battery. Drain the coolant.

2. Remove the air cleaner assembly and all attaching hoses.

3. Disconnect the throttle cable. On automatic transmission equipped vehicles, disconnect the kickdown cable.

4. Disconnect the EGR vacuum hose and remove the pipe between the EGR valve and manifold.

5. Remove the oil filler cap and cover the hole with a rag. Disconnect the PCV pipe(s) from the intake manifold.

6. Remove the front section of the intake manifold.

7. Disconnect the electrical connector and fuel line at the cold start injector. Disconnect the vacuum hose, both fuel lines. and the electrical connector from the control pressure regulator.

8. Disconnect the hose, pipe and electrical connector from the auxiliary air valve. Remove the auxiliary air valve.

9. Disconnect the electrical connector from the fuel distributor. Remove the wire loom from the intake manifolds. Disconnect the spark plug wires.

10. Disconnect the fuel injectors from their holders.

11. Disconnect the distributor vacuum hose, carbon filter hose and diverter valve hose from the intake manifold. Also, disconnect the power brake hose and heater hose at the intake manifold.

12. Disconnect the throttle control link from it pulley.

13. If equipped with an EGR vacuum amplifier, disconnect the wires from the throttle micro-switch and solenoid valve.

14. At the firewall, disconnect the fuel lines from the fuel filter and return line.

15. Remove the 2 attaching screws and lift out the fuel distributor and throttle housing assembly.

16. If not equipped with an EGR vacuum amplifier, disconnect the EGR valve hose from under the throttle housing.

17. Remove the cold start injector, rubber ring and pipe.

18. Remove the 4 retaining bolts and lift off the intake manifold. Remove the rubber rings.

19. Remove the splash guard under the engine.

20. If removing the left cylinder head, remove the air pump from its bracket.

21. Remove the vacuum pump and O-ring in the valve cover. Remove the vacuum hose from the wax thermostat.

22. If removing the right cylinder head, disconnect the upper radiator hose.

23. On air conditioned vehicles, remove the air conditioning compressor and secure it aside. Do not disconnect the refrigerant lines.

24. Disconnect the distributor leads and remove the distributor. Remove the EGR valve, bracket and pipe. At the firewall, disconnect the electrical connectors at the relays.

25. On air conditioned vehicles, remove the rear compressor bracket.

26. Disconnect the coolant hose(s) from the water pump to the cylinder head(s). If removing the left cylinder head disconnect the lower radiator hose at the water pump.

27. Disconnect the air injection system supply hose from the applicable cylinder head. Separate the air manifold at the rear of the engine. If removing the left cylinder head, remove the backfire valve and air hose.

28. Remove the valve cover(s).

29. On the left cylinder head, remove the Allen head screw and 4 upper bolts to the timing gear cover. On the right cylinder head, remove the 4 upper bolts to the timing gear cover and the front cover plate.

30. From under the vehicle, remove the exhaust pipe clamps for both header pipes.

31. If removing the right cylinder head, remove the retainer bracket bolts and pull the dipstick tube out of the crankcase.

32. Remove the applicable exhaust manifold(s).

33. Remove the cover plate at the rear of the cylinder head.

34. Rotate the camshaft sprocket, for the applicable cylinder head, into position so the large sprocket hole aligns with the rocker arm shaft. With the camshaft in this position, loosen the cylinder head bolts, in sequence, same sequence as tightening, and remove the rocker arm and shaft assembly.

35. Loosen the camshaft retaining fork bolt, directly in back of sprocket, and slide the fork away from the camshaft.

36. Next, it is necessary to hold the cam chain stretched during camshaft removal. Otherwise, the chain tensioner will automatically take up the slack, making it impossible to reinstall the sprocket on the cam without removing the timing chain cover to loosen the tensioner device. To accomplish this, a sprocket retainer tool 999 5104 is installed over the sprocket with 2 bolts in the top of the timing chain cover. A bolt is then screwed into the sprocket to hold it in place.

37. Remove the camshaft sprocket center bolt and push the camshaft to the rear, so it clears the sprocket.

38. Remove the cylinder head.

➡Do not remove the cylinder head by pulling straight up. Instead, lever the head off by inserting 2 spare head bolts into the front and rear inboard cylinder head bolt holes and pulling toward the applicable wheel housing. Otherwise, the cylinder liners may be pulled up, breaking the lower liner seal and leaking coolant into the crankcase. If any do pull up, new liner seals must be used and the crankcase completely drained. If the head(s) seem stuck, gently tap around the edges of the head(s) with a rubber mallet, to break the joint.

39. Remove the head gasket. Clean the contact surfaces with a plastic scraper and lacquer thinner.

40. If the head is going to be off for any length of time, install liner holders tool 999 5093 or 2 strips of thick stock steel with holes for the head bolts, so the liners stay pressed down against their seals. Install the holders width-wise between the middle 4 head bolt holes.

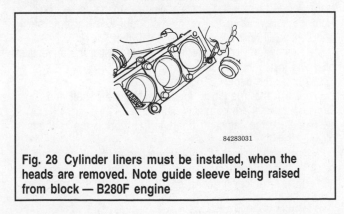

Fig. 28 Cylinder liners must be installed, when the heads are removed. Note guide sleeve being raised from block — B280F engine

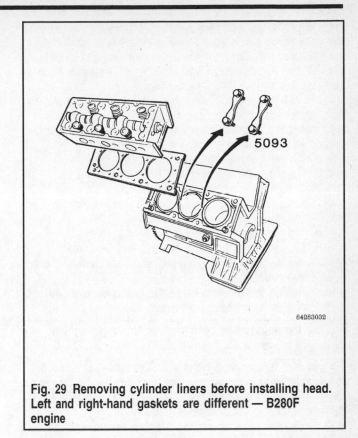

Fig. 29 Removing cylinder liners before installing head. Left and right-hand gaskets are different — B280F engine

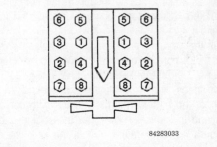

Fig. 30 Tightening sequence for cylinder head bolts — B280F engine

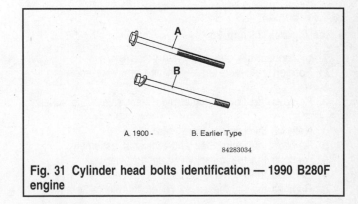

A. 1900 —   B. Earlier Type

Fig. 31 Cylinder head bolts identification — 1990 B280F engine

To install:

41. If the dowels at the outboard corners of the block have slipped down, use a pair of needle-nose pliers to retrieve

them. Prop them up with an ⅛ inch (3mm). Remember to keep the timing chain taunt during cylinder head installation.

42. Remove the liner holders and install the head gaskets. The left and right head gaskets are different, ensure the correct one is installed. Install the cylinder head.

43. Install the camshaft and remove the timing chain retainer tool. Install the head bolts finger tight after lubricating with oil.

44. On 1990 Asbestos-free gasket, with fixed-washer bolts, tighten all bolts in stages as follows:

   a. Tighten bolts to 44 ft. lbs. (60 Nm).
   b. Loosen bolts, tighten it to 30 ft. lbs. (40 Nm).
   c. Angle-tighten to 160-180 degrees.

45. Except 1990 Asbestos-free gasket, with fixed-washer bolts, tighten all bolts in stages as follows:

   a. Tighten bolts to 43 ft. lbs. (60 Nm).
   b. Loosen bolt 1, tighten it to 15 ft. lbs. (20 Nm).
   c. Angle-tighten to 106 degrees, using special tool (Tool 5098 or equivalent).
   d. Repeat this for remaining bolts in sequence shown. Loosen and tighten each bolt in turn.

➡**After the engine has been warmed-up, angle-tighten each bolt a further 45 degrees.**

46. Install the camshaft center bolt and tighten to 52-66 ft. lbs. Install the timing gear case and rear cylinder head covers. Check and adjust the valve lash. After adjusting valve lash, turn the engine to TDC on No. 1 piston.

47. Install the valve covers, air injection system, exhaust pipes and manifolds.

48. Install all coolant hoses, install the air conditioner compressor brackets, distributor, EGR valve, cold start injector and intake manifold.

49. Install the vacuum pump and lower splash shield. Connect all electrical connections previously disconnected.

50. Install the throttle linkage, fuel injectors and all fuel injection system hoses, lines and electrical connections.

51. Connect the battery. Fill the radiator with coolant, check the engine and transmission oil. Start the engine and allow it to reach operating temperature. Adjust the timing and check for leaks.

52. Allow the engine to cool for 2 hours; then, angle-tighten each cylinder head bolt a further 45 degrees.

B6304F Engine
▶ **See Figures 32 and 33**

1. Disconnect the negative battery cable.
2. Position a suitable drain pan and drain the cooling system.
3. Remove the front exhaust pipe, heat shield and exhaust manifold(s).
4. Remove the coolant pipe bolts.
5. Remove the timing belt and tensioner assembly.
6. Remove the transmission mounting plate bolt.
7. Remove the air mass meter and intake hose.
8. Remove the throttle pulley cover, throttle cable and cable bracket.
9. Disconnect the throttle switch lead and vacuum hoses at throttle housing and cruise control servo.
10. Remove the intake manifold (outer section).
11. Mark the positions and remove the ignition coils.

12. Mark the camshaft pulleys (intake and exhaust sides) and remove the pulleys, using Tool 5199 or equivalent.

13. Remove the camshaft sensor, ground terminals and temperature sensor connector. Remove the coolant hose at rear.

14. Carefully tap the top half of the cylinder head upwards, using a copper mallet.

15. Tap the joint lugs and camshaft front ends. Remove the camshafts.

16. Remove the cylinder head bolts, starting at the outside and working inwards. Lift the cylinder head from the engine. Remove the gasket.

17. Clean and inspect the cylinder head and block mating surface.

To install:

18. Align the crankshaft timing mark, by removing the starter motor and installing the crankshaft locking tool (5451 or equivalent). Turn the crankshaft until it is stopped by the tool.

19. Fit a new cylinder head gasket and install the bottom half of the cylinder head. Oil the cylinder head bolts; install and torque in sequence to specifications.

20. Install new O-rings in the spark plug wells and oil the camshaft bearing seats.

21. Apply sealing compound (Part No. 1161059-9 or equivalent) to the upper section of the cylinder head.

➡**Do not allow any compound to penetrate the coolant or oil passages.**

22. Oil the camshaft bearing seats and install the camshaft.

23. Place the upper section of the cylinder head into position. Install the press tools (5454 or equivalent) and tighten against the lower section. Install the bolts and working from the inside outwards, tighten to 13 ft. lbs. (17 Nm). Remove the tools.

24. Grease the camshaft front seal and tap the seal into place.

25. Place the upper timing cover into position. Install the camshaft pulleys while aligning the timing marks.

26. Install and tighten the pulley mounting bolts.

27. Remove the timing cover and install the mounting plate bolt.

28. Place the timing belt around the camshaft and right side idler. Place the belt over the camshaft pulleys, around the water pump and press over the tensioner pulley.

29. Install the belt tensioner. Tighten the tensioner mounting bolts to 18 ft. lbs. (25 Nm).

30. Slacken the camshaft pulley bolts and withdraw the tensioner locking pin. Insert the remaining camshaft pulley bolt. Hold the pulley, using the counterhold tool (5199 or equivalent) and tighten all bolts alternately to 15 ft. lbs. (20 Nm).

31. Remove the crankshaft locking tool. Install the protective plug and install the starter motor.

32. Install the upper timing cover.

33. Check that the timing marks on the crankshaft and camshaft pulleys are correctly aligned.

34. Grease the camshaft front seal and press the seal into place.

35. Install the camshaft sensor, ground terminals and temperature sensor connector. Install the coolant hose at rear.

36. Install the ignition coils, spark plug cover and auxiliaries drive belt.

37. Install the damper guard and splashguard.

38. Install the intake manifold

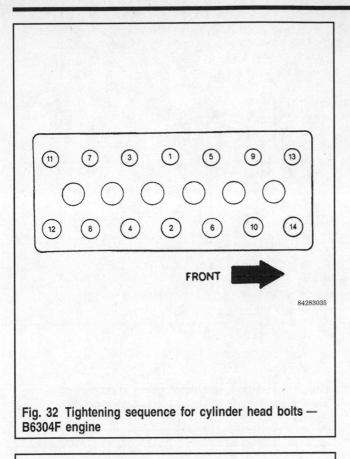

Fig. 32 Tightening sequence for cylinder head bolts — B6304F engine

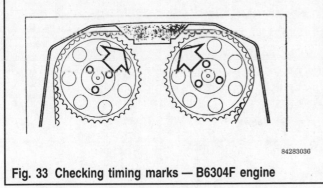

Fig. 33 Checking timing marks — B6304F engine

39. Install the exhaust manifold, using a new gasket. Install the heat shield and front exhaust pipe.

40. Connect the temperature sensor and coolant hose to the thermostat.

41. Loosen the catalytic convertor bolts and re-tighten to 18 ft. lbs. (25 Nm). This is necessary to prevent stress in the system.

42. Change the engine oil. Fill the cooling system.

43. Connect the negative battery lead. Start the engine and check for leaks.

44. Recheck the cooling system.

CLEANING AND INSPECTION

▶ See Figure 34

➡ **Be careful when handling the cylinder head. Do not allow the cylinder head gasket surface to become damaged.**

1. Clean the faces between the exhaust manifold and cylinder head. Use a soft putty knife and, if necessary, gasket solvent.

2. Check the cylinder head for distortion (warp), using a steel ruler and feeler gauge. Distortion must not exceed 0.02 inch (0.5mm) longitudinally and 0.01 inch (0.25mm) across the cylinder head.

➡ **Never machine a warped cylinder head. If distortion is greater than specified, the cylinder head must be replaced.**

3. Clean and check spark plug threads for damage. Clean the cylinder head bolt holes.

4. On B6304F engine, clean the cylinder block joint, coolant pipe joint and joint faces between the top and bottom halves of the cylinder head.

Valves, Valve Springs and Valve Stem Seals

REMOVAL & INSTALLATION

The following procedure is a general guide to reconditioning the B230F engine. It may be altered, as required, for most other engines. On all engines, the valve springs must be depressed and the retainers removed, so the valve can be removed from the cylinder head.

➡ **Be careful when handling the cylinder head. Do not allow the cylinder head gasket surface to become damaged.**

B230F Engine

▶ See Figures 35, 36 and 37

1. Remove the lifting eyelet, thermostat housing, thermostat and spark plugs from the cylinder head.

2. Remove the camshaft center cap. Install the press tool (5021 or equivalent) and depress the camshaft. Remove the remaining camshaft caps.

3. Remove the press tool, camshaft and camshaft seal.

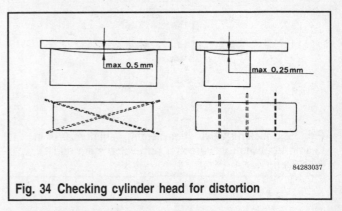

Fig. 34 Checking cylinder head for distortion

4. Remove the valve depressors and adjusting washers. Position the valve depressors in order, so they may be reinstalled in their original locations.

5. Remove the rubber seals from the valve stems.

6. Remove the valve cotters, upper spring seats, valve spring and valves.

7. Remove the valve stem seals from the inlet valve guides, using the correct tool (5219 or equivalent).

8. Remove the lower valve spring seats from the inlet valve guides after removing the valve stem seals.

➡**Do not interchange parts.**

To install:

9. Position the valves in the cylinder head.

  a. Position the valve stem height gauge (5222 or equivalent) in the camshaft bearing seats.

  b. Slide the measuring ring over the valve and at the same time press the valve against the valve seat with a finger. Measuring ring must not touch the valve. If the valve touches the measuring ring, stem must be ground shorter. Minimum 0.14 inch (3.5mm) between the valve cotter and valve stem end.

10. Install the lower valve spring seats. Place protective sleeve on the valve stem. Install new valve stem seals on the inlet valves, using tool (5219 or equivalent). Always use protective sleeve supplied with the gasket kit.

11. Install the valve spring, upper valve spring seat, valve cotters and rubber seal.

12. Oil and install the valve depressors and adjusting washers. Place them in their original locations.

13. Install the camshaft assembly. Install the front oil seal.

14. Adjust the valves.

B280F Engine

To gain access to the valves, the camshaft(s) must be removed from the head(s). Please refer to Camshaft Removal and Installation for detailed instructions.

1. To remove the valves, depress the valve spring with a valve spring compressor and remove the collets with a small magnet or similar tool.

2. Release the tension on the spring compressor and remove the valve spring, its parts and the valve.

3. Remove the valve guide seals.

4. To assemble, install new valve guide seals, being careful not to damaged them when installing. After lapping the valves,

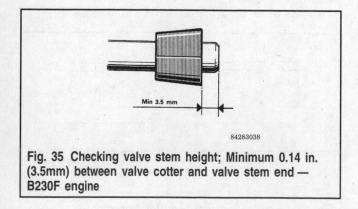

Fig. 35 Checking valve stem height; Minimum 0.14 in. (3.5mm) between valve cotter and valve stem end — B230F engine

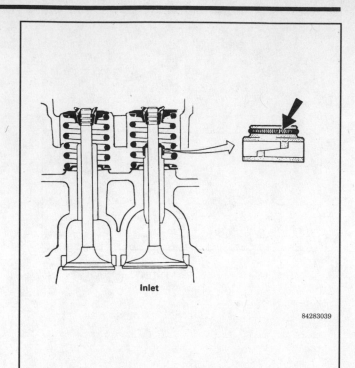

Fig. 36 Installing lower valve spring seats and valve stem seals. Only inlet valves have seals — B230F engine

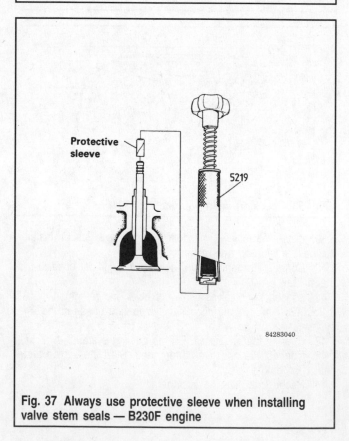

Fig. 37 Always use protective sleeve when installing valve stem seals — B230F engine

assemble the valve spring parts in the reverse order of removal.

INSPECTION

1. Clean the valve seats with a cutter. Inspect the valves and valve seats.

2. Remove all carbon deposit from the combustion chambers and valves.

3. If the valve seats are fractured or show signs of excessive wear they must be replaced.

SCRAPPING SODIUM-FILLED EXHAUST VALVES

▶ See Figure 38

✳✳CAUTION

Turbocharged engines have sodium-filled exhaust valves. Sodium in contact with water is explosive. When drilling, cutting or performing any form of work which involves separating sodium, be certain the sodium does not come in contact with water. These valves must not be mixed with ordinary scrap iron before first removing the sodium. Use the following procedure:

1. Drill a hole 0.16 inch (4.0mm) in the valve crown.

2. Drill a hole 0.16 inch (4.0mm) in the valve stem, or cut the stem approximately 25mm from the end.

3. Throw the valve into a bucket of water. Immediately move at least 10 feet (3 meters) from the bucket. A powerful reaction (explosive in nature) will occur. After the reaction subside, the valve can be mixed with ordinary scrap metal.

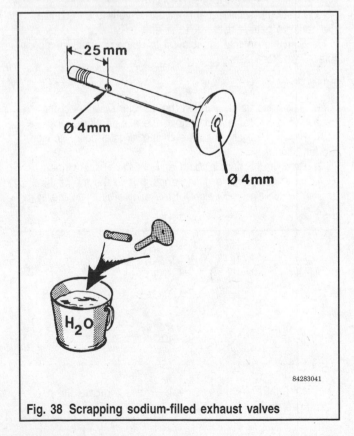

84283041

Fig. 38 Scrapping sodium-filled exhaust valves

LAPPING VALVES

Invert the cylinder head, lightly lubricate the valve stems, and install the valves in the head as numbered. Coat valve seats with fine valve grinding compound, moisten the suction cup on the lapping tool and attach the cup to a valve head.

Rotate the tool, changing position and lifting the tool often to prevent grooving. Lap the valve until a smooth, polished seat is evident. Remove the valve and tool, and rinse away all traces of grinding compound.

CHECKING VALVE SPRINGS

Check the valve spring for proper pressure at the specified spring lengths using a valve spring pressure tool. Weak valve springs cause poor performance; therefore, if the pressure of any spring is lower than the service limit replace the spring.

Springs should be ±5 lbs. of all other springs. Check each valve spring for squareness. Stand the spring on a flat surface next to a carpenter's square. Measure the height of the spring; rotate the spring slowly and observe the space between the top coil of the spring and the square. If the spring is out of square more than 5/64 inches (2mm) or the height varies (by comparison) by more than 1/16 inch (1.5mm), replace the spring.

Valve Seats and Valve Guides

If after cleaning and inspecting the valve seats and valve guides, you determined they must be replaced, it is recommended the valve seats and valve guides service be performed by a qualify machine shop.

✳✳WARNING

The use of the correct special tools or their equivalent is required for this procedure.

B230F Engine

The cylinder head, on B230F engine, requires heating to 212°; the installation tools are the same. If these tools are not available, press in the guides until the guide's height above the cylinder head surface, at the base of the guide, is 0.6061-0.6139 inch (15.4-15.6mm) for intake valve guides and 0.7051-0.7129 inch (17.9-18.1mm) for exhaust valve guides. When replacing the guides on the B230F engine, make sure the new guides have the same number of grooves at the end as the old guide. The number of grooves is an indication of the size of the guide.

B234F Engine

The cylinder head, on B234F engine, do not require heating but do require the guides to be installed under a minimum pressure of 2025 lbs. The pressing operation is conducted in three steps with three different drifts of exact size. The final installation step leaves the top of the guide projecting above

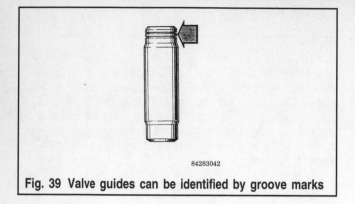

84283042

Fig. 39 Valve guides can be identified by groove marks

the head by 0.60 inch (15mm). The height is set by the installation tool.

After installing new guides, they must be reamed with a hand tool and the valves and seats must be ground (lapped).

B280F Engine

The cylinder heads, on B280F engine, require heating to about 300°F (149°C); it is generally outside the ability of the average home mechanic to safely deal with this level of heat. It is recommended that the head be taken to a machine shop for professional installation of new valve guides.

The·valve seats on all engines are removable. Since the usual method of removing and installing valve seats includes either freezing or heating the valve seat or the cylinder head, this job should be performed by a competent machine shop or garage. The intake valve seats on the B280F engine are of a new design and should not be replaced with the old style seats.

Valve Lifters

The B234F engine use hydraulic tappets to provide a means of maintaining the valve train in contact with the camshaft.

REMOVAL & INSTALLATION

B234F Engine

The camshaft(s) must first be removed, before the valve lifters can be remove from the camshaft carrier.

1. Remove the camshaft. See 'Camshaft' removal and installation in this section.
2. Remove the valve lifters from the camshaft carrier. A magnet or suction cup may be used to facilitate the lifters removal.

➡ **Do not interchange parts. Lifters must be replaced in original order.**

3. Inspect the lifters for signs of wear. Replace, as necessary.

➡ **Always store the lifters upside down to prevent drainage of oil.**

Oil Pan

REMOVAL & INSTALLATION

B230F Engine
▶ **See Figure 40**

1. Disconnect the negative battery cable. Raise and support the vehicle safely.
2. Drain the engine oil.
3. Remove the splash guard.
4. Remove the engine mount retaining nuts.
5. Remove the lower bolt and loosen the top bolt on the steering column yoke.
6. Slide the yoke assembly up on the steering shaft.
7. Raise and safely support the front of the engine.
8. Remove the retaining bolts for the front axle crossmember.
9. Remove the crossmember.
10. Remove the left engine mount.
11. Remove the pan support bracket.
12. Remove the pan bolts and remove the pan.

To install:

13. Clean the gasket mating surfaces thoroughly. Install the oil pan and using new gaskets, tighten the bolts to 8 ft. lbs. (11 Nm).
14. Lower the engine and install all engine mounts. Install the front crossmember and install the bolts.
15. Install the yoke assembly on the steering shaft and tighten the bolts to 18 ft. lbs. (24 Nm).
16. Install the splash guard, lower the vehicle and connect the negative battery cable. Fill the engine with oil.
17. Start the engine and allow it to reach operating temperature. Check for leaks.

B234F Engine

1. Raise and safely support the vehicle. Disconnect the negative battery cable and remove the engine oil dipstick.
2. Remove the air mass meter and air inlet hose. Loosen the fan shroud.
3. Remove the bolts at both ends of the crossmember.
4. Fit a chain hoist or lifting apparatus to the top of the engine and relieve the weight of the engine by lifting the at the front.

84283043

Fig. 40 Steering yoke removal; arrows indicate the retaining nuts

5. At the right motor mount, unbolt the bottom mounting plate from the crossmember. At the left motor mount, unbolt the upper mounting plate from the cylinder block.

6. Drain the engine oil and replace the drain bolt when the pan is empty. Use a new washer and tighten the bolt to 44 ft. lbs. (60 Nm).

7. Remove the splash guard from under the engine, the bottom nut for the left motor mount and the wiring harness bracket from the transmission cover.

8. At the steering shaft, remove the lower clamping bolt and loosen the upper bolt. Matchmark the position of the splined joint and slide the fitting up the steering shaft.

9. Remove the rubber bump-stop on the front crossmember and remove the reinforcing bracket between the engine and transmission.

10. Disassemble the bolted joint at the front of the catalytic converter.

11. Carefully elevate the engine with the hoist. Make very certain that no hoses or wires are strained and that clearance is maintained at the firewall. Raise the motor only enough to perform the next Steps of the procedure.

12. Remove the left motor mount.

13. Unbolt and remove the oil pan. It will need to be lifted and turned during removal.

To install:

14. Clean the gasket surfaces and install the new gasket so the small tab on the gasket is on the same side as the starter. Lift the pan into place, install the retaining bolts and tighten them to 8 ft. lbs. (11 Nm).

15. Install the reinforcing bracket between the engine and transmission. Attach it first to the transmission and then to the engine block. Tighten the bracket in stages so all the bolts pull up evenly.

16. Install the bump-stop on the front crossmember. Lift the crossmember into position against the side rails, install the bolts and tighten only a few turns to hold it in place.

17. When all the bolts are installed, tighten the crossmember bolts to 70 ft. lbs. (95 Nm). Install the left motor mount and secure the plate to the cylinder block. Don't forget to attach the cable clip on the upper bolt.

18. Paying close attention to the placement of the motor mounts, lower the engine into position. When the engine is correctly seated, the lifting equipment may be removed from the vehicle.

19. At the right motor mount, tighten the plate onto the crossmember. Check the connection of the air preheat tube at the exhaust manifold.

20. Tighten the fan shroud. Adjust the position of the bottom bracket as needed.

21. Reconnect the wiring harness bracket at the transmission, the bolted joint at the front of the catalytic converter and install the splashguard under the engine.

22. Tighten the left motor mount.

23. Observing the markings made earlier, reassemble the steering shafts. Insert and tighten the bottom bolt to 15 ft. lbs. (20 Nm). Tighten the upper bolt the same. Don't forget to install the small spring clips on the bolts.

24. Install the air mass meter and its hoses and connectors.

25. Fill the engine with the correct amount of oil and reinstall the dipstick.

26. Lower the vehicle, reconnect the battery cable and start the engine. Check for leaks.

B280F Engine

▶ **See Figure 41**

1. Disconnect the negative battery cable. Raise and support the vehicle safely. Remove the splash guard.

2. Drain the crankcase.

3. Remove the oil pan retaining bolts. Swivel the pan past the stabilizer bar and remove.

To install:

4. Clean the gasket mating surfaces thoroughly. Install the oil pan, using a new gasket, and tighten the bolts to 6-8 ft. lbs.

5. Install the splash guard, lower the vehicle and fill the crankcase with oil. Connect the negative battery cable. Start the engine and allow it to reach operating temperature. Check for leaks.

Oil Pump

REMOVAL

B230F Engine

▶ **See Figures 42 and 43**

1. Remove the oil pan.

2. Remove the 2 oil pump retaining bolts.

3. Remove the oil pump and pull the delivery tube from the block.

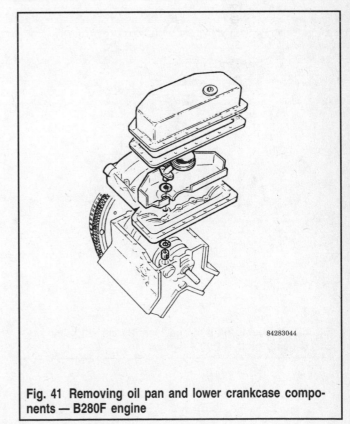

84283044

Fig. 41 Removing oil pan and lower crankcase components — B280F engine

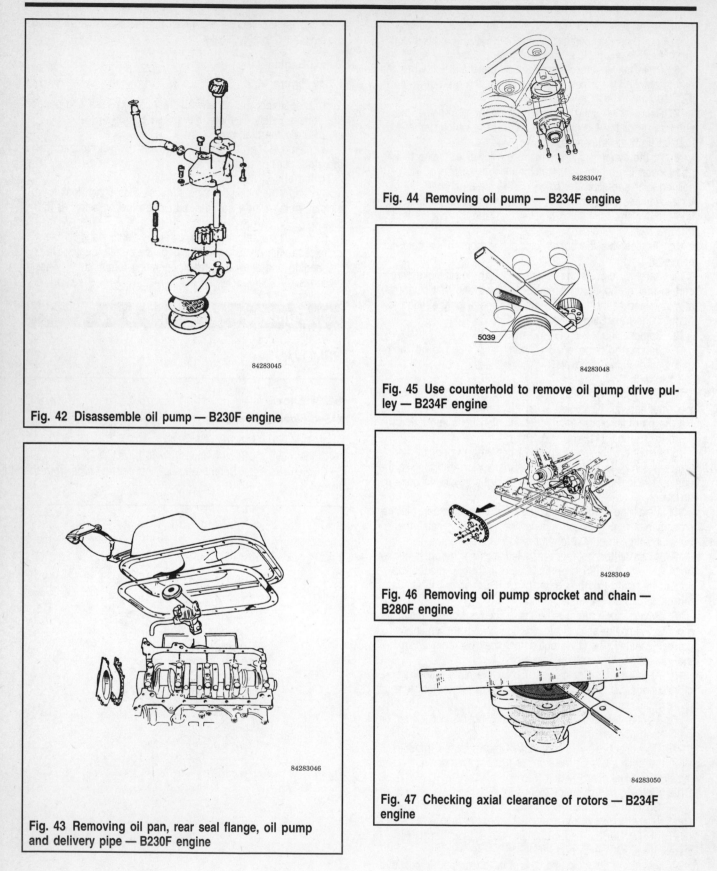

84283045

Fig. 42 Disassemble oil pump — B230F engine

84283046

Fig. 43 Removing oil pan, rear seal flange, oil pump and delivery pipe — B230F engine

84283047

Fig. 44 Removing oil pump — B234F engine

5039

84283048

Fig. 45 Use counterhold to remove oil pump drive pulley — B234F engine

84283049

Fig. 46 Removing oil pump sprocket and chain — B280F engine

84283050

Fig. 47 Checking axial clearance of rotors — B234F engine

B234F Engine

▶ **See Figures 44 and 45**

1. Remove the timing belt.
2. Using a counterholding tool 5039 or similar, remove the oil pump drive pulley.
3. Thoroughly clean the area around the oil pump. Place sheets of newspaper or a container on the splash guard to contain any spillage and remove the oil pump mounting bolts. Remove the pump from the engine.
4. Remove the seal from the groove in the block. Clean the area with solvent, making certain there are no particles of dirt trapped in the pump area.

B280F Engine

▶ **See Figure 46**

The oil pump body is cast integrally with the cylinder block. It is chain driven by a separate sprocket on the crankshaft and is located behind the timing chain cover. The pick-up screen and tube are serviced by removing the oil pan. To check the pump gears or remove the oil pump cover:

1. Disconnect the negative battery cable. Remove the air cleaner and valve covers.
2. Loosen the fan shroud and remove the fan. Remove the shroud.
3. Loosen the alternator, air pump, power steering pump, air conditioning compressor, if equipped, and remove their drive belts.
4. Block the flywheel from turning and remove the 36mm bolt and the crankshaft pulley.

➡ **Be careful not to drop key into crankcase.**

5. Remove the timing gear cover (25 bolts).
6. Remove the oil pump drive sprocket and chain.
7. Remove the oil pump cover and gears.

B6304F Engine

1. Disconnect the negative battery cable.
2. Drain the cooling system.
3. Remove the auxiliaries drive belt, front timing belt cover, cooling fan and splashguard. Remove the radiator.
4. Turn the crankshaft until the timing marks on the camshaft pulleys/timing belt cover mounting plate and crankshaft pulley/oil pump housing are aligned. Remove the upper timing belt cover.
5. Remove the vibration damper.
6. Remove the timing belt.
7. Remove the crankshaft pulley, using a suitable puller.
8. Remove the oil pump mounting bolts and remove the oil pump.

OVERHAUL AND INSPECTION

B230F Engine

1. Disassemble the oil pump and clean components thoroughly. Check all components for visible signs of wear or damage.

2. Check tooth flank clearance. Place a feeler gauge between the sides of the teeth while installed in the casing. Clearance should be 0.006-0.014 inch (0.15-0.35 mm).
3. Check axial clearance by laying a straight edge across the top of the housing and using a feeler gauge to measure the clearance between the top of the housing and the gears. Clearance should be 0.0008-0.0048 inch (0.02-0.12 mm).
4. Assemble the oil pump using new seals. Prime the pump by operating it while submersed in oil.

B234F Engine

▶ **See Figures 47, 48 and 49**

1. Disassemble the oil pump and clean components thoroughly. Check all components for visible signs of wear or damage.
2. Check the pump housing joint for distortion by laying a straight-edge across the top of the housing.
3. Check axial clearance by laying a straight edge across the top of the housing and using a feeler gauge to measure the clearance between the top of the housing and the gears. Clearance should be 0.0020-0.0040 inch (0.05-0.10 mm).
4. Assemble the oil pump using new seals. Prime the pump by operating it while submersed in oil.

B280F Engine

▶ **See Figure 50**

1. Check the backlash of the oil pump gears. Lock the rotating spindle by inserting a bolt in the carrier plate hose and tightening gently.
2. Mount either gear on the fixed spindle. Mount the pump housing on the block approximately 180 degrees from the normal position.

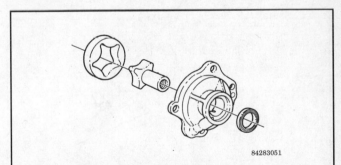

Fig. 48 Oil pump housing and components — B234F engine

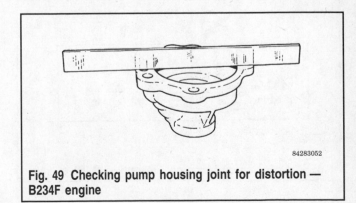

Fig. 49 Checking pump housing joint for distortion — B234F engine

3. Check gear backlash using a dial gauge. Backlash should be 0.0067-0.0106 in. (0.17-0.27 mm).

4. Remove the bolt from the carrier plate, oil all components and replace the pump.

B6304F Engine

1. Disassemble the oil pump. Clean and inspect all components.

2. Inspect for damage and wear, with particular attention to the half-moon insert (between the suction and delivery sides).

   a. Place the pump wheels in the housing, with the marking facing upwards. Place the small wheel in position.

   b. Check the clearance/play.

3. Replace the pump assembly, if there is evidence of wear, damage or excessive clearance/play.

4. Reassemble the pump.

INSTALLATION

B230F Engine

1. When installing, use new sealing rings at either end of the delivery tube.

2. Install the pump with the delivery tube attached. Align the pipe to the block so that the seal does not become damaged. Tighten the two oil pump retaining bolts.

3. Attach the clamp for the oil trap drain hose to the oil pump bolts. Make sure the hose is securely clamped behind the oil pump shoulder. Do not shorten the hose.

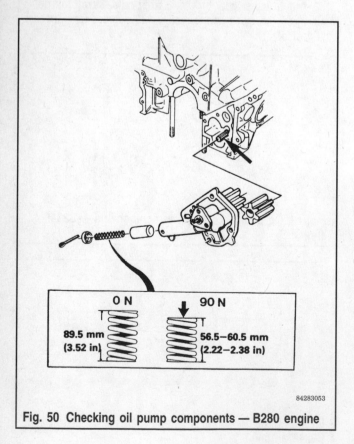

84283053

Fig. 50 Checking oil pump components — B280 engine

B234F Engine

1. Install the new seal in the groove and install the new oil pump. Lubricate the pump with clean engine oil before installation. Tighten the mounting bolts to 7.5 ft. lbs. (10 Nm).

2. Using the counterhold, install the drive pulley and tighten the center bolt to 15 ft. lbs. (20 Nm) plug 60 degrees of rotation.

3. Clean the area of any oil spillage; remove the paper or container from the splash guard.

4. Install the timing belt.

B280F Engine

1. Prime the pump, remove all air by filling it with clean engine oil and operating the pump by hands, before installation. Install the oil pump gears and cover. Install the oil pump drive sprocket and chain.

2. Install the timing gear cover, crankshaft pulley, alternator, air pump, power steering pump, air conditioning compressor and all accessory drive belts.

3. Remove the flywheel block and install the valve covers. Connect the negative battery cable.

B6304F Engine

1. Before installing the oil pump, thoroughly clean the mating surfaces.

2. Transfer the snow shield.

3. Place a new gasket into position; then install the oil pump, using tool 5455 or equivalent. Use the mounting bolts as a guide. Pull in the pump using the crankshaft center nut.

4. Apply thread locking compound to the pump mounting bolts and install the bolts. Tighten alternately to 7 ft. lbs. (10 Nm).

5. Install the crankshaft pulley, using the center bolt and spacer.

6. Install the timing belt.

7. Install the vibration damper. Tighten the center nut to 221 ft. lbs. (300 Nm).

8. Install the tensioner. Align the timing marks and install the ignition coil cover.

9. Install the radiator.

10. Install the front timing belt cover, cooling fan and splashguard. Install the auxiliaries drive belt.

Timing Belt Front Cover

REMOVAL & INSTALLATION

B230F Engine

1. Disconnect the negative battery cable. Loosen the fan shroud and remove the fan. Remove the shroud.

2. Loosen the alternator, power steering pump, if equipped, and air conditioning compressor, if equipped, and remove their drive belts.

3. Remove the water pump pulley.

4. Remove the 4 retaining bolts and lift off the timing belt cover.

To install:

5. Clean all gasket mating surfaces thoroughly. Install the timing belt cover using a new gasket. Tighten bolts to specification.

6. Install the water pump pulley, drive belts, air conditioning compressor, power steering pump and alternator.

7. Install the fan and shroud. Install the accessory drive belts. Connect the negative battery cable. Start the engine and check for leaks.

B234F Engine

1. Remove the negative battery cable and the alternator belt.

2. Remove the radiator fan, its pulley and the fan shroud.

3. Remove the drive belts for the power steering belts and the air conditioning compressor.

4. Remove the cover retaining bolts. Remove the covers, starting with the upper cover.

To install:

5. Install the lower; then upper timing belt cover.

6. Install the air conditioning compressor and power steering belts.

7. Install the radiator fan, its pulley and the fan shroud. Install the alternator belt.

8. Connect the negative battery, start the engine and check operation.

B6304F Engine

1. Disconnect the negative battery lead.

2. Remove the auxiliaries drive belt.

3. Remove the front (lower) timing belt cover, splashguard and vibration damper guard. Remove the ignition coil cover.

4. Remove the upper timing cover.

To install:

5. Install the upper timing belt cover. Install the ignition coil cover.

6. Install the front (lower) timing belt cover, splashguard and vibration damper guard.

7. Install the auxiliaries drive belt.

8. Connect the negative battery lead.

OIL SEAL REPLACEMENT

B234F Engine

1. Disconnect the negative battery cable.

2. Remove the timing/balance shaft belts as described in this section.

3. Remove the timing belt right-side idler.

4. Remove the crankshaft pulley, using a counterhold and guide (Tools 5284 and 5872 or equivalent) between the cylinder head, in right-hand idler bolt hole.

5. Carefully pry out the seal. Avoid damaging the sealing faces on the shaft and in seating flange.

To install:

6. Before installing the new seal, thoroughly clean the crankshaft end and seating flange.

7. Lubricate the new seal and tap the seal into the seating flange.

➡**Face of seal should normally be flush with the chamfered edge in the housing; however, if the shaft end shows sign of wear, seal may be located approximately 3mm further in.**

8. Install the balance shaft drive pulley. Guide must face outwards.

9. Install the timing belt pulley and guides.

10. Install the crankshaft damper/pulley. Tighten the crankshaft bolt in 2-stages. First tighten to 44 ft. lbs. (60 Nm); then tighten an additional 60 degree.

11. Turn the crankshaft to TDC on No. 1 cylinder.

12. Install the right-hand idler. Tighten to 18.5 ft. lbs. (25 Nm).

13. Install the timing/balance shaft belts as described in this section.

14. Connect the negative battery cable.

B6304F Engine

1. Disconnect the negative battery cable.

2. Remove the timing belt as described in this section.

3. Remove the crankshaft pulley, using a suitable puller.

4. Carefully pry out the old seal.

To install:

5. Before installing the new seal, thoroughly clean the crankshaft face.

6. Lubricate the new seal and tap the seal into place, using tool 5455 or equivalent.

7. Install the timing belt as described in this section.

8. Connect the negative battery cable.

Timing Chain Front Cover

REMOVAL & INSTALLATION

B280F Engine

1. Disconnect the negative battery cable. Remove the air cleaner and valve covers.

2. Loosen the fan shroud and remove the fan. Remove the shroud.

3. Loosen the alternator, air pump, power steering pump, air conditioning compressor, if equipped, and remove their drive belts.

4. Block the flywheel from turning, remove the crankshaft pulley nut (36mm) and the pulley.

➡**Do not drop the pulley key into the crankcase.**

5. Remove the power steering pump and place aside. Remove the pump bracket.

6. Remove the timing chain cover retaining bolts, 25-11mm hex bolts, tap and remove the cover.

To install:

7. Clean the gasket contact surfaces. Place the upper gasket on the cover and the lower gasket on the block. Install the cover and tighten to 7-11 ft. lbs. (10-15 Nm). Trim the gaskets flush with the valve cover.

8. Install a new crankshaft seal.

9. Block the flywheel, install the pulley, key and tighten the 36mm nut to 118-132 ft. lbs. (160-180 Nm).

10. Install the power steering pump, pump bracket, alternator, air pump, power steering pump and air conditioning compressor.

11. Install the fan and shroud. Install the accessory drive belts. Connect the negative battery cable. Start the engine and check for leaks.

Front Cover Oil Seal

REMOVAL & INSTALLATION

B280F Engine

1. Disconnect the negative battery cable. Remove the air cleaner and valve covers.

2. Loosen the fan shroud and remove the fan. Remove the shroud.

3. Loosen the alternator, air pump, power steering pump, air conditioning compressor, if equipped, and remove their drive belts.

4. Block the flywheel from turning, remove the crankshaft pulley nut (36mm) and the pulley.

➡**Do not drop the pulley key into the crankcase.**

5. Remove the seal, using a suitable puller (Tool 9 995 069-3 or equivalent).

➡**Be careful not to damage the timing chain cover contact surface.**

To install:

6. Fill the space between the seal lips with grease and install the new seal, using tool 5103 or equivalent.

7. Block the flywheel, install the pulley, key and tighten the 36mm nut to 118-132 ft. lbs. (160-180 Nm).

8. Install the power steering pump, pump bracket, alternator, air pump, power steering pump and air conditioning compressor.

9. Install the fan and shroud. Install the accessory drive belts. Connect the negative battery cable. Start the engine and check for leaks.

Timing Belt and Tensioner

REMOVAL & INSTALLATION

B230F Engine
▶ **See Figure 51**

1. Remove the timing belt cover.

2. To remove the tension from the belt, loosen the nut for the tensioner and press the idler roller back. The tension spring can be locked in this position by inserting the shank end of a 3mm drill through the pusher rod.

3. Remove the 6 retaining bolts and the crankshaft pulley.

4. Remove the belt, taking care not to bend it at any sharp angles. The belt should be replaced at 45,000 mile intervals, if it becomes oil soaked or frayed or if it is on a vehicle that has been sitting idle for any length of time.

To install:

5. If the crankshaft, idler shaft or camshaft were disturbed while the belt was out, align each shaft with is corresponding index mark to assure proper valve timing and ignition timing, as follows:

a. Rotate the crankshaft so the notch in the convex crankshaft gear belt guide aligns with the embossed mark on the front cover (12 o'clock position).

b. Rotate the idler shaft so the dot on the idler shaft drive sprocket aligns with the notch on the timing belt rear cover (4 o'clock position).

c. Rotate the camshaft so the notch in the camshaft sprocket inner belt guide aligns with the notch in the forward edge of the valve cover (12 o'clock position).

6. Install the timing belt (don't use any sharp tools) over the sprockets and then over the tensioner roller. New belts have yellow marks. The 2 lines on the drive belt should fit toward the crankshaft marks. The next mark should then fit toward the intermediate shaft marks, etc. Loosen the tensioner nut and let the spring tension automatically take up the slack. Tighten the tensioner nut to 37 ft. lbs. (51 Nm).

7. Rotate the crankshaft 1 full revolution clockwise and make sure the timing marks still align.

8. Install the drive belts, radiator fan and shroud. Connect the negative battery cable.

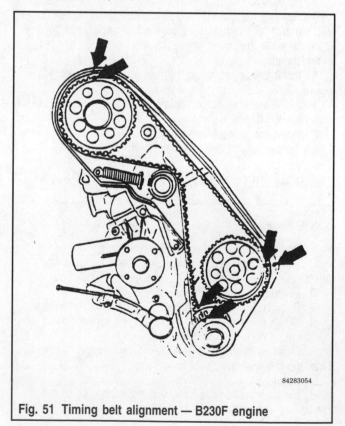

84283054

Fig. 51 Timing belt alignment — B230F engine

B234F Engine

▶ See Figures 52, 53, 54, 55, 56 and 57

➡ The B234F engine has 2 belts, one driving the camshafts and one driving the balance shafts. The camshaft belt may be removed separately; the balance shaft belt requires removal of the cam belt. During reassembly, the exact placement of the belts and pulleys must be observed.

1. Remove the negative battery cable and the alternator belt.

2. Remove the radiator fan, its pulley and the fan shroud.

3. Remove the drive belts for the power steering belts and the air conditioning compressor.

4. Beginning with the top cover, remove the retaining bolts and remove the timing belt covers.

5. Turn the engine to TDC, of the compression stroke, on cylinder No. 1. Make sure the marks on the cam pulleys align with the marks on the backing plate and that the marking on the belt guide plate (on the crankshaft) is opposite the TDC mark on the engine block.

6. Remove the protective cap over the timing belt tensioner locknut. Loosen the locknut, compress the tensioner, to release tension on the belts, and re-tighten the locknut, holding the tensioner in place.

7. Remove the timing belt from the camshafts. Do not crease or fold the belt.

➡ The camshafts and the crankshaft must not be moved when the belt is removed.

8. Check the tensioner by spinning it counterclockwise and listening for any bearing noise within. Check also that the belt contact surface is clean and smooth. In the same fashion, check the timing belt idler pulleys. Make sure the are tightened to 18.5 ft. lbs. (25 Nm).

9. If the balance shaft belt is to be removed:

   a. Remove the balance shaft belt idler pulley from the engine.

   b. Loosen the locknut on the tensioner and remove the belt. Slide the belt under the crankshaft pulley assembly. Check the tensioner and idler wheels carefully for any sign of contamination; check the ends of the shafts for any sign of oil leakage.

   c. Check the position of the balance shafts and the crankshaft after belt removal. The balance shaft markings on the pulleys should align with the markings on the backing plate and the crankshaft marking should still be aligned with the TDC mark on the engine block.

   d. When refitting the balance shaft belt, observe that the belt has colored dots on it. These marks assist in the critical placement of the belt. The yellow dot will align the right lower shaft, the blue dot will align on the crank and the other yellow dot will match to the upper left balance shaft.

   e. Carefully work the belt in under the crankshaft pulley. Make sure the blue dot is opposite the bottom (TDC) marking on the belt guide plate at the bottom of the crankshaft. Fit the belt around the left upper balance shaft pulley, making sure the yellow mark is opposite the mark on the pulley. Install the belt around the right lower balance shaft pulley and again check that the mark on the belt aligns with the mark on the pulley.

   f. Work the belt around the tensioner. Double check that all the markings are still aligned.

   g. Set the belt tension by inserting an Allen key into the adjusting hole in the tensioner. Turn the crankshaft carefully through a few degrees on either side of TDC to check that the belt has properly engaged the pulleys. Return the crank to the TDC position and set the adjusting hole just below the 3 o'clock position when tightening the adjusting bolt. Use the Allen wrench, in the adjusting hole, as a counter hold and tighten the locking bolt to 29.5 ft. lbs. (40 Nm).

   h. Use tool 998 8500 to check the tension of the belt. Install the gauge over the position of the removed idler pulley. The tension must be 1-4 units on the scale or the belt must be readjusted.

To install:

10. Reinstall the camshaft belt by aligning the double line marking on the belt with the top marking on the belt guide plate at the top of the crankshaft. Stretch the belt around the crank pulley and place it over the tensioner and the right side idler. Place the belt on the camshaft pulleys. The single line marks on the belt should align exactly with the pulley markings. Route the belt around the oil pump drive pulley and press the belt onto the left side idler.

11. Check that all the markings align and that the engine is still positioned at TDC, of the compression stroke, for cylinder No. 1.

12. Loosen the tensioner locknut.

13. Turn the crankshaft clockwise. The cam pulleys should rotate 1 full turn until the marks again align with the marks on the backing plate.

➡ The engine must not be rotated counterclockwise during this procedure.

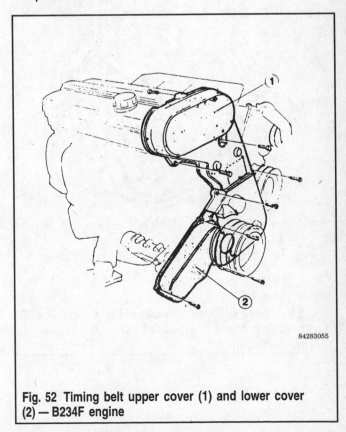

84283055

Fig. 52 Timing belt upper cover (1) and lower cover (2) — B234F engine

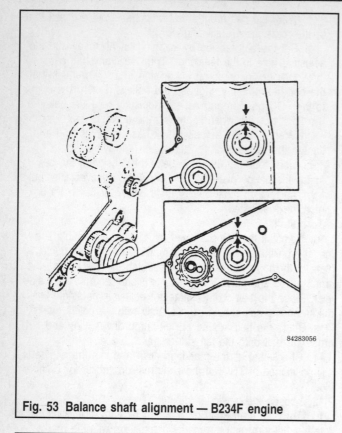

Fig. 53 Balance shaft alignment — B234F engine

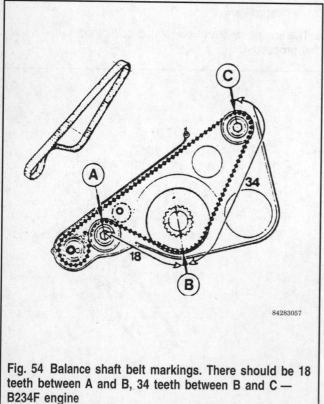

Fig. 54 Balance shaft belt markings. There should be 18 teeth between A and B, 34 teeth between B and C — B234F engine

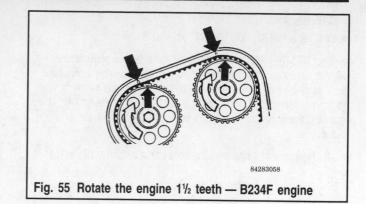

Fig. 55 Rotate the engine 1½ teeth — B234F engine

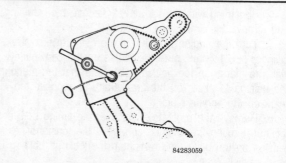

Fig. 56 Timing belt tensioner adjustment — B234F engine

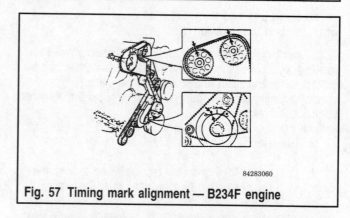

Fig. 57 Timing mark alignment — B234F engine

14. Smoothly rotate the crankshaft further clockwise until the cam pulley markings are 1½ teeth beyond the marks on the backing plate. Tighten the tensioner locknut.

15. Check the tension on the balance shaft belt; it should now be 3.8 units. If the tension is too low, adjust the tensioner clockwise. If the tension is too high, repeat Step 8g.

16. Check the belt guide for the balance shaft belt and make sure it is properly seated. Install the center timing belt cover, the one that covers the tensioner, the fan shroud, fan pulley and fan. Install all the drive belts and connect the battery cable.

17. Double check all installation items, paying particular attention to loose hoses or hanging wires, untightened nuts, poor routing of hoses and wires (too tight or rubbing) and tools left in the engine area.

18. Start the engine and allow it to run until the thermostat opens.

✳✳CAUTION

The upper and lower timing belt covers are still removed. The belt and pulleys are exposed and moving at high speed.

19. Turn the engine OFF and bring the engine to TDC, of the compression stroke, on cylinder No. 1.

20. Check the tension of the camshaft belt. Position the gauge between the right (exhaust) cam pulley and the idler. Belt tension must be 5.5 ± 0.2 units. If the belt needs adjustment, remove the rubber cap over the tensioner locknut, cap is located on the timing belt cover, and loosen the locknut.

21. Insert a suitable tool between the tensioner wheel and the spring carrier pin to hold the tensioner. If the belt needs to be tightened, move the roller to adjust the tension to 6.0 units. If the belt is too tight, adjust to obtain a reading of 5.0 units on the gauge. Tighten the tensioner locknut.

22. Rotate the crankshaft so the cam pulleys move through 1 full revolution and recheck the tension on the camshaft belt. It should now be 5.5 ± 0.2 units. Install the plastic plug over the tensioner bolt.

23. Final check the tension on the balance shaft belt by fitting the gauge and turning the tensioner clockwise. Only small movements are needed. After any needed readjustments, rotate the crankshaft clockwise through 1 full revolution and recheck the balance shaft belt. The tension should now be on the final specification of 4.9 ± 0.2 units.

24. Install the idler pulley for the balance shaft belt. Reinstall the upper and lower timing belt covers.

25. Start the engine and final check performance.

B6304F Engine

▶ **See Figure 58**

1. Disconnect the negative battery cable.
2. Remove the auxiliaries drive belts.
3. Remove the front timing belt cover.
4. Remove the splashguard, vibration damper guard and ignition coil cover.
5. Rotate the crankshaft clockwise, until the timing marks on the camshaft pulleys and timing belt mounting plate and crankshaft pulley/oil pump housing are aligned. Remove the upper timing belt cover.

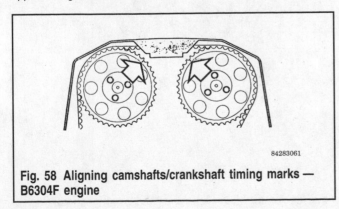

84283061

Fig. 58 Aligning camshafts/crankshaft timing marks — B6304F engine

6. Check the belt tensioner, as outlined in this section. Replace the tensioner, if required.
7. Remove the tensioner upper mounting bolts. Loosen the tensioner lower mounting bolt and twist the tensioner to free the plunger. Remove the lower mounting bolt and remove the tensioner.
8. Remove the timing belt.

➡**Do not rotate the crankshaft while the timing belt is removed.**

9. Check the tensioner and idler pulleys, as follows:
   a. Spin the pulleys and listen for bearing noise.
   b. Check that the pulley surfaces in contact with the belt are clean and smooth.
   c. Check the tensioner pulley arm and idler pulley mountings.
   d. Torque the tensioner pulley arm 30 ft. lbs. (40 Nm) and the idler pulley 18 ft. lbs. (25 Nm).

To install:

10. Place the belt around the crankshaft pulley and right-side idler. Place the belt over the camshaft pulleys. Position the belt around the water pump and press over tensioner pulley.
11. Insert the tensioner mounting bolts. Torque to 18 ft. lbs. (25 Nm).
12. Remove the locking pin. Install the front timing belt cover.
13. Turn the crankshaft through 2 revolutions and check that the timing marks on the crankshaft and camshaft pulleys are correctly aligned.
14. Install the ignition coil, front timing belt cover, auxiliaries drive belts, vibration damper guard and splashguard.
15. Connect the negative battery lead, start and check the engine operation.

➡**GREASING OF TIMING BELT** — the lever bushing, on the B234F and B6304F engines, must be greased everytime the belt is replace or the tensioner pulley removed. This is necessary to help prevent seizure of the bushing, with the possible risk of incorrect belt tension. Service the bushing, using the following procedure:

   a. Remove the lever mounting bolt, tensioner pulley and sleeve behind the bolt.
   b. Grease the surfaces of the bushing, bolt and sleeve, using Part No. 1161246-2 or equivalent.
   c. Install the sleeve, tensioner pulley and lever mounting bolt.
   d. Tighten the bolt 30 ft. lbs. (40 Nm).

ADJUSTMENT

B234F Engine

▶ **See Figure 59**

1. Place a tension gauge (9988500 or equivalent) between the exhaust camshaft drive pulley and tensioner.
2. Read the gauge. If the belt tension is correct, the gauge should read between 3.2-4.2 units.
3. If the reading is incorrect, remove the protective rubber cap in the timing belt cover. Slacken the locknut.

4. Turn the crankshaft clockwise through 1 revolution. Camshaft pulley markings should again coincide with the markings on the timing belt mounting plate.

➡**Do not turn the engine counter-clockwise during belt tensioning procedure.**

5. Turn the engine further clockwise until the camshaft pulley markings are 1½ teeth past the markings on the timing belt mounting plate. Tighten the tensioner locknut.

6. Turn the crankshaft clockwise to complete 1 revolution (TDC).

7. Check that all markings coincide.

8. Recheck the belt tension.

9. If the reading is still not correct, proceed as follows:

   a. Slacken the tensioner locknut.

   b. Install the measuring gauge. Insert a screwdriver between the tensioner pulley and the end of the spring carrier pin.

   c. Re-adjust the belt to obtain the specified tension. Tighten the tensioner locknut 37 ft. lbs. (50 Nm).

10. Install the protective rubber cap over the tensioner locknut. Install the upper timing belt cover.

B6304F Engine

1. Place a tension gauge (9988500 or equivalent) between the exhaust camshaft drive pulley and water pump.

2. Read the gauge. If the belt tension is correct, the gauge should read between 3.5-4.6 units.

3. If the reading is incorrect, replace the tensioner.

Timing Chain and Sprockets

REMOVAL & INSTALLATION

B280F Engine

▶ **See Figures 60, 61, 62, 63 and 64**

1. Remove the timing chain cover.

2. Remove the oil pump sprocket and drive chain.

3. Slacken the tension in both camshaft timing chains by rotating each tensioner lock ¼ turn counterclockwise and pushing the rubbing block piston.

4. Remove both chain tensioners. Remove the 2 curved and the 2 straight chain damper/runners.

5. Remove the camshaft sprocket retaining bolt, 10mm Allen head, and the sprocket and chain assembly. Repeat for the other side.

To install:

6. Install the chain tensioners and tighten to 5 ft. lbs. (7 Nm). Install the curved chain damper/runners and tighten to 7-11 ft. lbs. (10-15 Nm). Install the straight chain damper/runners and torque to 5 ft. lbs. (7 Nm).

7. First install the left (driver) side camshaft sprocket and chain:

   a. Rotate the crankshaft, using crankshaft nut, if necessary, until the crankshaft key is pointing directly to the left side camshaft and the left side camshaft key groove is pointing straight-up (12 o'clock).

   b. Place the chain on the left side sprocket so the sprocket notchmark is centered precisely between the 2 white lines on the chain.

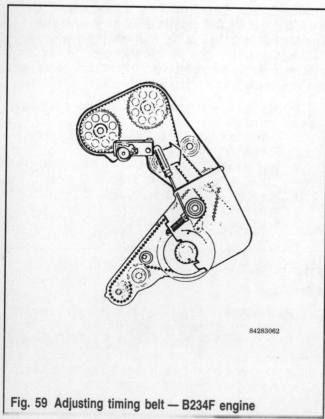

84283062

Fig. 59 Adjusting timing belt — B234F engine

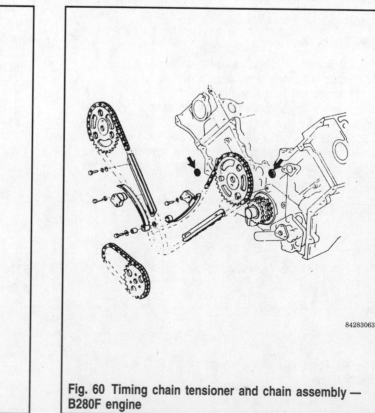

84283063

Fig. 60 Timing chain tensioner and chain assembly — B280F engine

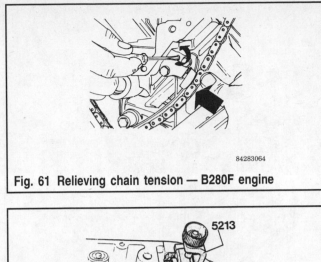

Fig. 61 Relieving chain tension — B280F engine

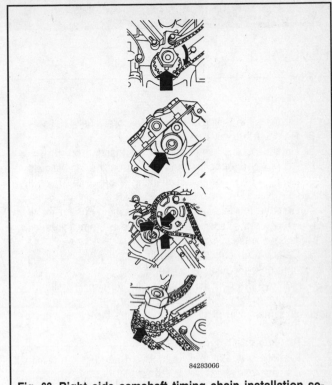

Fig. 63 Right side camshaft timing chain installation sequence — B280F engine

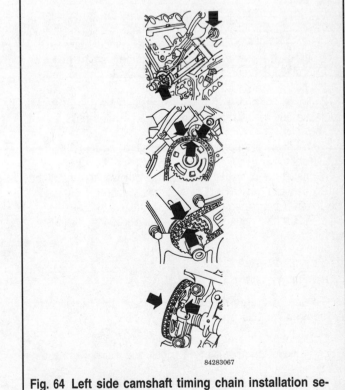

Fig. 62 Timing chain gear holding tool 5213 — B280F engine

c. Position the chain on the crankshaft sprocket (inner), making sure the other white line on the chain aligns with the crankshaft sprocket notch.

d. While holding the left side chain and sprockets in this position, install the sprocket and chain on the left side camshaft, chain stretched on tension side, so the sprocket pin fits into the camshaft recess.

e. Tighten the sprocket center bolt to 51-59 ft. lbs. (69-80 Nm); use a suitable tool to keep cam from turning.

8. To install the right side camshaft sprocket and chain:

a. Rotate the crankshaft clockwise until the crankshaft key points straight down (6 o'clock).

b. Align the camshaft key groove so it is pointing halfway between the 8 and 9 o'clock positions; at this position, the No. 6 cylinder rocker arms will rock.

c. Place the chain on the right side sprocket so the sprocket notchmark is centered precisely between the 2 white lines on the chain.

d. Then, position the chain on the middle crankshaft sprocket, making sure the other white line aligns with the crankshaft sprocket notch.

e. Install the sprocket and chain on the camshaft so the sprocket notch fits into the camshaft recess.

f. Tighten the sprocket nut to 51-59 ft. lbs. (69-80 Nm).

9. Rotate the chain tensioners ¼ turn clockwise each. The chains are tensioned by rotating the crankshaft 2 full turns clockwise. Recheck to make sure the alignment marks coincide.

10. Install the oil pump sprocket and chain.

11. Install the timing chain cover.

Fig. 64 Left side camshaft timing chain installation sequence — B280F engine

Camshaft

REMOVAL & INSTALLATION

B230F Engine

1. Remove the timing belt cover, as previously outlined.
2. Remove the valve cover.
3. Rotate the crankshaft so that the marking on the camshaft pulley is opposite the marking on the inner timing gear cover and the crankshaft marking is opposite '0" on the cover.
4. Remove the tensioner nut and washer. Pull on the timing belt to depress the tensioner spring. Use a 3mm drill to lock the tensioner spring.
5. Remove the camshaft gear and spacer washer, using the counterhold (5034 or equivalent).
6. Remove the camshaft center bearing cap. Install camshaft press tool 5021 over the center bearing journal to hold the camshaft in place while removing the other bearing caps.
7. Remove the 4 remaining bearing caps.
8. Remove the seal from the forward edge of the camshaft.
9. Release camshaft press tool and lift out the camshaft.

➡**Do not rotate the crankshaft while the camshaft is removed from the cylinder head.**

To install:

10. Apply sealant to the sealing surfaces toward cylinder head of front and rear caps. Lubricate and install camshaft into position. The guide pin for the timing gear should face up.
11. Install the rear bearing cap. Slide the camshaft back and forth to check the camshaft end-play. Endplay should be 0.004-0.016 in. (0.1-0.4mm).
12. Install the camshaft press tool. Install the camshaft seal. Lubricate and install the remaining caps. Tighten bolts to 14 ft. lbs. (20 Nm).
13. Lubricate the front seal and install, using tool 5025 or equivalent.
14. Install the camshaft gear and spacer washer. Install the timing belt and tensioner. Complete installation by reversing the removal procedure.
15. Adjust the valve clearance to specifications. Install the valve cover.

B234F Engine

▶ See Figure 65

➡**The use of the correct special tools or their equivalent is required for this procedure.**

1. Disconnect the negative battery cable.
2. Remove the alternator drive belt, the radiator fan and its pulley.
3. Remove the upper and lower timing belt covers.
4. Align the camshaft and crankshaft marks. Turn the engine to TDC, of the compression stroke, on cylinder No. 1 and make sure the pulley marks and the crank marks align with their matching marks on either the backing plate (cam pulleys) or the belt guide plate (crankshaft).

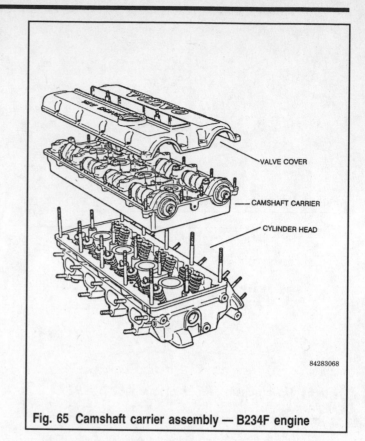

VALVE COVER

CAMSHAFT CARRIER

CYLINDER HEAD

84283068

Fig. 65 Camshaft carrier assembly — B234F engine

5. Remove the protective cap over the timing belt tensioner locknut. Loosen the locknut, compress the tensioner, to release tension on the belts, and re-tighten the locknut, holding the tensioner in place.
6. Remove the timing belt from the camshafts; do not crease or fold the belt.

➡**The camshafts and the crankshaft must not be moved when the belt is removed.**

7. Remove the timing belt idler pulleys.
8. Remove the camshaft drive pulleys. Use a counterhold wrench to prevent the cam from turning.
9. Remove the plate or panel behind the pulleys. Remove the cover plate for the ignition wires. Label and disconnect the ignition wiring from the spark plugs and the distributor cap; remove the coil wire from the distributor cap.
10. Remove the valve cover and gasket. Clean the surfaces of any gasket remains.
11. Remove the distributor housing from the camshaft carrier. Remove the ignition wire clip next to the left bolt.
12. Plug the spark plug holes with crumpled paper. Remove the center bearing cap for each camshaft. Mark the cam bearing caps for proper reinstallation.
13. Install a camshaft press tool 5021 or similar, on the exhaust side cam in place of the removed bearing cap. When it is securely in place, remove the remaining bearing caps and nuts. Remove the tool and remove the exhaust camshaft.
14. Remove the intake camshaft in identical fashion.

➡**Label or identify each cam and its bearing caps. All removed components should be kept in order.**

15. Using a magnet or a small suction cup, remove the tappets. Store them upside down, to prevent oil drainage, and keep them in order; they are not interchangeable.

To install:

16. Clean and inspect the camshaft carrier and tappet bores for any sign of wear or scoring.

17. Oil all matching surfaces on the cam carrier, bearing caps and tappets.

18. Insert the tappets; they must be inserted in their original order and place.

19. Install the exhaust side camshaft by placing it in the carrier with the pulley guide pin facing up. Using the rear bearing cap as a guide, press the cam into place with the press tool. Install the bearing caps in the original order.

20. Install the bearing cap nuts and tighten them in stages to 15 ft. lbs. (20 Nm). Remove the press tool and install the center bearing cap; tighten it in stages to 15 ft. lbs. (20 Nm).

21. Install the intake camshaft in the carrier with the pulley guide pin facing upwards.

22. Turn the distributor shaft to align the driver with the markings on the distributor housing. Install new O-rings on the housing and rotor shaft.

23. Using the rear bearing cap as a guide, press the cam into place with the press tool. Install the bearing caps in the original order.

24. Install the bearing cap nuts and tighten them in stages to 15 ft. lbs. (20 Nm).

25. Double check the tightness of all the camshaft bearing cap nuts. All should be 15 ft. lbs.; do not overtighten.

26. Reinstall the distributor, connect the coil wire and install the ignition wire clip at the left bolt. Remove the paper plugs from the spark plug holes.

27. Use a silicone sealer and apply to the front and rear camshaft bearing caps. Install new gaskets for the valve cover and the spark plug wells. Install the spark plug gasket with the arrow pointing towards the front of the vehicle and the word 'UP' facing up. Make sure the valve cover gasket is correctly positioned and install the valve cover.

28. Reconnect the ground wire at the distributor.

29. Install the ignition wires and the cover plate.

30. Using a compression seal driver tool 5025 or similar, install the oil seals for the front of each camshaft. Camshafts must not be allowed to turn during this operation.

31. Install the upper backing plate over the ends of the camshafts and adjust the plate so the cams are centered in the holes.

32. Replace the idler pulleys and tighten their mounts to 18.5 ft. lbs. (25 Nm).

33. Install the camshaft drive pulleys, using a counterhold to prevent the cams from turning.

34. Reinstall the camshaft belt by aligning the double line marking on the belt with the top marking on the belt guide plate at the top of the crankshaft. Stretch the belt around the crank pulley and place it over the tensioner and the right side idler. Place the belt on the camshaft pulleys. The single line marks on the belt should align exactly with the pulley markings. Route the belt around the oil pump drive pulley and press the belt onto the left side idler.

35. Check that all the markings align and that the engine is still positioned at TDC, of the compression stroke, for cylinder No. 1.

36. Loosen the tensioner locknut.

37. Turn the crankshaft clockwise. The cam pulleys should rotate 1 full turn until the marks again align with the marks on the backing plate.

➡️**The engine must not be rotated counterclockwise during this procedure.**

38. Smoothly rotate the crankshaft further clockwise until the cam pulley markings are 1½ teeth beyond the marks on the backing plate. Tighten the tensioner locknut.

39. Reinstall the fan pulley and fan. Install all the drive belts and connect the battery cable.

40. Double check all installation items, paying particular attention to loose hoses or hanging wires, untightened nuts, poor routing of hoses and wires (too tight or rubbing) and tools left in the engine area.

41. Start the engine and allow it to run until the thermostat opens.

✳✳CAUTION

The upper and lower timing belt covers are still removed. The belt and pulleys are exposed and moving at high speed.

➡️**This engine may be somewhat noisy when started. The noise will subside as oil reaches the tappets. Do not exceed 2500 rpm while the tappets are noisy.**

42. Shut the motor off and bring the motor to TDC, of the compression stroke, on cylinder No. 1.

43. Check the tension of the camshaft belt. Position the gauge between the right (exhaust) cam pulley and the idler. Belt tension must be 5.5 ± 0.2 units. If the belt needs adjustment, remove the rubber cap over the tensioner locknut and loosen the locknut.

44. Insert a suitable tool between the tensioner wheel and the spring carrier pin to hold the tensioner. If the belt needs to be tightened, move the roller to adjust the tension to 6.0 units. If the belt is too tight, adjust to obtain a reading of 5.0 units on the gauge. Tighten the tensioner locknut and remove the suitable tool.

45. Rotate the crankshaft so the cam pulleys move through 1 full revolution and recheck the tension on the camshaft belt. It should now be 5.5 ± 0.2 units. Install the plastic plug over the tensioner bolt.

46. Reinstall the remaining belt covers. Start the engine and final check performance.

B280F Engine

1. Remove the cylinder head.

2. Remove the camshaft rear cover plate.

3. Remove the camshaft retaining fork at the front of the cylinder head.

4. Pull the camshaft out the rear of the head.

To install:

5. Oil the camshaft and followers and install. Tighten the camshaft retaining bolt to 7-11 ft. lbs.

6. Install the camshaft retaining fork, install the rear cover plate and install the cylinder head.

B6304F Engine

◗ **See Figure 66**

1. Disconnect the negative battery cable.
2. Remove the accessories drive belt.
3. Remove the timing belt cover.
4. Remove the ignition coils cover.
5. Turn the crankshaft until the timing marks on the camshaft pulleys/transmission mounting plate and crankshaft pulley/oil pump housing are aligned.
6. Remove the tensioner and timing belt.

➡**Do not turn the crankshaft while the belt is removed.**

7. Remove the camshaft position sensor and shutter at right rear of camshaft assembly. Remove the switch holder and shield at left rear of assembly.
8. Remove the ignition coils. Mark their locations.
9. Remove the camshaft pulleys, using the counterhold (5199 or equivalent). Mark the pulleys; intake and exhaust side.
10. Remove the top half of the cylinder head. Tap the joint lugs ad camshaft front ends lightly.
11. Remove the camshafts.

To install:

12. Lubricate the camshafts and bearing seats. Place the camshafts into position. Install the holder (5453 or equivalent) to the front end and locking tool (5452 or equivalent) to the rear end of the cylinder head upper section.
13. Install the upper cylinder head section and tighten against the lower section, using 2 press tools (5454 or equivalent).
14. Install and tighten the retaining bolts 13 ft. lbs. (17 Nm), starting from the inside and working outwards. Remove the tools.
15. Lubricate the camshaft front seals and tap into place.
16. Install the camshaft pulleys. Tighten the bolts alternately to 15 ft. lbs. (20 Nm).
17. Install the timing belt, by placing around the crankshaft and right side idler. Place the belt over the camshaft pulleys, around the water pump and over the tensioner pulley.
18. Install the tensioner and tighten the bolts to 18 ft. lbs. (25 Nm). Check that the timing marks on the crankshaft and camshaft pulleys are correctly aligned.
19. Complete installation by reversing the removal procedure.

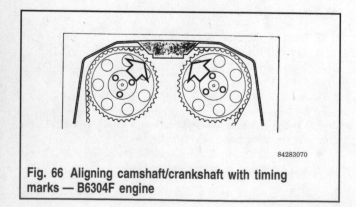

84283070

Fig. 66 Aligning camshaft/crankshaft with timing marks — B6304F engine

Balance Shafts

REMOVAL & INSTALLATION

B234 Engine

◗ **See Figures 67 and 68**

➡**The use of the correct special tools or their equivalent is required for this procedure.**

LEFT SHAFT AND HOUSING

1. Remove the timing and balance shaft belts.
2. Use a counterhold tool 5362 and remove the left side balance shaft pulley.
3. Remove the air mass meter and inlet hose.
4. Unfasten the bracket under the intake manifold and remove the bracket holding the alternator and power steering pump. These may be swung aside and tied with wire to the left shock tower.
5. Remove the bolts securing the balance shaft housing to the block. Using an extractor tool 5376 or similar, carefully separate the housing from the block. The housing must be removed evenly from both its front and rear mounts.

To install:

6. Clean the joint faces on the cylinder block. Place new O-rings in the grooves around the oil passages on the housing. The rings can be held in place with a light coating of grease.
7. Install the balance shaft housing. Make absolutely sure the housing is evenly mounted on the front and rear mountings. Tighten the bolts alternately in a diagonal pattern. Tighten each bolt ½ turn at a time; tighten them to 15 ft. lbs. (20 Nm). When all the bolts are at 15 ft. lbs. (20 Nm), loosen them individually and tighten each one to 7.5 ft. lbs. (10 Nm) plug 90 degrees of rotation.

➡**Make certain the shaft does not seize within the housing during installation.**

8. If the halves of the housing were split apart during the repair, tighten the joint bolts to 6 ft. lbs. (8 Nm).
9. Install the drive pulley. Use a counterholding tool. Note that the pulley has a slot which will align with the guide on the shaft. The shallow side of the pulley faces inward, toward the engine. Tighten the center bolt for the pulley to 37 ft. lbs. (50 Nm).
10. Install the bracket for the alternator and power steering pump. Double check their connections and hoses. Attach the support under the intake manifold and don't forget the wire clamp on the bottom bolt.
11. Install the air mass meter and its intake hose.
12. Install the balance shaft belt and camshaft belt.

RIGHT SHAFT AND HOUSING

1. Remove the timing and balance shaft belts.
2. Use a counterhold tool 5362 and remove the left side balance shaft pulley.
3. Remove the balance shaft belt tensioner and remove the bolt running through the backing plate to the balance shaft housing.

4. Remove the air mass meter and its air inlet hose.

5. Remove the air preheat hose from the bottom heat shield at the exhaust manifold. Remove the nuts holding the right engine mount to the crossmember.

6. Connect a hoist or engine lift apparatus to the top of the engine. Lift the engine at the right side, being careful to maintain clearance between the brake master cylinder and the intake manifold.

7. Remove the complete motor mount from the block, including the pad and lower mounting plate.

8. Remove the bolts securing the balance shaft housing to the block. Using a extractor tool 5376 or similar, carefully separate the housing from the block. The housing must be removed evenly from both its front and rear mounts.

To install:

9. Clean the joint faces on the cylinder block. Place new O-rings in the grooves around the oil passages on the housing. The rings can be held in place with a light coating of grease.

10. Install the balance shaft housing. Make absolutely sure the housing is evenly mounted on the front and rear mountings. Tighten the bolts alternately in a diagonal pattern. Tighten each bolt ½ turn at a time; tighten them to 15 ft. lbs. (20 Nm). When all the bolts are at 15 ft. lbs. (20 Nm), loosen them individually and tighten each one to 7.5 ft. lbs. (10 Nm) plus 90 degrees of rotation.

➡**Make certain the shaft does not seize within the housing during installation.**

11. If the halves of the housing were split apart during the repair, tighten the joint bolts to 6 ft. lbs. (8 Nm).

12. Install the drive pulley. Use a counterholding tool. Note that the pulley has a slot which will align with the guide on the shaft. The shallow side of the pulley faces inward, toward the engine. Tighten the center bolt for the pulley to 37 ft. lbs. (50 Nm).

13. Install the engine mount onto the block.

14. Using the studs on the crossmember as a guide, lower the engine into place on the front crossmember. When the engine is correctly seated, the lifting apparatus may be removed.

15. Reinstall the air mass meter and its air intake hose.

16. Reinstall the motor mount bolts and the air preheat tube at the lower part of the exhaust manifold.

17. Install the bolt through the backing plate and into the balance shaft housing. Reinstall the belt tensioner, tightening the bolt so the pulley is movable when the belt is in position.

18. Reinstall the balance shaft and camshaft belts.

Pistons and Connecting Rods

REMOVAL & INSTALLATION

1. Remove the engine from the vehicle, as previously outlined.

2. Secure the engine assembly in a holding fixture.

3. Disassembly the engine, by removing all components previously outlined.

4. Remove the flywheel or flexplate, as required.

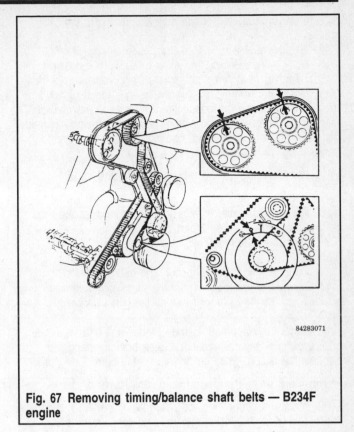

Fig. 67 Removing timing/balance shaft belts — B234F engine

84283071

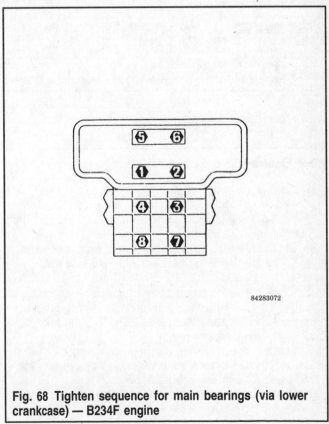

Fig. 68 Tighten sequence for main bearings (via lower crankcase) — B234F engine

84283072

5. Remove the support bracket, oil pan, rear seal flange, oil pump and delivery pipe, as required.

6. Install 2 flywheel bolts to facilitate turning of the crankshaft.

7. Remove any wear ridges from each cylinder.

8. Mark the connecting rod caps to facilitate installation.

9. Remove the connecting rod caps and carefully tap the piston assembly from each cylinder, using a brass or wooden mallet. Do not allow the connecting rod ends to rub against the cylinder walls when the piston assembly is being removed. Assemble the connecting rod, bearing and cap to prevent interchanging parts.

➡**Do not interchange the bearing shells and caps.**

To install:

10. Assemble the piston rings to the piston. Turn the rings so that the gaps are 120° apart.

11. Install the bearing shells in the connecting rods and caps.

12. Oil the cylinder bores, piston and bearing shells.

13. Turn the crankshaft so that the crank points straight downwards, for the cylinder to which the piston is being installed.

14. Generously apply oil to the cylinder wall and install the piston, using a ring compressor. Use a hammer handle to depress the piston, while guiding it into the correct position.

➡**The mark on the piston should face forward.**

15. Install the connecting rod cap, making certain the identification marks on the connecting rod and cap are the same. Torque to specifications.

➡**After installing each cap, check that the crankshaft can be turned.**

16. Install the remaining pistons.

17. Complete installation by installing all components previously removed.

CLEANING & INSPECTION

▶ **See Figures 69, 70, 71 and 72**

1. Remove the piston rings, using a piston ring pliers.

2. Remove all traces of carbon from the piston assembly. Scrape out the ring grooves, using a broken and ground piston ring or cleaner.

3. Check the piston for damage, sign of wear and cracks.

4. Check the ring to groove clearance, use new piston rings.

5. Check the piston ring gap: Insert the piston ring in the bore. Use an inverted piston to ensure that the ring takes up correct position. Measure the gap at 0.6 in. (15mm) from the lower edge, using a feeler gauge.

6. Check gudgeon (piston) pin fit in connecting rod. It should be possible to slide the pin through the bore with light thumb pressure, with any noticeable play.

7. Check gudgeon (piston) pin fit in piston. Pin should not be loose. It should be possible to press the pin through the hole with light thumb pressure. Oversized pins can be used if bore is worn.

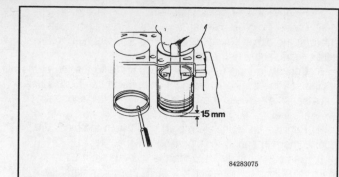
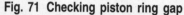

84283075

Fig. 71 Checking piston ring gap

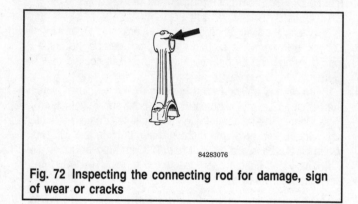

84283076

Fig. 72 Inspecting the connecting rod for damage, sign of wear or cracks

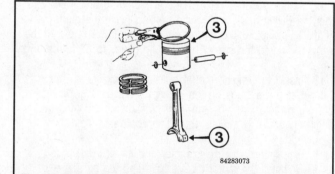

84283073

Fig. 69 Remove piston rings, using a piston ring pliers

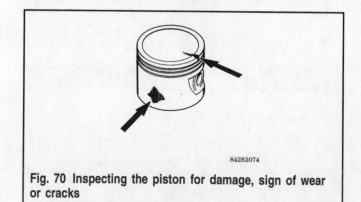

84283074

Fig. 70 Inspecting the piston for damage, sign of wear or cracks

8. Cylinder bores:

a. Measure the cylinder bores. Use an inside dial gauge (9639 or equivalent), micrometer (9704 or equivalent) and a micrometer stand.

b. Check for maximum wear at right-angles to the center line of the engine, immediately below Top Dead Center (TDC).

c. Check for minimum wear in direction of the center line at Bottom Dead Center (BDC).

9. In the event of excessive piston-to-bore clearance, the block must be hone bore to the next larger size.

Cylinder Liners and Seals

REMOVAL & INSTALLATION

B280F Engine

▶ See Figures 73 and 74

The B280F engine is equipped with wet cylinder liners, which are inserted into the block and are sealed off from the coolant jacket by the head gasket and a bottom shim. The tightness of the heads on the block seals the liners. After the pistons have been removed, the liners may be removed from the block. Check the mating surfaces and make sure they are clean and free of defects.

When installing liners, it is very important to obtain the correct liner height above the block. The correct height is 0.0063-0.0091 inch (0.16-0.23mm) with 0.0091 inch (0.23mm) preferred. This height is adjustable by using shims at the bottom of the liner.

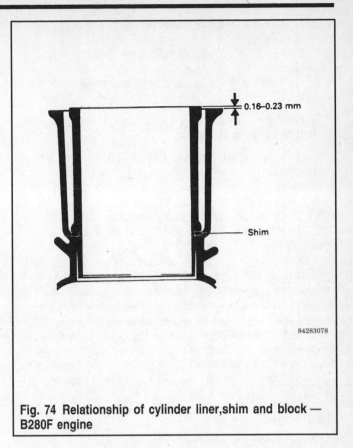

Fig. 74 Relationship of cylinder liner, shim and block — B280F engine

Install the new liner in cylinder number one and use the retainer bar finger tight to hold it in place. Measure the liner height at three different locations. Use the highest reading as a basis for calculating the proper shim height. Select a shim which is at or just under the calculated necessary thickness. Install the same size shim on all liners and install the liners in the motor. The color marking should face upward and be visible when the liner is installed. The tongues on the inside of the shim should fit into the groove in the liner. (In the diagram **A** is the color marking, **B** shows the tongues and **C** indicates the liner groove). Again measure the liner projection above the deck for EACH liner and exchange shims as necessary.

Rear Main Seal

REMOVAL & INSTALLATION

B230F and B234F Engines

1. Disconnect the negative battery terminal.
2. Remove the transmission.
3. Remove the clutch and pressure plate, if equipped.
4. Remove the pilot bearing snapring and remove the bearing.
5. Remove the flywheel or driveplate which ever is applicable.

➡Be careful not to press in the activator pins for the timing device.

6. Remove the rear oil pan brace.

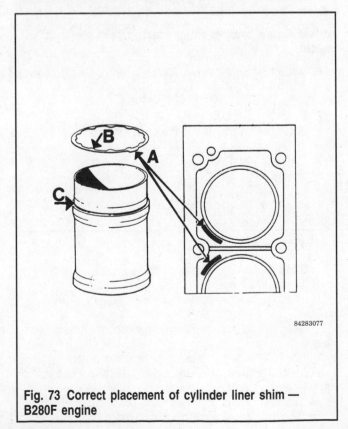

Fig. 73 Correct placement of cylinder liner shim — B280F engine

7. Remove the 2 center bolts from the pan that bolt into the seal housing.

8. Loosen 2 bolts on either side of the 2 in the seal housing.

9. Remove the 6 seal housing bolts and remove the seal housing.

➡**Be careful not to damage the oil pan gasket when removing the seal housing.**

10. Remove the seal using special tool 2817 or a suitable replacement.

To install:

11. Use a new gasket on the seal housing and coat the seal with oil prior to installation. Install the seal.

12. Install the seal housing and tighten the bolts to specification.

13. Install the rear oil pan brace and flywheel. Torque the flywheel to 47-54 ft. lbs. (64-73 Nm). When installing the flywheel turn the crankshaft to bring the No. 1 piston to TDC. The lower flywheel pin should be installed approximately 15 degrees from the horizontal and opposite the starter.

14. Install the pilot bearing. Install the clutch assembly and transmission, as required.

15. Connect the negative battery cable. Fill the transmission with fluid. Start the engine and allow it to reach operating temperature. Check for leaks.

B280F Engine

1. Disconnect the negative battery terminal.
2. Remove the transmission.
3. Remove the clutch and pressure plate, if equipped.
4. Remove the flywheel or driveplate, on automatic transmissions.

➡**On automatic transmissions remove the crankshaft spacer.**

5. Remove the 2 rear pan bolts.
6. Remove the bolts in the seal housing and then the housing.

➡**Carefully remove the housing so as not to damage the oil pan gasket.**

7. Using tool 5107, remove the old seal.

To install:

8. Using the seal tool, install the new seal. Install the seal housing and tighten the seal housing bolts to 7-11 ft. lbs. (10-15 Nm).

9. Install the rear oil pan bolts. Install the flywheel and clutch assembly, as required. Tighten the flywheel bolts to 33-37 ft. lbs. (45-50 Nm).

10. Install the transmission and connect the negative battery cable. Fill the transmission with oil. Start the engine and allow it to reach operating temperature. Check for leaks.

B6304F Engine

1. Disconnect the negative battery cable.
2. Remove the transmission from the vehicle.
3. Remove the flexplate.
4. Carefully pry out the seal, taking care not to damage the sealing faces on the shaft and in seat.

To install:

5. Before installing the seal, thoroughly clean the seat and inspect for signs of wear.

6. Lubricate the mating surface between the seat and seal. Oil the seal lips and press the new seal into place, using a suitable seal installer (Tool 5430 and 1801 or equivalent).

7. Install the flexplate. Use new bolts and thread locking compound. Tighten the bolts in 2 stages: First to 33 ft. lbs. (45 Nm); then tighten an additional 50 degree turn.

8. Install the transmission.

9. Connect the negative battery cable.

Crankshaft and Main Bearings

REMOVAL & INSTALLATION

1. Remove the engine from the vehicle, as previously outlined.

2. Remove the pistons and connecting rods, as previously outlined.

3. Mount a dial indicator at the rear of the crankshaft. Measure the crankshaft end-play by pressing the crankshaft against the end positions. Endplay should be 0.0032-0.0106 inches(0.08-0.27mm).

4. Mark the main bearing caps to facilitate installation. Remove the main bearing caps. Remove the thrust bearing, crankshaft and lower bearing halves.

➡**Do not interchange the bearing shells and caps.**

To install:

5. Install the main bearing shells into the block and caps. Lubricate the shells.

➡**Make certain bearing shells matched pairs are installed together.**

6. Install the crankshaft and thrust bearings. Oil the bearing seats and bolts. Install the main bearing caps. Torque to specifications.

7. Check the crankshaft end-play.

8. Install the pistons. Install the crankshaft front and rear seals.

9. Complete installation by installing all components previously removed.

CLEANING & INSPECTION

▶ See Figures 75 and 76

1. Clean all gasket material, sealing surfaces, bearing seats, oilways and holes for cylinder head bolts.

2. Clean the cylinder bores to remove the hard glossy surface.

3. Clean the crankshaft. Blow compressed air through the oilways.

4. Inspect the bearing caps, shells and thrust bearings.

5. Check the crankshaft main bearing journals and connecting rod journals for 'Out-of-Round' and 'Taper':

   a. Maximum out-of-round = 0.0016 (0.04mm)
   b. Maximum taper = 0.0016 (0.04mm)

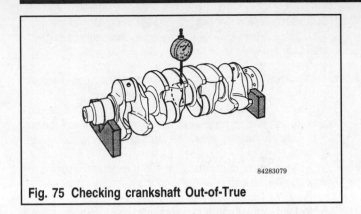

Fig. 75 Checking crankshaft Out-of-True

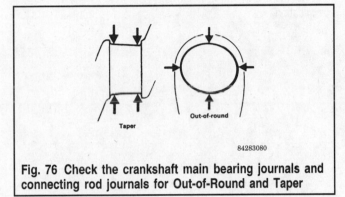

Fig. 76 Check the crankshaft main bearing journals and connecting rod journals for Out-of-Round and Taper

6. If measurements are out of specifications, journals can be ground to undersize.

7. If the crankshaft is suspected to be 'Out-of-True', check with a dial indicator, as follows:

   a. Support the crankshaft by the 2 outer main bearings on V-blocks.

   b. Mount a dial indicator, as shown.

   c. Rotate the crankshaft 1 turn and measure out-of-true on the center journal. Maximum out-of-true = 0.001 inch (0.025mm).

CHECKING BEARING CLEARANCE

♦ **See Figures 77 and 78**

Invert the engine on its stand and remove the cap from the bearing to be checked. Using a clean dry rag, thoroughly clean all oil from crankshaft journal and bearing insert.

➡**Plastigage® is soluble in oil; any oil on the journal or bearing could result in erroneous readings.**

Place a piece of Plastigage® along the full length of journal, reinstall cap, and torque to the specifications given in the chart earlier in this Section.

Remove bearing cap, and determine bearing clearance by comparing the width of Plastigage® to the scale on Plastigage® envelope. Journal taper is determined by comparing width of the Plastigage® strip near its ends. Rotate crankshaft 90° and retest, to determine journal eccentricity.

➡**Do not rotate crankshaft with Plastigage® installed.**

If bearing insert and journal appear intact and are within tolerances, no further main bearing service is required. If bearing or journal appear defective, cause of failure should be determined and repaired before replacement and reassembly.

Flywheel and Ring Gear

REMOVAL & INSTALLATION

♦ **See Figure 79**

The ring gear is contacted by the starter gear during engine start up. If any damage is found on the ring gear (broken or chipped teeth, cracks, etc.) the cause of the failure should be identified and repaired. The starter should be checked as a possible cause.

On vehicles with automatic transmission, the ring gear is an integral part of the flexplate and cannot be replaced. On vehicles with manual gearboxes, the ring gear on the flywheel can be removed and replaced. This replacement involves heating the ring to 450°F, and handling the heated ring. It is usually found to be easier to buy a complete flywheel and ring gear assembly than to attempt the replacement. If you possess the proper equipment for heating and handling the ring gear, the procedure is as follows:

1. Remove the transmission.
2. Remove the clutch plate and disc.
3. Remove the bolts attaching the flywheel to the crankshaft flange. Remove the flywheel.
4. Inspect the flywheel for cracks, and inspect the ring gear for burrs or worn teeth. Replace the flywheel or ring gear if any damage is apparent. Remove burrs with a mill file.

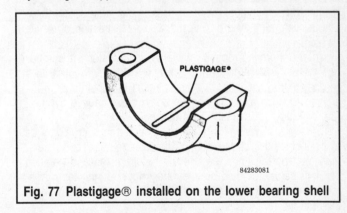

Fig. 77 Plastigage® installed on the lower bearing shell

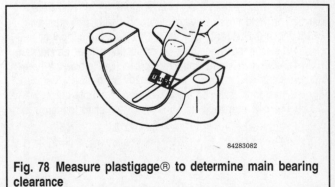

Fig. 78 Measure plastigage® to determine main bearing clearance

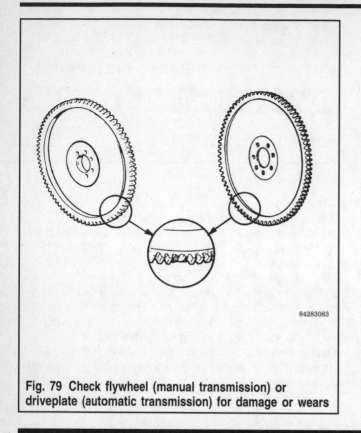

Fig. 79 Check flywheel (manual transmission) or driveplate (automatic transmission) for damage or wears

5. To replace a ring gear use the following steps.

a. Use a 10mm drill and drill a hole between two cogs (teeth) on the ring gear, being careful not to drill into the flywheel.

b. Mount the flywheel in a vise protected by soft jaws and split the ring gear at the hole with a chisel.

c. Heat the new ring gear to approximately 450°F. When handling the heated ring, wear heavy gloves and use tongs.

d. Position the ring gear with the bevelled side facing the flywheel.

e. Use a brass drift and tap the ring gear until flush. Allow to air cool before installation; do not attempt to cool the metal with water, oil or other fluids.

6. Install the flywheel. Install the bolts and torque to specification.

EXHAUST SYSTEM

The exhaust system serves to conduct and silence the flow of hot gasses out of the engine. While it appears to be simple plumbing, the science of exhaust flow is quite complex. Pipe diameter, bend radius, manifold design and internal structure of components all play a part in the efficient extraction of exhaust gasses.

When performing repairs on the exhaust system, it is important to use replacement parts which are virtually identical to the originals. Failure to do so may result in impaired or restricted function and/or a host of body rattles caused by improperly mounted pipes hitting the undercarriage.

The exhaust system is generally mounted in such a way as to be insulated from the body of the vehicle. Rubber hangers, washers and bushings are used to reduce noise and vibration. Their placement should be accurately noted during removal so that they can be properly reinstalled. If any rubber component has lost its flexibility, it should be replaced.

Working on an exhaust system is a project of mixed emotions; being held together with nuts and bolts, and generally not having easy access. Get yourself a healthy supply of rust penetrant and shop rags. In addition to the proper assortment of wrenches, you'll need good eye protection, gloves, a hammer, probably a cold chisel and possibly a small pry bar. On very old systems, it is sometimes easier to simply chisel the end off the bolt and replace it than to attempt to loosen the nut. New hardware and gaskets are always recommended during any exhaust repair.

✳✳CAUTION

Only work on the exhaust system when ALL components are cool to the touch. Catalytic converters can develop surface temperatures of 300°. Always wear eye protection and gloves. Make sure the vehicle is properly supported on jackstands.

REMOVAL & INSTALLATION

B230F and B230FT Engines

1. Disconnect the negative battery cable.
2. Raise and support the vehicle safely.
3. Remove the exhaust system parts, as required. Use the following general rules:
   - Always use new gaskets
   - The steel cone connectors should only be replace if damaged.
   - The exhaust pipe should project approximately 1.5 inch (40mm) into the muffler.
   - The rear silencer is marked 'IN' on the side to be connected to the exhaust pipe at rear axle.

• Clamps should be placed at the center of slotted section

• Clearance between the exhaust system and underside of chassis must not be less than 3/4 inch (20mm).

4. To avoid stressing in the exhaust system when installing, refer to the figure reference and use the following sequence:

a. Loosen mounting bolt A, between the exhaust pipe mounting bracket and transmission crossmember.

b. Align the exhaust system.

c. Tighten nut B, front pipe-manifold, muffler-pipe.

d. On B230F engine: Tighten mounting bolt C, bracket-front pipe. Make sure that the bracket on the pipe rests on the transmission crossmember.

e. On B230FT engine: Tighten mounting bolt C, bracket-front pipe.

f. Tighten bolt A.

g. Tighten muffler-pipe clamps D.

h. On B230F engine: Tighten catalytic converter, if equipped E.

i. On B230FT engine: Tighten catalytic converter, if equipped B.

j. On B230F engine: Tighten muffler-pipe clamp F.

k. On B230FT engine: Tighten muffler-pipe clamp E.

l. Make sure the exhaust system cannot strike the chassis. Adjust as required. Start the engine and check for exhaust leaks.

B234F Engine

1. Disconnect the negative battery cable.

2. Raise and support the vehicle safely.

3. Remove the exhaust system parts, as required. Use the following general rules:

• Always use new gaskets

• Replace the conical steel ring in clamped joint on the front exhaust pipe, only if damaged.

• Inspect the rubber mountings and replace, if necessary.

• The exhaust pipe should project approximately 1.5 inch (40mm) into the muffler.

• Clearance between the exhaust system and underside of chassis must not be less than 3/4 inch (20mm).

4. To avoid stressing in the exhaust system when installing, use the following sequence:

a. Install the front pipe and tighten bolted joint with manifold.

b. Insert and tighten the mounting bolts in the front pipe bracket.

c. Raise and align the other components.

d. Tighten pipe/silencer clamps.

e. Tighten nuts at front pipe pivot point.

f. Make sure the exhaust system cannot strike the chassis. Adjust as required. Start the engine and check for exhaust leaks.

B280F Engine

▶ **See Figure 80**

1. Disconnect the negative battery cable.

2. Raise and support the vehicle safely.

3. Remove the exhaust system parts, as required. Use the following general rules:

• Always use new gaskets. Install with bevelled face towards manifold.

• The steel cone connectors should only be replace if damaged.

• The exhaust pipe should project approximately 1.5 inch (40mm) into the muffler.

• Clearance between the exhaust system and underside of chassis must not be less than 3/4 inch (20mm).

4. To avoid stressing in the exhaust system when installing, refer to the figure reference and use the following sequence:

a. Loosen the gearbox bracket bolts.

b. Install the front pipe. Tighten nuts holding front pipe to manifold.

c. Install and tighten bolt for bracket-front pipe.

d. Tighten gearbox bracket bolts.

e. Hang and adjust all other parts.

f. Tighten clamps between silencer and pipes.

g. Tighten nuts at front pipe joint.

h. Make sure the exhaust system cannot strike the chassis. Adjust as required. Start the engine and check for exhaust leaks.

B6304 Engine

▶ **See Figure 81**

FRONT EXHAUST PIPE

1. Disconnect the negative battery cable.

2. Raise and support the vehicle safely.

3. Remove the front exhaust pipe-to-manifold joint nuts. Lower the front exhaust pipe and remove from the vehicle.

4. Installation is the reverse of the removal procedure. Before installing, clean the joint surfaces. Tighten the bolted joints to the manifold. Torque to 44 ft. lbs. (60 Nm) M10 or 30 ft. lbs. (40 Nm) M8.

5. Loosen the joint after the catalytic converter and re-tighten to 18 ft. lbs. (25 Nm). This is necessary to prevent stresses in the system.

6. Start the engine and check for exhaust leaks.

EXHAUST PIPE, RESONATOR/CONVERTER

Inspect the rubber mountings and replace as required. The pipe joints should overlap by approximately 40mm and clearance between the exhaust system and body should not be less than 20mm. Support and align all components. Tighten the clips retaining the rear silencer and pipe. Tighten the clips at the front pipe joint. Check the clearance between the system and body, adjust as required. Torque the spherical joints to 18 ft. lbs. (25 Nm). Upon completion, start the engine and check for exhaust leaks.

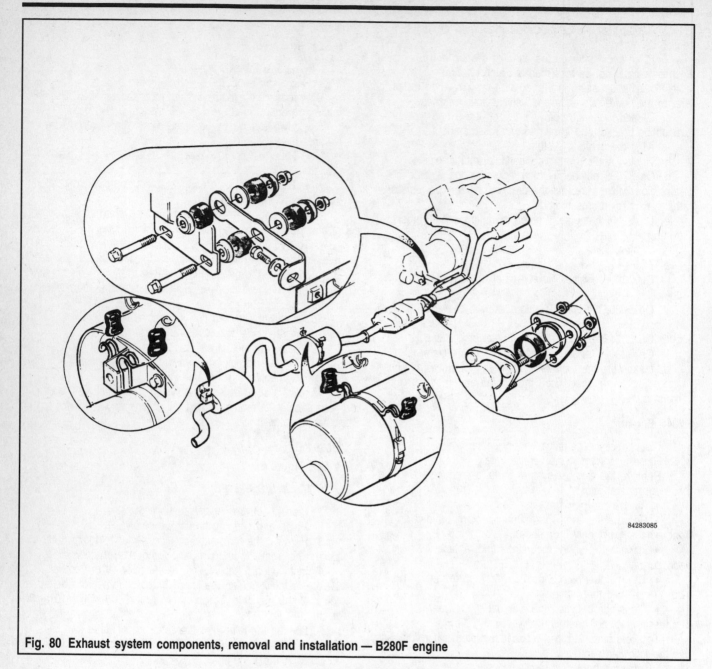

84283085

Fig. 80 Exhaust system components, removal and installation — B280F engine

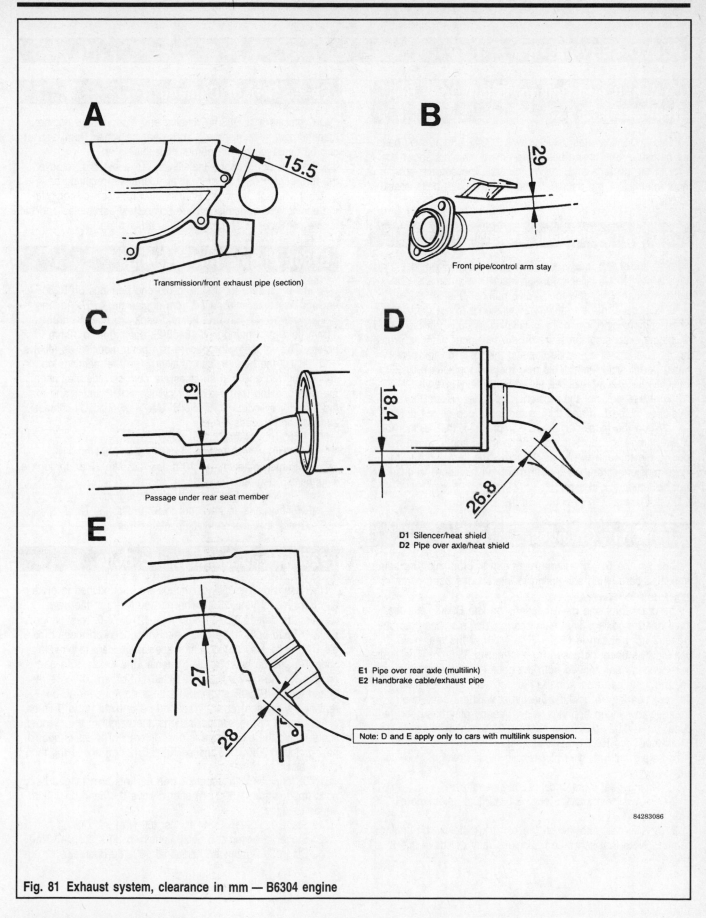

A Transmission/front exhaust pipe (section) — 15.5

B Front pipe/control arm stay — 29

C Passage under rear seat member — 19

D 18.4 / 26.8
D1 Silencer/heat shield
D2 Pipe over axle/heat shield

E 27 / 28
E1 Pipe over rear axle (multilink)
E2 Handbrake cable/exhaust pipe

Note: D and E apply only to cars with multilink suspension.

84283086

Fig. 81 Exhaust system, clearance in mm — B6304 engine

VOLVO SERVICE TIPS

Camshaft and Balance Shaft Drive Belt Replacement

Volvo 700-900 series vehicles with B234F engine may have the camshaft and timing belt replacement intervals shown in error in the owner's and service manual. The correct replacement interval for the camshaft and balance shaft belts is at 50,000 miles.

Cam Belt Automatic Tensioner Tool

Volvo 700-900 series, with B234F and B6304F engines, have a new tool available to help install the automatic cam belt tensioner. This new tool, Volvo number 999 5456-2 is used to ensure that the automatic tensioner is not damaged when compressing it prior to installation. A spring in the tool maintains a constant pressure on the tensioner plunger, pressing it into the cylinder while keeping the force on the seal within permissible limits. This new method replaces previous instructions to compress the tensioner directly in a vise.

Mount the tool, not the tensioner, in a vise. Place the belt tensioner in the tool and tighten the tool's central nut down fully. When the tensioner is fully compressed, that is, the hole in the plunger is opposite the hole in the cylinder, insert a locking pin through the holes. Unscrew the center nut to remove tensioner from the tool. Inspect the tensioner to ensure that no leakage is present.

Do not use a vise to compress the tensioner.

Crankshaft Changes

Although the B230F engine has been in production for some time, use care when attempting to interchange used parts for major engine repair.

The crankshaft and main bearings on late B230F engines have been modified. The main bearing diameter has been increased from 55mm to 63mm. The width of the rear main bearing has been increased from 29mm to 35.5mm. The thrust bearing has been moved from the center to the rear main bearing, changed from a half (180 degrees) to a full (360 degree) bearing. In addition the thrust washers have been changed to flanged bearings. Main bearing play has been reduced from 0.024-0.072mm (0.001-0.003 inches) to 0.024-0.061mm (0.001-0.002 inches).

To help identify engine blocks with these changes, look for the followings:

1. Timing gear case decal is marked with a **K**.
2. An **A** is cast into the engine block just below the oil filter.
3. A **K** is cast into the engine block just below the engine number. Note that some early engines may not have this **K** mark.

Speed Sensor Damage

On vehicles with B6304F engine and Motronic 1.8 engine management system, note that the engine speed (rpm) sensor can be damaged by the carrier plate during engine/transmission removal/installation. To avoid this, remove the rpm sensor prior to any repair operations requiring engine/transmission removal. Reinstall the rpm sensor only after the engine and transmission are completely assembled and the torque converter is attached to the carrier plate.

B280F Engine Rod Bearings

A new procedure for installing big end bearings on B280F engines has been introduced from engine no. 41672 (during model year 1990). Big end bearing caps are now secured with 11mm nuts (part number 1218403-2), compared to 13mm before. The tightening procedure has been modified as follows:

1. Install the bearing cap, making sure the markings on connecting rod and cap surfaces are correct. Side clearance must be oriented to the rear for cylinders 1, 2 and 3 and to the front for cylinders 4, 5 and 6. Use new nuts. Oil contact surfaces and threads.
2. Tighten in stages:
   a. Stage 1: tighten 1 nut to 18 ft. lbs. (25 Nm).
   b. Tighten other nut to 18 ft. lbs. (25 Nm), then through a further 75 degrees.
   c. Tighten the first nut through 75 degrees.
   d. Finally, tighten each nut to 37 ft. lbs. (50 Nm).
3. Check that the crankshaft rotates freely.

B280F Head Gaskets and Bolts

New asbestos-free cylinder heads were introduced in production from model year 1990. The part numbers of the new gaskets are: left-1218377-8 and right-1218378-6. New flanged cylinder head bolts have also been introduced on these models. The bolts are coated with a special lubricant to provide controlled friction when angle-tightening the heads. The part number for the new bolts is 1218366-1. Sixteen bolts are required for the B280F engine. The bolts do not need to be replaced with each repair. They can be re-used up to 5 times.

As a result of these modifications, the height of the cylinder liners above the block face is now different. The liners should now project 0.002-0.005 inches (0.05-0.12mm) above the face of the block.

B280F engines with asbestos-free gaskets and flanged head bolts (models from 1990 on) should have the head bolts tightened in stages.

1. Stage 1: tighten to 44 ft. lbs. (60 Nm).
2. Stage 2: loosen the bolts, tighten to 30 ft. lbs. (40 Nm).
3. Stage 3: Tighten an additional 160-180 degrees.

4. Adjust the valves. Re-torquing is not required with the new-type gaskets and bolts.

➡**The new-type head gaskets and bolts (both must be used together) can be installed in earlier B280F engines as long as the proper cylinder liner deck height is observed.**

TORQUE SPECIFICATIONS

Component	U.S.	Metric
Balance shaft housings		
B234 engine		
Step 1:	15 ft. lbs.[1]	20 Nm[1]
Step 2:	Loosen bolts	Loosen bolts
Step 3:	7.5 ft. lbs.	10 Nm
Step 4:	+ 90 degrees turn	+ 90 degrees turn
Camshaft retaining bolts		
Except B280F engine:	14 ft. lbs.	20 Nm
B280F engine:	7–11 ft. lbs.	9–15 Nm
Crankshaft damper bolt		
B230F, B230FT, B234F engines		
Step 1:	43 ft. lbs.	58 Nm
Step 2:	Tighten an additional 60 degrees	
B280F engine	177–206 ft. lbs.	240–280 Nm
B6304F engine	220 ft. lbs.	300 Nm
Cylinder head bolts		
B230F& 230FT engines		
Step 1:	14 ft. lbs.	20 Nm
Step 2:	30 ft. lbs.	41 Nm
Step 3:	+ 90 degrees turn	+ 90 degrees turn
B234F engine		
Step 1:	15 ft. lbs.	20 Nm
Step 2:	30 ft. lbs.	41 Nm
Step 3:	+ 115 degrees turn	+ 45 degrees turn
B280F engine		
With standard gasket		
Step 1:	43 ft. lbs.	60 Nm
Step 2:	15 ft. lbs.[2]	20 Nm[2]
Step 3:	+ 106 degrees turn	+ 106 degrees turn
Step 4:	See note 3	See note 3
Step 5:	+ 45 degrees turn	+ 45 degrees turn
With asbestos-free gasket		
Step 1:	44 ft. lbs.	60 Nm
Step 2:	Loosen bolts	Loosen bolts
Step 3:	30 ft. lbs.	40 Nm
Step 4:	+ 160–190 degrees turn	+ 160–190 degrees turn
B6304F		
Step 1:	15 ft. lbs.	20 Nm
Step 2:	44 ft. lbs.	60 Nm
Step 3:	+150 degrees turn	
Connecting rod bolts		
B230F, B230FT, B234F engines		
Step 1:	43 ft. lbs.	58 Nm
Step 2:	Tighten + 60 degrees	
B280F engine		
Step 1:	Tighten nut 1 to 18ft. lbs.	25 Nm
Step 2:	Tighten nut 2 to 18ft. lbs.	25 Nm
Step 3:	Tighten nut 2 additional 75 degrees	
Step 4:	Tighten nut 1 additional 75 degrees	
Step 5:	Tighten each nut in turn to 37 ft. lbs.	50 Nm
B6304F engine		
Step 1:	15 ft. lbs.	20 Nm
Step 2:	Tighten additional 90 degrees	

84283093

TORQUE SPECIFICATIONS

Component	U.S.	Metric
Exhaust manifold		
B230 engine:	10–20 ft. lbs.	14–27 Nm
B234F engine:	15 ft. lbs.	20 Nm
B280F engine:	7–11 ft. lbs.	10–15 Nm
B6304F engine:	15 ft. lbs.	20 Nm
Flywheel bolts (use new bolts, thread locking compound)		
B230F, B230FT, B234F engines:	50 ft. lbs.	70 Nm
B280F engine:	32–38 ft. lbs.	45–50 Nm
B6304F engine:		
Step 1:	33 ft. lbs.	45Nm
Step 2:	turn additional 50 degrees	
Fuel filter fittings:	22 ft. lbs.	30 Nm
Intake manifold		
B230 engine:	15 ft. lbs.	20 Nm
B234F engine:	15 ft. lbs.	20 Nm
B280F engine:	7–11 ft. lbs.	10–15 Nm
B6304 engine:	15 ft. lbs.	20 Nm
Main bearing bolts		
B230F, B230FT, B234F:	80 ft. lbs.	108 Nm
B280F		
Step 1:	22 ft. lbs.	30 Nm
Step 2:	Loosen nut 1, tighten it 22–26 ft. lbs.	
Step 3:	Angle tighten nut #1 +73–76 degrees	
Step 4:	Loosen and re-tighten the other nuts as in Step 2, in order	
Step 5:	Angle tighten the other nuts as in Step 3, in order	
Step 6:	Tighten side bolts to 14–18 ft. lbs.	20–25 Nm
Oil cooler hose fittings:	22 ft. lbs.	30 Nm
Oil pan bolts:	8 ft. lbs.	11 Nm
Spark plugs:		
B230F, B230FT, B234F engines:	18 ft. lbs.	24 Nm
B280F engine:	8–10 ft. lbs.	11–14 Nm
B6304F engine:	20 ft. lbs.	26 Nm
Starter-to-flywheel housing bolts:	25 ft. lbs.	34 Nm
Timing chain sprockets		
B280F engine:	51–59 ft. lbs.	69–80 Nm
Turbocharger-to-exhaust manifold bolts		
B230F turbocharged engine		
Step 1:	0.7 ft. lbs.	3 Nm
Step 2:	30 ft. lbs.	41 Nm
Step 3:	+ 120 degrees turn	+ 120 degrees turn
Valve cover bolts:	11 ft. lbs.	15 Nm
Vibration damper nut		
B6304F:	221 ft. lbs.	300 Nm
Water pump bolts:	11–15 ft. lbs.	20 Nm

1 – Tighten each bolt ½ turn at a time
2 – Loosen 1 bolt at a time and retorque
3 – Warm to operating temperature, shut down and cool 2 hours

ENGINE MECHANICAL SPECIFICATIONS

Component	U.S.	Metric
Displacement		
B230F/B230FT/B234F:	2.3L	2316cc
B280F:	2.8L	2849cc
B-6304F:	2.9L	2922cc
Number of Cylinders		
B230F/B230FT/B234F:	4	
B280F/B-6304F:	6	
Bore and Stroke		
B230F/B230FT/B234F:	3.78 x 3.15 inch	96.0 x 80.0mm
B280F:	3.58 x 2.87 inch	90.9 x 72.9mm
B-6304F:	3.27 x 3.54 inch	83.0 x 89.9mm
Camshaft		
Journal Diameter		
B230F/B230FT		
No. 1:	1.179–1.180 inch	29.950–29.972mm
No. 2:	1.179–1.180 inch	29.950–29.972mm
No. 3:	1.179–1.180 inch	29.950–29.972mm
No. 4:	1.179–1.180 inch	29.950–29.972mm
B234F:	N/A	N/A
B280F		
No.1:	1.592–1.593 inch	40.436–40.462mm
No.2:	1.616–1.617 inch	41.046–41.071mm
No.3:	1.639–1.640 inch	41.630–41.656mm
No.4:	1.663–1.664 inch	42.240–42.265mm
B-6304F:	N/A	N/A
Lobe Lift		
B230F/B230FT		
Intake:	0.374 inch	9.499mm
Exhaust:	0.414 inch	10.515mm
B234F		
Intake:	0.370 inch	9.398mm
Exhaust:	0.370 inch	9.398mm
B280F		
Intake:	0.235 inch	5.969mm
Exhaust:	0.214 inch	5.436mm
B-6304F		
Intake:	0.354 inch	8.992mm
Exhaust:	0.354 inch	8.992mm
Journal-to-Bearing Clearance		
B230F/B230FT/B234F:	0.0012–0.0028 inch	0.0304–0.0711mm
B280F:	0.0014–0.0034 inch	0.0356–0.0864mm
B-6304F:	N/A	N/A
End-play		
B230F/B230FT/B234F:	0.004–0.016 inch	0.102–0.406mm
B280F:	N/A	N/A
B-6304F:	0.002–0.008 inch	0.051–0.203mm

84283096

ENGINE MECHANICAL SPECIFICATIONS

Component	U.S.	Metric
Crankshaft and Connecting Rod		
Main Bearing Journal Diameter		
B230F/B230FT:	2.4981–2.4986 inch	63.4517–63.4644mm
B234F:	2.4803 inch	63.0000mm
B280F:	2.7576–2.7583 inch	70.0434–70.0608mm
B-6304F:	2.5590 inch	64.9986mm
Main Bearing Oil Clearance		
B230F/B230FT/B234F:	0.0011–0.0033 inch	0.0279–0.0838mm
B280F:	0.0035 inch	0.0889mm
B-6304F:	0.0009–0.0019 inch	0.0228–0.0483mm
End-play		
B230F/B230FT/B234F:	0.0015–0.0058 inch	0.0381–0.1473mm
B280F:	0.0028–0.0106 inch	0.0711–0.2692mm
B-6304F:	N/A	N/A
Main Bearing Oil Clearance		
Connecting Rod Journal Diameter		
B230F/B230FT:	2.1255–2.1260 inch	53.9877–54.0004mm
B234F:	2.0472–2.0476 inch	51.9989–52.0090mm
B280F:	2.3611–2.3618 inch	59.9719–59.9897mm
B-6304F:	1.9690 inch	50.0126mm
Connecting Rod, Bearing Oil Clearance		
B230F/B230FT/B234F:	0.0009–0.0028 inch	0.0228–0.0711mm
B280F:	0.0079–0.0150 inch	0.2007–0.3810mm
B-6304F:	N/A	N/A
Connecting Rod, Side Clearance		
B230F/B230FT:	0.006–0.014 inch	0.1524–0.3556mm
B234F:	0.006–0.018 inch	0.1524–0.4572mm
B280F:	0.0079–0.0150 inch	0.2007–0.3810mm
B-6304F:	0.005–0.017 inch	0.1270–0.4318mm
Valves		
Stem-to-Guide Clearance		
B230F/B230FT		
Intake:	0.0012–0.0024 inch	0.0305–0.0610mm
Exhaust:	0.0024–0.0036 inch	0.0610–0.0914mm
B234F		
Intake:	0.0012–0.0024 inch	0.0305–0.0610mm
Exhaust:	0.0016–0.0028 inch	0.0406–0.0711mm
B280F		
Intake[1]:	0.3150–0.3158 inch	8.0010–8.0213mm
Exhaust[1]:	0.3150–0.3158 inch	8.0010–8.0213mm
B-6304F		
Intake:	0.0012–0.0024 inch	0.0305–0.0610mm
Exhaust:	0.0012–0.0024 inch	0.0305–0.0610mm
Stem Diameter		
B230F/B230FT		
Intake:	0.3132–0.3138 inch	0.0305–0.0610mm
Exhaust:	0.3128–0.3134 inch	0.0610–0.0914mm
B234F:	N/A	N/A
B280F:	N/A	N/A
B-6304F:	N/A	N/A
Piston		
Piston-to-Cylinder Clearance		
B230F/B230FT/B234F:	0.0004–0.0012 inch	0.0101–0.0305mm
B280F:	0.0007–0.0015 inch	0.0177–0.0381mm

84283097

ENGINE MECHANICAL SPECIFICATIONS

Component	U.S.	Metric
B-6304F:	N/A	N/A
Ring Gap		
B230F/B230FT/B234F		
Top Compression:	0.0118–0.0217 inch	0.2997–0.5512mm
Bottom Compression:	0.0118–0.0217 inch	0.2997–0.5512mm
Oil Control:	0.0118–0.0256 inch	0.2997–0.6502mm
B280F		
Top Compression:	0.0158–0.0236 inch	0.4013–0.5994mm
Bottom Compression:	0.0158–0.0236 inch	0.4013–0.5994mm
Oil Control:	0.0158–0.0571 inch	0.4013–1.4503mm
B-6304F		
Top Compression:	0.0080–0.0160 inch	0.2032–0.4064mm
Bottom Compression:	0.0080–0.0160 inch	0.2032–0.4064mm
Oil Control:	0.0090–0.0200 inch	0.2286–0.5080mm
Ring Side Clearance		
B230F/B230FT/B234F		
Top Compression:	0.0024–0.0036 inch	0.0610–0.0914mm
Bottom Compression:	0.0016–0.0028 inch	0.0406–0.0711mm
Oil Control:	0.0012–0.0026 inch	0.0305–0.0660mm
B280F		
Top Compression:	0.0021–0.0029 inch	0.0533–0.0737mm
Bottom Compression:	0.0010–0.0021 inch	0.0254–0.0533mm
Oil Control:	0.0004–0.0092 inch	0.0102–0.2337mm
B-6304F		
Top Compression:	0.0020–0.0033 inch	0.0508–0.0838mm
Bottom Compression:	0.0012–0.0026 inch	0.0305–0.0660mm
Oil Control:	0.0008–0.0022 inch	0.0203–0.0559mm

1 = Tapered valve guide ID

84283098

4

EMISSION CONTROLS

EMISSION CONTROLS

Crankcase fumes, exhaust gasses, and gasoline evaporation are the three basic sources of gasoline engines pollutants. The pollutants formed from these substances fall into three categories:

- Unburned hydrocarbons (HC)
- Carbon monoxide (CO)
- Nitrogen oxides (NOx) In order to limit these source of pollutants, several methods have been introduce. These range from internal engine design (combustion chamber, heads, valves, camshaft, etc) to external added components (thermo vacuum valves, solenoids, relays and computers). As the emission laws of the US and other nations become stiffer, emission control systems change year to year to maintain the required balance of vehicle performance and driveability as well as reduced emissions.

Terms Used in This Section

A/C: Air Conditioner
CO: Carbon Monoxide
CTS: Coolant Temperature Sensor
DIS: Distributorless Ignition System
ECU: Electronic Control Unit
EGR: Exhaust Gas Recirculation
EZK: Elektrische Zundkontrolle   (Electronic ignition control)
HC: Hydrocarbons
MAP: Manifold Absolute Pressure
mV: millivolts
NOx: Oxides of Nitrogen
NTC: Negative Temperature Coefficient
PCB: Printed Circuit Board
PCV: Positive Crankcase Ventilation
PTC: Positive Temperature Coefficient
SRS: Supplemental Restraint System
TDC: Top Dead Center
TWC: Three-Way Catalytic Converter

Crankcase Ventilation System

All engines are equipped with a Positive Crankcase Ventilation (PCV) system. This system prevents crankcase gases from being release into the atmosphere but are directed to the intake manifold, where they are burned in the combustion process. The crankcase gases are removed from the crankcase by Positive Crankcase Ventilation (PCV). Engine vacuum draws the crankcase gases out, allowing fresh air to be drawn in.

The crankcase ventilation system consists of a controlled orifice or calibrated nipple, an oil trap, a flame guard (on non-turbocharged engines) and the hoses connecting the crankcase, intake manifold and air cleaner. The calibrated nipple regulates the crankcase gas flow and ensures that crankcase vacuum does not become excessive. The oil trap separates oil from the gases, reducing oil consumption and emissions. The flame guard prevents a possible backfire from entering the crankcase, possibly igniting blow-by gases.

At idle and at low engine loads, the vacuum in the intake manifold is high. Crankcase gases are then mixed with air

from the air cleaner, so vacuum does not increase. At high engine loads and/or large crankcase gas flow, vacuum in the intake manifold decreases. Crankcase gases then flow in 2 different directions, partly through the calibrated nipple and partly through the air cleaner.

SERVICE

Servicing the crankcase ventilation system consists of checking the hoses for cracks or vacuum leaks and checking the hoses, calibrated nipple and flame guard for clogging.

The PCV nipple should be removed and inspected every 60,000 miles (96,000 km).

Frequent oil changes and the use of a premium grade motor oil will help to ensure that the crankcase ventilation system functions properly. The flame guard for the B6034F engine is located at the air intake tube. Turn the guard to the left to remove it from the air intake.

REMOVAL & INSTALLATION

▶ **See Figures 1 and 2**

B230F Engine

1. Clean the nipple in the intake manifold.
2. Replace the flame trap. The flame trap should be positioned in T-piece.

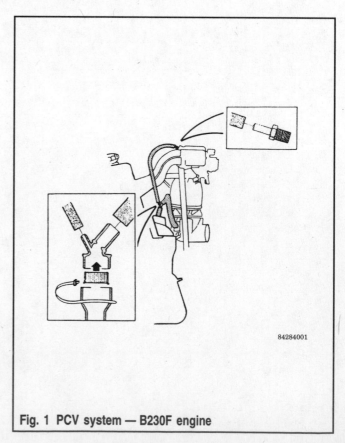

84284001

Fig. 1 PCV system — B230F engine

B6304F Engine

1. Rotate the flame trap casing approximately 0.59 inch (15mm) left (bayonet catch).
2. Pull out the flame trap and remove the oil filler cap.
3. Blow clean hoses down towards the crankcase ventilation.
4. Reinstall the flame trap in the inlet hose and rotate the flame trap outer casing back to its original position.

Evaporative Control System (EVAP)

OPERATION

▶ **See Figures 3 and 4**

The EVAP system controls the gases which evaporate from fuel in the fuel tank, preventing the gases from escaping into the atmosphere. Fuel vapor passes from the filter opening through a roll-over valve to a reservoir (canister, carbon filter). Fuel vapor is absorbed in the reservoir. The reservoir is equipped with EVAP valve which prevents leakage of fuel vapor when the engine is not running.

Fuel vapors from the fuel tank enter into the top of the carbon filter and are absorbed. Air is then pushed out through a channel from the bottom of the filter. If for any reason, the vehicle leans sideways at more than a 45 degree angle, a roll-over valve is incorporated into the system to prevent any fuel spills.

An EVAP valve is located at the top of the carbon filter and is closed when the engine is off. During idling, the EVAP valve is closed so that it does not interfere with the automatic idle settings or make the fuel mixture to rich. The EVAP valve closes using vacuum pressure taken from the intake manifold and from the throttle shutter positive terminal.

➡ **On B234F, the EVAP vacuum valve is replaced by an electrical valve placed between the canister and the intake manifold. The function is similar to the vacuum valve.**

Increased engine loads open the EVAP valve, allowing fuel vapor to flow from the carbon filter into the intake manifold, and at the same time air is drawn through the bottom channel. Under normal conditions, the filter discharges the fuel in approximately 15-20 minutes.

The 940 is equipped with a gas-evaporative control system. This system is comprised of an expansion chamber in the fuel tank, a roll-over valve on the cross member (front of the fuel

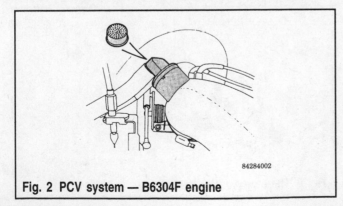

Fig. 2 PCV system — B6304F engine

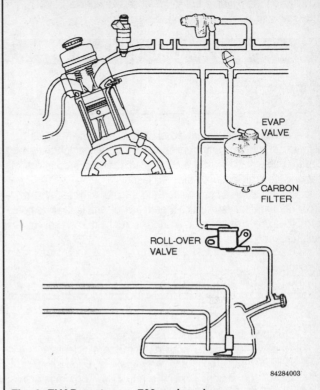

Fig. 3 EVAP system — 700 series shown

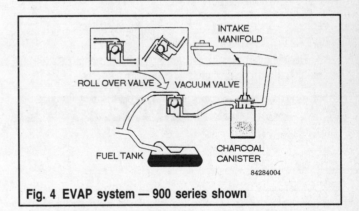

Fig. 4 EVAP system — 900 series shown

tank) and a charcoal canister with a built-in vacuum valve under the left front wheel housing.

SERVICE

The ability of the EVAP system to control gases from escaping into the atmosphere is dependent largely on a leak-free system.

1. Check for proper sealing of the fuel filler cap, which contains an O-ring type seals.
2. Check all evaporative hoses for tightness.
3. Check the conditions of all fuel lines under the vehicle. Repair as necessary.
4. Check the purge valve: Make sure fuel vapors do not pass through the purge valve when the engine is idling. This can be checked by crimping the evaporative hose between the

canister and the intake manifold, while the engine is idling. There should be no change in idle speed.

Thermostatic Air Cleaner Assembly

OPERATION

A thermostatically controlled shutter is housed in the air cleaner. The thermostat senses the intake air temperature and changes the position of the shutter, to vary the proportions of hot and cold air entering the air cleaner.

Intake air preheating provides the engine with nearly constant temperature intake air, regardless of ambient air temperature. This provides for smooth engine running and prevents ice build-up.

TESTING

▶ **See Figure 5**

1. Remove the air cleaner housing.
2. Remove the shutter housing from the air cleaner.
3. Check the bushings and the mounting of the shutter.
4. Check the shutter position at the following temperatures:
   a. 41°F (5°C) or less
   b. Approximately 50°F (10°C)
   c. 59°F (16°C) or more
5. Replace the thermostat if the shutter does not function as specified.
6. Reassemble and install the air cleaner, making sure the air cleaner housing and ducts are sealing properly.

Three-Way Catalytic (TWC) Converter

▶ **See Figure 6**

OPERATION

The catalytic converter is a supplementary device in the exhaust system, designed to reduce exhaust pollutants. The converter is mainly a ceramic material insert with channels, through which exhaust gases pass. The channel walls are covered by a thin layer of platinum-palladium. These metals act as catalysts, through a chemical reaction. Vehicles equipped with heated oxygen sensor, use a three-way catalytic converter containing platinum and rhodium.

The catalytic converter converts 90-95 % of the toxic substances to harmless substances. The pollutants are cleaned as follows:

- Unburned hydrocarbons (HC) — are oxidized to water vapor (H_2O) and carbon dioxide (CO_2)
- Carbon monoxide (CO) — is oxidized to carbon dioxide (CO_2)
- Nitrogen oxides (NOX) are reduced to nitrogen gas (N_2).

SERVICE

The catalytic converter, under normal circumstances, requires no service intervals. A properly tuned engine will help in avoiding malfunctions that could damage the TWC-converter.

During engine oil change and chassis lubrication intervals, inspect the catalytic converter condition and check for exhaust leaks. To prolong the life and operating performance of the catalytic converter, observe the followings:

— Always use unleaded fuel.
— Keep the engine properly tuned.
— Excessive starter cranking with an intermittently firing or flooded engine, can cause the TWC-converter to overheat.
— Do not continue to operate the vehicle if you detect engine misfire, noticeable loss of power or other unusual operating conditions.

✳✳WARNING

Do not park your vehicle over combustible materials, such as grass or leaves, which may come in contact with the hot exhaust system. Wind or other weather conditions can cause the hot exhaust to ignite these materials.

Heated Oxygen Sensor System

This is an emission control system designed to reduce emissions and improve fuel economy. Since the sensor functions only above a certain temperature, it is electrically heated. The heated oxygen sensor monitors the composition of the exhaust gases leaving the engine. The exhaust gas analysis is fed into an electronic control module. This adjusts the air/fuel ratio to provide optimum conditions for combustion and efficient reduction of the three major pollutants, by the TWC-converter.

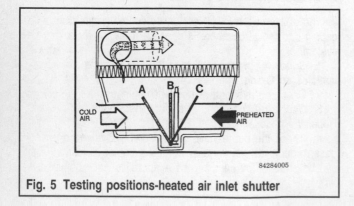

84284005

Fig. 5 Testing positions-heated air inlet shutter

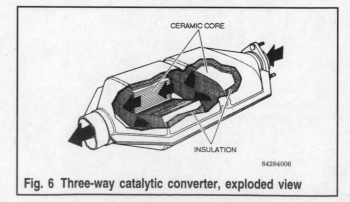

84284006

Fig. 6 Three-way catalytic converter, exploded view

SERVICE

The heated oxygen sensor does not require periodic replacement. If the sensor is suspected of being the cause of a driveability problem, measure the resistance of the pre-heater resistor. Replace, if the following values cannot be obtained.
— Cold sond, 68°F (20°C) = 3 ohms
— Hot sond, 660°F (350°C) = 13 ohms

REMOVAL & INSTALLATION

1. Disconnect the negative battery cable.
2. Raise and support the vehicle safely.
3. Disconnect the oxygen sensor connector. The sensor is located near the catalytic converter.
4. Remove the oxygen sensor, using a suitable wrench.
5. Installation is the reverse of the removal procedure. Before installing, apply 'Never Seez' paste (P/N 1 161 035-9) to the threaded section of the bond. Tighten to 40 ft. lbs. (55 Nm).

Pulsed Secondary Air Injection

OPERATION

This system, where equipped, adds air to the hot exhaust gases as they are expelled from the engine. This cause a secondary combustion of residual hydrocarbons and carbon monoxide, resulting in lower emissions levels in the exhaust gases.

Service Indicator Lamp

RESETTING

240/780 and 1990 740
▶ See Figure 7

The service reminder zeroing knob is located at the rear of the instrument panel. The indicator light illuminates after approximately 5,000 miles (8,000 km). It goes on for 2 minutes each time the engine is started until oil and filter have been changed and the counter reset.

Using a small screwdriver, depress the knob to reset.

Except 240/780 and 1990 740
▶ See Figure 8

The service reminder zeroing knob is located on the front of the instrument cluster, underneath a rubber grommet. The reminder light comes ON for two minutes after each start, after driving 5,000 miles (8,000 km) after previous oil change and accompanying resetting. To reset, remove the rubber grommet; then using a small screwdriver, depress the knob to reset.

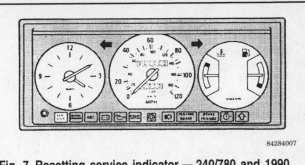

84284007

Fig. 7 Resetting service indicator — 240/780 and 1990 740

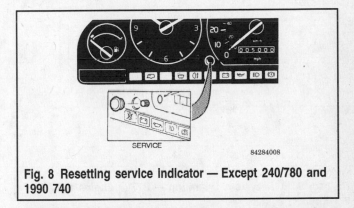

84284008

Fig. 8 Resetting service indicator — Except 240/780 and 1990 740

Exhaust Gas Recirculation (EGR) System (California Only)

GENERAL INFORMATION

▶ See Figure 9

This system has been introduced to meet California emission control standards. The function of the exhaust gas recirculation system is to help reduce Oxides of Nitrogen (NOx) gases. NOx occurs in the combustion chamber at high engine load and temperatures. The system is controlled by means of a solenoid valve supplied with signals by the EZ116K ignition system control unit. By mixing exhaust gas with the air/fuel mixture, the combustion chamber temperature is lowered.

The EGR system consists of the EGR valve, a vacuum booster, temperature sender, control unit and EGR pipe.

The system is not activated when the engine is cold or idling. Under these conditions, the NOx level is already low and recirculation would impair the running condition of the engine.

OPERATION

EGR Valve

The EGR valve controls flow of exhaust gases from the exhaust manifold to the intake manifold. The valve is operated by control pressure from the EGR vacuum booster. The EGR valve is located under the intake manifold.

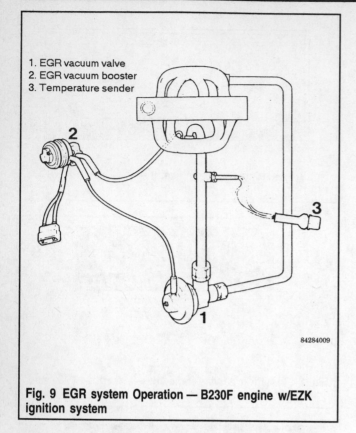

Fig. 9 EGR system Operation — B230F engine w/EZK ignition system

1. EGR vacuum valve
2. EGR vacuum booster
3. Temperature sender

84284009

EGR Vacuum Booster

The vacuum booster controls pressure in the vacuum line to the EGR valve by means of the admission valve (lower section). The pressure in the intake manifold is supplied to the reducing valve (upper section). The valve uses an electrical signal to maintain optimum control of the EGR valve. The unit is also designed to allow for ambient air pressure. The vacuum booster valve is located on the left-hand suspension strut tower.

Temperature Sender

The sensor measures the temperature of the exhaust gases returned to the intake manifold. This sensor have a positive temperature coefficient, which means that the resistance through the sensor will rise with the temperature. The sensor is designed to measure temperatures up to 930°F (500°C). Detection of the temperature variations enables the control unit to determine whether or not the EGR system is working. The sensor is located in the EGR upper pipe between the intake manifold and EGR valve.

SERVICE

The EGR valve should be inspected at 60,000 miles 96,000 km) and thereafter cleaned every 20,000 miles (32,000 km).

DIAGNOSTIC SYSTEM

The EGR system is equipped with a temperature sender which enables the control unit to determine whether or not the

EGR system is working. The control unit can activate two EGR fault codes.

Reading Fault Codes
▶ **See Figures 10 and 11**

TEST MODE 1

1. Connect the test lead probe to socket No. 6 on the diagnostic unit.
2. Turn the ignition switch **ON**.
3. Activate test mode 1 by pressing test button once.
4. Note all fault codes from the flashing light.
5. Code 2-4-1 indicates a system malfunction. The temperature sender detects that the EGR flow is too low.
6. Code 4-3-1 indicates the signal from the temperature sender is absent or faulty.
7. Erase codes when repair is completed.

Erasing Fault Codes

After reading and recording the fault codes, they should be erased.

1. Press the test button for more than 5 seconds, then release the button. After 3 seconds, the LED will come ON.
2. Press the test button for an additional 5 seconds. Release the button. The LED will go OFF.
3. Press the test button approximately 1 second. Code 1-1-1 will appear indicating that there are no remaining fault codes.

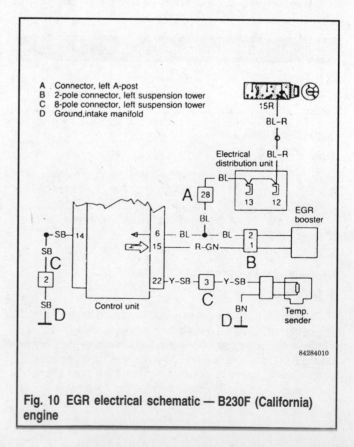

A Connector, left A-post
B 2-pole connector, left suspension tower
C 8-pole connector, left suspension tower
D Ground, intake manifold

Fig. 10 EGR electrical schematic — B230F (California) engine

84284010

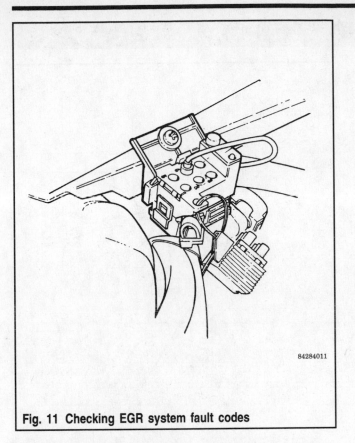

Fig. 11 Checking EGR system fault codes

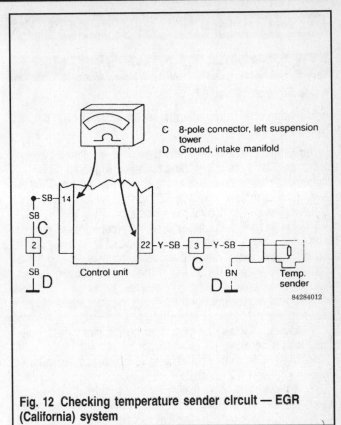

C 8-pole connector, left suspension tower
D Ground, intake manifold

Fig. 12 Checking temperature sender circuit — EGR (California) system

Checking Temperature Sender

▶ **See Figure 12**

1. Measure the resistance between terminals No. 14 and No. 22 of the ECU. The resistance should be 500-100 ohms.
2. If the value is different, check the wiring and harness connections.

Checking EGR Vacuum Booster

▶ **See Figures 13 and 14**

TEST MODE 3

1. Connect the test lead probe to socket No. 6 on the diagnostic unit.
2. Turn the ignition switch **ON**.
3. Press the test button on the diagnostic unit 3 times, each for more than 1 second. EGR vacuum booster should operate in step with flashing of the LED. If this occurs, vacuum booster circuit and wiring are intact.
4. If the EGR vacuum booster does not operate:
   a. Remove the booster connector and measure the voltage between terminal 2 and ground, of the connector.
   b. If 12 volts is not indicated, check the fuse and wiring between the ignition switch and vacuum booster. Reconnect the connector.
   c. Turn the ignition switch **OFF**.
   d. Measure the resistance between terminals 6 and 15 on the control unit connector. The resistance should be 75-95 ohms.
   e. If the reading is okay, the converter circuit and wiring are okay.

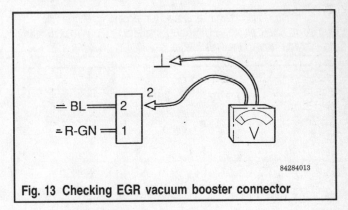

Fig. 13 Checking EGR vacuum booster connector

   f. Substitute another control unit.
5. If the reading is not within range, check the vacuum booster wiring and connections. Measure the vacuum booster resistance at the booster connector. Repair as required.

Checking Vacuum System

▶ **See Figure 15**

1. Open the EGR booster connector. Remove the lead directly opposite the black/white lead between pin No. 1 and ECU. Reconnect the connector.
2. Start the engine and run to normal operating temperature, allow engine to idle.
3. Ground the loose lead. Check to see if the EGR valve operates and the engine runs unevenly, if so the system is operating properly.

ELECTRONIC ENGINE CONTROLS

LH-Jetronic Fuel Injection System

▶ **See Figures 16 and 17**

➡ **For additional information, refer to SECTION 5 'Fuel System'.**

The LH-Jetronic Fuel Injection System is monitored by a self-diagnostic system that turns on a warning lamp on the instrument panel in the event of a component failure. The LH-Jetronic system also uses the EZK ignition system with a separate control unit to control the ignition circuit.

The LH-Jetronic system has a memory capability of up to 3 fault codes. Fault tracing can be carried out by actively utilizing the diagnostic procedure. A diagnostic socket is located behind the left strut tower. This socket is used for diagnosing various electronic systems.

Distinguishing features of the LH-Jetronic fuel injection system are:

1. Measures intake air mass through the mass meter, supplied with a hot wire.

2. Uses a separate cold start valve which supplies extra fuel, at or below 60°F (16°C).

3. It provides a richer fuel mixture to counteract knock when the fuel system anti-knock control system is unsuccessful at reducing knock by adjusting timing downward several degrees.

4. It is equipped with a Limp Home setting at the idle valve. In case of loss of current, the idle valve remains open to provide emergency air intake.

Fig. 15 Checking EGR vacuum system

5. It has an integrated shift indicator, related to vehicle speed and engine rpm. The indicator lamp turns on if the rpm for the next gear is higher than the pre-programmed limits.

CONTROL UNIT

The control unit incorporates a microprocessor that receives signals from the various sensors regarding operational conditions. It evaluates them in relation to pre-programmed values and calculates the correct injector opening durations.

The control unit governs idling rpm by regulating the amount of air bypassing the throttle valve. The most important function of the control unit is monitoring fault tracing through the diagnostic socket.

Control Unit Microprocessor Inputs

1. Exhaust gas oxygen content from the oxygen sensor.

2. RPM and crankshaft position information from the ignition system control unit. The fuel system will not function without this signal.

3. Engine temperature from the coolant temperature sensor.

4. Engine load information from the air mass meter.

5. Information from the throttle switch, indicates if the throttle plate is closed or wide open.

6. Electrical system voltage from the battery current.

7. A signal from the air conditioning switch informs if it is operating and the signal from the compressor connection indicates that the compressor is operating.

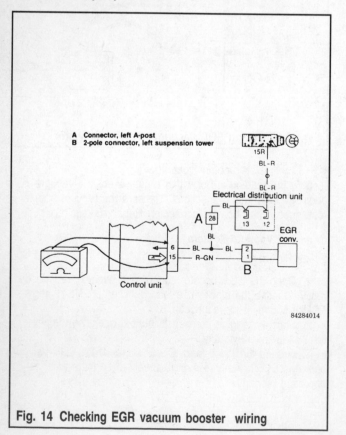

Fig. 14 Checking EGR vacuum booster wiring

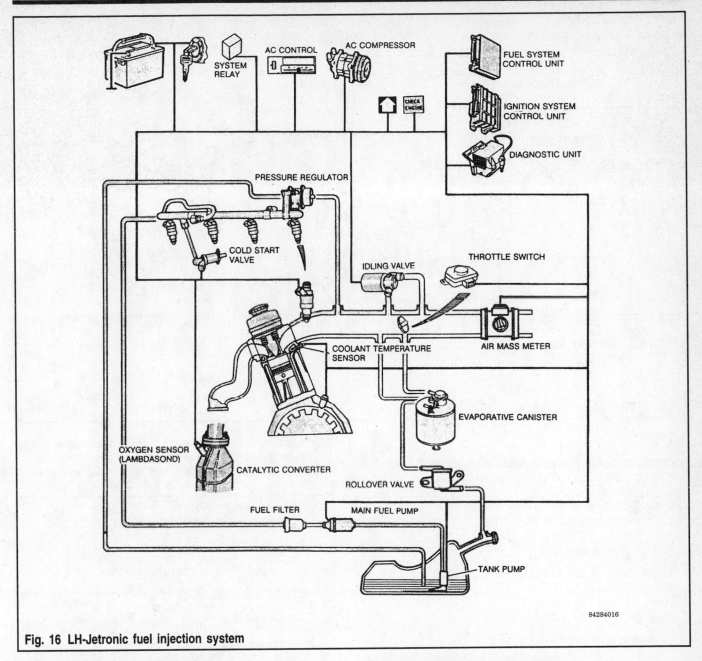

Fig. 16 LH-Jetronic fuel injection system

Control Unit Microprocessor Outputs

1. Sets system voltage by grounding the system relay.
2. Breaks system relay ground if engine turns over too slowly (engine stopped). This keeps the battery from being drained and cuts off fuel flow from the fuel pump.
3. Grounds injectors, which regulates opening, timing and injection duration.
4. Controls air valve for constant idle speed.
5. Provides the ignition system control unit with information.
6. Protects against engine over revving, shutting off the fuel injection until normal rpm is obtained.
7. Controls the check engine warning and shift indicator lamps.

Self-Adjusting Functions

The control unit is adaptive in that it adjusts its calculations according to input information.

Self-Adjusting Idle Speed Regulation

In time, wear will affect the operation of the throttle valve, causing less air to enter the intake system. Instead of working from a pre-programmed value, the idle valve receives a signal that is adapted to the experiences which the control unit has learned from previous driving conditions.

Self-Adjusting Oxygen Sensor

The oxygen sensor detects if the fuel mixture is rich or lean and adjusts the control unit's oxygen sensor regulator accordingly. This eliminates the need to adjust CO content and automatically compensates for the effects of tolerance and wear in the injection system or engine components.

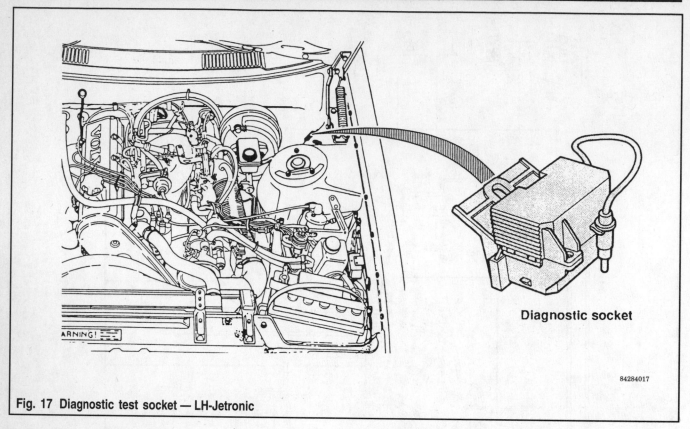

Diagnostic socket

84284017

Fig. 17 Diagnostic test socket — LH-Jetronic

Emergency Program

Incorporates a Limp Home function in the event of a malfunctioning component such as the signal from the air mass meter malfunctions. A pre-programmed value is used for fuel injection duration, allowing the vehicle to be driven with reduced power and performance.

FUEL SYSTEM PRESSURE

Testing

▶ **See Figures 18, 19 and 20**

1. Relieve the fuel system pressure:

   a. Remove the fuel pump relay. It is located next to the control unit on the 240 and in the fuse box behind the ash tray on 700 and 900 series. The relay is furthest to the left on the second row.

   b. Start the engine repeatedly until the engine will not start anymore, indicating that the fuel pressure is relieved.

2. Connect fuel pressure gauge 5011 or equivalent, between the fuel line and distribution pipe near the injectors. Block the free end of the gauge with a closed fitting.

3. Remove the panel under the right side of instrument panel and remove system relay.

4. Connect jumper lead across terminal No. 30 and terminal No. 87/2 of the system relay harness. Fuel pumps should now start to run.

5. Check to see if the main fuel pump is operating. The system pressure should be 42 psi (300 kPa).

   a. If the pressure is to high: remove the jumper wire, disconnect the return hose from the pressure regulator and

blow into the hose. Remove the vacuum hose from the regulator and blow into the hose. If both hoses are open, the regulator is defective. Replace and recheck the pressure.

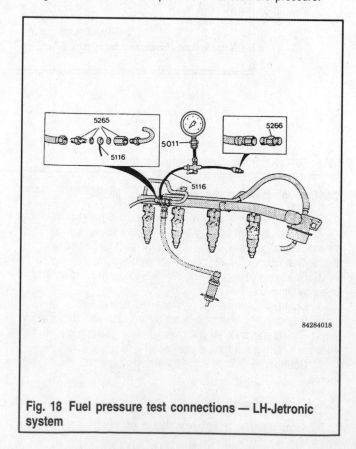

84284018

Fig. 18 Fuel pressure test connections — LH-Jetronic system

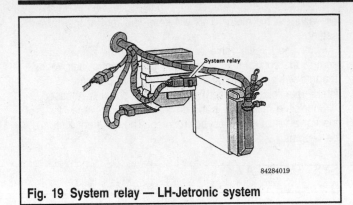

Fig. 19 System relay — LH-Jetronic system

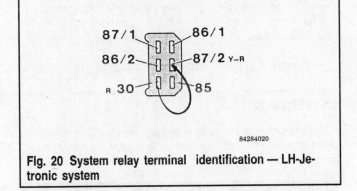

Fig. 20 System relay terminal identification — LH-Jetronic system

b. If the pressure is to low: squeeze the return hose and check that the pressure rises. Do not allow to go above 84 psi (600 kPa). If the pressure rises rapidly, replace the regulator and recheck pressure. If the pressure rises slowly, check the fuel filter, fuel pump strainer or lines for blockage.

c. If the pressure does not rise, the fuel pump is faulty. Replace and recheck pressure.

AIR MASS METER

Factors which affect air density, such as temperature, humidity and pressure are taken into consideration during measurement.

The sensor inside the air mass meter consists of a wire which is maintained at 250°F (120°C), above the temperature of the ambient air entering the engine. As the air mass passing over the wire increases, more current is required to maintain the correct temperature. The amount of current required is used to calculate the air mass taken in.

When the engine is turned off, any dirt on the wire is burned off electrically as the element is heated to a temperature of 1832°F (1000°C) for 1 second. Any dirt remaining on the wire would cause it to send incorrect signals to the control unit and result in an incorrect air/fuel mixture.

Check the resistance between terminals No. 2 and No. 3 of the sensor with the engine not running. The resistance should be 2.5-4.0 ohms. The mass air flow sensor is not an adjustable unit.

COOLANT TEMPERATURE SENSOR (CTS)

The coolant temperature sensor provides the injection and ignition control units with information regarding the engine temperature necessary for proper adjustment of injection duration. The CTS have a negative temperature coefficient, which means as the engine temperature rises the resistance through the sensor decreases.

Testing

Resistance across sensor terminals in ohms:
At 32°F (0°C): 7300 ohms
At 68°F (20°C): 2800 ohms
At 104°F (40°C): 1200 ohms
At 176°F (80°C): 300 ohms
At 212°F (100°C): 150 ohms

THROTTLE SWITCH

The throttle switch informs the ignition and injection control units whether the throttle valve is closed or fully opened for the purpose of fuel enrichment.

FUEL PRESSURE REGULATOR

The fuel pressure regulator ensures that fuel pressure remains constant at the injectors. Using a vacuum tube connected from the intake manifold to the pressure regulator the fuel pressure is kept at 42 psi at engine idle. At times of heavy engine load, no vacuum is present at the regulator thus raising fuel pressure slightly for fuel enrichment. Excess fuel is returned to the fuel tank through a return pipe.

INJECTORS

The injectors are fitted with a solenoid, a magnetic actuator and a fuel needle which opens or shuts a nozzle. The control unit sends current to the injectors in calculated time units, ensuring that all injectors spray a fine fuel mist. Injection occurs in the intake manifold near the intake valves.

COLD START VALVE

At cold start, fuel condenses on the cold surfaces in the form of drops. Some models are equipped with a cold start valve to improve engine cold starting. It is positioned farther away from the engine block than the injectors and delivers the fuel more as a gas than as drops. The cold start valve is controlled by the LH-Jetronic control unit, rather than the thermal switch. It operates when the temperature is approximately 5°F (-15°C) and when engine rpm is below 900 rpm. It cuts out when engine rpm exceeds the permissible limit. The cold start injector is not a serviceable unit, if defective replacement is the only option.

FUEL PUMP

The fuel pump is an electric pump, cooled by the fuel which flows through it. It incorporates a non-return valve and an overflow valve which opens when fuel pressure gets too high.

Both the primary pump and fuel pump operate when the starter motor or the engine is running. Should the engine stop while the ignition remains **ON**, the control unit will cut the current to the pumps.

IN-TANK FUEL PUMP (PRE-PUMP)

The in-tank fuel pump is an electric fuel pump that keeps pressure in the fuel line prior to the main fuel pump to prevent vapor lock. The pump incorporates a coarse strainer type filter and a non-return valve to maintain a constant amount of pressure in the system, even if the main pump is not operational.

FUEL FILTER

The fuel filter is adjacent to the main fuel pump and both are mounted on a plate under the vehicle on the drivers side.

IDLE AIR CONTROL VALVE

▶ **See Figure 21**

An idle valve is incorporated into the system to set the correct air valve opening and constant idle speed. The control unit uses information from the air mass meter regarding the amount of air entering the engine and from the ignition system control unit regarding rpm.

When current is off, a spring sets the idle valve opening for an idle speed between 1000-1100 rpm. When the engine is running, the control unit ensures that the idle valve opens at all engine speeds, in order to prevent a high negative pressure in the intake manifold when the throttle valve closes suddenly during deceleration.

The control unit receives a signal from the air conditioning control when the air conditioning is turned on or off, to enable the idle valve to be adjusted.

During idling, when the throttle plate switch is closed, the control unit receives a signal enabling it to send current to the air valve electric motor. This will keep idle rpm at the correct setting.

When the throttle valve switch is opened, no signals are sent to the control unit. When driving, the control unit keeps the idle valve partially open so the negative pressure in the intake manifold is reduced when the gas pedal is released.

Check the resistance between terminals No. 1 and No. 2 of the valve with the engine not running. The resistance should be 8 ohms.

SYSTEM RELAY

Controlled by the ECU, it provides current to the fuel pump, injectors, cold start valve, air mass meter and other control unit functions. The system relay and its functions are protected by a 20 amp fuse.

INJECTOR BALLAST RESISTOR PACK

▶ **See Figure 22**

The resistor cuts the voltage to each injector. The resistance between the center terminal and all 4 resistor terminals should be 5.5-6.5 ohms.

Volvo Regina Fuel Injection System

▶ **See Figure 23**

➡ **For additional diagnosis and testing, please refer to Section 5 'Fuel System'.**

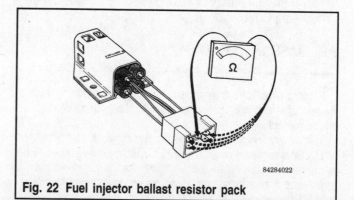

84284022

Fig. 22 Fuel injector ballast resistor pack

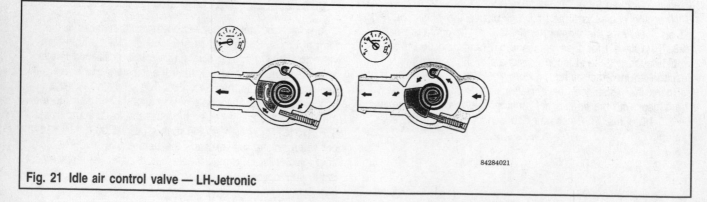

84284021

Fig. 21 Idle air control valve — LH-Jetronic

The Regina fuel injection system is a self diagnostic system that is capable of storing up to 3 fault codes in its memory. It is used in conjunction with the REX 1 ignition system. Both are adaptive systems, capable of multiple adjustments based on previous engine conditions. If a fault occurs, a warning lamp turns on at the instrument panel. Fault tracing can be carried out using the diagnostic program.

Regina fuel injection system components are generally color-coded yellow and the Volvo part number is imprinted. This is to reduce the possibility of using components from other similar injection systems by mistake.

Distinguishing features of the Regina fuel injection system are:

1. Engine load is calculated by measuring intake manifold pressure via a manifold absolute pressure (MAP) sensor.

2. Uses an intake air temperature sensor together with the manifold pressure sensor to calculate air intake volume.

3. Maintains a fuel pressure of 42 psi.

4. Uses a separate cold start valve, to ensure starting at low temperatures.

5. No adjustment of CO or minimum rpm is necessary.

6. Incorporates an automatic idle shut-off valve, if current is lost.

7. It has an integrated shift indicator, which is used according to vehicle speed and engine rpm. A warning lamp turns on, if the rpm for the next gear is higher than the pre-programmed limits.

8. Uses an induction sensor, mounted on the flywheel, to indicate rpm and crankshaft position through the ignition system control unit.

9. Uses an electrically heated oxygen sensor, which is affected by the oxygen concentration.

10. Incorporates a 3 way catalytic converter.

CONTROL UNIT

The Regina fuel system control unit is extremely compact and uses a double-sided printed circuit board. The multi-pin plug uses a filter to reduce interference and protect the electronics. It can operate at system voltage minimum of 6 volts. The microprocessor operates at a voltage of 5 volts.

The control unit incorporates a microprocessor that receives signals from various sensors regarding operational conditions, then evaluates them in relation to pre-programmed values and calculates the correct injector opening duration.

The control unit controls idling rpm by regulating the amount of air bypassing the throttle valve. It also controls other functions, such as the cold start valve, fuel pump and relay. The most important function is monitoring faults through the diagnostic unit.

Self-Adjusting Functions

The control unit adjusts its calculations according to pre-programmed values.

Self-Adjusting Idle Speed

In time, wear will affect the operation of the throttle valve, causing less air to enter the intake system. Instead of operating from a pre-programmed value, the idle valve receives a signal that is adapted to the condition which the control unit has learned from previous driving periods.

Self-Adjusting Oxygen Sensor

The oxygen sensor determines if the fuel mixture is rich or lean and adjusts the control unit's oxygen sensor regulator. The self-adjusting mechanism keeps the control unit function at mid point. Therefore, no adjustment is necessary for CO content and it automatically compensates for the effects and wear in the injection system. Whenever the vehicle is started and driven, the control unit will use the value that has been stored from previous engine operation.

Control Unit Micro-Processor Inputs

1. Signals from the pressure sensor and the air intake temperature sensor, regarding engine throttling.

2. RPM and crankshaft position information from the ignition system control unit.

➡ **If this information is not received, the system will not function.**

3. Engine temperature from the coolant temperature sensor.

4. Remaining oxygen level in the exhaust from the oxygen sensor.

5. Signals from the throttle switch, indicates if the throttle valve is closed or wide open.

6. System voltage from battery current.

7. A signal from the air conditioning switch to ensure that the switch is on and a signal from the compressor to indicate that the compressor is operating.

Emergency Program

Incorporates a Limp Home function for the pressure sensor, air temperature sensor and the coolant temperature sensor built into the control unit. If information is not obtained, the control unit uses 3 pre-programmed substitute values for intake manifold pressure. It results in the injection pattern being varied according to engine revolutions, allowing the vehicle to be driven without any major problems.

If the signal from the coolant temperature sensor is not present, the vehicle can still be driven as normal. However, there can be difficulties starting the engine since information on the engine temperature is used to adjust fuel mixture during cold start conditions.

Control Unit Micro-Processor Outputs

1. Sets system voltage by grounding the system relay.

2. Breaks the system relay ground if the engine turns over too slowly (has stopped). Prevents battery drain and cuts off fuel flow.

3. Regulates injector opening, timing and injection duration.

4. Controls the air valve for constant idle speed.

5. Controls the cold start injector.

6. Stores fault codes if faults are detected.

7. Provides load information to the ignition system.

8. Protects against engine over revving by cutting off the fuel injection until the engine rpm decreases.

9. Shuts off fuel injection during deceleration.

10. Controls indicator lamps (Check Engine and Gear Change).

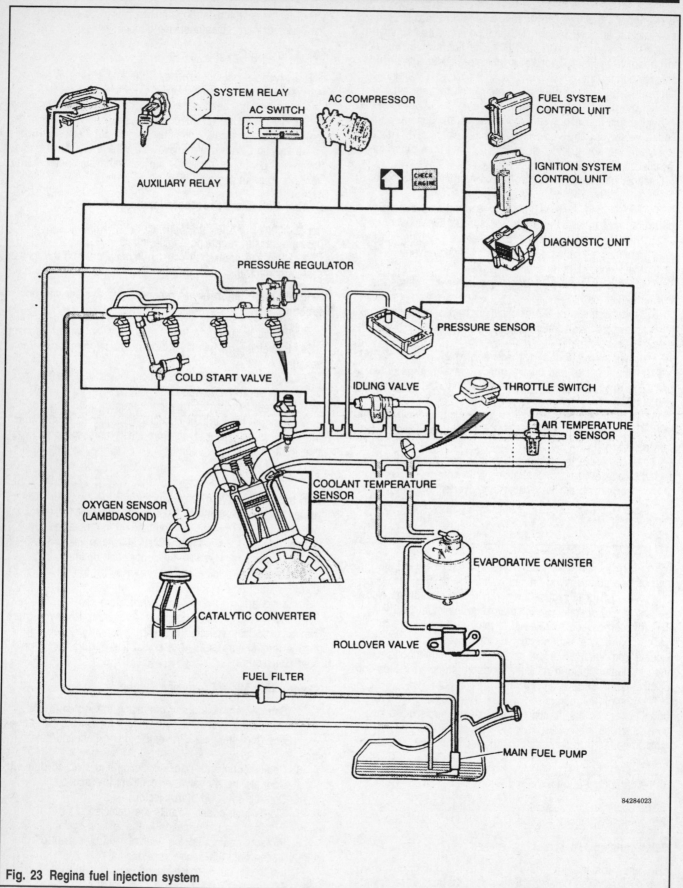

Fig. 23 Regina fuel injection system

FUEL SYSTEM PRESSURE TEST

▶ **See Figure 24**

1. Relieve the fuel system pressure:

   a. Remove the fuel pump relay from the electrical distribution unit. The relay is furthest to the left on the second row.

   b. Crank the engine until the engine will not start anymore, indicating that the fuel pressure is relieved. Reinstall the relay.

❊❊CAUTION

To avoid fire and personal injury, replace any plastic tie bands removed from the fuel lines.

2. Connect fuel pressure gauge 5011 or equivalent, between the fuel line and distribution pipe near the injectors. Block the free end of the gauge with a closed fitting.

3. Remove the system relay from the electrical distribution unit. This test will be performed easier if the seat belt reminder is disconnected.

4. Connect jumper lead across terminal No. 30 and terminal No. 87/2 of the system relay harness. Fuel pumps should now start to run.

5. Check to see if the main fuel pump is operating. The system pressure should be 42 psi (300 kPa).

   a. If the pressure is too high: remove the jumper wire, disconnect the return hose from the pressure regulator and blow into the hose. Remove the vacuum hose from the regulator and blow into the hose. If both hoses are open, the regulator is defective. Replace and recheck the pressure.

   b. If the pressure is too low: squeeze the return hose and check that the pressure rises. Do not allow to go above 84 psi (600 kPa). If the pressure rises rapidly, replace the regulator and recheck pressure. If the pressure rises slowly, check the fuel filter, fuel pump strainer or lines for blockage.

   c. If the pressure does not rise, the fuel pump is faulty. Replace and recheck pressure.

AIR PRESSURE SENSOR

▶ **See Figure 25**

The most important information for measuring engine fuel requirements comes from the pressure sensor. Using the pressure and temperature data, the micro-processor calculates the intake air mass. It is connected to the engine intake manifold through a hose and takes readings of the absolute pressure. A piezoelectric crystal changes a voltage input to an electrical output which reflects the pressure in the intake manifold.

Atmospheric pressure is measured both when the engine is started and when driving fully loaded, then the pressure sensor information is adjusted accordingly.

The pressure sensor terminal has 3 connectors A, B and C. A is ground, B carries the output signal to the control unit and C provides the pressure sensor with 5 volts of current from the control unit. The output varies between 0.5-5.0 volts depending on intake manifold pressure. When the engine is not running, atmospheric pressure will register at full potential. The sensor is sensitive to electrical disturbances, therefore it is protected by a metal cover. The signal strength should be about 4.4 volts at atmospheric pressure.

Testing

Test the output voltage at B terminal with the C terminal connected. Results should be as follows:

- 4.4 volts at 100 kPa
- 3.2 volts at 80 kPa
- 2.1 volts at 60 kPa
- 1.1 volts at 40 kPa
- 0.5 volts at 20 kPa

INTAKE AIR TEMPERATURE SENSOR

▶ **See Figure 26**

Information from this sensor is added to the pressure sensor information to calculate the air mass being sent to the cylinders. The air mass passes through holes in the sensor and over a bulb which sends a temperature signal to the control unit. The sensor have a negative temperature coefficient. As the temperature of the sensor rises the resistance across the sensor decreases.

Testing

The resistance at a specific temperature should be:

- At -40°F (-40°C): 45,000 ohms
- At -4°F (-20°C): 15,000 ohms at -4°F (-20°C)
- At 32°F (0°C): 8500 ohms at 32°F (0°C)
- At 68°F (20°C): 2500 ohms at 68°F (20°C)
- At 176°F (80°C): 330 ohms at 176°F (80°C)

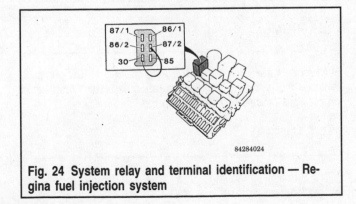

84284024

Fig. 24 System relay and terminal identification — Regina fuel injection system

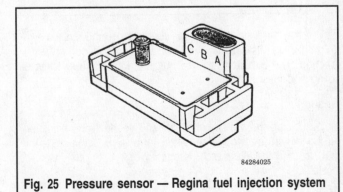

84284025

Fig. 25 Pressure sensor — Regina fuel injection system

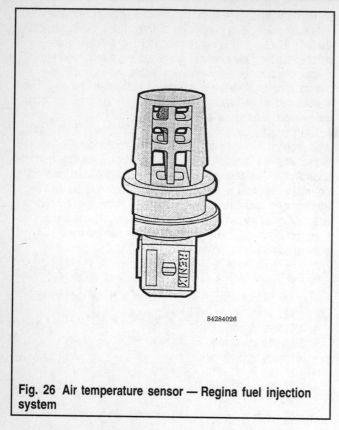

84284026

Fig. 26 Air temperature sensor — Regina fuel injection system

COOLANT TEMPERATURE SENSOR

While the engine is warming up, the mixture enrichment function is regulated by the control unit using information received from the coolant temperature sensor. Like the air temperature sensor, this sensor have a negative temperature coefficient. As the temperature of the sensor rises the resistance across the sensor decreases. The sensors output is used by the ignition and the injection control units.

Testing

The resistance from each terminal to ground should be:
- At 14°F (-10°C): 10,560-8260 ohms
- At 68°F (20°C): 2280-2720 ohms
- At 176°F (80°C): 290-364 ohms

THROTTLE SWITCH

The throttle switch informs the fuel system and ignition system control units whether the throttle valve is closed or fully opened. The throttle switch is equipped with micro-switches for idling and full load running.

Testing

1. Unplug the switch connector and connect an ohmmeter to the switch terminals. The center terminal is common, terminal No. 1 is the idle switch, terminal No. 3 is the full load switch.

2. The idle switch should be closed when the throttle is closed. Any movement of the throttle lever will open the switch just before the throttle plate actually opens. Operate the switch by hand if necessary to determine a faulty switch or faulty adjustment.

3. Connect the ohmmeter to the full load switch. The switch should close when the throttle lever is 70 degrees off idle, about ⅓ of full stroke.

4. If the switches are good but do not operate at the proper throttle angles, check throttle cable adjustment.

FUEL PRESSURE REGULATOR

The fuel pressure regulator ensures that fuel pressure remains constant at the injectors. Using a vacuum tube connected from the intake manifold to the pressure regulator the fuel pressure is kept at 42 psi at engine idle. At times of heavy engine load, no vacuum is present at the regulator thus raising fuel pressure slightly for fuel enrichment. Excess fuel is returned to the fuel tank through a return pipe.

FUEL INJECTORS

By activating the relay, the control unit sends current to the injectors. It controls injection duration by grounding the injectors. When the starter motor is operating, there are 2 injections per rotation to aid starting and 1 during normal driving. Injection occurs in the intake manifold near the intake valves.

While the Regina fuel injectors may appear similar to other injectors, they should never be interchanged. Regina injectors have different design characteristics and can be identified by yellow markings and Volvo part numbers.

COLD START VALVE

The cold start valve is operated directly by the control unit and is located under the intake manifold near the throttle valve. It is supplied with fuel through a hose connected to the distribution pipe.

At cold start, fuel condenses on the cold surfaces. Using a separate cold start valve improves engine cold starting. It is positioned farther away from the engine block then the injectors and delivers the fuel more in the form of vapor than in drops. It operates when the temperature is 5°F (-15°C) or below and when engine speed is below 1050 rpm. It cuts out when engine rpm exceeds the permissible limit.

FUEL PUMP

All models are equipped with a 2-stage electric fuel pump. It replaces the primary pump and the pre-pump which were used on previous models. It is located in the fuel tank.

FUEL FILTER

The fuel filter is mounted on a plate underneath the vehicle on the left side.

IDLE VALVE

▶ See Figure 27

The magnetic idle valve is mounted on a bracket under the intake manifold. As the control unit sends different current levels to the magnet actuator, a magnetized core is either drawn in or pushed out. A plate is attached to the core which allows a specific amount of air to pass. When no current is supplied, the idle valve is closed and the engine cannot idle.

The idle valve operates at all engine rpm. This prevents high negative pressure from forming in the intake manifold when the throttle valve is closed at high engine rpm.

The control unit uses information from engine rpm and the throttle valve position to determine the idle speed. The idle valve receives a control signal based on previous driving, instead of using a pre-programmed value stored in the control unit.

A built in system for increasing engine rpm causes the idle speed to increase slowly when the air conditioning is turned on. When the compressor cuts in, a load signal is sent to the control unit which compensates for the increased engine load to ensure that the rpm does not fluctuate.

Testing

The resistance between terminals No. 1 and No. 2 should be 4 ohms.

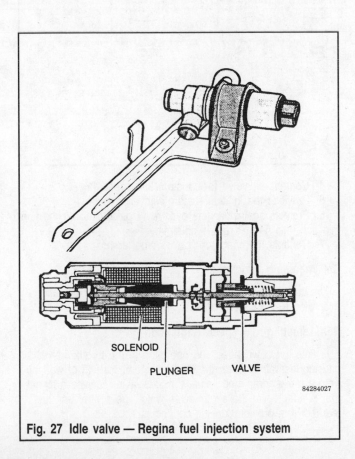

SOLENOID

PLUNGER   VALVE

84284027

Fig. 27 Idle valve — Regina fuel injection system

SYSTEM RELAY

The fuel injection system relay is located in the fuse/relay box and is controlled by the fuel system control unit. It supplies current to the fuel pumps and to certain control unit functions.

AUXILIARY RELAY

The auxiliary relay, mounted in the engine compartment, in front of the right shock tower, is controlled by the system relay. It supplies current to the injectors and the cold start valve. It diminishes the possibility of electrical interference by separating the cable harnesses from the system.

Motronic Fuel Injection System

▶ See Figure 28

➡ **For additional information, refer to SECTION 5 'Fuel System'.**

The Motronic fuel injection system, used in the Volvo 960, is equipped with a control unit which monitors the ignition and fuel injection functions by means of individual ignition coils and individual fuel injectors. Combining the control of these functions in a single unit conserves space and wiring.

Fault tracing is facilitated by the diagnostics incorporated in the Motronic system. Access to these is provided by the diagnostic unit in the engine compartment.

Apart from controlling the ignition and fuel injection functions, Motronic also:
- Determines whether or not the A/C compressor may be switched on.
- Reduces engine torque in response to a signal from the automatic transmission control unit, to ensure smooth engagement of the different gears.
- Provides a Limp Home mode to adapt to a failed component. The engine will perform with reduced power.
- Controls operation of the radiator fan.

The control unit is provided with adaptive Lambda control and idling control functions, with a timing retardation to eliminate engine knock. The service requirement is minimal, since neither the CO level nor the idling speed requires an adjustment.

CONTROL UNIT

The control unit incorporates a microprocessor that receives signals from the various sensors regarding operational conditions. It evaluates them in relation to pre-programmed values and calculates the correct injector opening durations.

The most important function of the control unit is monitoring fault tracing through the diagnostic socket. The control unit also governs idling rpm by regulating the amount of air bypassing the throttle valve.

Control Unit Microprocessor Inputs

1. Exhaust gas oxygen content from the oxygen sensor.

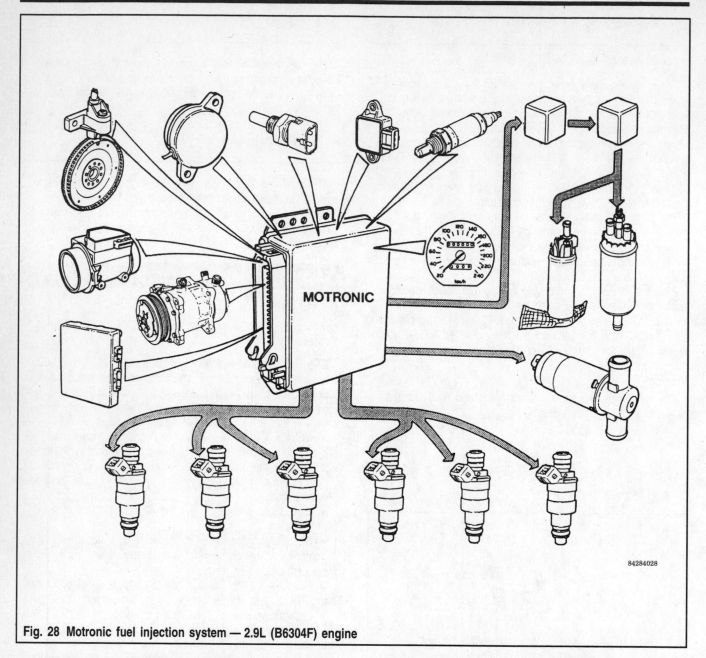

Fig. 28 Motronic fuel injection system — 2.9L (B6304F) engine

2. RPM and crankshaft position information.
3. Engine temperature from the coolant temperature sensor.
4. Engine load information from the air mass meter.
5. Information from the throttle switch, indicates if the throttle plate is closed or wide open.
6. Electrical system voltage from the battery current.
7. A signal from the air conditioning switch informs if it is operating and the signal from the compressor connection indicates that the compressor is operating.

Control Unit Microprocessor Outputs

1. Sets system voltage by grounding the system relay.
2. Breaks system relay ground if engine turns over too slowly (engine stopped). This keeps the battery from being drained and cuts off fuel flow from the fuel pump.
3. Grounds injectors, which regulates opening, timing and injection duration.

4. Controls air valve for constant idle speed.
5. Provides the ignition system with information.
6. Protects against engine over revving, shutting off the fuel injection until normal rpm is obtained.
7. Controls the check engine warning lamps.

Self-Adjusting Functions

The control unit is adaptive in that it adjusts its calculations according to input information.

Self-Adjusting Idle Speed Regulation

In time, wear will affect the operation of the throttle valve, causing less air to enter the intake system. Instead of working from a pre-programmed value, the idle valve receives a signal that is adapted to the experiences which the control unit has learned from previous driving conditions.

Self-Adjusting Oxygen Sensor

The oxygen sensor detects if the fuel mixture is rich or lean and adjusts the control unit's oxygen sensor regulator accordingly. This eliminates the need to adjust CO content and automatically compensates for the effects of tolerance and wear in the injection system or engine components.

Emergency Program

Incorporates a Limp Home function in the event of a malfunctioning component such as the signal from the air mass meter malfunctions. A pre-programmed value is used for fuel injection duration, allowing the vehicle to be driven with reduced power and performance.

FUEL SYSTEM PRESSURE

▶ **See Figures 29 and 30**

Testing

1. Relieve the fuel system pressure:
   a. With the ignition **OFF**, remove fuel pump fuses 30 and 31.
   b. Try starting and allowing the vehicle to run a few times until it will not stay running any more.
2. Connect fuel pressure gauge 5011 or equivalent, between the fuel line and distribution pipe near the injectors. Block the free end of the gauge with a closed fitting.
3. Remove the panel under the right side of instrument panel and remove fuses No. 30 and 31.
4. Connect jumper lead across right-hand fuse terminals. Fuel pumps should now star to run.

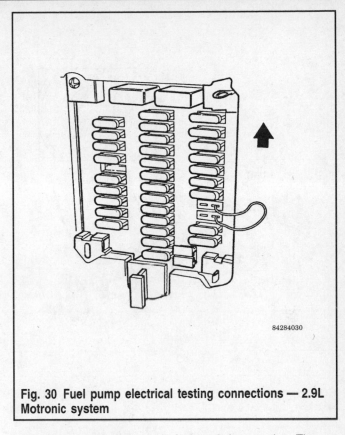

84284030

Fig. 30 Fuel pump electrical testing connections — 2.9L Motronic system

5. Check to see if the main fuel pump is operating. The system pressure should be 42 psi (300 kPa).
   a. If the pressure is too high: remove the jumper wire, disconnect the return hose from the pressure regulator and blow into the hose. Remove the vacuum hose from the regulator and blow into the hose. If both hoses are open, the regulator is defective. Replace and recheck the pressure.
   b. If the pressure is too low: squeeze the return hose and check that the pressure rises. Do not allow to go above 84 psi (600 kPa). If the pressure rises rapidly, replace the regulator and recheck pressure. If the pressure rises slowly, check the fuel filter, fuel pump strainer or lines for blockage.
   c. If the pressure does not rise, the fuel pump is faulty. Replace and recheck pressure.

AIR MASS METER

▶ **See Figure 31**

Factors which affect air density, such as temperature, humidity and pressure are taken into consideration during measurement.

The sensor inside the air mass meter consists of a wire which is maintained at 250°F (120°C), above the ambient air temperature of the air entering the engine. As the air mass passing over the wire increases, more current is required to maintain the correct temperature. The amount of current required is used to calculate the air mass taken in.

When the engine is turned off, any dirt on the wire is burned off electrically as the element is heated to a temperature of 1832°F (1000°C) for 1 second. Any dirt remaining on the wire

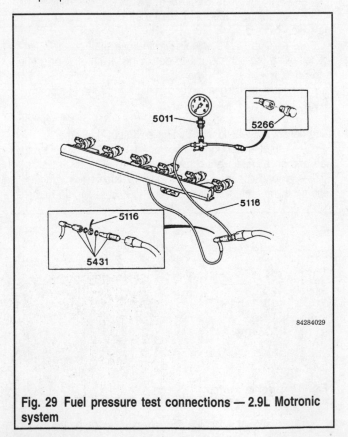

84284029

Fig. 29 Fuel pressure test connections — 2.9L Motronic system

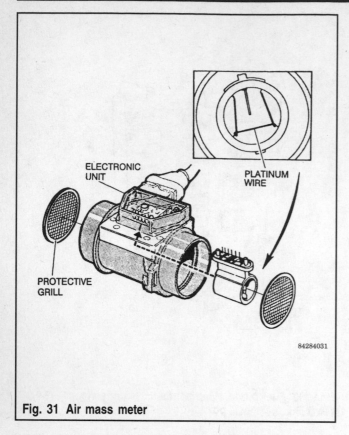

ELECTRONIC UNIT

PLATINUM WIRE

PROTECTIVE GRILL

84284031

Fig. 31 Air mass meter

would cause it to send incorrect signals to the control unit and result in an incorrect air/fuel mixture.

With the ignition **OFF**, check the resistance between terminals No. 2 and No. 3 of the sensor. The resistance should be 2.5-4.0 ohms. The mass air flow sensor is not an adjustable unit.

COOLANT TEMPERATURE SENSOR (CTS)

The coolant temperature sensor provides the control unit with information necessary for proper adjustment of injection duration. The CTS have a negative temperature coefficient, which means as the engine temperature rises the resistance through the sensor decreases.

Testing

Resistance across sensor terminals in ohms at:
- 32°F (0°C): 7300 ohms
- 68°F (20°C): 2800 ohms
- 104°F (40°C): 1200 ohms
- 176°F (80°C): 300 ohms
- 212°F (100°C): 150 ohms

THROTTLE SWITCH

▶ **See Figure 32**

The throttle switch informs the Motronic control unit whether the throttle valve is closed or fully opened for the purpose of

fuel enrichment. The resistance across terminals No. 1 and terminals No. 3 of the throttle switch should be 1000 ohms at idle and 700 ohms at full throttle. The throttle switch should be tested with the engine not running.

FUEL PRESSURE REGULATOR

The fuel pressure regulator ensures that fuel pressure remains constant at the injectors. By using a vacuum tube connected from the intake manifold to the pressure regulator, the fuel pressure is kept at 42 psi at engine idle. At times of heavy engine load, no vacuum is present at the regulator thus raising fuel pressure slightly for fuel enrichment. Excess fuel is returned to the fuel tank through a return pipe.

INJECTORS

The injectors are fitted with a solenoid, a magnetic actuator and a fuel needle which opens or shuts a nozzle. The control unit sends current to the injectors in calculated time units, ensuring that all injectors spray a fine fuel mist. The injector circuits are divided into 2 groups of 3 injectors each.

One group of injectors supplies fuel to cylinders No. 1, 2 and 4, while the second supplies fuel to injectors No. 3, 5 and 6. The two group arrangement has been adopted to ensure that fuel injection takes place as soon possible after injector opening.

Under normal conditions, each group of injectors is activated once every second crankshaft revolution. To compute the fuel injection the control unit uses:
— An engine load signal from the mass air sensor.
— An engine speed and crankshaft position signal from the timing pick-up.
— A piston stroke signal from the camshaft position sensor, enabling the control unit to determine which injector group is to be activated.
— The exhaust gas oxygen content from the Lambda (oxygen) sensor.
— An engine temperature signal from the coolant temperature sensor for functions including cold start enrichment.
— A throttle position signal from the throttle switch for full load and acceleration enrichment.
— A road speed signal from the speedometer for functions including fuel shut-off at speeds in excess of 140 mph.

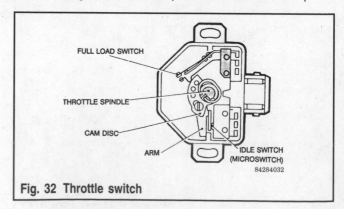

FULL LOAD SWITCH

THROTTLE SPINDLE

CAM DISC

ARM

IDLE SWITCH (MICROSWITCH)

84284032

Fig. 32 Throttle switch

CAMSHAFT SENSOR

▶ **See Figure 33**

The camshaft sensor is located at the rear of the cylinder head on the exhaust manifold side. The signal from this sensor is used to determine which pair of pistons (1-6, 5-2 or 3-4) is simultaneously approaching TDC. Together with the timing pick-up sensor, this enables the unit to identify the stroke being performed by each of the pistons in questions. The crankshaft sensor is a Hall effect sensor.

IGNITION COILS AND POWER UNITS

▶ **See Figures 34 and 35**

The ignition coils are mounted directly on the spark plugs. Two power units, mounted on the intake manifold for efficient cooling, are used to control the ignition coils. The front unit is connected to cylinders No. 1, 3 and 5, while the rear unit serves cylinders No. 2, 4 and 6. Each power unit incorporates three power stages, each connected to a coil assembly.

The use of an individual coil for each cylinder guarantees an extremely rapid voltage rise and an extremely high ignition voltage.

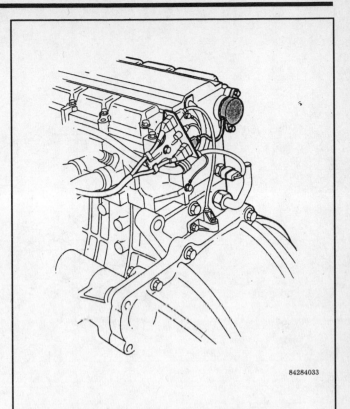

84284033

Fig. 33 Camshaft position sensor — 2.9L engine

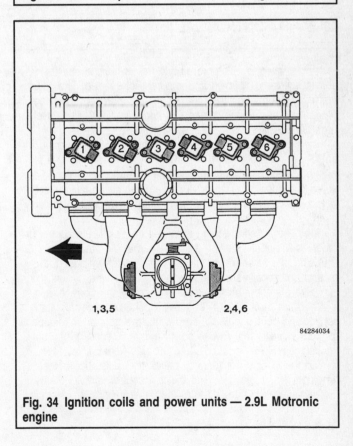

1,3,5   2,4,6

84284034

Fig. 34 Ignition coils and power units — 2.9L Motronic engine

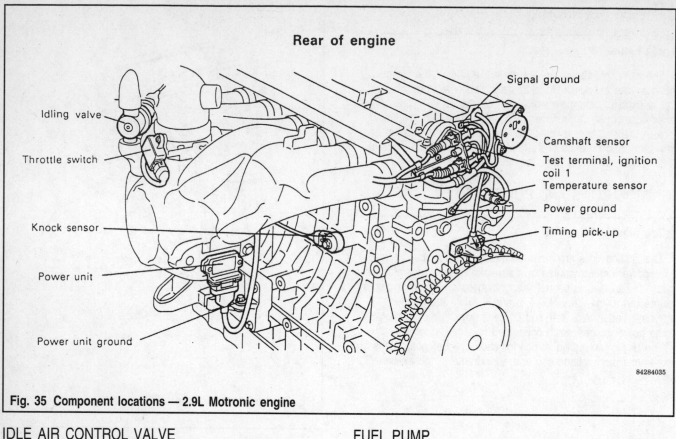

Rear of engine

Idling valve

Throttle switch

Knock sensor

Power unit

Power unit ground

Signal ground

Camshaft sensor

Test terminal, ignition coil 1

Temperature sensor

Power ground

Timing pick-up

84284035

Fig. 35 Component locations — 2.9L Motronic engine

IDLE AIR CONTROL VALVE

An idle valve is incorporated into the system to set the correct air valve opening and constant idle speed. The control unit uses information from the air mass meter regarding the amount of air entering the engine and from the ignition system regarding engine rpm.

When current is off, a spring sets the idle valve opening for an idle speed between 1000-1100 rpm. When the engine is running, the control unit ensures that the idle valve opens at all engine speeds, in order to prevent a high negative pressure in the intake manifold when the throttle valve closes suddenly during deceleration.

When the air conditioning is turned on or off, the control unit receives a signal enabling it to adjust the idle valve.

During idling, when the throttle valve switch is closed, the control unit receives a signal, enabling it to send current to the air valve electric motor to keep idle rpm at the correct setting.

When the throttle valve switch is opened, no signals are sent to the control unit. When driving, the control unit keeps the idle valve partially open so the negative pressure in the intake manifold is reduced when the gas pedal is released.

With the engine not running, check the resistance across terminals No. 1 and No. 3 of the idle control valve. Be sure to disconnect wiring harness from the valve for proper readings, the resistance should be 25 ohms.

FUEL PUMP

The fuel pump is an electric roller pump, cooled by the fuel which flows through it. It incorporates an in-line check valve and an overflow valve which opens when fuel pressure exceeds preset limits.

Both the primary in-tank pump and external fuel pump operate when the starter motor or the engine is running. Should the engine stop while the ignition remains **ON**, the control unit will stop the electrical current to the pumps.

IN-TANK FUEL PUMP (PRE-PUMP)

The electric in-tank fuel pump keeps pressure in the fuel line prior to the main fuel pump to prevent vapor lock. The pump incorporates a coarse strainer filter and a non-return or check valve to maintain a constant amount of pressure in the system, even if the main pump is not operating.

FUEL FILTER

The fuel filter is adjacent to the main fuel pump and both are mounted on a plate under the vehicle on the drivers side.

TROUBLE CODES

▶ **See Figures 36, 37 and 38**

For more information on system or component diagnosis,
please refer to Section 5 in this manual.

Code	Fault	Correction Test
1-1-1	No faults	—
1-1-2	Fault in control unit ①	Control unit
1-1-3	Fault in injector	Injector
1-2-1	Signal to/from air mass meter faulty	Air mass meter
1-2-3	Signal missing to/from coolant temperature sensor	Coolant temperature sensor
1-3-1	Ignition System RPM signal missing	RPM sensor
1-3-2	Battery voltage too low/high ②	Charging system
1-3-3	Throttle-Switch; idle setting faulty, possible grounding short	Throttle switch
2-1-2	Oxygen sensor signal missing or is faulty	Oxygen sensor or heater
2-1-3	Throttle-Switch; full load setting faulty possible grounding short	Throttle switch
2-2-1	Oxygen sensor not operating	Oxygen sensor or heater
2-2-3	Signal missing to/from idle valve	Idle valve
2-3-1	Self-adjusting oxygen sensor not operating	Air intake system or fuel system
2-3-2	Self-adjusting oxygen sensor not operating	Air intake system or fuel system
2-3-3	Idle valve closed, possibly leaking air	Idle valve
2-4-1	EGR system malfunction ③	EGR vacuum booster
3-1-1	Signal missing from speedometer	Speedometer signal
3-1-2	Signal missing for knock related fuel enrichment	Knock enrichment signal
3-2-2	Burn-off cleaning of hot wire in air mass meter not operating	Air mass meter hot wire
4-1-3	EGR temperature sensor signal absent or faulty ③	EGR temperature signal

① Change control unit
② Check battery and charging system
③ California

84285032

Fig. 36 Fault code descriptions — LH-Jetronic

Code	Fault	Correction Test
1-1-1	No faults	—
1-1-2	Fault in control unit ①	Control unit
1-1-3	Fault in injector	Injector
1-2-1	Signal missing or faulty, to/from pressure sensor	Pressure sensor
1-2-2	Signal missing or faulty, to/from air temperature sensor	Air temperature sensor
1-2-3	Signal missing to/from coolant temperature sensor, possible grounding short	Coolant temperature sensor
1-3-2	Battery voltage too low/high ②	Charging system
1-3-3	Throttle-Switch; idle setting faulty, possible grounding short	Throttle switch
2-1-2	Oxygen sensor signal missing or faulty	Oxygen sensor
2-1-3	Throttle-Switch; full load setting faulty, possible grounding short	Throttle switch
2-2-1	Oxygen sensor not operating	Oxygen sensor or air leak
2-2-2	Fault in system relay	System relay
2-2-3	Signal missing to/from idle valve	Idle valve
2-3-1	Self-adjusting oxygen sensor not operating	Intake air or fuel system
2-3-2	Self-adjusting oxygen sensor not operating	Intake air or fuel system
2-3-3	Idle valve closed	Idle valve
2-4-1	EGR system malfunction ③	EGR vacuum booster
3-1-1	Signal missing from speedometer	Speedometer signal
3-2-1	Signal missing or faulty to/from cold start valve	Auxiliary relay
4-1-3	EGR temperature sensor circuit ③	EGR temperature sensor

① Change control unit
② Check battery and charging system
③ California

84285069

Fig. 37 Diagnostic fault codes — Regina fuel system

Code	Fault	Correction Test
1-1-1	No faults	—
1-1-2	Fault in control unit	Control unit
1-1-3	Fault in injector	Injector
1-2-1	Air mass meter signal absent or faulty	Air mass meter
1-2-3	Engine temperature signal absent or faulty	Temperature sensor
1-3-1	No signal from timing pick-up	Timing pick-up
1-3-2	Battery voltage too low or too high ①	Battery voltage
1-4-3	Front knock sensor signal absent or faulty	Front knock sensor
2-1-2	Oxygen sensor signal absent or faulty	Oxygen sensor
2-1-4	Timing pick-up signal absent intermittently	Timing pick-up
2-2-3	Idling valve signal absent or faulty	Idle valve
2-3-1	Adaptive lambda control lean or rich in part-load range	Oxygen sensor
2-3-2	Adaptive lambda control lean or rich at idling	Oxygen sensor
2-3-3	Adaptive idling control outside control range	Idle speed
2-4-1	EGR system malfunction ②	EGR vacuum booster
2-4-3	Signal from throttle switch absent or faulty	Throttle switch
3-1-1	Speedometer signal absent	Speed sensor
3-1-4	Camshaft sensor signal absent	Camshaft sensor
3-2-2	Air mass meter burn-off signal absent	Air mass meter
4-3-1	Signal from EGR temperature sender absent or faulty ②	EGR temperature sensor
4-3-3	Rear knock sensor signal absent or faulty	Rear knock sensor

① Check charging system
② California

84285106

Fig. 38 Fault code descriptions — Motronic

VACUUM DIAGRAMS

▶ See Figures 39, 40 and 41

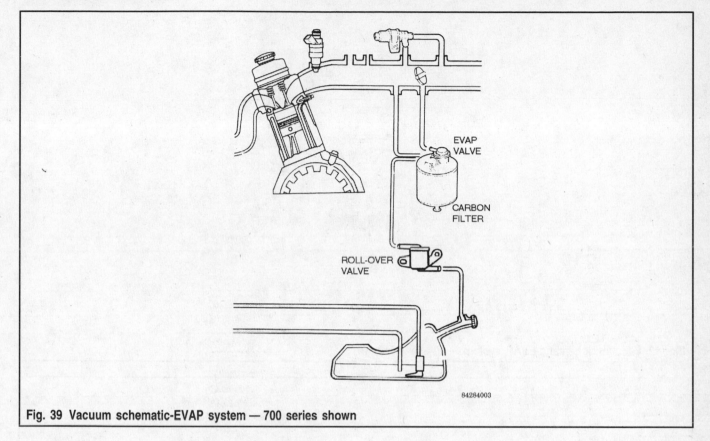

Fig. 39 Vacuum schematic-EVAP system — 700 series shown

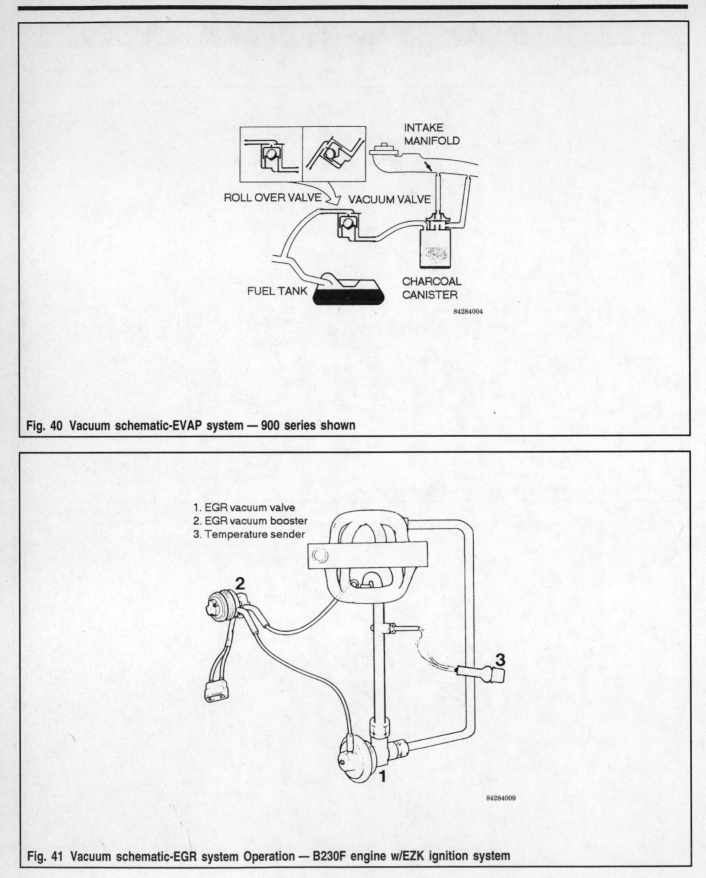

Fig. 40 Vacuum schematic-EVAP system — 900 series shown

1. EGR vacuum valve
2. EGR vacuum booster
3. Temperature sender

Fig. 41 Vacuum schematic-EGR system Operation — B230F engine w/EZK ignition system

5

FUEL
SYSTEM

FUEL INJECTION SYSTEM

Volvo uses three basic fuel injection systems on their 1990-93 models. These systems are as follows:
- Bosch LH-Jetronic Fuel System
- Bendix Regina Fuel System
- Bosch Motronic 1.8 Fuel System

Each system is covered individually. When service and/or repairs must be perform, refer to the specific system for your vehicle.

LH-JETRONIC FUEL INJECTION SYSTEM

Description and Operation

▶ **See Figure 1**

LH denotes that this is a 'hot wire' system. The system is fully electronically controlled and incorporate a number of sensors, whose signals are processed by a control unit. The LH Jectronic system is used in combination with the EZK ignition system and the turbocharged control system, where applicable. The LH fuel system is characterized by the following: — Measurement of intake air through the air mass meter of the hot wire type

— Use of a separate cold start valve that supplies extra fuel, at or below 60°F (16°C)

— Knock controlled fuel enrichment system

— Engine speed taken from the an inductive transmitter on the flywheel

— Lambda probe (oxygen sensor) providing oxygen content of the exhaust gases

— EVAP system to minimize evaporation from the fuel tank

— Three-way catalytic converter

Several sensors feed the control unit information to precisely control fuel injection. To accomplish this, the control unit evaluates: exhaust gas oxygen content from the oxygen sensor (Lambda-sond), engine RPM and crankshaft position information from the ignition system control unit (If information is not received, the fuel system control unit will not function), engine temperature from the coolant temperature sensor, engine load information from the air mass meter, information from the throttle switch, which indicates if the throttle is closed or wide open, electrical system voltage from the battery current and signals from the A/C switch and clutch, indicating whether they are operating.

System Components

Electronic Control Unit

The control unit incorporates a microprocessor that receives signals from the various sensors regarding operational conditions. It evaluates them in relation to pre-programmed values and calculates the correct injector opening durations.

The control unit governs idling rpm by regulating the amount of air by-passing the throttle valve. It also controls the cold start valve, the fuel pump and the fuel pump relay. An important function of the control unit is monitoring conditions leading to faults, accessible through the diagnostic unit.

Over a period of time the throttle valve will become worn, causing less air to enter the intake system. Instead of working

from a pre-programmed value, the idle valve receives a signal that is adapted to the experiences which the control unit has learned from previous driving conditions.

The limp home function allows the vehicle to be driven at a low speed in the event of an air mass meter malfunction, such as the hot wire breaking. A pre-programmed value is used for injection duration, allowing the vehicle to make its nearby destination safely.

DATA SENSORS

Air Mass Meter

This device measures the engine intake air mass. Factors that affect air density, such as temperature, humidity and pressure are compensated for during measurement.

The sensor inside the air mass meter consists of a wire which is maintained at 250°F (121°C) higher than the ambient air entering the engine. As the air mass passing over the wire increases, more current is required to maintain the correct temperature. The amount of current required to maintain this temperature is used to calculate the intake air mass.

When the engine is turned off, any dirt on the wire is burned off electrically by heating the wire to 1800°F (1000°C). If dirt were to remain on the wire, it would cause incorrect signals to be sent to the control unit and result in an incorrect air/fuel mixture.

Engine Temperature Sensor
▶ **See Figure 2**

The engine temperature sensor, located in the cylinder head, provides the control unit with information necessary for proper adjustment of injection duration and the idle speed in relationship to the engine temperature.

Throttle Switch
▶ **See Figure 3**

The throttle switch sends signals to the control unit for the fuel and ignition systems on whether the throttle valve is closed. It does not function as a variable resistor. It also indicates whether the throttle valve is fully open, except on turbocharged models.

Lambda Sond Probe (Oxygen Sensor)

The oxygen sensor is mounted in the catalytic converter. It produces a measurable current by comparing the amount of oxygen in the exhaust gas with the amount in the ambient air.

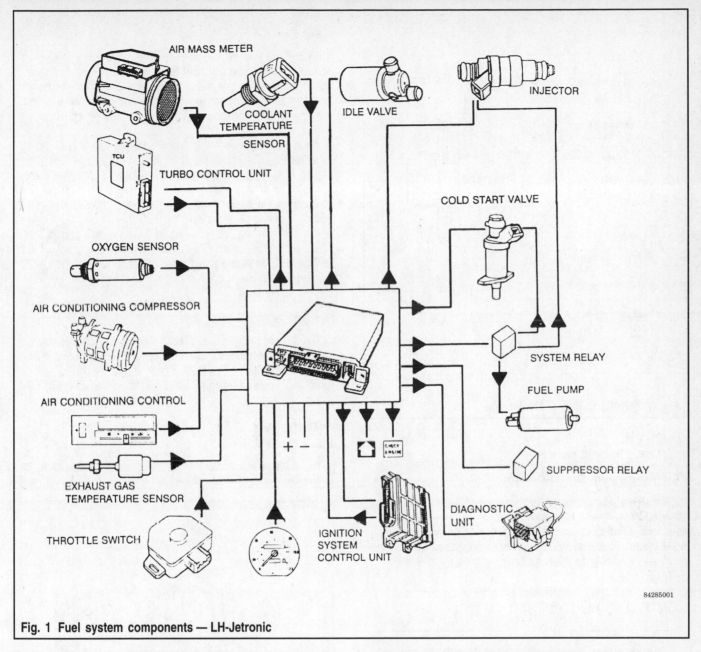

Fig. 1 Fuel system components — LH-Jetronic

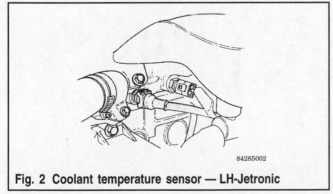

Fig. 2 Coolant temperature sensor — LH-Jetronic

Under normal conditions, the optimum air/fuel ratio is 14.7:1. This ratio is monitored by post-combustion measurement of the oxygen content in the exhaust gas using the oxygen sensor.

The oxygen sensor operating temperature ranges from 545°-1530°F (285°-832°C). It is electrically heated to enable it to reach operating temperature quickly. When ignition is turned to the **ON** position, current is sent to a resistor whose resistance increases with rising temperature. As a result the oxygen sensor quickly reaches operating temperature, even at low exhaust gas temperature.

The exhaust gases reach the outer surface of the sensor through slits in the protective sleeve. Ambient air reaches the sensors inner surface through channels. The sensor consists of a platinum covered zirconium-oxide pipe.

The signal strength is in direct proportion to the amount of oxygen in the exhaust gases. This depends on the air/fuel ratio. The Lambda value of 1, represents the theoretically perfect ratio. A rich mixture results in higher voltage and a lean mixture results in lower voltage. The current sent by the oxygen sensor to the control unit varies between 0.1-1.0 volt. The difference between high and low voltage occurs when the

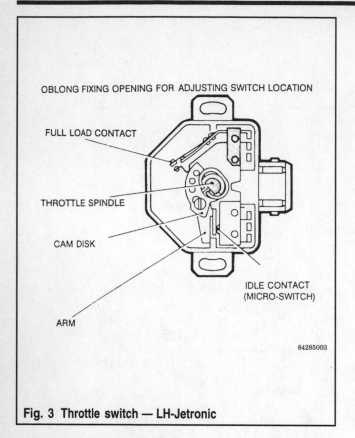

OBLONG FIXING OPENING FOR ADJUSTING SWITCH LOCATION

FULL LOAD CONTACT

THROTTLE SPINDLE

CAM DISK

ARM

IDLE CONTACT
(MICRO-SWITCH)

84285003

Fig. 3 Throttle switch — LH-Jetronic

Lambda value is at 1. The control unit uses this information to adjust the amount of fuel injected.

EGR Temperature Sensor(California Only)

This sensor measures the temperature of the exhaust gases returned to the intake manifold. Detection of the temperature variations enables the control unit to determine whether the EGR system is operating. Its resistance increases with temperature and it is able to measure temperatures up to 930°F (500°C).

CONTROLLED OUTPUTS

In response to various operating conditions, the control unit sends commands to maintain efficient operation:

1. Provides system voltage by grounding the system relay.
2. Breaks the system relay ground if engine is stopped. This prevents the fuel pump from continuing to run and prevents the battery from being drained.
3. Grounds injectors, which regulates opening, timing and injection duration.
4. Controls air valve for constant idle speed.
5. Provides the ignition system control unit with information.
6. Protects against too high rpm by shutting off fuel injection until normal rpm is obtained.
7. Controls the check engine warning and shift indicator lamps.

Idle Valve
▶ **See Figure 4**

An idle valve is incorporated into the system to set the correct air valve opening, and thereby achieve constant idle speed under all engine load. The control unit uses information from the air mass meter regarding the amount of air entering the engine, and from the ignition system control unit regarding rpm.

When the engine is off, a spring sets the idle valve opening for a starting idle speed between 1000-1100 rpm. When the engine is running, the control unit ensures that the idle valve opens at all engine speeds in order to prevent a high negative pressure in the intake manifold when the throttle shutter closes suddenly during deceleration.

The control unit receives a signal from the A/C control unit when the A/C is turned ON or OFF, to enable it to adjust the idle valve. Signals are sent to the control unit from the A/C compressor so the idle valve can be adjusted when the compressor is engaged.

System Relay

The system relay, which is controlled by the control unit, provides current directly, or indirectly, to the fuel pump, injectors, cold start valve, air mass meter and other control unit functions. The system relay and its functions are protected by a fuse.

Auxiliary Relay
▶ **See Figure 5**

The auxiliary relay, mounted in the engine compartment, just in front of the right shock tower, is controlled by the system

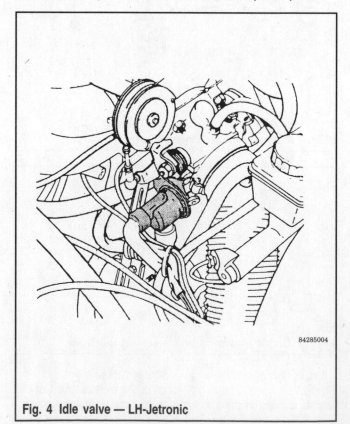

84285004

Fig. 4 Idle valve — LH-Jetronic

relay. It supplies current to the injectors and the cold start valve. It diminishes the possibility of electrical interference, by isolating the cable harnesses from the system.

EGR Vacuum Booster

▶ See Figure 6

This component is found on California vehicles. It controls the pressure in the vacuum line to the EGR valve by means of the admission valve (lower section of the valve). The vacuum in the intake manifold is supplied to the reducing valve (upper section of the valve). The vacuum booster processes the electrical signal from the control unit and the vacuum signal from the intake manifold to maintain optimum control of the EGR valve. The unit is also designed to compensate for changes in atmospheric pressure. It is mounted on the left strut tower.

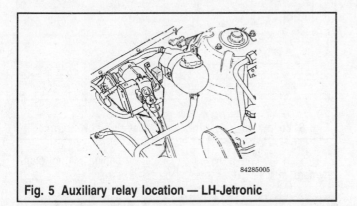

Fig. 5 Auxiliary relay location — LH-Jetronic

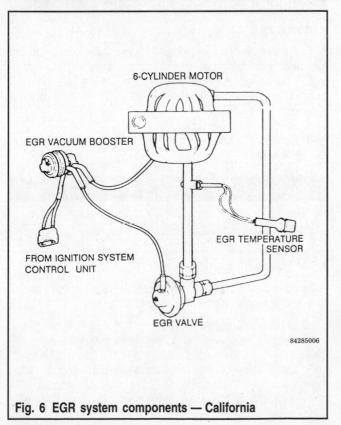

Fig. 6 EGR system components — California

FUEL DELIVERY SYSTEM

Fuel Pressure Regulator

The fuel pressure regulator ensures that fuel pressure remains at a constant 42 psi at idle at the injectors. Using a vacuum tube connected to the engine intake manifold, fuel pressure is gradually increased as intake manifold vacuum decreases. Because of this, adequate pressure is maintained, regardless of throttle position. The amount of fuel injected largely depends on injection duration. Excess fuel is returned to the fuel tank through a return pipe.

Injectors

The fuel injectors as designed as electric solenoids. While the starter motor is operating, there are 2 injections per engine rotation. This is reduced to 1 during normal driving. Injection occurs in the intake manifold near the intake valves.

Cold Start Valve

The cold start valve is used on certain models. It improve engine cold start performance. At cold start, fuel condenses on the cold surfaces in the form of drops. The valve is positioned farther away from the engine block than the injectors and delivers the fuel more as a gas than as drops. The cold start valve is controlled by the control unit, rather than the thermal switch. It operates when the temperature is approximately 5°F (-15°C), and when engine rpm is below 900 rpm.

Fuel Pump

The fuel pump is an electric pump, cooled by the fuel that flows through it. It incorporates a check valve and an overflow valve that opens when fuel pressure gets too high.

Both the primary pump and secondary pump operate when the starter motor or the engine is running. Should the engine stop while the ignition remains on, the control unit will cut the current to the pumps.

The in-tank fuel pump is an electric fuel pump that keeps pressure in the fuel line prior to the main fuel pump to prevent vapor lock. The pump incorporates a coarse strainer type filter and a non-return valve to maintain a constant amount of pressure in the system, even if the main pump is not operational.

Fuel Filter

The fuel filter is adjacent to the main fuel pump, which is mounted on a plate underneath the vehicle on the left side.

SERVICE PRECAUTIONS

▶ See Figures 7 and 8

• Safety is the most important factor when performing not only fuel system maintenance, but any type of maintenance. Failure to conduct maintenance and repairs in a safe manner may result in serious personal injury or death.
• Use caution when working around ignition system components. the ignition system operates at high power with dangerous voltages in both the low-tension and high-tension circuits, including connectors and similar fittings.

• Do not operate the fuel pumps when the fuel lines are empty.

• Do not arc weld on the vehicle unless all the control units have been removed.

• The control unit must not be exposed to temperatures above 175°F (80°C), such as in a paint booth.

• Make sure that the ignition switch is **OFF** before connecting or disconnecting the control unit, ignition coil, spark plug wiring or test instruments.

• Always use new gaskets and seals when remaking a fuel connection.

• When running a compression test, remove the electrical leads from connection 1 on the ignition coil (to prevent arcing) and remove the connectors from the injectors (to prevent flooding).

• Make sure all control unit connectors are fastened securely. A poor connection can cause an extremely high surge voltage, resulting in damage to integrated circuits.

• Keep any control unit harness at least 4 in. away from adjacent harnesses to prevent a system malfunction due to external electronic interference.

• Switch **OFF** the radio before disconnecting or connecting the battery ground lead to prevent radio damage.

• Keep all parts and harnesses dry during service.

• Before attempting to remove any parts, turn off the ignition switch and disconnect the battery ground cable.

• Always use a 12 volt battery as a power source.

• Do not attempt to disconnect the battery cables with the engine running.

• Do not attempt to disassemble a control unit under any circumstances.

• If a battery cable is disconnected, the memory will be erased.

• Always disconnect the yellow SRS (air bag) connector when performing any other diagnostic, trouble shooting or service procedure not associated with the SRS system. Failure to do so can cause damage to the crash sensor. Also, make sure the ignition switch is **OFF** when disconnecting the connector.

Relieving Fuel System Pressure

▶ **See Figures 9 and 10**

1. Remove the fuel pump relay. It is located next to the control unit on the 240 and in the fuse box behind the ash tray on 700 and 900 series. The relay is furthest to the left on the second row.

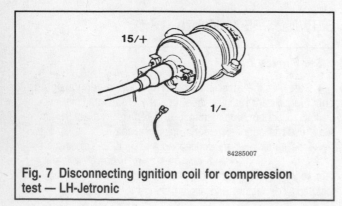

84285007

Fig. 7 Disconnecting ignition coil for compression test — LH-Jetronic

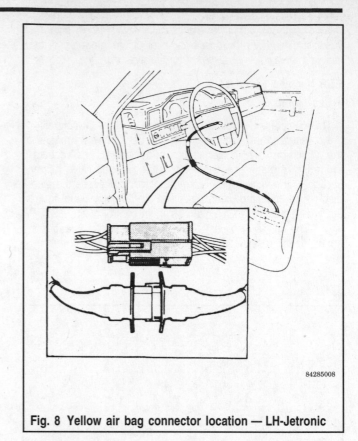

84285008

Fig. 8 Yellow air bag connector location — LH-Jetronic

2. Start the engine repeatedly until the engine will not start anymore, indicating that the fuel pressure is relieved.

Draining Fuel Lines and Filter

▶ **See Figure 11**

1. Remove the protective cap from the valve located on the fuel injection manifold between injectors 1 and 2.

2. Connect adapter hose/union to the fuel drainage unit. Use the special tools 999-5484, 981-2270, 2273, 2282 or their equivalent.

3. Start the fuel drainage.

4. Connect the hose/union to locked/closed valve. Unlock/open valve.

Fuel Injectors

REMOVAL & INSTALLATION

▶ **See Figures 12 and 13**

➡**Remove and install the fuel distribution pipe, the injectors and the cold start valve as one unit.**

1. Unbolt the pressure regulator from the fuel rail bracket.

2. Remove the fuel rail bolts without distorting the metal of the rail.

3. Use 2 line wrenches and separate the line fittings, then remove the injector assembly.

4. Installation is the reverse of removal. Use new O-rings and lubricate with petroleum jelly.

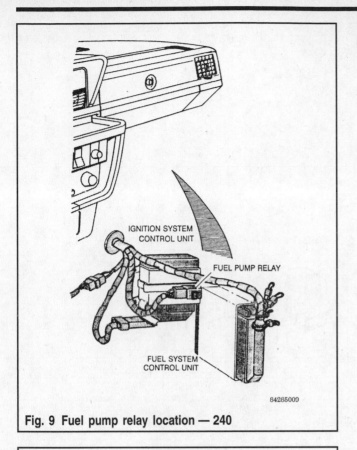

IGNITION SYSTEM
CONTROL UNIT

FUEL PUMP RELAY

FUEL SYSTEM
CONTROL UNIT

84285009

Fig. 9 Fuel pump relay location — 240

84285010

Fig. 10 Fuel pump relay location — Except 240

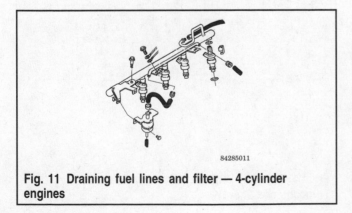

84285011

Fig. 11 Draining fuel lines and filter — 4-cylinder engines

TESTING

Resistance Testing

▶ **See Figures 14 and 15**

1. Test fuel injectors as follows:

a. On 700 and 900 series, remove auxiliary relay from its socket, then connect a jumper wire between pin 2 and pin 3 on the auxiliary relay socket.

b. Connect an ohmmeter between connections pin 9 and pin 18 on the control unit connector. Ohmmeter should read 4 ohms.

c. If reading obtained is higher, current is not going through the injectors.

d. If on non-turbocharged vehicles the ohmmeter reads 5.3 ohms, fault is in 1 injector or its leads. If ohmmeter reads 8 ohms, fault is in 2 injectors or their leads. If ohmmeter reads 16 ohms, fault is in 3 injectors or their leads.

e. If on turbocharged vehicles the ohmmeter reads 2.9 ohms, fault is in 1 injector or its leads. If ohmmeter reads 4.4 ohms, fault is in 2 injectors or their leads. If ohmmeter reads 8.5 ohms, fault is in 3 injectors or their leads.

f. If measured resistance is wrong, remove injector connectors and test them individually. Ohmmeter should read for each injector 16 ohms for non-turbocharged engines and 2 ohms for turbocharged engines.

2. On turbocharged engines disconnect the ballast resistor connector.

3. When measuring between the center pin and each of the other pins the resistance should be 5.5-6.5 ohms.

Operation Testing

Check fuel injectors as follows:

1. Turn ignition switch to the **ON** position, then remove diagnostic socket cover and enter Control Function 3. The injectors will begin to operate at this point.

2. The diagnostic socket LED will flash in a continuous pattern. The control function will repeat itself until interrupted by changing the control systems or turning the ignition switch to the **OFF** position.

3. Listen to and feel by hand each injector to ensure injectors are operating correctly. If an injector is not operating, change injector connector to a injector that's operating. If fault moves to the injector that was operating previously, then the fault is in the connector head.

4. If the injector is still not operating, the fault is in the injector. Check injector separately by connecting an ohmmeter between the injector pins. The ohmmeter should read 16 ohms for non-turbocharged engines and 2 ohms for turbocharged engines. If not, replace injector.

Lambda Sond (Oxygen Sensor)

REMOVAL & INSTALLATION

1. Disconnect the negative battery cable.
2. Raise and support the vehicle safely.
3. Disconnect the oxygen sensor connector. The sensor is located at the catalytic converter.

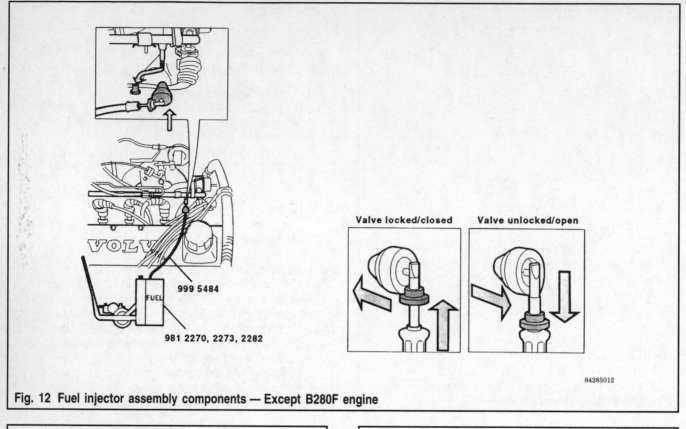

Fig. 12 Fuel injector assembly components — Except B280F engine

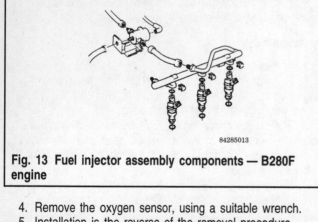

Fig. 13 Fuel injector assembly components — B280F
engine

4. Remove the oxygen sensor, using a suitable wrench.
5. Installation is the reverse of the removal procedure.
Before installing, apply 'Never Seez' paste (P/N 1 161 035-9)

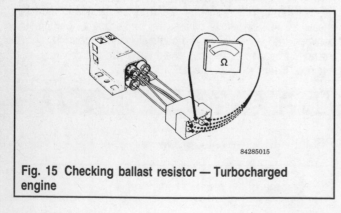

Fig. 15 Checking ballast resistor — Turbocharged
engine

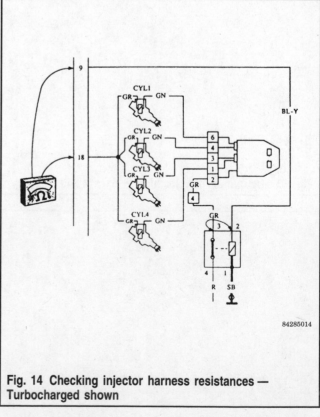

Fig. 14 Checking injector harness resistances —
Turbocharged shown

to the threaded section of the sond. Tighten to 40 ft. lbs. (55
Nm).

Lambda Sond (Oxygen Sensor) Heater

1. On 700 and 900 series, remove panels from under instrument panel right side, then remove glove compartment. Disconnect control unit connector. Connect a voltmeter between ground and pin 8 in the 25 terminal connector.

2. On the 240, ground pin 20 and pin 21 on the control unit connector in order to start fuel pumps. Connect a voltmeter between ground and the Yellow/Red cable in the 2 terminal connector at the right wheel housing. Voltmeter should read 12 volts.

3. On the 240, connect an ohmmeter between ground and the Yellow/Red cable in the 2 terminal connector at the right wheel housing.

4. The ohmmeter should read 3 ohms with the oxygen sensor at 68°F (20°C) and 13 ohms with oxygen sensor at 660°F (349°C).

Throttle Switch

REMOVAL & INSTALLATION

1. Turn the ignition switch to the **OFF** position.
2. Disconnect the throttle switch connector.
3. Remove the throttle switch retaining screws and remove the throttle switch.
4. Installation is the reverse of the removal procedure. Adjust the throttle, as required.

TESTING

1. Turn the ignition switch to the **ON** position. Open the diagnostic unit cover and install selector plug into socket No. 2.

2. Turn the throttle control to the full load position.
3. Enter Control Function 2.
4. Release the throttle control. If the LED flashes diagnostic code 3-3-3, the function of the throttle switch is correct in the full load position.

5. If the LED continues to flash rapidly, proceed as follows:

  a. Check the throttle switch setting by opening the throttle slightly and listen to the switch. A click should be heard when the shutter opens (idle switch). If not, adjust throttle switch by loosening the mounting bolts, turn switch slightly clockwise, then counterclockwise until the switch clicks. Tighten mounting bolts and check setting.

  b. Turn the ignition switch to the **OFF** position.

  c. Remove control unit connector, then the connector protective sleeve.

  d. Check the throttle switch by connecting a ohmmeter between ground and pin 2 on the control unit connector. The reading should be 0 ohms (throttle switch closed).

  e. Depress gas pedal slightly. The resistance should increase to 2-3 kilo-ohms (throttle switch opens).

  f. Connect an ohmmeter between ground and pin 3 on the control unit connector. Ohmmeter should read infinity.

Depress gas pedal fully. Ohmmeter should read 0 ohms. If a fault occurs, check the resistances at the throttle switch, and check the ground connections at intake manifold.

6. Turn the throttle slightly. If LED turns off, then flashes diagnostic code 3-3-2, the throttle switch is operating correctly in the idle position. If LED continues to flash, check throttle switch to see if the fault is in the switch or in its leads. Check ground connections at intake manifold.

ADJUSTMENTS

1. Open the throttle slightly and listen to the switch. There should be a click when the shutter opens, if the adjustment is correct.
2. Loosen the throttle switch mounting bolts.
3. Turn the switch slightly clockwise.
4. Turn the switch counter-clockwise until the switch clicks, then tighten the mounting bolts.
5. Recheck the setting.

Engine Temperature Sensor

REMOVAL & INSTALLATION

1. Turn the ignition switch to the **OFF** position.
2. Drain the cooling system.
3. Disconnect the temperature sensor connector and remove the temperature sensor.
4. Installation is the reverse of the removal procedure.

TESTING

1. Connect an ohmmeter between ground and the pin 13 in the control unit connector. Ohmmeter should read as follows:
  — 14°F (-9°C), 8,260-10,560 ohms
  — 68°F (20°C), 2,280-2720 ohms
  — 176°F (79°C), 290-364 ohms
2. If specifications are not as specified, check coolant temperature sensor to see if fault is in sensor or its leads. Check ground connections at intake manifold.

RPM Sensor

REMOVAL & INSTALLATION

The sensor is located at the rear of the engine block, above the flywheel.
1. Turn the ignition switch to the **OFF** position.
2. Disconnect the engine speed sensor connector.
3. Remove the speed sensor retaining screws and remove the speed sensor.
4. Installation is the reverse of the removal procedure.

TESTING

1. Check rpm sensor lead from the ignition system control unit by connecting a voltmeter between ground and pin 1 on the control unit connector.

2. Run starter motor.

3. Voltmeter should read 12 volts (on 240 series) or 5-7 volts (on 700 series).

4. Start the engine and enter Control Function 2.

5. If LED turns off, then flashes diagnostic code 3-3-1, the rpm signal from the ignition system is correct.

6. On vehicles equipped with B230F engines, if the engine does not start, run starter motor until diode light goes off. On models equipped with the B234F engine, if the engine does not start, run starter motor until the diagnostic code flashes out.

7. If the LED continues to flash, check for faults in the ignition system.

8. If no faults are found in the ignition system, proceed as follows:

   a. Check control unit grounds near the control unit.

   b. Make sure the ignition switch is in the **OFF** position, then disconnect control unit connector and remove protective sleeve.

   c. Make sure that there is 12 volts between ground and pin 4 on the control unit connector. If there is not, check the wire between the control unit connector and fuse 1 in the fuse box.

   d. Check the diagnostic unit itself.

   e. Check ignition lock voltage by turning ignition switch to the **ON** position. Connect voltmeter between ground and the pin 35 on the control unit connector. Voltmeter should read 12 volts. Ensure voltage exists when starter motor is running. Turn ignition switch to the **OFF** position.

   f. Check ground connections by connecting a ohmmeter between ground and pins 5, 17, 19 and 29 on the control unit connector. Ohmmeter reading at all connections should be 0 ohms. All leads are grounded to the intake manifold.

   g. Ensure that the oxygen sensor lead is connected to the pin 5 on the control unit connector.

   h. Check the rpm sensor lead from the ignition system control unit by connecting a voltmeter between ground and the pin 1 on the control unit connector. Run starter motor and note reading. Voltmeter should read 12 volts.

Air Mass Meter

REMOVAL & INSTALLATION

1. Turn the ignition switch to the **OFF** position.

2. Disconnect the air mass meter electrical connector. Loosen the clamps and remove the retaining screws, as required.

3. Remove the air mass meter.

4. Installation is the reverse of the removal procedure.

TESTING

▶ **See Figure 16**

1. Connect an ohmmeter between pin 6 and pin 7 on the control unit connector. Ohmmeter should read 2.5-4.0 ohms.

2. Slide back the rubber boot from the air mass meter connector. Connect a voltmeter between ground (connect a jumper wire from ground to pin 21 on the control unit connector) and the pin 5 on the air mass meter connector. The voltmeter should show approximately 12 volts.

3. Connect voltmeter between pin 1 (ground) and pin 5 (current feed from system relay) on air mass meter connector. Voltmeter should read 12 volts.

4. Remove jumper wire from pin 21 on the control unit connector. Start and allow engine to reach normal operating temperature.

5. Connect a voltmeter between pin 1 and pin 4. Rev engine up to 2100 rpm, then turn engine off. After approximately 4 seconds, the voltmeter indicator should swing back and forth for approximately 1 second (burn-off cleaning). Remove voltmeter and slide back rubber boot.

Fuel Filter

REMOVAL & INSTALLATION

1. Disconnect the negative battery cable.

2. Relieve the fuel system pressure.

3. Raise and safely support the vehicle safely.

4. Place a container under the filter to catch the excess fuel.

5. Using a shop rag to prevent fuel spray, remove the fuel lines, mounting bracket nut and the filter.

   To install:

➡ **Fuel flow direction arrow is marked on the new (and old) filter. Arrow follows direction from fuel tank to engine.**

6. Install the new filter in the proper direction. Tighten the fittings 15-25 ft. lbs. (20-35Nm).

7. Connect the negative battery cable, turn the ignition **ON** and check for leaks.

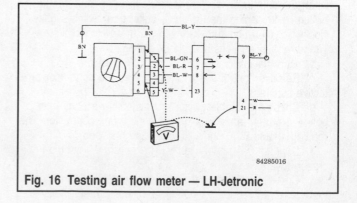

84285016

Fig. 16 Testing air flow meter — LH-Jetronic

FUEL SYSTEM TESTING

▶ **See Figures 17, 18 and 19**

Pressure Relief

1. Remove the fuel pump relay. It is located next to the control unit on the 240 and in the fuse box behind the ash tray on 700 and 900 series. The relay is furthest to the left on the second row.

2. Start the engine repeatedly until the engine will not start anymore, indicating that the fuel pressure is relieved.

3. Refer to 'Draining the fuel lines and filter' in this section.

Pressure Check

1. Relieve the fuel pressure.

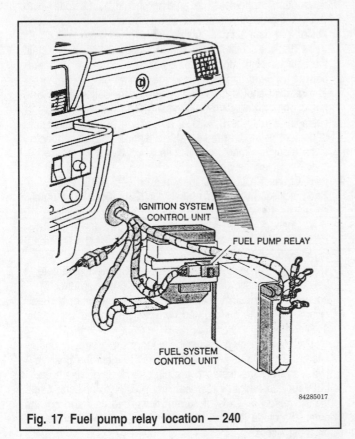

Fig. 17 Fuel pump relay location — 240

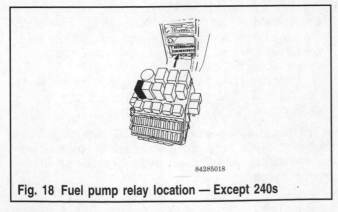

Fig. 18 Fuel pump relay location — Except 240s

2. Connect a fuel pressure gauge. Hold a shop towel under the fuel line to catch any spilled fuel when it is disconnected.

3. With the fuel pump relay still removed, remove the seat belt reminder on 700 and 900 series, since this makes the test more easily performed. It is located in the middle of the top row in the fuse box.

4. Start the fuel pump by connecting an electrical lead between terminals 30 and 87/2 on the relay socket. Verify pump operation by removing the fuel cap and listening.

5. The fuel pressure should be 42 psi (300 kPa).

6. Remove the lead between terminals 30 and 87/2.

7. Relieve the fuel pressure and remove the pressure gauge, catching any spilled fuel with a shop towel.

8. Reinstall the relay.

> ## ✳✳CAUTION
>
> **To avoid fire and personal injury, replace any plastic tie bands removed from the fuel lines.**

Pump Inoperative

1. If the fuel pump does not start, remove the lead between terminals 30 and 87/2.

2. Check for voltage at terminal 30. If there is none, check the lead between the relay and the battery.

3. Connect an electrical lead between terminals 30 and 87/2 on the relay socket. If the pump still does not start, check the lead between the pump and the relay. Check the lead between 87/1 and 85 for continuity with an ohmmeter.

Pressure Too High

1. Remove the lead between terminals 30 and 87/2 on the relay socket.

2. Remove the return hose from the pressure regulator and blow air into the hose.

3. Remove the vacuum hose from the pressure regulator and blow air into the hose.

4. If both hoses are open, the pressure regulator is faulty. Replace it and recheck the fuel pressure.

Pressure Too Low

1. Squeeze the return hose by hand, not with a tool, and check if the pressure rises.

> ## ✳✳CAUTION
>
> **To avoid personal injury and fire, do not allow the pressure to exceed 84 psi (600 kPa).**

2. If the pressure rises rapidly, the pump and hoses are good. Replace the regulator and recheck the pressure.

3. If the pressure rises slowly, the fuel filter, pump strainer or the fuel lines are clogged or blocked.

4. If the pressure does not rise, the fuel pump is faulty.

Pressure Regulator

1. Connect a vacuum pump to the pressure regulator.

2. Apply vacuum to the regulator and check that the fuel pressure falls as more vacuum is applied.

3. Remove the lead between terminals 30 and 87/2.

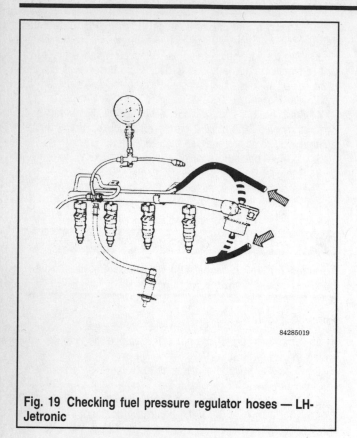

84285019

Fig. 19 Checking fuel pressure regulator hoses — LH-Jetronic

4. Relieve the fuel pressure and remove the pressure gauge, catching any spilled fuel with a shop towel.
5. Reinstall the relay.

✳✳✳CAUTION

To avoid fire and personal injury, replace any plastic tie bands removed from the fuel lines.

Fault Tracing

TESTING

Diagnostic Unit
▸ **See Figures 20 and 21**

1. Remove the diagnostic unit cover and install selector plug into socket No. 2.
2. Turn ignition switch to the **ON** position.
3. Enter Control Function 1 by pressing the button once. Hold the button for at least 1 second, but not more than 3 seconds.
4. Watch the LED and count the number of flashes in the 3 flash series corresponding to a fault code. The flash series are separated by 3 second intervals. Note fault codes (Refer to Fig. 31 in this section).

➡**If there are no fault codes in the diagnostic unit, the LED will flash 1-1-1. Proceed to Control Function 2.**

5. If LED does not flash when button is pressed, or no code is flashed, proceed as follows:
   a. Check ground connections on the intake manifold, and the ground connection for the oxygen sensor at the right front mudguard.
   b. Check fuse 4 and the in-line fuse on the 240, fuses 1 and 11 on 740, 780 and 940 and fuses 30 and 31 on the 760 for the pump relay and the primary pump. The 240 main fuse box is located in front of the left front door pillar and the in-line fuse is in the engine compartment. On 700 and 900 series, the fuse box is located behind the ash tray in the center console.
   c. Remove glove compartment, and check control unit ground connections.
   d. Turn ignition switch to the **OFF** position. Remove control unit connector and connector protective sleeve.
   e. Connect a voltmeter between ground and pin 4 on the control unit connector. The reading should be 12 volts. If no voltage is present, check the wire between control unit connector and fuse 1 in the fuse/relay box.
   f. Turn the ignition switch to the **ON** position, and install the selector plug into the No. 2 socket. Connect a voltmeter between ground and pin 12 on the control unit connector. The reading should be 12 volts. Press the button on diagnostic unit and note voltage reading. The reading on the voltmeter should be 0 volts. If no voltage at the control unit is present, take the reading at the diagnostic unit connector. If the reading remains at 12 volts when button is pressed, check the diagnostic unit.
   g. Connect a voltmeter between ground and the Red/Black lead on the diagnostic unit connector. The reading should be 12 volts.
   h. Connect an ohmmeter between ground and the Brown/Black lead in the diagnostic unit connector. The reading should be 0 ohms.
   i. Turn ignition to the **OFF** position. Connect ohmmeter between diagnostic unit selector plug and the pin directly underneath the selector button. The ohmmeter should read infinity. Press the button, and note the reading. It should be 0 ohms.
   j. Connect a diode tester between the pin directly underneath the LED and the selector plug: Connect the positive test lead from the tester to the pin directly underneath the LED and the negative test lead from tester to selector cable, then reverse the leads. If current flows one way and not the other, the diode is good. If current flows both ways, replace diagnostic socket.
   k. Check the system relay by connecting a voltmeter between ground and pin 9 on the control unit connector, then connect a jumper wire between ground and pin 21 on the control unit connector. The relay should activate and the reading should be 12 volts.

6. Enter Control Function 1 again and check for any fault codes. If the LED flashes Code 1-1-1, there are no other codes in the memory.

➡**The diagnostic system memory is full when it contains 3 fault codes. Until those codes are corrected and the memory erased, the system cannot give information on any other problems.**

7. When all fault codes have been read and corrected, erase the diagnostic system memory and recheck for codes.

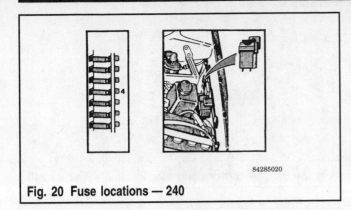

Fig. 20 Fuse locations — 240

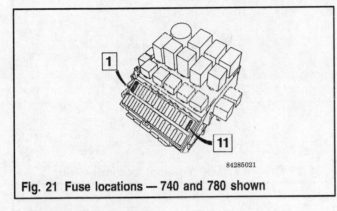

Fig. 21 Fuse locations — 740 and 780 shown

Air Conditioning Switch

1. Enter Control Function 2.

2. On vehicles equipped with A/C, check the on/off function of the compressor by placing A/C controls in the **ON** position. If the LED turns off, then flashes diagnostic code 1-1-4, the A/C switch is operating properly.

3. If LED continues to flash, check the lead from A/C control unit by connecting an ohmmeter between ground and pin 15 on the control unit connector. With A/C switch **OFF**, ohmmeter should read 1 kilo-ohm. With A/C switch **ON**, ohmmeter should read 10 ohms.

4. The LED will return to rapid flashes prior to A/C compressor turning on. When the compressor turns on the diode light should go off and then flash diagnostic code 1-3-4.

5. If LED continues to flash rapidly, check lead to A/C compressor by connecting an ohmmeter between ground and pin 14 connection on the control unit connector. Ohmmeter should read 0-5 ohms.

6. Turn engine **OFF**.

Neutral Switch

1. Enter Control Function 2.

2. On vehicles equipped with automatic transmission, depress brake pedal and place gear selector lever in position **D** and then in position **N**. The LED should go off and then flash diagnostic code 1-2-4.

3. If LED continues to flash, check gear selector signal by placing gear selector in the **N** position.

4. Connect an ohmmeter between ground and pin 30 on control unit connector. Ohmmeter should read 0 ohms.

5. Move gear selector into position **D**. Ohmmeter should read infinity. On vehicles equipped with manual transmissions, ohmmeter should read 0 ohms in all gears.

Carbon Filter Solenoid Valve

This test applies to vehicles with the B234F engine.

1. Enter Control Function 3.

2. While the LED continues to flash, the injectors, idle valve and carbon filter solenoid valve should all begin to operate.

3. If carbon filter solenoid valve does not operate, connect an ohmmeter between pin 9 and pin 27 on the control unit. Ohmmeter should read approximately 45 ohms.

Air Intake System

1. Check the air mass meter area for leaks.

2. Check intake manifold between the air filter and the manifold, hoses and hose connections to the intake manifold, and bolted joints and seals (throttle housing).

Idle Valve

1. Check idle valve by connecting an ohmmeter between connections pin 9 and pin 33 on the control unit connector.

2. Ohmmeter should read approximately 8 ohms.

3. Enter Control Function 3 for a function check.

4. If idle valve does not operate, but LED flashes, connect an ohmmeter between pin 9 and pin 33 on the control unit connector. Ohmmeter should read 8 ohms.

Speedometer Signal
▶ See Figure 22

1. Remove access panel from under the instrument panel on the drivers side.

2. On the 240, disconnect connector from speedometer and connect an ohmmeter between the Blue cable and pin 34 on the control unit connector.

3. On 700 and 900 series, disconnect connector from speedometer and connect an ohmmeter between Violet/White cable and pin 34 on the control unit connector.

4. The ohmmeter should read 0 ohms. If Fault Code 3-1-1 has flashed and ohmmeter reads 0 ohms, replace speedometer assembly.

System Relay
▶ See Figure 23

1. Check the system relay/primary relay by connecting a voltmeter between ground and the pin 9 on the control unit connector, then connect a jumper wire from ground to pin 21 on the control unit connector. The relay should activate and voltmeter reading should be 12 volts.

2. With pin 21 still grounded, connect voltmeter between ground and pin 9 on control unit connector, then a jumper wire from ground to pin 20 of control unit connector. The pump relay should close and fuel pumps activate.

3. On the 740 and 940, connect voltmeter between ground and pin 8 in the 25-terminal connector located at the right A-post. Voltmeter should read approximately 12 volts.

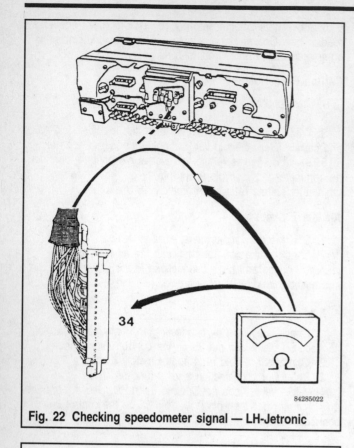

Fig. 22 Checking speedometer signal — LH-Jetronic

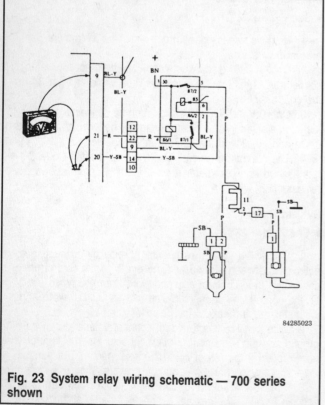

Fig. 23 System relay wiring schematic — 700 series shown

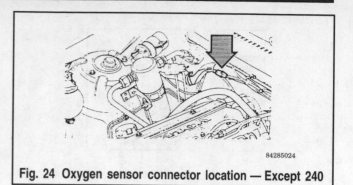

Fig. 24 Oxygen sensor connector location — Except 240

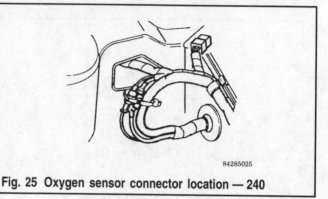

Fig. 25 Oxygen sensor connector location — 240

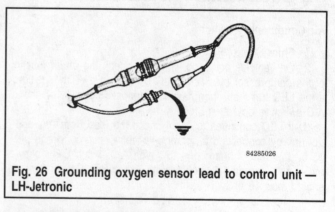

Fig. 26 Grounding oxygen sensor lead to control unit — LH-Jetronic

Exhaust Carbon Monoxide Content

▶ **See Figures 24, 25 and 26**

1. Check carbon monoxide content by removing the tapped plug on the catalytic converter.

2. Warm the engine and check the carbon monoxide content. If carbon monoxide content is not within specification, check the oxygen sensor.

3. Check oxygen sensor by disconnecting oxygen sensor electrical connector. Ground the lead coming from the control unit. Carbon monoxide content reading should rise, indicating that the control unit and its connections are good.

4. Connect a voltmeter to the oxygen sensor electrical connector. The reading should move back and forth to indicate the functioning of the oxygen sensor. Reading on voltmeter with correct carbon monoxide content should be approximately 0.5 volts.

Air Mass Meter Hot Wire

1. Start and run engine until normal operating temperature has been obtained, then slide back rubber boot from the air mass meter connector.

2. Connect a voltmeter between the pin 1 and pin 4 connections. Rev engine up to 2100 rpm. Turn engine OFF. After approximately 4 seconds, the voltmeter indicator should swing back and forth for approximately 1 second (indicating burn-off cleaning).

Knock Enrichment Signal

1. Turn ignition switch to the **ON** position.

2. Connect a voltmeter between ground and the pin 28 connection on the control unit connector. Voltmeter reading should be 0.7 volts. Turn ignition switch **OFF**.

EGR Vacuum Booster(California Only)

On California vehicles an EGR system malfunction is indicated by Fault Code 2-4-1. It results when the EGR temperature sensor detects that the exhaust gas recirculation flow is too low.

1. Turn the ignition switch **ON**.

2. Enter Control Function 3. The lamp should flash according as the EGR converter is activated.

3. Turn the ignition switch **OFF**.

4. If the EGR converter is not activated, measure the resistance between pins 6 and 15 in the control unit connector. The resistance should be approximately 75-95 ohms.

5. If the value is different, check the wiring and connection.

EGR System Check(California Only)

▶ **See Figure 27**

1. Open the EGR converter connector. Remove the lead directly opposite the black-white lead between pin 1 and the control unit. Reconnect the connector.

2. Start and warm the engine to operating temperature.

3. Ground the loose lead. If the engine starts to run unevenly, the EGR system is operating.

EGR Temperature Sensor(California Only)

If the signal from the EGR temperature sensor is absent or faulty, Fault Code 4-3-1 will result.

➡**The sensor is extremely sensitive to shock and impact. When replacing, torque to 5-10 ft. lbs. (7-13 Nm).**

1. Measure the resistance between terminal 14 (ground) and terminal 22 on the control unit connector. It should be 500-1000 ohms.

2. If the value is different, check the leads and connections, the ground terminal on the intake manifold and the resistance of the sensor connector.

READING CODES

Control Function 1

▶ **See Figure 28**

The fuel system incorporates a built-in self-diagnostic system. It is located behind the left spring strut tower in the

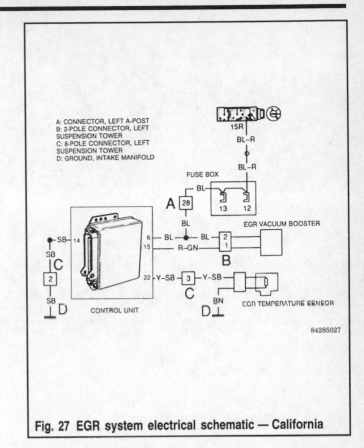

A: CONNECTOR, LEFT A-POST
B: 2-POLE CONNECTOR, LEFT SUSPENSION TOWER
C: 8-POLE CONNECTOR, LEFT SUSPENSION TOWER
D: GROUND, INTAKE MANIFOLD

Fig. 27 EGR system electrical schematic — California

engine compartment. The diagnostic system uses socket No. 2 for the fuel system and socket No. 6 for the ignition system and EGR system (California).

There are many possible fault codes in the diagnostic system, and the system is capable of storing up to 3 system faults at 1 time. When the engine is running, the fuel system control unit continuously checks the control units internal functions, oxygen sensor, battery current, coolant temperature sensor, air temperature sensor, pressure sensor, throttle valve, engine rpm, speedometer and the idle speed according to the air valve position.

The following procedure is for retrieving FAULT codes.

1. Open the diagnostic socket cover in the driver's side rear of the engine compartment and install the selector cable into socket No. 2 for ignition or fuel system codes, or into socket No. 6 for EGR system codes on California vehicles.

2. Turn ignition to the **ON** position.

3. Enter Control Function 1 by pressing the button once. Hold the button for at least 1 second, but not more than 3 seconds.

4. Watch the light emitting diode (LED) and count the number of flashes in each of the 3 flash series, which will indicate a fault code. The flash series are separated by 3 second intervals. Note the fault codes.

➡**If there are no fault codes in the diagnostic unit, the LED will flash 1-1-1 and the fuel system is operating correctly.**

5. Depress the button again. If the same code is repeated, there are no additional codes stored. If the code is different,

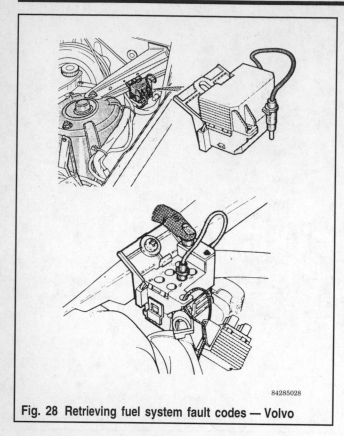

84285028

Fig. 28 Retrieving fuel system fault codes — Volvo

depress the button a third time and record the code, if different.

➡The diagnostic memory is full when it contains 3 fault codes. Until those 3 are rectified and the memory erased, the system cannot give information on any other problems.

Control Function 2

This function is activated by pressing the button twice (between 1-3 seconds between operations), causing the LED to flash. The control unit delivers a diagnostic code (not a fault code) acknowledging the receipt of a signal from each of the following items:

Diagnostic Code 3-3-2: Throttle switch, when the throttle is moved from the fully closed position

Diagnostic Code 3-3-3: Throttle switch, when the throttle is moved from the full-load position

Diagnostic Code 3-3-1: Rpm signal from the ignition system

Diagnostic Code 1-1-4: ECC control panel, when the A/C button is depressed or released

Diagnostic Code 1-3-4: Air conditioning compressor

Diagnostic Code 1-2-4: Testing idle speed compensation on automatic transmission vehicles. When depressing the brake pedal and placing the gear selector lever in **D** and then moved to **N** again.

Control Function 3

This function is activated by turning the ignition **ON**, installing the selector cable into socket No. 2. and pressing the button 3 times, allowing between 1-3 seconds between each

pressing. The control unit then responds by activating the injectors, idle valve, cold start valve, auxiliary relay (radio interference suppression relay) and fuel pump.

CLEARING CODES

▶ **See Figures 29, 30, 31 and 32**

When all the fault codes have been read and corrected, the diagnostic system memory can be erased as follows:

1. Turn ignition switch to the **ON** position.
2. Read fault codes again.
3. Press and hold diagnostic socket button for more than 5 seconds. Release button. After 3 seconds, the LED should light.
4. While the LED is lit, press button again for more than 5 seconds. Release button. The LED should go out. Memory is cleared.

➡**To ensure that the memory has been erased, press button again for 1 second but not more than 3 seconds. The LED should flash 1-1-1, indicating that the memory is erased.**

5. Start and run the engine. If it will not start, enter Control Function 2.
6. Recheck for fault codes. If Code 1-1-1 comes up, there are no additional system fault codes.

ADJUSTMENTS

Base Idle

▶ **See Figure 33**

1. Loosen the throttle locknut.
2. Loosen the adjustment screw until the throttle is completely closed.
3. Tighten the adjustment screw until it just touches the linkarm, then turn a half a turn further.
4. Tighten the locknut without changing the adjusting screw position.

➡**It may be necessary to loosen the throttle switch before setting the throttle.**

Throttle Control Pulley and Cable

1. Disconnect the linkarm and make sure that the pulley moves smoothly.
2. Make sure that the throttle cable is fully extended in the idle position without affecting the pulley position. The pulley should hit the idle stop.
3. Adjust the cable if the pulley is not hitting the idle stop.
4. Depress the accelerator pedal all the way and check that the pulley hits the full throttle stop.
5. Reconnect the linkarm and adjust it as follows:
   a. Insert a 1mm feeler gauge between the control pulley and the idle stop.
   b. The play between the throttle lever and the adjustment screw should be 0.1-0.3mm.
   c. Adjust the linkarm to bring into specifications.

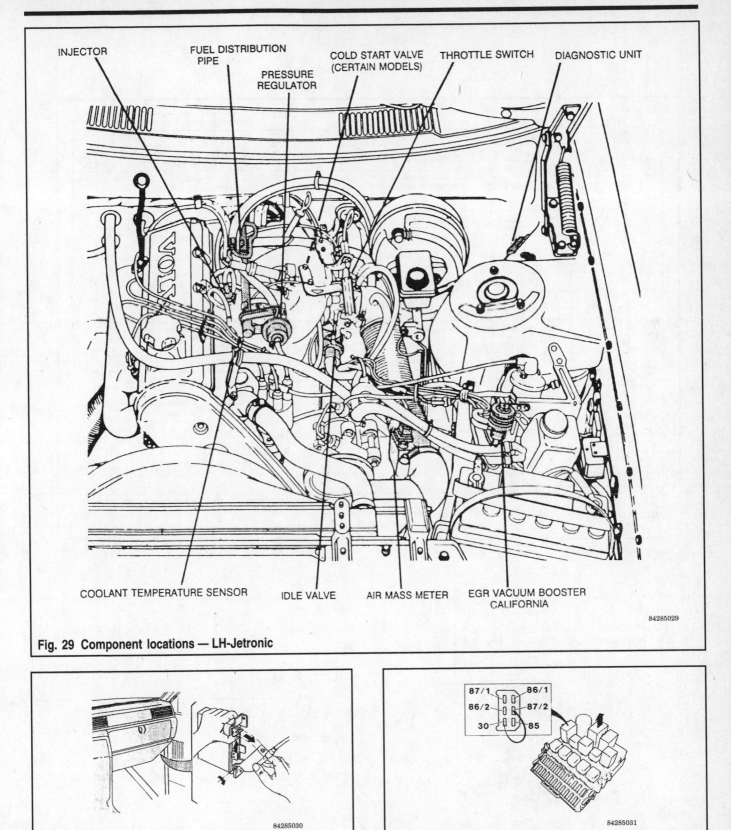

INJECTOR FUEL DISTRIBUTION PIPE PRESSURE REGULATOR COLD START VALVE (CERTAIN MODELS) THROTTLE SWITCH DIAGNOSTIC UNIT

COOLANT TEMPERATURE SENSOR IDLE VALVE AIR MASS METER EGR VACUUM BOOSTER CALIFORNIA

84285029

Fig. 29 Component locations — LH-Jetronic

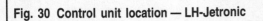

84285030

Fig. 30 Control unit location — LH-Jetronic

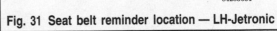

84285031

Fig. 31 Seat belt reminder location — LH-Jetronic

Code	Fault	Correction Test
1-1-1	No faults	—
1-1-2	Fault in control unit ①	Control unit
1-1-3	Fault in injector	Injector
1-2-1	Signal to/from air mass meter faulty	Air mass meter
1-2-3	Signal missing to/from coolant temperature sensor	Coolant temperature sensor
1-3-1	Ignition System RPM signal missing	RPM sensor
1-3-2	Battery voltage too low/high ②	Charging system
1-3-3	Throttle-Switch; idle setting faulty, possible grounding short	Throttle switch
2-1-2	Oxygen sensor signal missing or is faulty	Oxygen sensor or heater
2-1-3	Throttle-Switch; full load setting faulty possible grounding short	Throttle switch
2-2-1	Oxygen sensor not operating	Oxygen sensor or heater
2-2-3	Signal missing to/from idle valve	Idle valve
2-3-1	Self-adjusting oxygen sensor not operating	Air intake system or fuel system
2-3-2	Self-adjusting oxygen sensor not operating	Air intake system or fuel system
2-3-3	Idle valve closed, possibly leaking air	Idle valve
2-4-1	EGR system malfunction ③	EGR vacuum booster
3-1-1	Signal missing from speedometer	Speedometer signal
3-1-2	Signal missing for knock related fuel enrichment	Knock enrichment signal
3-2-2	Burn-off cleaning of hot wire in air mass meter not operating	Air mass meter hot wire
4-1-3	EGR temperature sensor signal absent or faulty ③	EGR temperature signal

① Change control unit
② Check battery and charging system
③ California

84285032

Fig. 32 Fault code descriptions — LH-Jetronic

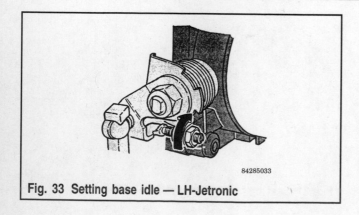

84285033

Fig. 33 Setting base idle — LH-Jetronic

IDLE SPEED

◆ **See Figures 34, 35, 36, 37, 38, 39, 40 and 41**

Adjustment

After other throttle related adjustments have been made, idle speed is controlled by the idle valve and is not adjustable.

1. Battery
2. Ignition switch
4. Ignition coil
29. Positive terminal test point
31. Ground connection rail in central electrical unit
84. Coolant temperature sensor
135. Relay, fuel injection
187. Lambda sond
196. Air control valve
198. Throttle switch LH-Jetronic

210. Tank pump 1.6A
211. Fuel pump 6.5A
217. Control unit LH-Jetronic
219. Test point Lambda sond system
220. Test point CIS system
260. Control unit, ignition system
284. Air mass meter
361-366. Injectors
464. Radio interference relay
886. Bridge connector.

A. Connector right A post
B. Connector left A post
C. Connector right suspension tower
D. Connector right suspension tower
E. Connector left A post
F. Connector left suspension tower
G. Connector right suspension tower
H. Ground point on intake manifold
J. Ground point in trunk
K. Connector on firewall
L. Connector in central electrical unit
M. Ground point, right A post
N. Ground point right front wing

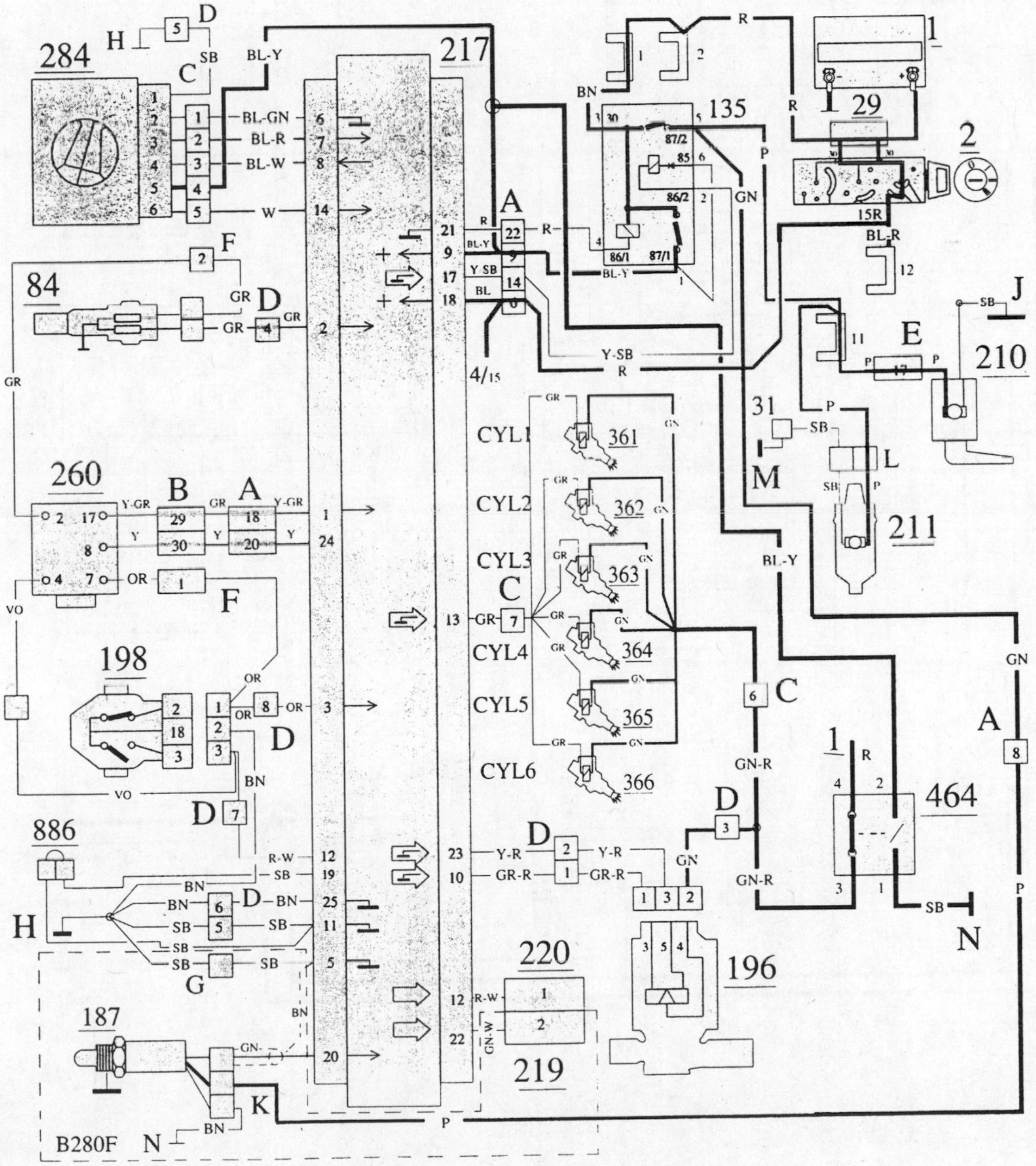

Fig. 34 LH-Jetronic 2.2 component terminal identification — 780 with B280F engine

84285037

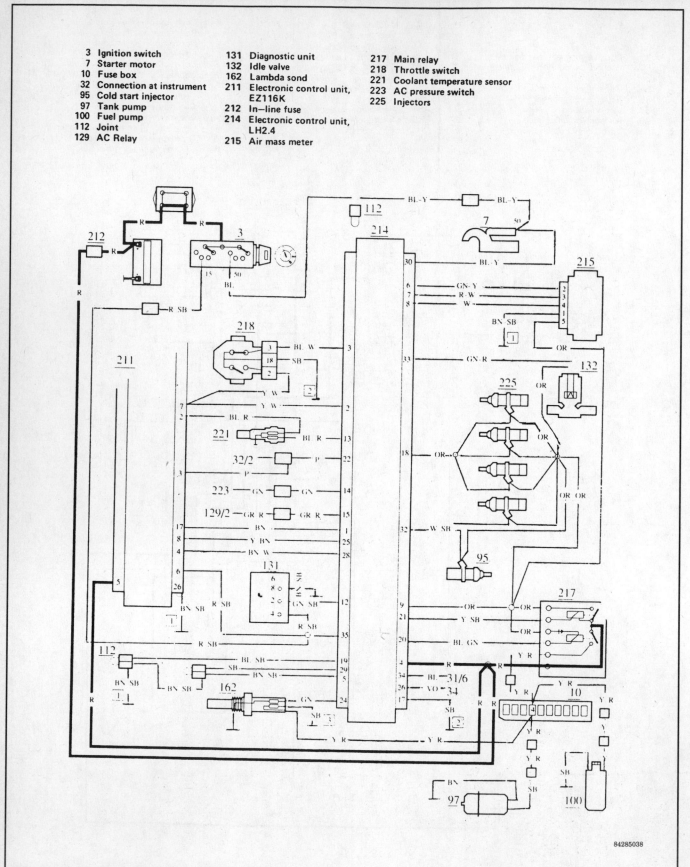

3 Ignition switch
7 Starter motor
10 Fuse box
32 Connection at instrument
95 Cold start injector
97 Tank pump
100 Fuel pump
112 Joint
129 AC Relay

131 Diagnostic unit
132 Idle valve
162 Lambda sond
211 Electronic control unit, EZ116K
212 In–line fuse
214 Electronic control unit, LH2.4
215 Air mass meter

217 Main relay
218 Throttle switch
221 Coolant temperature sensor
223 AC pressure switch
225 Injectors

84285038

Fig. 35 LH-Jetronic System wiring diagram — 240

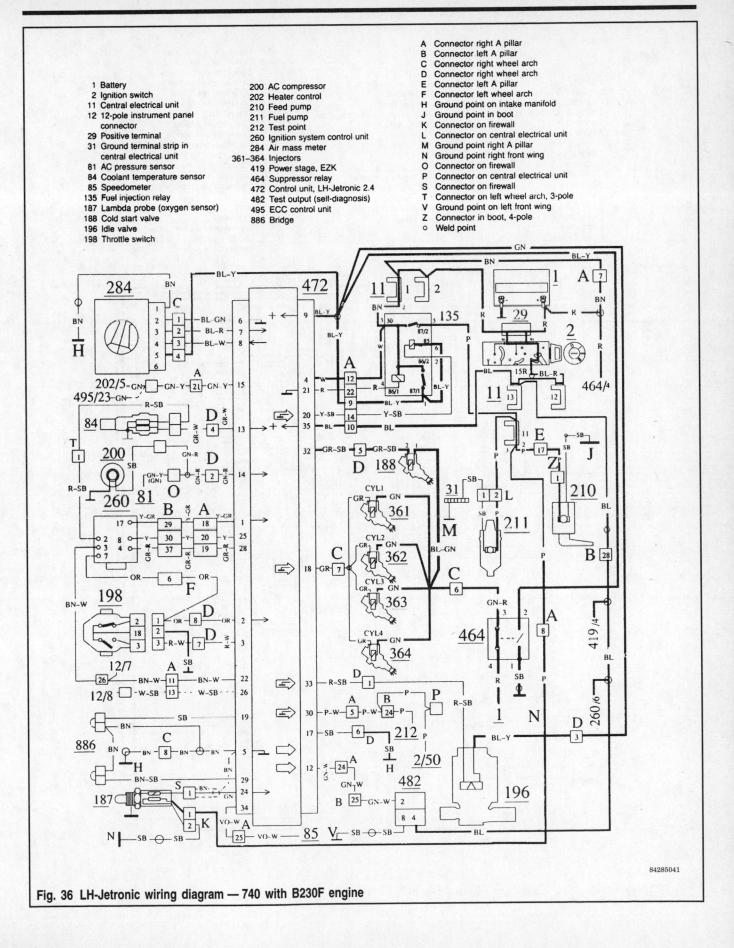

Fig. 36 LH-Jetronic wiring diagram — 740 with B230F engine

1 Battery
2 Ignition switch
11 Central electrical unit
12 12-pole instrument panel connector
29 Positive terminal
31 Ground terminal strip in central electrical unit
81 AC pressure sensor
84 Coolant temperature sensor
85 Speedometer
135 Fuel injection relay
187 Lambda probe (oxygen sensor)
188 Cold start valve
196 Idle valve
198 Throttle switch

200 AC compressor
202 Heater control
210 Feed pump
211 Fuel pump
212 Test point
260 Ignition system control unit
284 Air mass meter
361–364 Injectors
419 Power stage, EZK
464 Suppressor relay
472 Control unit, LH-Jetronic 2.4
482 Test output (self-diagnosis)
495 ECC control unit
886 Bridge

A Connector right A pillar
B Connector left A pillar
C Connector right wheel arch
D Connector right wheel arch
E Connector left A pillar
F Connector left wheel arch
H Ground point on intake manifold
J Ground point in boot
K Connector on firewall
L Connector on central electrical unit
M Ground point right A pillar
N Ground point right front wing
O Connector on firewall
P Connector on central electrical unit
S Connector on firewall
T Connector on left wheel arch, 3-pole
V Ground point on left front wing
Z Connector in boot, 4-pole
o Weld point

84285041

1 Battery
2 Ignition switch
11 Central electrical unit
12 12-pole instrument panel
    connector
29 Positive terminal
31 Ground terminal strip in
    central electrical unit
81 AC pressure sensor
84 Coolant temperature sensor
85 Speedometer
135 Fuel injection relay
187 Lambda probe (oxygen sensor)
188 Cold start valve
196 Idle valve
198 Throttle switch
200 AC compressor
202 Heater control

210 Feed pump
211 Fuel pump
212 Test point
260 Ignition system control unit
284 Air mass meter
361–364 Injectors
376 Ballast resistor
377 PTC resistor
419 Power stage, EZK
464 Suppressor relay
472 Control unit, LH-Jetronic 2.4
482 Test output (self-diagnosis)
495 ECC control unit
886 Bridge

A Connector right A pillar
B Connector left A pillar
C Connector right wheel arch
D Connector right wheel arch
E Connector left A pillar
F Connector left wheel arch
H Ground point on intake manifold
J Ground point in boot
K Connector on firewall
L Connector on central electrical unit
M Ground point right A pillar
N Ground point right front wing
O Connector on firewall, single-pole
P Connector on central electrical unit
S Connector on firewall
T Connector on left wheel arch
U Accessory
V Ground point on left front wing
Z Connector in boot, 4-pole
o Weld point

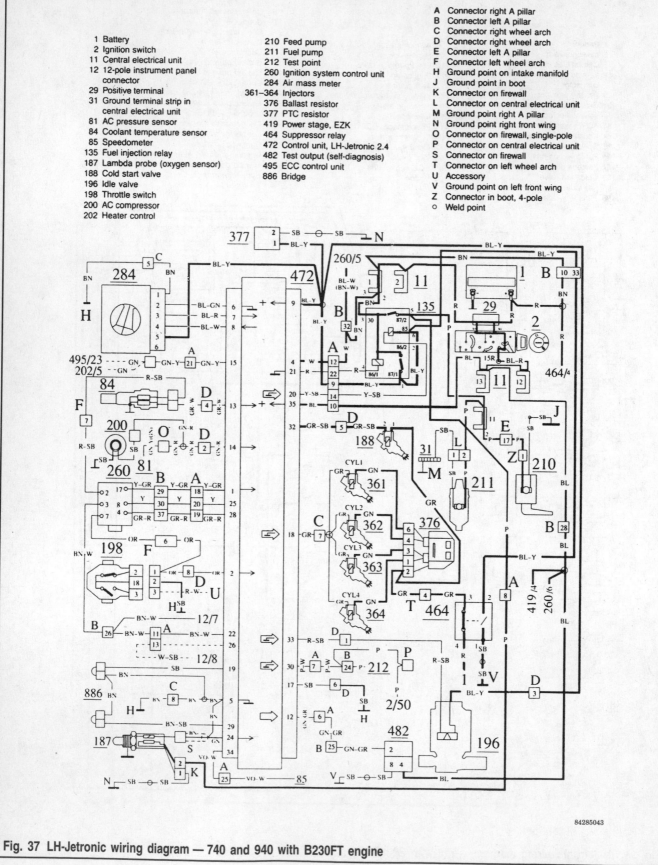

Fig. 37 LH-Jetronic wiring diagram — 740 and 940 with B230FT engine

1 Battery
2 Ignition switch
11 Central electrical unit
12 12-pole instrument panel connector
29 Positive terminal
31 Ground terminal strip in central
   electrical unit
81 AC pressure sensor
84 Coolant temperature sensor
85 Speedometer
120 AC cut-out relay
135 Fuel injection relay
183 Solenoid, charcoal filter (only B 234 F)
187 Lambda probe (oxygen sensor)
    (only B 234 F)
196 Idle valve
198 Throttle switch

202 Heater control
210 Feed pump
211 Fuel pump
212 Test point
260 Ignition system control unit
284 Air mass meter
361–364 Injectors
419 Power stage, EZK
464 Suppressor relay
472 Control unit, LH-Jetronic 2.4
482 Test output (self-diagnosis)
495 ECC control unit
886 Bridge

A Connector right A pillar
B Connector left A pillar
C Connector right wheel arch
D Connector right wheel arch
E Connector left A pillar
F Connector left wheel arch
H Ground point on intake manifold
J Ground point in boot
K Connector on firewall
L Connector on central electrical unit
M Ground point right A pillar
N Ground point right front wing
O Connector on firewall, single-pole
P Connector on central electrical unit
S Connector on firewall
T Connector on left wheel arch, 3-pole
V Ground point on left front wing
Z Connector in boot, 4-pole
○ Weld point

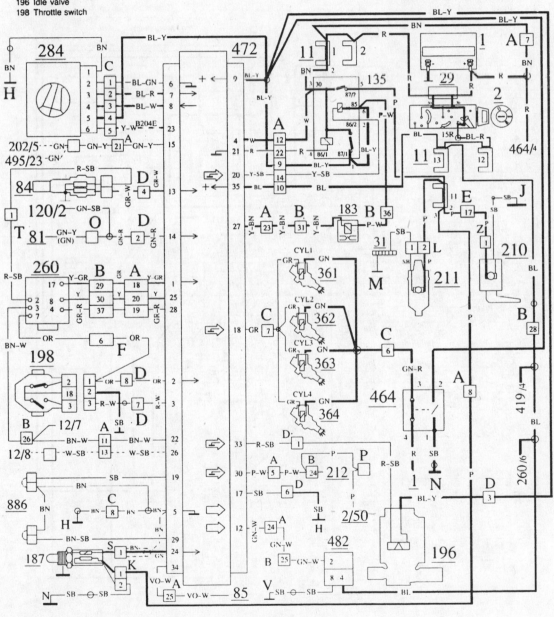

Fig. 38 LH-Jetronic wiring diagram — 740 and 940 with B234F engine

84285045

1/1 Battery (1)
2/12 Suppressor relay (464)
2/13 Fuel injection relay (135)
3/1 Ignition switch (2)
3/50 Throttle switch (198)
4/6 ECC control unit (495)
4/10 Ignition system control unit (260)
4/15 Power stage, EZK (419)
4/23 Control unit, LH-Jetronic 2.4 (472)
5/1E Speedometer (85)
5/18 18-pole connector on instrument panel (18)
6/31 Fuel pump (211)
6/32 Feed pump (210)
7/13 AC pressure sensor (81)
7/15 Lambda probe (oxygen sensor) (187)
7/15 Lambdasond (187)

7/16 Coolant temperature sensor (84)
7/17 Air mass meter (284)
7/47 PTC resistor (235)
8/3 AC compressor (200)
8/5 Idle valve (196)
8/6–8/9 Injectors (361–364)
8/12 Cold start valve (188)
11/1–35 Fuses
14/105 Bridge (886)
15/1 Positive terminal (78)
17/7 Test output (self-diagnosis) (482)
17/11 Test point (212)
20/15 Ballast resistor (376)
31/31 Ground terminal strip in central relay unit (31)

A Connector right A pillar
B Connector left A pillar
C Connector right wheel arch
D Connector right wheel arch
E Connector left A pillar
F Connector left wheel arch
G Connector, 10-pole on instrument panel
H Ground point on intake manifold
J Ground point in boot
K Connector on firewall
L Connector on central electrical unit
M Ground point in central relay unit
N Ground point right front wing
O Connector on firewall
P Connector, 3-pole, right wheel arch
Q Connector, 12-pole on instrument panel
R Connector, 10-pole on instrument panel
S Connector on firewall
T Connector on left wheel arch
V Ground point on left front wing
Z Connector in boot, 4-pole
○ Weld point

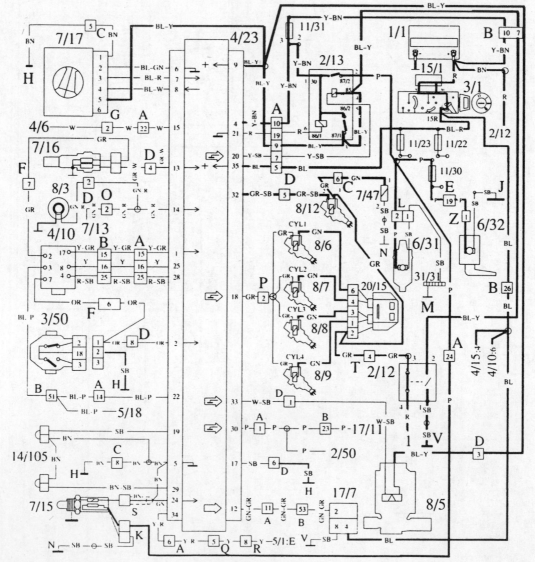

84285047

Fig. 39 LH-Jetronic wiring diagram — 760 with B230FT engine

1 Battery
2 Ignition switch
11 Central electrical unit
12 12-pole instrument panel
   connector
29 Positive terminal
31 Ground terminal strip in
   central electrical unit
81 AC pressure sensor
84 Coolant temperature sensor
85 Speedometer
135 Fuel injection relay
187 Lambda probe (oxygen sensor)
188 Cold start valve
196 Idle valve
198 Throttle switch
200 AC compressor

210 Feed pump
211 Fuel pump
212 Test point
259 High power system control unit
260 Ignition system control unit
284 Air mass meter
361–364 Injectors
376 Ballast resistor
419 Power stage, EZK
420 Throttle switch test point
464 Suppressor relay
472 Control unit, LH-Jetronic 2.4
482 Test output (self-diagnosis)
495 Control unit, ECC
886 Bridge

A Connector right A pillar
B Connector left A pillar
C Connector right wheel arch
D Connector right wheel arch
E Connector left A pillar
F Connector left wheel arch
H Ground point on intake manifold
J Ground point in boot
K Connector on firewall
L Connector on central electrical unit
M Ground point right A pillar
N Ground point right front wing
O Connector on firewall, single-pole
P Connector on central electrical unit
S Connector on firewall
T Connector left wheel arch
V Ground point on left front wing
Z Connector in boot, 4-pole
○ Weld point

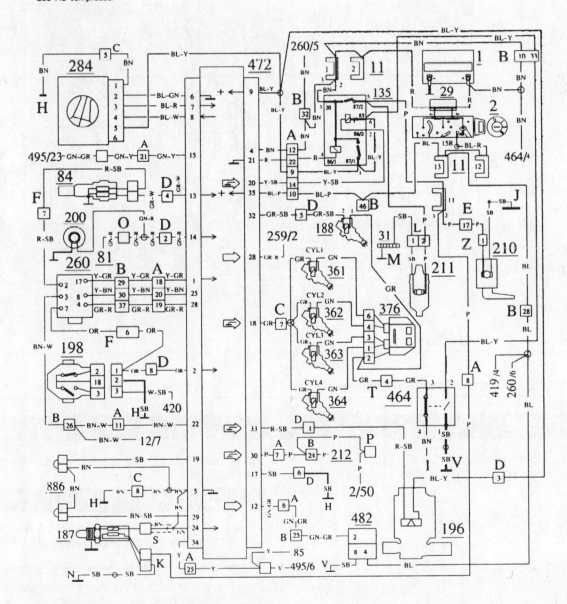

Fig. 40 LH-Jetronic wiring diagram — 780 with B230FT engine

84285049

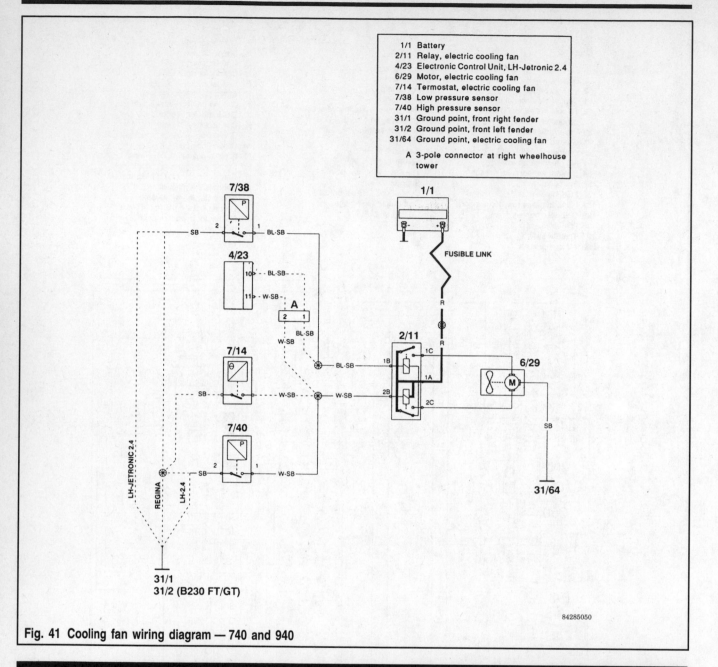

1/1	Battery
2/11	Relay, electric cooling fan
4/23	Electronic Control Unit, LH-Jetronic 2.4
6/29	Motor, electric cooling fan
7/14	Termostat, electric cooling fan
7/38	Low pressure sensor
7/40	High pressure sensor
31/1	Ground point, front right fender
31/2	Ground point, front left fender
31/64	Ground point, electric cooling fan
A	3-pole connector at right wheelhouse tower

Fig. 41 Cooling fan wiring diagram — 740 and 940

FUEL TANK

The feed pump is located in the fuel tank. The fuel pump and filter is located underneath the vehicle.

REMOVAL & INSTALLATION

1. Disconnect the negative battery cable.
2. Raise and support the vehicle safely.

3. Release the fuel system pressure. Drain the fuel tank completely.

✳✳CAUTION

When performing this procedure, always have a dry-chemical fire extinguisher handy. Fuel vapors are extremely explosive.

4. In the trunk, remove the panels which cover the filler hose. It may be necessary to remove the spare tire on some vehicles. Roll back the carpet and remove the access panel cover.

5. Disconnect the fuel filler pipe connection. Label and disconnect all fuel lines leading to the fuel tank. Label and disconnect all electrical connectors at the fuel tank.

6. Position a floorjack under the tank, using a large piece of wood as a cushion between the fuel tank and the floorjack. Raise the jack so that it just contacts the tank.

7. Remove any shields or protective covers on the tank. Loosen and remove the tank retaining bolts. Lower the jack slowly and inspect for any obstructions.

To install:

8. Install the protective shields and raise the fuel tank into position. Install and tighten the attaching bolts.

9. Remove the floorjack. Connect all fuel and electrical lines leading to the fuel tank.

10. Install the protective panel in the trunk and replace the spare tire (as required) and the carpet.

11. Lower the vehicle.

12. Connect the negative battery cable. Turn the ignition key **ON** and check for leaks.

Feed Pump and Sending Unit

REMOVAL & INSTALLATION

1. Disconnect the negative battery cable.
2. Raise and support the vehicle safely.
3. Relieve the fuel system pressure.
4. Remove the fuel tank.
5. Loosen the lock-ring at the top of the fuel tank and remove the sending unit with the transfer pump attached. Note the direction of the float in the tank.
6. Remove the transfer pump from the sending unit.

To install:

7. Install the transfer pump on the sending unit. Install the sending unit in the fuel tank and tighten the lock-ring to specification. Do not overtighten the lock-ring as the plastic threads on some fuel tanks are easily stripped.
8. Install the fuel tank in the vehicle.
9. Lower the vehicle.
10. Connect the negative battery cable, start the engine and check for leaks.

REGINA FUEL INJECTION SYSTEM

Description and Operation

▶ **See Figures 42 and 43**

The Regina fuel injection system is a self-diagnosing system that is capable of storing up to 3 fault codes in its memory. It is used in conjunction with the REX 1 ignition system. Both are adaptive systems that are capable of multiple adjustments based on previous driving. If a fault occurs, a warning lamp lights up the instrument panel. Fault tracing can be carried out using the diagnostic program.

The Regina fuel system is characterized by the followings:
— Utilizing a pressure sensor for measuring engine load
— An air mass meter for measuring air intake volume
— Utilizing a separate cold start valve to ensure starting at low temperatures
— Incorporation of an automatic idle shut-off valve if power is lost
— Utilization of an induction sensor, which is mounted on the flywheel to indicate rpm and crankshaft position through the ignition system control unit
— Use of an electrically heated oxygen sensor (Lambda-sond)
— EVAP system to minimize evaporation from the fuel tank
— Three-way catalytic converter

Various input sensors feed information that is interpreted by the control unit to achieve optimum efficiency. The control unit receives signals from the pressure sensor, air intake temperature sensor and receives crankshaft position information from the ignition control unit, without which the system will not function. The coolant temperature sensor, oxygen sensor and throttle switch also send information to the control unit.

System Components

Control Unit

▶ **See Figure 44**

The Regina fuel system control unit is extremely compact and uses a double-sided Printed Circuit Board (PCB). Discrete components are soldered to one side of the PCB and surface mounted components are on the other side. The multi-pin plug uses a filter to reduce interference and protect the electronics. It can operate at system voltage down to a minimum of 6 volts. The microprocessor operates at a voltage of 5 volts.

The control unit incorporates a microprocessor that receives signals from various sensors regarding operational conditions, then evaluates them in relation to pre-programmed values and calculates the correct injector opening duration.

The control unit controls idling rpm by regulating the amount of air bypassing the throttle valve. It also controls other functions, such as the cold start valve, fuel pump and the relay. The most important function is monitoring faults through the diagnostic unit.

In time, wear will affect the operation of the throttle valve, causing less air to enter the intake system. Instead of operating from a pre-programmed value, the idle valve receives a signal that is adapted to the condition which the control unit has learned from previous driving periods.

The oxygen sensor determines if the fuel mixture is rich or lean and adjusts the control unit's Lambda regulator. The self-adjusting mechanism keeps the control unit function at mid point. Therefore, no adjustment is necessary for carbon monoxide content and automatically compensates for the effects of tolerances and wear in the injection system. Whenever the

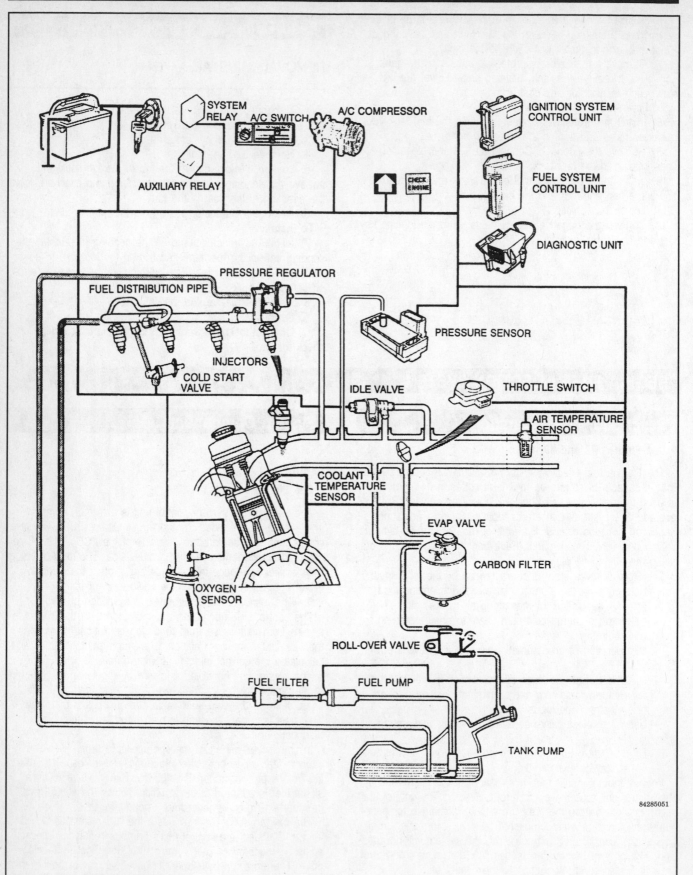

Fig. 42 Fuel system components — Regina

84285051

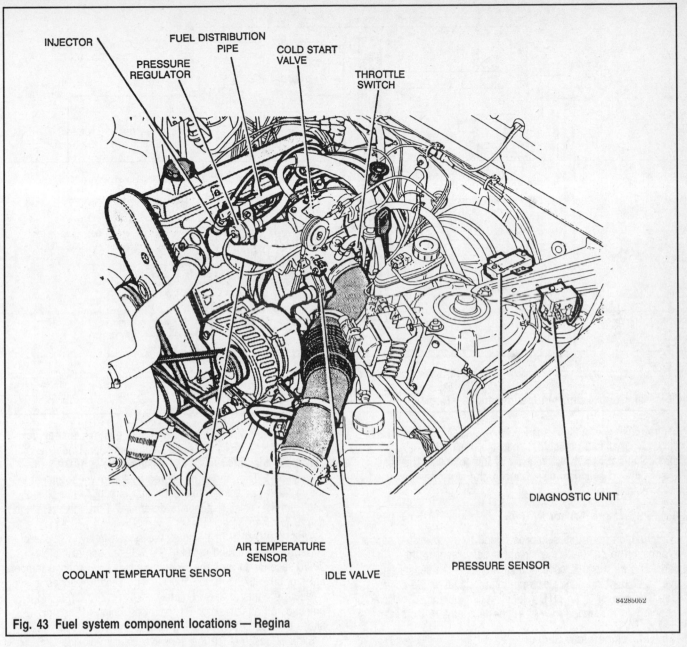

INJECTOR

PRESSURE REGULATOR

FUEL DISTRIBUTION PIPE

COLD START VALVE

THROTTLE SWITCH

DIAGNOSTIC UNIT

AIR TEMPERATURE SENSOR

COOLANT TEMPERATURE SENSOR

IDLE VALVE

PRESSURE SENSOR

84285052

Fig. 43 Fuel system component locations — Regina

vehicle is started and driven, the control unit will use the value that has been stored from previous driving.

Incorporated is a limp home function for the pressure sensor, air temperature sensor and the coolant temperature sensor. If no load information is obtained, the control unit uses 3 pre-programmed substitute values for intake manifold pressure. It results in the injection pattern being varied according to engine revolutions, allowing the vehicle to be driven without any major problems.

If the signal from the coolant temperature sensor stops, the vehicle can still be driven without a problem. However, there can be difficulties when starting the engine since information on engine temperature is used to adjust the fuel mixture through the cold start system.

DATA SENSORS

Pressure Sensor

The most important information for measuring engine fuel comes from the pressure sensor. Using the pressure and temperature data, the micro-processor calculates the intake air mass. It is connected to the engine intake manifold through a hose and takes its reading there of the present pressure. A piezo-electric crystal changes a voltage input to an electrical output that reflects the pressure in the intake manifold.

Atmospheric pressure is measured when the engine is started and when driving fully loaded, then the pressure sensor information is adjusted accordingly.

The pressure sensor connector has 3 terminals: A, B and C. A is ground, B carries the output signal to the control unit and C provides the pressure sensor with 5 volts of current from the

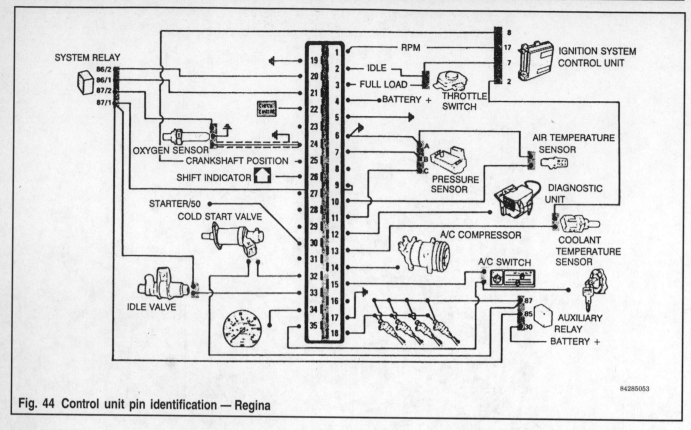

Fig. 44 Control unit pin identification — Regina

control unit. The output varies between 0.5-5 volts depending on intake manifold pressure. When the engine is not running, atmospheric pressure will register at full potential. The sensor is sensitive to electrical disturbances, therefore it is protected by a metal cover.

Air Temperature Sensor

Information from this sensor is added to the pressure sensor information to calculate the air mass being sent to the cylinders. The air mass passes through holes in the sensor and over a bulb which sends a temperature signal to the control unit. The sensor is an NTC (Negative Temperature Coefficient), meaning its resistance lowers as the temperature increases.

Coolant Temperature Sensor

While the engine is warming up, the choke mixture enrichment function is regulated by the control unit using information received by the coolant temperature sensor. This sensor is also a NTC type (Negative Temperature Coefficient), meaning resistance lowers as temperature increases. The sensor has 2 resistors. The second is connected to the ignition system's control unit and is grounded to the engine block.

Throttle Switch

The throttle switch tells the fuel system and ignition system control units whether the throttle valve is closed or fully opened. The throttle switch is equipped with micro-switches for idling and full load running.

Lambda Sond (Oxygen Sensor)

The purpose of the oxygen sensor is to maintain the air/fuel mixture value so that the catalytic converter can operate most

effectively. It is mounted in the exhaust gas manifold approximately 6 inch in front of the catalytic converter. Under normal conditions, the optimum air/fuel mixture ratio is 14.7:1 (Lambda=1). The ratio is monitored by the oxygen content in the exhaust gas using information that is sent to the control unit from the oxygen sensor to determine if the mixture is too rich or too lean.

When the control unit signals the system relay, 12 volts of current is sent through resistor R1. It takes approximately 20-30 seconds to heat the oxygen sensor to a working temperature of 392°-572°F (200°-300°C). The sensor reaches a level of about 9 ohms at approximately 1292°F (700°C). Current branches off after resistor R1, with part going to resistor R2 and a constant 1.2 volts being sent to the oxygen sensor.

Exhaust gases reach the sensitive titanium-dioxide film through slits in the exhaust manifold sleeve pipe. The resistance of the titanium-dioxide film rises or drops in direct relationship to the amount of oxygen present.

The control unit disregards the oxygen sensor signal, during and after a choke assisted start-up. At full load, the oxygen sensor signal is blocked by the throttle switch. This enables the control unit to enrich the fuel mixture and prevent overheating of the engine, oxygen sensor and the catalytic converter.

EGR Temperature Sensor(California Only)

This sensor, found on California vehicles, measures the temperature of the exhaust gases returned to the intake manifold. Detection of the temperature variations enables the control unit to determine whether the EGR system is operating. It is able to measure temperatures up to 500°C (930°F). Before this limit the resistance increases with temperature.

CONTROLLED OUTPUTS

Based on information provided by the input sensors, the control unit sets system voltage by grounding the system relay, removes the system relay ground if the engine turns over too slowly (has stopped), thus preventing battery drain from unnecessary fuel pump operation, regulates opening, timing and injection duration, controls the air valve for constant idle speed, controls the cold start injector, stores fault codes if faults are detected, provides load information to the ignition system, protects against overrevving of the engine by disabling the injectors, shuts off fuel injection during deceleration and controls indicator lamps (Check Engine and Gear Change).

Idle Valve

The magnetic idle valve is mounted on a bracket under the intake manifold. As the control unit sends different current levels to the magnet actuator, a magnetized core is either drawn in or pushed out. A plate is attached to the core which allows a chosen amount of air to pass. When no current is supplied, the idle valve is closed and the engine cannot idle.

The idle valve operates at all engine rpm. This prevents high negative pressure from forming in the intake manifold if the throttle valve is closed at high engine rpm by braking the engine.

The control unit uses information from engine rpm and the throttle valve to determine when the idle valve will open, in order to provide a constant idle speed. The idle valve receives a control signal based on previous driving, instead of using a pre-programmed value stored in the control unit. A built in system for increasing engine rpm causes the idle speed to increases slowly when the A/C is turned to the **ON** position. Thus, creating an immediate rpm increasing function. When the compressor cuts in, a load signal is sent to the control unit which compensates for the increased engine load to ensure that the rpm does not fluctuate.

System Relay

The fuel injection system relay is located in the fuse/relay box, mounted in the center console underneath the radio, and is controlled by the fuel system control unit. It supplies current to the fuel pump and certain control unit functions, and controls the auxiliary relay.

Auxiliary Relay

The auxiliary relay, mounted in the engine compartment, just in front of the right shock tower, is controlled by the system relay. It supplies current to the injectors and the cold start valve. It diminishes the possibility of electrical interference, by separating the cable harnesses from the system.

EGR Vacuum Booster
▶ See Figure 45

This component is found on California vehicles. It controls the pressure in the vacuum line to the EGR valve by means of the admission valve (lower section). The converter processes the electrical signal from the intake manifold to maintain optimum control of the EGR valve. The unit is also designed to

allow for the ambient air pressure. It is mounted on the left strut tower.

FUEL DELIVERY SYSTEM

Fuel Pressure Regulator

The fuel pressure regulator which is mounted on the distribution pipe, ensures that the fuel pressure remains constant at the injectors. Using a vacuum hose connected to the engine intake manifold, fuel pressure is kept at approximately 42 psi to ensure that the pressure over the injectors is kept constant, regardless of throttle position. The amount of fuel injected depends entirely on the injection time. Excess fuel is returned to the fuel tank through a return pipe.

Injectors

By activating the relay, the control unit sends current to the injectors. It controls injection duration by grounding the injectors. When the starter motor is operating, there are 2 injections per rotation, and 1 during normal driving. Injection occurs in the intake manifold near the intake valves.

Cold Start Valve

The cold start valve is controlled directly by the control unit, and is located under the intake manifold near the throttle valve. It is supplied with fuel through a hose connected to the distribution pipe.

At cold start, fuel condenses on the cold surfaces in the form of drops. Using a separate cold start valve improves engine cold starting. Its positioned farther away from the engine block than the injectors and delivers the fuel more in the

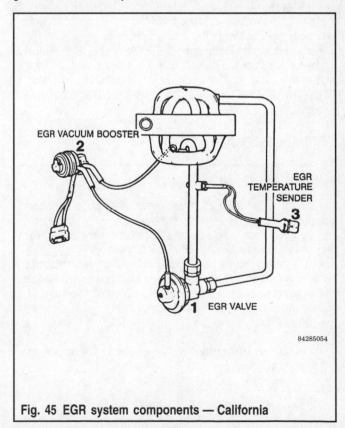

84285054

Fig. 45 EGR system components — California

form of vapor than in drops. It operates when the temperature is below freezing and when engine rpm is below 1050. It cuts out when engine rpm exceeds the permissible limit.

Fuel Pump

All models are equipped with a 2-stage electric fuel pump. It replaces the primary pump and the pre-pump which were used on previous models. It is located in the fuel tank.

Fuel Filter

The fuel filter is mounted on a plate underneath the vehicle on the left side.

Evaporative Control System (EVAP)

▶ **See Figure 46**

This system controls the gases that result from normal fuel tank evaporation, keeping them from polluting the air. Fuel vapor passes from the filter opening through a roll-over valve to a reservoir (canister, carbon filter). Fuel vapor is absorbed in the reservoir. The reservoir is equipped with EVAP valve which prevents leakage of fuel vapor when the engine is not running.

Fuel vapors from the fuel tank enter into the top of the carbon filter and are absorbed. Air is then pushed out through a channel from the bottom of the filter. Depending on temperature and other conditions, the filter can store approximately 90 grams of fuel. If for any reason, the vehicle leans sideways at more than a 45 degree angle, a roll-over valve is incorporated into the system to prevent any fuel spills.

An EVAP valve is located at the top of the carbon filter and is closed when the engine is off. During idling, the EVAP valve is closed so that it does not interfere with the automatic idle settings or make the fuel mixture to rich. The EVAP valve closes using vacuum pressure taken from the intake manifold and from the throttle shutter positive terminal.

Increased engine loads open the EVAP valve, allowing fuel vapor to flow from the carbon filter into the intake manifold, and at the same time air is drawn through the bottom channel. Under normal conditions, the filter discharges the fuel in approximately 15-20 minutes.

SERVICE PRECAUTIONS

▶ **See Figures 47 and 48**

• Safety is the most important factor when performing not only fuel system maintenance, but any type of maintenance. Failure to conduct maintenance and repairs in a safe manner may result in serious personal injury or death.

• Use caution when working around ignition system components. the ignition system operates at high power with dangerous voltages in both the low-tension and high-tension circuits, including connectors and similar fittings.

• Do not operate the fuel pump when the fuel lines are empty.

• Do not arc weld on the vehicle unless all the control units have been removed.

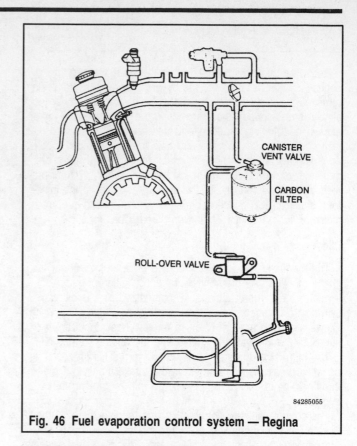

Fig. 46 Fuel evaporation control system — Regina

• The control units must not be exposed to temperatures above 175°F (80°C), such as in a paint booth.

• Make sure that the ignition switch is **OFF** before connecting or disconnecting the control unit, ignition coil, spark plug wiring or test instruments.

• Always use new gaskets and seals when remaking a fuel connection.

• When performing a compression test, disconnect the wire from terminal 1 on the ignition coil (to prevent arcing) and remove the connectors from the injectors (to avoid flooding).

• Make sure all control unit connectors are fastened securely. A poor connection can cause an extremely high surge voltage, resulting in damage to integrated circuits.

• Keep any control unit harness at least 4 in. away from adjacent harnesses to prevent a system malfunction due to external electronic interference.

• Keep all parts and harnesses dry during service.

• Before attempting to remove any parts, turn off the ignition switch and disconnect the battery ground cable.

• Always use a 12 volt battery as a power source.

• Do not attempt to disconnect the battery cables with the engine running.

• When using a tester probe on the control unit connector, first remove the protective sleeve, then always gently check connections through the numbered holes on the connector side.

• Do not attempt to disassemble a control unit under any circumstances.

• If a battery cable is disconnected, the memory will be erased.

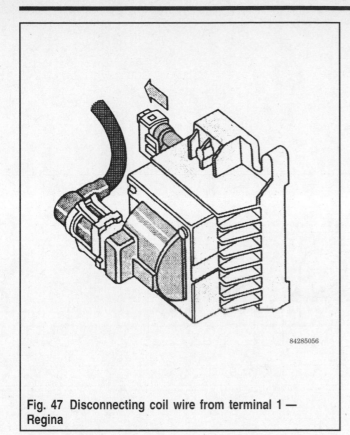

Fig. 47 Disconnecting coil wire from terminal 1 — Regina

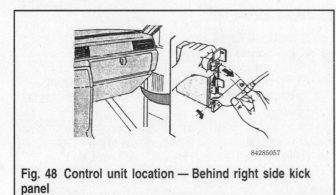

Fig. 48 Control unit location — Behind right side kick panel

Relieving Fuel System Pressure

▶ **See Figure 49**

1. Remove the fuel pump relay from the electrical distribution unit. The relay is furthest to the left on the second row.
2. Crank the engine until the engine will not start anymore, indicating that the fuel pressure is relieved.
3. Reinstall the relay.

❋❋CAUTION

To avoid fire and personal injury, replace any plastic tie bands removed from the fuel lines.

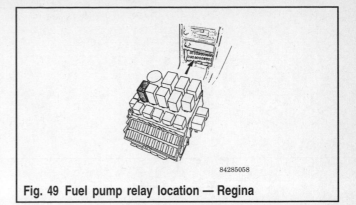

Fig. 49 Fuel pump relay location — Regina

Draining Fuel Lines and Filter

▶ **See Figure 50**

1. Remove the protective cap from the valve located on the fuel injection manifold between injectors 1 and 2.
2. Connect adapter hose/union to the fuel drainage unit. Use the special tools 999-5484, 981-2270, 2273, 2282 or their equivalent.
3. Start the fuel drainage.
4. Connect the hose/union to locked/closed valve. Unlock/open valve.

Fuel Injectors, Distribution Pipe and Pressure Regulator

REMOVAL & INSTALLATION

▶ **See Figure 51**

➡**Remove and install the fuel distribution pipe, the injectors and the cold start valve as one unit.**

1. Unbolt the pressure regulator from the fuel rail bracket.
2. Remove the fuel rail bolts without distorting the metal of the rail.
3. Use 2 line wrenches and separate the line fittings, then remove the injector assembly.
4. Installation is the reverse of removal. Use new O-rings and lubricate with petroleum jelly.

TESTING

Injector Resistance Check

1. Turn the ignition switch **OFF**. Disconnect auxiliary relay from its connector.
2. Connect a jumper wire between pin 2 (BL/Y) and pin 3 (GN/R) on the auxiliary relay connector.
3. Connect an ohmmeter between pin 9 and pin 18 on the control connector. Ohmmeter should read 4 ohms.
4. If ohmmeter reads approximately 5.3 ohms, fault is in 1 injector or its leads; 7 ohms, fault is in 2 injectors or its leads; 14 ohms, fault is in 3 injectors or its leads.

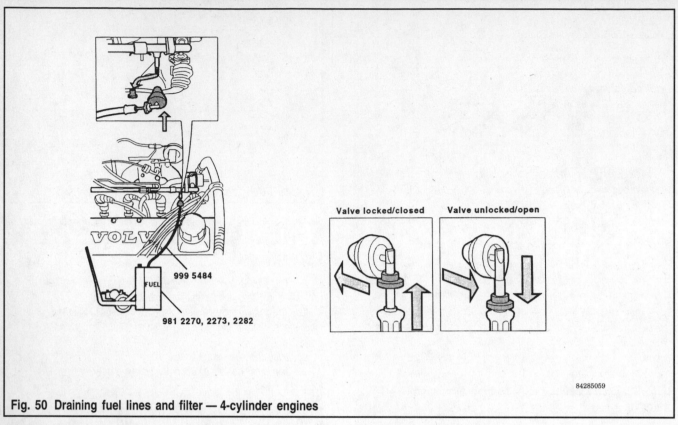

Fig. 50 Draining fuel lines and filter — 4-cylinder engines

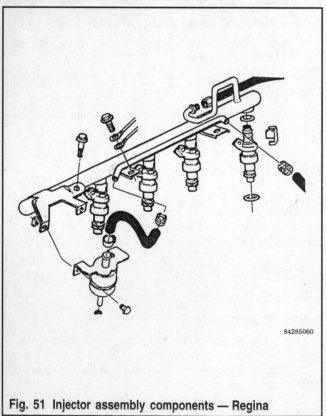

Fig. 51 Injector assembly components — Regina

5. If measured resistance is not as indicated, disconnect injector connectors and test separately. Reading for individual injectors should be 14 ohms.

Control Function 3 Test

1. Turn the ignition switch to the **ON** position.
2. Open diagnostic cover and enter Control Function 3.
3. The injectors should begin to operate, followed by the idle valve and the LED should flash a continuous pattern.
4. Listen and feel by hand each injector to ensure they all are operating.
5. If an injector is not operating, change connector from an injector that's operating. If the fault moves to the injector that was operating, then the fault is in the connector lead.
6. If the injector is still not operating, then the injector is faulty.
7. Test injector separately, by connecting an ohmmeter between the injector pins. Ohmmeter should read approximately 14 ohms.

Lambda-Sond (Oxygen Sensor)

REMOVAL & INSTALLATION

1. Disconnect the negative battery cable.
2. Raise and support the vehicle safely.
3. Disconnect the oxygen sensor connector. The sensor is located near the catalytic converter.
4. Remove the oxygen sensor, using a suitable wrench.
5. Installation is the reverse of the removal procedure. Before installing, apply 'Never Seez' paste (P/N 1 161 035-9) to the threaded section of the sond. Tighten to 40 ft. lbs. (55 Nm).

TESTING

1. Disconnect oxygen sensor electrical connector.
2. Ground the lead coming from the control unit. carbon monoxide content should rise, indicating that the control unit and its connections are operating correctly.
3. Connect a voltmeter between ground and the connector coming from the oxygen sensor. Reading at correct carbon monoxide content should be approximately 0.5 volts.

Throttle Switch

REMOVAL & INSTALLATION

1. Turn the ignition switch to the **OFF** position.
2. Disconnect the throttle switch connector.
3. Remove the throttle switch retaining screws and remove the throttle switch.
4. Installation is the reverse of the removal procedure. Adjust the throttle, as required.

ADJUSTMENTS

1. Open the throttle slightly and listen to the switch. There should be a click when the shutter opens, if the adjustment is correct.
2. Loosen the throttle switch mounting bolts.
3. Turn the switch slightly clockwise.
4. Turn the switch counter-clockwise until the switch clicks, then tighten the mounting bolts.
5. Recheck the setting.

TESTING

1. Turn ignition switch to the **OFF** position.
2. Check the throttle switch by connecting an ohmmeter between ground and pin 2 on the control unit connector. ohmmeter should read 0 ohms (switch closed).
3. Depress gas pedal slightly, resistance should increase to 2000-3000 ohms (switch opens).
4. Connect an ohmmeter between ground and pin 3 connection on the control unit connector. Ohmmeter should read infinity. (full load switch open).
5. Depress gas pedal all the way. Ohmmeter should read 0 ohms.
6. If specifications are not as specified, check at throttle switch to see if fault is in throttle switch or its leads. Check ground connections at intake manifold.

Coolant Temperature Sensor

REMOVAL & INSTALLATION

1. Turn the ignition switch to the **OFF** position.

2. Drain the cooling system.
3. Disconnect the temperature sensor connector and remove the temperature sensor.
4. Installation is the reverse of the removal procedure.

TESTING

1. Turn ignition switch to the **OFF** position.
2. Check the coolant temperature sensor by connecting an ohmmeter between ground and pin 13 on the control unit connector. Ohmmeter reading various depending on temperature.
   a. At 14°F, reading should be between 8,260-10,560 ohms.
   b. At 68°F, reading should be between 2,280-2,720 ohms.
   c. At 176°F, reading should be between 290-364 ohms.
3. If specifications are not as specified, test the coolant temperature sensor to see if fault is in the sensor or its leads.
4. Check ground connections at the intake manifold.

Pressure Sensor

REMOVAL & INSTALLATION

1. Turn the ignition switch **OFF**.
2. Disconnect the pressure sensor connector.
3. Remove the sensor mounting screws and remove the sensor from the vehicle.
4. Installation is the reverse of the removal procedure.

TESTING

1. Check that the ignition switch is in the **OFF** position. Disconnect the pressure sensor hose.
2. Install the control unit connector loosely on the control unit.
3. Turn ignition switch to the **ON** position.
4. Connect a voltmeter between ground and pin 7 connection on the control unit connector. Voltmeter should read approximately 5 volts.
5. Connect voltmeter between ground and pin 11 on the control unit connector. Voltmeter should read approximately 5 volts.
6. Connect a hand operated vacuum pump to the pressure sensor. Connect a voltmeter between pin 7 and pin 11 on the control unit connector then apply vacuum. Voltage should drop, indicating proper operation of the sensor. If voltage does not drop, replace pressure sensor.

Fuel Filter

REMOVAL & INSTALLATION

1. Disconnect the negative battery cable.
2. Relieve the fuel system pressure.
3. Raise and safely support the vehicle safely.

4. Place a container under the filter to catch the excess fuel.

5. Using a shop rag to prevent fuel spray, remove the fuel lines, mounting bracket nut and the filter.

To install:

➡**Fuel flow direction arrow is marked on the new (and old) filter. Arrow follows direction from fuel tank to engine.**

6. Install the new filter in the proper direction. Be sure to use the new sealing rings and torque the fuel lines to the filter to 14 ft. lbs. (20 Nm).

7. Connect the negative battery cable, turn the ignition **ON** and check for leaks.

FUEL SYSTEM TESTING

Pressure Check

▶ **See Figure 52**

1. Relieve the fuel pressure. Also, refer to 'Draining the fuel lines and filter' in this section.

2. Connect fuel pressure gauge 5011, or equivalent, holding a shop towel under the fuel line to catch any spilled fuel.

3. With the fuel pump relay still removed, remove the seat belt reminder, since this makes the test more easily performed. It is located in the middle on the top row.

4. Start the fuel pump by connecting an electrical lead between terminals 30 and 87/2 on the relay base. Verify pump operation by removing the fuel cap and listening.

5. The fuel pressure should be 300 kPa (42 psi).

6. Remove the lead between terminals 30 and 87/2.

7. Relieve the fuel pressure and remove the pressure gauge, catching any spilled fuel with a shop towel.

8. Reinstall the relay.

✴✴CAUTION

To avoid fire and personal injury, replace any plastic tie bands removed from the fuel lines.

Pump Inoperative

1. If the fuel pump does not start, remove the lead between terminals 30 and 87/2.

2. Check for voltage at terminal 30. If there is none, check the lead between the relay and the battery.

3. Connect an electrical lead between terminals 30 and 87/2 on the relay base. If the pump still does not start, check the lead between the pump and the relay. Check the lead between 87/1 and 85 for breaks with an ohmmeter.

Pressure Too High

▶ **See Figure 53**

1. Remove the lead between terminals 30 and 87/2 on the relay base.

2. Remove the return hose from the pressure regulator and blow into the pipe.

3. Remove the vacuum hose from the pressure regulator and blow into the pipe.

4. If both hoses are open, the pressure regulator is faulty. Replace and recheck.

Pressure Too Low

1. Squeeze the return hose by hand, not with a tool, and check if the pressure rises.

✴✴CAUTION

To avoid personal injury and fire, do not allow the pressure to exceed 600 kPa (84 psi).

2. If the pressure rises rapidly, the pump and hoses are good. Replace the regulator and recheck the pressure.

3. If the pressure rises slowly, the fuel filter, pump strainer or the fuel lines are clogged or blocked.

4. If the pressure does not rise, the fuel pump is faulty.

Pressure Regulator

1. Connect a vacuum pump to the pressure regulator.

2. Apply vacuum to the regulator and check that the fuel pressure falls as more vacuum is applied.

3. Remove the lead between terminals 30 and 87/2.

4. Relieve the fuel pressure and remove the pressure gauge, catching any spilled fuel with a shop towel.

5. Reinstall the relay.

✴✴CAUTION

To avoid fire and personal injury, replace any plastic tie bands removed from the fuel lines.

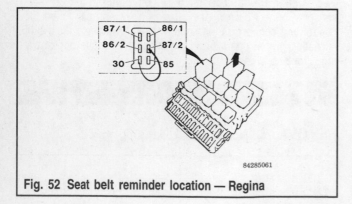

84285061

Fig. 52 Seat belt reminder location — Regina

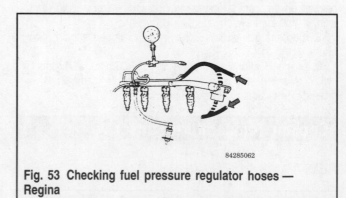

84285062

Fig. 53 Checking fuel pressure regulator hoses — Regina

Fault Tracing

TESTING

Diagnostic Unit
▶ **See Figure 54**

1. Enter Control Function 1. If the LED does not flash when the button is pressed, or if no code is flashed, continue the diagnostic unit test.

➡**If there are no fault codes the LED should flash fault code 1-1-1, which indicates that no other fault codes are stored.**

2. Check ground connections at the intake manifold. Poor ground connections can cause different fault symptoms.

3. Check oxygen sensor ground connection, located at the right front mud guard.

4. Check the pump relay fuse (fuse 1), located in the fuse/relay box.

5. Remove panels from under the instrument panel right side, in front of right firewall side, then remove glove compartment. Check control unit grounds.

6. Disconnect control unit electrical connector, then remove the protective sleeve.

7. Check diagnostic unit by connecting a voltmeter between ground and pin 4 on the control unit connector. Voltmeter should read 12 volts. If no voltage is present, check lead between the control unit connector and fuse 1 in the fuse/relay box.

8. Turn the ignition switch to the **ON** position, then install selector plug into socket No. 2 on the diagnostic unit.

9. Connect a voltmeter between ground and pin 12 on the control unit connector. Voltmeter should read 12 volts.

10. Press the button on the diagnostic unit. Voltmeter should read 0 volts. If no voltage is present at the control unit, take reading at the diagnostic unit connector. If voltmeter remains reading 12 volts when button is pressed, check the diagnostic unit.

11. Disconnect the diagnostic unit electrical connector, then connect a voltmeter between ground and the blue lead on the diagnostic unit connector. Voltmeter should read 12 volts.

12. Connect an ohmmeter between ground and the black lead in the diagnostic unit connector. Ohmmeter should read 0 ohms. Turn ignition switch to the **OFF** position.

13. Connect an ohmmeter between the diagnostic unit selector plug and the pin under the selector button (on bottom of diagnostic unit). Ohmmeter should read infinity. Press button. Ohmmeter should read 0 ohms.

14. Connect a diode tester between the selector plug and the diagnostic unit LED pin: Connect the positive test lead from the tester to the pin directly underneath the LED and the negative test lead from the tester to the selector plug, then reverse the leads. If current flows only one way, the diode is good. If current flows both ways, replace diagnostic unit.

15. Check the pressure sensor by disconnecting the pressure sensor vacuum hose, then connect the control unit connector. Turn the ignition switch to the **ON** position.

16. Connect a voltmeter between the control unit ground and pin 7 on the control unit connector. Voltmeter should read approximately 5 volts.

17. Connect a voltmeter between the control unit ground and pin 11 on the control unit connector. Voltmeter should read approximately 5 volts.

18. Connect a hand operated vacuum pump to the pressure sensor. Connect a voltmeter between pin 7 and pin 11 on the control unit connector. Apply vacuum to the pressure sensor. Voltage should drop, which indicates proper operation of the pressure sensor. If voltage does not drop, replace pressure sensor. Turn ignition switch to the **OFF** position and disconnect the control unit connector.

19. Press the diagnostic unit button again. Check to see if any additional fault codes are stored.

20. Press the diagnostic unit button for the third time to see if any fault codes are stored in the memory. If fault code 1-1-1 flashes, then there are no other fault codes in the memory.

➡**The diagnostic system memory is full when it contains 3 fault codes. Until those 3 are rectified and the memory erased, the system can not give information on any other problems.**

TESTING IN CONTROL FUNCTION 2

Throttle Control
▶ **See Figure 55**

1. Open the diagnostic unit cover, then install selector cable into socket No. 2.

2. Turn the throttle control to the full load position.

3. Enter control system 2, by pressing the diagnostic unit button 2 times. Hold button down for at least 1 second, but not more than 3 seconds. The LED should begin to flash.

4. Release throttle control. If diagnostic code 3-3-3 flashes, function of the shutter switch is correct in the full load position.

5. If the LED continues to flash, proceed as follows:

   a. Check throttle switch setting by opening the throttle slightly and listening to the switch. A click should be heard when the shutter opens (idle switch).

   b. Turn switch slightly clockwise, then counterclockwise until the switch clicks. Tighten mounting bolts and check setting.

   c. Test the throttle switch by disconnecting the control unit electrical connector. Connect an ohmmeter between

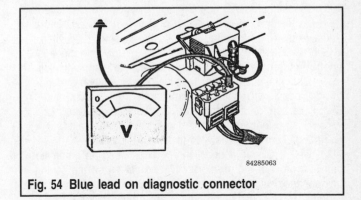

84285063

Fig. 54 Blue lead on diagnostic connector

ground and pin 2 on the control unit connector. Ohmmeter reading should be 0 ohms (switch closed).

d. Depress gas pedal slightly. Resistance should increase to 2000-3000 ohms (switch opens).

e. Connect an ohmmeter between ground and pin 3 on the control unit connector. Ohmmeter should read infinity (full load switch open).

f. Depress gas pedal all the way. Ohmmeter should read 0 ohms. If a fault appears, take reading at throttle switch to see if fault is in the throttle switch or its leads. Also, check the ground connections at the intake manifold.

6. Start the engine. If LED goes off, then flashes diagnostic code 3-3-1, the rpm signal from the ignition system is correct. If the engine does not start, run the starter motor until the LED goes off.

7. If the LED continues to flash rapidly, the ignition system has faults that must be repaired. If the ignition system has no faults, continue testing.

8. Check control unit ground connections.

9. Disconnect control unit electrical connector and remove protective sleeve.

10. Check diagnostic unit by connecting a voltmeter between ground and pin 4 on the control unit connector. Voltmeter should read 12 volts.

11. If no voltage is present, check lead between the control unit connector and fuse 1 in the fuse/relay box (located in center console).

12. Turn the ignition switch to the **ON** position, then install selector plug into socket No. 2 on the diagnostic unit.

13. Connect a voltmeter between ground and pin 12 on the control unit connector. Voltmeter should read 12 volts.

14. Press the button on the diagnostic unit. Voltmeter should read 0 volts. If no voltage is present at the control unit, take reading at the diagnostic unit connector. If voltmeter remains reading 12 volts when button is pressed, check the diagnostic unit.

15. Disconnect the diagnostic unit electrical connector, then connect a voltmeter between ground and the blue lead on the diagnostic unit connector. Voltmeter should read 12 volts.

16. Connect an ohmmeter between ground and the black lead in the diagnostic unit connector. Ohmmeter should read 0 ohms. Turn ignition switch to the **OFF** position.

17. Connect an ohmmeter between the diagnostic unit selector plug and the pin under the selector button (on bottom of diagnostic unit). Ohmmeter should read infinity. Press diagnostic button. Ohmmeter should read 0 ohms.

18. Connect a diode tester between the selector plug and the diagnostic unit LED pin: Connect the positive test lead from the tester to the pin directly underneath the LED and the negative test lead from the tester to the selector plug, then switch the leads. If current flows one way only, the diode is good. If current flows both ways, replace the diagnostic unit.

19. Check ignition lock voltage by turning ignition switch to the **ON** position. Connect a voltmeter between ground and pin 35 on the control unit connector. Voltmeter should read 12 volts. Ensure that voltage exists when the starter motor is operating. Turn ignition switch to the **OFF** position.

20. Check ground connections by connecting an ohmmeter between ground and pin 5, pin 17 and pin 19 on the control unit connector. Ohmmeter reading at all connections should be 0 ohms. Pin 5, pin 17 and pin 19 are ground leads at the intake manifold.

21. Ensure that the oxygen sensor wire is connected to pin 5 on the control unit connector.

22. Check the rpm sensor lead from the ignition system control unit by connecting a voltmeter between ground and pin 1 on the control unit connector. Turn ignition switch to the **ON** position. Voltmeter should read 12 volts.

23. Turn ignition switch to the **OFF** position. Check the throttle switch by connecting an ohmmeter between ground and pin 2 on the control unit connector. Ohmmeter should read 0 ohms (switch closed). Depress gas pedal slightly. Resistance should increase 2-3 kilo-ohm (switch opens).

24. Connect an ohmmeter between ground and pin 3 connection on the control unit. Ohmmeter should infinity (full load switch open). Depress gas pedal all the way. Ohmmeter should read 0 ohms. If specifications are not as specified, measure at throttle switch to see if fault is in the switch or its leads. Also, check ground connections at intake manifold..

25. Check the air temperature sensor by connecting an ohmmeter between pin 6 and pin 10 on the control unit connector. Ohmmeter reading depends on temperature; at -4°F (-20°C), reading should be 15000 ohms, at 68°F (20°C), reading should be 2500 ohms and at 212°F (100°C), reading should be 160 ohms. It is possible to check the coolant temperature sensor resistance at various temperatures by warming the sensor using a hot air gun. If specifications are not as specified, measure the air temperature sensor to see if fault is in the sensor or its leads.

26. Check the pressure sensor by disconnecting pressure sensor hose. Ensure that the ignition switch is in the **OFF** position, then install control unit connector loosely.

27. Turn ignition switch to the **ON** position. Connect a voltmeter between ground and pin 7 on the control unit connector. Voltmeter should read approximately 5 volts. Then, connect voltmeter between ground and pin 11 connection on the control unit connector. Voltmeter reading should be approximately 5 volts.

28. Install a hand operated vacuum pump to pressure sensor. Connect a voltmeter between pin 7 and pin 11 on the control unit connector and apply vacuum. Voltage should drop, indicating proper operation of the pressure sensor. If voltage does not drop, replace pressure sensor.

29. Turn ignition switch to the **OFF** position, then disconnect connector from control unit.

30. Test system relay/primary relay by connecting a voltmeter between ground and pin 9 on the control until connector, then a jumper wire from ground to pin 21 on the control unit connector. Relay should activate and voltmeter reading should read approximately 12 volts.

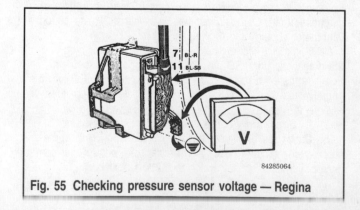

84285064

Fig. 55 Checking pressure sensor voltage — Regina

31. If fault has not been found, proceed to Control Function 3.

TESTING IN CONTROL FUNCTION 3

Air Conditioning Functions

On vehicles equipped with A/C, check the on/off function of the compressor as follows:

1. Turn ignition switch and A/C switch to the **ON** positions.

2. If LED goes off and then flashes fault code 1-1-4, A/C switch is operating correctly.

3. If the LED continues to flash rapidly, check lead from A/C control unit. Connect an ohmmeter between ground and pin 15 on the control unit connector. Note reading. Position A/C controls to A/C position. Resistance should change.

4. The LED will now return to rapid flashes, prior to the A/C compressor turning on. When the A/C compressor turns on, the LED light should go off and then flash fault code 1-3-4. If LED continues to flash rapidly, check lead from A/C compressor. Connect an ohmmeter between ground and pin 15 on the control unit connector. Ohmmeter should read 0-5 ohms. Turn ignition switch to the **OFF** position.

Idle Speed Compensation

1. Depress brake pedal and place selector lever into the **D** position and then into the **N** position. The LED should go off, then flash fault code 1-2-4.

2. If LED continues to flash rapidly, place gear selector lever into the **N** position. Connect ohmmeter between ground and pin 30 on the control unit connector. Ohmmeter should read 0 ohms.

3. Depress brake pedal and place gear selector lever into the **D** position. Ohmmeter should read infinity. On vehicles equipped with manual transmissions, ohmmeter should read 0 ohms in all gears.

Injectors

If injectors are not operating, but the LED flashes, proceed as follows:

1. Disconnect auxiliary relay.

2. Install a jumper wire between pin 2 (BL/Y) and pin 3 (GN/R) on the auxiliary relay socket.

3. Connect an ohmmeter between pin 9 and pin 18 on the control unit connector. Ohmmeter should read 4 ohms. If reading obtained is higher, current is not going through the injectors.

4. If ohmmeter reading is approximately 5.3 ohms, fault is in 1 injector or its leads; 7 ohms, fault is in 2 injectors or its leads; 14 ohms, fault is in 3 injectors or its leads.

5. If measured resistance is not as indicated, remove injector connectors and test them separately. Ohmmeter reading for individual injectors should be 14 ohms.

Idle Valve

If the idle valve is not operating, but the LED flashes, connect an ohmmeter between pin 9 and pin 33 on the control unit connector. Ohmmeter reading should be approximately 4 ohms.

Cold Start Valve

If the cold start valve is not operating, but the LED flashes, connect an ohmmeter between pin 9 and pin 32 on the control unit connector. Ohmmeter should read 10 ohms.

Auxiliary Relay

If the auxiliary relay is not operating, but the LED flashes, proceed as follows:

1. Connect a jumper wire from ground to pin 21 on the control unit.

2. Connect a voltmeter between ground and pin 18 on the control unit connector.

3. Both the system relay and auxiliary rely should operate and voltmeter reading should be approximately 12 volts. Remove jumper wire from pin 21.

Fuel Pump

▶ **See Figure 56**

If the fuel pump is not operating, but the LED flashes, proceed as follows:

1. Connect a jumper wire from ground to terminal 20 on the control unit connector. The fuel pump relay should close and the fuel pump should start to operate.

2. Connect a voltmeter between ground and pin 8 connection in the 25 terminal connector, located at the right A-post.

3. Voltmeter should read approximately 12 volts. Remove jumper wires from pin 20 and pin 21 from the control unit connector.

Air Temperature Sensor

1. Turn ignition switch to the **OFF** position.

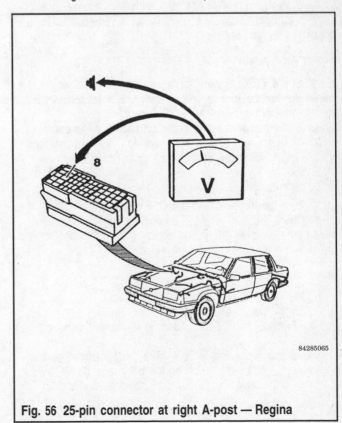

84285065

Fig. 56 25-pin connector at right A-post — Regina

2. Check the air temperature sensor by connecting an ohmmeter between pin 6 and pin 10 on the control unit connector. Ohmmeter should read as follows:

    a. At -4°F (-20°C), approximately 15,000 ohms.

    b. At 68°F (20°C), approximately 2,500 ohms.

    c. At 212°F (100°C), approximately 160 ohms.

3. To check the sensor at various temperatures, heat the sensor using a hot air gun.

4. If specifications are not as specified, test the air temperature sensor to see if fault is in the sensor or its leads.

System Relay

1. Turn ignition switch to the **OFF** position.

2. Check the system relay/primary relay as follows:

    a. Connect a voltmeter between ground and pin 9 connection on the control unit connector.

    b. Install a jumper wire from ground to pin 21 on the control unit connector. Relay should operate and voltmeter should read approximately 12 volts.

3. Check the system relay/pump relay as follows:

    a. Install a jumper wire from ground to pin 20 on the control unit connector. The pump relay should close and start the fuel pumps.

    b. Connect a voltmeter between ground and pin 8 in the 25 terminal connector located at the right A-post. Voltmeter should read approximately 12 volts. Remove jumper wires from pin 20 and pin 21.

Exhaust Carbon Monoxide Content

1. Check carbon monoxide content by inserting a carbon monoxide meter probe into the tapped hole on the catalytic converter.

2. Start and run engine. Check carbon monoxide content.

3. If carbon monoxide content is not within specifications, check the oxygen sensor.

Intake Air System

Check the intake system for leaks. System air leaks could cause the fuel mixture to be too lean. Check for leaks in the following locations:

1. Intake manifold between the air filter and the manifold.

2. All hoses and hose connections to the intake manifold.

3. The intake manifold and the throttle housing.

Idle Valve

1. Turn ignition switch to the **OFF** position.

2. Check the idle valve by connecting an ohmmeter between pin 9 and pin 33 on the control unit connector. Ohmmeter should read approximately 4 ohms.

Speedometer Signal

1. Turn ignition switch to the **OFF** position.

2. Check the speedometer signal as follows:

    a. Remove panel from under the instrument panel on the drivers side.

    b. Disconnect cable (VO/W) from the speedometer, then connect an ohmmeter between the cable and pin 34 on the control unit connector. Ohmmeter should read 0 ohms.

    c. If fault code 3-1-1 flashes and ohmmeter reads 0 ohms, the speedometer signal is missing. Replace speedometer assembly.

Auxiliary Relay

1. Remove auxiliary relay from its connector. Install a jumper wire between pin 2 (BL/Y) and pin 3 (GN/R) on the auxiliary relay socket.

2. Check the cold start valve by connecting an ohmmeter between pin 9 and pin 32 on the control unit connector. Ohmmeter reading should be approximately 10 ohms.

EGR Vacuum Booster

On California vehicles an EGR system malfunction is indicated by Fault Code 2-4-1. It results when the EGR temperature sensor detects that the exhaust gas recirculation flow is too low.

1. Turn the ignition switch **ON**.

2. Enter Control Function 3. The lamp should flash according as the EGR converter is activated.

3. Turn the ignition switch **OFF**.

4. If the EGR converter is not activated, measure the resistance between pins 6 and 15 in the control unit connector. The resistance should be approximately 75-95 ohms.

5. If the value is different, check the wiring and connection.

Exhaust Gas Recirculation (EGR) System(California Only)

▶ **See Figure 57**

1. Open the EGR vacuum booster connector. Remove the lead directly opposite the black-white lead between pin 1 and the control unit. Reconnect the connector.

2. Start and warm the engine to operating temperature.

3. Ground the loose lead. If the engine starts to run unevenly, the EGR system is operating.

EGR Temperature Sensor(California Only)

If the signal from the EGR temperature sensor is absent or faulty, Fault Code 4-3-1 will result.

➡**The sensor is extremely sensitive to shock and impact. When replacing, torque to 5-10 ft. lbs. (7-13 Nm).**

1. Measure the resistance between terminal 14 (ground) and terminal 22 on the control unit connector. It should be 500-1000 ohms.

2. If the value is different, check the leads and connections, the ground terminal on the intake manifold and the resistance of the sensor connector.

READING CODES

Control Function 1

▶ **See Figure 58**

The fuel system incorporates a built-in self-diagnostic system. It is located behind the left spring strut tower in the engine compartment. The diagnostic system uses socket No. 2

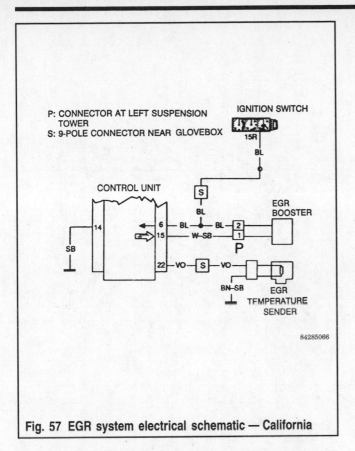

Fig. 57 EGR system electrical schematic — California

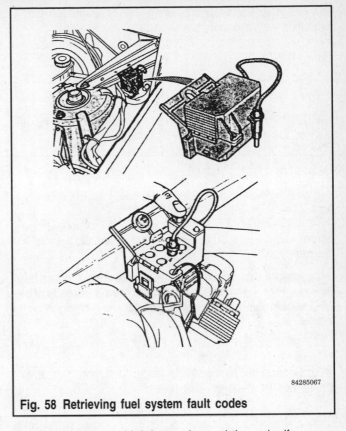

Fig. 58 Retrieving fuel system fault codes

for the fuel system and socket No. 6 for the ignition system and EGR system (California).

There are many possible fault codes in the diagnostic system, and the system is capable of storing up to 3 system faults at 1 time. When the engine is running, the fuel system control unit continuously checks the control unit internal functions, oxygen sensor, battery voltage, coolant temperature sensor, air temperature sensor, pressure sensor, throttle position, engine rpm and the idle speed through the air valve

The following procedure is for retrieving fault codes.

1. Open the diagnostic unit cover in the driver's side rear of the engine compartment and install the selector plug into socket No. 2 for ignition or fuel system codes, or into socket No. 6 for EGR system codes (California).

2. Turn ignition to the **ON** position.

3. Enter Control Function 1 by pressing the button once. Hold the button for at least 1 second, but not more than 3 seconds.

4. Watch the LED and count the number of flashes in each of the 3 flash series, which will indicate a fault code. The flash series are separated by 3 second intervals. Note the fault codes.

➡If there are no fault codes in the diagnostic unit, the LED will flash 1-1-1 and the fuel system is operating correctly.

5. Depress the button again. If the same code is repeated, there are no additional codes stored. If the code is different, depress the button a third time and record the code, if different.

➡The diagnostic memory is full when it contains 3 fault codes. Until those 3 are rectified and the memory erased, the system cannot give information on any other problems.

Control Function 2

This function is activated by pressing the button twice (between 1-3 seconds between operations), causing the LED to flash. The control unit delivers a diagnostic code (not a fault code) acknowledging the receipt of a signal from each of the following items:

Diagnostic Code 3-3-2: Throttle switch, when the throttle is moved from the fully-closed position

Diagnostic Code 3-3-3: Throttle switch, when the throttle is moved from the full-load position

Diagnostic Code 3-3-1: Rpm signal from the ignition system

Diagnostic Code 1-1-4: Electronic Climate Control (ECC) panel, when the A/C button is depressed or released

Diagnostic Code 1-3-4: Air conditioning compressor

Diagnostic Code 1-2-4: Testing idle speed compensation on automatic transmission vehicles. When depressing the brake pedal and placing the gear selector lever in **D** and then moved to **N** again.

Control Function 3
▶ See Figure 59

This function is activated by turning the ignition **ON**, installing the selector plug into socket No. 2. and pressing the button 3 times (between 1-3 seconds between operations). The control unit then responds by activating the injectors, idle valve, cold start valve, auxiliary relay (radio interference suppression relay) and fuel pump.

CLEARING CODES

▶ **See Figures 60 and 61**

When all the fault codes have been read and corrected, the diagnostic system memory can be erased as follows:

1. Turn ignition switch to the **ON** position.
2. Read fault codes again.
3. Press and hold diagnostic unit button for more than 5 seconds. Release button. After 3 seconds, the LED should light.
4. While the LED is lit, press button again for more than 5 seconds. Release button. The LED should go out. Memory is cleared.

➡**To ensure that the memory has been erased, press button again for 1 second but not more than 3 seconds. The LED should flash 1-1-1, indicating that the memory is erased.**

5. Start and run the engine. If it will not start, see Control Function 2.
6. Recheck for fault codes. If Code 1-1-1 comes up, there are no additional system fault codes.

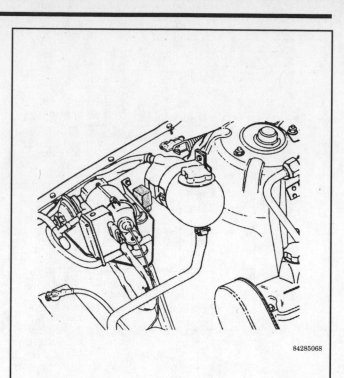

84285068

Fig. 59 Auxiliary relay location — Regina

Code	Fault	Correction Test
1-1-1	No faults	—
1-1-2	Fault in control unit ①	Control unit
1-1-3	Fault in injector	Injector
1-2-1	Signal missing or faulty, to/from pressure sensor	Pressure sensor
1-2-2	Signal missing or faulty, to/from air temperature sensor	Air temperature sensor
1-2-3	Signal missing to/from coolant temperature sensor, possible grounding short	Coolant temperature sensor
1-3-2	Battery voltage too low/high ②	Charging system
1-3-3	Throttle-Switch; idle setting faulty, possible grounding short	Throttle switch
2-1-2	Oxygen sensor signal missing or faulty	Oxygen sensor
2-1-3	Throttle-Switch; full load setting faulty, possible grounding short	Throttle switch
2-2-1	Oxygen sensor not operating	Oxygen sensor or air leak
2-2-2	Fault in system relay	System relay
2-2-3	Signal missing to/from idle valve	Idle valve
2-3-1	Self-adjusting oxygen sensor not operating	Intake air or fuel system
2-3-2	Self-adjusting oxygen sensor not operating	Intake air or fuel system
2-3-3	Idle valve closed	Idle valve
2-4-1	EGR system malfunction ③	EGR vacuum booster
3-1-1	Signal missing from speedometer	Speedometer signal
3-2-1	Signal missing or faulty to/from cold start valve	Auxiliary relay
4-1-3	EGR temperature sensor circuit ③	EGR temperature sensor

① Change control unit
② Check battery and charging system
③ California

84285069

Fig. 60 Diagnostic fault codes — Regina fuel system

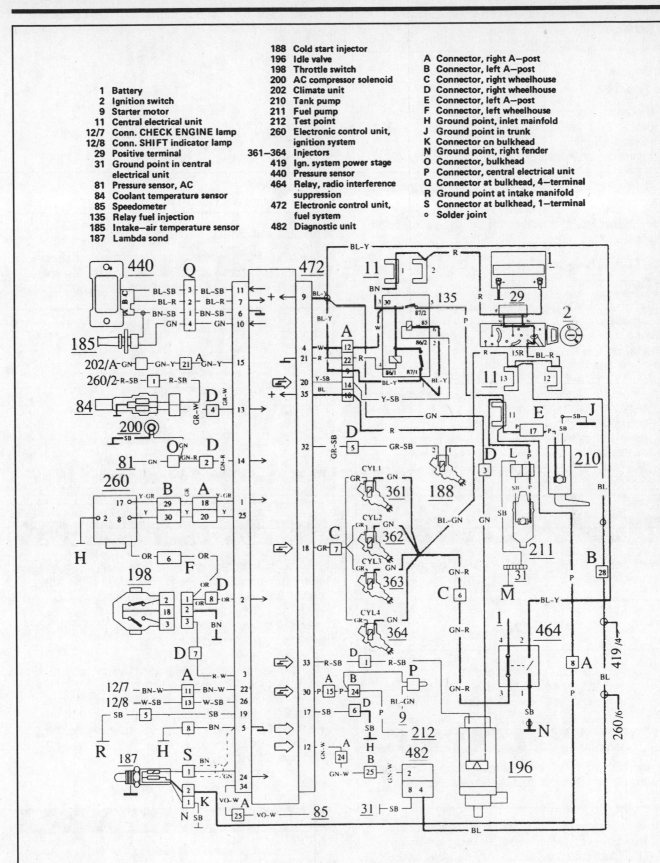

1 Battery
2 Ignition switch
9 Starter motor
11 Central electrical unit
12/7 Conn. CHECK ENGINE lamp
12/8 Conn. SHIFT indicator lamp
29 Positive terminal
31 Ground point in central electrical unit
81 Pressure sensor, AC
84 Coolant temperature sensor
85 Speedometer
135 Relay fuel injection
185 Intake—air temperature sensor
187 Lambda sond

188 Cold start injector
196 Idle valve
198 Throttle switch
200 AC compressor solenoid
202 Climate unit
210 Tank pump
211 Fuel pump
212 Test point
260 Electronic control unit, ignition system
361—364 Injectors
419 Ign. system power stage
440 Pressure sensor
464 Relay, radio interference suppression
472 Electronic control unit, fuel system
482 Diagnostic unit

A Connector, right A—post
B Connector, left A—post
C Connector, right wheelhouse
D Connector, right wheelhouse
E Connector, left A—post
F Connector, left wheelhouse
H Ground point, inlet mainfold
J Ground point in trunk
K Connector on bulkhead
N Ground point, right fender
O Connector, bulkhead
P Connector, central electrical unit
Q Connector at bulkhead, 4—terminal
R Ground point at intake manifold
S Connector at bulkhead, 1—terminal
o Solder joint

Fig. 61 Regina wiring diagram — 740 and 940

84285071

ADJUSTMENTS

Base Throttle
▶ See Figure 62

1. Loosen the throttle locknut.
2. Loosen the adjustment screw until the throttle is completely closed.
3. Tighten the adjustment screw until it just touches the linkarm, then turn a half a turn further.
4. Tighten the locknut without changing the adjusting screw position.

➡ **It may be necessary to loosen the throttle switch before setting the throttle.**

Throttle Control Pulley and Cable
▶ See Figure 63

1. Disconnect the linkarm and make sure that the pulley moves smoothly.
2. Make sure that the throttle cable is fully extended in the idle position without affecting the pulley position. The pulley should hit the idle stop.
3. Adjust the cable if the pulley is not hitting the idle stop.
4. Depress the accelerator pedal all the way and check that the pulley hits the full throttle stop.
5. Reconnect the linkarm and adjust it as follows:
   a. Insert a 1mm feeler gauge between the control pulley and the idle stop.
   b. The play between the throttle lever and the adjustment screw should be 0.1-0.3mm.
   c. Adjust the linkarm to bring into specifications.

Fig. 62 Setting base idle — Regina

Idle Speed and Mixture

After other throttle related adjustments have been made, there are no other provisions for adjustment. The idle speed and mixture are feedback controlled and not adjustable.

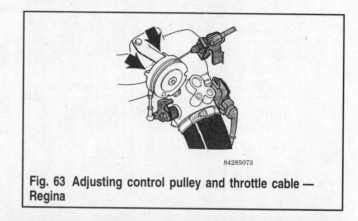

Fig. 63 Adjusting control pulley and throttle cable — Regina

FUEL TANK

The fuel tank on all vehicles contain the fuel pump and sending unit assembly.

REMOVAL & INSTALLATION

1. Disconnect the negative battery cable.
2. Raise and support the vehicle safely.
3. Release the fuel system pressure. Drain the fuel tank completely.

✳✳CAUTION

When performing this procedure, always have a dry-chemical fire extinguisher handy. Fuel vapors are extremely explosive.

4. In the trunk, remove the panels which cover the filler hose. It may be necessary to remove the spare tire on some vehicles. Roll back the carpet and remove the access panel cover.
5. Disconnect the fuel filler pipe connection. Label and disconnect all fuel lines leading to the fuel tank. Label and disconnect all electrical connectors at the fuel tank.

6. Position a floorjack under the tank, using a large piece of wood as a cushion between the fuel tank and the floorjack. Raise the jack so that it just contacts the tank.
7. Remove any shields or protective covers on the tank. Loosen and remove the tank retaining bolts. Lower the jack slowly and inspect for any obstructions.
To install:
8. Install the protective shields and raise the fuel tank into position. Install and tighten the attaching bolts.
9. Remove the floorjack. Connect all fuel and electrical lines leading to the fuel tank.
10. Install the protective panel in the trunk and replace the spare tire (as required) and the carpet.
11. Lower the vehicle.
12. Connect the negative battery cable.
13. Turn the ignition key **ON** and check for leaks.

Fuel Pump

Vehicles equipped with Bendix Regina fuel system uses a new two-stage fuel pump. The new pump replaces the two individual unit on earlier models.

REMOVAL & INSTALLATION

1. Disconnect the negative battery cable.
2. Raise and support the vehicle safely.
3. Relieve the fuel system pressure.
4. Remove the fuel tank.
5. Loosen the lock-ring at the top of the fuel tank and remove the sending unit with the transfer pump attached. Note the direction of the float in the tank.

6. Remove the transfer pump from the sending unit.
To install:
7. Install the transfer pump on the sending unit. Install the sending unit in the fuel tank and tighten the lock-ring to specification. Do not overtighten the lock-ring as the plastic threads on some fuel tanks are easily stripped.
8. Install the fuel tank in the vehicle.
9. Lower the vehicle.
10. Connect the negative battery cable, start the engine and check for leaks.

MOTRONIC 1.8 FUEL INJECTION

▶ See Figures 64 and 65

Description and Operation

The Motronic 1.8 fuel injection system, found on 1992-93 960 models, is equipped with a powerful control unit that controls the ignition and fuel injection functions by means of individual ignition coils and injectors.

In addition to controlling the ignition and fuel injection functions, Motronic also:
• Determines whether the A/C compressor may be switched in;
• Reduces the engine torque in response to a signal from the automatic transmission control unit, to insure smooth en-

gagement of the different gears and also supplies the transmission control unit with information on engine running conditions for computing gear changes;
• Controls the operation of the radiator fan.

The control unit is provided with adaptive Lambda control and idling control functions as well as timing retardation function to eliminate knock. The service requirement is minimal, since neither the carbon monoxide level nor the idling speed require adjustment.

CONNECTIONS

Conn.	Function	Type of signal			
1	Ignition signal, cylinder 1	output	29	Rear knock sensor signal	input
2	Ignition signal, cylinder 3	output	30	Sensor ground	ground
3	Fuel pump relay signal	output	31	Ignition signal, cylinder 4	output
4	Idling valve opening coil	output	32	Spare	
5	Spare		33	Spare	
6	Speed signal	output	34	Radiator fan, full speed	output
7	Air mass meter signal	input	35	Spare	
8	Camshaft sensor signal	input	36	Main relay signal	output
9	Speedometer signal	input	37	Busbar 15 supply from main relay	supply
10	Camshaft sensor + supply	output	38	Spare	
11	Front knock sensor signal	input	39	Load signal to transmission	output
12	Throttle switch + supply	output	40	AC idling compensation	input
13	Ignition signal, cylinder 2	output	41	AC request from ECC	input
14	Radiator fan, half speed	output	42	Drive/neutral idling compensation	input
15	Environmental warning lamp	output	43	Timing retardation response to transmission	output
16	Injectors, group 1	output	44	Spare	
17	Injectors, group 2	output	45	Temperature sensor signal	input
18	Busbar 30 supply	supply	46	Spare	
19	Signal ground	ground	47	Timing pick-up signal	input
20	Ignition signal, cylinder 5	output	48	Timing pick-up ground	ground
21	Ignition signal, cylinder 6	output	49	Throttle position information to transmission	output
22	Idling valve closing coil	output	50	Timing retardation request from transmission	input
23	AC on/off control signal	output	51	Timing retardation request from transmission	input
24	Power ground	ground	52	Spare	
25	Air mass meter burn-off	output	53	Throttle switch signal	input
26	Air mass meter ground	ground	54	Sprare	
27	Busbar 15 supply	supply	55	Diagnostic lead	
28	Oxygen sensor (Lambdasond) signal	input			

84285124

Fig. 64 Motronic control unit pin identification — 960. Use this key to identify system components illustrated in this Section.

1/1	Battery (1)		11/1–35	Fuses
2/10	ECC power unit (499)		17/7	Diagnostic unit
2/11	Relay, radiator fan (131)		17/8	Service terminal, coil terminal 1, No. 1 cylinder
2/12	Main relay (464)		20/3–8	Ignition coils and spark plugs 1–6
2/13	Relay, fuel pump (135)		31/14	Ground terminal on relay board
2/46	Relay, ignition coils (134)		31/31	Ground, busbar 31 on relay board
4/3	Control unit, cruise control (226)		31/32	Ground, engine (power)
4/6	Control unit, ECC (495)		31/33	Ground, engine (instrument)
4/12	Control unit, Motronic (216)		31/36	Ground, oxygen sensor
4/28	Transmission control unit (414/415)			
4/38	Power unit 1 (290)			
4/39	Power unit 2 (291)			
5/1	Combined instrument			
6/31	Fuel pump (211)			
7/15	Oxygen sensor (Lambdasond) (187)		A	Connector, LH A-post
7/16	Coolant temperature sensor (84)		B	Connector, driver's A-post
7/17	Air mass meter (284)		C	Connector, 10-pole
7/21	Camshaft sensor (214)		D	Connector at LH suspension strut tower
7/23	Knock sensor 2 (218)		E	Connector, 2-pole, for oxygen sensor
7/24	Knock sensor 1 (218)		F	Connector, 2-pole, for oxygen sensor (screened)
7/25	Timing pick-up (412)		G	Connector for transfer box (at control unit)
7/38	Low-speed pressure switch, radiator fan (82)		H	Connector at rear of engine
7/39	Safety and high-speed pressure switch, radiator fan (83)		J	Connector at electrical distribution unit
7/54	Throttle switch		K	Connector at rear of engine
8/3	AC compressor solenoid (200)		L	Connector, I-pole, at LH engine mounting
8/5	Idling (CIS) valve (196)		M	Connector, 4-pole, luggage compartment
8/6–8/11	Injectors (361–366)		N	Ground, power unit 4/38
			O	Ground, power unit 4/39

84285125

Fig. 65 Motronic wiring diagram component key — 960. Use this key to identify wiring diagram components illustrated in this Section.

DATA SENSORS

▶ **See Figure 66**

Air Mass Meter

The air mass meter measures the engine intake air mass. Factors that affect air density, such as temperature, humidity and pressure are compensated for during measurement.

The sensor inside the air mass meter consists of a wire which is maintained at 250°F (121°C) higher than the ambient air entering the engine. As the air mass passing over the wire increases, more current is required to maintain the correct temperature. The amount of current required to maintain this temperature is used to calculate the intake air mass.

When the engine is turned off, any dirt on the wire is burned off electrically by heating the wire to 1800°F (1000°C). Any dirt remaining on the wire would cause it to send incorrect signals to the control unit and result in an incorrect air/fuel mixture.

Coolant Temperature Sensor

The coolant temperature sensor provides the control unit with information necessary for proper adjustment of injection duration.

Throttle Switch

The throttle switch indicates to the fuel system whether the throttle valve is closed. It does not function as a variable resistor. It also indicates whether the throttle valve is fully open.

Oxygen Sensor (Lambda-Sond)

The oxygen sensor is mounted in the exhaust manifold in front of the catalytic converter. It produces a measurable current by comparing the amount of oxygen in the exhaust gas with the amount in the ambient air.

Under normal conditions, the optimum air/fuel ratio is 14.7:1. This ratio is monitored by post-combustion measurement of the oxygen content in the exhaust gas using the oxygen sensor.

The oxygen sensor operating temperature ranges from 545°-1530°F (285°-832°C). It is electrically heated to enable it to reach operating temperature quickly. When ignition is turned to the **ON** position, current is sent to a PTC resistor (Positive Temperature Coefficient) whose resistance increases with rising temperature. Due to this system, the oxygen sensor quickly reaches operating temperature, even at low exhaust gas temperature.

The exhaust gases reach the outer surface of the sensor through slits in the protective sleeve. Ambient air reaches the sensors inner surface through channels. The sensor consists of a platinum covered zirconium-oxide pipe.

The signal strength is in direct proportion to the amount of oxygen in the exhaust gases. This depends on the air/fuel ratio. The Lambda value of 1, represents the theoretically perfect ratio. A rich mixture results in higher voltage and a lean mixture results in lower voltage. The current sent by the oxygen sensor to the control unit varies between 0.1-1.0 volt. The difference between high and low voltage occurs when the Lambda value is at 1. The control unit uses this information to adjust the amount of fuel used.

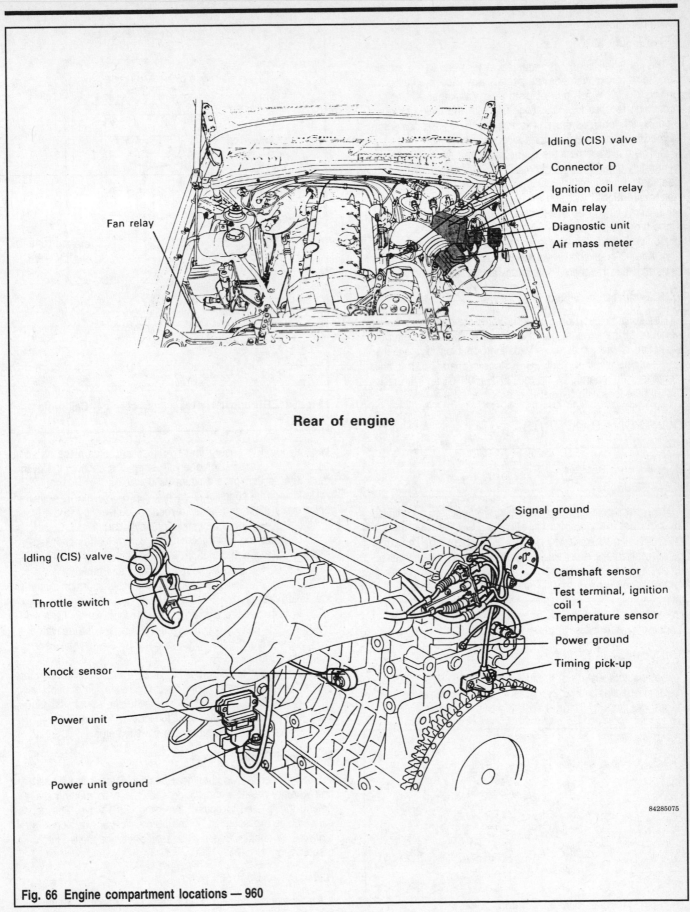

Idling (CIS) valve

Connector D

Ignition coil relay

Main relay

Diagnostic unit

Air mass meter

Fan relay

Rear of engine

Idling (CIS) valve

Throttle switch

Knock sensor

Power unit

Power unit ground

Signal ground

Camshaft sensor

Test terminal, ignition coil 1

Temperature sensor

Power ground

Timing pick-up

84285075

Fig. 66 Engine compartment locations — 960

Camshaft Sensor

▶ **See Figure 67**

The camshaft sensor is mounted at the rear of the cylinder head on the exhaust side. Its signals are used by the control unit to identify which pair of pistons is simultaneously approaching top dead center. Together with the timing pick-up signals, this enables the unit to identify the stroke being performed by each of the pistons in question.

The main components of the camshaft sensor are a Hall generator, trigger rotor and cover. As the rotor rotates with the camshaft, it alternately shields and exposes the Hall element, generating high 5 volt and low 0 volt signals in turn. Since the vane and opening on the rotor are of the same width, and since the camshaft rotates at only half the crankshaft speed, the output signal changes only after a full crankshaft revolution. After 2 crankshaft revolutions, the signal from the Hall generator has reached 1 maximum and 1 minimum.

EGR Temperature Sensor

This sensor, found on California vehicles, measures the temperature of the exhaust gases returned to the intake manifold. Detection of the temperature variations enables the control unit to determine whether the EGR system is operating. It is able to measure temperatures up to 930°F (500°C) and the resistance increases with temperature.

CONTROLLED OUTPUTS

EGR Vacuum Booster

▶ **See Figure 68**

This component is found on California vehicles. It controls the pressure in the vacuum line to the EGR valve by means of the admission valve (lower section of the booster). The pressure in the intake manifold is supplied to the reducing valve (upper section of the booster). The vacuum booster processes the electrical signal from the intake manifold to maintain optimum control of the EGR valve. The unit is also designed to compensate for changes in atmospheric pressure. It is mounted on the left strut tower.

Fuel Control

The injectors are divided into 2 groups of 3. One group of injectors supplies fuel to cylinders 1, 2 and 4, while the second serves cylinders 3, 5 and 6. The 2-group arrangement has

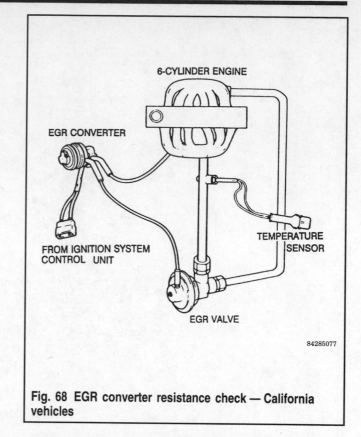

Fig. 68 EGR converter resistance check — California vehicles

been adopted to ensure that fuel injection takes place as soon as possible after injector opening, supplying each of the cylinders with as uniform a mixture as possible.

Under normal conditions, each group of injectors is activated once every other crankshaft revolution, delivering the full fuel charge required for combustion in 1 cylinder.

To compute the fuel injection, the control unit is supplied with the following information:

1. An engine load signal by the air mass meter.
2. An engine speed signal and crankshaft position signal by the timing pick-up.
3. A piston stroke signal by the camshaft sensor, enabling the unit to determine which injector group is to be activated.
4. The exhaust gas oxygen content by the oxygen sensor (Lambda Sond).
5. An engine temperature signal by the coolant temperature sensor, for functions including fuel enrichment on starting.
6. A throttle position signal by the throttle switch, for functions including acceleration and full-load enrichment.
7. A road speed signal by the speedometer.

Idle Speed Control

Factors such as whether gear position **D** or **P** is selected, and whether the air conditioning compressor is running are among those used to control the idling (CIS) valve. The necessary signals are supplied by the automatic transmission control unit and air conditioning compressor electromagnetic clutch respectively.

Radiator Fan Control

A fully-electric radiator fan is operated by a relay, either in response to the engine temperature signal supplied to the Mo-

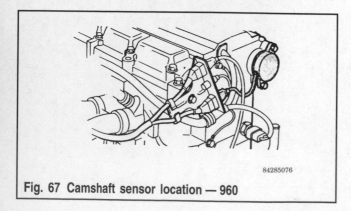

Fig. 67 Camshaft sensor location — 960

tronic control unit or directly by the pressure switches mounted in the A/C high-pressure circuit. The fan relay is mounted on a bracket in front of the battery.

If the coolant temperature is unusually high when the engine is switched **OFF**, the Motronic control unit will keep the fan running for a further period not exceeding 5 minutes. (The fan cannot, however, be restarted until some time has elapsed after stopping the engine.)

Air Conditioning Compressor Control

The Motronic control unit controls the operation of the A/C compressor electromagnetic clutch by means of a relay in the electronic climate control (ECC) power unit. A request to start the A/C compressor is initiated from the ECC control panel.

The control unit prevents the compressor from starting under the following conditions, to reduce the load on the engine at full load and to prevent overheating:

1. When the throttle is fully open, using the signal from the throttle switch.

2. When the coolant temperature approaches 239°F (115°C), in order to remain safely within the boiling point of approximately 275°F (134°C). The signal from the coolant temperature sensor is used for this purpose.

EGR System Control(California Only)
▶ **See Figure 69**

The EGR electrical circuit is equipped with a temperature sensor that enables the control unit to determine if the EGR system is operating as intended. The purpose of the sensor is to detect the temperature variations that occur when the system is in operation. The sensor is connected to the control unit, which can activate 2 EGR fault codes. The sensor has no effect on system operation, only on the diagnostic function.

FUEL DELIVERY SYSTEM

Fuel Pressure Regulator

The fuel pressure regulator ensures that fuel pressure remains at approximately 43.5 psi (300 kPa) at idle at the injectors. Using a vacuum tube connected to the engine intake manifold, fuel pressure is gradually increased as intake manifold vacuum decreases. Because of this, adequate pressure is maintained, regardless of throttle position. The amount of fuel injected largely depends on injection duration. Excess fuel is returned to the fuel tank through a return pipe.

Injectors

The fuel injectors as designed as electric solenoids. While the starter motor is operating, there are 2 injections per engine rotation. This is reduced to 1 during normal driving. Injection occurs in the intake manifold near the intake valves.

Fuel Pump

The fuel pump is an electric pump, cooled by the fuel that flows through it. It incorporates a check valve and an overflow valve that opens when fuel pressure gets too high.

Both the primary pump and secondary pump operate when the starter motor or the engine is running. Should the engine

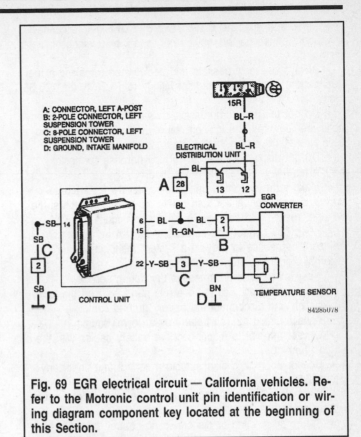

A: CONNECTOR, LEFT A-POST
B: 2-POLE CONNECTOR, LEFT SUSPENSION TOWER
C: 8-POLE CONNECTOR, LEFT SUSPENSION TOWER
D: GROUND, INTAKE MANIFOLD

Fig. 69 EGR electrical circuit — California vehicles. Refer to the Motronic control unit pin identification or wiring diagram component key located at the beginning of this Section.

stop while the ignition remains on, the control unit will cut the current to the pumps.

The in-tank fuel pump is an electric fuel pump that keeps pressure in the fuel line prior to the main fuel pump to prevent vapor lock. The pump is part of the fuel level transmitter assembly and incorporates a coarse strainer type filter and a non-return valve to maintain a constant amount of pressure in the system, even if the main pump is not operational.

Fuel Filter

The fuel filter is adjacent to the main fuel pump, which is mounted on a plate underneath the vehicle on the left side.

SERVICE PRECAUTIONS

▶ **See Figures 70 and 71**

- Safety is the most important factor when performing not only fuel system maintenance, but any type of maintenance. Failure to conduct maintenance and repairs in a safe manner may result in serious personal injury or death.
- Use caution when working around ignition system components. The ignition system operates at high power with dangerous voltages in both the low-tension and high-tension circuits, including connectors and similar fittings.
- Do not operate the fuel pump when the fuel lines are empty.
- Do not arc weld on the vehicle unless all the control units have been removed.
- The control units must not be exposed to temperatures above 175°F (80°C), such as in a paint booth.

• Make sure that the ignition switch is **OFF** before connecting or disconnecting the ignition coil, spark plug wiring or test instruments.

• Always use new gaskets and seals when remaking a fuel connection. Torque the fuel filter fittings to 15-26 ft. lbs. (20-35 Nm).

• Do not test the compression on the 960 until the ignition coils are removed, the ignition coil relay is disconnected and fuse No. 31 (to disarm fuel pumps) is removed.

• Do not disconnect the control unit harness connector before fuse No. 24 has been removed.

• Make sure all control unit connectors are fastened securely. A poor connection can cause an extremely high surge voltage, resulting in damage to integrated circuits.

• Keep any control unit harness at least 4 in. away from adjacent harnesses to prevent a system malfunction due to external electronic interference.

• Keep all parts and harnesses dry during service.

• Before attempting to remove any parts, turn off the ignition switch and disconnect the battery ground cable.

• Always use a 12 volt battery as a power source.

• Do not attempt to disconnect the battery cables with the engine running.

• Do not attempt to disassemble a control unit under any circumstances.

• If a battery cable is disconnected, the fault code memory will be erased.

• Before connecting or disconnecting control unit ECU harness connectors, make sure the ignition switch is **OFF** and the negative battery cable is disconnected to avoid the possibility of damage to the control unit.

• A spare location in the fuse box is used as a test terminal for air bag diagnostics on the 960. Never install a fuse in this position or connect accessories to this terminal.

RELIEVING FUEL SYSTEM PRESSURE

▶ **See Figure 72**

1. With the ignition **OFF**, remove fuel pump fuses 30 and 31.

2. Try starting and allowing the vehicle to run a few times until it will not stay running any more.

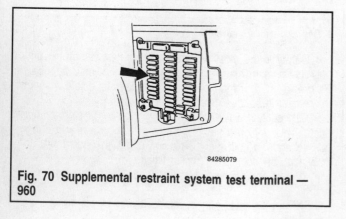

Fig. 70 Supplemental restraint system test terminal — 960

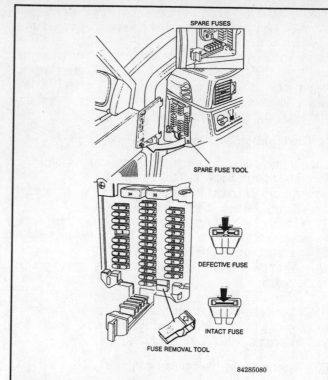

Fig. 71 Fuse box location — far left side of the dash board on 960

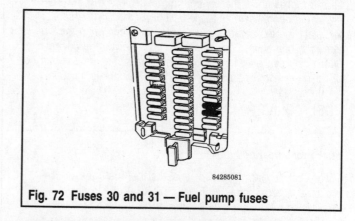

Fig. 72 Fuses 30 and 31 — Fuel pump fuses

DRAINING THE FUEL LINES AND FILTER

▶ **See Figure 73**

1. Remove the protective cap located at the rear end of the fuel injection manifold.

2. Connect adapter hose/union to the fuel drainage unit. Use the special tools 999-5484, 981-2270, 2273, 2282 or their equivalent.

3. Start the fuel drainage.

4. Connect the hose/union to locked/closed valve. Unlock/open valve.

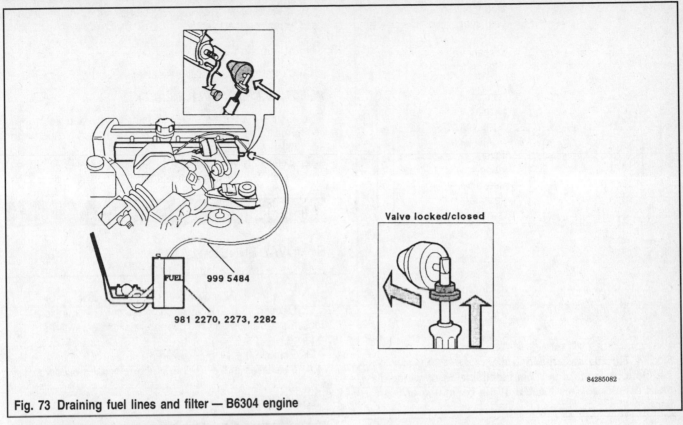

Fig. 73 Draining fuel lines and filter — B6304 engine

Throttle Switch

REMOVAL & INSTALLATION

1. Turn the ignition switch to the **OFF** position.
2. Disconnect the throttle switch connector.
3. Remove the throttle switch retaining screws and remove the throttle switch.
4. Installation is the reverse of the removal procedure. Adjust the throttle, as required.

TESTING

▶ See Figures 74 and 75

The function of the throttle switch is to detect the throttle position from fully closed to fully open. If the switch signal is constantly below 0.06 volt or above 4.9 volts, the control unit will interpret this as a fault and will report the Fault Code 2-4-3. Under these conditions, a substitute value equivalent to an opening of approximately 20 degrees will be adopted.

Control Function 2 Testing

1. Enter Control Function 2.
2. Turn the throttle slightly. If flashing Diagnostic Code 3-3-2 is displayed, the throttle function is correct in the idling position.
3. Turn the throttle to the full-load position and release. If flashing Diagnostic Code 3-3-3 is displayed, the throttle function is correct in the full-load position.

Throttle Switch Signal Check

Turn the ignition **ON** and connect a voltmeter across terminals 30 and 53 of the control unit. Instrument should indicate approximately 0.5 volt at idling and approximately 4.5 volts at full load.

Absent or Faulty Signal Check

1. Turn the ignition **ON** and check for a 5 volts reference signal at terminal 12 of the control unit.
2. With the ignition **ON** connect the voltmeter across terminals 12 and 30 of the control unit. There should be 5 volts.
3. Ensure that terminal 30 is grounded. Connect an ohmmeter across terminals 19 and 30 of the control unit. There should be approximately 0 ohms.

Absent or Faulty Reference Signal Check

1. With the ignition **OFF**, check the resistance between terminals 53 and 30 of the control unit. The resistance should be approximately 1000 ohms at idling and approximately 700 ohms at full load.
2. Check vehicles with automatic transmissions in Control Function 1 if speed signal fault code is displayed.

Injector

TESTING

▶ See Figure 76

If the difference in current consumption between the injector groups is excessive, the control unit will interpret the condition

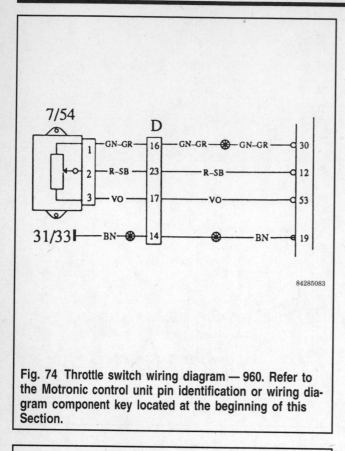

Fig. 74 Throttle switch wiring diagram — 960. Refer to the Motronic control unit pin identification or wiring diagram component key located at the beginning of this Section.

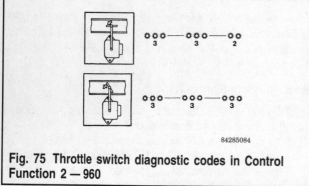

Fig. 75 Throttle switch diagnostic codes in Control Function 2 — 960

as an injector open-circuit or short-circuit, and will store the fault code. The entire group will be isolated in the event of a short-circuit, while the injectors not affected will continue to operate in the event of an open-circuit. Lambda control will become inactive once the fault code is reported.

Resistance Across Injector Groups Check

1. With the ignition switch **OFF**, connect an ohmmeter across terminals 16 and 37. The resistance should be approximately 5.3 ohms.
2. With the ignition switch **OFF**, connect an ohmmeter across terminals 17 and 37. The resistance should be approximately 5.3 ohms.

Individual Injector Resistance Check

1. With the ignition switch **OFF**, measure the resistance of each injector.

2. If the resistance of each injector is not 16 ohms at 68°F (20°C), replace the injector.

Control Function 3 Check

Check the operation of the injectors in Control Function 3.

INJECTOR INPUT SIGNALS CHECK

1. Connect a voltmeter across terminals 16 and 24 of the control unit. The voltmeter should indicate battery voltage with the ignition switch **ON**.
2. Connect a voltmeter across terminals 17 and 24 of the control unit. The voltmeter should indicate battery voltage **ON**.

Air Mass Meter

REMOVAL & INSTALLATION

1. Turn the ignition switch to the **OFF** position.
2. Disconnect the air mass meter electrical connector. Loosen the clamps and remove the retaining screws, as required.
3. Remove the air mass meter.
4. Installation is the reverse of the removal procedure.

TESTING

Since the injection period is largely determined be the computed air mass, the system is dependent on this signal. If the signal is absent, and thus setting Fault Code 1-2-1, the injec-

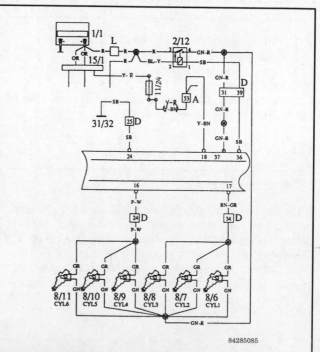

Fig. 76 Injector wiring schematic — 960. Refer to the Motronic control unit pin identification or wiring diagram component key located at the beginning of this Section.

tion period is computed on the basis of the throttle switch angle (Limp-home Mode). Oxygen feedback control and idling control are disabled under these conditions.

Burn-off to clean the air mass meter element should occur if the engine speed has exceeded 1800 rpm and the coolant temperature has exceeded 140°F (60°C). Approximately 4 volts is delivered to the platinum wire in the air mass meter from control unit terminal 5, returning to terminal 7. The fault code 3-2-2 is recorded if the voltage between ground and terminal 7 does not exceed 2.5 volts.

Ground Check

▶ **See Figure 77**

1. Make sure that the ignition switch is **OFF**.
2. Connect an ohmmeter between terminals 19 and 26. There should be approximately 0 ohms.
3. Connect an ohmmeter between air mass meter connector terminal 1 and ground. The resistance should also be approximately 0 ohms.

Resistance Check

1. Make sure that the ignition switch is **OFF**.
2. Measure the resistance between terminals 7 and 26 on the control unit connector. The resistance should be approximately 2.5-4.0 ohms.
3. If the resistance is not as specified, measure the resistance across the air mass meter itself.

Signal Check

1. Turn the ignition switch **ON**.

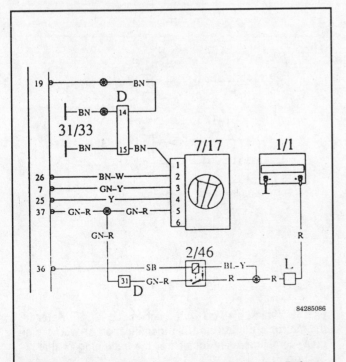

Fig. 77 Air mass meter wiring schematic — 960. Refer to the Motronic control unit pin identification or wiring diagram component key located at the beginning of this Section.

84285086

2. Connect a voltmeter across terminals 7 and 19. The reading should be approximately 1.4 volts.
3. Start the engine.
4. The voltage should be between 2.3-2.6 volts when idling, depending on engine temperature, with the air conditioning OFF. The voltage should be 2.3 volts with the engine hot.

Burn-Off Function Check

The engine temperature must be above 140°F (60°C) and the engine speed must have exceeded 1800 rpm.

1. While the engine is running, connect a voltmeter across terminals 7 and 19.
2. Stop the engine and read the voltmeter. The value should rise to 2.5 volts.
3. If the reading is too low or no voltage is indicated, connect a voltmeter across terminals 25 and 19.
4. Start the engine and increase the engine speed to 1800 rpm.
5. Stop the engine and read the voltmeter. It should read approximately 4 volts.
6. Check Control Function 1 for automatic transmission (if equipped) if load signal fault code is displayed.

Coolant Temperature Sensor

REMOVAL & INSTALLATION

1. Turn the ignition switch to the **OFF** position.
2. Drain the cooling system.
3. Disconnect the temperature sensor connector and remove the temperature sensor.
4. Installation is the reverse of the removal procedure.

TESTING

▶ **See Figures 78 and 79**

The coolant temperature signal to the control unit has a great influence on the computed injection period and on radiator fan control. For example, when the engine is being started and when it is cold, the amount of injected fuel must be relatively large.

If the control unit receives a signal higher than 302°F (150°C) or lower than -40°F (-40°C), it will interpret the signal as a fault and report a fault code. In this case, the control unit will assume a substitute value corresponding to 32°F (0°C) on starting and 68°F (20°C) when the engine has started. The radiator fan will be operated at half speed and adaptive control of the injection period interrupted. Knock control will be permitted at idling.

Signal Check

1. With the control unit connected, connect a voltmeter across terminals 30 and 45.
2. Turn the ignition switch **ON**.
   At 68°F (20°C) the voltage should be 1.7 volts.
   At 122°F (50°C) the voltage should be 0.8-3.9 volts.
   At 194°F (90°C) the voltage should be 2.2 volts.

➡At 122°F (50°C), the control unit alters the voltage range for better signal resolution.

Absent or Faulty Signal Check

1. Make sure that the ignition switch is **OFF**.
2. Remove fuse No. 24 before disconnecting the control unit, then disconnect it.
3. Measure the resistance between terminals 30 and 45. If the sensor does not match specifications at several different temperatures, replace the temperature sensor.
4. Reconnect the control unit and reinstall the fuse.

Timing Pickup

TESTING

◆ **See Figure 80**

Fault Code 1-3-1 is reported if no signal is received from the camshaft sensor pick-up for 10 engine revolutions. The engine will not start as a result of this.

Fault Code 2-1-4 is reported only if a fault occurs when the engine is running. The code is set if what the control unit computes and what it actually sees are different. A slight jerk may be a symptom felt in this event.

Testing In Control Function 2

1. Enter Control Function 2 and operate the starter motor.
2. Diagnostic Code 1-4-1 should be displayed, indicating a timing pick-up signal.

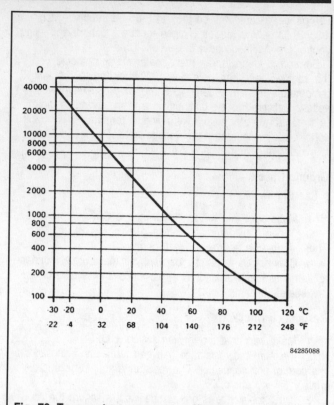

Fig. 79 Temperature sensor specifications — 960

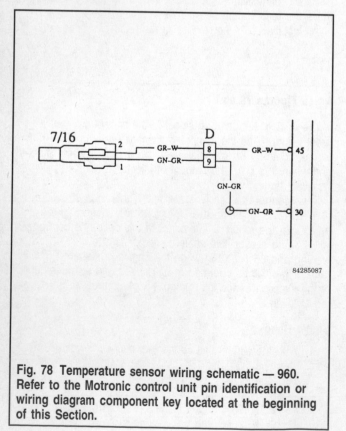

Fig. 78 Temperature sensor wiring schematic — 960. Refer to the Motronic control unit pin identification or wiring diagram component key located at the beginning of this Section.

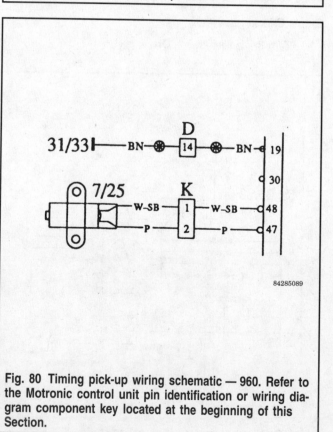

Fig. 80 Timing pick-up wiring schematic — 960. Refer to the Motronic control unit pin identification or wiring diagram component key located at the beginning of this Section.

Timing Pick-up Signal Check

1. Connect a voltmeter across terminals 47 and 48, and set on the AC millivolt scale.
2. Operate the starter motor and check that the voltmeter displays 300-400 millivolts.

Absent or Faulty Signal Check

1. With the ignition switch **OFF**, remove fuse No. 24 and disconnect the control unit.
2. Connect an ohmmeter between terminals 47 and 48.
3. Check that the ohmmeter reads 200-400 ohms, depending on the temperature.
4. Reconnect the control unit.
5. Measure the resistance between terminals 48 and 19. The resistance should be 0 ohms.
6. Measure the resistance between terminals 48 and 30. The resistance should be 0 ohms.
7. On vehicles with automatic transmissions, check in Control Function 1 if speed signal fault is displayed.

Knock Sensor

TESTING

▶ **See Figures 81 and 82**

Fault Codes 1-4-3 and 4-3-3 indicate that the front and rear knock sensor signals, respectively, are absent or faulty. The fault codes will be reported if the following 2 conditions are fulfilled:

1. The engine speed is at least 2970 rpm and a certain engine load has been exceeded.
2. The signal from either of the knock sensors to the control unit falls below 255 millivolts during 96 successive ignitions.

The control unit will then safety-retard the timing.

Wiring Check

The knock sensors themselves cannot be checked; only the wiring can.

1. Disconnect the knock sensor connector and connect a jumper wire between the connector terminals.
2. Remove fuse No. 24 and disconnect the control unit.
3. Connect an ohmmeter between terminal 2 and terminal 11 or 29, depending on which knock sensor is affected. The reading should be 0 ohms.
4. Replace the knock sensor if the reading is correct. Do not replace it if the reading is incorrect. Torque the sensor to 15 ft. lbs. (20 Nm).
5. Reconnect the control unit.

Oxygen Sensor (Lambda Sond)

REMOVAL & INSTALLATION

1. Disconnect the negative battery cable.
2. Raise and support the vehicle safely.

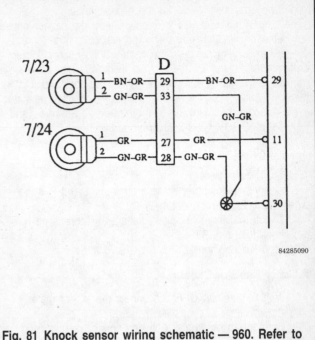

Fig. 81 Knock sensor wiring schematic — 960. Refer to the Motronic control unit pin identification or wiring diagram component key located at the beginning of this Section.

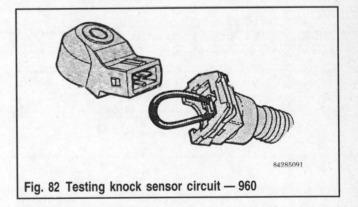

Fig. 82 Testing knock sensor circuit — 960

3. Disconnect the oxygen sensor connector. The sensor is located at the catalytic converter.
4. Remove the oxygen sensor, using a suitable wrench.
5. Installation is the reverse of the removal procedure. Before installing, apply 'Never Seez' paste (P/N 1 161 035-9) to the threaded section of the sond. Tighten to 40 ft. lbs. (55 Nm).

TESTING

▶ **See Figures 83 and 84**

Fault Code 2-1-2 indicates that the oxygen sensor signal is absent or faulty. The control unit cannot exercise Lambda (feedback) control if the signal is absent. The fault code will be reported if the sensor signal is constantly below 0.9 volts or above 1.1 volts, or varies from its mid-point value (0.5 volt) for

3 minutes after the engine temperature has exceeded 167°F (75°C) and a certain load has been maintained. Lambda control will become inactive under these conditions.

The control unit receives information from the oxygen sensor on whether the fuel/air mixture is too rich or too lean in the part-load and idling ranges. The control unit adaptive system compensates for this by making the mixture leaner or richer as required to maintain Lambda = 1. When the control unit is obliged to apply almost the maximum compensation permitted by the adaptive function, this is interpreted as abnormal and Fault Codes 2-3-1 or 2-3-2 are reported.

Supply Voltage Check

1. Start the engine.
2. Connect a voltmeter across terminals 1 and 2 in the starter motor 2-pole connector.
3. Check that there is battery voltage. If there is no voltage, check fuse No. 30.
4. Stop the engine.

Preheater Resistor Check

1. With the ignition **OFF**, disconnect the starter motor connector.
2. Connect an ohmmeter between connector terminal 1 and terminal 2.
3. Check that the ohmmeter indicates 3-13 ohms, depending on the resistor temperature.

Signal Check

1. Start the engine.
2. Connect a voltmeter across terminals 28 and 30. It should begin to oscillate between 0.1-1.0 volts after a short

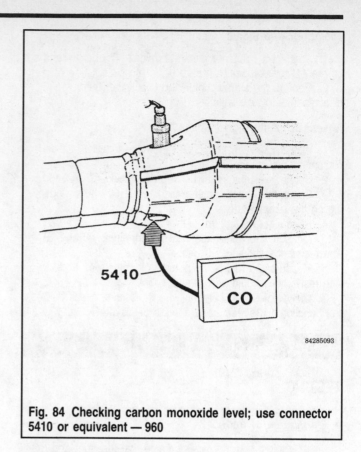

Fig. 84 Checking carbon monoxide level; use connector 5410 or equivalent — 960

time. If the voltage remains constant at 0 volts, the sensor is interpreting the fuel/air mixture as lean. If the voltage remains constant at 1 volt, the sensor is interpreting the fuel/air mixture as rich.

3. If either Fault Code 2-3-1 or 2-3-2 is displayed although the meter is oscillating between 0.1-1.0 volt, Lambda control may be successfully adjusting the carbon monoxide content to the correct level although the control unit is indicating a fault.

Basic Carbon Monoxide Adjustment Check

1. Insert a carbon monoxide meter probe into the tapped hole on the catalytic converter by means of special connector tool 5410, or equivalent.

❋❋CAUTION

To avoid personal injury, be aware that the catalytic converter area may be extremely hot.

2. Run the engine up to normal operating temperature.
3. Disconnect the oxygen sensor to ensure that feedback control does not correct for the fault that has been set.
4. Reset adaptability by displaying, recording and clearing the fault codes. The adaptive system is reset when the diagnostic system memory is erased.
5. Check the carbon monoxide content after the memory has been erased.
   a. If the meter indicates low carbon monoxide content, the engine is running lean and the system is having to enrich the mixture to compensate. Check for an air leakage problem, for example.
   b. If the meter indicates high carbon monoxide content (over 2.5%), the engine is running rich and the system is

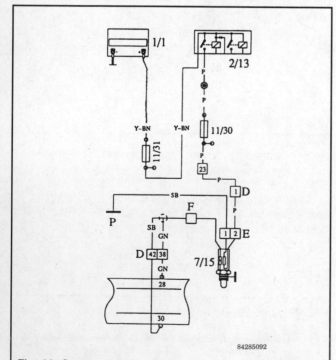

Fig. 83 Oxygen sensor wiring schematic — 960. Refer to the Motronic control unit pin identification or wiring diagram component key located at the beginning of this Section.

having to make the mixture leaner to compensate. Check for high fuel pressure or fuel leakage, for example.

Camshaft Sensor

TESTING

▶ **See Figure 85**

The camshaft sensor is mounted at the end of the camshaft and enables the control unit to determine which cylinder requires fuel and ignition. As the camshaft performs a revolution every 2 crankshaft revolutions, the sensor signal goes high on 1 crankshaft revolution and low on the next. Fault Code 3-1-4 is reported if the signal remains constantly high or low for more than 30 seconds. Under these conditions, the control unit supplies double injection and double ignition while safety-retarding the timing.

Signal Check

1. Remove fuse No. 31 to prevent the engine from starting.
2. Connect a voltmeter across terminals 8 and 19 of the control unit.
3. Operate the starter motor.
4. Check that the reading oscillates between 0.1-0.5 volts.

Absent or Faulty Signal

1. Check that the voltage across terminals 10 and 30 of the control unit is approximately 11 volts.
2. Check that terminal 30 is grounded.
3. Connect an ohmmeter between terminals 30 and 19 of the control unit. It should read 0 ohms.

FUEL SYSTEM TESTING

▶ **See Figure 86**

Main Fuel Pump

The main fuel pump is located on a shelf underneath the vehicle, under rear seat. The pump discharge capacity at a line pressure of 43.5 psi (300 kPa) and a temperature of 68°F (20°C) is 34 oz. (1 liter) in 30 seconds.

The current draw of the under-car pump at a line pressure of 43.5 psi (300 kPa), a temperature of 68°F (20°C) and at 12 volts is 3-4 amps.

In-Tank Pump

The current draw of the tank pump is 6.5 amps.

Fuel Pressure Testing

▶ **See Figure 87**

1. Turn the ignition switch **ON**. The pumps should run for 3 seconds.
2. Turn the ignition switch **OFF**.
3. Connect a fuel gauge between the fuel line and the distribution manifold.
4. Remove fuses 30 and 31.

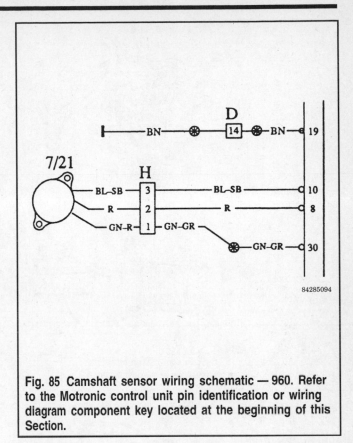

Fig. 85 Camshaft sensor wiring schematic — 960. Refer to the Motronic control unit pin identification or wiring diagram component key located at the beginning of this Section.

5. Connect a jumper lead across the right-hand terminals in the fuse cavities. The fuel pumps should now start and be clearly audible.
6. Measure the fuel pressure, which should be 43.5 psi (300 kPa).

LINE PRESSURE TOO HIGH

1. Disconnect the jumper lead between the fuse terminals.
2. Disconnect and blow air through the pressure regulator return line.
3. Disconnect and blow through the vacuum line.
4. If both lines are clear, replace the pressure regulator and recheck the pressure.

LINE PRESSURE TOO LOW

1. Clamp the return line by hand and check whether the pressure rises.

✳✳CAUTION

Do not allow the pressure to exceed 87 psi (600 kPa) to avoid fire and personal injury.

2. If the pressure rises rapidly, the pump and lines are fault-free. Replace the regulator and recheck the line pressure.
3. If the pressure rises slowly, the fuel filter, pump strainer or lines are blocked.
4. If the pressure does not rise, replace the fuel pump.

Fuel Pressure Regulator Testing

1. Connect a vacuum pump to the regulator.

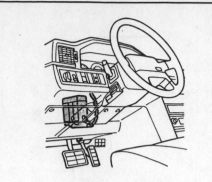

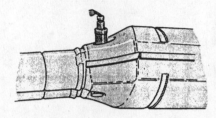

Control unit (Motronic 1.8)
INSIDE PANEL ON DRIVER'S SIDE

Oxygen sensor (Lambdasond)
INSTALLED IN CATALYTIC CONVERTER

Fuel pump relay
IN ELECTRICAL DISTRIBUTION UNIT

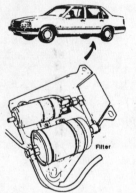

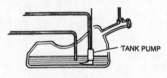

TANK PUMP

Tank pump
INSTALLED IN TANK (AS PART OF FUEL LEVEL TRANSMITTER ASSEMBLY)

Filter

Main fuel pump and fuel filter
ON SHELF UNDERNEATH CAR, UNDER REAR SEAT

84285095

Fig. 86 Component locations — 960

2. Check that the line pressure falls by the same amount as that in the regulator.

3. Disconnect the jumper, check and install the fuses.

4. The residual pressure should not fall below 29 psi (200 kPa) in less than 20 minutes.

❋❋CAUTION

If removed, the plastic tape securing the fuel lines must be re-secured to prevent fire and personal injury.

Fault Tracing

Battery Voltage Test
▶ See Figure 88

Fault Code 1-3-2 will set if the battery voltage falls below 8 volts or exceeds 16 volts for 5 seconds after the engine has started.

VOLTAGE CHECK

1. Connect a voltmeter across terminals 18 and 19 of the control unit.

2. Start the engine and read the battery voltage.

3. Check the battery and charging system if the voltage is in abnormal range.

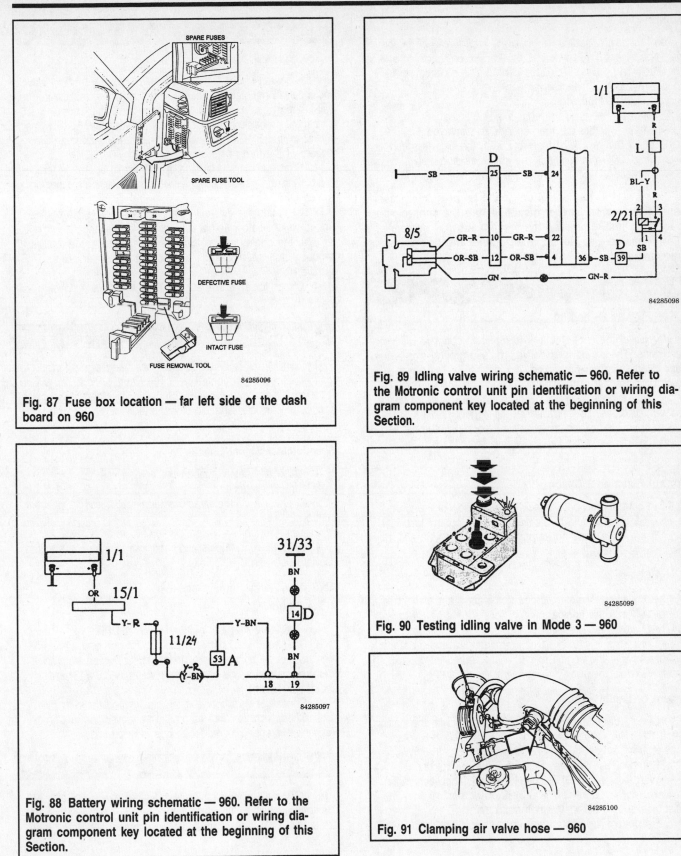

Fig. 87 Fuse box location — far left side of the dash board on 960

Fig. 88 Battery wiring schematic — 960. Refer to the Motronic control unit pin identification or wiring diagram component key located at the beginning of this Section.

Fig. 89 Idling valve wiring schematic — 960. Refer to the Motronic control unit pin identification or wiring diagram component key located at the beginning of this Section.

Fig. 90 Testing idling valve in Mode 3 — 960

Fig. 91 Clamping air valve hose — 960

Control Unit

The Motronic control unit checks its program when the engine is switched **OFF**, whereas the knock control circuit is checked while driving. The fault code 1-1-2 is displayed if this check reveals that a fault is present.

1. Clear the fault code.
2. Start and shut off the engine a few times.
3. Check whether the fault code is re-displayed.
4. Drive the vehicle at high load with the engine speed exceeding 3000 rpm to check the knock sensor circuit.
5. Replace the control unit if the fault code recurs.

➡**The power to the control unit must be completely dissipated when connecting or disconnecting the connector or measuring unit, otherwise the component may be damaged. Remove fuse No. 24 when connecting or disconnecting.**

Idle Valve

▶ **See Figures 89 and 90**

The role of the control unit is to maintain constant idling conditions. The control unit delivers pulsed ground signals to both idling valve coils (opening and closing). If the signal is absent, or if either of the coil circuits is open or shorted, the control unit cannot exercise idling control. In this case, no ground pulses will be delivered by the control unit and the engine speed will be controlled by the spring-loaded function 6, which maintains a small valve opening at all times.

Control Function 3 Check

1. In control function 3 check the operation of the idling valve. The valve should be activated by the control unit.
2. If the valve does not operate, check the wiring and the supply to and from the valve.

Signal Check

1. Connect a voltmeter across terminals 4 and 24 of the control unit with the engine idling. There should be approximately 11 volts with the engine hot.
2. Connect a voltmeter across terminals 22 and 24 of the control unit with the engine idling. There should be approximately 7.5 volts.

Absent or Faulty Signal

1. Check for voltage at terminals 4 and 22 with the ignition switch **ON**. The voltage should be approximately 8-9 volts.
2. If there is no voltage, check the supply to the valve.
3. Remove fuse 24 and disconnect the control unit.
4. With the ignition **OFF**, check the resistance across the idle valve coils at terminals 4 and 22 of the control unit. The resistance should be approximately 25 ohms.
5. Reconnect the control unit and replace the fuse.

Idle Speed

▶ **See Figure 91**

If the control unit is forced to open or close the idling valve too much to maintain constant idling conditions, the control unit will interpret this as a fault and record the Fault Code 2-3-3. The most probable causes are incorrect measurement by the air mass meter or air leakage into the intake manifold downstream of the throttle housing.

1. Start and run the engine up to normal operating temperature, with the gear selector lever in **N** and the air conditioning switch **OFF**.
2. Clamping the air valve hose and observing the engine speed will indicate whether air leakage is present.
3. If the engine speed exceeds 600-700 rpm, the fault is probably due to air leakage or incorrect adjustment of the throttle disc.
4. Check for air leakage and adjust the throttle housing as required.

Speed Sensor

The control unit is dependent on the speed signal for full-load enrichment, fan control, etc. The Fault Code 3-1-1 will be reported if the speed exceeds 3390 rpm, the load signal corresponds to part load and the signal is absent for 3 seconds.

Speedometer Signal Check

1. Raise and safely support the vehicle with the rear wheels freely suspended.
2. Connect a voltmeter across terminals 9 and 19 of the control unit.
3. Turn the ignition switch **ON**.
4. Spin the rear wheels and read the voltmeter. It should oscillate between 0.1-12 volts.

Absent or Faulty Signal Check

▶ **See Figure 92**

1. Make sure that the ignition switch is **OFF**.
2. Check the lead between the control unit and the instrument cluster by connecting an ohmmeter between terminal 9 and the terminal at the rear of the cluster (Gn/Or). There should be 0 ohms.
3. Check the wire between the cluster and the rear axle.
4. Check vehicles with automatic transmissions in Control Function 1 if speed signal fault code is displayed.

EGR Vacuum Booster

An EGR system malfunction is indicated by Fault Code 2-4-1 (California vehicles). It results when the EGR temperature sensor detects that the exhaust gas recirculation flow is too low.

EGR Vacuum Booster Check

▶ **See Figures 93 and 94**

1. Turn the ignition switch **ON**.

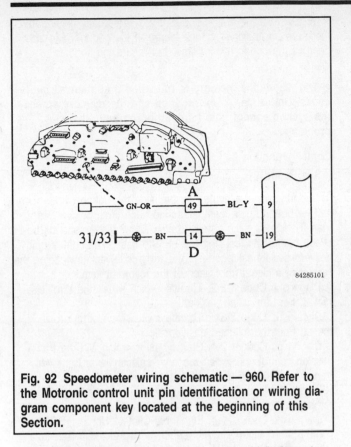

Fig. 92 Speedometer wiring schematic — 960. Refer to the Motronic control unit pin identification or wiring diagram component key located at the beginning of this Section.

2. Enter Control Function 3. The lamp should flash as the EGR vacuum booster is activated.

3. Turn the ignition switch **OFF**.

4. If the EGR vacuum booster is not activated, measure the resistance between pins 6 and 15 in the control unit connector. The resistance should be approximately 75 95 ohms.

5. If the value is different, check the wiring and connection.

EGR System Operational Check

1. Open the EGR converter connector. Remove the lead directly opposite the Black/White lead between pin 1 and the control unit. Reconnect the connector.

2. Start and warm the engine to operating temperature.

3. Ground the loose lead. If the engine starts to run unevenly, the EGR system is operating.

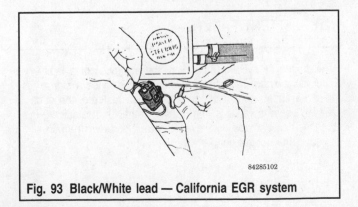

Fig. 93 Black/White lead — California EGR system

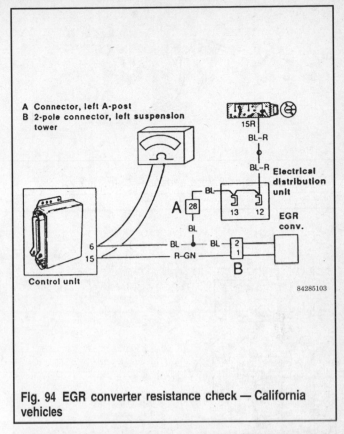

Fig. 94 EGR converter resistance check — California vehicles

EGR Temperature Sensor

▶ See Figures 95 and 96

If the signal from the EGR temperature sensor is absent or faulty, Fault Code 4-3-1 will result (California vehicles).

➡**The sensor is extremely sensitive to shock and impact. When replacing, torque to 7-13 Nm (5-10 ft. lbs.).**

1. Measure the resistance between terminal 14 (ground) and terminal 22 on the control unit connector. It should be 500-1000 ohms.

2. If the value is different, check the leads and connections, the ground terminal on the intake manifold and the resistance of the sensor connector.

READING CODES

Control Function 1

▶ See Figure 97

Faults stored in the memory are read through a series of flashes from the diagnostic socket LED. All fault codes have 3 digits, each capable of ranging from 1 through 9. The fault codes are read from the series of flashes delivered by the LED. Each code requires 3 series of uninterrupted flashes, with a 3 second interval between each series of flashes to make the codes easy to read.

The following procedure is for retrieving fault codes.

1. Open the diagnostic socket cover in the left side rear of the engine compartment and install the selector plug into

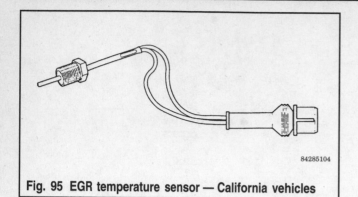

84285104

Fig. 95 EGR temperature sensor — California vehicles

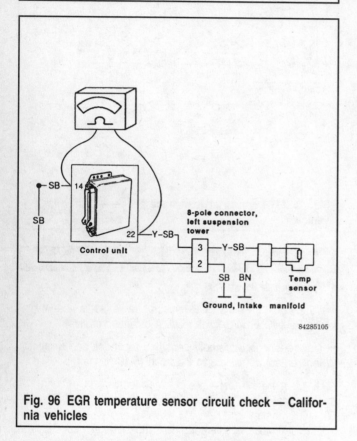

84285105

Fig. 96 EGR temperature sensor circuit check — California vehicles

socket No. 2 for ignition or fuel system codes, or into socket No. 6 for EGR system codes on California vehicles.

2. Turn ignition to the **ON** position.

3. Enter Control Function 1 by pressing the button once. Hold the button for at least 1 second, but not more than 3 seconds.

4. Watch the LED and count the number of flashes in each of the 3 flash series, which will indicate a fault code. The flash series are separated by 3 second intervals. Note the fault codes.

➡**If there are no fault codes in the diagnostic unit, the LED will flash 1-1-1 and the fuel system is operating correctly.**

5. Depress the button again. If the same code is repeated, there are no additional codes stored. If the code is different, depress the button a third time and record the code, if different.

➡**The diagnostic memory is full when it contains 3 fault codes. Until those 3 are rectified and the memory erased, the system cannot give information on any other problems.**

Control Function 2
▶ **See Figure 97**

This function is activated by pressing the button twice, holding the button for at least 1 second each time, but not more than 3 seconds each time and also allowing 1-3 seconds between operations, causing the LED to flash. The control unit delivers a diagnostic code (not a fault code) acknowledging the receipt of a signal from each of the following items:

Diagnostic Code 3-3-2: Throttle switch, when the throttle is moved from the idling position

Diagnostic Code 3-3-3: Throttle switch, when the throttle is moved from the full-load position

Diagnostic Code 1-2-4: Start inhibitor switch, via the transmission control unit, when the gear selector lever is moved from 1 of the drive positions to the **N** or **P** position

Diagnostic Code 1-4-1: Timing pick-up, when the starter motor is running

Diagnostic Code 1-1-4: Electronic Climate Control (ECC) control panel, when the A/C button is depressed or released

Diagnostic Code 1-3-4: Relay in ECC power unit and, as a result, A/C compressor electromagnetic clutch, when A/C is switched **ON**

Control Function 3
▶ **See Figure 97**

This function is activated by pressing the button 3 times, holding the button for at least 1 second each time, but not more than 3 seconds each time and also allowing 1-3 seconds between operations. The control unit then responds by activating, in order:

1. Radiator fan at half speed for 3 seconds
2. Radiator fan at full speed for 3 seconds
3. Injectors at 13 Hz
4. Idling (CIS) valve at 1 Hz
5. Relay in ECC power unit and, as a result, A/C compressor electromagnetic clutch, at 1 Hz.

This activation is repeated twice.

INTERMITTENT FAULTS

All diagnostic system faults, with the exception of a faulty knock sensor, are reversible. In other words, once a signal which has been absent or faulty has been restored, the control unit will begin to reuse it immediately rather that remaining in the 'limp-home' mode. However, the fault code will remain stored in the control unit.

CLEARING CODES

When all the fault codes have been read and corrected, the diagnostic system memory can be erased as follows:

1. Turn ignition switch to the **ON** position.
2. Read fault codes again.
3. Press and hold diagnostic socket button for approximately 5 seconds. Release button. After 3 seconds, the LED should light.
4. While the LED is lit, press button again for approximately 5 seconds. Release button. The LED should go out. Memory is cleared.

➡**To ensure that the memory has been erased, press button again for 1 second but not more than 3 seconds. The LED should flash 1-1-1, indicating that the fuel system is operating properly.**

ENGINE SYMPTOM TESTS

Engine Does Not Start
GROUND CONNECTIONS CHECK
▶ **See Figures 98 and 99**

1. With the ignition key **OFF**, connect an ohmmeter between ground and terminals 19, 24, 26, 30 and 48 of the control unit. The meter should indicate approximately 0 ohms in all cases.
2. Check the power unit ground connections under each unit. Connect an ohmmeter between ground and terminal 4 on front power unit connector, then between ground and terminal 4 on rear power unit connector. The meter should indicate approximately 0 ohms in both cases.
3. If high resistance is indicated, check the connectors and the wiring.

VOLTAGE CHECK
▶ **See Figure 100**

1. With the ignition switch **OFF**, check for voltage supply to terminal 18 across fuse 24 and to terminal 36 across the main relay.
2. Connect a voltmeter across terminals 18 and 19, then across terminals 36 and 19 of the control unit. The voltmeter should indicate battery voltage in both cases. Check the fuse, wiring and the relay if no reading is obtained.
3. Turn the ignition switch **ON** and check that the voltage falls from battery voltage to approximately 0.1 volt at terminal 36.

FUEL PUMP OPERATION CHECK

1. Remove the fuel tank filler cap.
2. Check that the fuel pumps operate for 3 seconds when the ignition is turned **ON**, listening for noise.
3. If the pumps do not operate when the ignition is turned **ON**, connect a voltmeter across terminals 3 and 19 of the control unit. Battery voltage should be indicated.
   a. If there is no voltage, check the wiring and the supply to the pump relay.
   b. If there is voltage, check the wiring and the supply to the fuel pump.

Code	Fault	Correction Test
1-1-1	No faults	—
1-1-2	Fault in control unit	Control unit
1-1-3	Fault in injector	Injector
1-2-1	Air mass meter signal absent or faulty	Air mass meter
1-2-3	Engine temperature signal absent or faulty	Temperature sensor
1-3-1	No signal from timing pick-up	Timing pick-up
1-3-2	Battery voltage too low or too high ①	Battery voltage
1-4-3	Front knock sensor signal absent or faulty	Front knock sensor
2-1-2	Oxygen sensor signal absent or faulty	Oxygen sensor
2-1-4	Timing pick-up signal absent intermittently	Timing pick-up
2-2-3	Idling valve signal absent or faulty	Idle valve
2-3-1	Adaptive lambda control lean or rich in part-load range	Oxygen sensor
2-3-2	Adaptive lambda control lean or rich at idling	Oxygen sensor
2-3-3	Adaptive idling control outside control range	Idle speed
2-4-1	EGR system malfunction ②	EGR vacuum booster
2-4-3	Signal from throttle switch absent or faulty	Throttle switch
3-1-1	Speedometer signal absent	Speed sensor
3-1-4	Camshaft sensor signal absent	Camshaft sensor
3-2-2	Air mass meter burn-off signal absent	Air mass meter
4-3-1	Signal from EGR temperature sender absent or faulty ②	EGR temperature sensor
4-3-3	Rear knock sensor signal absent or faulty	Rear knock sensor

① Check charging system
② California

84285106

Fig. 97 Fault code descriptions — Motronic

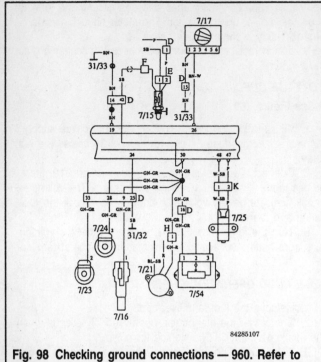

Fig. 98 Checking ground connections — 960. Refer to the Motronic control unit pin identification or wiring diagram component key located at the beginning of this Section.

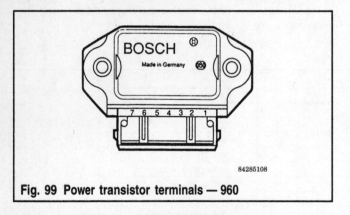

84285108

Fig. 99 Power transistor terminals — 960

BUSBAR NUMBER 15 SUPPLY CHECK

1. Connect a voltmeter across terminals 27 and 19, then across terminals 37 and 19 of the control unit.
2. Turn the ignition switch **ON**. The meter should indicate battery voltage in both cases.
3. Check the wiring to the control unit if no reading is obtained.

INJECTOR SUPPLY CHECK

1. Connect a voltmeter across terminals 16 and 24, then across terminals 17 and 24 of the control unit.
2. Turn the ignition switch **ON**. The meter should indicate battery voltage in both cases.
3. Check the wiring and the connectors if no reading is obtained.

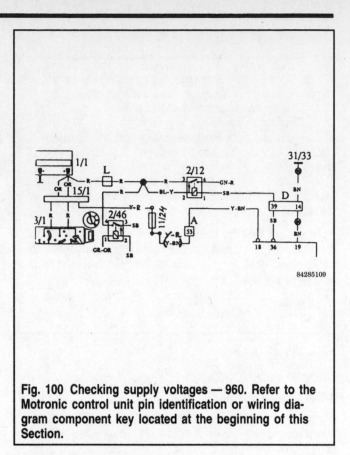

84285109

Fig. 100 Checking supply voltages — 960. Refer to the Motronic control unit pin identification or wiring diagram component key located at the beginning of this Section.

IGNITION COIL VOLTAGE SUPPLY CHECK

♦ See Figure 101

1. Turn the ignition switch **ON**.
2. Connect a voltmeter between ground and the test terminal at the rear of the engine. The reading should be battery voltage.
3. If the reading is not battery voltage, check the coil relay, wiring and the connectors up to the ignition coils.
4. Attempt to start the engine.
5. If the engine still does not start, remove the ignition coil cover and remove one coil.
6. Fit a spare spark plug in the ignition coil and crank the engine.
7. If no spark is obtained, check the timing pick-up as per Fault Code 1-3-1.

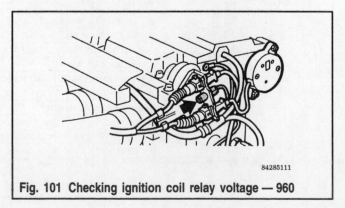

84285111

Fig. 101 Checking ignition coil relay voltage — 960

INJECTOR OPERATION CHECK

1. If the pick-up is intact, check that the control unit is operating the injectors.
2. Connect a milli-voltmeter between supply terminal 37 and terminal 16 of the control unit.
3. Crank the engine. The meter should indicate approximately 500 millivolts.
4. Test with a new control unit if no reading is obtained.

Engine Starts But Does Not Fire On All Cylinders

MISSING CYLINDER IDENTIFICATION

1. Idle the engine.
2. Disconnect and reconnect 1 injector at a time. If the engine speed drops appreciably when connector is disconnected, the cylinder is firing normally.

IGNITION OR FUEL SYSTEM IDENTIFICATION

▶ **See Figures 102 and 103**

1. Use a voltmeter to check the injectors.
2. The voltage should be approximately 250-400 millivolts when the engine is hot.
3. If the voltage is correct, either the fault is in the ignition system or the injector is blocked. Check the fuel system for fault codes.

FIRING PULSE AT COIL CHECK

1. Use test diode 999-5280 or equivalent. Make an adaptor to fit between the ignition coil connector and the test diode.
2. Connect the test diode.

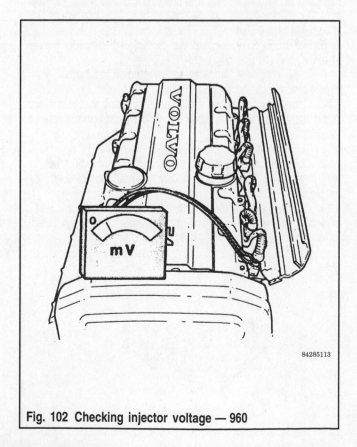

Fig. 102 Checking injector voltage — 960

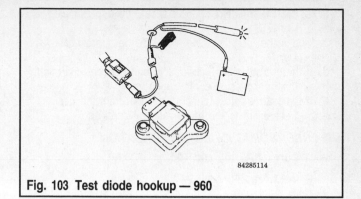

Fig. 103 Test diode hookup — 960

3. Start the engine. The LED should flash when a signal is present.
   a. If there is no signal, check the signal output from the control unit.
   b. If there is a signal present, replace the ignition coil or spark plug.

CONTROL UNIT SIGNAL OUTPUT CHECK

1. Connect a voltmeter between ground and the control unit terminal that is connected to the ignition coil.
2. Start the engine.
3. The meter should indicate between 60-100 millivolts if the signal is correct.
4. If the reading is approximately 3.5 volts, there is an open circuit present between the control unit and the ignition coil.
5. If the signal is present, check the power unit and wiring. Stop the engine.

POWER UNIT AND WIRING CHECK

1. With the ignition switch **OFF**, connect the diode tester with the positive side connected to the control unit terminal for cylinder to be checked and to terminal 1 on corresponding ignition coil connector. Also check in reverse direction.
2. Connect the diode tester with the positive side connected to ground and to terminal 1 on the ignition coil connector. Also check in the reverse direction.
3. Check the wiring if a faulty diode is found.

Idling Speed Drops When Drive Is Engaged Or When A/C Is Switched In

IDLING COMPENSATION IN DRIVE CHECK

1. Start the engine.
2. Enter Control Function 2.
3. Move the gear select lever to **D**, then to **N**, and await response.
4. Code 1-2-4 indicates contact between the transmission control unit and the Motronic control unit.
5. If no code is displayed, check the voltage signal and the wiring.
6. Switch the ignition **OFF**.

VOLTAGE SIGNAL AND WIRING CHECK

1. Connect a voltmeter across terminals 42 and 19 of the control unit.
2. Turn the ignition switch **ON**.

3. Check the meter reading. It should be approximately 5.5 volts in **P** or **N**.

4. Check the meter reading. It should be approximately 0.5 volts in **D** or **R**.

5. If there is no signal, check the lead between the control unit and the transmission control unit.

6. If the lead is intact, check the signal from the gear selector mechanism to the transmission control unit.

AIR CONDITIONING IDLING COMPENSATION

▶ **See Figures 104, 105 and 106**

1. Enter Control Function 2.
2. Start the engine.
3. Disconnect the low-pressure switch connector on the dryer bottle.
4. Switch the blower motor **ON**, otherwise the A/C will not operate.
5. Depress and release the A/C button.
6. If Diagnostic Code 1-1-4 is displayed, go to step 8.
7. If no code is displayed, go to step 12.
8. Reconnect the low-pressure switch connector.
9. Diagnostic Code 1-3-4 should be displayed when the A/C compressor clutch operates.
10. If the code is not displayed or if it is displayed without the operation of the compressor, go to step 19.
11. Turn **OFF** the engine.
12. If Diagnostic Code 1-1-4 was absent, start the engine.
13. Connect a voltmeter across terminals 41 and 19.
14. Depress the A/C OFF button.
15. The instrument should indicate approximately 11 volts.
16. Release the A/C OFF button (A/C request position). The compressor should start after a brief interval and the voltage should fall drastically to a value below 1 volt.
17. If there is no voltage on A/C request, check the lead between the control unit and ECC control.
18. Turn **OFF** the engine.
19. If Diagnostic Code 1-3-4 is absent, enter Control Function 3.

➡ **As the last operation in Control Function 3, the control unit will operate the ECC power unit relay, causing the A/C compressor clutch to engage and disengage (once per second).**

20. If neither the relay nor the compressor clutch operates, check the supply to the control unit terminal 40.

21. Connect a voltmeter across terminals 23 and 19. It should indicate battery voltage.

22. If there is no voltage, check the wiring and the supply to the ECC power unit.

23. If voltage is present, connect a voltmeter across terminals 40 and 19. Ground terminal 23.

24. The voltmeter should indicate battery voltage. If not, the fault is in the A/C system.

Electric Radiator Fan Testing

▶ **See Figure 107**

1. Enter Control Function 3.

➡ **As the first operation in Control Function 3, the control unit will operate the radiator fan relay at half-speed for 3 seconds, and then at full speed for a further 3 seconds.**

2. If the fan does not operate, check the wiring and the relay.

3. Connect a voltmeter across terminals 14 and 19 of the control unit. It should indicate battery voltage.

4. Connect the voltmeter across terminals 14 and 19. It should indicate battery voltage.

5. If there is no voltage to the control unit, check the supply to the relay.

6. If voltage is present, check the wiring between the fan motor, the relay and ground.

Diagnostic Unit Testing

▶ **See Figures 108, 109, 110, 111 and 112**

1. Turn the ignition switch **ON**.
2. Connect the test lead to socket 2 on the diagnostic unit.
3. Connect a voltmeter across terminals 55 and 19 on the control unit connector. The instrument should indicate 12 volts.
4. Press the button on the control unit. The instrument should indicate 0 volt.
5. If there is no voltage at the control unit, measure instead at the diagnostic unit connector.
6. If the voltmeter indicates 12 volts when the button is depressed, check the diagnostic unit.
7. Connect a voltmeter between ground and the blue lead in the diagnostic unit connector. It should read approximately 12 volts.
8. Turn the ignition switch **OFF**.
9. Connect an ohmmeter between ground and the black lead in the diagnostic unit connector. It should indicate approximately 0 ohms.
10. Connect an ohmmeter between the diagnostic unit test plug and the pin that is directly underneath the function selector button. The instrument should indicate infinity.

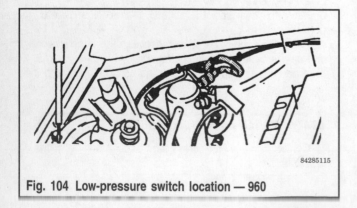

84285115

Fig. 104 Low-pressure switch location — 960

84285116

Fig. 105 Electronic climate control power relay — 960

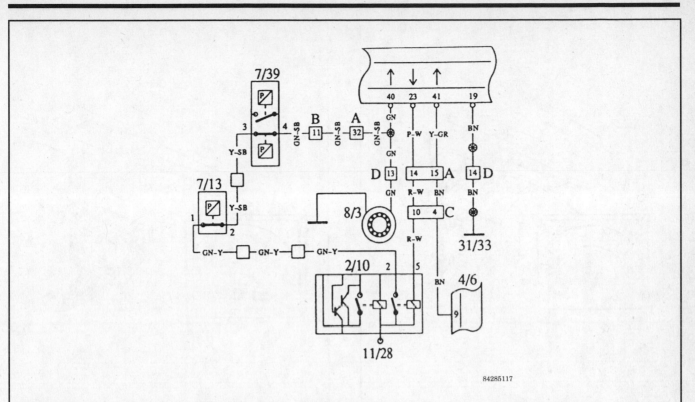

Fig. 106 Air conditioning clutch wiring schematic — 960. Refer to the Motronic control unit pin identification or wiring diagram component key located at the beginning of this Section.

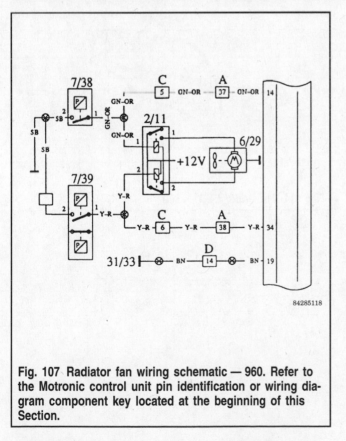

Fig. 107 Radiator fan wiring schematic — 960. Refer to the Motronic control unit pin identification or wiring diagram component key located at the beginning of this Section.

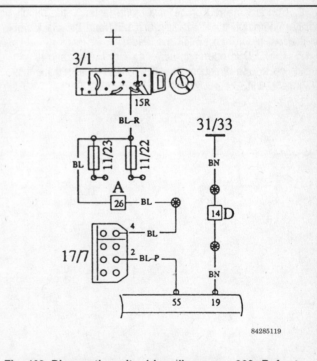

Fig. 108 Diagnostic unit wiring diagram — 960. Refer to the Motronic control unit pin identification or wiring diagram component key located at the beginning of this Section.

11. Depress the selector button. The ohmmeter should indicate 0 ohms.

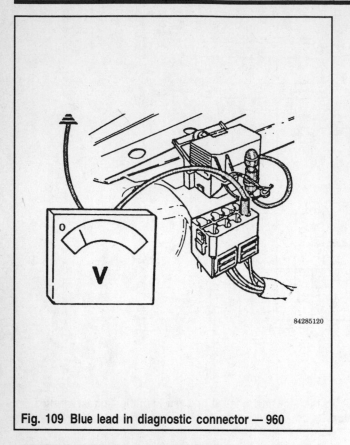

Fig. 109 Blue lead in diagnostic connector — 960

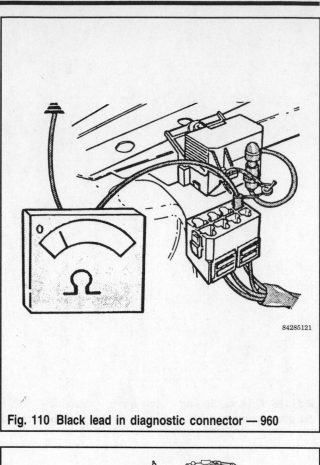

Fig. 110 Black lead in diagnostic connector — 960

12. Connect the red probe of a diode tester to the pin directly underneath the diagnostic unit LED and the black probe to the test plug, then switch the leads.

13. The LED is operating correctly if the tester shows an indication in one direction only. If it is defective, replace the diagnostic unit.

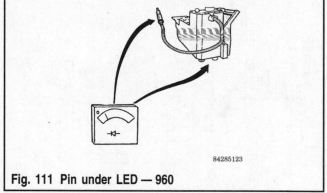

Fig. 111 Pin under LED — 960

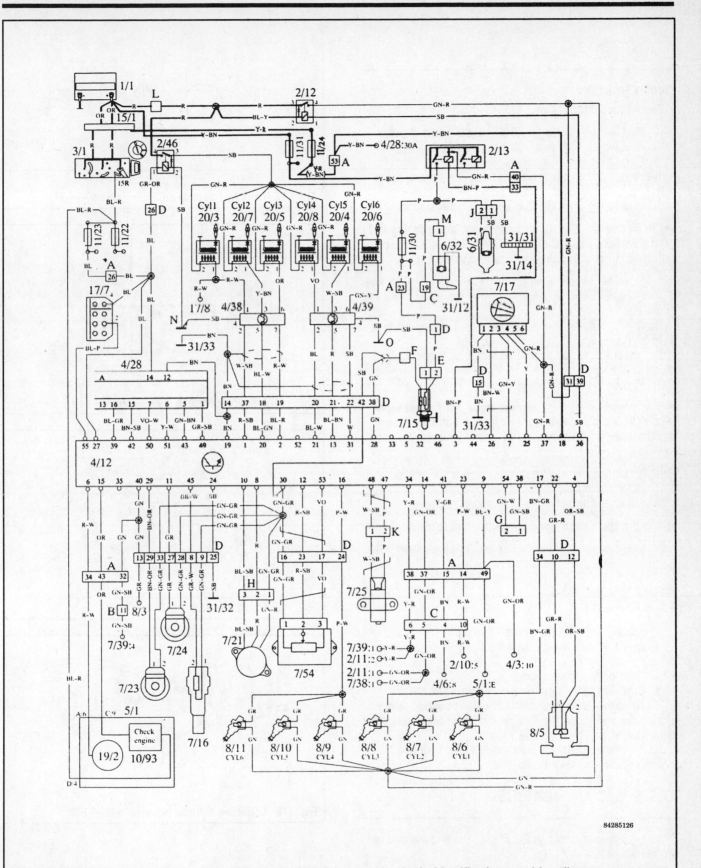

Fig. 112 Motronic system wiring — 960. Refer to the Motronic control unit pin identification or wiring diagram component key located at the beginning of this Section.

84285126

ADJUSTMENTS

Throttle Housing

▶ **See Figures 113, 114 and 115**

1. Remove the throttle housing from the intake manifold.
2. Remove the throttle switch from the housing.
3. Carefully clean the housing.
4. Loosen the adjusting screw so that the throttle closes fully.
5. Loosen the 2 throttle disc retaining screws slightly.

➡**Check that the disc is correctly installed or facing in the right direction. Since the edges of the disc are thin, careful observation is required to detect chamfering.**

6. Open the throttle approximately one-third using the lever.
7. Release the lever suddenly so that the disc centers itself in the throttle opening.
8. Check that the throttle spindle can be moved easily forward and backward.
9. Adjust the throttle spindle so that it protrudes 12.5mm outside the housing.
10. Tighten the disc retaining screws.

➡**It is important that the spindle does not project more than 12.5mm, otherwise it may foul the bottom of the throttle switch.**

11. Screw in the adjusting screw until it just touches the arm. Tighten a further half turn, then tighten the locknut.
12. Mount the throttle switch on the spindle.
13. Install and tighten the switch retaining screws.

➡**The throttle switch does not require adjustment.**

14. Mount the throttle housing on the intake manifold, then reconnect all hoses.

Throttle Housing Pulley

▶ **See Figure 116**

1. Attach the link to the throttle housing.
2. Adjust the link exactly to fit the ball joint on pulley and press into position.
3. Tighten the adjusting nuts.
4. Check that the pulley moves freely without sticking.
5. The cable should be taut in the idling position, without altering the pulley position. The pulley should bear against the idling stop. Adjust the pulley as required.
6. Press the accelerator pedal itself to the floor and check that the pulley reaches full-load stop.

IDLE SPEED AND MIXTURE

The predetermined idle speed of 750 rpm and the mixture are not adjustable.

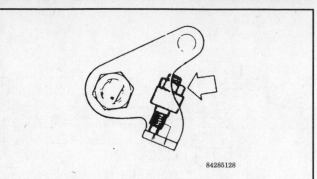

84285128

Fig. 113 Throttle housing adjusting screw — 960

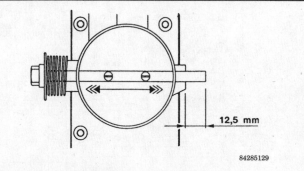

12,5 mm

84285129

Fig. 114 Adjusting throttle disk — 960

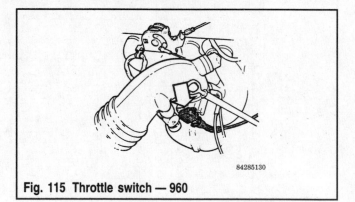

84285130

Fig. 115 Throttle switch — 960

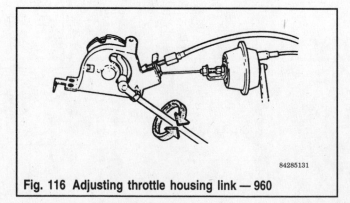

84285131

Fig. 116 Adjusting throttle housing link — 960

6

CHASSIS ELECTRICAL

UNDERSTANDING AND TROUBLESHOOTING ELECTRICAL SYSTEMS

The following section outlines basic diagnosis techniques for dealing with the automotive electrical systems. A general explanation of the various types of test equipment available to aid in servicing the automotive electronic systems and basic repair techniques for wiring harnesses and connectors are also given. Read the basic information before attempting any repairs or testing on any computerized system, to provide the background of information necessary to avoid the most common and obvious mistakes that can cost both time and money. Although the replacement and testing procedures are simple in themselves, the systems are not, and unless one has a thorough understanding of all components and their function within a particular computerized control system, the logical test sequence these systems demand cannot be followed. Minor malfunctions can make a big difference, so it is important to know how each component affects the operation of the overall electronic system to find the ultimate cause of a problem without replacing good components unnecessarily.

Safety Precautions

❊❊CAUTION

Whenever working on or around any computer based microprocessor control system, always observe these general precautions to prevent the possibility of personal injury or damage to electronic components.

• Never install or remove battery cables with the key ON or the engine running. Jumper cables should be connected with the key OFF to avoid power surges that can damage electronic control units. Engines equipped with computer controlled systems should avoid both giving and getting jump starts due to the possibility of serious damage to components from arcing in the engine compartment when connections are made with the ignition ON.

• Always remove the battery cables before charging the battery. Never use a high output charger on an installed battery or attempt to use any type of 'hot shot' (24 volt) starting aid.

• Exercise care when inserting test probes into connectors to insure good connections without damaging the connector or spreading the pins. Always probe connectors from the rear (wire) side, NOT the pin side, to avoid accidental shorting of terminals during test procedures.

• Never remove or attach wiring harness connectors with the ignition switch ON, especially to an electronic control unit.

• Do not drop any components during service procedures and never apply 12 volts directly to any component (like a solenoid or relay) unless instructed specifically to do so. Some component electrical windings are designed to safely handle only 4 or 5 volts and can be destroyed in seconds if 12 volts are applied directly to the connector.

• Remove the electronic control unit if the vehicle is to be placed in an environment where temperatures exceed approximately 176°F (80°C), such as a paint spray booth or when arc or gas welding near the control unit location in the car.

ORGANIZED TROUBLESHOOTING

When diagnosing a specific problem, organized troubleshooting is a must. The complexity of a modern automobile demands that you approach any problem in a logical, organized manner. There are certain troubleshooting techniques that are standard:

1. Establish when the problem occurs. Does the problem appear only under certain conditions? Were there any noises, odors, or other unusual symptoms?

2. Isolate the problem area. To do this, make some simple tests and observations; then eliminate the systems that are working properly. Check for obvious problems such as broken wires, dirty connections or split or disconnected vacuum hoses. Always check the obvious before assuming something complicated is the cause.

3. Test for problems systematically to determine the cause once the problem area is isolated. Are all the components functioning properly? Is there power going to electrical switches and motors? Is there vacuum at vacuum switches and/or actuators? Is there a mechanical problem such as bent linkage or loose mounting screws? Doing careful, systematic checks will often turn up most causes on the first inspection without wasting time checking components that have little or no relationship to the problem.

4. Test all repairs after the work is done to make sure that the problem is fixed. Some causes can be traced to more than one component, so a careful verification of repair work is important to pick up additional malfunctions that may cause a problem to reappear or a different problem to arise. A blown fuse, for example, is a simple problem that may require more than another fuse to repair. If you don't look for a problem that caused a fuse to blow, for example, a shorted wire may go undetected.

Experience has shown that most problems tend to be the result of a fairly simple and obvious cause, such as loose or corroded connectors or air leaks in the intake system; making careful inspection of components during testing essential to quick and accurate troubleshooting. Special, hand held computerized testers designed specifically for diagnosing the system are available from a variety of aftermarket sources, as well as from the vehicle manufacturer, but care should be taken that any test equipment being used is designed to diagnose that particular computer controlled system accurately without damaging the control unit (ECU) or components being tested.

➡**Pinpointing the exact cause of trouble in an electrical system can sometimes only be accomplished by the use of special test equipment. The following describes commonly used test equipment and explains how to put it to best use in diagnosis. In addition to the information covered below, the manufacturer's instructions booklet provided with the tester should be read and clearly understood before attempting any test procedures.**

TEST EQUIPMENT

Jumper Wires

Jumper wires are simple, yet extremely valuable, pieces of test equipment. Jumper wires are merely wires that are used to bypass sections of a circuit. The simplest type of jumper wire is merely a length of multistrand wire with an alligator clip at each end. Jumper wires are usually fabricated from lengths of standard automotive wire and whatever type of connector (alligator clip, spade connector or pin connector) that is required for the particular vehicle being tested. The well equipped tool box will have several different styles of jumper wires in several different lengths. Some jumper wires are made with 3 or more terminals coming from a common splice for special purpose. Whenever working on or around any computer based microprocessor control system, always observe these general precautions to prevent the possibility of personal injury or damage to electronic components.

• Never install or remove battery cables with the key ON or the engine running. Jumper cables should be connected with the key OFF to avoid power surges that can damage electronic control units. Engines equipped with computer controlled systems should avoid both giving and getting jump starts due to the possibility of serious damage to components from arcing in the engine compartment when connections are made with the ignition ON.

• Always remove the battery cables before charging the battery. Never use a high output charger on an installed battery or attempt to use any type of 'hot shot' (24 volt) starting aid.

• Exercise care when inserting test probes into connectors to insure good connections without damaging the connector or spreading the pins. Always probe connectors from the rear (wire) side, NOT the pin side, to avoid accidental shorting of terminals during test procedures.

• Never remove or attach wiring harness connectors with the ignition switch ON, especially to an electronic control unit.

• Do not drop any components during service procedures and never apply 12 volts directly to any component (like a solenoid or relay) unless instructed specifically to do so. Some component electrical windings are designed to safely handle only 4 or 5 volts and can be destroyed in seconds if 12 volts are applied directly to the connector.

• Remove the electronic control unit if the vehicle is to be placed in an environment where temperatures exceed approximately 176°F (80°C), such as a paint spray booth or when arc or gas welding near the control unit location in the car.

ORGANIZED TROUBLESHOOTING

When diagnosing a specific problem, organized troubleshooting is a must. The complexity of a modern automobile demands that you approach any problem in a logical, organized manner. There are certain troubleshooting techniques that are standard:

1. Establish when the problem occurs. Does the problem appear only under certain conditions? Were there any noises, odors, or other unusual symptoms?

2. Isolate the problem area. To do this, make some simple tests and observations; then eliminate the systems that are working properly. Check for obvious problems such as broken wires, dirty connections or split or disconnected vacuum hoses. Always check the obvious before assuming something complicated is the cause.

3. Test for problems systematically to determine the cause once the problem area is isolated. Are all the components functioning properly? Is there power going to electrical switches and motors? Is there vacuum at vacuum switches and/or actuators? Is there a mechanical problem such as bent linkage or loose mounting screws? Doing careful, systematic checks will often turn up most causes on the first inspection without wasting time checking components that have little or no relationship to the problem.

4. Test all repairs after the work is done to make sure that the problem is fixed. Some causes can be traced to more than one component, so a careful verification of repair work is important to pick up additional malfunctions that may cause a problem to reappear or a different problem to arise. A blown fuse, for example, is a simple problem that may require more than another fuse to repair. If you don't look for a problem that caused a fuse to blow, for example, a shorted wire may go undetected.

Experience has shown that most problems tend to be the result of a fairly simple and obvious cause, such as loose or corroded connectors or air leaks in the intake system; making careful inspection of components during testing essential to quick and accurate troubleshooting. Special, hand held computerized testers designed specifically for diagnosing the system are available from a variety of aftermarket sources, as well as from the vehicle manufacturer, but care should be taken that any test equipment being used is designed to diagnose that particular computer controlled system accurately without damaging the control unit (ECU) or components being tested.

➡Pinpointing the exact cause of trouble in an electrical system can sometimes only be accomplished by the use of special test equipment. The following describes commonly used test equipment and explains how to put it to best use in diagnosis. In addition to the information covered below, the manufacturer's instructions booklet provided with the tester should be read and clearly understood before attempting any test procedures.

TEST EQUIPMENT

Jumper Wires

Jumper wires are simple, yet extremely valuable, pieces of test equipment. Jumper wires are merely wires that are used to bypass sections of a circuit. The simplest type of jumper wire is merely a length of multistrand wire with an alligator clip at each end. Jumper wires are usually fabricated from lengths of standard automotive wire and whatever type of connector (alligator clip, spade connector or pin connector) that is required for the particular vehicle being tested. The well equipped tool box will have several different styles of jumper wires in several different lengths. Some jumper wires are made with three or more terminals coming from a common splice for special purpose testing. In cramped, hard-to-reach areas it is advisable to have insulated boots over the jumper wire terminals in order to prevent accidental grounding, sparks, and possible fire, especially when testing fuel system components.

Jumper wires are used primarily to locate open electrical circuits, on either the ground (-) side of the circuit or on the hot (+) side. If an electrical component fails to operate, connect the jumper wire between the component and a good ground. If the component operates only with the jumper installed, the ground circuit is open. If the ground circuit is good, but the component does not operate, the circuit between the power feed and component is open. You can sometimes connect the jumper wire directly from the battery to the hot terminal of the component, but first make sure the component uses 12 volts in operation. Some electrical components, such as fuel injectors, are designed to operate on about 4 volts and running 12 volts directly to the injector terminals can burn out the wiring. By inserting an in-line fuseholder between a set of test leads, a fused jumper wire can be used for bypassing open circuits. Use a 5 amp fuse to provide protection against voltage spikes. When in doubt, use a volt meter to check the voltage input to the component and measure how much voltage is being applied normally. By moving the jumper wire successively back from the lamp toward the power source, you can isolate the area of the circuit where the open is located. When the component stops functioning, or the power is cut off, the open is in the segment of wire between the jumper and the point previously tested.

✳✳CAUTION

Never use jumpers made from wire that is of lighter gauge than used in the circuit under test. If the jumper wire is of too small gauge, it may overheat and possibly melt. Never use jumpers to bypass high resistance loads (such as motors) in a circuit. Bypassing resistances, in effect, creates a short circuit which may, in turn, cause damage and fire. Never use a jumper for anything other than temporary bypassing of components in a circuit.

12 Volt Test Light

The 12 volt test light is used to check circuits and components while electrical current is flowing through them. It is used for voltage and ground tests. Twelve volt test lights come in different styles but all have three main parts; a ground clip, a probe, and a light. The most commonly used 12 volt test lights have pick-type probes. To use a 12 volt test light, connect the ground clip to a good ground and probe wherever necessary with the pick. The pick should be sharp so that it can penetrate wire insulation to make contact with the wire, without making a large hole in the insulation. The wrap-around light is handy in hard to reach areas or where it is difficult to support a wire to push a probe pick into it. To use the wrap around light, hook the wire to probed with the hook and pull the trigger. A small pick will be forced through the wire insulation into the wire core.

✳✳CAUTION

Do not use a test light to probe electronic ignition spark plug or coil wires. Never use a pick-type test light to probe wiring on computer controlled systems unless

specifically instructed to do so. Any wire insulation that is pierced by the test light probe should be taped and sealed with silicone after testing.

Like the jumper wire, the 12 volt test light is used to isolate opens in circuits. But, whereas the jumper wire is used to bypass the open to operate the load, the 12 volt test light is used to locate the presence of voltage in a circuit. If the test light glows, you know that there is power up to that point; if the 12 volt test light does not glow when its probe is inserted into the wire or connector, you know that there is an open circuit (no power). Move the test light in successive steps back toward the power source until the light in the handle does glow. When it does glow, the open is between the probe and point previously probed.

➡**The test light does not detect that 12 volts (or any particular amount of voltage) is present; it only detects that some voltage is present. It is advisable before using the test light to touch its terminals across the battery posts to make sure the light is operating properly.**

Self-Powered Test Light

The self-powered test light usually contains a 1.5 volt penlight battery. One type of self-powered test light is similar in design to the 12 volt test light. This type has both the battery and the light in the handle and pick-type probe tip. The second type has the light toward the open tip, so that the light illuminates the contact point. The self-powered test light is dual purpose piece of test equipment. It can be used to test for either open or short circuits when power is isolated from the circuit (continuity test). A powered test light should not be used on any computer controlled system or component unless specifically instructed to do so. Many engine sensors can be destroyed by even this small amount of voltage applied directly to the terminals.

Open Circuit Testing

To use the self-powered test light to check for open circuits, first isolate the circuit from the vehicle's 12 volt power source by disconnecting the battery or wiring harness connector. Connect the test light ground clip to a good ground and probe sections of the circuit sequentially with the test light (start from either end of the circuit). If the light is out, the open is between the probe and the circuit ground. If the light is on, the open is between the probe and end of the circuit toward the power source.

Short Circuit Testing

By isolating the circuit both from power and from ground, and using a self-powered test light, you can check for shorts to ground in the circuit. Isolate the circuit from power and ground. Connect the test light ground clip to a good ground and probe any easy-to-reach test point in the circuit. If the light comes on, there is a short somewhere in the circuit. To isolate the short, probe a test point at either end of the isolated circuit (the light should be on). Leave the test light probe connected and open connectors, switches, remove parts, etc., sequentially, until the light goes out. When the light goes out, the short is between the last circuit component opened and the previous circuit opened.

➡ **The 1.5 volt battery in the test light does not provide much current. A weak battery may not provide enough power to illuminate the test light even when a complete circuit is made (especially if there are high resistances in the circuit). Always make sure that the test battery is strong. To check the battery, briefly touch the ground clip to the probe; if the light glows brightly the battery is strong enough for testing. Never use a self-powered test light to perform checks for opens or shorts when power is applied to the electrical system under test. The 12 volt vehicle power will quickly burn out the 1.5 volt light bulb in the test light.**

Voltmeter

A voltmeter is used to measure voltage at any point in a circuit, or to measure the voltage drop across any part of a circuit. It can also be used to check continuity in a wire or circuit by indicating current flow from one end to the other. Voltmeters usually have various scales on the meter dial and a selector switch to allow the selection of different voltages. The voltmeter has a positive and a negative lead. To avoid damage to the meter, always connect the negative lead to the negative (-) side of circuit (to ground or nearest the ground side of the circuit) and connect the positive lead to the positive (+) side of the circuit (to the power source or the nearest power source). Note that the negative voltmeter lead will always be black and that the positive voltmeter will always be some color other than black (usually red). Depending on how the voltmeter is connected into the circuit, it has several uses.

A voltmeter can be connected either in parallel or in series with a circuit and it has a very high resistance to current flow. When connected in parallel, only a small amount of current will flow through the voltmeter current path; the rest will flow through the normal circuit current path and the circuit will work normally. When the voltmeter is connected in series with a circuit, only a small amount of current can flow through the circuit. The circuit will not work properly, but the voltmeter reading will show if the circuit is complete or not.

Available Voltage Measurement

Set the voltmeter selector switch to the 20V position and connect the meter negative lead to the negative post of the battery. Connect the positive meter lead to the positive post of the battery and turn the ignition switch ON to provide a load. Read the voltage on the meter or digital display. A well charged battery should register over 12 volts. If the meter reads below 11.5 volts, the battery power may be insufficient to operate the electrical system properly. This test determines voltage available from the battery and should be the first step in any electrical trouble diagnosis procedure. Many electrical problems, especially on computer controlled systems, can be caused by a low state of charge in the battery. Excessive corrosion at the battery cable terminals can cause a poor contact that will prevent proper charging and full battery current flow.

Normal battery voltage is 12 volts when fully charged. When the battery is supplying current to one or more circuits it is said to be 'under load'. When everything is off the electrical system is under a 'no-load' condition. A fully charged battery may show about 12.5 volts at no load; will drop to 12 volts under medium load; and will drop even lower under heavy load. If the battery is partially discharged the voltage decrease under heavy load may be excessive, even though the battery shows 12 volts or more at no load. When allowed to discharge further, the battery's available voltage under load will decrease more severely. For this reason, it is important that the battery be fully charged during all testing procedures to avoid errors in diagnosis and incorrect test results.

Voltage Drop

When current flows through a resistance, the voltage beyond the resistance is reduced (the larger the current, the greater the reduction in voltage). When no current is flowing, there is no voltage drop because there is no current flow. All points in the circuit which are connected to the power source are at the same voltage as the power source. The total voltage drop always equals the total source voltage. In a long circuit with many connectors, a series of small, unwanted voltage drops due to corrosion at the connectors can add up to a total loss of voltage which impairs the operation of the normal loads in the circuit.

INDIRECT COMPUTATION OF VOLTAGE DROPS

1. Set the voltmeter selector switch to the 20 volt position.
2. Connect the meter negative lead to a good ground.
3. Probe all resistances in the circuit with the positive meter lead.
4. Operate the circuit in all modes and observe the voltage readings.

DIRECT MEASUREMENT OF VOLTAGE DROPS

1. Set the voltmeter switch to the 20 volt position.
2. Connect the voltmeter negative lead to the ground side of the resistance load to be measured.
3. Connect the positive lead to the positive side of the resistance or load to be measured.
4. Read the voltage drop directly on the 20 volt scale.

Too high a voltage indicates too high a resistance. If, for example, a blower motor runs too slowly, you can determine if there is too high a resistance in the resistor pack. By taking voltage drop readings in all parts of the circuit, you can isolate the problem. Too low a voltage drop indicates too low a resistance. If, for example, a blower motor runs too fast in the MED and/or LOW position, the problem can be isolated in the resistor pack by taking voltage drop readings in all parts of the circuit to locate a possibly shorted resistor. The maximum allowable voltage drop under load is critical, especially if there is more than one high resistance problem in a circuit because all voltage drops are cumulative. A small drop is normal due to the resistance of the conductors.

HIGH RESISTANCE TESTING

1. Set the voltmeter selector switch to the 4 volt position.
2. Connect the voltmeter positive lead to the positive post of the battery.
3. Turn on the headlights and heater blower to provide a load.
4. Probe various points in the circuit with the negative voltmeter lead.

5. Read the voltage drop on the 4 volt scale. Some average maximum allowable voltage drops are:

    FUSE PANEL — 7 volts
    IGNITION SWITCH — 5volts
    HEADLIGHT SWITCH — 7 volts
    IGNITION COIL (+) — 5 volts
    ANY OTHER LOAD — 1.3 volts

➡**Voltage drops are all measured while a load is operating; without current flow, there will be no voltage drop.**

Ohmmeter

The ohmmeter is designed to read resistance (ohms) in a circuit or component. Although there are several different styles of ohmmeters, all will usually have a selector switch which permits the measurement of different ranges of resistance (usually the selector switch allows the multiplication of the meter reading by 10, 100, 1000, and 10,000). A calibration knob allows the meter to be set at zero for accurate measurement. Since all ohmmeters are powered by an internal battery (usually 9 volts), the ohmmeter can be used as a self-powered test light. When the ohmmeter is connected, current from the ohmmeter flows through the circuit or component being tested. Since the ohmmeter's internal resistance and voltage are known values, the amount of current flow through the meter depends on the resistance of the circuit or component being tested.

The ohmmeter can be used to perform continuity test for opens or shorts (either by observation of the meter needle or as a self-powered test light), and to read actual resistance in a circuit. It should be noted that the ohmmeter is used to check the resistance of a component or wire while there is no voltage applied to the circuit. Current flow from an outside voltage source (such as the vehicle battery) can damage the ohmmeter, so the circuit or component should be isolated from the vehicle electrical system before any testing is done. Since the ohmmeter uses its own voltage source, either lead can be connected to any test point.

➡**When checking diodes or other solid state components, the ohmmeter leads can only be connected one way in order to measure current flow in a single direction. Make sure the positive (+) and negative (-) terminal connections are as described in the test procedures to verify the one-way diode operation.**

In using the meter for making continuity checks, do not be concerned with the actual resistance readings. Zero resistance, or any resistance readings, indicate continuity in the circuit. Infinite resistance indicates an open in the circuit. A high resistance reading where there should be none indicates a problem in the circuit. Checks for short circuits are made in the same manner as checks for open circuits except that the circuit must be isolated from both power and normal ground. Infinite resistance indicates no continuity to ground, while zero resistance indicates a dead short to ground.

RESISTANCE MEASUREMENT

The batteries in an ohmmeter will weaken with age and temperature, so the ohmmeter must be calibrated or 'zeroed' before taking measurements. To zero the meter, place the selector switch in its lowest range and touch the two ohmmeter leads together. Turn the calibration knob until the meter needle is exactly on zero.

➡**All analog (needle) type ohmmeters must be zeroed before use, but some digital ohmmeter models are automatically calibrated when the switch is turned on. Self-calibrating digital ohmmeters do not have an adjusting knob, but its a good idea to check for a zero readout before use by touching the leads together. All computer controlled systems require the use of a digital ohmmeter with at least 10 meagohms impedance for testing. Before any test procedures are attempted, make sure the ohmmeter used is compatible with the electrical system or damage to the on-board computer could result.**

To measure resistance, first isolate the circuit from the vehicle power source by disconnecting the battery cables or the harness connector. Make sure the key is OFF when disconnecting any components or the battery. Where necessary, also isolate at least one side of the circuit to be checked to avoid reading parallel resistances. Parallel circuit resistances will always give a lower reading than the actual resistance of either of the branches. When measuring the resistance of parallel circuits, the total resistance will always be lower than the smallest resistance in the circuit. Connect the meter leads to both sides of the circuit (wire or component) and read the actual measured ohms on the meter scale. Make sure the selector switch is set to the proper ohm scale for the circuit being tested to avoid misreading the ohmmeter test value.

✳✳CAUTION

Never use an ohmmeter with power applied to the circuit. Like the self-powered test light, the ohmmeter is designed to operate on its own power supply. The normal 12 volt automotive electrical system current could damage the meter.

Ammeters

An ammeter measures the amount of current flowing through a circuit in units called amperes or amps. Amperes are units of electron flow which indicate how fast the electrons are flowing through the circuit. Since Ohms Law dictates that current flow in a circuit is equal to the circuit voltage divided by the total circuit resistance, increasing voltage also increases the current level (amps). Likewise, any decrease in resistance will increase the amount of amps in a circuit. At normal operating voltage, most circuits have a characteristic amount of amperes, called 'current draw' which can be measured using an ammeter. By referring to a specified current draw rating, measuring the amperes, and comparing the two values, one can determine what is happening within the circuit to aid in diagnosis. An open circuit, for example, will not allow any current to flow so the ammeter reading will be zero. More current flows through a heavily loaded circuit or when the charging system is operating.

An ammeter is always connected in series with the circuit being tested. All of the current that normally flows through the circuit must also flow through the ammeter; if there is any other path for the current to follow, the ammeter reading will not be accurate. The ammeter itself has very little resistance to current flow and therefore will not affect the circuit, but it will measure current draw only when the circuit is closed and electricity is flowing. Excessive current draw can blow fuses and drain the battery, while a reduced current draw can cause motors to run slowly, lights to dim and other components to not operate properly. The ammeter can help diagnose these conditions by locating the cause of the high or low reading.

Multimeters

Different combinations of test meters can be built into a single unit designed for specific tests. Some of the more common combination test devices are known as Volt/Amp testers, Tach/Dwell meters, or Digital Multimeters. The Volt/Amp tester is used for charging system, starting system or battery tests and consists of a voltmeter, an ammeter and a variable resistance carbon pile. The voltmeter will usually have at least two ranges for use with 6, 12 and 24 volt systems. The ammeter also has more than one range for testing various levels of battery loads and starter current draw and the carbon pile can be adjusted to offer different amounts of resistance. The Volt/Amp tester has heavy leads to carry large amounts of current and many later models have an inductive ammeter pickup that clamps around the wire to simplify test connections. On some models, the ammeter also has a zero-center scale to allow testing of charging and starting systems without switching leads or polarity. A digital multimeter is a voltmeter, ammeter and ohmmeter combined in an instrument which gives a digital readout. These are often used when testing solid state circuits because of their high input impedance (usually 10 megohms or more).

The tach/dwell meter combines a tachometer and a dwell (cam angle) meter and is a specialized kind of voltmeter. The tachometer scale is marked to show engine speed in rpm and the dwell scale is marked to show degrees of distributor shaft rotation. In most electronic ignition systems, dwell is determined by the control unit, but the dwell meter can also be used to check the duty cycle (operation) of some electronic engine control systems. Some tach/dwell meters are powered by an internal battery, while others take their power from the car battery in use. The battery powered testers usually require calibration much like an ohmmeter before testing.

Special Test Equipment

A variety of diagnostic tools are available to help troubleshoot and repair computerized engine control systems. The most sophisticated of these devices are the console type engine analyzers that usually occupy a garage service bay, but there are several types of aftermarket electronic testers available that will allow quick circuit tests of the engine control system by plugging directly into a special connector located in the engine compartment or under the dashboard. Several tool and equipment manufacturers offer simple, hand held testers that measure various circuit voltage levels on command to check all system components for proper operation.

These computerized testers can allow quick and easy test measurements while the engine is operating or while the vehicle is being driven. In addition, the on-board computer memory can be read to access any stored trouble codes; in effect allowing the computer to tell you where it hurts and aid trouble diagnosis by pinpointing exactly which circuit or component is malfunctioning. In the same manner, repairs can

be tested to make sure the problem has been corrected. The biggest advantage these special testers have is their relatively easy hookups that minimize or eliminate the chances of making the wrong connections and getting false voltage readings or damaging the computer accidentally.

➡**It should be remembered that these testers check voltage levels in circuits; they don't detect mechanical problems or failed components if the circuit voltage falls within the preprogrammed limits stored in the tester PROM unit. Also, most of the hand held testers are designed to work only on one or two systems made by a specific manufacturer.**

Wiring Harnesses

The average automobile contains about ½ mile of wiring, with hundreds of individual connections. To protect the many wires from damage and to keep them from becoming a confusing tangle, they are organized into bundles, enclosed in plastic or taped together and called wire harnesses. Different wiring harnesses serve different parts of the vehicle. Individual wires are color coded to help trace them through a harness where sections are hidden from view.

A loose or corroded connection or a replacement wire that is too small for the circuit will add extra resistance and an additional voltage drop to the circuit. A ten percent voltage drop can result in slow or erratic motor operation, for example, even though the circuit is complete. Automotive wiring or circuit conductors can be in any one of three forms:

1. Single strand wire
2. Multistrand wire
3. Printed circuitry

Single strand wire has a solid metal core and is usually used inside such components as alternators, motors, relays and other devices. Multistrand wire has a core made of many small strands of wire twisted together into a single conductor. Most of the wiring in an automotive electrical system is made up of multistrand wire, either as a single conductor or grouped together in a harness. All wiring is color coded on the insulator, either as a solid color or as a colored wire with an identification stripe. A printed circuit is a thin film of copper or other conductor that is printed on an insulator backing. Occasionally, a printed circuit is sandwiched between two sheets of plastic for more protection and flexibility. A complete printed circuit, consisting of conductors, insulating material and connectors for lamps or other components is called a printed circuit board. Printed circuitry is used in place of individual wires or harnesses in places where space is limited, such as behind instrument panels.

Wire Gauge

Since computer controlled automotive electrical systems are very sensitive to changes in resistance, the selection of properly sized wires is critical when systems are repaired. The wire gauge number is an expression of the cross section area of the conductor. The most common system for expressing wire size is the American Wire Gauge (AWG) system.

Wire cross section area is measured in circular mils. A mil is $\frac{1}{1000}$" (0.001"); a circular mil is the area of a circle one mil in diameter. For example, a conductor ¼" in diameter is 0.250 in. or 250 mils. The circular mil cross section area of the wire is 250 squared (250²)or 62,500 circular mils. Imported car models usually use metric wire gauge designations, which is simply the cross section area of the conductor in square millimeters (mm²).

Gauge numbers are assigned to conductors of various cross section areas. As gauge number increases, area decreases and the conductor becomes smaller. A 5 gauge conductor is smaller than a 1 gauge conductor and a 10 gauge is smaller than a 5 gauge. As the cross section area of a conductor decreases, resistance increases and so does the gauge number. A conductor with a higher gauge number will carry less current than a conductor with a lower gauge number.

➡**Gauge wire size refers to the size of the conductor, not the size of the complete wire. It is possible to have two wires of the same gauge with different diameters because one may have thicker insulation than the other.**

12 volt automotive electrical systems generally use 10, 12, 14, 16 and 18 gauge wire. Main power distribution circuits and larger accessories usually use 10 and 12 gauge wire. Battery cables are usually 4 or 6 gauge, although 1 and 2 gauge wires are occasionally used. Wire length must also be considered when making repairs to a circuit. As conductor length increases, so does resistance. An 18 gauge wire, for example, can carry a 10 amp load for 10 feet without excessive voltage drop; however if a 15 foot wire is required for the same 10 amp load, it must be a 16 gauge wire.

An electrical schematic shows the electrical current paths when a circuit is operating properly. It is essential to understand how a circuit works before trying to figure out why it doesn't. Schematics break the entire electrical system down into individual circuits and show only one particular circuit. In a schematic, no attempt is made to represent wiring and components as they physically appear on the vehicle; switches and other components are shown as simply as possible. Face views of harness connectors show the cavity or terminal locations in all multi-pin connectors to help locate test points.

If you need to backprobe a connector while it is on the component, the order of the terminals must be mentally reversed. The wire color code can help in this situation, as well as a keyway, lock tab or other reference mark.

WIRING REPAIR

Soldering is a quick, efficient method of joining metals permanently. Everyone who has the occasion to make wiring repairs should know how to solder. Electrical connections that are soldered are far less likely to come apart and will conduct electricity much better than connections that are only 'pig-tailed' together. The most popular (and preferred) method of soldering is with an electrical soldering gun. Soldering irons are available in many sizes and wattage ratings. Irons with higher wattage ratings deliver higher temperatures and recover lost heat faster. A small soldering iron rated for no more than 50 watts is recommended, especially on electrical systems where excess heat can damage the components being soldered.

There are three ingredients necessary for successful soldering; proper flux, good solder and sufficient heat. A soldering flux is necessary to clean the metal of tarnish, prepare it for soldering and to enable the solder to spread into tiny crevices. When soldering, always use a resin flux or resin core solder which is non-corrosive and will not attract moisture once the job is finished. Other types of flux (acid core) will leave a residue that will attract moisture and cause the wires to corrode. Tin is a unique metal with a low melting point. In a molten state, it dissolves and alloys easily with many metals. Solder is made by mixing tin with lead. The most common proportions are 40/60, 50/50 and 60/40, with the percentage of tin listed first. Low priced solders usually contain less tin, making them very difficult for a beginner to use because more heat is required to melt the solder. A common solder is 40/60 which is well suited for all-around general use, but 60/40 melts easier, has more tin f or a better joint and is preferred for electrical work.

Soldering Techniques

Successful soldering requires that the metals to be joined be heated to a temperature that will melt the solder — usually 360-460°F (182-238°C). Contrary to popular belief, the purpose of the soldering iron is not to melt the solder itself, but to heat the parts being soldered to a temperature high enough to melt the solder when it is touched to the work. Melting flux-cored solder on the soldering iron will usually destroy the effectiveness of the flux.

➡**Soldering tips are made of copper for good heat conductivity, but must be 'tinned' regularly for quick transference of heat to the project and to prevent the solder from sticking to the iron. To 'tin' the iron, simply heat it and touch the flux-cored solder to the tip; the solder will flow over the hot tip. Wipe the excess off with a clean rag, but be careful as the iron will be hot.**

After some use, the tip may become pitted. If so, simply dress the tip smooth with a smooth file and 'tin' the tip again. An old saying holds that 'metals well cleaned are half soldered.' Flux-cored solder will remove oxides but rust, bits of insulation and oil or grease must be removed with a wire brush or emery cloth. For maximum strength in soldered parts, the joint must start off clean and tight. Weak joints will result in gaps too wide for the solder to bridge.

If a separate soldering flux is used, it should be brushed or swabbed on only those areas that are to be soldered. Most solders contain a core of flux and separate fluxing is unnecessary. Hold the work to be soldered firmly. It is best to solder on a wooden board, because a metal vise will only rob the piece to be soldered of heat and make it difficult to melt the solder. Hold the soldering tip with the broadest face against the work to be soldered. Apply solder under the tip close to the work, using enough solder to give a heavy film between the iron and the piece being soldered, while moving slowly and making sure the solder melts properly. Keep the work level or the solder will run to the lowest part and favor the thicker parts, because these require more heat to melt the solder. If the soldering tip overheats (the solder coating on the face of the tip burns up), it should be retinned. Once the soldering is completed, let the soldered joint stand until cool.

Tape and seal all soldered wire splices after the repair has cooled.

Wire Harness and Connectors

The on-board computer (ECM) wire harness electrically connects the control unit to the various solenoids, switches and sensors used by the control system. Most connectors in the engine compartment or otherwise exposed to the elements are protected against moisture and dirt which could create oxidation and deposits on the terminals. This protection is important because of the very low voltage and current levels used by the computer and sensors. All connectors have a lock which secures the male and female terminals together, with a secondary lock holding the seal and terminal into the connector. Both terminal locks must be released when disconnecting ECM connectors.

These special connectors are weather-proof and all repairs require the use of a special terminal and the tool required to service it. This tool is used to remove the pin and sleeve terminals. If removal is attempted with an ordinary pick, there is a good chance that the terminal will be bent or deformed. Unlike standard blade type terminals, these terminals cannot be straightened once they are bent. Make certain that the connectors are properly seated and all of the sealing rings in place when connecting leads. On some models, a hinge-type flap provides a backup or secondary locking feature for the terminals. Most secondary locks are used to improve the connector reliability by retaining the terminals if the small terminal lock tangs are not positioned properly.

Molded-on connectors require complete replacement of the connection. This means splicing a new connector assembly into the harness. All splices in on-board computer systems should be soldered to insure proper contact. Use care when probing the connections or replacing terminals in them as it is possible to short between opposite terminals. If this happens to the wrong terminal pair, it is possible to damage certain components. Always use jumper wires between connectors for circuit checking and never probe through weatherproof seals.

Open circuits are often difficult to locate by sight because corrosion or terminal misalignment are hidden by the connectors. Merely wiggling a connector on a sensor or in the wiring harness may correct the open circuit condition. This should always be considered when an open circuit or a failed sensor is indicated. Intermittent problems may also be caused by oxidized or loose connections. When using a circuit tester for diagnosis, always probe connections from the wire side. Be careful not to damage sealed connectors with test probes.

All wiring harnesses should be replaced with identical parts, using the same gauge wire and connectors. When signal wires are spliced into a harness, use wire with high temperature insulation only. With the low voltage and current levels found in the system, it is important that the best possible connection at all wire splices be made by soldering the splices together. It is seldom necessary to replace a complete harness. If replacement is necessary, pay close attention to insure proper harness routing. Secure the harness with suitable plastic wire

clamps to prevent vibrations from causing the harness to wear in spots or contact any hot components.

➡**Weatherproof connectors cannot be replaced with standard connectors. Instructions are provided with replacement connector and terminal packages. Some wire harnesses have mounting indicators (usually pieces of colored tape) to mark where the harness is to be secured.**

In making wiring repairs, it's important that you always replace damaged wires with wires that are the same gauge as the wire being replaced. The heavier the wire, the smaller the gauge number. Wires are color-coded to aid in identification and whenever possible the same color coded wire should be used for replacement. A wire stripping and crimping tool is necessary to install solderless terminal connectors. Test all crimps by pulling on the wires; it should not be possible to pull the wires out of a good crimp.

Wires which are open, exposed or otherwise damaged are repaired by simple splicing. Where possible, if the wiring harness is accessible and the damaged place in the wire can be located, it is best to open the harness and check for all possible damage. In an inaccessible harness, the wire must be bypassed with a new insert, usually taped to the outside of the old harness.

When replacing fusible links, be sure to use fusible link wire, NOT ordinary automotive wire. Make sure the fusible segment is of the same gauge and construction as the one being replaced and double the stripped end when crimping the terminal connector for a good contact. The melted (open) fusible link segment of the wiring harness should be cut off as close to the harness as possible, then a new segment spliced in as described. In the case of a damaged fusible link that feeds two harness wires, the harness connections should be replaced with two fusible link wires so that each circuit will have its own separate protection.

➡**Most of the problems caused in the wiring harness are due to bad ground connections. Always check all vehicle ground connections for corrosion or looseness before performing any power feed checks to eliminate the chance of a bad ground affecting the circuit.**

Repairing Hard Shell Connectors

Unlike molded connectors, the terminal contacts in hard shell connectors can be replaced. Weatherproof hard-shell connectors with the leads molded into the shell have non-replaceable terminal ends. Replacement usually involves the use of a special terminal removal tool that depress the locking tangs (barbs) on the connector terminal and allow the connector to be removed from the rear of the shell. The connector shell should be replaced if it shows any evidence of burning, melting, cracks, or breaks. Replace individual terminals that are burnt, corroded, distorted or loose.

➡**The insulation crimp must be tight to prevent the insulation from sliding back on the wire when the wire is pulled. The insulation must be visibly compressed under the crimp tabs, and the ends of the crimp should be turned in for a firm grip on the insulation.**

The wire crimp must be made with all wire strands inside the crimp. The terminal must be fully compressed on the wire strands with the ends of the crimp tabs turned in to make a firm grip on the wire. Check all connections with an ohmmeter to insure a good contact. There should be no measurable resistance between the wire and the terminal when connected.

SUPPLEMENTAL RESTRAINT SYSTEM (SRS)

General Information

The air bag system used on Volvo vehicles is referred to as Supplemental Restraint System (SRS). The SRS system provides additional protection for the driver, if a forward collision of sufficient force is encountered. The SRS assists the normal seatbelt restraining system by deploying an air bag, via the steering wheel and dashboard (960 models).

The system also includes a knee bolster at the lower steering column area. It is used to absorb energy and control the driver's forward movement during an accident by limiting leg movement.

The system also includes a battery voltage check. The SRS warning lamp will illuminate, if the voltage falls below 9 volts. When the voltage rises above 9 volts again, the lamp will be go out after approximately 10 seconds.

The SRS system is monitored continuously by a microprocessor in the crash sensor. Any faults which is detected, is stored in the memory and the SRS warning lamp will turn ON.

SYSTEM OPERATION

Under normal conditions, the SRS warning lamp will come ON when the ignition switch is turned to the **ON** position. If the engine is not started, the lamp will be extinguished after approximately 10 seconds. Failure of the warning lamp to go OFF, while driving, indicates a fault in the SRS system. The warning lamp will remain lit until the fault is corrected and the memory cleared.

The crash sensor records a combination of G-force and prolong deceleration. When a sufficiently high G-force and prolong deceleration are simultaneously recorded, the power unit will deliver a current which will trigger the gas generator of the inflatable bag. The bag will be filled in a few hundredths of a second with non-toxic nitrogen. Immediately after the collision, the gas is released through a ventilation hole and the air bag slowly collapses. The entire sequence of inflation and collapse takes approximately 0.2 seconds.

SYSTEM COMPONENTS

▶ **See Figure 1**

Inflatable Bag

The inflatable bag is mounted in an assembly in the center of the steering wheel and in the dashboard (960 models). It incorporates a gas generator which inflates the bag.

Crash Sensor

The crash sensor, mounted under the driver's seat, monitors deceleration of the vehicle and also functions as a diagnostic unit. It incorporates an electrical sensor to detect deceleration, a mercury switch, a microprocessor and a memory which retains information even after the power supply has failed.

Contact Reel

The contact reel, mounted between the steering column, assures the most reliable contact between the gas generator and the crash sensor.

Stand-by Power Unit

The stand-by power unit consists of a voltage converter and capacitor which operates the system with the necessary power if the normal power supply is interrupted. However, this energy is only stored for about a second after the supply has failed.

Knee Bolster

The knee bolster is used to absorb energy and control the driver's forward movement during an accident by limiting leg movement.

SERVICE PRECAUTIONS

➡**Since the Supplemental Restraint System (SRS) is such a complex and critical safety system (which requires special precautions when repairs are being made), Volvo recommends that all repairs to the SRS system be performed by SRS-trained Volvo technicians.**

✳✳CAUTION

To avoid deployment when servicing the SRS system or components in the immediate area, do not use electrical test equipment such as battery or A.C. powered voltmeter, ohmmeter, etc. or any type of tester other than specified. Do not use a non-powered probe tester. To avoid personal injury all precautions must be strictly adhered to.

• All work which includes removing or replacing the air bag assembly must be carried out with the battery disconnected and with the ignition turned OFF for the duration of work. This is to ensure that the air bag does not accidentally inflate during service repairs and that no faults codes will register, requiring subsequent cancellation.

• When working around the instrument panel or steering column, take special care to ensure that the SRS wirings are not pinched, chafed or penetrated by bolts/screws etc. This is most likely to happen when installing the sound insulation, knee bolsters, ignition lock or steering column cover.

• For air bag fault tracing purposes and/or to check the system, use multimeter 999 6525 and test resistor 998 86595 or their equivalent.

• Do not disassemble or tamper with the air bag assembly.

• Always store a removed air bag assembly with the pad surface upwards.

• Never install used SRS parts from another vehicle.

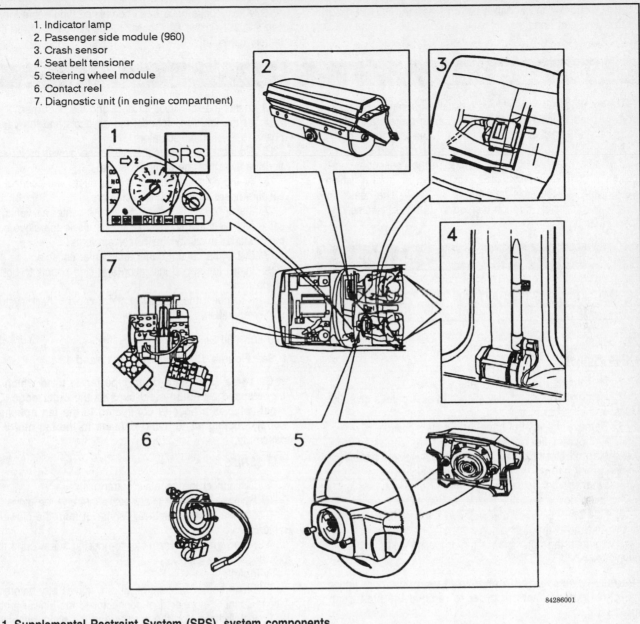

1. Indicator lamp
2. Passenger side module (960)
3. Crash sensor
4. Seat belt tensioner
5. Steering wheel module
6. Contact reel
7. Diagnostic unit (in engine compartment)

84286001

Fig. 1 Supplemental Restraint System (SRS), system components

• Never replace the original steering wheel with any other design, since it will make it impossible to properly install the air bag.

• Always disconnect the yellow SRS connector when performing any diagnostic troubling shooting or service procedure associated with the SRS system.

• When repairs are made to the front suspension and steering, be aware that the contact reel can only withstand being turned 3 turns in either direction.

• Never install an air bag assembly that shows signs of being dropped or improperly handled, such as dents, cracks or deformation.

• When replacing a sensor, the replacement unit should be installed with the directional arrow oriented.

• Do not energize the system until all components are connected. A failure code may appear.

• Always wear gloves and safety glasses when handling the air bag assembly. Wash hands with mild soap and water afterwards.

• Always store the air bag assembly on a secure flat surface, away from high heat source and free of oil, grease, detergent or water.

• Never disconnect any electrical connection with the ignition switch **ON** unless instructed to do so in a test.

• Before disconnecting the negative battery cable, make a record of the contents memorized by each memory system (ex: audio, seats, etc.). Then when service or repairs are completed, make certain to reset these memory systems.

DISARMING AND ENABLING THE SYSTEM

1. Turn the ignition switch to the **OFF** position.

2. Disconnect the negative battery cable AND TAPE the end of the lead end.

3. After repairs have been completed, verify that the ignition switch is in the **OFF** position, then re-connect the negative battery cable.

HEATING SYSTEM

The heating unit assembly is basically the same configuration as used in the heating/air conditioning system and the removal and installation procedures are basically the same.

The heater core and blower motor are contained in the heater box (fresh air housing) located in the passenger compartment under the dashboard. The blower fan is of a turbine design and is accessible from under the dash. The heater core is mostly accessible through the removal and disassembly of the heater box.

Blower Motor

REMOVAL & INSTALLATION

240 Series
▶ See Figures 2, 3, 4 and 5

1. Disconnect the negative battery cable.
2. Remove the sound insulation and side panels on both sides of the radio, if equipped.
3. Remove the control panel and center console.
4. Remove or disconnect as required, the center air vents, the cable and electrical connectors from the clock, the glove compartment and air ducts for the center air vents.
5. From the right side, remove the air ducts and disconnect the vacuum hoses from the shutter actuators.
6. Fold back the floor mat, remove the rear floor duct screw and move the duct aside.
7. Remove the outer blower motor casing and the blower motor wheel.

➡It may be necessary to remove the support from under the glove compartment in order to remove the blower motor casing.

8. Disconnect the blower motor switch from the center console and the electrical leads from the switch.
9. From the left side, disconnect the air ducts and the vacuum hoses from the shutter actuators.
10. Remove or disconnect the inner blower motor casing, the vacuum hose from the rear floor shutter actuator, the electrical connector and the blower motor.

➡Should the blower motor need to be replaced, a modified replacement unit is available. Certain modifications must be done and instructions are included with the new assembly.

To install:
11. Clean heater housing of all dirt, leaves etc. before installation. Install the blower motor, the electrical connector, the vacuum hose to the rear floor shutter actuator and the inner blower motor casing.
12. Install the blower motor wheel and the outer blower motor casing.

13. Install the rear floor air duct and the floor mat.
14. At the left side, connect the air ducts and the vacuum hoses to the shutter actuators.
15. Connect the electrical leads to the blower motor switch and the switch to the center console.
16. At the right side, install the air ducts and connect the vacuum hoses to the shutter actuators.
17. Install or connect as required the center air vents, the cable and electrical connectors to the clock, the glove compartment and air ducts for the center air vents.
18. Install the control panel and center console.
19. Install the sound insulation and side panels to both sides of the radio.
20. Reconnect the negative battery cable. Check system for proper operation.

700 and 900 Series
▶ See Figures 6, 7, 8, 9, 10, 11, 12 and 13

➡On some vehicles, a drum type fan is used which can be balanced by fitting steel clips to the outer edge. On most vehicles a hose is connected to the fan housing to supply cooling air to avoid damage to the fan motor assembly.

740 SERIES
1. Disconnect the negative battery cable.
2. Remove the lower glove box panel and the glove box.
3. Disconnect the electrical connector from the blower motor.
4. Remove the blower motor-to-housing screws and the blower motor assembly.

To install:
5. Clean heater housing of all dirt, leaves etc. before installation. Connect the electrical connector to the blower motor.
6. Install the motor, the screws and the panel beneath the glove compartment.
7. Connect the negative battery cable and check the blower motor operation.

760, 780 AND 940 SERIES/AUTOMATIC CLIMATE CONTROL (ACC)
1. Disconnect the negative battery cable.
2. Remove the lower glove box panel.
3. From the right side, remove the instep moulding.
4. Remove the panel from above the control unit; be careful not damage it upon removal.
5. Disconnect the electrical connector from the control unit.
6. Remove the control unit-to-bracket bolts and the control unit. Remove the bracket-to-chassis bolts and the bracket.
7. Disconnect the electrical connector from the blower motor.
8. Remove the ventilation pipe, the blower motor-to-housing screws and the blower motor.

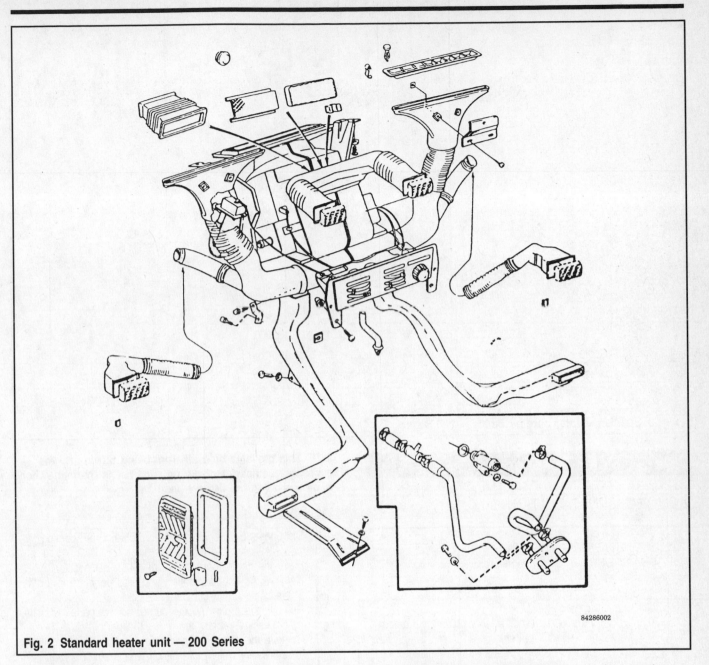

84286002

Fig. 2 Standard heater unit — 200 Series

To install:

9. Clean heater housing of all dirt, leaves etc. before installation. Install the blower motor and the ventilation pipe.

10. Connect the electrical connector to the blower motor.

11. Install the control unit bracket and the control unit.

12. Connect the electrical connector to the control unit.

13. Install the panel above the control unit, the instep panel and the lower glove box panel.

14. Connect the negative battery cable and check the blower motor operation.

760, 780 AND 940 SERIES/ELECTRONIC CLIMATE CONTROL (ECC)

1. Disconnect the negative battery cable.

2. From the right side, remove the lower glove box panel and the glove box.

3. Disconnect the electrical connector and the mounting bracket from the blower motor housing.

4. Disconnect the electrical connector from the blower motor.

5. Remove the blower motor-to-housing screws and the motor.

To install:

6. Clean heater housing of all dirt, leaves etc. before installation. Install the rubber seal to the blower motor and install assembly.

7. Connect the electrical connector to the blower motor and the positive terminal to the housing.

8. Connect the negative battery cable and check all blower motor speeds.

9. Install the glove box and the lower panel.

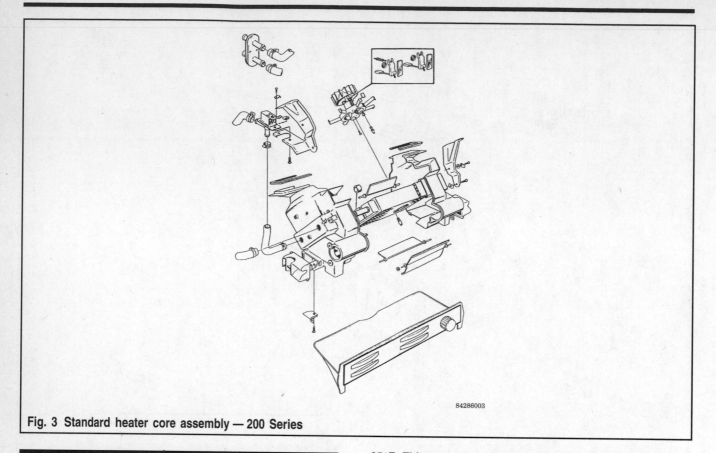

Fig. 3 Standard heater core assembly — 200 Series

84286003

Blower Motor Resistor

REMOVAL & INSTALLATION

1. Disconnect the negative cable.
2. Disconnect the electrical connector from the blower resistor assembly.
3. Remove mounting screw and remove the blower resistor assembly from the case.
4. Installation is the reverse of the service removal procedure. Reconnect the negative battery cable. Check the blower motor for proper operation at all speeds after installation.

➡**Some vehicles may be prone to high fan noise in fan speed No. 1. This condition is due to too high a fan speed. Noise level can be lowered by installing an additional resistor in series with the positive lead of the fan switch.**

Heater Core

REMOVAL & INSTALLATION

➡**On vehicles equipped with ACC (Automatic Climate Control), a thermal switch is located on the outlet hose from the heater core. It switches on and starts the fan motor only when the water temperature exceeds approximately 95°F. This prevents cold air from being blown into the passenger compartment during winter. The thermal switch is by passed in the defrost position.**

240 Series

1. Disconnect the negative battery cable. Drain cooling system.
2. Move the heater controls to the CLOSED position.
3. Remove the sound proofing and side panels from both sides of the center dash console.
4. Remove the radio and the center control panel. Disconnect any necessary cables and move the panel aside.
5. Remove the glove box assembly and the strip below the right air vent by carefully prying it off with a small prybar.
6. Remove the steering wheel casing (column cover) and disconnect the choke control with the cover plate.
7. Remove the strip from under the left air vent, the instrument panel lighting intensity and the light switch knobs; do not remove the switch.
8. Remove the speedometer drive cable and any electrical connectors from the instrument panel cover plate and the cover plate.
9. Remove the storage compartment, the center air vents and the instrument panel frame.
10. From the left side, disconnect the windshield wiper connectors.
11. Disconnect the air duct between the heater and the center air vents.
12. Disconnect the electrical connector from the glove box courtesy light and the rubber straps from the defroster vents.
13. Remove the dashboard unit from the dash assembly, as necessary.

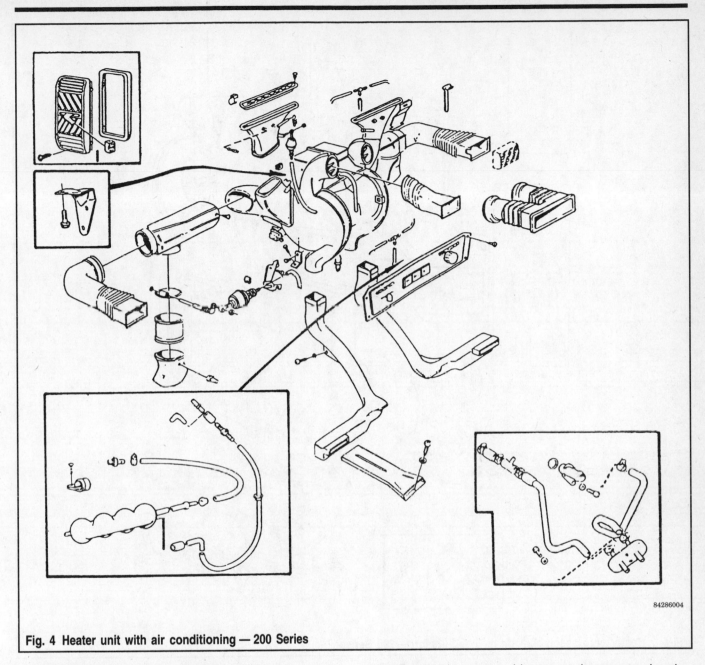

84286004

Fig. 4 Heater unit with air conditioning — 200 Series

14. Remove or disconnect the rear floor air duct screws and lower the duct slightly.

15. Remove or disconnect the following:
   a. The lower heater mount screws
   b. The vacuum hose from the vacuum tank
   c. The cable from the control valve
   d. The upper and lower center console screws
   e. The center support screws located on the console
   f. The fan motor ground electrical connector
   g. The inlet hose from the control valve

16. Disconnect the upper hose from the heater core tube and the vacuum hoses from the shutter actuators.

17. Loosen the upper housing screws.

18. From the right side, disconnect the vacuum hoses from the shutter actuators.

19. Disconnect and remove the air ducts.

20. Disconnect the hoses from the vacuum tank. Remove the rear floor duct screws and lower the duct slightly.

21. Remove the upper and lower console screws and position it aside.

22. Remove the right support screws and the support.

23. Disconnect the electrical connector from the heater fan switch and the positive lead.

24. Disconnect the REC shutter vacuum hose from the control panel.

25. Disconnect the input vacuum hose from the T connection-to-floor shutter actuators.

26. Remove the upper heater housing retaining assembly screws and remove the assembly from the vehicle.

27. Place the assembly on a cleared area and remove or disconnect the following:
   a. The upper hose from the heater core.
   b. The air inlet rubber seal from the top of the housing.
   c. The REC shutter clips, from the left side.
   d. The rubber seals from both defroster vents.

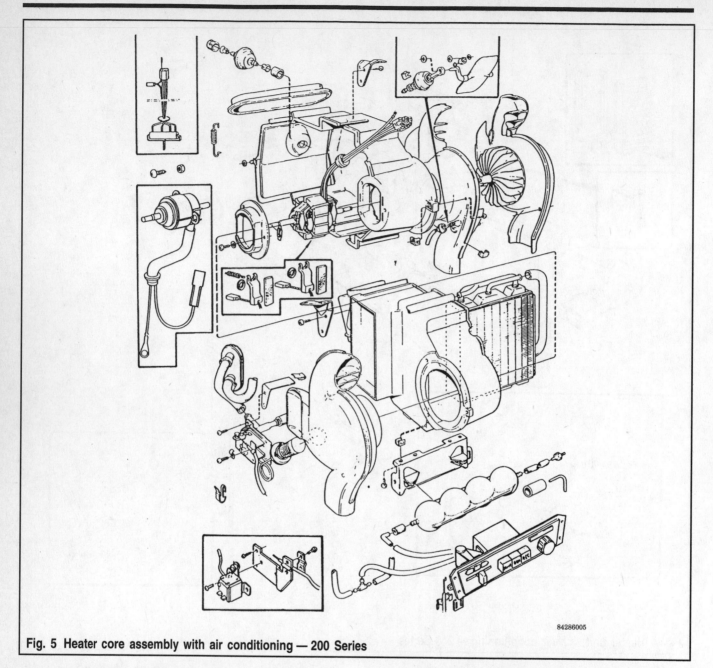

Fig. 5 Heater core assembly with air conditioning — 200 Series

84286005

e. All outer blower motor casing clips and the casing from the assembly.

28. Remove the blower motor wheel locking clips (from both sides) and the blower motor wheels.

29. Remove the heater core drain hose and the vacuum tank assembly. The vacuum tank bracket screws from the left side. The REC shutter spring and heater housing clips.

30. Remove the blower motor screws and the heater control valve capillary tube from the T joint.

31. Pull the heater housing apart from the middle.

32. Remove the blower motor and the heater core assembly.

To install:

33. Install the blower and heater core in the housing assembly. Make sure that the fan motor is correctly positioned in the housing. Install fan motor hose.

34. Using a suitable sealant, coat mating surface of the heater housing and assemble the case.

35. Install the heater control valve capillary tube to the T joint and the blower motor screws.

36. Install the heater housing clips and REC shutter spring. At the left side, install vacuum tank assembly, the vacuum tank bracket screws and the heater core drain hose.

37. Install the blower motor wheel and the blower motor wheel locking clips to both sides.

38. Install or connect the following items:

a. The outer blower motor casing clips to the assembly.

b. The rubber seals to both defroster vents.

c. The REC shutter clips to the left side.

d. The air inlet rubber seal to the top of the housing.

e. The upper hose to the heater core.

39. Install the heater assembly into the vehicle.

➡Before installation, be sure all sealing flanges are correctly sealed to prevent air leakage during the system operation.

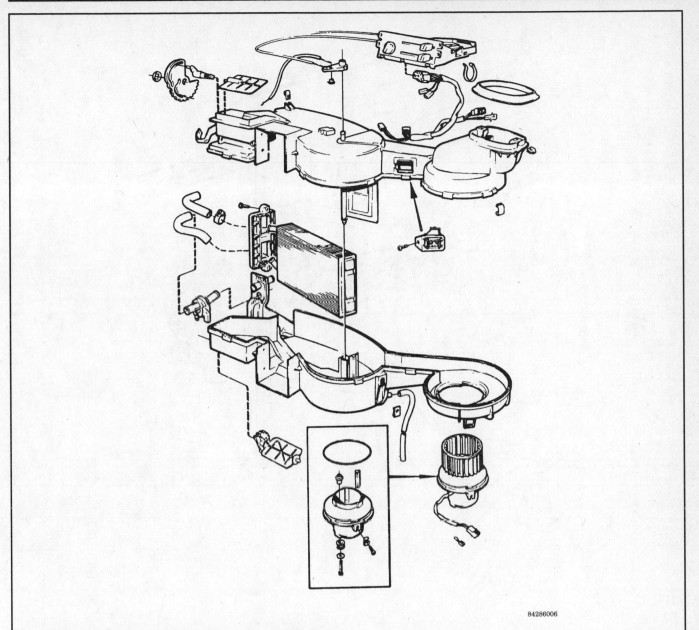

84286006

Fig. 6 Standard heater core assembly — 700 and 900 Series

40. Install the upper housing retaining screws.

41. Connect the REC shutter vacuum hose to the control panel.

42. Connect the electrical connector to the heater fan switch and the positive lead. Install protective cover.

43. Install the right support and console.

44. Install the heater assembly lower mount and the rear floor duct. Connect the hoses to the vacuum tank.

45. Install the air ducts. At the right side, connect the vacuum hoses to the shutter actuators.

46. Connect the upper hose to the heater core tube and the vacuum hoses to the shutter actuators.

47. Install or connect the following items:
   a. The inlet hose to the control valve
   b. The fan motor ground electrical connector
   c. The console center support and the center console screws
   d. The cable to the control valve

   e. The vacuum hose to the vacuum tank
   f. The lower heater mount screws

48. Install the rear floor air and the dashboard unit to the dash assembly.

49. Connect the electrical connector to the glove box courtesy light and the rubber straps to the defroster vents.

50. Connect the windshield wiper connectors, the air duct between the heater housing and the center air vents.

51. Install the instrument panel, the storage compartment, the center air vents and the instrument panel frame.

52. Install the speedometer cable and any electrical connectors to the instrument panel.

53. Install the strip from under the left air vent, the instrument panel lighting intensity and the light switch knobs.

54. Install the steering wheel casing and connect the choke control with the cover plate.

55. Install the glove box assembly and the strip below the right air vent.

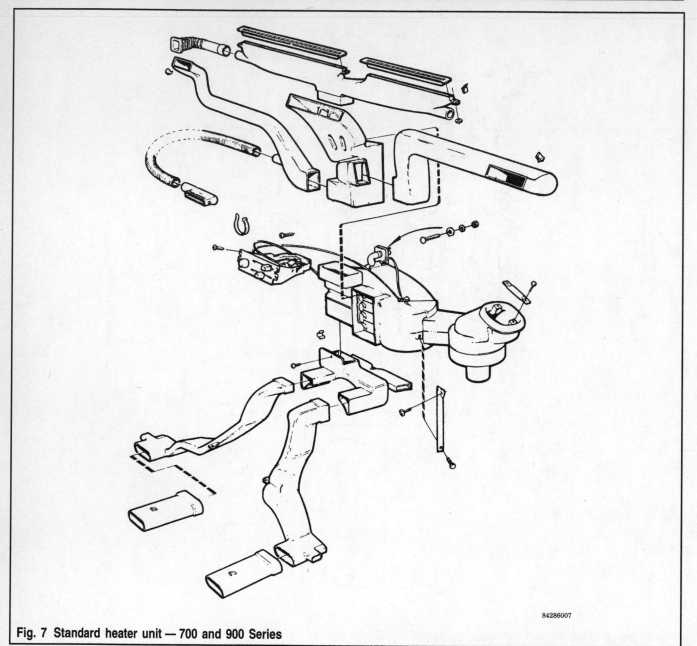

Fig. 7 Standard heater unit — 700 and 900 Series

84286007

56. Install the center control panel and the radio.

57. Install the sound proofing and side panels to both sides of the center dash console.

58. Move the heater controls to the OPEN position.

59. Refill the cooling system. Connect the negative battery cable.

60. Start the engine, allow it to reach normal operating temperatures and check for leaks. Check system for proper operation.

740 Series

1. Disconnect the negative battery cable. Remove the throttle cable from the pulley assembly.

2. Drain cooling system. Disconnect all heater hoses.

3. From the left side of the dash, remove the lower panel. Remove the hose from the panel air vent.

4. At the control panel, move the selector to the FLOOR position.

5. Remove the following items:
   a. The accelerator pedal.
   b. The ignition system control unit and bracket.
   c. The cruise control connector, if equipped.
   d. The water valve hose and the grommet.

6. Remove both hoses from the water valve and the clip from the water valve control cable.

7. To remove the water valve, turn it right, pull it out and disconnect the cable.

8. Remove the heater core cover and the heater core assembly.

To install:

9. Clean heater core housing of all dirt, leaves etc. before installation. Install the heater core assembly and the cover. Connect the water valve.

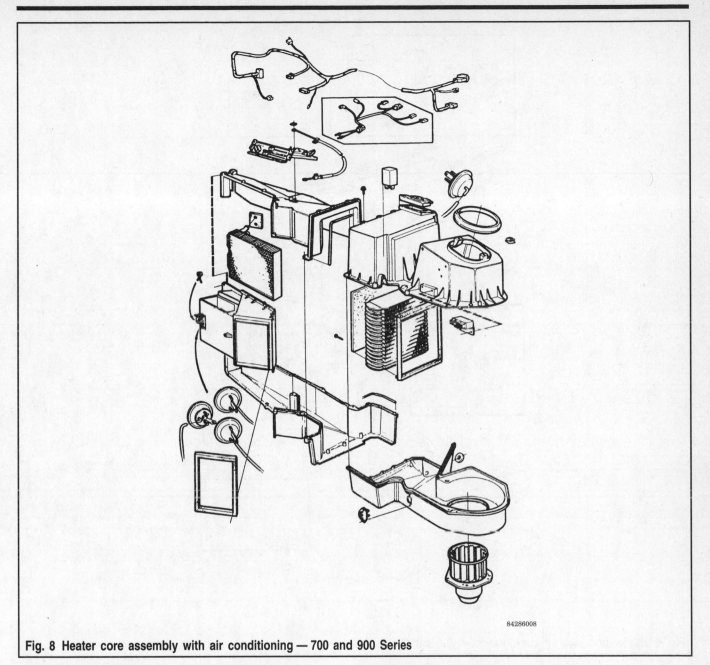

84286008

Fig. 8 Heater core assembly with air conditioning — 700 and 900 Series

10. Install the water valve control cable clip, turn the valve left, adjust the cable and install the clip. Connect the hoses to the water valve and the heater core.

11. Install the following items:
   a. The grommet and the water valve.
   b. The cruise control connector, if equipped.
   c. The ignition system bracket and control unit.
   d. The accelerator pedal.

12. Connect the hose the panel vent below the dash and the lower panel.

13. Reconnect the throttle cable to the pulley assembly. Reconnect the negative battery cable.

14. Refill the cooling system. Start the vehicle, allow it to reach normal operating temperatures, check for leaks. Check system for proper operation.

760, 780 and 900 Series

WITH AUTOMATIC CLIMATE CONTROL (ACC) SYSTEM

1. Disconnect the negative battery cable.

2. Drain the cooling system. Disconnect the heater hoses from the heater core assembly.

3. Remove the ashtray, the ashtray holder, the cigarette lighter and console's storage compartment.

4. Remove the console assembly from the gearshift lever and the parking brake.

5. Disconnect the electrical connector. Remove the rear ashtray, the console and light.

6. Remove the screws beneath the plastic cover in the bottom of the storage compartment and the parking brake console.

7. From the left side of the passenger compartment, re-move the panel from under the dashboard.

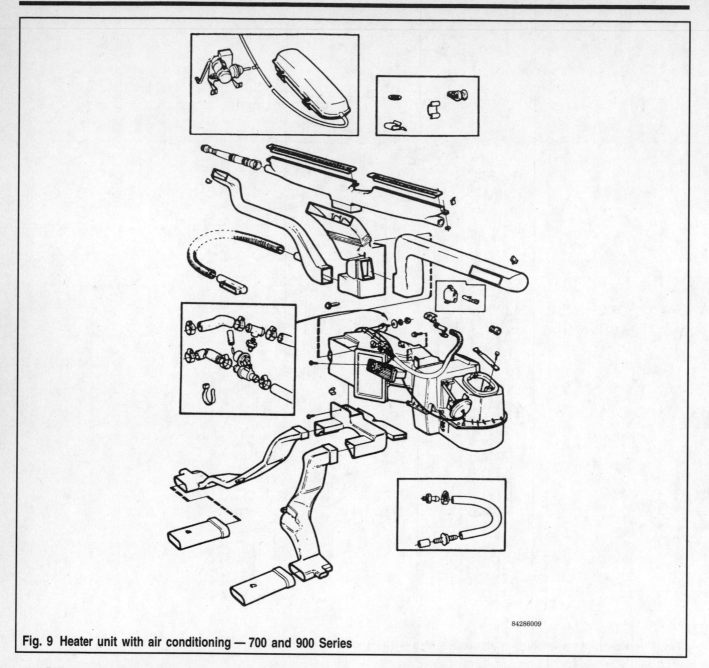

84286009

Fig. 9 Heater unit with air conditioning — 700 and 900 Series

8. Pull down the floor mat and remove the side panel screws, front and rear edge.

9. From the right side of the passenger compartment, remove the panel from under the glove compartment and the glove compartment box with lighting.

10. Pull down the floor mat on the right side and remove the side panel screws, front and rear edge.

11. Remove the radio compartment assembly screws.

12. Remove the screws from the heater control, the radio compartment assembly console and the control panel.

13. Loosen the heater control head assembly retaining screws and remove the assembly and mount from the dash.

14. Remove the center dash panel, the distribution duct screw and the air duct-to-panel vents/distribution duct screws.

15. Remove the screws holding the air ducts top-to-rear seats and the air distribution duct section-to-rear seat ducts.

16. Remove the vacuum hoses from the vacuum motors and the hose from the aspirator, if equipped with an ACC unit.

17. Remove the distribution unit housing from the vehicle.

18. Remove the retaining clips and the heater core assembly.

19. If the vacuum motors must be replaced, remove the panel from the distribution unit and replace the vacuum motor.

To install:

20. Clean heater core housing of all dirt, leaves etc. before installation. Install the heater core assembly and the retaining clips.

21. Install the distribution unit into the vehicle.

22. Connect the vacuum hoses to the vacuum motors and the hose to the aspirator, if equipped with an ACC unit.

23. Install the air ducts top-to-rear seats and the air distribution duct section-to-rear seat ducts.

24. Install the center dash panel, the distribution duct screw and the air duct-to-panel vents/distribution duct screws.

25. Install the heater control head assembly unit and the mount to the dash.

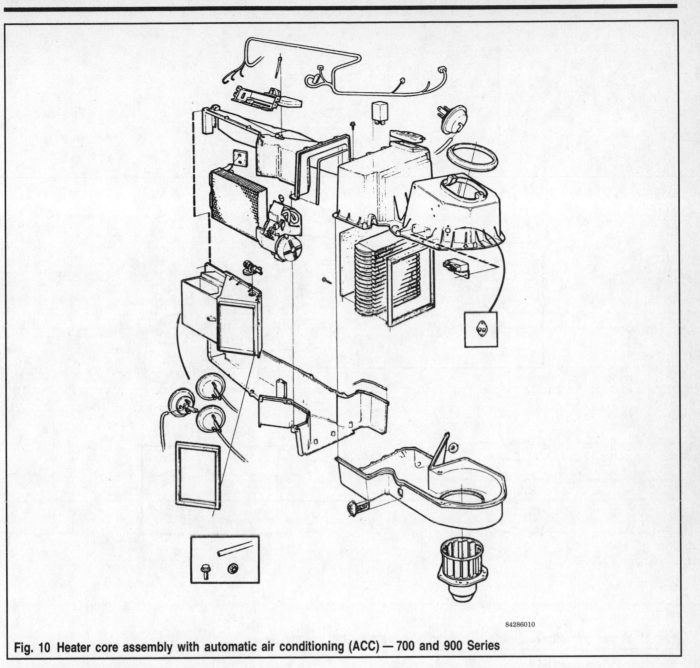

Fig. 10 Heater core assembly with automatic air conditioning (ACC) — 700 and 900 Series

84286010

26. Install the heater control, the radio compartment console and the control panel.

27. Install the radio compartment screws.

28. At the right side of the passenger compartment, install the panel under the glove compartment and the glove compartment box with lighting.

29. Install the side panel screws, front and rear edge.

30. At the left side of the passenger compartment, install the panel under the dashboard.

31. Install the plastic cover in the bottom of the storage compartment and the parking brake console.

32. Connect the electrical connector. Install the rear ashtray, the console and light.

33. Install the console assembly to the gearshift lever and the parking brake.

34. Install the ashtray holder, the ashtray, the cigarette lighter and console's storage compartment.

35. Reconnect the heater core hoses. Refill the cooling system and charge the air conditioning system.

36. Connect the negative battery cable. Start the engine, allow it to reach normal operating temperatures. Check system for proper operation.

WITH ELECTRONIC CLIMATE CONTROL (ECC) SYSTEM
▶ See Figures 14, 15 and 16

1. Disconnect the negative battery cable.

2. Drain cooling system. Disconnect the heater hoses from the heater core assembly. Remove the heater core cover plate.

3. Remove the dashboard by performing the following procedures:

   a. From the right side, remove the lower glove box panel, the glove box, the footwell panel and the A post panel.

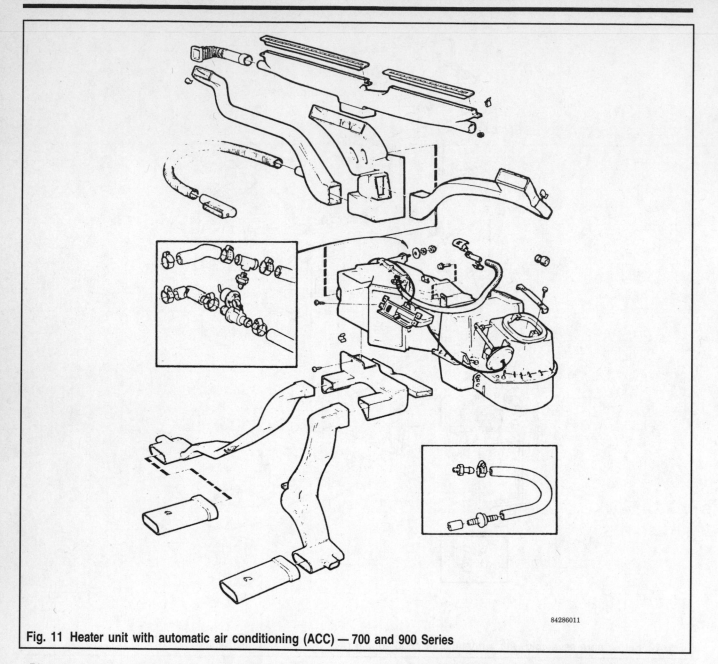

84286011

Fig. 11 Heater unit with automatic air conditioning (ACC) — 700 and 900 Series

Disconnect the solar sensor electrical connector and cut the cable ties.

b. From the left side, remove the lower steering wheel sound-proofing, the knee bolster (leave bracket attached to bolster), the footwell panel and the A post panel.

c. From the left side, remove the defroster grille, the plastic fusebox screws, the ashtray, the dashboard-to-center console screws, the parking brake-to-console screws (move console rearward) and the lower center console screws (located below the ashtray).

➡**Before performing the next procedure, be sure the front wheels are in the straight ahead position.**

d. If not an SRS equipped vehicle, remove the steering wheel, the steering wheel adjustment assembly (Allen wrench), the upper steering column cover panels and the steering column combination switch assembly.

e. If an SRS equipped vehicle, remove the steering column adjuster (Allen), the steering column covers, the air bag assembly (Torx), the steering wheel center bolt, the plastic tape label screw from the steering wheel hub (use the lock screw, label attached, to lock the contact reel through the steering wheel hub hole) and lift off the steering wheel. Remove the contact reel and the steering column combination switch assembly.

➡**After securing the contact reel, do not turn the steering wheel for it will shear of the contact reel pin.**

f. From the left side of the steering column, push out the light switch panel. Remove the small trim mouldings and the light switch.

g. From the right side of the steering column, push out the switch panel. Remove the ECC control panel, the radio console and the small trim moulding.

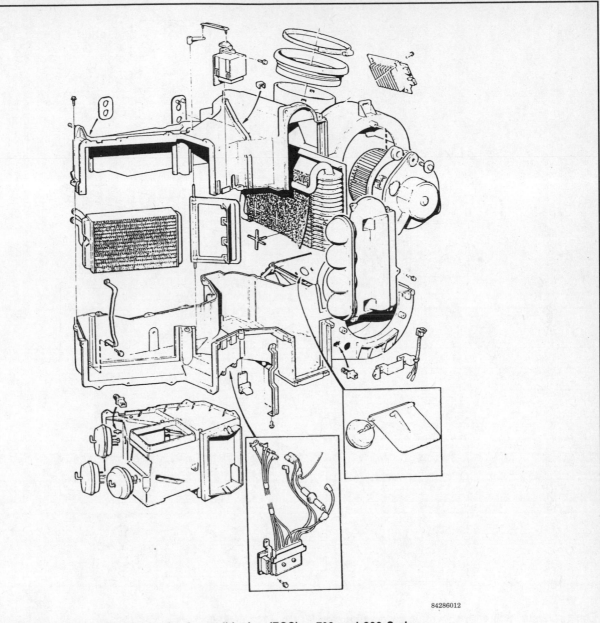

84286012

Fig. 12 Heater core assembly with electronic air conditioning (ECC) — 700 and 900 Series

h. Remove the outer air vent grille by lifting it upwards, grasp it at the bottom and pull it upwards to release it. Remove the instrument panel cover-to-dash screws and the cover.

i. Remove the combined instrument assembly-to-dash screws and the assembly; disconnect any electrical connectors and/or vacuum hoses.

j. From the rear of the dashboard, cut the cable ties.

k. At the dashboard-to-firewall area, turn the retaining clips {i/₃ turn (to release), pull the dash out slightly and pass the fuse box through the opening. Disconnect the cable harnesses from the dashboard and carefully lift it from the vehicle.

4. From the left side of the heater housing, remove the lower duct. Disconnect the vacuum hoses from the diaphragms and the electrical connector. Remove the heater core cover-to-housing screws and the cover.

5. Remove the heater core-to-housing bracket and carefully remove the heater core.

To install:

6. Clean heater housing of all dirt, leaves etc. installation. Install the heater core and the bracket.

7. Install the heater core cover to the housing. Connect the electrical connector and the vacuum hoses. Install the lower duct to the housing assembly.

8. Install the dash by performing the following procedures:

a. Install the dash, connect the cable harnesses, pass the fuse box through the opening. Secure the dash clips by turning them 1/₃ turn.

b. Install the combined instrument assembly to the dash. Install the instrument panel cover and the outer air vent grille.

c. Install the small trim moulding, the radio console, the ECC control panel and the right side switch panel.

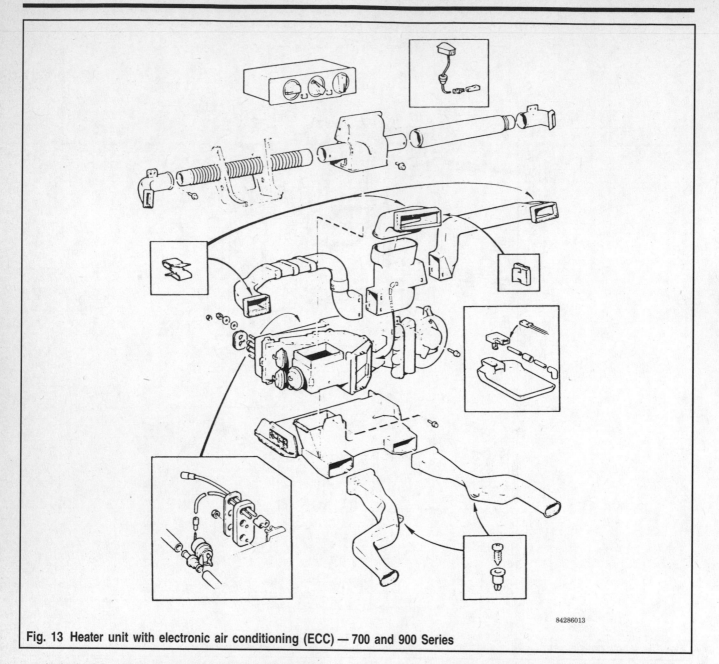

Fig. 13 Heater unit with electronic air conditioning (ECC) — 700 and 900 Series

d. At the left side of the steering column, install the light switch, the small trim mouldings and the light switch panel.

e. If an SRS equipped vehicle, install the steering column combination switch assembly and the contact reel. Install the steering wheel and remove the lock screw. Install the steering wheel center bolt, the air bag assembly and the steering column adjuster.

f. If not an SRS equipped vehicle, install the steering column combination switch assembly, the steering column covers, the steering wheel adjustment assembly and the steering wheel.

g. At the left side, install the lower center console screw, the parking brake-to-console screws, the dashboard-to-center console screws, the ashtray, the plastic fusebox screws and the defroster grille.

h. At the left side, install the A post panel, the footwell panel, the knee bolster (with bracket) and the lower steering wheel sound-proofing.

i. At the right side, connect the solar sensor electrical connector, install the A post panel, the footwell panel, the glove box and the lower glove box panel.

9. Install the heater core cover plate and connect the heater hoses to the heater core.

10. Refill the cooling system. Connect the negative battery cable.

11. Start the engine, allow it to reach normal operating temperatures. Check the heater operation and the system for leaks.

AIR CONDITIONING SYSTEM

The purpose of the air conditioning unit is to reduce the temperature in the passenger compartment to an acceptable level when ambient temperatures are high. The unit operates on the principle that heat is always transferred from a hot medium to a cold one. In practice, warm air from the passenger compartment is circulated passed an evaporator which contains a cold liquid. Heat is therefore transferred from the air to the liquid and the cooler air is blown into the passenger compartment.

A direct relationship exists between the pressure, temperature and volume of the refrigerant. By allowing the refrigerant to circulate in a closed system and altering the pressure and volume conditions, it is possible to get the refrigerant to boil (evaporate). For this purpose the warm air in the passenger compartment is directed through an evaporator, in which the refrigerant circulates. Heat is absorbed by the refrigerant and in doing so the warm air is cooled down and the refrigerant boils. It is this cold air which is blown into the passenger compartment by the fan. The heat which is absorbed by the refrigerant in the evaporator is transferred to the condenser in the engine compartment, where it is cooled by air flow with the aid of the engine and the electric fans. A compressor is used to circulate the refrigerant within the system.

240 Series

Two Climate Units (CU) are used and are of common construction, one for the use of a heating system only and the

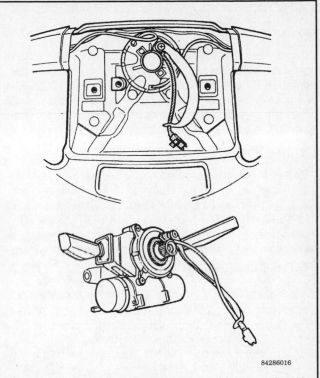

Fig. 15 Removing the steering wheel vehicles equipped with SRS — 700 and 900 Series

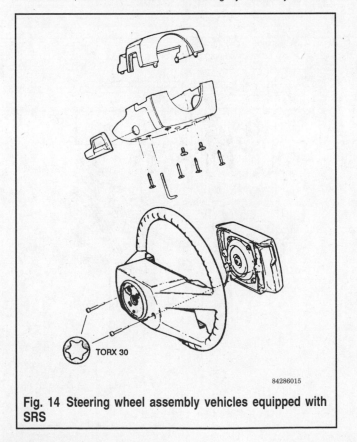

Fig. 14 Steering wheel assembly vehicles equipped with SRS

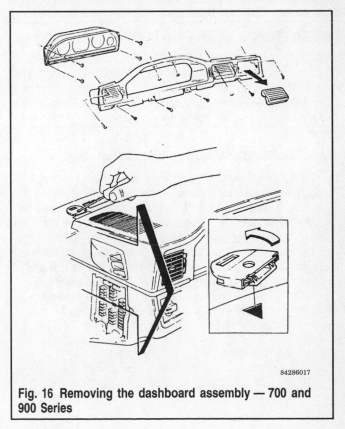

Fig. 16 Removing the dashboard assembly — 700 and 900 Series

other for the use of both a heating unit and an air conditioning unit combined. The removal and installation of the heating system components and the air conditioning/heating system components are basically the same for both CU units.

700 and 900 Series

Three types of climate units are used and are of common construction: the Combined Unit (CU), the Automatic Climate Control (ACC) and the Electronic Climate Control (ECC). The difference in the units lie in the equipment used, such as with or without air conditioning and the manner in which the unit is controlled, either manually or automatic.

CLIMATE UNIT WITHOUT AIR CONDITIONING

This is a manually controlled heater and fresh air unit. The unit is prepared for the installation of an air conditioning unit. The panel vents and the water valve are controlled by vacuum and the air mix shutter is controlled by a cable, connected to the temperature control lever. The same control panel is used on vehicles with manually controlled air conditioning systems.

CLIMATE UNIT WITH AIR CONDITIONING

The climate unit is identical to the heater climate unit but with air conditioning included. This unit has 4 control positions, MAX, NORM, B/L and DEFROST. The positions are controlled manually from the control panel where the mode, fan speed and temperature can be selected. The wiring, vacuum and the air flow schematics are basically the same as the CU unit without air conditioning. If the mode selector is in one of the air conditioning positions and the fan speed is in the ON position, the fan will operate automatically in low speed to prevent evaporator ice build-up.

AUTOMATICALLY CONTROLLED CLIMATE UNIT (ACC)

With the ACC unit, the passenger compartment is kept at a preset temperature regardless of the ambient temperature. The unit is set at the control panel but is controlled by a programmer located behind the instrument controlled unit. However, the wiring, vacuum and air flow schematics are different from the other units.

ELECTRONIC CLIMATE CONTROL UNIT (ECC)

The ECC system incorporates a self-diagnosis function; faults are indicated by a series of flashing codes when the A/C button is pushed. The control unit is programmed to make the best of the situation if a fault is detected. If a fault is detected, the unit ignores the faulty signal and selects an alternative pre-programmed value. The control unit is also designed to prevent the delivery of faulty outputs. The presence of a fault(s) is indicated by flashing of the A/C button. In the workshop, any such fault code may be requested by setting the controls to a specified configuration. The absence of a fault code is not a guarantee that the system is fault-free.

Service Valve Location

York Compressor System
▶ **See Figure 17**

The service valve location for high pressure side is at compressor's DISCH valve. The service valve location for the low pressure side is at compressor's suction valve.

Except York Compressor System

The high pressure service valve is located on the compressor. The low pressure service valve is located on the receiver/drier assembly.

✳✳WARNING

Please read the 'SAFETY WARNINGS', under Air Conditioning System in Section 1 of this manual.

System Discharging

R-12 refrigerant is a chlorofluorocarbon which, when mishandled, can contribute to the depletion on the ozone layer in the upper atmosphere. Ozone filters out harmful radiation from the sun. In order to protect the ozone layer, an approved R-12 Recovery/Recycling machine that meets SAE standard J1991 should be employed when discharging the system. Follow the operating instructions provided with the approved equipment exactly to properly discharge the system.

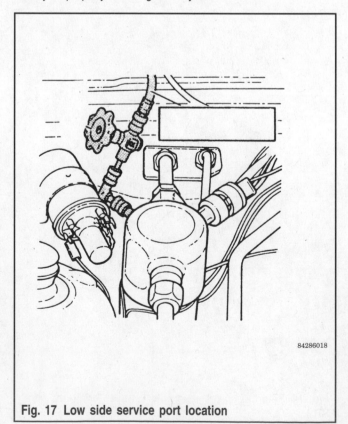

84286018

Fig. 17 Low side service port location

System Evacuating

If the air conditioning system has been opened to the atmosphere, it should be air and moisture free before being recharged with refrigerant. Moisture and air mixed with refrigerant will raise the compressor head pressure, possibly damage the system's components and will reduce the performance of the system. To evacuate the system, perform the following procedure:

1. Leak test the system and repair any leaks found.
2. Connect an approved charging station, Recovery/Recycling machine or manifold gauge set and vacuum pump to the discharge and suction ports. The red hose is normally connected to the discharge (high pressure) line and the blue hose is connected to the suction (low pressure) line.
3. Open the discharge and suction ports and start the vacuum pump. If the pump is not able to pull at least 26 in. Hg of vacuum, there is a leak that must be repaired before evacuation can occur.
4. Once the system has reached at least 26 in. Hg of vacuum, allow the system to evacuate for at least 30 minutes. The longer the system is evacuated, the more contaminants will be removed.
5. Close all valves and turn the pump off. If the system loses more than 2 in. Hg of vacuum after 15 minutes, there is a leak that should be repaired.

System Charging

1. Connect an approved charging station, Recovery/Recycling machine or manifold gauge set to the discharge and suction ports. The red hose is normally connected to the discharge (high pressure) line and the blue hose is connected to the suction (low pressure) line.
2. Follow the instructions provided with the equipment and charge the system with the specified amount of refrigerant.
3. Perform a leak test.

Condenser

REMOVAL & INSTALLATION

240 Series

1. Disconnect the negative battery cable.
2. Recover refrigerant (discharge system) from refrigeration system.
3. Remove the radiator grille and headlight frames. Remove the center stay and the horn bracket.
4. Remove the electric cooling fan assembly as applicable.
5. Remove all refrigerant system connections. Cap open fittings immediately.
6. Remove the condenser mounting retaining bolts. Remove the condenser assembly.
   To install:
7. Drain and measure the amount of refrigerant oil from the condenser and install the same amount of new oil in the replacement condenser.

8. Install the condenser (transfer air seals-install air seals in correct position). Using new O-ring seals, lubricated with refrigerant oil, install the refrigerant lines to the condenser assembly.
9. Install the electric cooling fan assembly as applicable.
10. Install horn bracket, center stay and headlight frames. Install the radiator grille assembly.
11. Reconnect the battery cable. Evacuate, charge and test refrigerant system.

700 and 900 Series

1. Disconnect the negative battery cable.
2. Recover refrigerant (discharge system) from refrigeration system.
3. Remove the radiator grille, the support stay from in front of the condenser and the upper radiator member bolts.
4. Remove the hood release cable from the upper radiator member.
5. Remove the air guide panel from the upper radiator member.
6. Remove the upper condenser retaining screws and the upper radiator member. From under the bumper, remove the air guide panel.
7. Recover refrigerant (discharge system) from refrigeration system.
8. Remove all refrigerant system connections. Cap open fittings immediately.
9. Remove the lower condenser nuts and the condenser assembly from the vehicle.
   To install:
10. Drain and measure the amount of refrigerant oil from the condenser and install the same amount of new oil in the replacement condenser.
11. Install the condenser (transfer air seals-install air seals in correct position). Using new O-ring seals, lubricated with refrigerant oil, install the lines to the condenser.
12. Install the lower air guide panel under the bumper and the upper air guide panel to the upper radiator member.
13. Install the hood release cable to the upper radiator member.
14. Install the upper radiator member, the stay support in front of the condenser and the radiator grille.
15. Reconnect the negative battery cable.
16. Evacuate, charge and test refrigerant system. Check system for leaks.

Compressor

REMOVAL & INSTALLATION

Except York Compressor System

1. Disconnect the negative battery cable.
2. Recover refrigerant (discharge system) from refrigeration system.
3. Remove all refrigerant system connections. Cap open fittings immediately.
4. Loosen the compressor and mounting brackets bolts. Disconnect the electrical connector from the compressor.

5. Remove the drive belt from the compressor, the mounting bolts and the compressor assembly.

To install:

6. Drain the refrigerant oil from the compressor and measure so the same amount can be installed in the compressor, if replacing the unit.

7. Mount the compressor on the mounting brackets and install the mounting bolts. Install compressor assembly.

8. Immediately upon opening the service connection ports, attach the hoses and tighten securely.

9. Install the drive belt. Adjust the drive belt so it not possible to depress it by more than 0.2-0.4 in. for Sankyo and Kiki or 0.04-0.08 in. for Delco at the middle of the longest belt span between pulleys.

10. Connect the negative battery cable.

11. Evacuate, check for proper refrigerant oil level and charge the system.

12. Start the engine, allow it to reach normal operating temperatures and the check the system operation.

York Compressor System

▶ **See Figures 18 and 19**

1. Disconnect the negative battery cable.

2. Recover refrigerant (discharge system) from refrigeration system.

3. Disconnect both the suction and the discharge service valves from the compressor head. Cap open fittings immediately.

4. At the crankshaft pulley, loosen the tensioner plate nuts and remove the drive belt.

5. Disconnect the electrical connection from compressor assembly.

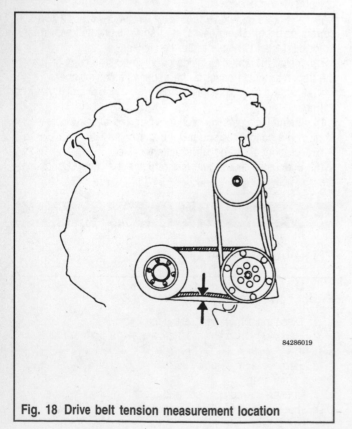

Fig. 18 Drive belt tension measurement location

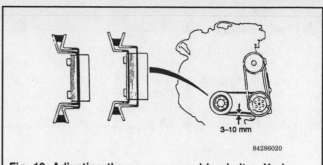

Fig. 19 Adjusting the compressor drive belt — York compressor system

6. Remove the compressor-to-bracket retaining bolts and the compressor assembly.

To install:

7. Drain the refrigerant oil from the compressor and measure so the same amount can be installed in the compressor, if replacing the unit.

8. Install compressor assembly. Install the compressor-to-bracket retaining bolts and torque to 28 ft. lbs.

9. Remove the tensioner plate and outer split pulley half from the crankshaft pulley.

10. Install the drive belt, the split pulley half and the tensioner plate. To adjust the drive belt tension, remove or add shims to the assembly until the deflection is 0.1-0.4 in. between the pulleys. Install any extra shims between the outer split pulley and tensioner plate.

11. Torque the tensioner plate-to-crankshaft nuts to 15 ft. lbs.

12. Reconnect the electrical connection to compressor assembly.

13. Connect both the suction and the discharge service lines to the compressor assembly.

14. Connect the negative battery cable.

15. Evacuate, check for proper refrigerant oil level and charge the system.

16. Start the engine, allow it to reach normal operating temperatures and the check the system operation.

Receiver/Drier

REMOVAL & INSTALLATION

▶ **See Figures 20 and 21**

1. Disconnect the negative battery cable.

2. Recover refrigerant (discharge system) from refrigeration system.

3. Disconnect, cap or plug the refrigerant lines to the receiver/drier assembly.

4. Disconnect the electrical connector from the receiver/drier pressure sensor.

5. Remove the receiver/drier from the bracket.

➡**Before replacement of a new receiver/drier, drain the refrigerant oil from the old unit, measure the amount of oil and add the same amount of new oil into the new receiver/drier assembly.**

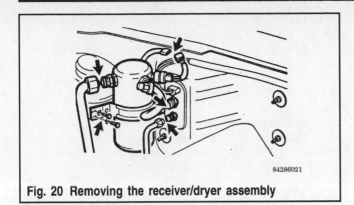

Fig. 20 Removing the receiver/dryer assembly

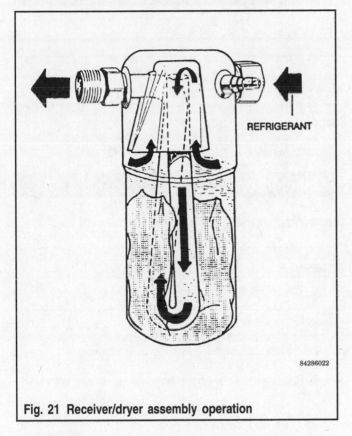

Fig. 21 Receiver/dryer assembly operation

To install:

6. Install the receiver/drier assembly into the bracket.

7. Connect the electrical connector to the receiver/drier pressure sensor.

8. Remove the line caps and install the refrigerant lines to the receiver/drier assembly.

9. Evacuate, check for proper refrigerant oil level and charge the air conditioning system.

10. Connect the negative battery cable.

11. Start the engine, allow it to reach normal operating temperatures and check the system operation.

Expansion Valve

REMOVAL & INSTALLATION

➡ The 240 series are equipped with an expansion valve. The 740, 760, 780 and 940 series are equipped with a fixed orifice tube.

240 Series

◆ See Figure 22

1. Disconnect the negative battery cable.

2. Recover refrigerant (discharge system) from refrigeration system.

3. Remove the right side sound proofing panel from under the glove box. Remove the console side panel from the right side.

4. Remove the evaporator cover and the evaporator outlet insulation.

5. Remove the expansion valve from the evaporator tube.

6. Carefully remove the capillary tube with the expansion valve. Using new O-rings lubricated with refrigerant oil, carefully install the expansion valve and the capillary tube.

7. Installation is the reverse of the removal procedure. Evacuate, check for proper refrigerant oil level and charge the system. Check the system for proper operation.

Fixed Orifice Tube

REMOVAL & INSTALLATION

➡ The orifice tube is located in the evaporator inlet and regulates the amount of refrigerant flowing into the evaporator assembly.

700 and 900 Series

1. Disconnect the negative battery cable.

2. Recover refrigerant (discharge system) from refrigeration system.

3. Remove the inlet tube from the evaporator, separated the rubber and remove the fix orifice tube.

4. Lubricate the tube with refrigerant oil, position the short filtered end (outlet filter) towards the evaporator and install the tube assembly.

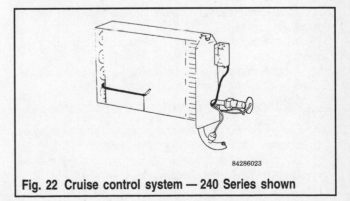

Fig. 22 Cruise control system — 240 Series shown

5. Reconnect the negative battery cable. Evacuate, check for proper refrigerant oil level and charge the system. Check the system for proper operation.

Evaporator

REMOVAL & INSTALLATION

240 Series

1. Disconnect the negative battery cable. Recover refrigerant (discharge system) from refrigeration system.
2. Remove the glove box, panel below the glove box and side panel next to heater assembly. Remove the right side defroster vent and duct.
3. Remove the expansion valve. Remove the insulation and evaporator cover assembly.
4. Remove all refrigerant system connections. Cap open fittings immediately. Remove the evaporator assembly.
5. Installation is the reverse of the service removal procedure. Install new evaporator seal (insulation) and O-rings at refrigerant system connections. Evacuate, charge and test refrigerant system. Check system for leaks.

700 and 900 Series

MANUAL LEVER AND AUTOMATIC CLIMATE CONTROL TYPE SYSTEMS

1. Disconnect the negative battery cable.
2. Recover refrigerant (discharge system) from refrigeration system.
3. Remove the glove box and panel below the glove box assembly.
4. Remove all refrigerant system connections. Cap open fittings immediately.
5. Remove the right side instep moulding and panel covering the control unit.
6. Remove the control unit and mounting bracket.
7. Remove all electrical connections and 2 lower screws of fan housing. Remove the evaporator housing cover from the assembly. Remove the evaporator assembly.
   To install:
8. Transfer rubber seal and filter to evaporator. Apply sealer to lower casing and position the evaporator in the assembly. Install evaporator housing cover.
9. Reconnect all electrical connections. Position wiring harness to housing cover.
10. Install control unit and bracket. Install panel and right side instep moulding.
11. Install the glove box and panel below the glove box assembly.
12. Reconnect the negative battery cable. Evacuate, charge and test refrigerant system. Check system for leaks.

ELECTRONIC CLIMATE CONTROL TYPE SYSTEM

1. Disconnect the negative battery cable. Recover refrigerant (discharge system) from refrigeration system.
2. Disconnect the electrical connector and unscrew the receiver/drier from the wheel house.

3. Disconnect the electrical connectors from the firewall. Remove the cover plate and the foam rubber seal.
4. From the right side, remove the lower glove box panel and the glove box.
5. Disconnect the vacuum lines from the tank and remove the evaporator cover. Remove the evaporator assembly from the housing.
6. Installation is the reverse of the service removal procedure. Install new evaporator seal (insulation) and O-rings at refrigerant system connections. Evacuate, charge and test refrigerant system. Check system for leaks.

Refrigerant Lines

REMOVAL & INSTALLATION

1. Disconnect the negative battery cable. Recover refrigerant (discharge system) from refrigeration system.
2. Remove and replace defective line. Install new O-rings, as required.
3. Reconnect the negative battery cable. Evacuate, charge and test refrigerant system. Check system for leaks.

Manual Control Head

REMOVAL & INSTALLATION

240 Series

1. Disconnect the negative battery cable.
2. Remove the sound proofing and side panels from both sides of the center dash console.
3. Remove the radio assembly. Remove the center control panel. Position the control assembly as far forward as possible.
4. Remove the lever knob, cable from lever and control assembly.
5. Install is the reverse of the service removal procedure. Adjust cable as necessary.

700 and 900 Series

1. Disconnect the negative battery cable.
2. Remove the trim panel. Remove the control assembly from the dashboard.
3. Disconnect control cable clip, vacuum connections and electrical connections.
4. Install is the reverse of the service removal procedure. Adjust cable, as necessary.

Manual Control Cables

ADJUSTMENT

On all vehicles make sure the air mix shutter assembly touches both end stops when the control cable is moved between COOL and WARM positions on the manual control head assembly.

REMOVAL & INSTALLATION

240 Series

1. Disconnect the negative battery cable.
2. Remove the sound proofing and side panels from both sides of the center dash console.
3. Remove the radio assembly. Remove the center control panel. Position the control assembly as far forward as possible.
4. Remove the (upper end) cable from lever on the control assembly.
5. Disconnect (lower end) from the unit assembly. Note location and position for correct installation. Remove the control cable.
6. Install is the reverse of the service removal procedure. Adjust cable, as necessary.

700 and 900 Series

1. Disconnect the negative battery cable. Remove the glove box and panel below the glove box assembly.
2. Position the heater control to the WARM position.
3. Remove the trim panel. Remove the control assembly from the dashboard. Position the control assembly as far forward as possible.
4. Remove the (upper end) cable from lever on the control assembly.
5. Disconnect (lower end) from the unit assembly. Note location and position for correct installation. Remove the control cable.

6. Install is the reverse of the service removal procedure. Adjust cable, as necessary.

Electronic Control Head

REMOVAL & INSTALLATION

700 and 900 Series

PROGRAMMER ASSEMBLY

1. Disconnect the negative battery cable. Remove the panel beneath the glove box and the glove box.
2. Remove the outer panel vents and the air ducts.
3. Disconnect the air mix shutter rod from the programmer assembly.
4. Disconnect the electrical connector from the left side of the programmer assembly.
5. Remove the clips for the vacuum hose connections and disconnect the hoses.
6. Remove the programmer assembly.
To install:
7. Install the programmer assembly.
8. Connect the electrical connector to the left side of the programmer and connect the junction.
9. Install the control rod (air mix rod) and adjust as follows:
   a. Start the engine to obtain vacuum, if necessary.
   b. Set the temperature dial to MAX HEAT on the thumbwheel. Pull control rod until it reaches end position. Secure rod to programmer assembly.
10. Install the air ducts and panel vents.
11. Install the glove box unit and the lower panels.
12. Reconnect the negative battery cable. Check system for proper operation.

CRUISE CONTROL

General Description

The cruise control system maintains the vehicle speed at a setting selected by the driver by means of mechanical, electrical, and vacuum operated devices.

The cruise control unit receives an immediate electrical input from the ignition switch, therefore, the cruise circuit is ready for operation whenever the ignition switch is turned on. Actual activation of the cruise control is accomplished by lifting up and holding the control switch in the direction of ACCEL/SET or DECEL/SET until the desired speed is attained. The control unit also receives information about operating conditions from the brake switch, the distributor, speed sensor, the clutch switch (with manual transmission), or the shift lever position switch (with automatic transmission). The cruise control unit, in turn, sends operational signals to the devices that regulate the throttle position. The throttle position maintains the selected vehicle speed. The cruise control compares the actual speed of the vehicle to the selected speed. Then, the control unit uses the result of that comparison to open or close the throttle.

The control unit will disengage the instant the driver depresses the brake pedal. The brake switch sends an electronic signal to the control unit when the brake pedal is depressed; the control unit responds by allowing the throttle to close. The shift lever position switch (automatic transmission) or the clutch switch (manual transmission) sends a disengage signal input to the control unit that also allows the throttle to close.

➡The use of the speed control is not recommended when driving conditions do not permit maintaining a constant speed, such as in heavy traffic or on roads that are winding, icy, snow covered or slippery.

SYSTEM OPERATION

▶ See Figure 22

The cruise control system will set and automatically maintain any speed above 25 mph (40 kph). When the desired speed is attained, a brief tapping against the switch toward the ACCEL/SET or DECEL/SET, will keep the speed constant until a new speed is selected or if the brake pedal is depressed. To match this set speed, hold the switch in direction of

ACCEL/SET or DECEL/SET until the desired speed is attained. Upon releasing the switch the new speed is held constant.

Short tapping against the switch towards the OFF position or depressing the brake or clutch pedal, will switch off the cruise control system. However, the system remains ready for operation until the ignition switch is off. If the system is disengaged temporarily by the brake switch, clutch switch or deceleration and the vehicle speed is still above 25 mph, tap the switch toward RESUME. The vehicle will automatically return to the previous set speed retained in memory.

If the vehicle is accelerated above the set speed, the vehicle will return to the set speed when the pedal is released. While driving with the cruise control system, do not engage the selector lever in **N** position, vehicles with automatic transmission, since this will speed up the engine.

SERVICE PRECAUTIONS

❊❊CAUTION

If equipped with an air bag system, the system must be fully disabled before performing repairs, following all safety precautions. Failure to disarm the system could result in personal injury and/or property damage.

- Never disconnect any electrical connection with the ignition switch **ON**.
- Avoid touching module connector pins.
- Leave new components and modules in the shipping package until ready to install them.
- Always touch a vehicle ground after sliding across a vehicle seat or walking across vinyl or carpeted floors to avoid static charge damage.
- Never allow welding cables to lie on, near or across any vehicle electrical wiring.
- Do not operate the cruise control or the engine with the drive wheels off the ground.

Directional Indicator/Cruise Control Switch

REMOVAL & INSTALLATION

▶ See Figure 23

1. Disconnect the negative battery cable.
2. Remove the upper and lower steering column covers. There is no need to remove the steering wheel.
3. Remove the switch and disconnect the switch connector.
4. Reconnect the switch connector and refit the new switch.
5. Install the upper and lower steering column covers.
6. Reconnect the negative battery cable.

Fig. 23 Replacing directional indicator/cruise control switch — 240 shown

Control Unit

REMOVAL & INSTALLATION

▶ See Figure 24

1. Disconnect the negative battery cable.
2. Remove the knee bolster access panel. Remove the screws and remove the bolster.
3. Fold down the sound proofing. Remove the control unit retaining screws, disconnect the control unit connector and remove the control unit from the vehicle.
4. Reconnect the control unit connector and fit the unit into position.
5. Install the knee bolster. Reconnect the negative battery cable.

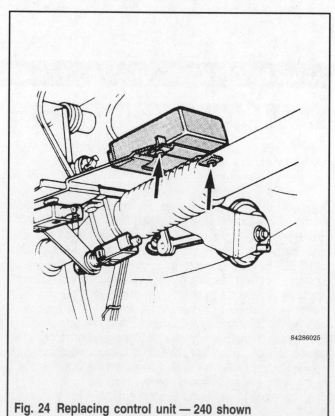

Fig. 24 Replacing control unit — 240 shown

6. Road test the vehicle and check the cruise control system operation.

Vacuum Servo

REMOVAL & INSTALLATION

▶ **See Figure 25**

1. Disconnect the negative battery cable.
2. Remove the knee bolster access panel. Remove the screws and remove the bolster.

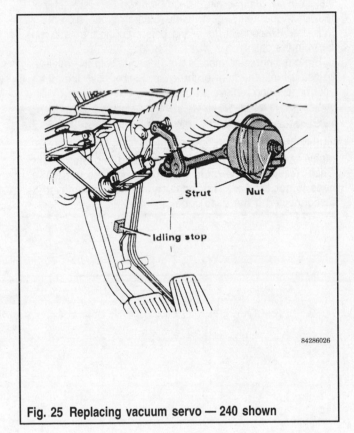

84286026

Fig. 25 Replacing vacuum servo — 240 shown

3. Fold down the sound proofing.
4. Remove the vacuum servo strut. Matchmark the locking strut position. Disconnect the hose and remove the rod. Remove the vacuum servo.
5. Install the replacement vacuum servo. Adjust the strut so that the throttle pedal reaches the idling stop without play in the joints. Tighten the nut to 13 ft. lbs. (18 Nm).
6. Install the sound proofing and knee bolster.
7. Reconnect the negative battery cable.
8. Road test the vehicle and check the cruise control system operation.

Vacuum Valve

REMOVAL & INSTALLATION

▶ **See Figure 26**

1. Disconnect the negative battery cable.
2. Remove the knee bolster access panel. Remove the screws and remove the bolster.
3. Fold down the sound proofing.
4. Disconnect the connector, hose and clip. Remove the vacuum valve.
5. To install, reverse the removal procedure. Adjust the new valve as shown. Vehicle with automatic transmission have only 1 vacuum valve.

Vacuum Pump

REMOVAL & INSTALLATION

▶ **See Figure 27**

1. Disconnect the negative battery cable.
2. Disconnect the vacuum hose. Disconnect the connector and remove the vacuum pump retaining screws.
3. Remove the vacuum pump.
4. Installation is the reversal of the removal procedure.

RADIO

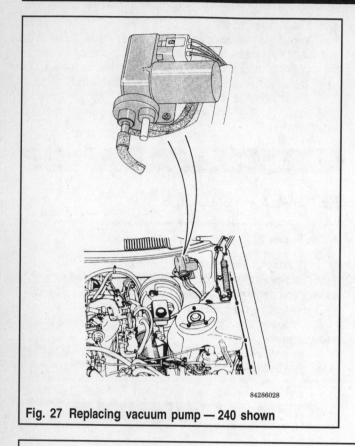

84286028

Fig. 27 Replacing vacuum pump — 240 shown

REMOVAL & INSTALLATION

On most models, the radio is held in by 2 clips in the console. Remove the side covers and locate the 2 access holes (one on each side) in line with the radio case. Insert a small probe or very small screwdriver into each hole and push gently. This releases the clip and the radio may be removed from the front of the console.

Other models have the same style clips, but they are released by inserting a thin, flat probe down each side of the radio from the front. Again, release the clips and slide the radio free. Disconnect the wiring before pulling the radio too far from the dash.

The radio on some models are designed with the releases being built into the front of the case. Simply push the tabs with your fingers and remove the radio.

❋❋WARNING

Although these radios are relatively simple to removed, many have a security code programmed into the circuitry. Once reinstalled, the radio will not work if the correct code is not entered. The radio should not be removed or disconnected if the user code is not available.

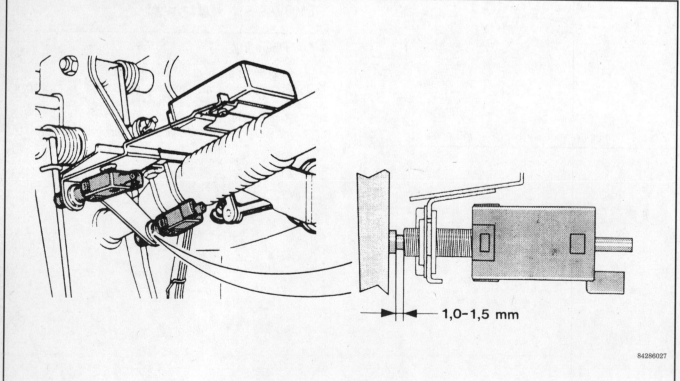

1,0–1,5 mm

84286027

Fig. 26 Replacing vacuum valve — 240 shown

WINDSHIELD WIPERS AND WASHERS

Wiper Blade

REMOVAL & INSTALLATION

▶ **See Figure 28**

1. Lift the wiper arm and blade clear of the glass. Hold the blade assembly at right angles to the arm.
2. Pinch in the end of the plastic clip at the back of the arm.
3. Slide the blade assembly down the arm until it clears the 'U' at the end.
4. Move the blade slightly to the side and remove it from the arm.
5. When reinstalling, pay attention! It is possible to get the blade on the arm backwards, resulting In strange positioning against the glass. The blade should seal on the arm with a distinct click and should then be able to be folded down parallel to the arm so that it sits flush against the glass over its entire length.

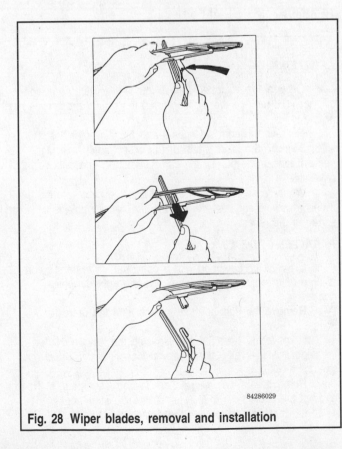

84286029

Fig. 28 Wiper blades, removal and installation

Wiper Arms

REMOVAL & INSTALLATION

▶ **See Figure 29**

1. Pry up or lift the plastic or metal spindle cover at the base of the arm.
2. Unscrew and remove the axle nut.
3. Gently lift the blade and arm from the glass and remove the arm from the drive axle.
4. When reassembling, tighten the axle nut to 10-13 ft. lbs. Do not overtighten or the splines will be damaged. Make sure the wiper blade will be in the correct position on the glass before tightening the nut.

Windshield Wiper Motor

REMOVAL & INSTALLATION

240 Series

➡**This procedure includes wiper drive link REMOVAL & INSTALLATION.**

1. Disconnect the negative battery cable.
2. Remove the right side-panel and remove the panel under the dashboard (beneath the glove box).
3. Remove the defroster hoses and remove the glove box.
4. Remove the wiper arms.
5. Disconnect the wiper assembly and lift it out through the glove box opening.
6. Reverse the above procedure to install.

700 Series

▶ **See Figures 30 and 31**

1. Disconnect the negative battery cable
2. Remove the wiper arms and remove the rubber boot at the base of the arm.
3. Lift the hood to its uppermost position by pushing the catch on the hood hinges.

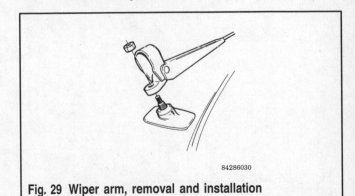

84286030

Fig. 29 Wiper arm, removal and installation

4. Release the washer hoses from the clips along the edge of the cowl. Unscrew the cowl retaining bolts. Older vehicles may use plastic clips instead of bolts to hold the cowl in place. Lower the hood to its normal position.

5. Remove the cowl by pulling it forward and then rotating the front edge upward. Close the hood.

6. Unscrew the bolts which hold the linkage assembly. One of the bolts is hidden beneath a rubber cap.

7. Remove the cover from the wiper motor, cut the cable tie and disconnect the plug to the motor.

8. Unscrew the spindle nut on the motor and the 3 bolts holding the motor to the linkage. Lift the motor free of the linkage.

9. When reassembling, make sure the wipers are in the park position.

10. After the motor is secure on the linkage and the linkage is mounted on the vehicle, visually check for any possible interference between the moving parts and the wiring. Always reinstall the wire tie on the motor harness.

11. Make sure the cowl is properly seated before installing the bolts. Install the washer hoses in their clips, replace the rubber boots and install the wiper arms. Connect the negative battery cable.

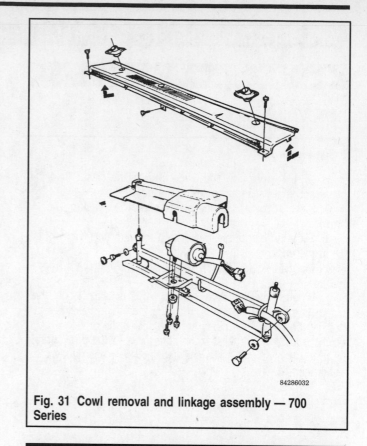

84286032

Fig. 31 Cowl removal and linkage assembly — 700 Series

Wiper Linkage

REMOVAL & INSTALLATION

DRIVE LINK

1. On vehicles equipped with a combination heater-air conditioner unit, remove the glovebox and the right defroster nozzle.

2. Remove the right side panel and the defroster hoses.

3. Remove the locking tab for the wiper motor lever connection, loosen the nut for the cable stretcher, and remove the drive link.

4. When reassembling, carefully place the cable around the wiper arm drive segment. Make sure the cable nipple is inserted in the recess.

PARALLEL DRIVE LINK

1. On vehicles equipped with a combination heater-air conditioner unit, remove the glovebox and the right defroster nozzle.

2. Remove the right-hand side panel and the defroster hoses.

3. Remove the drive link by releasing the locking tab for the wiper motor lever connection and loosening the cable stretcher.

4. Remove each cable stretcher nut and disconnect both ends of the cable from their wiper arm drive segments.

5. Lift forward and remove the parallel drive link.

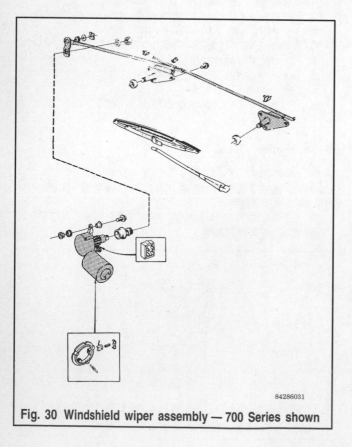

84286031

Fig. 30 Windshield wiper assembly — 700 Series shown

6. Reverse the above procedure to install. Carefully place each cable end around its wiper drive arm segment. The cable nipple must be inserted in the segment recess.

CABLE

1. Remove the drive link and parallel drive link as described above.

2. Pry up and remove the cable retaining lockwasher. Remove the old cable.

3. Position the new cable on its wiper arm drive segments and secure it with a new retaining lockwasher.

4. Install the cable stretcher on the drive link. The tensioning nut should not be tightened until the drive link and parallel drive link are installed.

5. Install the drive link and parallel drive link. Tighten the tensioning nut.

Tailgate Windshield Wiper

REMOVAL & INSTALLATION

240 Series

▶ **See Figure 32**

1. Disconnect the negative battery cable.
2. Remove the upholstered finish panel on the inside of the tailgate.
3. Remove the bolts for the wiper motor protection plate.
4. Disconnect the ball-and-socket wiper arm link at the motor.
5. Fold the protection plate aside and lift out the wiper motor.
6. Mark the wires and disconnect them at the motor.

➡**The brushes in the motor are replaceable. Remove the motor cover, unhook the brush springs and remove the brushes from the holders. Be careful not to damage the brush holders. Install the new brushes and attach the springs.**

7. When reinstalling, make certain that the motor is in the park position before installing. Connect the wiring to the motor and install the motor and the protection plate.
8. Reattach the connecting link to the motor and install the retaining screws for the protection plate.
9. Install the trim panel on the inside of the tailgate and connect the negative battery cable.

700 Series

▶ **See Figure 33**

1. Disconnect negative battery cable.
2. Remove the inner trim pad on the tailgate.
3. Loosen and remove the center nut on the motor and remove the linkage from the motor.
4. Remove the bolts holding the motor and remove the motor. Disconnect the wiring from the motor.
5. When reassembling, make certain that the motor is in the park position.
6. Attach the wiring and mount the motor to the door.

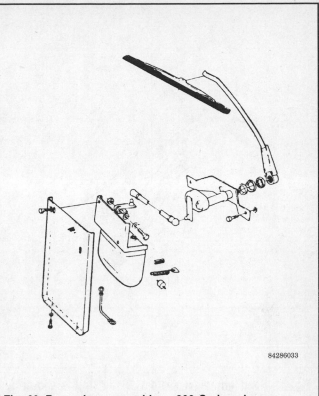

84286033

Fig. 32 Rear wiper assembly — 200 Series shown

7. Attach the linkage to the motor and tighten the center nut.
8. Replace the trim pad and attach the negative battery cable.

Headlight Wiper Blades

REMOVAL & INSTALLATION

▶ **See Figure 34**

The small blades for the headlight wipers found on the 700 Series are removed in the same fashion as the windshield wiper blades. Pull the wiper away from the light, lift the spindle cover, remove the shaft nut and remove the blade and arm. It is necessary to disconnect the washer tube from the blade assembly when removing the arm.

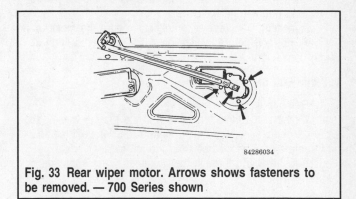

84286034

Fig. 33 Rear wiper motor. Arrows shows fasteners to be removed. — 700 Series shown

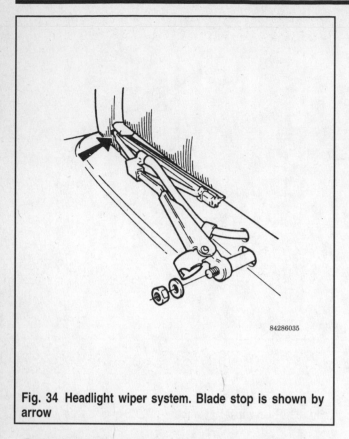

Fig. 34 Headlight wiper system. Blade stop is shown by arrow

During installation, place the wiper blade below the park stop on the light. Tighten the shaft nut and reposition the blade above the stop. The blade should rest firmly on the stop. Don't forget to reattach the washer line.

Headlight Wiper Motor

REMOVAL & INSTALLATION

740 and 760 models

▶ **See Figure 35**

1. Remove the wiper arm.
2. Disconnect wiring connector and the ground wire (2 separate connectors) for the motor. Connectors for both left and right motors may be located near the left fender
3. Loosen the nut on the motor shaft, slide off the plastic tubing and remove the motor.
4. Reassemble in reverse order. Make sure the motor is in the park position before installation. Insure a secure fit on all wiring connectors.

780 and 900 Series

1. Remove the wiper arm.
2. Disconnect wiring connector and the ground wire (2 separate connectors) for the motor. Connectors for both left and right motors may be located near the left fender.
3. Pull the wiring through the grommet in the front side panel.

4. For the LEFT wiper motor:
   a. Remove the foglight or auxiliary light cluster and turn aside.
   b. Loosen the nut on the motor shaft, remove the plastic tubing, and remove the motor through the front side panel.
   c. Reassemble in reverse order. Make sure the motor is in the park position before installation. Insure a secure fit on all wiring connectors.
5. For the RIGHT wiper motor:
   a. Tie a five foot piece of string to the wiring connectors. This will ease reinstallation.
   b. Remove the grille.
   c. Carefully lift the lower part of the spoiler and release the two clips holding the wiring harness.
   d. Pull the wiring through the front of the spoiler, allowing the string to follow the wire path. When the wiring is clear of the spoiler, untie the string but allow it to remain in place in the vehicle.
   e. Remove the foglight or auxiliary light cluster and turn aside.
   f. Loosen the nut on the motor shaft, remove the plastic tubing, and remove the motor.
   g. When reassembling, remove the sleeves from the terminals of the new motor.
   h. Install the motor and tie the string to the wiring harness. Position and attach the foglight assembly.
   i. Using the string, pull the wiring through the spoiler and into position. Install new cable ties and/or clips as necessary; the cables and pipes across the front of the vehicle must be held in place.
   j. Reinstall the grille.
   k. Remove the string and connect the electrical connectors, making sure they are clean and tight. Reinstall the wiper arm.

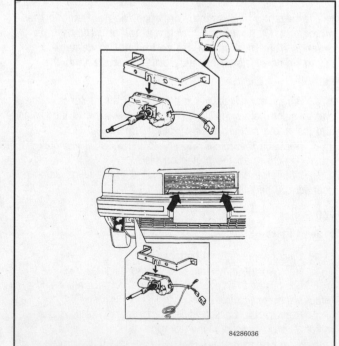

Fig. 35 Headlight wiper assemblies. Above: 740 and 760 models. Below: Right side of 780 model. Large arrows show wire harness clips to be released during removal

INSTRUMENTS AND SWITCHES

Service Precautions

❊❊CAUTION

To avoid personal injury, all SRS precautions must be strictly adhered to. Refer to SRS system precautions at the beginning of this section.

- The battery must be disconnected when replacing any electrical components
- The radio must be switched OFF before disconnecting the battery negative lead to avoid damage to the microprocessor (microprocessor radio).
- All vehicles are equipped with a Supplemental Restraint System (SRS). To avoid deployment when servicing components in the immediate area, do not use electrical test equipment such as battery or A.C. powered voltmeter, ohmmeter, etc. or any type of tester other than specified. Do not use a non-powered probe tester.

Instrument Cluster

REMOVAL & INSTALLATION

240 Series

1. Disconnect the negative battery cable.
2. Remove the molded plastic casings from the steering column.
3. Remove the bracket retaining screw and lower the bracket toward the steering column.
4. Remove the cluster attaching screws.
5. Disconnect the speedometer cable.
6. Tilt the cluster out of its snap fitting and disconnect the plug. On vehicles equipped with a tachometer, disconnect the tachometer sending wire.
7. Lift the cluster out of the dashboard.
8. When reinstalling, make sure wiring and speedometer cable is reconnected before replacing the cluster. Also make sure the cluster engages its snap fittings when placed in the dash.
9. Install the cluster attaching screws and replace the bracket and retaining screw.
10. Install the molded plastic casings on the steering column and connect the negative battery cable.

Except 240 Series

1. Disconnect the negative battery cable.

❊❊CAUTION

Refer to the SRS (air bag) system 'Safety Precautions' listed earlier in this section.

2. Remove the soundproofing above the foot pedals.

3. Remove the two cover panels and screws holding the instrument panel.
4. Lift the instrument cluster away from the dashboard.
5. Remove the connector seal on the back of the cluster and remove the electrical connectors.
6. When reinstalling, remember to hook up all the wiring before installation. Always use a new connector seal.
7. If the wiring harness was cut away from the air duct (step 3, above) always re-tie it to prevent chafing. Use a new wire tie and anchor securely.
8. Install the two retaining screws and replace the covers.
9. Install the soundproofing panel.

Windshield Wiper Switch/Turn Signal Switch

REMOVAL & INSTALLATION

❊❊CAUTION

This procedure requires removal of the steering wheel. If the vehicle is equipped with the SRS (air bag) system, refer to the safety precautions listed earlier in this section. DO NOT remove the wheel until these precautions have been followed.

1. Turn the steering wheel to the straight ahead position.
2. Remove the center pad from the wheel.
3. Remove the steering wheel retaining bolt. If possible, matchmark the wheel and steering shaft.   If the vehicle is equipped with SRS, pull out the locking screw and the long tape label from its station in the steering wheel hub. Use the lock screw (with the tape flag attached) to lock the contact reel through the hole in the steering wheel hub. Do not turn the steering wheel once the bolt is removed; the pin in the contact reel will shear.
4. Remove the steering wheel and the upper and lower steering column casings.
5. To remove the wiper switch, simply remove the screws holding it to the column and unplug the connector. The turn signal switch is on the opposite side and is also held to the column by two or three screws.
6. When reassembling, remember to check the position of all the wires so that nothing is pinched in casings.
7. Reinstall the column casings and then reinstall the steering wheel. Check that the steering wheel position is true to the position of the wheels.   If the vehicle is SRS equipped, do not turn the steering wheel until the center bolt is reinstalled and tight; doing so will shear the pin in the contact reel. Remove the locking bolt with its flag and store it in the extra hole on the left side of the wheel.
8. Tighten the steering wheel bolt to 24 ft. lbs. Reinstall the center pad.
9. If equipped with the SRS system, make the necessary connections to reactivate the system.

Rear Window Wiper Switch

The tailgate washer/wiper controls are mounted on the same control stalk as the front wipers. The components are not individually replaceable for the rear system. To replace the switch assembly, follow the directions given for Windshield Wiper Switch, REMOVAL & INSTALLATION.

Headlight Switch (Lighting Selector)

REMOVAL & INSTALLATION

240 Series

1. Disconnect the negative battery cable.
2. Disconnect the hose from the left side dash vent.
3. Carefully remove the trim below the vent, remove the screws holding the vent in place and remove the vent assembly.
4. Using a very small screwdriver, loosen the set-screw holding the selector knob onto the shaft. If no set screw is evident, simply pull on the knob until it comes free of the shaft.
5. Remove the shaft nut from the switch and remove the switch through the back of the dash. Remove the plug from the back of the switch assembly.
6. When reassembling, remember to connect the new switch to the wiring harness and remember to tighten the small set-screw holding the knob to the shaft. Reconnect the battery and check the switch function.

Except 240 Series

1. Remove the selector knob by pulling it free of the shaft.
2. Disconnect the wiring connector by reaching under the dash. It may be necessary to loosen or remove the under dash pad to gain access.
3. Remove the shaft nut from the switch and remove the switch through the back of the dash.
4. Reassemble in reverse order.

Rocker Switches

REMOVAL & INSTALLATION

The dash or console mounted rocker switches are easily removed. Depending on the model, it may be necessary to remove the trim panel surrounding the switch. After this is done, reach behind the switch and disconnect the wire harness running to the switch. While your hand is back there, grasp each side of the switch, compress the retaining clips and remove the switch through the front of the panel.

If length allows, the wire harness may be brought out through the panel (after the switch is removed) for circuit testing. When reinstalling, make sure the wiring is properly routed and not crimped or pinched. The switch should engage the panel with a definite click when in place. Reinstall the trim panel.

Ignition Switch

REMOVAL & INSTALLATION

On all models, the ignition key lock is mounted on the steering column and incorporates a steering wheel lock to deter vehicle theft. The lock is attached to the steering column by shearbolts, whose heads break off when the proper tightness is reached. Removing the lock requires removing these bolts, either by cutting slots in their tops and using a screwdriver to extract them, or by drilling them out. If they are drilled out, the lock housing will probably be damaged. On many models, removing the ignition lock also requires loosening or removing the steering column. Because of the complexity of these operations, repairs are best left to a professional repair facility.

1. Disconnect the negative battery cable.
2. Provide access to the back of the ignition switch by removing panels and covers as necessary.
3. Remove the round multi-wire connector at the back of the switch, then unfasten and remove the electrical unit (sometimes called the start contact) from the back of the lock assembly.

➡ **This unit is generally held on with 2 small screws, but they are in a difficult location and an awkward position — have patience. When reassembling, make certain that the new unit is properly seated against the pin from the ignition lock. Also insure that the wiring connector is firmly attached to the new start contact.**

Speedometer Cable

REMOVAL & INSTALLATION

240 Series

On 200 series, the speedometer is cable driven by the transmission. The cable is connected to a drive gear in the transmission case and connects to the dashboard unit which interprets the number of cable revolutions into an expression of speed and distance.

The speedometer cable is unscrewed from the rear of the speedometer (it may be necessary to remove the instrument cluster for access) and from the transmission case. When installing a new cable, seat the ends of the inner cable in both the speedometer and transmission. Cable routing is critical; at no point should the bends in the cable be any sharper than a 4 inch radius. A crimped or binding cable can cause noise, vibration and possible damage to the speedometer unit.

➡ **A tamper-proof seal is installed on both the speedometer connection and the transmission connection. The speedometer connection has a plastic collar which must be broken to remove the cable. The retaining bolt for the transmission side of the cable is covered by a plastic cap which must be broken in order to remove the bolt.**

Except 240 Series

These vehicles uses an electric inductive pick-up in the differential to generate speed data. The number of electrical pulses varies with the speed; the speedometer unit transforms the pulses into a readable display of speed.

LIGHTING

When installing Halogen bulbs, do not touch the glass with your fingers. Grease, oil or any other impurities can be carbonized onto the bulb and damage the reflector.

Always use bulbs of the correct type and voltage. Failure to do so could activate the bulb failure warning light (if equipped).

Headlights

REMOVAL & INSTALLATION

▶ **See Figures 36 and 37**

1. Raise and support the hood. Working from inside the engine compartment, separate the socket contact from the bulb holder.
2. Unscrew and remove the bulb holder retaining ring.
3. Pull out the bulb holder assembly and replace it as a unit.
4. Installation is the reverse of the removal procedure.

➡**It may be necessary, on some models, to remove the washer fluid reservoir fill tube in order to gain access to the bulb holder.**

Signal and Marker Lights (Front)

REMOVAL & INSTALLATION

240

1. Loosen the lens retaining screws, using a Phillips screwdriver.

❄❄WARNING

When using a screwdriver to pry plastic components, use care and avoid scratching or breaking. If necessary, wear eye protection whenever possible.

2. Press in on the bulbs and turn them slightly counterclockwise. Remove the bulb.
3. Installation is the reverse of the removal procedure. When reinstalling the lens, check that the gasket is in position.

700 and 900 Series

1. Raise and support the hood. Working from inside the engine compartment, turn the lamp holder 1/4 turn counterclockwise and remove the bulb holder.

➡**Do not remove the connector from the bulb holder.**

2. Press the bulb in and turn it 1/4 turn counterclockwise and remove the bulb.

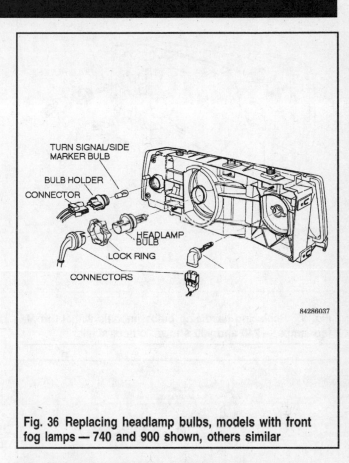

Fig. 36 Replacing headlamp bulbs, models with front fog lamps — 740 and 900 shown, others similar

3. Replace the bulb and reinstall the unit in the reverse order.

Tail Lamp

REMOVAL & INSTALLATION

240 Sedan

▶ **See Figure 39**

All tail lamp bulbs are replaced from inside the trunk.
1. Open the trunk. Remove the tail lamp inside cover.
2. Unscrew and remove the tail lamp inside cover. The cover is hooked at the upper edge. Lift the lower end out and up, then unhook the upper edge.
3. Turn the bulb holder approximately 3/8 inch (1 cm) counterclockwise and remove it from the tail lamp.
4. Depress the bulb in the holder, turn it slightly counterclockwise and remove it from the holder.
5. Install a new bulb in the holder and install the holder to the tail lamp. Turn the bulb holder clockwise.

➡**One of the bulb holder tabs is wider and fits only in its corresponding recess.**

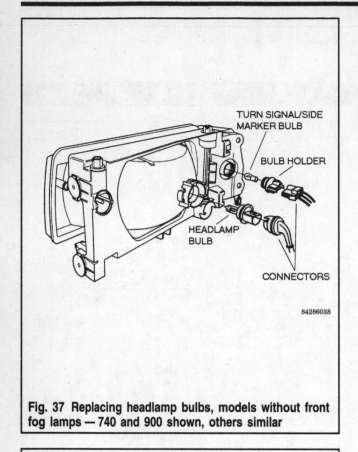

Fig. 37 Replacing headlamp bulbs, models without front fog lamps — 740 and 900 shown, others similar

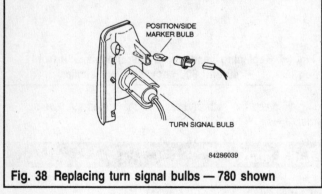

Fig. 38 Replacing turn signal bulbs — 780 shown

240 Wagon

▶ See Figure 40

All bulbs in the tail light cluster are removed from inside the trunk.

1. Left-hand: Remove the spare tire cover and the spare wheel assembly.

2. Right-hand: Remove the stowage cover. Loosen the clip and move the panel aside.

3. Depress the bulb, turn it slightly counterclockwise and remove it.

4. When reinstalling, hold the bulb holder with the word 'Volvo' turned towards the center of the vehicle.

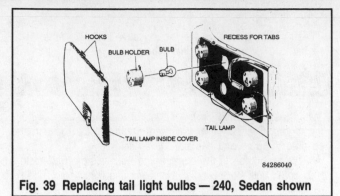

Fig. 39 Replacing tail light bulbs — 240, Sedan shown

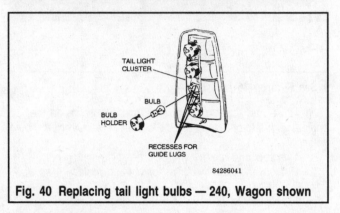

Fig. 40 Replacing tail light bulbs — 240, Wagon shown

700 and 900 Series

▶ See Figures 41 and 42

All bulbs in the tail light cluster are removed from inside the trunk. To avoid confusion, replace bulbs one at a time.

1. Unscrew and remove the tail lamp inside cover. Note that the inside cover is hooked at the lower edge.

2. Remove the plastic screw and remove the bulb holder and bulb as a unit.

3. Depress the bulb in the bulb holder, turn it slightly counterclockwise and remove it.

4. Install a new bulb. Install the bulb holder in the tail lamp.

5. Check that the bulb lights. Replace the tail lamp inside cover.

License Plate Light

REMOVAL & INSTALLATION

240 Series

SEDAN

1. Slide the bulb housing backwards until it is released from the front edge.

2. Pull out the lamp housing and remove the bulb.

3. Install a new bulb. Insert the front edge of the lamp housing and press up the rear edge by hand.

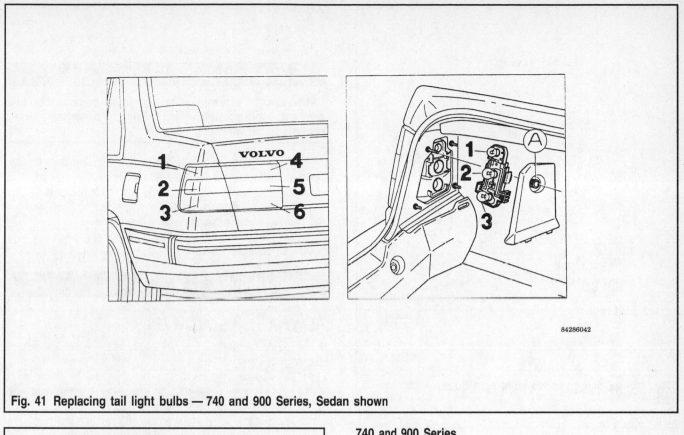

Fig. 41 Replacing tail light bulbs — 740 and 900 Series, Sedan shown

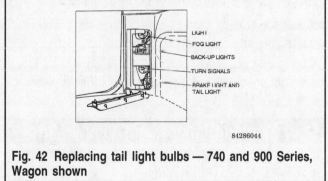

Fig. 42 Replacing tail light bulbs — 740 and 900 Series, Wagon shown

WAGON

1. Insert a screwdriver through the opening in the housing and depress the catch tab.

❋❋WARNING

When using a screwdriver to pry plastic components, use care and avoid scratching or breaking. If necessary, wear eye protection whenever possible.

2. Pull out the housing assembly.
3. Installation is the reverse of the removal procedure.

740 and 900 Series

▶ See Figure 43

Remove the screws from the light housing. Insert a screwdriver and pry off the light assembly. Replace the bulb and re-install the light housing.

780 Series

▶ See Figure 44

1. Slide the bulb housing backwards until it is released from the front edge.
2. Pull out the lamp housing and remove the bulb.
3. Install a new bulb. Insert the front edge of the lamp housing and press up the rear edge by hand.

High-Mounted Stop Light

REMOVAL & INSTALLATION

240 Series

1. On sedans, use a screwdriver to depress the catch, then pull the plastic cover up and away from the light assembly.

❋❋WARNING

When using a screwdriver to pry plastic components, use care and avoid scratching or breaking. If necessary, wear eye protection whenever possible.

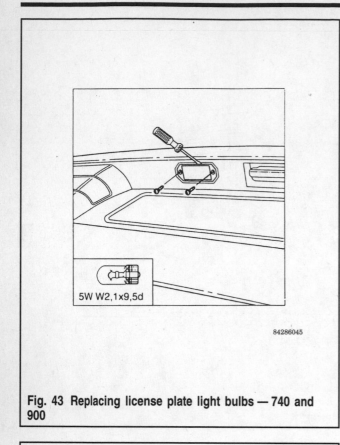

Fig. 43 Replacing license plate light bulbs — 740 and 900

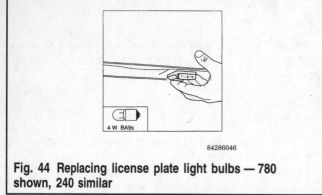

Fig. 44 Replacing license plate light bulbs — 780 shown, 240 similar

2. On wagons, depress the marked areas on the side of the housing and pull it away from the light assembly.

3. Press in the reflector catch to release the reflector assembly. Swing out the reflector and remove the bulb.

4. Install a new bulb and snap the reflector into position. Check that the bulb light when the brake pedal is depressed.

5. Align the light assembly catches with the holes in the lamp housing and press it into place.

700 and 900 Series

▶ See Figure 45

1. Depress the catch with a screwdriver.

❋❋WARNING

When using a screwdriver to pry plastic components, use care and avoid scratching or breaking. If necessary, wear eye protection whenever possible.

2. Grasp the cover with both hands and pull it towards you. Depress the catches and fit a new bulb.

3. Install the reflector and check that the light works.

4. On Sedan models, press the cover into position, noting the position of the alignment pin at the top.

5. On Wagon models, align the catches and press the cover into position.

Interior Light

REMOVAL & INSTALLATION

240 Series

1. Insert a screwdriver through the opening in the right side of the housing and depress the catch tab.

2. Pull out the housing assembly and remove the bulb.

3. Installation is the reverse of the removal procedure.

700 and 900 Series

▶ See Figure 46

Take hold of the front section of the light and pull the housing straight down. Replace the bulb and check its operation. Install the bulb housing.

Door Warning Lamps and Vanity Mirror

REMOVAL & INSTALLATION

▶ See Figures 47 and 48

Insert a screwdriver and turn it to remove the lens. Replace the bulb and press the lens back into place.

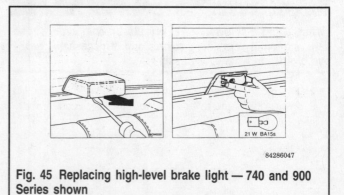

Fig. 45 Replacing high-level brake light — 740 and 900 Series shown

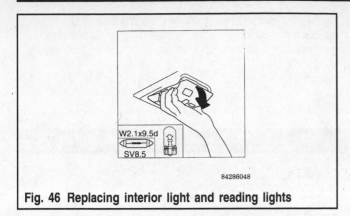

Fig. 46 Replacing interior light and reading lights

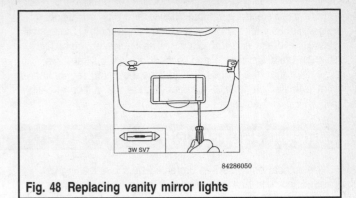

Fig. 48 Replacing vanity mirror lights

Engine Compartment and/or Trunk Light

REMOVAL & INSTALLATION

1. Remove the lamp assembly retaining screws. Lift out and remove.
2. Replace the bulb.
3. Reinstall by first inserting the guides into one side, then press in the light assembly.
4. Install the retaining screws.

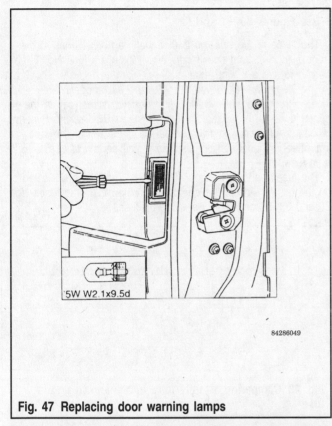

Fig. 47 Replacing door warning lamps

TRAILER WIRING

Wiring the vehicle for towing is fairly easy. There are a number of good wiring kits available and these should be used, rather than trying to design your own. All trailers will need brake lights and turn signals as well as tail lights and side marker lights. Most states require extra marker lights for overly wide trailers. Also, most states have recently required back-up lights for trailers, and most trailer manufacturers have been building trailers with back-up lights for several years.

Additionally, some Class I, most Class II and just about all Class III trailers will have electric brakes.

Add to this number an accessories wire, to operate trailer internal equipment or to charge the trailer's battery, and you can have as many as seven wires in the harness.

Determine the equipment on your trailer and buy the wiring kit necessary. The kit will contain all the wires needed, plus a plug adapter set which included the female plug, mounted on the bumper or hitch, and the male plug, wired into, or plugged into the trailer harness.

When installing the kit, follow the manufacturer's instructions. The color coding of the wires is standard throughout the industry.

One point to note, some domestic vehicles, and most imported vehicles, have separate turn signals. On most domestic vehicles, the brake lights and rear turn signals operate with the same bulb. For those vehicles with separate turn signals, you can purchase an isolation unit so that the brake lights won't blink whenever the turn signals are operated, or, you can go to your local electronics supply house and buy four diodes to wire in series with the brake and turn signal bulbs. Diodes will isolate the brake and turn signals. The choice is yours. The isolation units are simple and quick to install, but far more expensive than the diodes. The diodes, however, require more work to install properly, since they require the cutting of each bulb's wire and soldering in place of the diode.

One final point, the best kits are those with a spring loaded cover on the vehicle mounted socket. This cover prevents dirt and moisture from corroding the terminals. Never let the vehicle socket hang loosely. Always mount it securely to the bumper or hitch.

CIRCUIT PROTECTION

All electrical equipment is protected from overloading by fuses. Each fuse has an amperage rating that will allow it to transmit a predetermined amount of current before its filament melts, thereby stopping the excessive current flow. By providing this engineered 'weak spot' in the circuit, the first failure will occur at a known location (the fuse), eliminating hours of tracing wiring harnesses to locate a problem.

If a fuse blows repeatedly, the trouble is probably in the electrical component that the fuse protects. NEVER replace a fuse with another of a higher ampere rating. Sometimes a fuse will blow when all of the electrical equipment protected by the fuse is operating, especially under severe weather conditions. For this reason, it is wise to carry a few spare fuses of each type in the car.

When tracking down an inoperative electrical circuit, follow a logical pattern. Wiring itself is rarely the problem. Remember that in some cases a fuse can look good but not be capable of passing an electrical load. Either remove the fuse and check it with an ohmmeter or simply replace it with a new one. Always have the ignition switched off when removing and replacing fuses. On all models, the circuit that each fuse protects is given either on the fuse box cover or in the owners manual.

Fuses

▶ See Figure 49

A blown fuse is indicated by the failure of all units protected by it. It is caused by overloading the circuits. Examine the curved metal wire, on the inside of the fuse, to see if it is broken. If so, replace with a new fuse of the same color and amperage.

LOCATION

240 Series

▶ See Figures 50, 51 and 52

The fuses and relays, on 240 models, are positioned in the front of the left front door pillar. When installing fuse No. 1, be certain to use a 8 amp fuse.

The fuses and relays, on the 780 and 940 models, are located in the central electrical unit behind the ashtray in the center console. In addition, a fuse for the ABS Braking System is located under the instrument panel, to the left of the steering wheel. When installing fuse No. 5, be certain to use a 15 amp fuse.

The fuses and relays, on 740 and 960 models, are located on the far left side of the dashboard. When installing fuses No. 26 and 33, be certain to use 10 amp fuses.

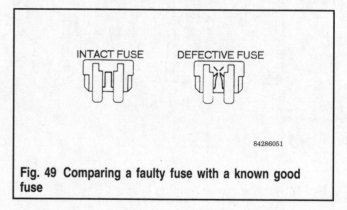

84286051

Fig. 49 Comparing a faulty fuse with a known good fuse

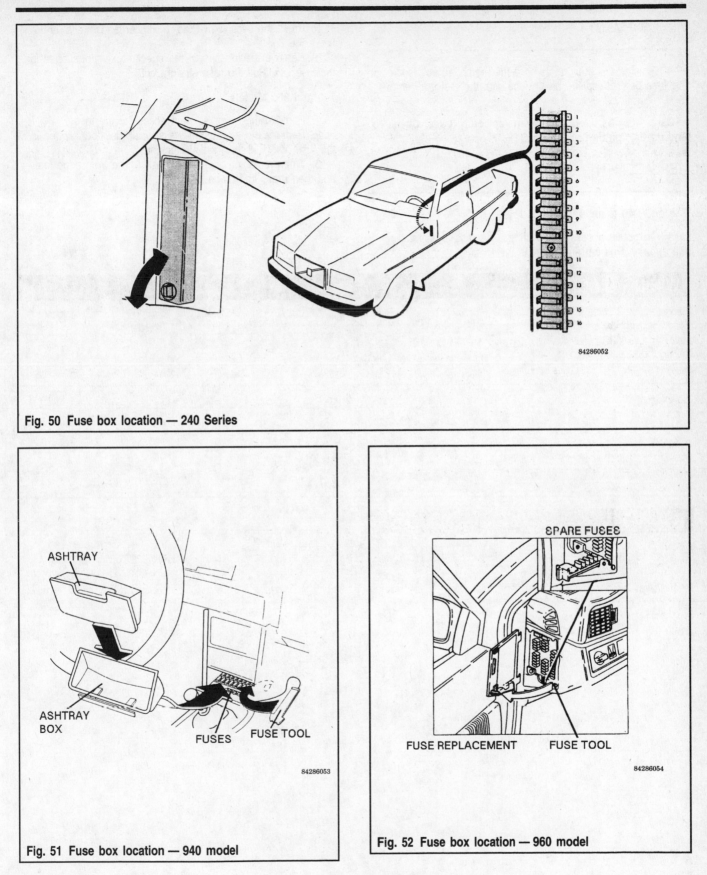

Fig. 50 Fuse box location — 240 Series

84286052

Fig. 51 Fuse box location — 940 model

ASHTRAY

ASHTRAY BOX

FUSES

FUSE TOOL

84286053

Fig. 52 Fuse box location — 960 model

SPARE FUSES

FUSE REPLACEMENT

FUSE TOOL

84286054

REPLACEMENT

All vehicles are equipped with a fuse removal tool, located in the fuse box. Grasp the blown fuse with the tool and remove it.

➡**Care must be exercised when replacing fuses. Check to ensure the ignition switch is OFF.**

REPLACEMENT

780 and 940 Models

1. To obtain access to the central electrical unit, remove the ashtray. Pull out and depress the tongue.

2. Press the section marked 'electrical fuses-press' and remove the unit.

3. Remove the fuse using the special fuse tool clipped in the fuse box. Pull the fuse straight out.

740 and 960 Models

1. Remove the cover, to gain access to the fuses.

2. Remove the fuse using the special fuse tool clipped in the fuse box. Pull the fuse straight out.

3. When replacing the cover, push in the front edge first and then press into place.

WIRING DIAGRAMS

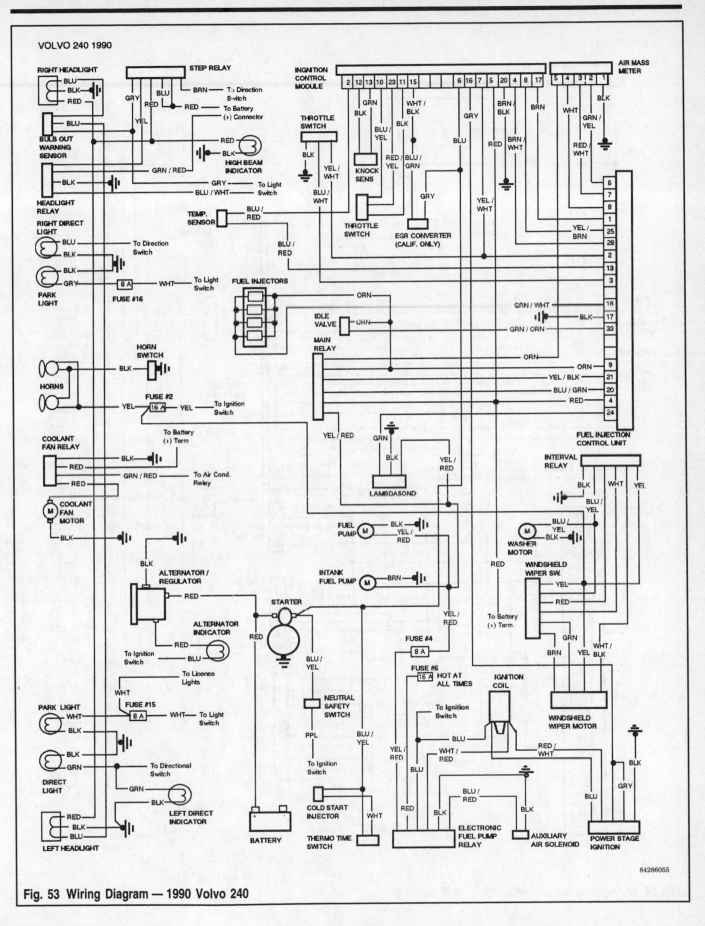

Fig. 53 Wiring Diagram — 1990 Volvo 240

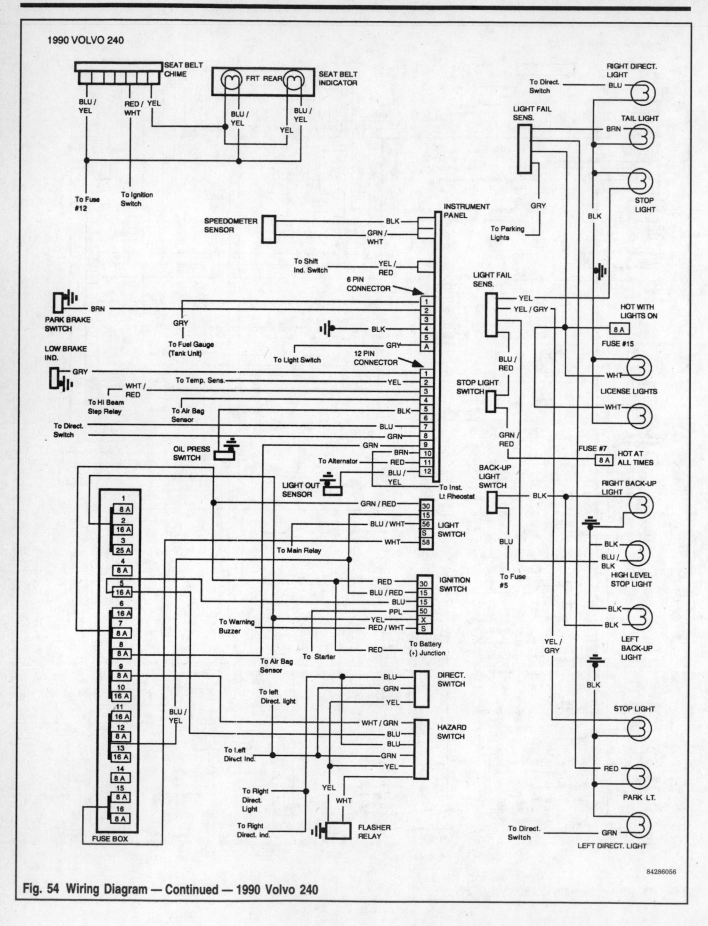

Fig. 54 Wiring Diagram — Continued — 1990 Volvo 240

84286056

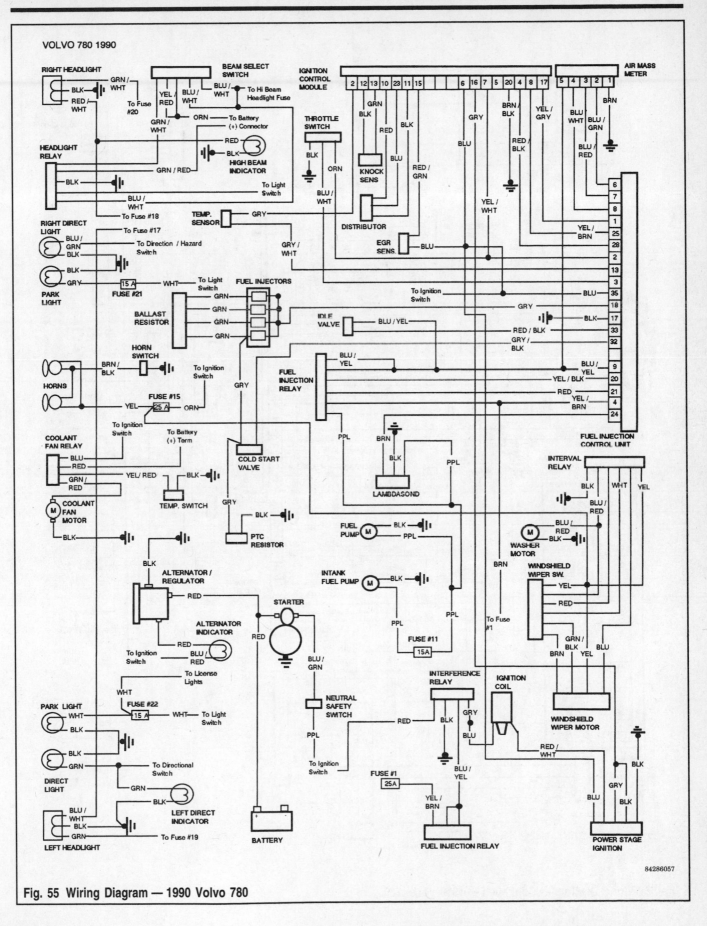

Fig. 55 Wiring Diagram — 1990 Volvo 780

84286057

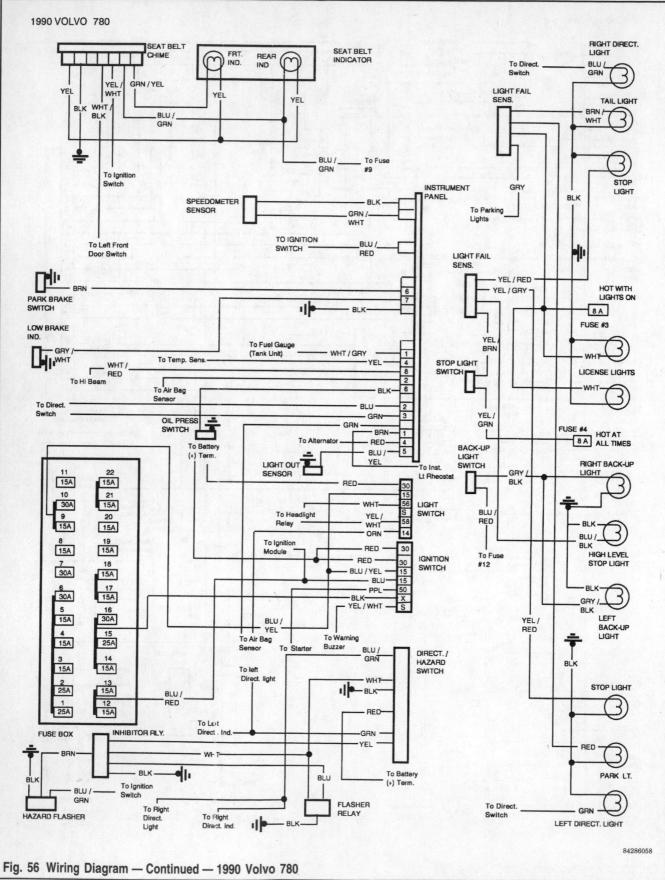

Fig. 56 Wiring Diagram — Continued — 1990 Volvo 780

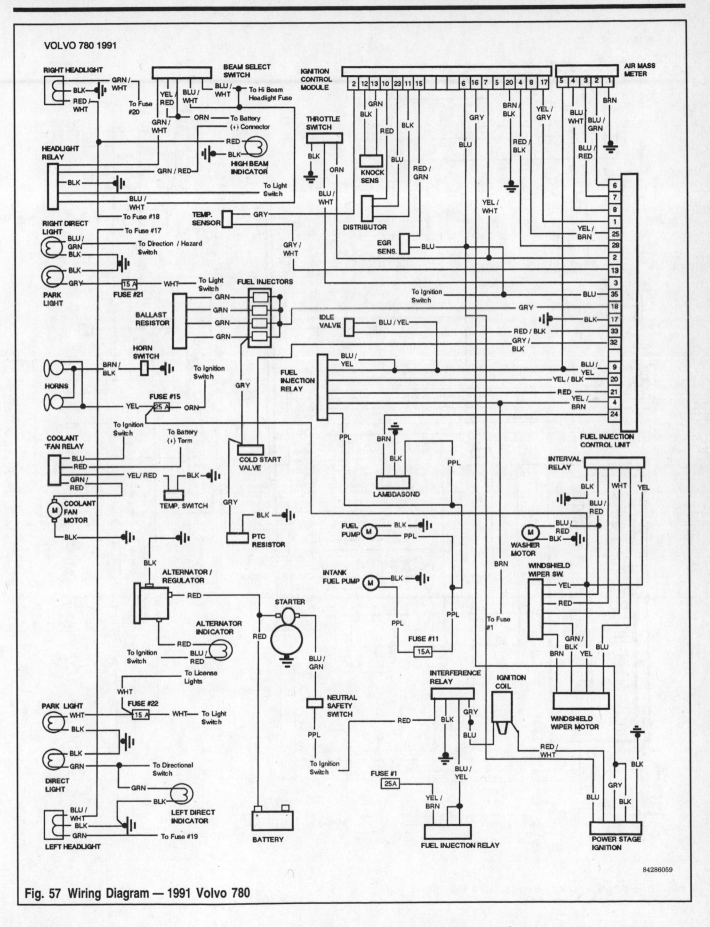

Fig. 57 Wiring Diagram — 1991 Volvo 780

84286059

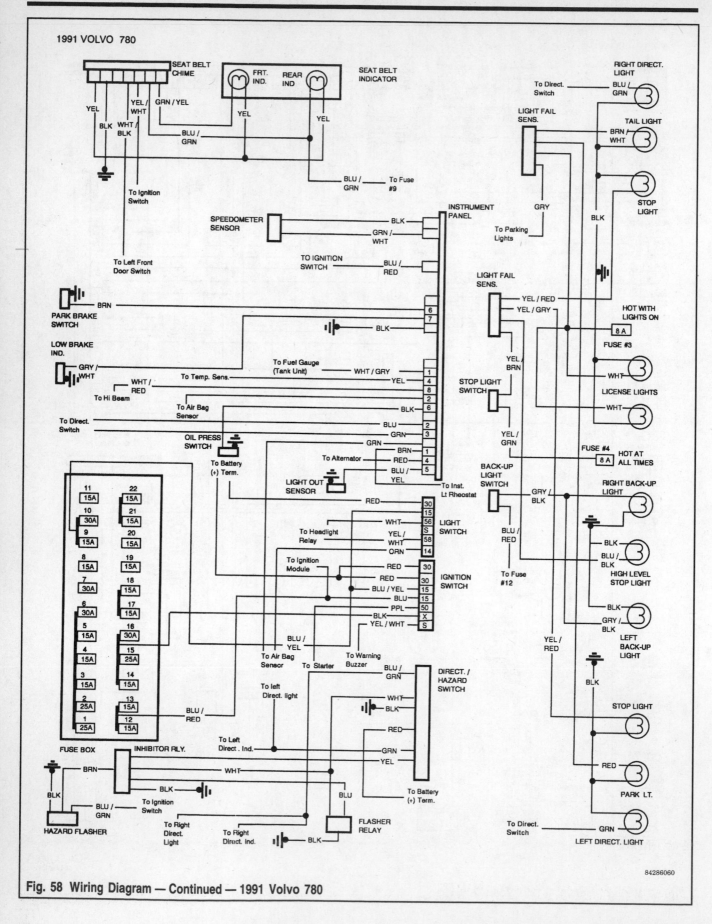

1991 VOLVO 780

Fig. 58 Wiring Diagram — Continued — 1991 Volvo 780

84286060

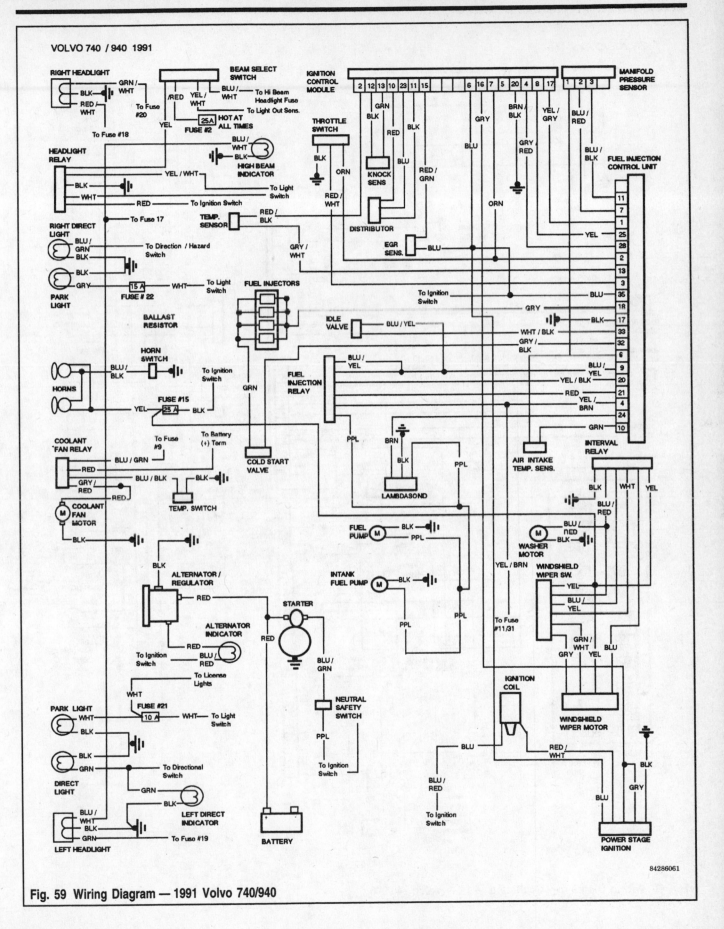

Fig. 59 Wiring Diagram — 1991 Volvo 740/940

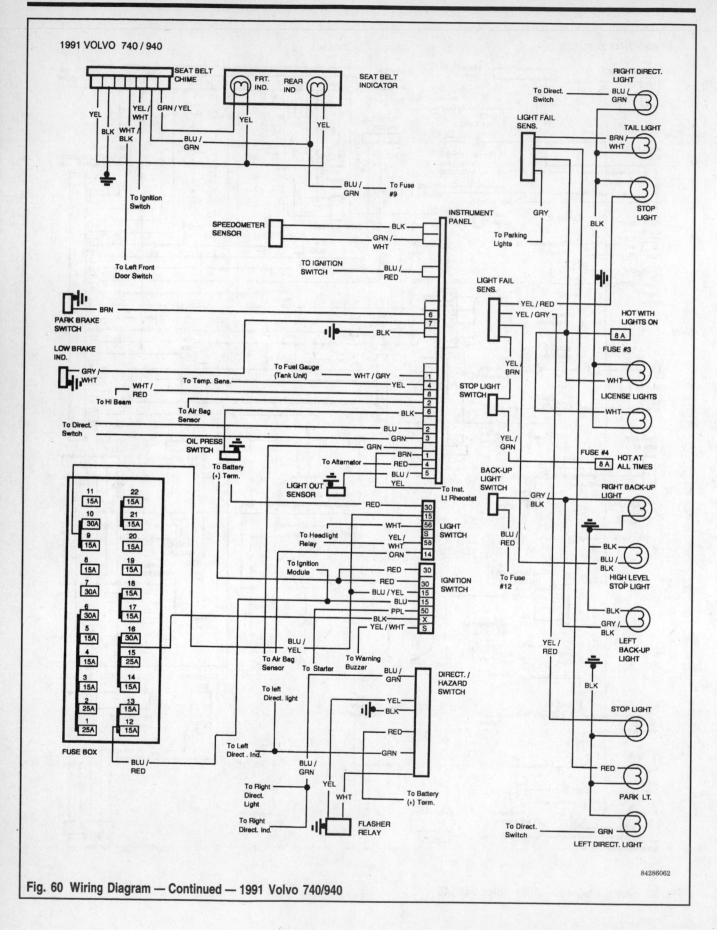

Fig. 60 Wiring Diagram — Continued — 1991 Volvo 740/940

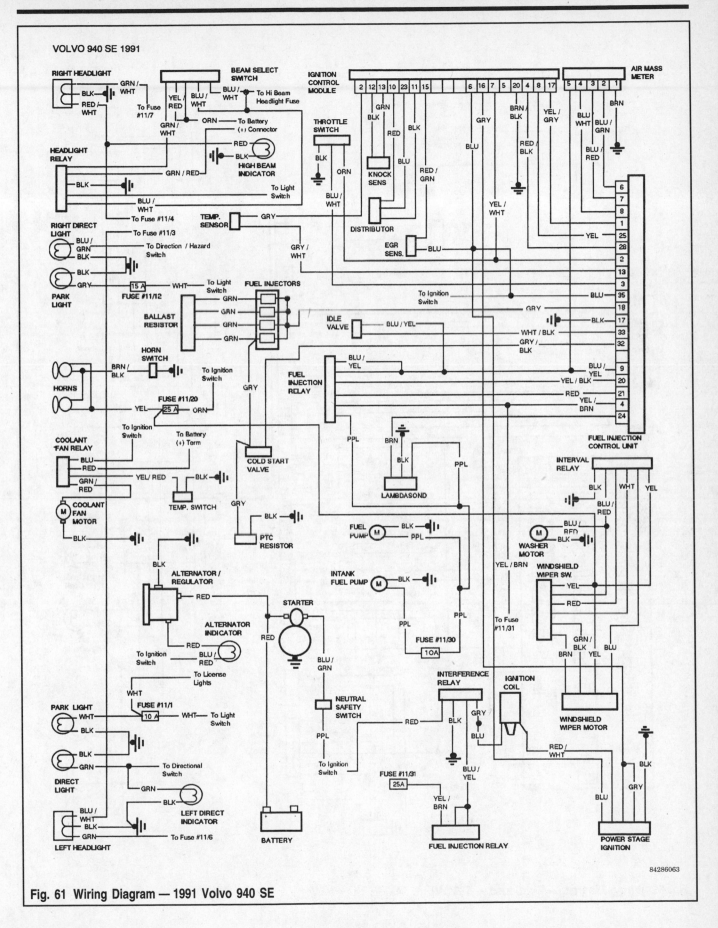

Fig. 61 Wiring Diagram — 1991 Volvo 940 SE

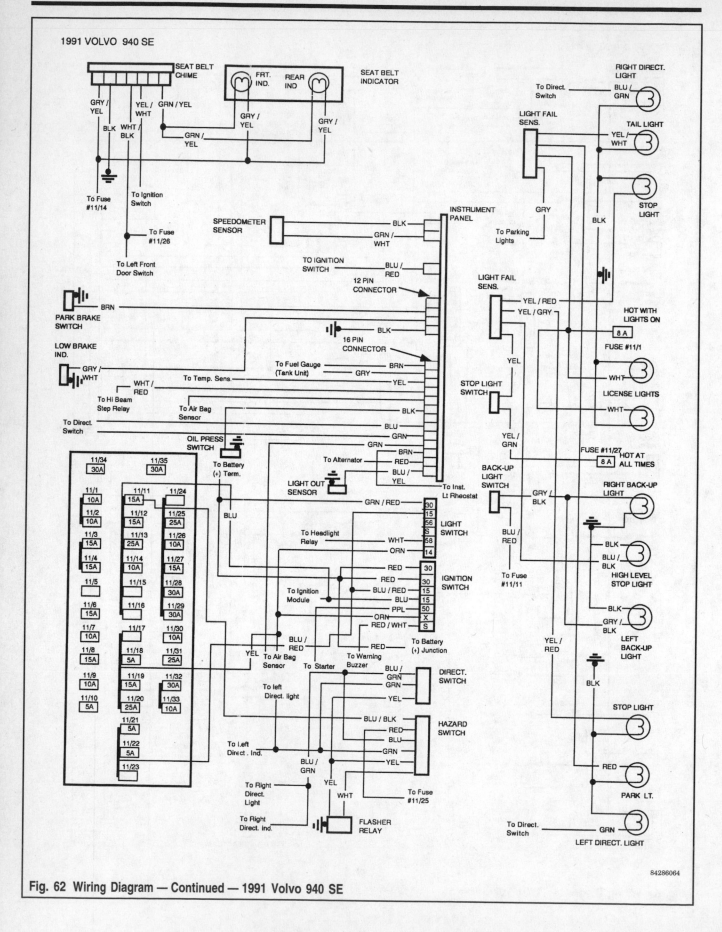

Fig. 62 Wiring Diagram — Continued — 1991 Volvo 940 SE

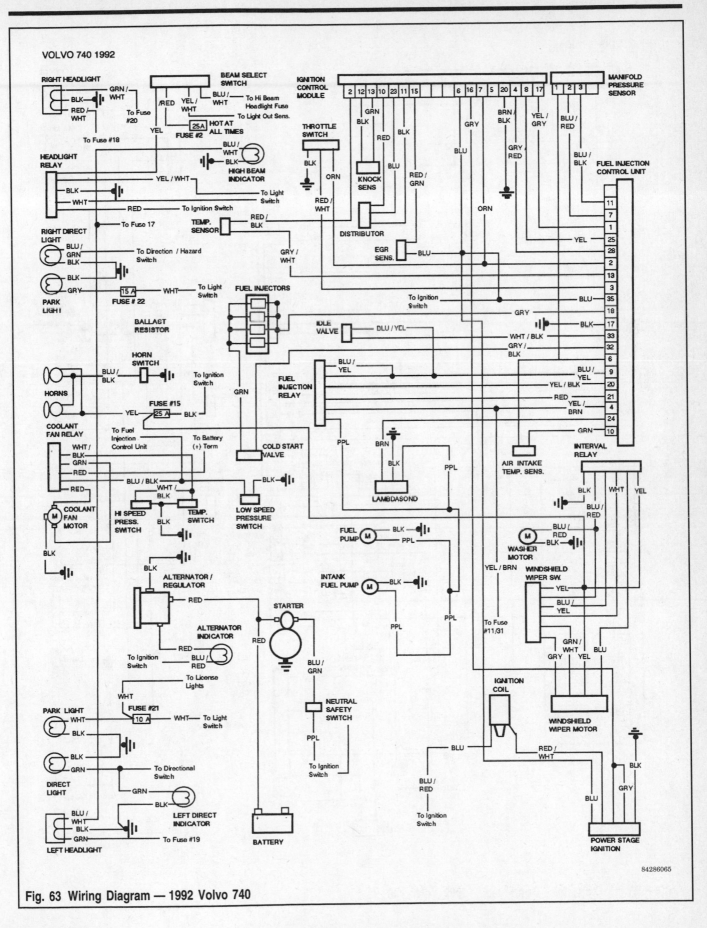

Fig. 63 Wiring Diagram — 1992 Volvo 740

84286065

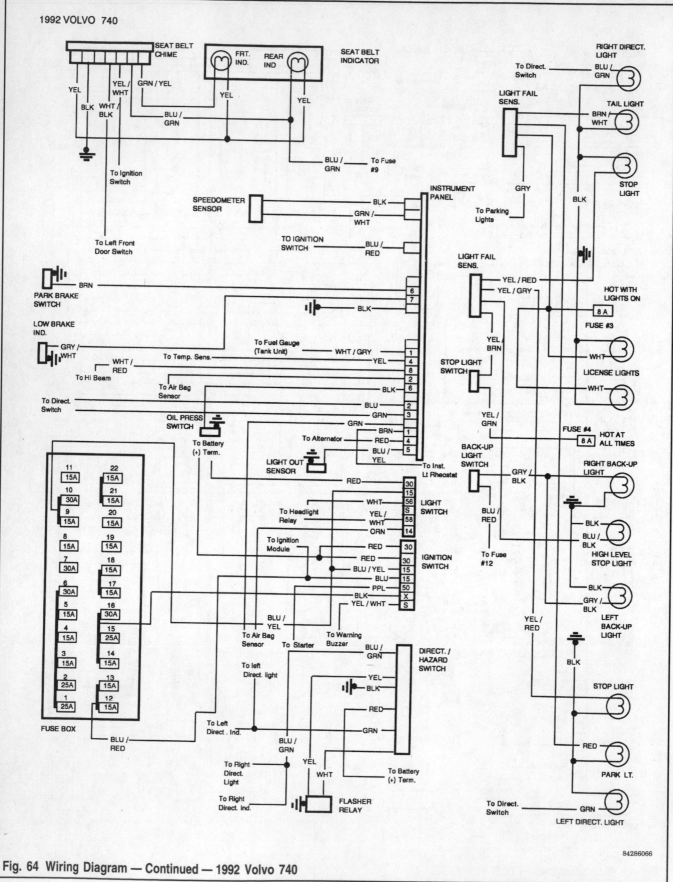

Fig. 64 Wiring Diagram — Continued — 1992 Volvo 740

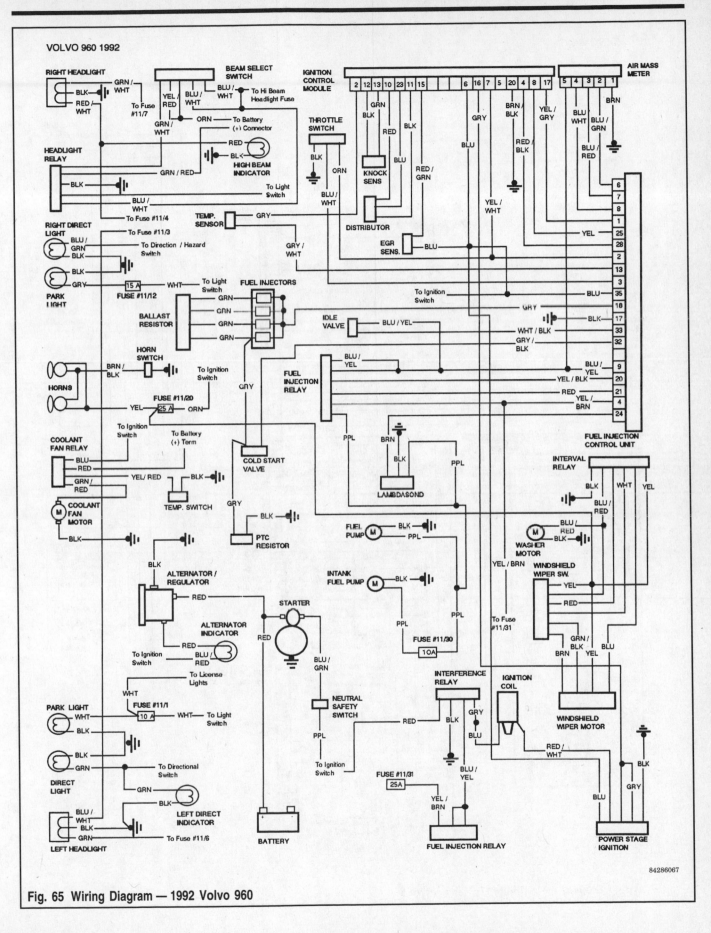

Fig. 65 Wiring Diagram — 1992 Volvo 960

84286067

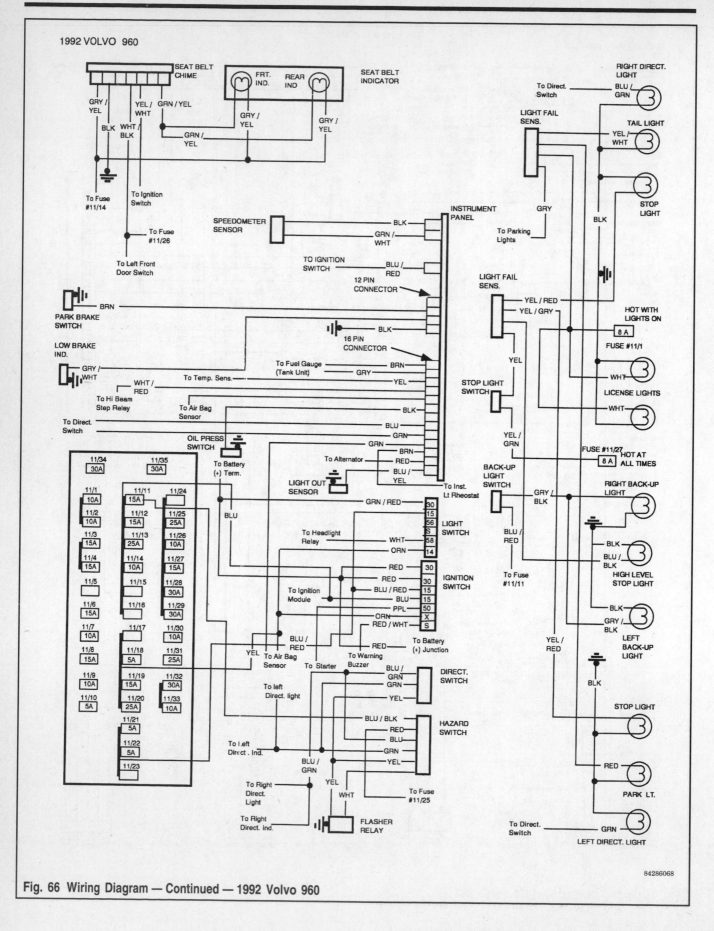

Fig. 66 Wiring Diagram — Continued — 1992 Volvo 960

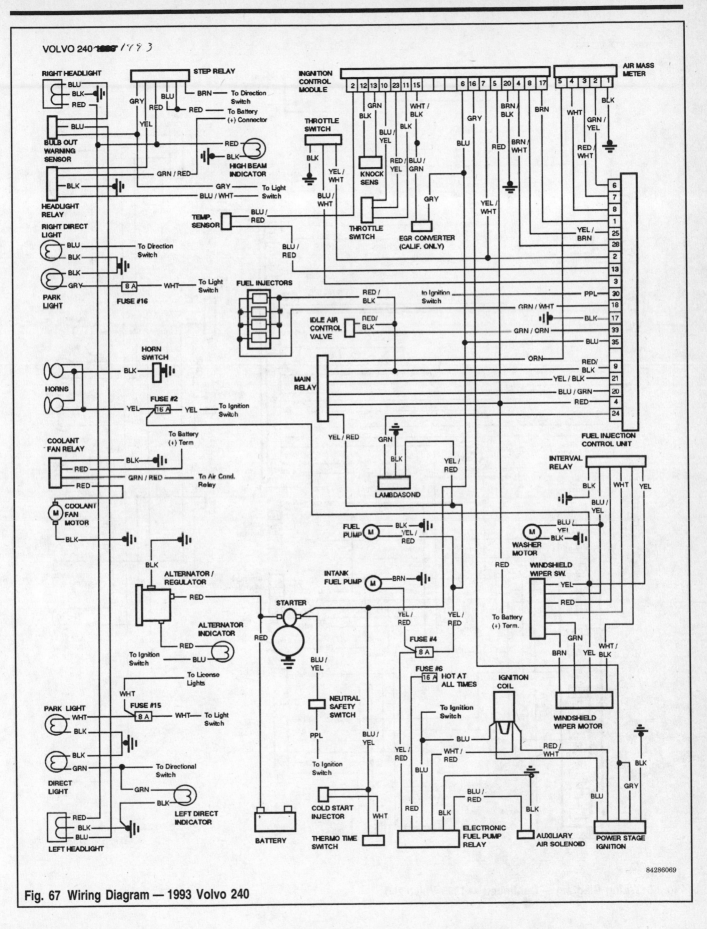

Fig. 67 Wiring Diagram — 1993 Volvo 240

84286069

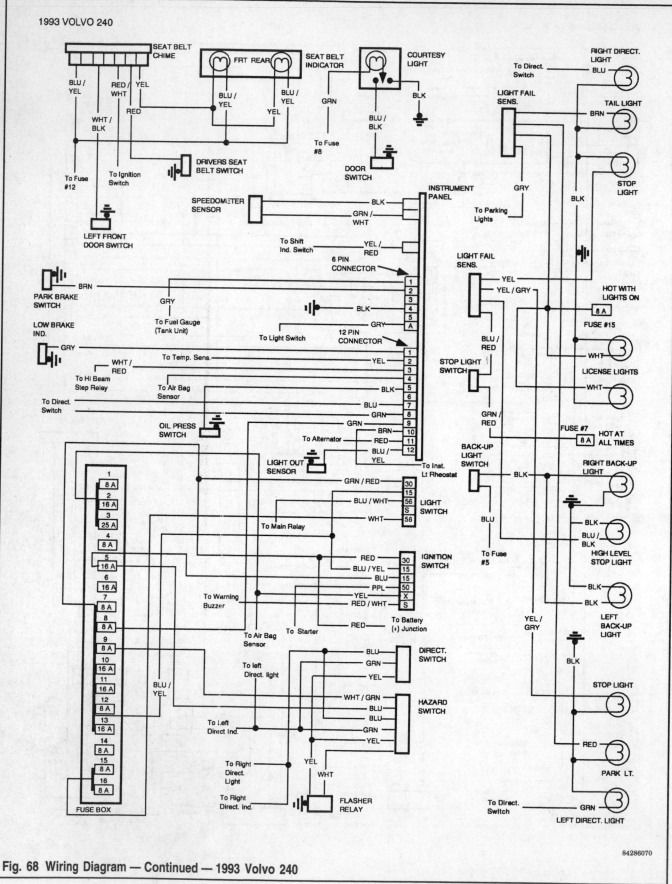

Fig. 68 Wiring Diagram — Continued — 1993 Volvo 240

7

DRIVE
TRAIN

MANUAL TRANSMISSION

Understanding the Manual Transmission

Because of the way an internal combustion engine breathes, it can produce torque, or twisting force, only within a narrow speed range. Most modern, overhead valve engines must turn at about 2,500 rpm to produce their peak torque. By 4,500 rpm they are producing so little torque that continued increases in engine speed produce no power increases.

The manual transmission and clutch are employed to vary the relationship between engine speed and the speed of the wheels so that adequate engine power can be produced under all circumstances. The clutch allows engine torque to be applied to the transmission input shaft gradually, due to mechanical slippage. The vehicle can, consequently, be started smoothly from a full stop.

The transmission changes the ratio between the rotating speeds of the engine and the wheels by the use of gears. The lower gears allow full engine power to be applied to the rear wheels during acceleration at low speeds.

The transmission contains a mainshaft which is separated at one point, so that front and rear portions can turn at different speeds.

Power is transmitted by a countershaft in the lower gears and reverse. The gears of the countershaft mesh with gears on the mainshaft, allowing power to be carried from one to the other. All the countershaft gears are integral with that shaft, while several of the mainshaft gears can either rotate independently of the shaft or be locked to it. Shifting from one gear to the next causes one of the gears to be freed from rotating with the shaft and locks another to it. Gears are locked and unlocked by internal dog clutches which slide between the center of the gear and the shaft. The forward gears usually employ synchronizers; friction members which smoothly bring gear and shaft to the same speed before the toothed dog clutches are engaged.

Identification

▶ See Figures 1 and 2

The manual transmissions, used on 240 and 740 models, can be identified by referring to the Service Designation Number plate, found on the upper right side radiator support. A 10-digit Vehicle Identification Code (VIC), located in the upper right-hand corner of the Service Designation Number plate, contains information on the type of transmission used. The 9th digit of the VIC designate the transmission type and can be termed as follows:

2 = M46 (4-speed manual transmission, with controlled overdrive fifth gear)

3 = M47 (5-speed manual transmission)

The M46 transmission is used in combination with B230FT and 234F engines. The M47 is used in combination with B230F engine.

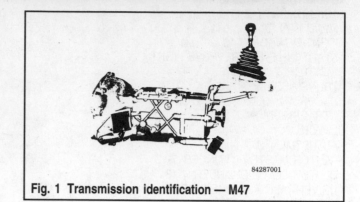

Fig. 1 Transmission identification — M47

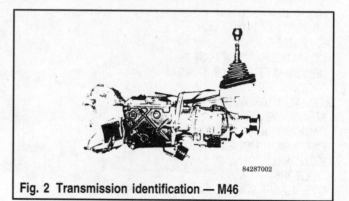

Fig. 2 Transmission identification — M46

Both the M46 and M47 have the same 4-speed basic gear unit. Consequently when comparing the transmissions, only the 5th gear housing is taken into consideration. M47 differs from M46 as follows:

• A 5th gear housing containing 2 gear wheels with gear dogteeth, synchronizing ring and sleeve
• Additional selector shaft for 5th gear
• Modified gear selector shaft for 5th gear
• Modified gear selector plate
• Input shaft O-bearing is a press fit in the transmission
• Countershaft front bearing is a cylindrical roller bearing and not a taper roller bearing
• Countershaft is longer and consists of 2 parts with an extra journal
• Shim for adjusting countershaft end float is in a different position
• Mainshaft has an extra journal comprising a roller bearing in the rear casing

Adjustments

SHIFT LINKAGE

Shift linkage adjustments are neither necessary nor possible on Volvo manual transmissions. The linkage is mounted internally and is permanently bathed in oil.

Back-up Light Switch

REMOVAL & INSTALLATION

▶ **See Figure 3**

1. Raise the vehicle and support it safely on jackstands.
2. Matchmark and remove the front driveshaft from the transmission or overdrive unit; lower the shaft out of the way.
3. Position and support the transmission with a jack or transmission hoist.
4. Loosen, but do not separate the exhaust joint at the right side of the transmission case.
5. Carefully remove the transmission crossmember from the body.
6. Lower the rear end of the transmission.
7. Disconnect the wiring from the switch. Thoroughly clean the area around the switch before removing it. Remove the switch using a suitable socket (5250 or equivalent).

To install:

8. Installation is the reverse of the removal procedure. After replacing the switch and connecting the wiring, check its function before reassembling everything.
9. Raise the transmission back into position and install the crossmember. Position and tighten the exhaust joint.
10. Reinstall the driveshaft. Lower the vehicle from its stands.

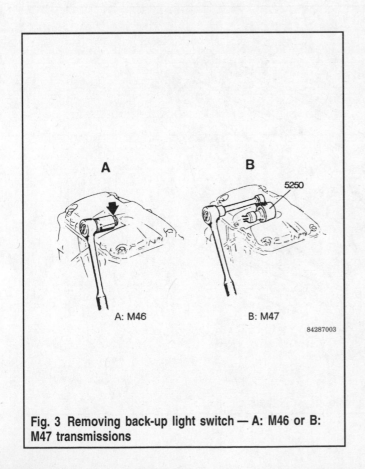

Fig. 3 Removing back-up light switch — A: M46 or B: M47 transmissions

Extension Housing Seal

REMOVAL & INSTALLATION

1. Disconnect the negative battery cable.
2. Raise and support the vehicle safely.
3. Matchmark the driveshaft with the coupling.
4. Disconnect the driveshaft. Use tool (5244 or equivalent) for a round coupling flange.
5. Remove the coupling flange nut. Use spanner (5149 or equivalent) to prevent the flange from rotating. Remove the coupling flange, using a suitable puller (2261 or equivalent).
6. Carefully pry the seal from the housing.

To install:

7. Clean the sealing areas thoroughly. Install a new seal using a suitable drift (2412 for M46 or 5064 for M47 or their equivalent).
8. Press the coupling flange into place, using tool 1845 or equivalent.
9. Install the coupling flange nut. Torque to 126 ft. lbs. (175 Nm) — on the M46 or 65-80 ft. lbs. (90-110 Nm) on the M47.
10. Complete installation in the order of the removal procedure.

Transmission

REMOVAL & INSTALLATION

▶ **See Figure 4**

240

1. Disconnect the battery. At the firewall, disconnect the back-up light connector.
2. Raise the front of the vehicle and install jackstands. Under the vehicle: Loosen the setscrew and drive out the pin for the shifter rod. Disconnect the shift lever from the rod.
3. Inside the vehicle: Pull up the shift boot. Remove the fork for the reverse gear detent. Remove the snapring and lift up the shifter. If overdrive-equipped, disconnect the engaging switch wire.
4. Disconnect the clutch cable and return spring at the fork.
5. Disconnect the exhaust pipe bracket(s) from the flywheel cover. Remove the oil pan splash guard.
6. Using a floor jack and a block of wood, support the engine beneath the oil pan. Remove the transmission support crossmember.
7. Disconnect the driveshaft. Disconnect the speedometer cable. If so equipped, disconnect the overdrive wire.
8. Remove the starter retaining bolts and pull the starter free of the flywheel housing. Leave the starter wiring connected and secure the starter out of the way.

✳✳CAUTION

The transmission is heavy. Support its weight with a second jack or hoist before removing. Do not allow the transmission to hang partially removed on the shaft.

9. Support the transmission using another floor jack. Remove the flywheel (bell) housing-to-engine bolts and remove the transmission by pulling it straight back.

To install:

10. Prior to installation, inspect the condition of the clutch and throwout bearing. Replace the bearing if it is scored or has been noisy in operation.

11. After reinstalling the transmission, tighten the mounting bolts to 30 ft. lbs. Secure the starter to the bellhousing. Fill the transmission with fluid to the proper level.

12. Connect the driveshaft, the speedometer cable and if necessary, the overdrive wiring.

13. Reinstall the transmission cross member. When secure, remove the jack from beneath the engine. Replace the splash guard and attach the exhaust bracket to the bell housing.

14. Reconnect the clutch cable and return spring to the fork.

15. Inside the vehicle: Connect the shifter and the reverse gear detent fork. Connect the wiring for the overdrive switch and install the shift boot and cover.

16. Under the vehicle: Connect the shifter rod to the shift lever. Don't forget to tighten the setscrew.

17. Connect the reverse light wiring and attach the negative battery cable.

700 Series

1. If possible, support the engine with a hoist or support apparatus such as Volvo tool 5006 or equivalent. The purpose of supporting the rear of the engine is to prevent damage to the fan, radiator or front engine mounts by limiting the downward travel of the engine when the transmission crossmember is removed. If no lifting apparatus is available, place a jack with a protective wooden block beneath the engine oil pan. Do not place the jack under the flywheel (clutch) housing.

2. Disconnect the battery ground cable. Remove the ashtray and holder assembly. Remove the trim box around the gear shift lever.

3. Disconnect the shift lever cover from the floor. Remove the snapring at the base of the shift lever.

4. Raise the vehicle and safely support it with jackstands. From underneath the vehicle, disconnect the gear shift rod at the gear shift lever. Remove the lock screw, and press out the pivot pin. Push up on the shift lever, and pull it up and out of the vehicle.

5. Matchmark the driveshaft and transmission flanges for later assembly. Disconnect the driveshaft from the transmission.

6. Separate the exhaust pipe at the joint under the vehicle. Detach the bracket from the front end of the exhaust pipe (near the bend).

7. Unbolt the transmission crossmember; at the same time, detach it from the rear support (rubber bushing).

8. Remove the rear support from the transmission. Lower the transmission, as required.

9. Tag and disconnect the electrical connectors from the overdrive, back-up light connector and the solenoid.

10. Cut the plastic clamp at the gear shift assembly from the wiring harness.

11. Remove the starter motor retaining bolts. Remove the cover plate under the bellhousing and the cover plate from the other starter motor opening, as required.

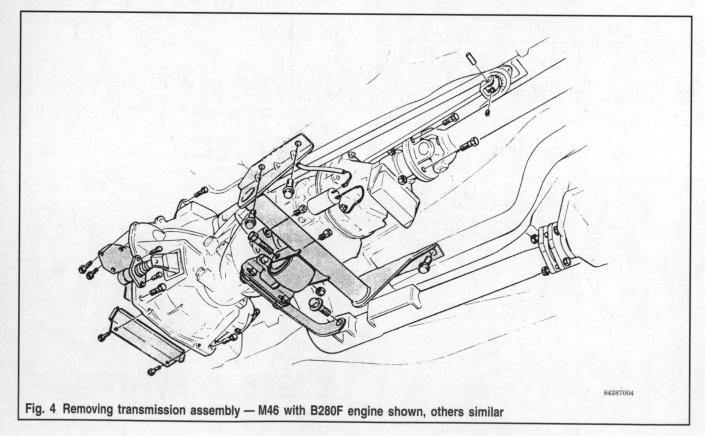

84287004

Fig. 4 Removing transmission assembly — M46 with B280F engine shown, others similar

12. Remove the slave cylinder from the bellhousing and upper bolts holding the bellhousing.

✳✳CAUTION

The transmission is heavy. Support its weight with a second jack or hoist before removing. Do not allow the transmission to hang partially removed on the shaft.

13. Place a transmission jack or a hydraulic floor jack underneath the transmission so that the transmission is resting on the jack pad. If possible, have another person steadying and guiding the transmission on the jack as it is lowered. Remove the lower bolts holding the bellhousing, and lower the transmission a few inches as you roll it back so the input shaft will clear. Stop the jack and make sure all wires and linkage are disconnected, then lower the transmission the rest of the way.

To install:

14. When installing the transmission, make sure the release bearing is correctly positioned in the shift fork, and that the input shaft is aligned in the clutch disc.

15. Install the upper bolts in the bellhousing. Raise the end of the transmission and attach the gear lever.

16. Attach the slave cylinder or clutch cable to its mounts.

17. Reinstall the starter motor.

18. Remount the gear lever to the transmission. Secure the connectors for the reverse lights, the solenoid and (on M46) the overdrive unit.

19. Replace the transmission crossmember. Set the engine back to its normal position.

20. Tighten the exhaust pipe joint, attach its bracket and attach the gear shift rod to the gear shift lever.

21. Install and tighten the driveshaft. Refill the transmission with the proper amount of fluid.

22. Connect the gear shift rod to the gear shift lever. Inside the vehicle, mount and secure the shifter assembly.

23. Double check all installation items, paying particular attention to loose hoses or hanging wires, untightened nuts, poor routing of hoses and wires (too tight or rubbing) and tools left in the work area.

24. Lower the vehicle. Install the ashtray, interior trim and shifter boot.

25. Reconnect the negative battery cable.

Overdrive

M46 Transmission

▶ **See Figure 5**

The overdrive unit is a planetary gear type and is mounted on the rear of the transmission. When the overdrive is in the direct drive position (overdrive switched off), power from the transmission mainshaft is transmitted through the freewheel rollers and uni-directional clutch to the overdrive output shaft.

When the vehicle is backing up or during periods of engine braking, torque is transmitted through the clutch sliding member which is held by spring pressure against the tapered portion of the output shaft.

When the overdrive is actuated, the clutch sliding member is pressed by hydraulic pressure against the brake disc (ring), which locks the sun wheel. As a result, the output shaft of the overdrive rotates at a higher speed than the mainshaft, thereby accomplishing a 20% reduction in engine speed in relation to vehicle speed.

REMOVAL & INSTALLATION

To prevent internal damage and facilitate removal, the vehicle should first be driven in 4th gear with the overdrive engaged, and then coasted for a few seconds with the overdrive disengaged and the clutch pedal depressed. This can be done with the rear wheels elevated and the vehicle on jackstands; however, make certain that the stands are properly located and on a very firm base. The overdrive unit can be removed with the transmission in the vehicle.

The internal workings of the overdrive are similar to an automatic transmission. The need for special pressure and clearance measuring tools puts this repair outside the scope of this book. Disassembly and internal repair of the overdrive is best left to a qualified technician.

1. Disconnect the negative battery cable. Raise and support the vehicle safely on jackstands.

2. Disconnect the driveshaft from the overdrive flange.

3. Support the engine from below with a jack. Use a block of wood to protect the oil pan.

4. Remove the transmission crossmember and lower the engine/transmission assembly about an inch. Check that the distributor does not hit the firewall.

5. Disconnect the wiring at the overdrive solenoid.

6. Position a second jack or transmission dolly under the overdrive unit. Remove the bolts holding the overdrive to the

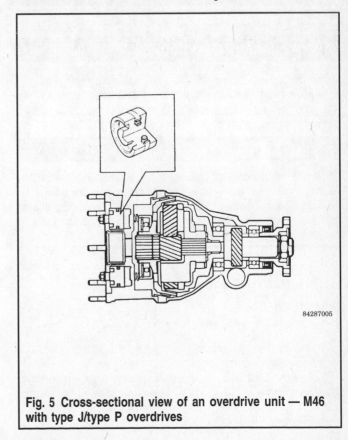

84287005

Fig. 5 Cross-sectional view of an overdrive unit — M46 with type J/type P overdrives

transmission and pull the overdrive unit straight back until free of the transmission output shaft.

To install:

7. When reinstalling, make sure that the overdrive unit is fitted straight onto the transmission shaft. At no time should it hang on the shaft partially installed.

8. Install the retaining bolts and torque to 5-8 ft. lbs. Reconnect the solenoid wiring. Raise the motor back to its proper position and install the transmission crossmember.

9. Reconnect the driveshaft to the output flange.

10. Lower the vehicle and reconnect the battery cable. If the overdrive was drained, refill the unit with the correct amount of fluid. Check the vehicle operation and recheck the fluid level. Top up if needed.

Overdrive Solenoid

REMOVAL & INSTALLATION

▶ See Figure 6

➡️ The solenoid and operating valve are one unit, and are replaced together.

1. Disconnect the wire clips from the solenoid unit.
2. Unscrew the solenoid from the side of the overdrive unit.
3. When installing, use a new seal and new O-rings. Immerse the O-rings in automatic transmission fluid prior to installation. Screw the solenoid into the overdrive by hand until snug. Using a crow's-foot open-end wrench attachment on a torque wrench, torque the solenoid unit to 37 ft. lbs.
4. Attach the wire clips, check overdrive oil level and check operation.

Transmission Overhaul

The procedures below refer to a manual transmission which is removed from the vehicle. If the unit has been removed with the overdrive attached, remove the overdrive unit before carrying out these procedures.

✳✳WARNING

The use of the correct special tools or their equivalent is required for this procedure. Do not begin repairs unless equipped with bearing pullers, hub pullers, snaring pliers, and variously sized bearing drivers and installation tools. Access to a press will also be required.

M46 and M47 Transmissions

DISASSEMBLE

▶ See Figures 7, 8, 9, 10, 11, 12, 13, 14 and 15

1. Mount the transmission securely on the workbench or attach to a transmission stand.
2. Unscrew the bolts for the transmission cover and remove the cover. Remove the spring and interlock (detent) ball for the shift forks. Remove the reverse light switch and the overdrive switch (except M47).

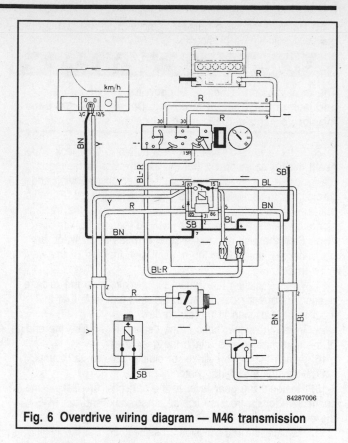

84287006

Fig. 6 Overdrive wiring diagram — M46 transmission

3. Remove the selector plate assembly and the return spring. Remove the gasket and clean the gasket surface.

4. Remove the glide washers for the selector plate assembly. Remove the locking pin for the shifter.

5. On M46 units, remove the overdrive unit.

6. Remove the gear shift carrier assembly.

7. Remove the sleeve for the gear shift rod joint. Tap out the rear pin in the gear shift rod, rotate the rod and remove the front pin. Remove the gear shift rod.

8. Unbolt and remove the intermediate housing; remove the gasket and shims.

9. Remove the gear selector rails, the shifter and the shift forks.

10. On M46 units, remove the eccentric for the overdrive oil pump by removing the lock ring and pulling off the eccentric. Catch the locking key as it falls clear.

11. Remove the lock ring and spacer for the mainshaft bearing.

12. Install a counterhold (Volvo 2985 or similar) between the input shaft and the front synchronizer. Remove the spacer ring and remove the mainshaft bearing. Remove the bearing thrust washer.

13. Remove the clutch fork, spacer and release bearing. Then remove the bolts for the clutch casing (bell housing) and remove the casing.

14. Remove the outer races for the intermediate shaft bearings. On cast iron housings, tap the shaft backwards until the rear outer bearing race comes free. Then tap the shaft forward until the front outer race can be removed. On aluminum cases (How can you tell? Use a magnet!) tap the shaft only enough to expose the race, then affix a puller (5177 or equivalent) and extract the race. Continued thumping on the shaft will crack the case. Don't risk it.

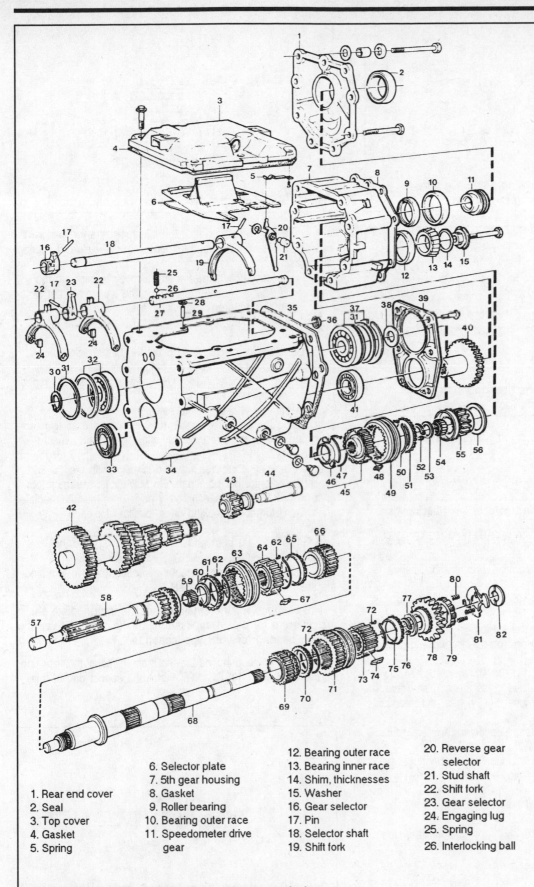

27. Selector shaft
28. Sliding washer
29. Guide pin
30. Lock ring
31. Shim, thicknesses
32. Ball bearing
33. Roller bearing
34. Transmission housing
35. Gasket
36. Seal
37. Ball bearing
38. Shim, thicknesses
39. Bearing holder
40. Drive gear
41. Roller bearing
42. Intermediate shaft
43. Reverse gear wheel
44. Stud shaft
45. Synchronizer hub
46. Drive flange
47. Spring
48. Sliding key ("dog")
49. Spring
51. Synchronizer ring
52. Lock ring
53. Spacer
54. Needle bearing
55. 5th gear wheel
56. Spacer
57. Sleeve
58. Input shaft
59. Needle bearing
60. Lock ring
61. Synchronizer ring
62. Spring
63. Operating sleeve
64. Synchronizer hub
65. Synchronizer ring
66. 3rd gear wheel
67. Sliding key
68. Mainshaft
69. 2nd gear wheel
70. Synchronizer ring
71. Operating sleeve
72. Spring
73. Synchronizer hub
74. Sliding key
75. Synchronizer ring
76. Lock ring
77. Washer
78. 1st gear wheel
79. Damper cone
80. Spring
81. Drive flange
82. Thrust washer (if not equipped with damper)

1. Rear end cover
2. Seal
3. Top cover
4. Gasket
5. Spring
6. Selector plate
7. 5th gear housing
8. Gasket
9. Roller bearing
10. Bearing outer race
11. Speedometer drive gear
12. Bearing outer race
13. Bearing inner race
14. Shim, thicknesses
15. Washer
16. Gear selector
17. Pin
18. Selector shaft
19. Shift fork
20. Reverse gear selector
21. Stud shaft
22. Shift fork
23. Gear selector
24. Engaging lug
25. Spring
26. Interlocking ball

84287008

Fig. 7 Components exploded view — M47 transmission

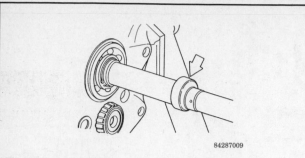

84287009

Fig. 8 Eccentric for overdrive oil pump. Be sure to catch the small locking pin during removal.

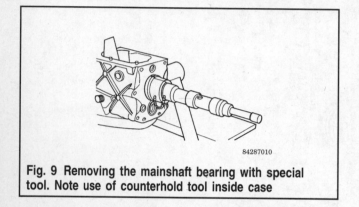

84287010

Fig. 9 Removing the mainshaft bearing with special tool. Note use of counterhold tool inside case

15. Pull out the input shaft and remove the 4th gear synchronizer ring.

16. Lift out the mainshaft.

17. Lift out the intermediate shaft, and on M47 units, the intermediate shaft extension.

18. Using a punch, tap the reverse gear shaft backwards and remove the gear and shaft.

19. Remove the reverse gear shift fork and remove the seal for the selector rail.

20. Using a suitable puller, remove the intermediate shaft bearings from the shaft.

21. Remove 1st gear and its synchronizer ring from the mainshaft.

22. Remove the lock ring for the 1st-2nd synchronizer hub. Using a press, support the hub and press the hub and gear off the shaft.

23. Remove the lock ring for the 3rd-4th synchronizer hub. Using a press, support the hub and press the hub and gear off the shaft. On M47 units, remove the 5th gear synchronizer, hub and gear.

24. Remove the locking ring and spacer ring for the input shaft bearing.

25. Again using the press and supporting the bearing, remove the bearing on the input shaft.

26. Remove the rubber ring from the gear shift rod joint.

27. Remove the gear shift rod bushings and the bell housing seal.

28. Disconnect the synchronizer hubs by pushing the hubs out of the sleeves.

ASSEMBLE

Before reassemble, clean all parts in solvent and examine the gears carefully for any signs of cracks or scoring, particu-

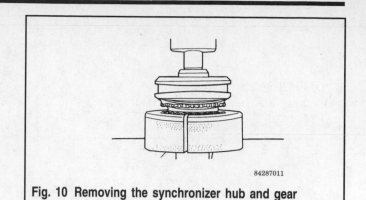

84287011

Fig. 10 Removing the synchronizer hub and gear

larly in the tooth areas. Check the synchronizers for excessive wear, and examine the bearings closely for any sign of scoring or cracks.

1. Begin assembling the transmission by building up the synchronizer hubs. Position the hub in the sleeve so that slots align with the chamfered teeth within the sleeve. Insert the dogs (3 in each synchro) and lock them in place with the springs.

2. Using the proper drivers, install the bell housing seal, position a new rubber ring in the shifter joint and install new bushings on the gear shift rod. Use grease to retain the rubber ring on the right side of the shifter rod.

3. Install a new seal for the selector rail in the case.

4. Using the press, assemble the 3rd gear and its synchronizer ring and install the assembly with the 3rd-4th synchronizer hub onto the main shaft. Repeat the procedure for the 2nd gear and synchronizer hub and install it with the 1st-2nd synchronizer onto the mainshaft. On M47 units, assemble 5th gear and its attendant synchronizer parts onto the intermediate shaft. Don't forget the locking rings (circlips) for each assembly.

5. Install the 1st gear and synchronizer ring onto the mainshaft.

6. Using a drift of the correct size, install the two intermediate shaft bearings onto the shaft.

➡**The bearings for the small end of the intermediate shaft are different for diesel applications. Make sure you use the correct bearing for your application.**

7. Install the bearing on the input shaft. Install the lock ring on the input shaft but DO NOT install the spacer ring at this

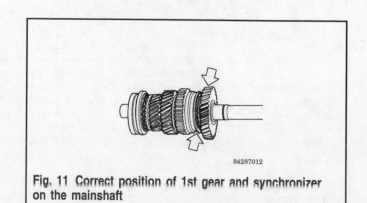

84287012

Fig. 11 Correct position of 1st gear and synchronizer on the mainshaft

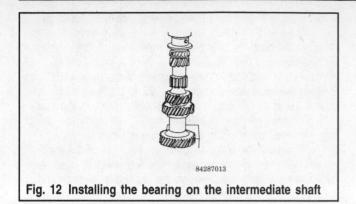

84287013

Fig. 12 Installing the bearing on the intermediate shaft

time. It will be installed later in the procedure. **Follow this subprocedure only if transmission case is aluminum:**

a. Position the intermediate shaft in its housing. Position the outer races for the intermediate shaft bearings in the case.

b. Install the bell housing with its gasket and torque its bolts to 30 ft. lbs.

c. Turn the transmission to a vertical position. Eliminate any play in the intermediate shaft bearings by tapping the bearing race until the clearance is gone and the shaft does not rotate easily.

d. Using an accurate metric depth gauge, measure the distance between the (intermediate shaft bearing) outer race and the rear surface of the case.

e. Calculate the thickness of shims for the intermediate shaft. Keep all your measurements and calculations in millimeters; replacement shims are not referenced in inch units.   Start with the depth just measured — let's say 1.50mm — and add 0.25mm for the gasket thickness. (1.50 + 0.25 = 1.75mm) The shaft free play spec is 0.03-0.08mm, so add that to your total. (1.75 + 0.03 to 0.08 = 1.78 to 1.83mm). Since shims are available only in multiples of 5, we choose in our example shims totalling 1.80mm.   Select the shims and set them aside; don't install them yet.

f. Since this was only for the purposes of preliminary measurement, remove the bellhousing and its gasket, remove the outer races for the intermediate shaft bearings and lift out the intermediate shaft.

8. Install the reverse gear shifter and lock ring. Install reverse gear and its shaft.

9. Check and adjust the position of the reverse gear shaft in the case. It should be 0.002 inches (0.05mm) below the housing face.

10. Adjust the clearance between reverse gear and the shift fork. Correct clearance is 0.004-0.04 inches (0.1-1.0mm). Perform adjustments by tapping the shift fork pivot pin with a punch to move it.

11. Position the intermediate shaft (and its extension for M47) in the bottom of the transmission case.

12. Position the main shaft in its housing.

13. Put the thrust washer and bearing on the mainshaft. The bearing should have its positioning ring in place.

14. Using tool 2831 or equivalent, press the mainshaft bearing into position. Press so that reverse gear is loaded towards the center of the transmission. Make sure that gears do not contact each other and cause damage.

15. Install the lock ring for the mainshaft bearing.

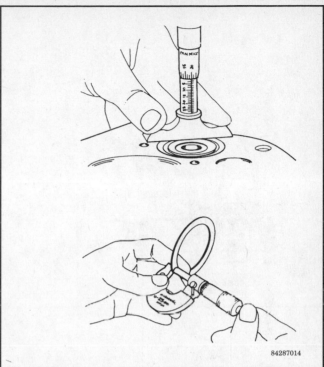

84287014

Fig. 13 Use a metric depth gauge to take necessary measurements, then select correct shim(s) based on calculations

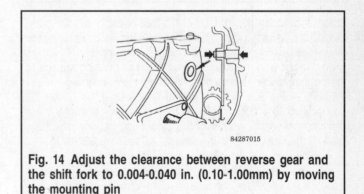

84287015

Fig. 14 Adjust the clearance between reverse gear and the shift fork to 0.004-0.040 in. (0.10-1.00mm) by moving the mounting pin

16. For M46 units, place the locking key in the mainshaft keyway and install the overdrive oil pump eccentric and its locking ring.

17. Coat the bearing with grease and install the roller bearing into the input shaft.

18. Place the 4th gear synchronizer ring in the hub.

19. Attach the input shaft to the mainshaft and push it in all the way. Lift up the intermediate shaft so that the bearings are correctly positioned in the housing.

20. Pull out the input shaft so that the spacer ring can be positioned on the bearing. Push the shaft back in; the spacer should lie against the housing.

21. Install the outer races for the intermediate shaft bearings. On units in aluminum cases, use a drift of the correct diameter.

22. Using a metric depth gauge, measure the distance between the front end of the input shaft bearing and the front surface of the case. Record this number. Now measure the

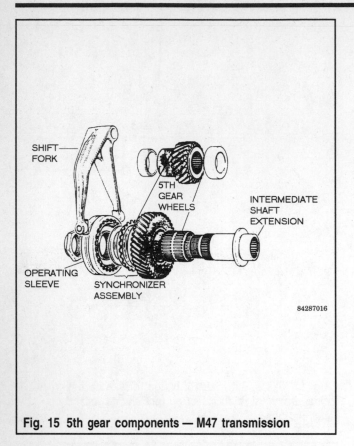

SHIFT FORK

5TH GEAR WHEELS

INTERMEDIATE SHAFT EXTENSION

OPERATING SLEEVE

SYNCHRONIZER ASSEMBLY

84287016

Fig. 15 5th gear components — M47 transmission

shaft by using a drift to tap the bearing race until the shaft has noticeable drag when turning. For units with iron cases, measure the distance between the outer race of the intermediate shaft bearing and the surface of the housing. To this measurement, add the known thickness of the gasket, 0.25mm. Subtract the allowable clearance, 0.025 to 0.10mm, and choose the shim or combination of shims closest to the total.

26. For both iron and aluminum cases, determine and select shims for the mainshaft in the following manner:

a. Measure the distance between the front of the mainshaft bearing and the surface of the transmission case. Also measure the distance between the rear cover surface and the bottom of the bearing seat.

b. Beginning with the rear measurement (cover-to-bearing seat), add the known thickness of the gasket, 0.25mm.

c. From that total, subtract the front bearing-to-case surface measurement.

d. From that result, subtract the allowable clearance (free-play), 0.01 to 0.20mm. Select the shim closest to the total.

27. Install the shift forks; make sure the lugs are in their correct position. Install the shifter and the gear selection rails.

28. Position the gasket and shim pack for the intermediate shaft. (For aluminum cases, this shim thickness was computed in step 35. For iron units, it was computed in step 53).

29. Position the mainshaft shim pack in the intermediate housing or, on M45, the rear cover.

30. Install the cover (M45) or the housing (M46), and secure with the two lower bolts finger-tight. On M45 units, install the drive flange and tighten the bolts to 65-75 ft. lbs. On M45, install the speedometer gear and O-ring at this time.

31. Install the gear shift rod. Tighten the bolts to 30 ft. lbs.

32. Install and tighten remaining bolts for rear cover or intermediate housing. Correct torque is 30 ft. lbs.

33. Install the lock pin for the shifter, install the selector plate assembly and the return spring.

34. Install the gear shift lever (without its lockscrew and lockring) on the transmission. Hold the selector plate assembly with the palm of your hand and move the shifter through all the gears. Check for proper engagement and release of each gear. Make necessary corrections before proceeding. Remove the shifter.

35. Install the detent ball and spring; install a new gasket for the top cover.

36. Install the top cover and tighten the bolts to 15 ft. lbs.

37. Reinstall the overdrive switch, the reverse light switch and the wiring at the solenoid. The unit may be refilled with oil now or after installation in the vehicle.

distance between the surface of the bell housing and the bottom of the bearing case. The following calculation will compute the necessary thickness of the shims for the input shaft. Start with the distance from the bell housing surface to the bottom of the bearing seat — for example, let's say 5.60mm — and add to it the known thickness of the gasket, 0.25mm. (5.60 + 0.25 = 5.85) From the result, subtract the distance between the front of the input shaft bearing and the front of the case — for our example, 4.71mm. (5.85 - 4.71 = 1.04) Now subtract the allowable free-play in the shaft — 0.01 to 0.15mm — to get the final shim thickness. (1.04 - 0.01 to 0.15 = 1.03 to 0.89). The nearest shim thickness to our need is 0.90mm.

23. Install the bell housing with its gasket; for aluminum cases, install the clutch fork and spacer. Tighten the bolts to 30 ft. lbs.

24. Install the clutch release (throw-out) bearing.

25. Turn the transmission to a vertical position. For aluminum cased units, remove any free play in the intermediate

CLUTCH

The purpose of the clutch is to disconnect and connect engine power at the transmission. A vehicle at rest requires a lot of engine torque to get all that weight moving. An internal combustion engine does not develop a high starting torque (unlike steam engines), so it must be allowed to operate without any load until it builds up enough torque to move the vehicle. Torque increases with engine rpm. The clutch allows the engine to build up torque by physically disconnecting the engine from the transmission, relieving the engine of any load or resistance. The transfer of engine power to the transmission

(the load) must be smooth and gradual; if it weren't, drive line components would wear out or break quickly. This gradual power transfer is made possible by gradually releasing the clutch pedal. The clutch disc and pressure plate are the connecting link between the engine and transmission. When the clutch pedal is released, the disc and plate contact each other (clutch engagement), physically joining the engine and transmission. When the pedal is pushed in, the disc and plate separate (the clutch is disengaged), disconnecting the engine from the transmission.

The clutch assembly consists of the flywheel, the clutch disc, the clutch pressure plate, the throwout bearing and fork, the actuating linkage and the pedal. The flywheel and clutch pressure plate (driving members) are connected to the engine crankshaft and rotate with it. The clutch disc is located between the flywheel and pressure plate, and splined to the transmission shaft. A driving member is one that is attached to the engine and transfers engine power to a driven member (clutch disc) on the transmission shaft. A driving member (pressure plate) rotates (drives) a driven member (clutch disc) on contact and in so doing, turns the transmission shaft. There is a circular diaphragm spring within the pressure plate cover (transmission side). In a relaxed state (when the clutch pedal is fully released), this spring is convex; that is, it is dished outward toward the transmission. Pushing in the clutch pedal actuates an attached linkage rod. Connected to the other end of this rod is the throwout bearing fork. The throwout bearing is attached to the fork. When the clutch pedal is depressed, the clutch linkage pushes the fork and bearing forward to contact the diaphragm spring of the pressure plate. The outer edges of the spring are secured to the pressure plate and are pivoted on rings so that when the center of the spring is compressed by the throwout bearing, the outer edges bow outward and, by so doing, pull the pressure plate in the same direction — away from the clutch disc. This action separates the disc from the plate, disengaging the clutch and allowing the transmission to be shifted into another gear. A coil type clutch return spring attached to the clutch pedal arm permits full release of the pedal. Releasing the pedal pulls the throwout bearing away from the diaphragm spring resulting in a reversal of spring position. As bearing pressure is gradually released from the spring center, the outer edges of the spring bow outward, pushing the pressure plate into closer contact with the clutch disc. As the disc and plate move closer together, friction between the two increases and slippage is reduced until, when full spring pressure is applied (by fully releasing the pedal), The speed of the disc and plate are the same. This stops all slipping, creating a direct connection between the plate and disc which results in the transfer of power from the engine to the transmission. The clutch disc is now rotating with the pressure plate at engine speed and because it is splined to the transmission shaft, the shaft now turns at the same engine speed. Understanding clutch operation can be rather difficult at first; if you're still confused after reading this, consider the following analogy. The action of the diaphragm spring can be compared to that of an oil can bottom. The bottom of an oil can is shaped very much like the clutch diaphragm spring and pushing in on the can bottom and then releasing it produces a similar effect. As mentioned earlier, the clutch pedal return spring permits full release of the pedal and reduces linkage slack due to wear. As the linkage wears, clutch free-pedal travel will increase and free-travel will decrease as the clutch wears. Free-travel is actually throwout bearing lash.

The diaphragm spring type clutches used are available in two different designs: flat diaphragm springs or bent spring.

The bent fingers are bent back to create a centrifugal boost ensuring quick re-engagement at higher engine speeds. This design enables pressure plate load to increase as the clutch disc wears and makes low pedal effort possible even with a heavy-duty clutch. The throwout bearing used with the bent finger design is 1¼ in. (31.75mm) long and is shorter than the bearing used with the flat finger design. These bearings are not interchangeable. If the longer bearing is used with the bent finger clutch, free-pedal travel will not exist. This results in clutch slippage and rapid wear.

The transmission varies the gear ratio between the engine and rear wheels. It can be shifted to change engine speed as driving conditions and loads change. The transmission allows disengaging and reversing power from the engine to the wheels.

Adjustments

The clutch is operating properly if:
- It will stall the engine when released with the vehicle held stationary.
- The shift lever can be moved freely between 1st and reverse gears when the vehicle is stationary and the clutch disengaged.

CLUTCH NEGATIVE PLAY

240 Series

▶ **See Figure 16**

The 240 Series are equipped with mechanical clutch linkage. The throwout bearing has a small preload applied by a spring at the pedal bracket. Pedal and clutch fork must have a free movement rearward (negative play) to prevent slipping as the clutch wears. If required, adjust to obtain approximately 5/64 inch (2mm) free movement rearward.

700 Series

The 700 Series are equipped with hydraulic clutch linkage. The control system is self-adjusting and requires no service adjustments.

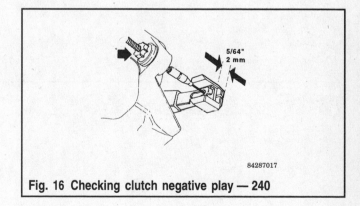

84287017

Fig. 16 Checking clutch negative play — 240

Driven Disc and Pressure Plate

❊❊CAUTION

The clutch driven disc contains asbestos, which has been determined to be a cancer causing agent. Never clean clutch surfaces with compressed air! Avoid inhaling dust particles from all clutch surfaces! When cleaning clutch surfaces, use a commercially available brake cleaning fluid.

REMOVAL & INSTALLATION

▶ **See Figure 17**

1. Remove the transmission as outlined under 'Removal & Installation'.

2. Scribe alignment marks on the clutch and flywheel. In order to prevent warpage, slowly loosen the bolts holding the clutch to the flywheel in a diagonal pattern. Remove the bolts and lift off the clutch and pressure plate.

3. Inspect the clutch assembly as outlined under 'Clutch Inspection'.

To install:

4. When ready to install, wash the pressure plate and flywheel with solvent to remove any traces of oil, and wipe them clean with a cloth.

5. Position the clutch assembly (the longest side of the hub facing backward or away from the engine) to the flywheel and align the bolt holes. Insert a centering drift (5111 or equivalent) or an input shaft from an old transmission of the same type, through the clutch assembly and flywheel. This centers the assembly and pilot bearing.

6. Install the clutch retaining bolts and tighten them in a diagonal pattern, a few turns at a time. After all the bolt are tightened, remove the pilot shaft (centering mandrel).

7. Install the transmission as outlined under 'Removal & Installation'.

8. Bleed the clutch hydraulic system, if necessary.

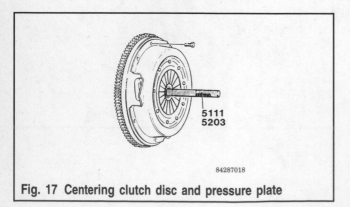

84287018

Fig. 17 Centering clutch disc and pressure plate

CLUTCH INSPECTION

▶ **See Figure 18**

Check the pressure plate for heat damage, cracks, scoring, or other damage to the friction surface. Check the curvature of the pressure plate with a steel ruler.

Place the ruler diagonally over the pressure plate friction surface and measure the distance between the straight edge of the ruler and the inner diameter of the pressure plate. This measurement must not be greater than 0.008 inch (0.2mm). In addition, there must be no clearance between the straight edge of the ruler and the outer diameter of the pressure plate. This check should be made at several points. Additionally, inspect the tips of the diaphragm springs (fingers) for any sign of wear.

Replace the clutch as a unit (disc, pressure plate and throwout bearing) if any fault is found.

Check the throwout bearing by rotating it several times while applying finger pressure, so that the ball bearings roll against the inside of the races. If the bearing does not turn easily or if it binds at any point, replace it as a unit. Also make sure that the bearing slides easily on the guide sleeve from the transmission.

Inspect the clutch disc for signs of slippage (burns) or oil contamination. Make sure the rivets are not loose and that the clutch contact surfaces are well above the rivet heads. The thickness of the disc above the rivet heads is the 'remaining life' of the disc; always replace the disc if in doubt.

When reassembling, apply grease to the splines and end shaft, the throwout bearing and the pivot ball and seat of the clutch fork.

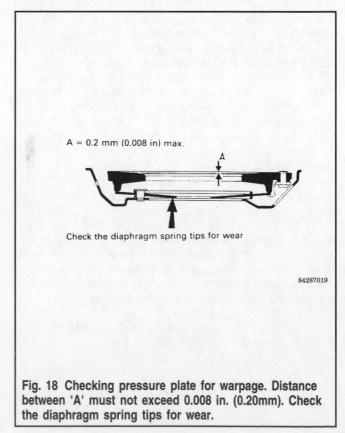

A = 0.2 mm (0.008 in) max.

Check the diaphragm spring tips for wear

84287019

Fig. 18 Checking pressure plate for warpage. Distance between 'A' must not exceed 0.008 in. (0.20mm). Check the diaphragm spring tips for wear.

Clutch Master Cylinder

REMOVAL & INSTALLATION

1. Drain the clutch reservoir with a bulb syringe. Be careful not to drip brake fluid on any painted surfaces.
2. Remove the underdash panel and remove the lockring and pin from the clutch pedal.
3. Remove the hose from the master cylinder. Use a clean jar to collect spillage.
4. Remove the retaining bolts and remove the master cylinder.
5. Installation is the reverse of the removal procedure. When reinstalling, make sure that the clearance (free play) between the pushrod and piston is 0.04 inch (1mm). Make certain the hose is correctly threaded and secure. Top up the fluid and bleed the system as explained below.

Clutch Slave Cylinder

REMOVAL & INSTALLATION

1. Raise and support the front end on jackstands.
2. Disconnect the fluid line at the cylinder.
3. Unbolt the cylinder from the flywheel housing.
4. Installation is the reverse of removal. Be sure to bleed the system after installation.

Hydraulic Clutch Bleeding

▶ See Figure 19

The hydraulic clutch system should be bled any time the hoses have been loosened or any component replaced. The bleeding process is quite simple and eliminates any air which has become trapped within the lines. The clutch system may be bleed usIng Tool 998 5876 or equivalent, or with the help of an assistant.

AUTOMATIC TRANSMISSION

Identification

The automatic transmissions, used in your vehicle, can be identified by referring to the Service Designation Number plate, found on the upper right side radiator support. A 10-digit Vehicle Identification Code (VIC), located in the upper right-hand corner of the Service Designation Number plate, contains information on the type of transmission used. The 9th digit of the VIC designate the transmission type and can be termed as follows:
- = AW70 (4-speed automatic transmission, without lock-up clutch (controlled forth gear 'overdrive')
6 = AW70L (4-speed automatic transmission, with lock-up clutch — controlled forth gear 'overdrive')
7 = AW71 (4-speed automatic transmission, without lock-up clutch — controlled forth gear 'overdrive')

Add brake fluid to the reservoir. Attach a length of hose to the bleeder nipple on the slave cylinder (at the transmission) and put the other end in a clear glass jar. Put enough brake fluid in the jar to cover the end of the hose.

Have an assistant press the clutch pedal to the floor and open the bleed screw on the slave cylinder. Close off the bleeder while the pedal is still depressed and repeat the process with another application of the clutch pedal. As the bleeder is released each time, observe the fluid in the jar. When no bubbles are coming out of the hose, the system is bled. Secure the fitting, remove the hose and jar, and top up the brake fluid to its proper level.

84287020

Fig. 19 Bleeding clutch system with tool 998 5876

6 = AW72L (Basically the same transmission as the AW70L, but designed for heavier applications.)
- = AW30-40 (4-speed automatic transmission, with torque converter lock-up function (Electronically Controlled)

The transmission type designation, serial number and part number also appears on a product plate (metal plate), affix to the left-hand side of the transmission, just above the transmission pan. The transmission 'type code' is a single letter, located in the lower center of the product plate and can be interpret as follows:
C = AW70
K = AW70L
F = AW71
P = AW72L
- = AW30-40

AW70L

The AW70L transmission is used in combination with B230F engine. The unit is a 4-speed automatic transmission, with lockup clutch. The 4th gear is automatically engaged after the transmission has shifted through the first 3 gears.

The 4th gear (overdrive) can be disengaged by depressing the button on the side of the gear selector. This condition provides a three-speed transmission suitable for towing or mountain driving. When the 4th gear is disengaged, a reminder light on the instrument panel illuminates. The transmission can revert to a four-speed transmission by depressing the button on the gear selector again.

AW71

The AW71 transmission is used in conjunction with B230FT and B280F engines. The unit is a four-speed automatic transmission, with no lockup. The 4th gear is automatically engaged after the transmission has shifted through the first 3 gears.

The 4th gear (overdrive) can be disengaged by depressing the button on the side of the gear selector. This condition provides a three-speed transmission suitable for towing or mountain driving. When the 4th gear is disengaged, a reminder light on the instrument panel illuminates. The transmission can revert to a four-speed transmission by depressing the button on the gear selector again.

AW72L

The AW72L transmission is used in conjunction with the B234 engine. The unit is basically the same transmission as the AW70L, but designed for heavier applications.

AW 30-40

▶ **See Figure 20**

The AW 30-40 transmission is used in combination with B6304F engine. The unit is a 4-speed transmission with torque converter, lockup function operating in the top 3-speeds. All gear changes and lockup functions are controlled by an Electronic Control Unit (ECU). The driver now has the capabilities to select alternative gear change programs (or, in simpler terms, different driving styles) with the aid of a selector switch along-side the selector lever.

The ECU uses information on clutch and brake slip (a normal feature of these components), as well as signals from the torque converter lockup function, to compute the instant at which a particular gear should be engaged. The ECU also uses signals from the engine electronic management system and the speedometer. The ECU is supplied with speed signal from a sun wheel in the front planetary train by the speed pickup mounted in the front section of the transmission.

To aid in fault tracing, the ECU is equipped with diagnostic facilities (accessible through socket 1 on the diagnostic unit), which enable faults to be recorded and stored for later display.

A special emergency program (flashing of a warning lamp on the instrument panel) ensures that the vehicle can be driven to a repair shop, in the event of a major fault.

Understanding the Automatic Transmission

The automatic transmission allows engine torque and power to be transmitted to the rear wheels within a narrow range of engine operating speeds. The transmission will allow the engine to turn fast enough to produce plenty of power and torque at very low speeds, while keeping it at a sensible rpm at high vehicle speeds. An automatic transmission performs these functions entirely without the driver assistance. The transmission uses a light fluid as the medium for the transmission of power. This fluid also works in the operation of various hydraulic control circuits and as a lubricant. Because the transmission fluid performs all of these functions, trouble within the unit can easily travel from one part to another. For this reason, and because of the complexity and unusual operating principles of the transmission, a very sound understanding of the basic principles of operation will simplify troubleshooting.

TORQUE CONVERTER

▶ **See Figure 21**

The torque converter serves as both a clutch and a hydraulic gear, linking the engine to the transmission. It has three functions:

1. It allows the engine to idle with the vehicle at a standstill, even with the transmission in gear.

2. It allows the transmission to shift from range to range smoothly, without requiring that the driver close the throttle during the shift.

3. It multiplies engine torque to an increasing extent as vehicle speed drops and throttle opening is increased. This has the effect of making the transmission more responsive and reduces the amount of shifting required.

The torque converter consists of the following:

- An impeller — connected to the engine crankshaft
- A turbine — connected to the input shaft of the transmission
- A stator — mounted in a one-way clutch.

The AW70L, AW72L and the AW30-40 transmissions have a mechanical lock-up unit which is very similar to a manual transmission clutch. The unit locks the impeller to the turbine when the transmission is operating in 4th gear and the vehicle is being driven above a certain speed and thereby eliminates power loss.

PLANETARY GEARS

▶ **See Figure 22**

The ability of the torque converter to multiply engine torque is limited. Also, the unit tends to be more efficient when the turbine is rotating at relatively high speeds. Therefore, a planetary gear-set is used to vary the power output of the transmission.

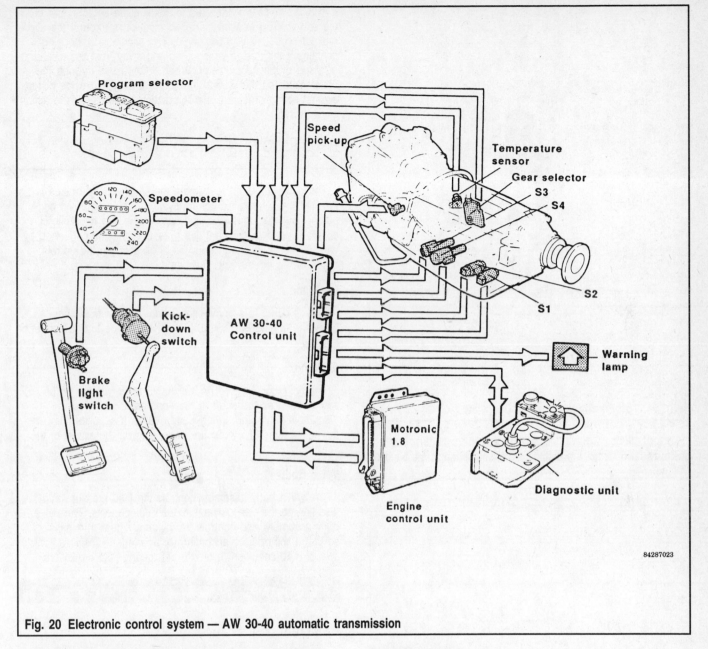

Fig. 20 Electronic control system — AW 30-40 automatic transmission

In the center of the planetary gear-set is a sun gear shaft around which are assembled planetary gears. The planetary gears are mounted on a carrier and are in mesh with a ring gear (annulus). They transfer power from the sun gear to the ring gear or vise versa. In some cases they are stationary in relation to the sun and ring gears.

Front gear ratios can be obtained by preventing 1 of the 3 units from rotating. The greatest advantage of the planetary gear unit, is that because the gears are in constant mesh, it is possible to change gears ratio without declutching.

CLUTCHES

Multi-disc clutches, operated by hydraulic pistons, are used to connect the torque converter to the various gear sets.

BRAKE BANDS

Brake bands, operated by hydraulic servos, hold different parts of the gear set stationary. The brake bands do not need adjustments.

FREEWHEELS

The freewheels or one-way clutches freewheel in 1 direction and prevent gear wheel rotation in the opposite.

SERVOS AND ACCUMULATORS

The servos are hydraulic pistons and cylinders. They resemble the hydraulic actuators used on many familiar machines,

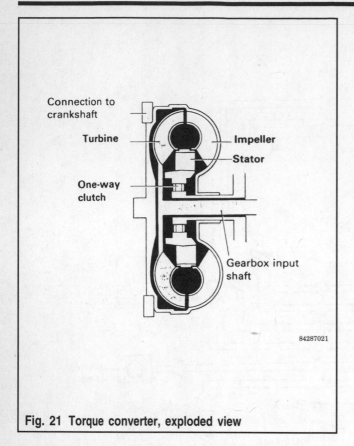

Fig. 21 Torque converter, exploded view

such as bulldozers. Hydraulic fluid enters the cylinder, under pressure, and forces the piston to move to engage the band or clutches.

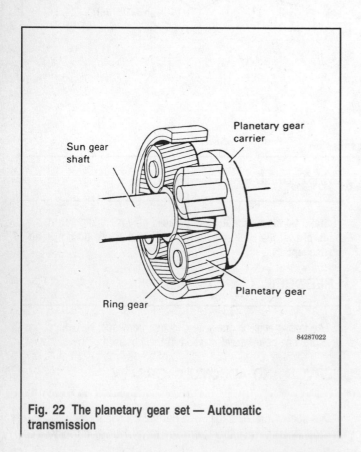

Fig. 22 The planetary gear set — Automatic transmission

The accumulators are used to cushion the engagement of the servos. The transmission fluid must pass through the accumulator on the way to the servo. The accumulator housing contains a thin piston which is sprung away from the discharge passage of the accumulator. When fluid passes through the accumulator on the way to the servo, it must move the piston against spring pressure, and this action smooths out the action of the servo.

HYDRAULIC CONTROL SYSTEM

The power required to operate the clutches and brakes is provided by a hydraulic control system consisting of an oil pump, governor and valve body assembly. The hydraulic circuits are under a constant line pressure which is converted by various valves to bring about the application, in the correct order, of the brakes and clutches.

Oil Pump

The oil pump is a conventional gear pump which operates when the engine is running. It is driven by the torque converter hub.

Governor

The governor, located on the output shaft, rotates at the same speed as the shaft. It functions as a combined centrifugal valve and spring-loaded valve. It supplies fluid to the shift valves at a pressure depending on the speed of the vehicle.

Valve Body

The valve body assembly controls the fluid pressure and fluid flow to the various transmission components. The valve body assembly also controls the planetary gear transmission so that it will operate according to: accelerator position, vehicle speed, road condition (hills etc) and gear selector position.

Fluid Pan

REMOVAL & INSTALLATION

✳✳CAUTION

If the vehicle has been driven within the last 3-5 hours the fluid may be scalding hot. Use extreme caution when draining fluid or handling components.

1. Raise the vehicle and support it safely.
2. If the fluid pan is equipped with a drain plug, remove the plug and drain the fluid.
3. On fluid pan without drain plug, remove the return oil cooler pipe connection at the side of the transmission. Connect a transparent plastic tube to the pipe and drain the fluid.
4. Remove the fluid pan retaining bolts and lower the pan and gasket. Some fluid will remain in the pan.
5. Inspect the magnet for metal particles. Check the filter screen for the pump. Remove any gum or sludge from the bottom of the pan. Clean and dry the pan.

6. Installation is the reverse of the removal procedure. Install the pan using a new gasket. Torque the fluid pan retaining bolts to 3 ft. lbs. (4 Nm). Torque the drain plug bolt 13-17 ft. lbs. (18-23 Nm).

FILTER SERVICE

1. Remove the pan as outlined above.
2. Remove the bolts which retain the strainer to the valve body, and lower the strainer.
3. Clean the strainers in an alcohol-based solvent solution.
4. Position the strainers to the valve body and install the retaining screws and bolts. Torque the bolt(s) to 8-12 ft. lbs. (6-9 Nm).
5. Install the pan with a new gasket as outlined in the 'Removal & Installation' section.

Adjustments

Before performing any adjustments, the following checks should be made: — Check that the engine can be started, only with the selector lever in position **P** and with the brake pedal depressed. The selector lever should stand vertically when in position **P**. — Check that the backup lights illuminate, only when the selector lever is in position **R**. — On AW 70/71/72 transmissions, check that the clearance from position **D** towards **N** is the same or smaller than the clearance between position **3** towards **2**. — On AW 30-40 transmission, check that there is a noticeable play from position **D** towards **N**; however, that play should not be greater than the play from position **3** towards **L**.

SHIFT CONTROL

AW 70/71/72 Transmissions
▶ **See Figure 23**

1. Set the selector lever in position **P**. Loosen the retaining nuts for the shift control rod 'A' and retaining arm 'B'.
2. Check that the lever on the transmission is at position **P** (first step seen from the rear). Turn the transmission output shaft until it locks.
3. Set the lever in the vertical position on the shift control rod, or just facing forward; tighten the nut. Push the retaining arm lightly to the rear until slight resistance is felt. Temporarily torque the retaining nut to 3.5 ft. lbs. (5 Nm).
4. Check that the clearance from position **D** towards **N** is the same or smaller than the clearance between position **3** towards **2**.
5. If incorrect:
   a. If the gear selector lever is stiff in position **D**, move the connecting rod 5/64 inch (2mm) to the rear.
   b. If the gear selector lever is stiff in position **3**, move the connecting rod 1/8 inch (3mm) to the front.
6. When the adjustment is correct, torque the retaining nut 13-17 ft. lbs. (17-23 Nm).

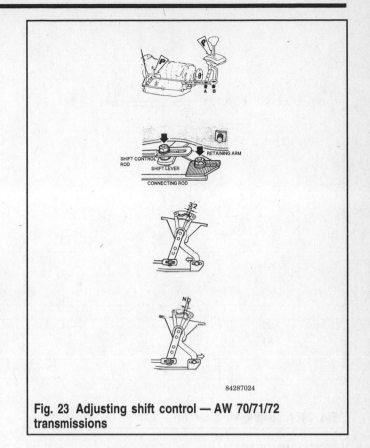

Fig. 23 Adjusting shift control — AW 70/71/72 transmissions

7. After adjustment, check that the engine can be started, only with the selector lever in position **P** and with the brake pedal depressed. The backup lights should illuminate, only when the selector lever is in position **R**.

AW 30-40 Transmission
▶ **See Figure 24**

1. Place the selector lever in position **P**.
2. Loosen the nuts on the control rod and reaction strut.
3. Make sure the selector link arm on the transmission is in position **P** (rearmost gear position).
4. Make sure the gear lever arm 'A' is vertical (or slightly forward) and tighten the nut.
5. Press the reaction arm 'B' gently backwards until slight resistance is felt. Tighten the nut approximately 4 ft. lbs. (5 Nm).
6. Check that the play from position **D** towards **N**; is the same as the play from position **3** towards **L**.
7. If incorrect:
   a. If there is no play in position **D**, move the reaction arm backwards approximately 0.08 inches (2mm).
   b. If there is no play in position **3**, move the reaction arm forwards approximately 0.12 inches (3mm).
8. When the adjustment is correct, torque the retaining nut 13-17 ft. lbs. (17-23 Nm).
9. After adjustment, check that the engine can be started, only with the selector lever in positions **P** or **N**. The backup lights should illuminate, only when the selector lever is in position **R**.

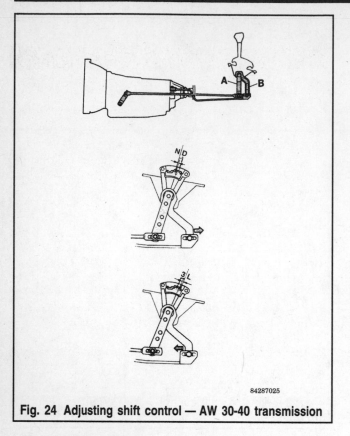

Fig. 24 Adjusting shift control — AW 30-40 transmission

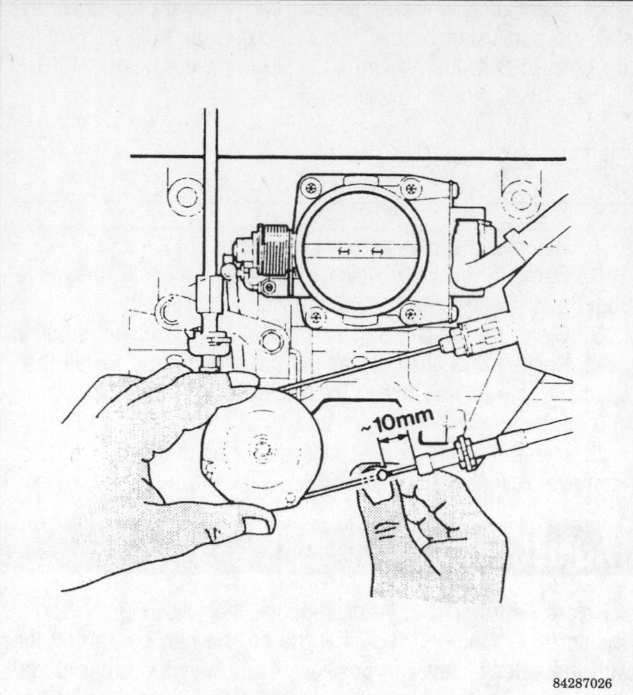

84287025

KICKDOWN CABLE

AW 70/71/72 Transmissions
▶ **See Figures 25 and 26**

1. Check that the wire is tensioned at idle setting, without tensioning against the throttle pulley, and that it is in the pulley groove and runs smoothly.

2. Pull the wire out approximately 0.39 inch (10mm) and release suddenly. A mechanical click should be heard from the throttle cam, when it reaches standby setting. Adjust with the wire tensioner.

   a. If no clicking is heard, the wire is too firmly tensioned.

   b. If no kickdown can be obtained, the wire is too slack.

3. Check the cable sheath adjustment with the throttle pedal in the vehicle depressed, not by actuating the linkage by hand. When depressing the throttle pedal fully, distance from the cable sheath to clip should be 2.02 inches (51.5mm); 1.98-2.06 inches (50.4-52.6mm) is permitted. If required, adjust the distance on the cable sheath.

Start Inhibitor/Reverse Light Switch

REMOVAL & INSTALLATION

The start inhibitor (neutral safety switch) also serves to illuminate the reverse lights. The switch is found on the left side of the gear shift selector.

1. Remove the ashtray and panel in the center console.

84287026

Fig. 25 Checking and adjusting kick-down cable, with wire tensioner — AW 70/71/72 transmissions

2. Remove the faceplate with the gear position symbols.

3. Remove the start inhibitor/reverse light switch. Open the connector and lift off the switch.

To install:

4. Install the new switch and connect the wiring. Make sure that the tab on the selector lever enters the slot on the switch. Don't forget the prism which fits onto the top of the new switch.

5. Reinstall the holder and the shifter faceplate.

6. Install the panel and the ashtray in the center console.

Transmission

REMOVAL & INSTALLATION

▶ **See Figure 27**

❈❈CAUTION

If the vehicle has been driven within the last 3-5 hours, the transmission oil can be scalding hot. Use extreme care when draining the oil or handling components.

Except 240 and 960

1. Disconnect the battery ground cable.

2. Place the gear selector in the **P** position. Disconnect the kickdown cable at the throttle pulley on the engine.

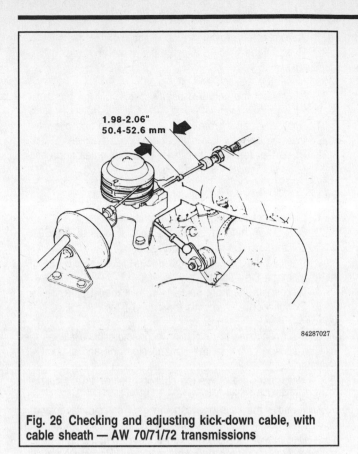

1.98-2.06"
50.4-52.6 mm

84287027

Fig. 26 Checking and adjusting kick-down cable, with cable sheath — AW 70/71/72 transmissions

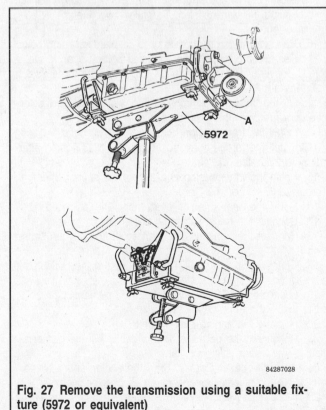

5972

A

84287028

Fig. 27 Remove the transmission using a suitable fixture (5972 or equivalent)

3. Disconnect the oil filler tube at the oil pan, and drain the transmission oil.

✳✳CAUTION

The oil will be scalding hot if the vehicle was recently driven.

4. Disconnect the control rod at the transmission lever, and disconnect the reaction rod at the transmission housing.

5. On AW71 transmission, disconnect the wire at the solenoid (slightly to the rear of the transmission-to-driveshaft flange).

6. Matchmark the transmission-to-driveshaft flange and unbolt the driveshaft.

7. Place a jack or transmission dolly under the transmission and support the unit. Remember that the transmission will be heavier at the front end than the rear. Remove the transmission crossmember assembly.

8. Disconnect the exhaust pipe at the joint and remove the exhaust pipe bracket from the exhaust pipe. Remove the rear engine mount with the exhaust pipe bracket.

9. Remove the starter motor.

10. Remove the cover plate at the torque converter housing.

11. Disconnect the oil cooler lines at the transmission.

12. Remove the upper bolts at the torque converter cover. Remove the oil filler tube.

➡It is helpful to have another person steadying and guiding the transmission during the removal process.

13. Remove the lower bellhousing bolts.

14. Remove the bolts retaining the torque converter to the drive plate. Pry the torque converter back from the drive plate with a small prybar.

15. Slowly lower the transmission as you pull it back to clear the input shaft.

✳✳WARNING

Do not tilt the transmission forward, or the torque converter may slide off.

To install:

16. When reinstalling, install the two lower bolts in the casing as soon as the transmission is in place. For B280 engine, adjust the panel between the starter motor and torque converter casing and install the bolts for the starter.

17. Mount the oil filler tube at the oil pan but do not tighten the nut.

18. Install the tube bracket and the two upper bolts in the converter casing. Now tighten the nut for the oil tube to 65 ft. lbs.

19. Install the bolts for the coupling flange; tighten the bolts hand-tight first, then tighten in a crisscross pattern to 32 ft. lbs.

20. Reinstall the rear engine mount with the exhaust pipe bracket and reconnect the exhaust system.

21. Reinstall the transmission crossmember; when it is securely bolted in place, the supporting jack may be removed.

22. Reinstall the driveshaft.

23. Making sure that both the transmission linkage and the shift selector in the vehicle are in the **P** position. Attach the

actuator rod and the reaction rod. Adjust the shift linkage as necessary.

24. On AW71 models, install and connect the wiring to the solenoid valve.

25. Connect the kickdown cable at the throttle pulley. Adjust the cable if necessary.

26. Fill the transmission with oil. Connect the negative battery cable.

27. Apply the parking brake. Start the engine and allow to idle. Move the selector lever through all gear positions.

28. Place the selector lever in **P**. Wait 2 minutes and check the fluid level. Top up, as required.

240

1. Disconnect the negative battery cable. Remove the dipstick and filler pipe clamp.

2. Remove the bracket and throttle cable from the dashboard and throttle control.

3. Disconnect the exhaust pipe at the manifold flange.

4. Raise the vehicle and support on jackstands at the front and rear axles.

5. Drain the fluid into a clean container.

6. Disconnect the driveshaft from the transmission flange.

7. Disconnect the selector lever controls (shift linkage) and the pan reinforcing bracket.

8. Remove the converter attaching bolts.

9. Support the transmission with a jack or a transmission dolly and holding fixture.

10. Remove the rear crossmember.

11. Disconnect the exhaust pipe brackets and remove the speedometer cable from the case.

12. Remove the filler pipe.

13. Install a wooden block between the engine and firewall; lower the jack until the engine contacts the block.

14. Make sure no tension is put on the battery cable.

15. Disconnect all electrical wiring at the transmission case.

16. Disconnect the starter cable and remove the starter.

17. Remove the converter housing bolts.

18. Pull the transmission backwards to clear the guide pins. Lower and remove the transmission assembly from the vehicle.

To install:

19. When reinstalling, load the transmission straight onto the engine and install the converter housing bolts. Tighten the converter-to-drive plate bolts to 35 ft. lbs.

20. Install the starter and connect its cable; hook up all other wiring to the transmission case.

21. Using the jack, elevate the transmission and engine into their proper position. Install the speedometer cable and the filler pipe.

22. Reconnect the exhaust pipe and the rear engine mount brackets.

23. Install the rear crossmember and tighten its bolts to 18 ft. lbs. When the crossmember is secure, the jack may be removed.

24. Install the converter attaching bolts. Connect the selector lever controls and the pan reinforcing bracket.

25. Connect the driveshaft to the transmission flange.

26. Lower the vehicle from its stands and refill the transmission fluid.

27. Reconnect the exhaust pipe at the manifold flange.

28. Reinstall the bracket and throttle cable and adjust if necessary.

29. Install the dipstick and filler pipe.

30. Reconnect the negative battery cable. Fill the transmission to the proper level with fluid.

31. Apply the parking brake. Start the engine and allow to idle. Move the selector lever through all gear positions.

32. Place the selector lever in **P**. Wait 2 minutes and check the fluid level. Top up, as required.

960

1. Disconnect the negative battery cable.

2. Support the engine, using the special tools (5006, 5033, 5115, 5429 and 5186 or their equivalent).

3. Remove the preheater pipe under the engine. Be careful not to damage the O-ring.

4. Disconnect the front section of the exhaust pipe.

5. Disconnect the transmission cooler lines. Plug the openings.

6. Disconnect the transmission connectors (3). Release the oxygen sensor lead from the transmission unit and support member.

7. Matchmark the driveshaft coupling halves to aid during re-assemble. Disconnect the driveshaft.

8. Remove the clips between the gear selector lever and control rod/reaction arm. Withdraw the rods from the mounting.

9. Disconnect the transmission support member from the transmission bump stop and side members. Position a service jack beneath the transmission. Carefully lower the transmission.

10. Remove the torque convertor-to-flexplate retaining bolts.

11. Remove the transmission housing bolts. Separate the torque convertor from the flexplate and lower the transmission.

To install:

12. Lift the transmission into position, while aligning the torque convertor with the flexplate.

13. Install the transmission housing mounting bolts.

14. Install the torque convertor retaining bolts. Tighten alternately to 22 ft. lbs. (30 Nm).

15. Raise the transmission and secure the support member. Torque to 37 ft. lbs. (50 Nm).

16. Install the gear selector lever. Install the locking clips.

17. Connect the transmission oil cooler lines.

18. Connect the transmission connectors and oxygen sensor lead.

19. Connect the driveshaft. Check to ensure the matchmarks are aligned.

20. Lubricate the O-ring and install the preheater pipe.

21. Install the front exhaust pipe.

22. Remove the engine support tools.

23. Reconnect the negative battery cable. Fill the transmission to the proper level with fluid.

24. Apply the parking brake. Start the engine and allow to idle. Move the selector lever through all gear positions.

25. Place the selector lever in **P**. Wait 2 minutes and check the fluid level. Top up, as required.

DRIVELINE

▶ **See Figure 28**

The driveshaft is a two-piece tubular unit, connected by an intermediate universal joint. The rear end of the front section of the driveshaft contains a splined sleeve. A splined shaft forming one of the yokes for the intermediate U-joint fits into this sleeve.

The front section is supported by a bearing contained in an insulated rubber housing attached to the bottom of the driveshaft tunnel. The front section is connected to the transmission flange, and the rear section is connected to the differential housing flange by universal joints.

Each joint consists of a spider with 4 ground trunnions in the flange yokes by needle bearings.

Driveshaft and Universal Joints

REMOVAL & INSTALLATION

▶ **See Figure 29**

1. Raise the vehicle and install safety stands.
2. Mark the relative positions of the driveshaft yokes on the transmission and differential housing flanges for purposes of assembly. Remove the nuts and bolts which retain the front and rear driveshaft sections to the transmission and differential housing flanges. Remove the support bearing housing from the driveshaft tunnel, and lower the driveshaft and universal joint assembly as a unit.
3. Pry up the lock washer and remove the support bearing retaining nut. Pull off the rear section of the drivshaft with the intermediate universal joint and splined shaft of the front section. The support bearing may now be pressed off from the driveshaft.
4. Remove the support bearing from its housing.
5. For removal of the universal joints from the driveshaft, refer to 'Universal Joint Overhaul' in this section.
6. Inspect the driveshaft sections for straightness. Using a dial indicator, or rolling the shafts along a flat surface, make sure that the driveshaft out-of-round does not exceed 0.010 inches (0.25mm). Do not attempt to straighten a damaged shaft. Any shaft exceeding 0.010 inches (0.25mm) out-of-round will cause substantial vibration, and must be replaced. Also,

inspect the support bearing by pressing the races against each other by hand and turning them in opposite directions. If the bearing binds at any point, it must be discarded and replaced.

7. Install the support bearing into its housing.
8. Press the support bearing and housing onto the front driveshaft section. Push the splined shaft of the rear section (with the intermediate universal joint and rear driveshaft section) into the splined sleeve of the front section. Install the retaining nut and lock washer for the support bearing.

➡ **Pay particular attention to the placement of the yokes at the end of the shaft. They must be in the same alignment front and rear or driveline vibration will be induced.**

9. Taking note of the alignment marks made prior to removal, position the driveshaft and universal joint assembly to its flange and install but do not tighten its retaining nuts and bolts. Position the support bearing housing to the driveshaft tunnel and install the retaining nut. Tighten the nuts which retain the driveshaft sections to the transmission and differential housing flanges to a torque of 25-30 ft. lbs.
10. Remove the safety stands and lower the vehicle. Road test the vehicle and check for driveline vibrations.

UNIVERSAL JOINT OVERHAUL

▶ **See Figures 30, 31, 32 and 33**

1. Remove the driveshaft and universal joint assembly as outlined above.

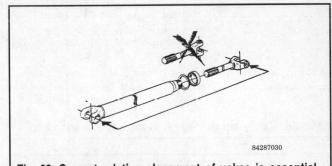

84287030

Fig. 29 Correct relative placement of yokes is essential to eliminating driveline vibrations

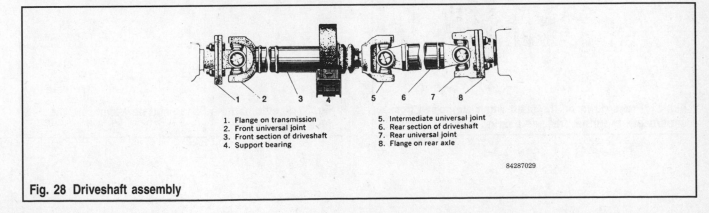

1. Flange on transmission
2. Front universal joint
3. Front section of driveshaft
4. Support bearing
5. Intermediate universal joint
6. Rear section of driveshaft
7. Rear universal joint
8. Flange on rear axle

84287029

Fig. 28 Driveshaft assembly

2. Clean off the dirt from the surrounding area and remove the snaprings, which secure the needle bearings in the yokes, with a snapring pliers. If the rings are difficult to loosen, apply rust penetrant and tap the ring lightly with a hammer and punch.

3. Lightly mount the shaft in a vise and adjust its position so that the yoke is supported by the jaws. If at all possible, do not tighten the vise onto the tubular shaft; it can be easily deformed.

4. Using a plastic mallet, tap on the shaft flange until the bearing cup(s) protrude about 0.2 inch (5mm). Do not tap on the tubular shaft.

5. Leaving the flange clamped in the vise, lift the driveshaft and insert a piece of wood or a hammer handle under the shaft. Gently press down on the driveshaft; this will lever the bearing cap upwards. Once all are removed, clean the seats in the driveshaft and flange. Clean the spider and needle bearings completely. Check the contact surfaces for wear. Replace any worn or broken parts. If the old needle bearings and spider are to be reused, fill them with molybdenum disulfide chassis grease, and make sure that the rubber seals are not damaged. If new needle bearings are used, fill them half-way with the grease.

6. Remove the bearing caps and seals from the new spider. Make sure that the needle bearings and seals are in place within the cups.

7. Position the spider into the flange yoke. Place one of the bearing cups on the spider and tap the cup until it is firmly seated.

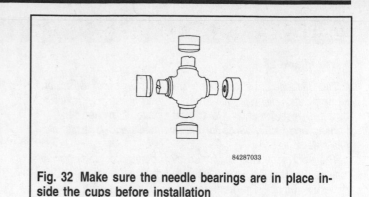

Fig. 32 Make sure the needle bearings are in place inside the cups before installation

8. Using the vise and a sleeve of proper size, press the cup into place in the yoke. The cup should project through the yoke about 0.1-0.2 inch (2.5-5.0mm). Install the snapring (circlip). Make sure the spider is centered within the yoke.

9. Repeat the previous pressing operation on the opposite side of the flange yoke. Note that when the second bearing cup is pressed into place, the first bearing cup is pressed against its snapring.

10. Fit the spider into the driveshaft yoke. Place and press each bearing cup into place following the procedures above.

11. Release the assembly from the vise. Check the new joint for free motion in all dimensions. If any stiffness or binding is present, remount the assembly in the vise (as described previously) and LIGHTLY tap the spider ends with a plastic mallet.

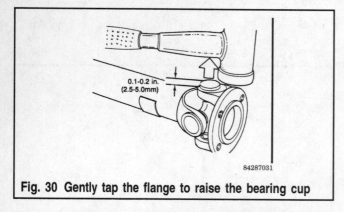

Fig. 30 Gently tap the flange to raise the bearing cup

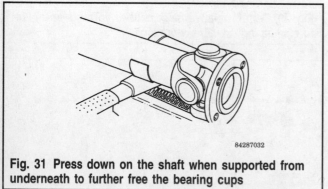

Fig. 31 Press down on the shaft when supported from underneath to further free the bearing cups

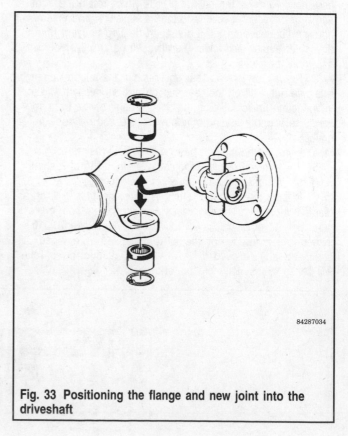

Fig. 33 Positioning the flange and new joint into the driveshaft

Center Bearing

REMOVAL & INSTALLATION

♦ **See Figures 34, 35 and 36**

The center support bearing must rotate freely with no noise or binding. It not a serviceable component; if it is noisy or binds it must be replaced. Use of a press with the appropriate blocks and sleeves is required for replacement.

240

1. Remove the front driveshaft and center bearing assembly as outlined above.
2. Press the bearing out of the rubber mount. The bearing will stay attached to the driveshaft.
3. Using a drift or a press if necessary, remove the bearing from the driveshaft. Take vehicle not to damage the dust cover around the bearing.
4. Install the new bearing by pressing it onto the shaft. Install the rubber mount. Observe correct placement of the bearing within the mount.
5. Reassemble the driveshaft halves. If the splines are dry, lightly coat them with grease.
6. When reinstalling the driveshaft and central bearing in the vehicle, check that the spring and washer are positioned correctly in the rubber mount. Also make sure that the bearing is centered in its mounts before final tightening.

Except 240

1. Remove the front driveshaft section as outlined above.
2. Remove the protective rubber boot. Using a sleeve of suitable size, mount the shaft in a press and remove the shaft from the bearing assembly.
3. Remove the bearing from the 'cage' by using the press and a sleeve.

➡ **There are several different types of bearings used. When buying the new bearing, have the old one along for comparison and make sure the replacement is identical in every respect.**

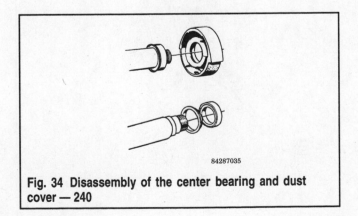

Fig. 34 Disassembly of the center bearing and dust cover — 240

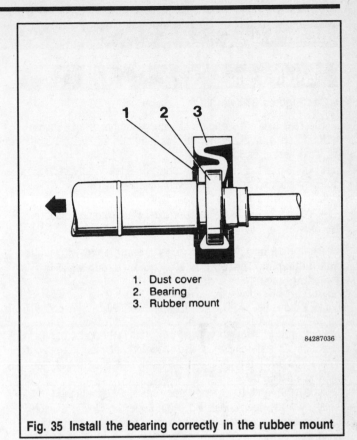

1. Dust cover
2. Bearing
3. Rubber mount

84287036

Fig. 35 Install the bearing correctly in the rubber mount

4. Install the new bearing into the cage. Support the cage as necessary and use a drift when pressing the bearing into place.
5. Tap the protective ring (dust cover) onto the driveshaft, then use the press as needed to install the bearing assembly onto the shaft. Install the rear dust cover, tapping it evenly so that it seats straight.
6. Check the bearing for free motion, silent operation and lack of binding.
7. Install the rubber boot on the back part of the bearing. Lubricate it with a light coat of petroleum jelly. Make sure the boot is properly held in place.
8. Making sure that the yokes are placed in identical positions, reassemble the front and rear driveshaft halves. Install the small rubber boot (if any) on the rear driveshaft section.
9. Reinstall the driveshaft as outlined previously.

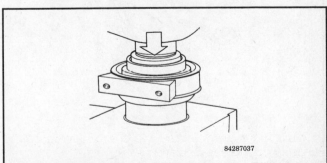

84287037

Fig. 36 Installing the bearing into the cage. Tool shown above and below

REAR AXLE

Identification

▶ **See Figures 37 and 38**

The rear axle ratio and identification number (Part Number) is found on a label, located on the left-hand side of the axle housing and is as follows:

- Volvo 1041 = Beam type rear axle (Heavy-duty version of the discontinued 1030 and 1031 rear axles)
- Volvo 1035 = Multi-link rear axle
- Volvo 1045 = Multi-link rear axle, with automatic differential lock

➡️ **Type 1030 and 1031 rear axles are equipped with limited slip (anti-spin). These axles are equipped with steel inspection cover.**

Type 1041 rear axle (beam type) is attached to the body by support arms, a torque arm and a torque arm frame. A panhard rod is installed between the rear axle and crossmember. An anti-roll bar is also mounted between the support arms. The 1041 rear axle can be easily identified by its aluminum inspection cover.

Type 1035 and 1045 rear axles (multi-link) is attached to the body by a member consisting of an upper and lower section. The upper links extend from the upper member. The lower links and 2 track rods are mounted between the lower section of the axle member and the wheel bearing housings. The wheel bearing housings and body are connected by the support arms.

Certain rear axle variants are equipped with Automatic Differential Lock. The locking mechanism is controlled by a centrifugal governor. This device operates automatically when 1 of the drive wheels is spinning and the speed of the vehicle is less than 25 mph (40 km/h). When the vehicle is driven at a steady speed and both driveshafts are rotating at the same speed, the differential functions exactly as a conventional type.

Understanding the Rear Axle

The rear axle is a special type of transmission that reduces the speed of the drive from the engine and transmission and divides the power to the rear wheels. Power enters the rear axle from the driveshaft via the companion flange. The flange is mounted on the drive pinion shaft. The drive pinion shaft and gear carries the power into the differential. The gear on the end of the pinion shaft drives a large ring gear the axis of rotation of which is 90 degrees away from the of the pinion. The pinion and gear reduce the gear ratio of the axle, and change the direction of rotation to turn the axle shafts which drive both wheels. The rear axle gear ratio is found by dividing the number of pinion gear teeth into the number of ring gear teeth.

The ring gear drives the differential case. The case provides the 2 mounting points for the ends of a pinion shaft on which are mounted two pinion gears. The pinion gears drive the 2 side gears, one of which is located on the inner end of each axle shaft (beam type axle) or inner driveshafts (multi-link axle).

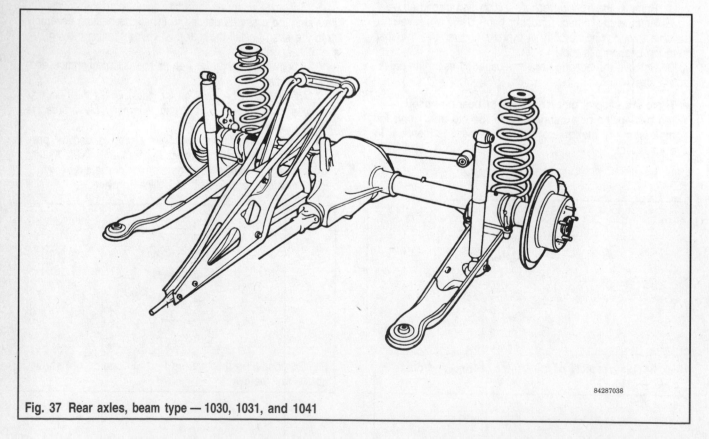

84287038

Fig. 37 Rear axles, beam type — 1030, 1031, and 1041

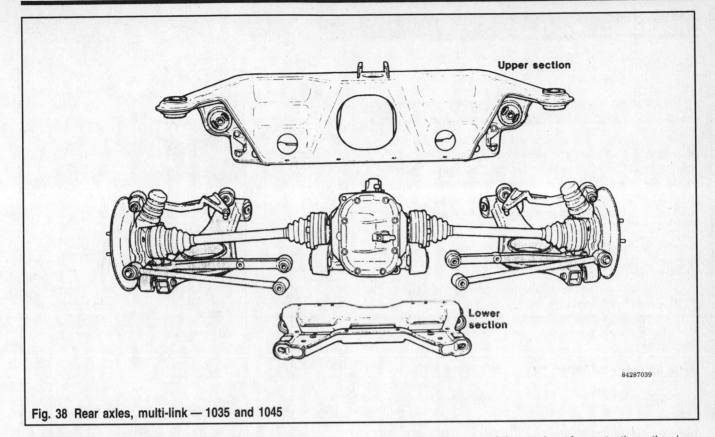

Fig. 38 Rear axles, multi-link — 1035 and 1045

By driving the axle shafts through the arrangement, the differential allows the outer drive wheel to turn faster than the inner drive wheel in a turn.

The main drive pinion and the side bearings, which bear the weight of the differential case, are shimmed to provide proper bearing preload, and to position the pinion and ring gears properly.

➡ **The proper adjustment of the relationship of the ring and pinion gears is critical. It should be attempted only by those with extensive equipment and/or experience.**

Limited-slip differentials include clutches which tend to link each axle shaft to the differential case. Clutches may be engaged either by spring action or by pressure produced by the torque on the axles during a turn. During turning on a dry pavement, the effects of the clutches are overcome, and each wheel turns at the required speed. When slippage occurs at either wheel, however, the clutches will transmit some of the power to the wheel which has the greater amount of traction. Because of the presence of clutches, limited-slip units require a special lubricant.

Determining Axle Ratio

The drive axle is said to have a certain axle ratio. This number (usually a whole number and a decimal fraction) is actually a comparison of the number of gear teeth on the ring gear and the pinion gear. For example, a 4.11 rear means that theoretically, there are 4.11 teeth on the ring gear for each tooth on the pinion gear. By dividing the number of teeth on the pinion gear into the number of teeth on the ring gear, the numerical axle ratio (4.11) is obtained. This also provides a good method of ascertaining exactly what axle ratio one is dealing with.

Another method of determining gear ratio is to jack up and support the vehicle so that both rear wheels are off the ground. Make a chalk mark on the rear wheel and the driveshaft. Put the transmission in neutral. Turn the rear wheel one complete turn and count the number of turns that the driveshaft makes. The number of turns that the driveshaft makes in one complete revolution of the rear wheel is an approximation of the rear axle ratio.

The final drive is of the hypoid design, with the drive pinion lying below the ring gear. On the solid axle models, each axle shaft is indexed into a splined sleeve for the differential side gears, and supported at its outer end in a tapered roller bearing. Bearing clearance is not adjustable by use of shims, but instead is determined by bearing thickness. Both sides of the axle bearings are protected by oil seals.

On vehicles with the Multi-Link suspension, the axles are actually halfshafts, bolted to the differential. Each halfshaft has a constant velocity (CV) joint at each end, allowing a full range of motion as the vehicle passes over bumps and depressions.

Axle Shaft, Bearing and Oil Seal

REMOVAL & INSTALLATION

> ❊❊**CAUTION**
>
> This procedure requires removal of the rear brake pads or shoes. Brake pads and shoes contain asbestos, which has been determined to a cancer causing agent. Never clean the brake surfaces with compressed air! Avoid inhaling and dust from brake surfaces! When cleaning brakes, use commercially available brake cleaning fluids.

Except Multi-Link Suspension

▶ **See Figures 39, 40 and 41**

1. Raise the vehicle and safely support it on jackstands.
2. Remove the applicable wheel.
3. Remove the brake caliper mounting bolts and remove the caliper. Secure the caliper, with a piece of stiff wire, to the rear springs.

➡ **Do not allow the caliper to hang by the brake line.**

4. Remove the brake disc and parking brake shoes.
5. Remove the thrust washer bolts through the holes in the axle shaft flange. Using a puller (slide hammer), remove the axle shaft, bearing and oil seal assembly. If a slide hammer is not available, the brake disc may be bolted onto the axle backwards (remember to mount the nuts tapered side out) and used to pull the axle free.
6. Remove the inner oil seal using a suitable puller or small prybar. Clean the inside of the rear axle tube.
7. Press off the toothed wheel. Use 2 V-block.
8. Raise up the seal and pressure plate on the axle shaft so that the divided press plate can be placed on the bearing. Place the press yoke over the press plate. Removing the bearing together with the snapring. Use press tool 5212 or equivalent.

To install:

9. Pack the new bearing with grease before installation. The preferred method is with a bearing packer (a low cost tool available at most automotive supply shops) but it may be done by hand if necessary. The bearing must be packed from one side until the grease comes out the other side.

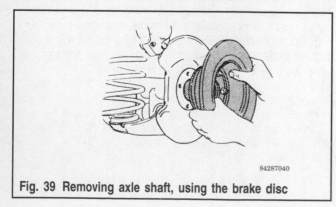

84287040

Fig. 39 Removing axle shaft, using the brake disc

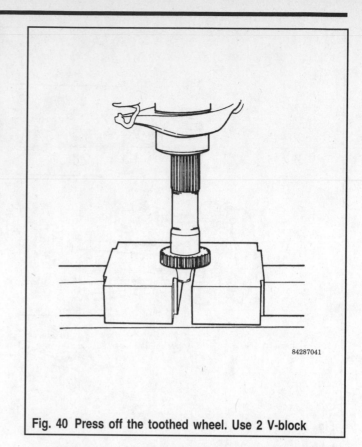

84287041

Fig. 40 Press off the toothed wheel. Use 2 V-block

10. Fill the space between the lips of the new oil seal with wheel bearing grease. Position the new seal on the axle shaft. Using a press, install the bearing with a new locking ring, onto the axle shaft.

> ❊❊**WARNING**
>
> When reinstalling the additional toothed gear on axles, the gear must be installed precisely 116mm onto the shaft. The acceptable margin is ± 0.1mm. If at all possible, use Volvo tool 2412 which will allow precise location of this gear. If this gear is not properly located, the vehicle may not run properly.

11. Install the inner oil seal in the axle shaft housing using a seal installation tool (such as Volvo 5009 or similar) and drift.
12. Install the axle shaft into the housing, rotating it so that it aligns with the differential. Install the bolts for the thrust washer and tighten to 29 ft. lbs. (40 Nm)
13. Install the parking brake shoes, brake disc, caliper and pads. Use new bolts and torque to 58 Nm. Make sure the brake disc rotates free of the brake pads.
14. Install the wheel and adjust the parking brake. Lower the vehicle.

Multi-link Suspension

▶ **See Figures 42, 43 and 44**

Because of the nature of the Multi-Link suspension, component position and bolt tightening values (torque) are critical to ride quality and rear wheel alignment. When installing components, exact location must be achieved — close doesn't count.

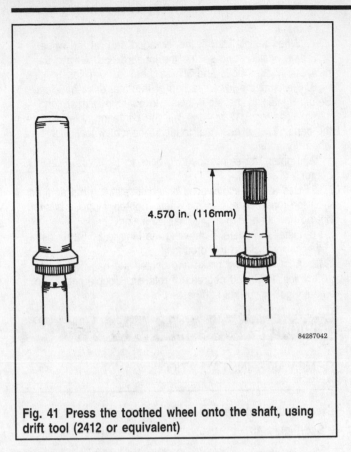

Fig. 41 Press the toothed wheel onto the shaft, using drift tool (2412 or equivalent)

4.570 in. (116mm)

84287042

Tightening specifications must be followed exactly or component function will be impaired.

1. Disconnect the negative battery cable.

2. Raise and support the vehicle safely. Do not allow the rear lifting arms to interfere with the support arms.

3. Remove the wheels. Remove the brake caliper mounting bolts and use a piece of wire to hang the caliper out of the way.

4. Mark the position of the brake disc relative to its small locating pin, then remove the disc. Remove the brake shoes.

5. Disconnect and remove the parking brake cable from the wheel bearing housing.

6. Remove the retaining bolt for the support arm at the housing. Tap the support arm loose.

7. Remove the nut and bolt holding the lower link arm to the housing.

8. Remove the retaining bolt for the track rod (Panhard rod) at the bearing housing and use a small claw-type puller to remove the track rod.

9. Loosen and remove the large nut holding the end of the driveshaft within the bearing housing.

10. Remove the retaining nut for the upper link at the bearing housing. The wheel bearing housing can now be removed as a unit.

➡ **There are shims between the bearing housing and the upper link arm. Collect them when the housing is removed.**

11. Mount the housing assembly in a vise. Place a counterhold tool (5340 or equivalent) between the hub and bearing housing. Press out the hub with a proper sized drift.

12. Remove the circlip retaining the bearing in the wheel bearing housing. Press the bearing out of the wheel bearing housing, using a counterhold tool (5341 or equivalent) and a suitable drift. Apply the drift to the inner ring.

13. Use a bearing puller (2722 or equivalent) and a counterhold (5310 or equivalent) to pull the inner ring off the hub.

To install:

14. Press in the new bearing using the drift and counterhold. Install the circlip.

15. Using a counterhold below the inner ring, press the hub into place.

❋❋WARNING

If the counterhold (support) is not applied to the inner ring, the wheel bearing will be destroyed during the hub installation.

16. Install the wheel bearing housing onto the driveshaft and install the driveshaft retaining nut. Secure the nut, but don't torque it; that will be done later.

17. Install the shims between the upper link and the wheel bearing housing and then install the retaining nut at the upper link.

18. Pull the wheel bearing housing outwards at the top and tighten the upper link arm nut to 85 ft. lbs. This pulling out is essential to insure correct wheel alignment when completed.

19. Tilt the bearing housing outwards at the bottom (as necessary) to refit the lower link arm and it retaining bolt. When in place, pull the bottom of the bearing housing inwards (towards the center of the vehicle) and tighten the link arm to 36 ft.lbs. PLUS an additional 90 degrees of rotation.

20. Install the support arm and its bolt. Tighten the nut to 44 ft. lbs. PLUS an additional 90 degrees of rotation.

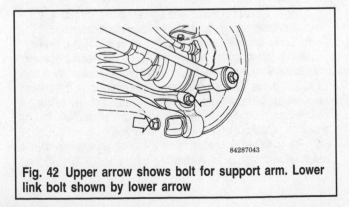

84287043

Fig. 42 Upper arrow shows bolt for support arm. Lower link bolt shown by lower arrow

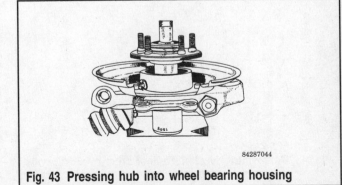

84287044

Fig. 43 Pressing hub into wheel bearing housing

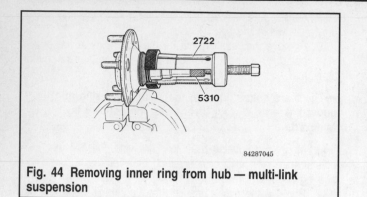

84287045

Fig. 44 Removing inner ring from hub — multi-link suspension

21. Install the track rod (Panhard rod) and tighten to 63 ft. lbs.

22. Reinstall the parking brake cable at the bearing housing.

23. Reinstall the brake shoes, the brake disc as marked and the brake caliper. Tighten the caliper mounting bolts to 44 ft. lbs.

24. Install the wheel, tightening the lugs to 60-62 ft. lbs. Lower the vehicle.

25. Tighten the driveshaft nut to 103 ft. lbs. PLUS 60 degrees of rotation.

Halfshafts (Multi-link Suspension)

REMOVAL & INSTALLATION

▶ **See Figure 45**

1. Loosen the lug nuts for the appropriate wheel. Loosen the large halfshaft retaining nut in the center of the wheel bearing housing.

2. Block the front wheels and safely elevate and support the rear of the vehicle.

3. Remove the wheel and remove the halfshaft retaining nut.

4. At the center of the vehicle, remove the eight bolts holding the upper and lower sections of the final drive housing.

5. Remove the bolts holding the halfshaft to the final drive unit (differential) and remove the shaft from the wheel bearing housing.

6. When the shaft is removed, inspect the rubber boots for any sign of splitting or cracking. The boots must be intact and waterproof or the joint within is at risk. A light coat of silicone or vinyl protectant applied to a CV boot will extend its life.

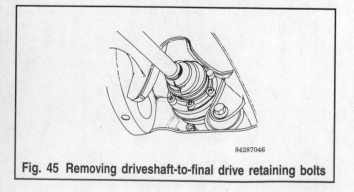

84287046

Fig. 45 Removing driveshaft-to-final drive retaining bolts

To install:

7. When reinstalling, fit the threaded end (at the wheel) first, then position and secure the inboard end. Always use new, lightly oiled bolts and tighten them to 70 ft. lbs.

8. Reinstall the lower section of the final drive housing. Before tightening the eight mounting bolts, install two long 12mm bolts (or 2 12mm drifts) in the centering holes and align the panel. This is essential to insure correct wheel alignment when finished.

9. Tighten the eight mounting bolts to 52 ft. lbs. PLUS 30 degrees of rotation.

10. Use a new, lightly oiled halfshaft retaining nut and install it on the threaded end of the shaft. Tighten it until it is snug but do not attempt to apply final tightening.

11. Install the wheel, tightening the lugs to 60-62 ft. lbs. Lower the vehicle to the ground.

12. Apply the hand brake and tighten the halfshaft nut to 103 ft. lbs. PLUS 60 degrees of rotation. Double check the wheel lugs for correct tightness.

Pinion Seal

REMOVAL & INSTALLATION

Except Multi-Link Suspension

▶ **See Figure 46**

1. Disconnect the driveshaft at the final drive unit (differential).

2. Loosen and remove the large center nut in the center of the pinion flange. The use of a counterhold device is highly recommended. (Volvo 5149 or similar)

3. Use a puller to remove the flange from the housing.

4. Remove the old seal from the inside of the casing and discard it.

5. Clean and check the sealing surfaces. Replace the coupling flange if the sealing surface is worn.

To install:

6. Prepare the new seal by greasing the lip area and greasing the small spring to hold it in place during installation. Install the seal using suitable drivers; do not crimp or gouge the seal during installation.

7. With an installation tool (Volvo 5156 or similar), reinstall the flange in the housing.

8. Check the serial number on the rear axle. If it begins with an 'S', follow Step 8b, below. If it does not contain an S prefix, continue with 8a below.

   a. Install the center nut and tighten it to 145-180 ft. lbs. Use a counterhold to hold the flange while tightening.

   b. Axles denoted by the S prefix in their serial number contain a compression sleeve within the differential housing. On these vehicles, install the center nut and carefully tighten it to 1.3 ft. lbs. (finger-tight only). Make sure that the brakes are not applied and turn the flange at about 1 revolution per second so as to tighten the nut. As an alternative, the nut may be tightened with a wrench to at least 130 ft. lbs.

9. Reinstall the driveshaft. Check the oil level within the final drive and top up as necessary.

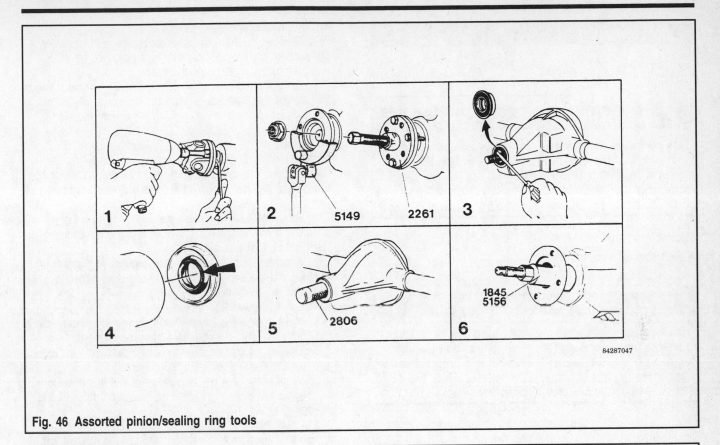

Fig. 46 Assorted pinion/sealing ring tools

Multi-Link Suspension

◗ See Figure 47

1. Matchmark the driveshaft flange and the final drive (differential) flange. Remove the bolts and separate the shaft from the final drive.

2. Loosen and remove the large center nut in the center of the pinion flange. The use of a counterhold device is highly recommended. (Volvo 5149 or similar). Remove the 1 additional bolt from the flange. This bolt is a weight which serves to balance the rotational forces of the driveshaft.

3. Matchmark or etch reference marks on the flange and its center shaft.

4. Drain the oil from the housing.

5. Use a puller to remove the flange from the housing.

6. Remove the old seal from the inside of the casing and discard it.

7. Clean and check the sealing surfaces. Replace the coupling flange if the sealing surface is worn.

To install:

8. Prepare the new seal by greasing the lip area and greasing the small spring to hold it in place during installation. The use of a seal puller such as Volvo 5069 is highly recommended.

9. Install the seal using suitable drivers; do not crimp or gouge the seal during installation.

10. Position the flange so that the marks align. With an installation tool (Volvo 5156 or similar), reinstall the flange in the housing.

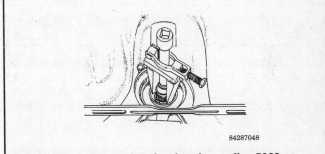

Fig. 47 Removing seal, using bearing puller 5069 or equivalent

11. Install a new, lightly oiled center nut and tighten it to 132-145 ft. lbs.

✳✳WARNING

Do not overtighten the center nut. The pinion bearings will become over-adjusted and fail prematurely.

12. Install the bolt for weight in its original position.

13. Install the driveshaft, observing correct placement as shown by the matchmarks. Use new nuts and bolts and tighten them to 36 ft. lbs.

14. Refill the final drive unit with oil.

Axle Housing

REMOVAL & INSTALLATION

✴✴WARNING

This operation requires removal of a substantial amount of weight from the rear of the vehicle. Position the jack-stands at front end, under the control arm brackets and at rear, under the jack mounts. If the vehicle is not supported as described, it may become front heavy.

Except Multi-Link
▶ See Figures 48 and 49

1. Raise the vehicle and support it safely.

✴✴WARNING

This operation requires removal of a substantial amount of weight from the rear of the vehicle. Position the jack-stands at front end, under the control arm brackets and at rear, under the jack mounts. If the vehicle is not supported as described, it may become front heavy.

2. On the 240 Series, remove the rear axle vent hose and the brake line brackets. Do not loosen any brake lines; they will be left intact.

3. Remove the brake calipers and secure them to the upper spring mount with a piece of stiff wire.

4. Remove the axle shafts, as outlined in this section.

5. Position the jacks or cradle below the rear axle so that the axle is supported.

6. If the exhaust system runs under the axle housing, disconnect the first joint forward of the axle, disconnect any hangers or brackets behind the axle and remove the rear section of the exhaust system.

7. Disconnect the reaction rods or torque rod from the axle housing.

8. Disconnect the panhard rod from the rear axle.

9. Remove the parking brake cables and mounting brackets from the rear axle.

10. Disconnect the connector for the speedometer transmitter and if equipped, the connectors for the ETC system.

11. Loosen and remove the bolts attaching the driveshaft to the pinion flange.

12. Double check that the axle assembly is firmly supported by the jacks or cradle. Remove the bolts which hold the lower mount of the shock absorber.

13. On the 240 Series:
   a. Remove the adjacent bolt which holds the anti-roll bar (sway bar).
   b. Loosen, but do not remove the trailing arm bolts at the front of the trailing arm.
   c. Lower the jacks or cradle and allow the axle assemble to pivot downwards on the trailing arms. When clear of the vehicle and well supported on the jacks or cradle, remove the trailing arm mounts at the axle housing.
   d. Remove the rear axle assembly.

14. On the 700 and 900 Series:
   a. Remove the front brackets for the support arms. Pry the support arms loose from the front mounts.
   b. Remove the rear axle assembly.
   c. Once the axle assembly is clear of the vehicle, remove the anti-roll bar (sway bar). Mark the support arms for the left and right sides and remove the arms from the axle housing.

To install:
15. On the 240 Series:
   a. Position the axle unit under the vehicle and attach the trailing arm mounts. Tighten the bolts only enough to hold and still allow motion.
   b. Raise the axle and align the springs to their upper mounts. Install the anti-roll bar bolts and the bolts for the lower shock absorber mounts
   c. Attach the torque rods to their mounts and attach the Panhard rod to its mount. Tighten these bolts only enough to hold and still allow motion.

16. On the 700 and 900 Series:
   a. Make sure the left and right markings are observed. Fit the bushings within the clamps and fit the clamps.
   b. Tighten the clamps in a crisscross pattern to 33 ft. lbs. and reinstall the anti-roll bar if so equipped.
   c. Position the axle on its jacks or cradle and elevate it so the support arms align with both their front mounts and the spring seats.
   d. Install the front brackets for the support arms and tighten the two bolts to 35 ft. lbs. Tighten the nut to 62 ft. lbs.
   e. Install the lower shock absorber bolts and tighten to 62 ft. lbs.

17. Reinstall the driveshaft to the pinion flange.

18. Connect the wiring for the ETC sensor and/or the speedometer sensor, as required.

19. Install the parking brake cables and brackets. Adjust the parking brake.

20. Reinstall the exhaust system, as necessary.

21. Complete installation by reversing the removal procedure. Tighten all components to the specifications in this section.

22. Check oil level in differential.

Multi-Link Suspension
▶ See Figure 50

Because of the nature of the Multi-Link suspension, component position and bolt tightening values (torque) are critical to ride quality and rear wheel alignment. When installing components, exact location must be achieved — close doesn't count. Tightening specifications must be followed exactly or component function will be impaired.

1. Raise the vehicle and support it firmly with stands. Locate front lifting arms as far forward as possible. Make sure the rear lifting arms do not interfere with the support arms. Remove the rear wheels.

2. On one side only, remove the bolt holding the support arm to the wheel bearing housing. Drive out the support arm.

3. Remove the nut and bolt holding the lower link arm to the wheel bearing housing.

4. Remove the bolts holding the track rod (Panhard rod) to the wheel bearing housing. Use a small claw puller and an M12 bolt 50mm long to move the rod away from the housing.

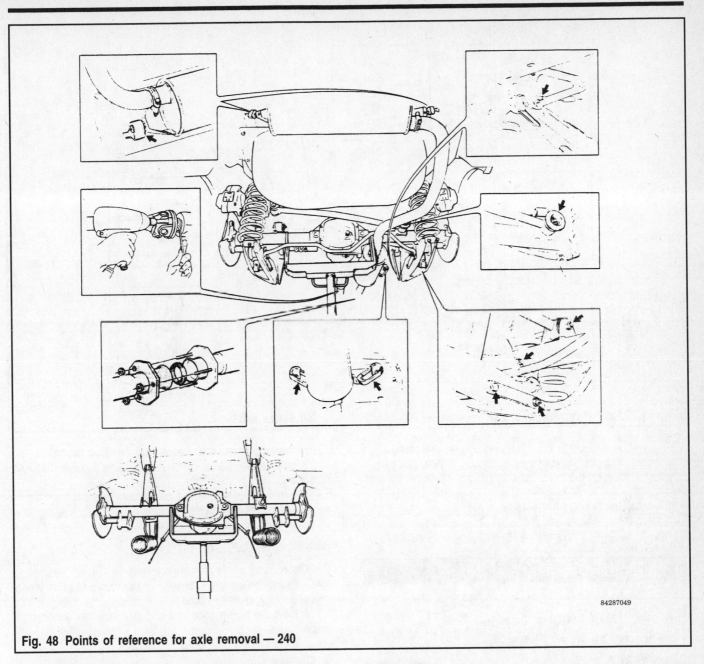

Fig. 48 Points of reference for axle removal — 240

5. Remove the bolts joining the upper and lower sections of the rear axle housing.

6. Swing the lower part of the wheel bearing housing outwards and swing down the lower part of the axle housing. It will still have the arms attached to it and will be attached to the vehicle by the arms on the opposite side.

7. Matchmark the flanges at the rear of the driveshaft. Remove the four bolts and lower the driveshaft.

8. Place a jack or cradle under the center of the final drive (differential) unit. Raise the jack and support the unit.

9. Remove the bolts holding the final drive to the upper housing.

10. Lower the final drive slightly. Remove the wiring to the impulse sender.

11. Remove the bolts holding the axles to the final drive. Carefully lower the final drive unit and remove it from under the vehicle.

To install:

12. Raise the final drive unit almost to its final position under the vehicle and connect the impulse sender cable. Tighten the bolt to 7 ft. lbs.

13. Raise the unit to its final position and install the three bolts to the upper housing. Tighten the bolts. When the bolts are secure, the jack or cradle may be removed.

14. Attach the halfshafts to the final drive. Tighten the bolts to specifications.

15. Install the driveshaft to the pinion flange. Remember to observe the matchmarks made earlier and position the driveshaft properly.

16. Raise the lower section of the axle housing. Loosely install the bolts which retain it to the upper housing. Before tightening the mounting bolts, install 2 long 12mm bolts (or 2 12mm drifts) in the centering holes and align the panel. This is essential to insure correct wheel alignment when finished. Tighten the mounting bolts to specifications.

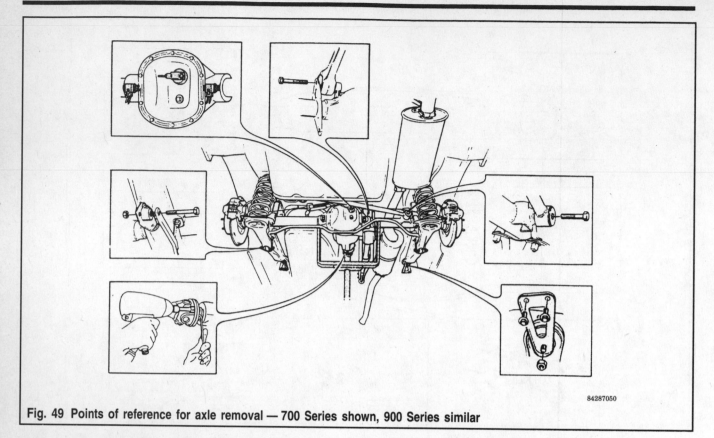

Fig. 49 Points of reference for axle removal — 700 Series shown, 900 Series similar

84287050

17. Position and install the lower link arm on the wheel bearing housing. Before tightening the nut and bolt, pull the housing in towards the center of the vehicle. When all the play is out of the mount, tighten the link bolt to specifications.

18. Install the support arm and track rod.

19. Install the wheels and lower the vehicle from its stands. Check the oil level in the final drive and top up as necessary.

Differential Overhaul

Type 1030, 1031 (1041) Rear Axles
▶ **See Figures 51, 52, 53, 54 and 55**

DISASSEMBLE

1. Mount the axle in a suitable fixture (2522 or equivalent).

2. Remove inspection cover and drain oil into a suitable container.

3. Remove the driveshaft pressure plates and driveshafts. Use brake disc to remove driveshafts.

4. Check the differential housing clamp markings and remove the clamps. Attach an expander and holder (2394 and 2601 or equivalent). Expand the tool until it engages the holes. Turn the screw until the differential can be lifted out.

5. Remove the drive pinion nut and remove the pinion flange, using a suitable puller.

6. Tap out the pinion with a plastic mallet. Remove the pinion seal, oil thrower plate and bearing.

7. Remove the pinion bearing outer race, using a brass drift. If equipped, discard the shim fitted under the rear bearing race.

8. Press the rear pinion bearing off the drive pinion.

9. Remove the differential bearings, using a puller (2483 or equivalent). Retain the shims.

10. Remove the bolts from the ring gear and separate the ring gear from its mounting, if required.

11. Remove the driveshaft seals.

CLEANING & INSPECTION

- Clean and inspect all components.
- Replace the complete bearing, if the rollers or races show sign of scoring or other damage.
- Inspect the pinion gear and ring gear teeth for scoring, gouging, etc.
- Inspect sealing face on drive flange.

ASSEMBLE

➡**Oil all surfaces before assembling.**

1. Install the pinion bearing outer races. Make sure the bearing races are fully seated.

2. Install the rear pinion bearing and shims, if required. Use shims of thickness 0.0394 inch (1.0mm). Press on the bearing using a suitable sleeve.

3. Install the pinion:

   a. Type without compression sleeve: Install a 0.0295 inch (0.75mm) shim and almost one turn of soldering wire approximately 0.0591 inch (1.5mm) in thickness.

   b. Type with compression sleeve: Do not install sleeve at this point, but proceed to Step 8.

4. Insert the pinion and press on the front bearing. Use the pinion nut and tighten to obtain a bearing preload of 1.8-2.6 ft. lbs. (2.5-3.5 Nm) for new bearing or 1.1-1.8 ft. lbs. (1.5-2.5

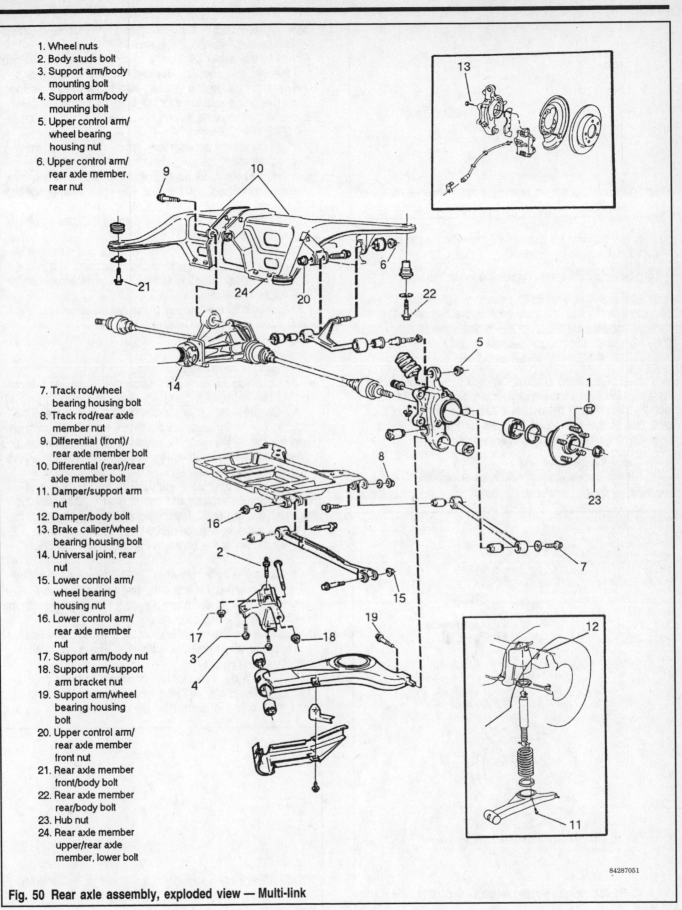

1. Wheel nuts
2. Body studs bolt
3. Support arm/body mounting bolt
4. Support arm/body mounting bolt
5. Upper control arm/wheel bearing housing nut
6. Upper control arm/rear axle member, rear nut
7. Track rod/wheel bearing housing bolt
8. Track rod/rear axle member nut
9. Differential (front)/rear axle member bolt
10. Differential (rear)/rear axle member bolt
11. Damper/support arm nut
12. Damper/body bolt
13. Brake caliper/wheel bearing housing bolt
14. Universal joint, rear nut
15. Lower control arm/wheel bearing housing nut
16. Lower control arm/rear axle member nut
17. Support arm/body nut
18. Support arm/support arm bracket nut
19. Support arm/wheel bearing housing bolt
20. Upper control arm/rear axle member front nut
21. Rear axle member front/body bolt
22. Rear axle member rear/body bolt
23. Hub nut
24. Rear axle member upper/rear axle member, lower bolt

84287051

Fig. 50 Rear axle assembly, exploded view — Multi-link

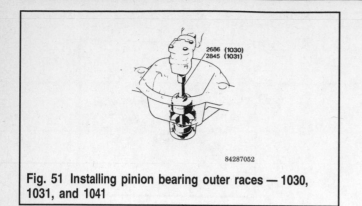

Fig. 51 Installing pinion bearing outer races — 1030, 1031, and 1041

Nm) for run-in. Turn the pinion until the rollers have been centered and torque is steady.

➡**Turn at approximately 1 revolution per second.**

5. Pinion Height Setting: The pinion must be set at a certain distance (A) from the centerline of the ring gear. This distance should be 2.25±0.0012 inch. (plus the deviation tolerance marked on the pinion. Example: If the pinion is marked 30, A=57.15 + 0.30 = 57.45mm ±0.03mm.

➡**In case of a pinion marked '30' or not provided with a marking, the face of the gauge must be 0.0118±0.0012 inch (0.30±0.30mm) below the measuring surface of the tool. The pinion setting is adjusted by installing a shim (B) between the pinion end and rear bearing.**

6. Check the pinion setting:
   a. Place the measuring tool (2393 or equivalent) in the differential bearing seat and on the pinion. Check that the

tool is fully seated in the bearing seat and that the gauge is in firm contact with the pinion end.
   b. Place a holder (2284 or equivalent) and a dial indicator on the rear axle housing. Measure the difference in height between the gauge and smaller diameter of the measuring tool. The gauge should be below the face of the smaller diameter by the same amount as marking on the pinion ±0.0012 inch (0.03mm).
   c. If adjustment is necessary, remove the rear pinion bearing. Measure the shim thickness. If the difference is positive, add shims as needed. If the difference is negative, reduce until tolerance is reached. Example: If difference is +0.10, add 0.05-0.12. Select a 0.08mm shim.

7. Adjustment of pinion bearing preload: (applies to pinions without compression sleeve)
   a. Measure the total thickness of shim and soldering wire.
   b. If the piston setting difference is positive, add same amount as when adjusting setting. If the difference is negative, subtract the same amount.

8. Insert the pinion and install the compression sleeve or shims. Press on the front bearing.

9. Lubricate the seal lips and spring. Install the seal and oil thrower plate.

10. Install the drive flange and nut.
   a. On pinion without compression sleeve, tighten the nut to 148-184 ft. lbs. (200-250 Nm). Check the bearing preload.
   b. On pinion with compression sleeve, tighten the nut in stages. Turn the pinion until the rollers have been centered and the torque is steady. Conclude when the correct bearing preload has been reached. Replace the compression sleeve, if preload is exceeded.

11. Check that the mating surfaces of the ring gear and mounting flange are clean and free of grease. Oiled new bolts and install the ring gear. Tighten bolts alternately to 26 ft. lbs. (35 Nm) + angle tighten through 60 degrees.

12. Adjustment of the backlash and differential bearing preload:
   a. Mount the assembly rings (2595 or equivalent) on the differential housing. Lubricate the ring seating surfaces. Mount the rings on the bearing seats of the housing with the black ring on the ring gear side.
   b. Install the differential housing in ;the case. Pry apart the assembly rings until the differential housing is seated firmly without preload.
   c. Mount a dial indicator into position with the plunger resting on the ring gear wheel tooth approximately 3mm from the big end of tooth. Hold the pinion and move the ring

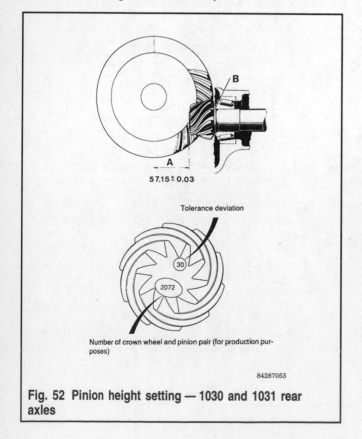

Fig. 52 Pinion height setting — 1030 and 1031 rear axles

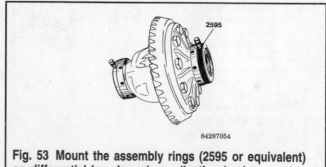

Fig. 53 Mount the assembly rings (2595 or equivalent) on differential housing when adjusting backlash/differential bearing preload

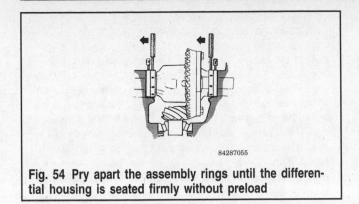

Fig. 54 Pry apart the assembly rings until the differential housing is seated firmly without preload

gear forwards and backwards against the plunger. Backlash should vary between 0.0039-0.0063 inches (0.10-0.16mm).

d. Adjust the clearance by using pins to turn both assembly rings in the same directional. Lock the rings when the backlash is correct. Remove the differential housing and assembly rings.

e. Measure the thickness of the shims.

➡**Check that the correct bearings and shims are located on either side of the differential housing, otherwise the backlash will be incorrect.**

f. Place the bearing (ring gear side) in the fixture, 2600 or equivalent, with the outer race facing upward, along with mount plate, spring and nut. Flat side of nut must face downwards. Turn the plate and bearing forwards and backwards a few times to ensure the rollers assume correct position.

g. Mount an assembly ring (1) on the fixture. Mount the holder, 2284 or equivalent, on the dial indicator. Place the dial indicator plunger on the assembly ring and zero the gauge. Next, place the plunger against the bearing and read the gauge.

h. Use a micrometer to measure the shims with combined thickness equal to indicated value plus 0.0028 inch (0.07mm) for new bearing and 0.0016 inch (0.04mm) for used bearing. This will give correct differential bearing preload.

i. Place the shims and measured bearing aside, then repeat Steps 12a-12h for the other side.

13. Install the differential bearings: Place the shims and locking plate in position. Make sure the locking plate is not jammed between the bearing and housing.

14. Install the differential housing: Mount the expander (2394 or equivalent) and holder (2601 or equivalent). Expand the tool

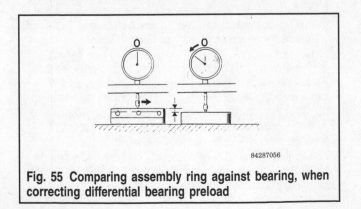

Fig. 55 Comparing assembly ring against bearing, when correcting differential bearing preload

until it engages and make 2.5 additional turns. Place the differential and bearings in the housing. Remove the tool.

15. Install the clamps, using new bolts. Note the markings made previously.

16. Recheck that the backlash is within specifications.

17. Install the inspection cover. Tighten the bolts 15-22 ft. lbs. (20-30 Nm).

18. Install the driveshaft seals.

19. Install the driveshafts along with the parking brake retaining springs. Tighten the driveshaft pressure plates to 30 ft. lbs. (40 Nm).

Type 1035 (1045) Rear Axles

▶ **See Figures 56 and 57**

DISASSEMBLE

1. Remove the weight from the housing. Mount the differential in a fixture (5370 or equivalent).

2. Remove the brackets for the rear bushings in the housing. Lever out the driveshafts and remove the cover.

3. Remove the screws that secure the locks washers on the differential bearing adjusting nuts. Remove the adjusting nuts and differential housing.

4. Remove the drive flange retaining nut, using a counterhold (5149, 5426 or equivalent). Mark the location of the drive flange in relation to the pinion.

5. Using a puller (5304 or equivalent), remove the drive flange.

6. Using a puller and counterhold, remove the seal.

7. Using a brass drift, remove the pinion bearing races.

8. Remove the rear pinion bearing slightly, using a puller (2844 or equivalent). Place the ring (5214 or equivalent) in a press. Place the half-rings (5216 or equivalent) around the bearing. Press off the bearing.

9. Remove the differential bearings, using a suitable puller. Inspect the bearing and gear set.

10. If necessary, remove the tooth wheel.

➡**The tooth wheel must be replaced if removed.**

11. Remove the spring pin (roll pin) and tap the pinion shaft out.

12. Rotate the differential pinions (gear shaft) through the quarter turn. Remove the differential gear set and washers.

13. Inspect all components and replace any components showing wear.

ASSEMBLE

➡**Oil all components before assembling.**

1. Place the spring washer on the differential gears. Place the pinions facing each other and rotate into position.

2. Install the pinion shaft. Use puller (5069 or equivalent) as an expander to pry apart the differential gears.

3. Insert the support washers behind the pinions. Install the spring pin and lock by punching edge of hole.

4. If removed, press on a new tooth wheel.

5. Install the shims behind the pinion bearing races. Check that the shims are properly seated. Oil the bearing races and install.

6. Install the rear pinion bearing, using a sleeve (2842 or equivalent). The shims must be located under the bearing race in housing when adjusting the pinion height.

7. Install the pinion without the compression sleeve. Press on the bearing, using the nut and special wrench (2404 or equivalent). The wrench must be modified as illustrated.

8. Tighten nut to obtain a bearing preload of 0.9-2.1 ft. lbs. (1.2-2.8 Nm). Turn the pinion until rollers are centered. Use a torque meter and turn 1 revolution per second.

9. Pinion height setting: The pinion must be set at a certain distance (A) from the centerline of the ring gear. This distance should be 2.25±0.0012 inch. (plus the deviation tolerance marked on the pinion. Example: If the pinion is marked 30, A=57.15 + 0.30 = 57.45mm ±0.03mm.

➡**In case of a pinion marked "30" or not provided with a marking, the face of the gauge must be 0.0118±0.0012 inch (0.30±0.30mm) below the measuring surface of the tool. The pinion setting is adjusted by installing a shim (C) between the bearing inner race and housing.**

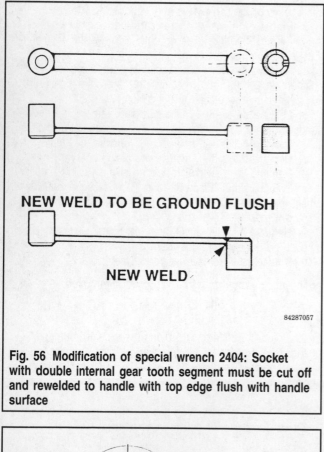

84287057

Fig. 56 Modification of special wrench 2404: Socket with double internal gear tooth segment must be cut off and rewelded to handle with top edge flush with handle surface

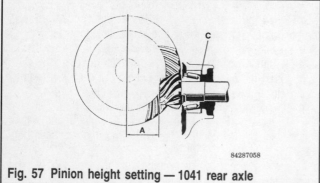

84287058

Fig. 57 Pinion height setting — 1041 rear axle

10. Check the pinion setting:

   a. Install the adjusting nuts in housing with original O-rings. Lubricate the nuts and mating surfaces in housing. Tighten the nuts edge to edge. Set up measuring too (2393 or equivalent).

   b. Place a holder (2284 or equivalent) and a dial indicator on the rear axle housing. Measure the vertical distance between the plug gauge and smaller diameter of the measuring tool. The gauge should be below measuring surface of the smaller diameter by the distance marked on pinion±0.0012 inch (0.03mm).

   c. If adjustment is necessary, tap out the bearing race. Measure the shim thickness. If the difference is negative, reduce shim thickness until tolerance is reached.

11. Install the bearing race and shim.

12. Install pinion and compression sleeve. Press on the front bearing.

13. Lubricate the seal. Install the seal and oil thrower plate.

14. Install the drive flange. Use a new nut and tighten in stages. Turn the pinion until the bearing rollers have been centered. Quit tightening when the correct bearing preload is reached. Value for new, oiled bearing is 0.89-2.07 ft. lbs. (1.2-2.8 Nm). Nut torque should be between 133-207 ft. lbs. (180-280 Nm). Replace compression sleeve if preload is exceeded.

15. Check that the mating surfaces of the ring gear and mounting flange are clean and free of grease. Oiled new bolts and install the ring gear. Tighten bolts alternately to 26 ft. lbs. (35 Nm) + angle tighten through 60 degrees.

16. Press on the differential bearings. Check that the locking plate is correctly located in housing.

17. Adjustment of the backlash and differential bearing preload:

   a. Install the differential housing in the case. Install the adjusting nuts with new O-rings and seals. Lubricate the seal and oil the nut. Install the nuts together with bearing races.

   b. Install washer (5791 or equivalent) for 1 adjusting nut. Mount a dial indicator into position with the plunger at opposite side of housing.

   c. Using a suitable wrench, tighten the nuts until a small backlash is felt at the ring gear and the dial indicator just begins to indicate.

   d. Rotate the differential housing a few turns until the bearing rollers are centered. Adjusting nuts are now tightened as far as possible without imposing bearing preload.

18. Adjust and check backlash:

   a. Mount the dial indicator in position and position the plunger on the ring gear tooth approximately 0.12 in. (3mm) from the outer end of the tooth. Hold the pinion and move the ring gear towards and away from the plunger. Flank clearance may vary between 0.0039-0.0063 in. (0.10-0.16mm).

   b. Adjust by moving nut in or out. If nut is adjuster outwards, the other nut should be adjusted inwards by the same amount. Adjust until the correct backlash is achieved.

19. Coat the rear cover faces with liquid sealing compound (P/N 1-161-059-9 or equivalent) and install the rear cover. Tighen the bolts 15-22 ft. lbs. (20-30 Nm).

20. Tighten adjusting nuts a further notch on each side.

21. Tighten the adjusting nuts to 30-41 ft. lbs. (40-56 Nm). Lock the adjusting nuts with lock washers.

22. Install the side brackets. Tighten nuts to 30-41 ft. lbs. (40-56 Nm).

23. Install the driveshafts. Install the weight and tighten to 15-21 ft. lbs. (20-28 Nm).

24. Fill the differential with oil prior to installation.

Reconditioning of Automatic Differential Lock(Type 1041 and 1045 Rear Axles)

▶ See Figure 58

DISASSEMBLE

1. Mount the axle in a suitable fixture (2522 or equivalent).

2. Remove inspection cover and drain oil into a suitable container.

3. Remove the driveshaft pressure plates and driveshafts. Use brake disc to remove driveshafts.

4. Remove the bearing caps and remove the differential from the rear axle.

5. Attach an expander and holder (2394 and 2601 or equivalent). Expand the tool until it engages the holes. Turn the screw until the differential can be lifted out.

➡Note the location of the bearing races to ensure that these are reinstalled in the same position.

6. Remove the differential bearings and locking plate, using a puller (2483 or equivalent). Retain the shims.

7. Remove the bolts from the ring gear and separate the ring gear from its mounting, if required.

8. Slacken the bolts securing the differential housing-to-flange. Tap the bolt heads lightly to separate endplate from the housing. Turn the housing upside down and remove the bolts. Lift off the endplate. Differential gear adjusting washer may remain attached to plate.

9. Lift out the differential gear on the ring gear side, completely with plate assembly, guides and adjusting washer (if not already removed with endplate. Remove engagement/disengagement mechanism.

10. Remove the pinion shaft (differential gear) locking pin, using a long 3/16 inch (4mm) drift. Place the differential housing on the counterhold (2861 or equivalent) with 1 of the recesses opposite the locking pin hole.

11. Tap out the pinion shaft from the opposite locking pin hole.

12. Remove the reaction block and differential gear set and pressure plates.

➡If the gear set is to be replaced, mark the gears to ensure that they are reinstalled in the correct positions when reassembling.

13. Remove the locking ring securing the plate assembly on the ring gear side.

14. Remove the plate assembly and guides. Remove the cam wheel from the differential gear.

15. Wash all components and inspect for wear, cracking and other damage.

ASSEMBLE

➡Oil all components, with final drive oil, before assembling.

1. Install the plate assembly on the inner differential gear. Use grease to hold the guides in position on the plate assembly.

2. Install the differential gear and plate assembly in housing: Before installing differential gear and plate assembly, place new adjusting washer of the same thickness as original in the housing.

3. Install the differential pinions (check markings) and thrust washers, reaction block and pinion shaft (differential gear). Tap the shaft in until it engages the hole at the other end.

➡The pinion shaft is smaller in diameter at one end.

4. Mount a C-clamp in a vice and center the reaction block between the differential pinions. Use the C-clamp to clamp the differential housing between the reaction block and differential gear bearing seat.

5. Measure the backlash between the differential gear and pinion at inner side of housing:

   a. Mount a magnetic stand and dial indicator on the differential housing face. Measure the backlash of both pinions. Correct value is 0.0098-0.0591 inch (0.025-0.15mm). If clearance is required, shims of different thicknesses are available.

   b. Place the dial indicator plunger in the middle of the tooth. Press the pinion in the direction of the thrust washer while measuring the clearance.

   c. If adjusting, repeat Steps 11 and 12 under 'DISASSEMBLE' and Steps 5a and 5b above, then recheck clearance.

6. Tap out the pinion shaft from the opposite locking pin hole. Remove the reaction block and differential gear set and pressure plates.

7. Install the differential pinions. Make sure that each pinion is located on the correct side after measurement. Install the thrust washers, reaction block, pinion shaft in correct direction.

8. Position the differential gear on the ring gear side in engagement with pinions in differential housing. Install the new shim of the same thickness as original at end of differential gear. Use grease to hold the shims in position.

9. Install the differential housing endplate and housing joint bolts. Tighten to 6-8 ft. lbs. (8-10 Nm).

10. Mount the differential housing, as before, in the C-clamp.

11. Measure the backlash between the differential pinions and differential gear on the ring gear side:

   a. Mount plate (5971 or equivalent) in position using 1 of the ring gear bolt holes. Mount a magnetic stand and dial indicator in position.

   b. Measure the backlash of the differential gears. Correct clearance should be 0.0984-0.1693 inch (0.25-0.43mm). If clearance is required, shims of different thicknesses are available.

   c. Remove the magnetic stand, plate, bolts in endplate, differential gear on ring gear side, shim, pinion shaft, differential pinions, thrust washers and reaction block.

12. Tighten the differential gear at inner end of housing, completely with correct shim and plate assembly and differential gear at ring gear end with shim in endplate.

➡When tightening, use 2 M12 bolts, 2 large flat washers, nuts and modified washers. Place the washers against the differential gears.

13. Assemble the differential housing and housing endplate. Tighten bolts to 6-8 ft. lbs. (8-10 Nm).

14. Measure the clearance between the axial faces of the differential gears. Use an internal caliper.

15. Measure the thickness of the reaction block, using a micrometer. Clearance between the gears and reaction block should be 0.0039-0.0945 inch (0.10-0.24mm). If clearance is incorrect, select a reaction block of a different width.

16. Remove the housing endplate, bolts, complete with washers and nuts, securing differential gears.

17. Check that the differential gear, together with plate assembly, guides and shim are correctly seated in the differential housing.

18. Install the pinions (gear shafts) noting the markings. Install the thrust washers, reaction block (with flat face towards large opening in housing) and pinion shaft. Align the locking pin hole in the shaft with hole in housing. Use a 3/16 inch (4.5mm) drill bit.

19. Install a new lock pin from the flat face of the differential housing. Check that the pin is seated approximately 0.0197 inch (0.5mm) below face.

20. Install the weighted latch and centrifugal weights. Check that the latch spring is positioned on the correct side of the governor weight axle.

21. Install the tooth cam wheel and weight assembly on the differential gear at ring gear end. Use grease to hold the guides in position.

22. Install the differential gear at ring gear end in the housing, completely with plate assembly and guides. Use grease to hold the guides in position.

23. Make sure that the mating surfaces of the differential housing and housing endplate are degreased. Use methylated (mineral) spirits or similar.

24. Install the differential housing endplate. Tighten the bolts to 6-8 ft. lbs. (8-10 Nm).

25. Tooth Wheel (Speed Sensor) Replacement: Use a pair of snips to cut off the toothed wheel. Oil the new wheel and seating surface on the differential housing. Tap on the wheel lightly using a rubber mallet. Check that the wheel is straight. Place the differential housing on the counterhold (2861 or equivalent) and press on the wheel until housing meets the tool.

26. Make sure that the mating surfaces of the differential housing and housing endplate are degreased. Use methylated (mineral) spirits or similar. Install the ring gear. Use new mounting bolts and tighten to 26 ft. lbs. (35 Nm)+ angle-tighten through 60 degrees.

27. On 1041 rear axle only: Install the locking plate and differential bearings with associated shim.

28. Install the differential housing: Mount the expander (2394 or equivalent) and holder (2601 or equivalent). Expand the tool until it engages and make 2.5 additional turns. Place the differential and bearings in the housing. Remove the tool.

29. Install the clamps, using new bolts. Note the markings made previously.

30. Recheck that the backlash is within specifications.

31. Install the inspection cover. Tighten the bolts 15-22 ft. lbs. (20-30 Nm).

32. Install the driveshaft seals.

33. Install the driveshafts along with the parking brake retaining springs. Tighten the driveshaft pressure plates to 30 ft. lbs. (40 Nm).

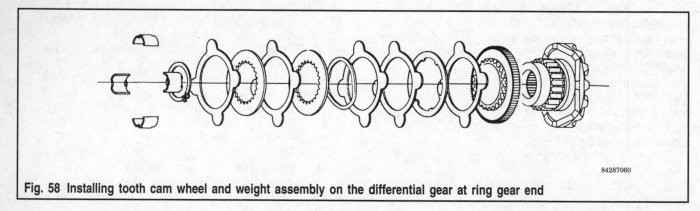

84287060

Fig. 58 Installing tooth cam wheel and weight assembly on the differential gear at ring gear end

TORQUE SPECIFICATIONS

Component	English	Metric
Transmission overdrive unit, retaining bolts		
M46:	5–8 ft. lbs.	7–11 Nm
Overdrive solenoid unit, retaining bolt		
M46:	37 ft. lbs.	50 Nm
Transmission-to-bellhousing (bolts)		
M46:	30 ft. lbs.	40 Nm
M47:	30 ft. lbs.	40 Nm
Clutch fork and spacer, mounting bolts		
M46:	30 ft. lbs.	40 Nm
M47:	30 ft. lbs.	40 Nm
Gearshift rod, retaining bolts		
M46:	30 ft. lbs.	40 Nm
M47:	30 ft. lbs.	40 Nm
Selector plate, top cover (bolts)		
M46:	15 ft. lbs.	20 Nm
M47:	15 ft. lbs.	20 Nm
Automatic transmissions		
Fluid pan (bolts):	3 ft. lbs.	4 Nm
Drain plug bolt:	13–17 ft. lbs.	18–23 Nm
Strainer-to-valve body (bolts):	6–9 ft. lbs.	8–12 Nm
Converter-to-flexplate (bolts)		
Except 960 Series:	35 ft. lbs.	48 Nm
960 Series::	22 ft. lbs.	30 Nm

84287061

MULTI-LINK REAR SUSPENSION TORQUE SPECIFICATIONS

Component	U.S.	Metric
Wheel nuts:	62 ft. lbs.	85 Nm
Body studs bolt:	51 ft. lbs.	70 Nm
Support arm/body mounting bolt:	35 ft. lbs.	48 Nm
Upper control arm/wheel bearing housing nut:	84 ft. lbs.	115 Nm
Upper control arm/rear axle member, rear nut:	62 ft. lbs.	85 Nm
Track rod/wheel bearing housing bolt:	62 ft. lbs.	85 Nm
Track rod/rear axle member nut:	51 ft. lbs.	70 Nm
Differential (front)/rear axle member bolt:	116 ft. lbs.	160 Nm
Differential (rear)/rear axle member bolt:	116 ft. lbs.	160 Nm
Damper/support arm nut:	41 ft. lbs.	56 Nm
Damper/body bolt:	62 ft. lbs.	85 Nm
Brake caliper/wheel bearing housing bolt:	44 ft. lbs.	60 Nm
Universal joint, rear nut:	37 ft. lbs.	50 Nm
Lower control arm/wheel bearing housing nut:	37 ft. lbs. (3)	50 Nm (3)
Lower control arm/rear axle member nut:	37 ft. lbs. (3)	50 Nm (3)
Support arm/body nut:	51 ft. lbs. (3)	70 Nm (3)
Support arm/support arm bracket nut:	91 ft. lbs. (4)	125 Nm (4)
Support arm/wheel bearing housing bolt:	44 ft. lbs. (3)	60 Nm (3)
Upper control arm/rear axle member front nut:	51 ft. lbs. (2)	70 Nm (2)
Rear axle member front/body bolt:	51 ft. lbs. (2)	70 Nm (2)
Rear axle member rear/body bolt:	51 ft. lbs. (2)	70 Nm (2)
Hub nut:	102 ft. lbs. (2)	140 Nm (2)
Rear axle member upper/rear axle member, lower bolt:	51 ft. lbs. (2)	70 Nm (1)

1 = Torque + angle-tightened joints 30 degrees
2 = Torque + angle-tightened joints 60 degrees
3 = Torque + angle-tightened joints 90 degrees
4 = Torque + angle-tightened joints 120 degrees

84287062

8

SUSPENSION AND STEERING

WHEELS

Wheels

Factory installed tires and wheels are designed to operate satisfactorily with loads up to an including full-rated load capacity when inflated to recommended inflation pressures.

Replacement wheels must be equal to the original equipment wheels in load capacity, diameter, width, offset and mounting configuration. Improper wheels may affect wheel and bearing life, ground and tire clearance, or speedometer and odometer calibrations.

REMOVAL & INSTALLATION

1. Raise the vehicle and support it safely. Place jackstands under the jack attachments.
2. Mark the position of the wheel stud nearest to the valve. Wheel is marked to facilitate installation and to avoid the need for rebalancing.
3. Remove the wheel nuts and remove the wheel assembly.

To install:

4. Before installing the wheel assembly, it must be inspected (See 'INSPECTION' in this Section).
5. Clean the dirt from the hub or drum mounting surface.
6. Install the wheel on the hub assembly, while aligning the marking made earlier. Alternately tighten the nuts to specifications.
7. Lower the vehicle.

INSPECTION

Whenever the wheel and tire assembly is removed from the vehicle, it should be carefully inspected. Wheels must be replaced when they are bent, dented or heavily rusted, have air leaks or elongated bolt holes, and have excessive lateral or radial runout. Such conditions may cause high-speed vehicle vibration. If any of these are found, replace the wheel.

CARE OF SPECIAL WHEELS

Occasionally check the rims for cracking, impact damage or air leaks. If any of these are found, replace the wheel. In order to prevent this type of damage, and the costly replacement of a special wheel, observe the following precautions:

• Use extra care not to damage the wheels during removal, installation, balancing, etc. After removal of the wheels from the vehicle, place them on a mat or other protective surface.
• While driving, watch for sharp obstacles.
• When washing, use a mild detergent and water. Avoid cleansers with abrasives or the use of hard brushes. There are many cleaners and polishes for special wheels. Use them.

• If possible, remove your special wheels from the vehicle during the winter months. Salt and sand used for snow removal can severely damage the finish.
• Make sure that the recommended lug nut torque is never exceeded or the wheel may crack. Never use snow chains on special wheels; severe scratching will occur.

TIRE AND WHEEL BALANCE

▶ **See Figures 1 and 2**

There are 2 types of wheel and tire balance:
• Static balance — is the equal distribution of weight around the wheel. This condition cause a bouncing action called 'wheel tramp'.
• Dynamic balance — is the equal distribution of weight on each side of the centerline so that when the tire spins there is no tendency for the assembly to move from side to side. This condition cause wheel shimmy.

Wheel Studs

REMOVAL & INSTALLATION

1. Raise the vehicle and support it safely.
2. Mark the position of the wheel stud nearest to the valve. Wheel is marked to facilitate installation and to avoid the need for rebalancing.

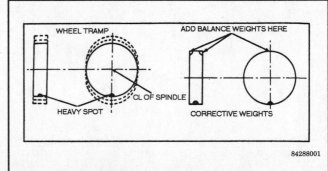

Fig. 1 Static balancing

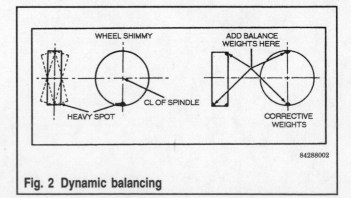

Fig. 2 Dynamic balancing

3. Remove the wheel assembly.

4. Remove the brake caliper retaining bolts and lift off the caliper. Using a piece of wire, hang the caliper up to avoid damaging the hoses.

5. Mark the position of the brake disc in relationship to the guide pin. Remove the guide pin and remove the brake disc.

6. Remove the protective cap and hub nut. DO NOT reuse the hub nut.

➡**If the vehicle is equipped with Anti-Lock Brake (ABS) and the toothed wheel is not being replaced, the damaged wheel stud can be removed without removing the hub. Use a large spanner as a brace and press the damaged stud from the hub, using tool 2862 or equivalent. Press the new stud into place, making certain that the stud is pressed against the contact surface in the hub.**

7. Fit the locking socket (5408 or equivalent) against the end of the spindle axle and carefully pull off the hub.

➡**To prevent the inner bearing ring from falling out, brace against the inner bearing ring as soon as there is enough space.**

8. If equipped with Anti-Lock Brake (ABS) and removing the toothed wheel, support the hub with a suitable holding tool and withdraw the toothed wheel.

9. Press the damaged wheel stud from the hub.

To install:

10. Clean the spindle and install the hub. Use a suitable socket (5294 or equivalent) to tighten the inner ring of the outer bearing. The locking socket used in disassembly will be pressed out by the spindle axle.

➡**There is no need to put grease in the hub. It is prepacked with the correct amount of special grease.**

11. Install a new hub nut and tighten to the point where the axial play disappears. Torque the nut to 74 ft. lbs. (100 Nm) PLUS angle tighten nut 45 degrees.

12. Install the protective cap.

13. Install the brake disc according to the mark made earlier. Install the guide pin.

14. Install the brake caliper.

15. Install the wheel on the hub assembly, while aligning the marking made earlier. Alternately tighten the nuts to specifications.

16. Lower the vehicle.

FRONT SUSPENSION

▶ **See Figures 3 and 4**

The front suspension is the MacPherson type, which means that the wheels are independently sprung. The spring strut consists of a tube, the lower end of which is affixed to the wheel spindle. The shock absorber is located in a tube and is retained by a threaded screw in an upper mount, which is fixed to the wheel housing, and by its seating at the bottom. The upper end of the spring is fixed to the wheel arch and bears on the upper mount, through the upper mount seat. The seating for the lower end of the spring is welded to the top of the tube.

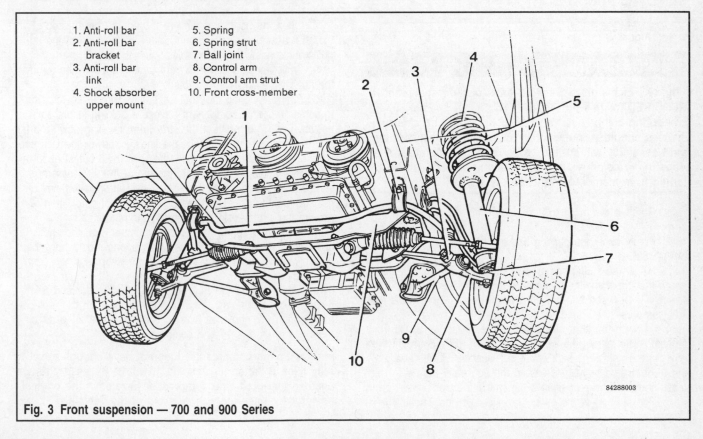

1. Anti-roll bar
2. Anti-roll bar bracket
3. Anti-roll bar link
4. Shock absorber upper mount
5. Spring
6. Spring strut
7. Ball joint
8. Control arm
9. Control arm strut
10. Front cross-member

84288003

Fig. 3 Front suspension — 700 and 900 Series

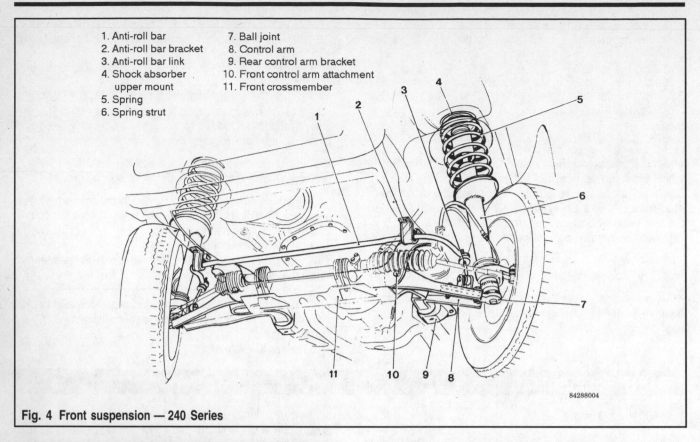

1. Anti-roll bar
2. Anti-roll bar bracket
3. Anti-roll bar link
4. Shock absorber
   upper mount
5. Spring
6. Spring strut
7. Ball joint
8. Control arm
9. Rear control arm bracket
10. Front control arm attachment
11. Front crossmember

84288004

Fig. 4 Front suspension — 240 Series

Coil Springs

REMOVAL & INSTALLATION

▶ See Figure 5

❊❊CAUTION

The use of the correct special tools or their equivalent is REQUIRED for this procedure. To remove the spring, a coil spring compressor must be used. Under no circumstances should you attempt to lower and disassemble the strut assembly without the proper spring compressor. Serious injury could result. Spring compressors can be rented from many repair and supply shops.

1. Remove the hub cap and loosen the lug nuts a few turns.
2. Firmly apply the parking brake and place blocks in back of the rear wheels.
3. Install the spring compressor on the spring directly beneath the upper mount. Make sure that at least 3 coils of the spring are between the tool attachment points. Tighten the tool and compress the spring.
4. Jack up the front of the vehicle at the center of the front crossmember. When the wheels are 2-3 in. (50-75mm) off the ground, the vehicle is high enough. Place jackstands beneath the front jacking points. Remove the floor jack from the crossmember, and reposition it beneath the lower control arm to provide support at the outer end. Remove the wheel.

5. Using a ball joint puller, disconnect the steering rod from the steering arm.
6. Disconnect the stabilizer bar at the upper link.
7. Remove the bolt holding the brake line bracket to the fender well.
8. Open the hood and remove the cover from the top of the strut assembly upper mount. Mark the position of the upper mounts relative to their holes.
9. While keeping the strut from turning, loosen and remove the nut for the upper strut mount.
10. Before lowering the strut assembly, wire or tie the strut to some stationary component (or use a holding fixture such as Volvo 5045) to prevent the strut from traveling down too far and damaging the hydraulic brake lines. Lower the jack supporting the lower arm and allow the strut to tilt out at about a 60 degree angle. At this angle, the top of the strut assembly should just protrude past the wheel well, allowing removal of the strut components from the top. Take great care when removing the strut. Avoid damaging to the fender.
11. Lift off the spring seat, rubber bumper, and the shock absorber protector. Remove the upper spring mount from the shaft. Remove the coil spring and compressor assembly from the strut.
12. Slowly relieve the tension on the compressor and remove it from the spring. Place the compressor on the replacement spring (making sure at least 3 coils separate the attachment points as before) and compress.

➡**If the spring compressor does not have enough travel to fully release the spring tension, it will be necessary to use another sandwich type compressor to remove the original compressor once the spring is out of the vehicle.**

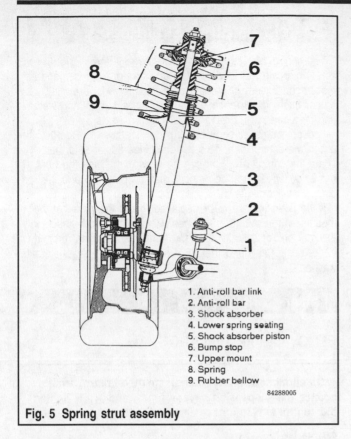

1. Anti-roll bar link
2. Anti-roll bar
3. Shock absorber
4. Lower spring seating
5. Shock absorber piston
6. Bump stop
7. Upper mount
8. Spring
9. Rubber bellow

84288005

Fig. 5 Spring strut assembly

To install:

13. Position the new spring and compressor on the strut assembly. Install the upper spring mount. Make sure the spring end is properly aligned with the lower mount.

➡**Make sure that the compressor bolts face downwards.**

14. Install the rubber bumper and the shock absorber protector. Position the spring seat on the spring, making sure it is aligned with the spring.

15. Carefully lift and guide the strut assembly into its upper attachment in the spring tower. Connect the stabilizer bar to the stabilizer link.

16. Guide the shock absorber spindle into the upper attachment and raise the jack beneath the lower control arm. Install the washer and nut on top of the shock absorber spindle. Position the upper mount according to marks made during removal.   Tighten the upper mounting bolts. The smaller outer nuts should be tightened to 15-25 ft. lbs. The large center nut should be tightened to 90-100 ft. lbs. Install the cover.

17. Attach the brake line bracket to its mount. Make sure that the brake lines sit properly in their mounts. Tighten the nut holding the stabilizer bar to the link. Connect the steering rod at the steering arm.

18. Release the coil spring compressor and install the wheel and tire assembly. Remove the jackstands and lower the vehicle. Bounce the suspension a few times and then road test.

Ball Joint

INSPECTION

Check the ball joint axial play. Maximum axial play permitted is 0.12 inch (3mm). Check the radial play. Maximum radial play permitted is 0.02 inch (0.5mm).

REMOVAL & INSTALLATION

Except 240 Series

1. Raise the vehicle and support it safely.
2. Mark the position of the wheel stud nearest to the valve. Wheel is marked to facilitate installation and to avoid the need for rebalancing. Remove the wheel and tire assembly.
3. Remove the bolt which holds the anti-roll bar link to the control arm. Remove the cotter pin, nut and washer for the ball joint stud.
4. Pull the control arm from the ball joint using a suitable puller (5259 or equivalent).
5. Remove the bolts holding the ball joint to the spring strut. Press the control arm downwards and remove the ball joint.

To install:

6. Install the new ball joint. Use new bolts and apply sealing fluid to the threads. Check that the bolt heads sit flat on the ball joint. Torque the bolts to 22 ft. lbs. (30 Nm) PLUS angle-tighten 90 degrees.
7. Install the control arm to ball joint. Install the washer and nut. Tighten ball joint stud (nut) to 44 ft. lbs. 60 Nm. Install the cotter pin.
8. Install the anti-roll bar.
9. Install the wheel on the hub assembly, while aligning the marking made earlier. Alternately tighten the nuts to specifications.
10. Lower the vehicle.

240 Series

1. Raise the vehicle and support it safely.
2. Mark the position of the wheel stud nearest to the valve. Wheel is marked to facilitate installation and to avoid the need for rebalancing. Remove the wheel and tire assembly.
3. Remove the 4 bolts which retains the ball joint and remove the ball joint from the control arm.
4. Remove the ball joint retaining nut and press the ball joint out of attachment.

To install:

➡**Ball joints are different for right and left sides. It is therefore important that the correct ball joint is installed on the correct side.**

5. Attach the ball joint to the attachment and tighten to 44 ft. lbs. (60 Nm).
6. Install the ball joint attachment to the spring strut using new locking bolts and lock washers, if used. Tighten bolts to 17 ft. lbs. (23 Nm).

7. Install the ball joint to the control arm and torque to 85 ft. lbs. (115 Nm).

8. Install the wheel on the hub assembly, while aligning the marking made earlier. Alternately tighten the nuts to specifications.

9. Lower the vehicle.

Anti-Roll Bar (Sway Bar)

The sway bar, variously called the anti-roll bar or stabilizer bar, serves to control the sideways roll of the body during cornering. While the bar itself rarely fails, the links and bushings around it are prone to wear. If the bar is not rigidly mounted to the vehicle, it cannot do its job properly.

Sway bars of different diameters (thicknesses) can stiffen or soften the roll characteristics of a vehicle. Bushings are easily replaced and well worth the effort in terms of restoring proper cornering manners to your vehicle.

REMOVAL & INSTALLATION

All Models

1. Raise the vehicle and support it safely.

2. Mark the position of the wheel stud nearest to the valve. Wheel is marked to facilitate installation and to avoid the need for rebalancing. Remove the wheel and tire assembly.

3. Remove the underside splash guard panel, if equipped.

4. Remove the upper nut securing the anti-roll bar to the struts (link).

5. Remove the upper link nut on the opposite side. The bar now hangs by its two forward brackets.

6. Remove the bolts for the two retaining brackets and remove the bar.

7. If the link bushings are worn, remove the lower link bolts and remove the entire link. Inspect all the bushings for compression or elongation. Replace any that are not almost perfect. The two U-shaped bushings from the front brackets are particularly prone to deforming.

To install:

8. Reconnect the lower link to the arm on each side, if removed.

9. Hold the bar in position and install the front brackets with their bushings. Make sure the slot in the bushing faces forward.

10. Install the bar to the link on one side of the vehicle but do not tighten more than a few turns. Connect the bar to the link on the opposite side and install the bushings and nut.

11. Tighten each upper link nut until 1.65 inches (42mm) can be measured between the outer surfaces of the upper and lower washers.

12. Reinstall the underside splash panel. if required.

13. Install the wheel on the hub assembly, while aligning the marking made earlier. Alternately tighten the nuts to specifications.

14. Lower the vehicle.

Control Arm Strut (Strut Rod)

The control arm strut, also called the radius rod or strut rod, serve to locate the lower control arm and prevent fore-and-aft movement. Except for impact damage, the rods rarely fail. The rubber bushings on each end are prone to fatigue and wear and may need to be replaced after a few years.

Loosen the rod-to-body bolt but don't remove it. Remove the nut at the control arm. This is sometimes easier said than done; the control arm bolt can be very tight. Once the front nut is loosened, the back mount may be removed and the rod placed on a workbench.

If the bushings are to be replaced, press them free of their mounts and install the new ones. Reinstall the rod, attaching the rear bolt first. Make sure the front bushings seat properly in the control arm and that the front nut draws tight against its washer.

Lower Control Arm

REMOVAL & INSTALLATION

➡**On all models, always fully install the control arm, bounce the suspension several times, and THEN tighten the control arm to crossmember mounting nuts or bolts.**

240 Series

▶ **See Figure 6**

1. Raise the vehicle and support it safely. Mark the position of the wheel stud nearest to the valve. Wheel is marked to facilitate installation and to avoid the need for rebalancing.

2. Disconnect the stabilizer (sway bar) link at the control arm.

3. Remove the control arm from the ball joint. (Helpful tips can be found in 'Lower Ball Joint Removal & Installation' in this Section.)

4. Remove the control arm rear attachment plate.

5. Remove the control arm front retaining bolt.

6. Remove the control arm.

To install:

7. If bushings are to be replaced, note that the right and left bushings are not interchangeable. The right side bushing should be turned so that the small slots point horizontally when installed.

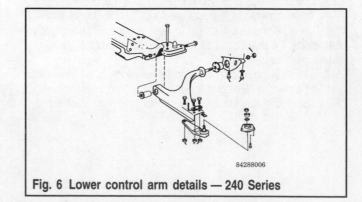

84288006

Fig. 6 Lower control arm details — 240 Series

8. Install the bracket onto the control arm. The nut should be tightened only enough to hold securely. The washer should be able to be turned with your fingers after the nut is on.

9. Attach the control arm. Install the front retaining bolt and nut; tighten the nut only a few turns onto the bolt.

10. Guide the stabilizer link into position. Attach it loosely with its nut and bolt.

11. Install the ball joint and its mount. Tighten the 3 mounting bolts to specifications.

12. Install the rear bracket to the vehicle. Tighten the three bolts to 25-35 ft. lbs.

13. Tighten the stabilizer link.

14. Install the wheel on the hub assembly, while aligning the marking made earlier. Alternately tighten the nuts to specifications.

15. Lower the vehicle. Jounce the front of the vehicle up and down. This 'normalizes' the front suspension and allows the control arm to seek its final position.

16. Tighten the rear mount nut to 38-44 ft. lbs. Tighten the front mount to 55 ft. lbs.

700 and 900 Series

▶ See Figure 7

1. Raise the vehicle and support it safely. Mark the position of the wheel stud nearest to the valve. Wheel is marked to facilitate installation and to avoid the need for rebalancing.

2. Remove the cotter pin from the ball joint and remove the ball joint nut.

3. Disconnect the stabilizer (sway bar) link at the control arm.

4. Disconnect the strut bolt and remove the front bushing.

5. Use a ball joint puller and separate the ball joint from the control arm. Make sure the puller is properly located and that the rubber boot is not damaged during removal.

6. Unbolt the control arm at the crossmember and remove the arm.

7. If the bushings are to be replaced, use a press and support the arm from below. The new bushings should always be pressed in from the front side of the arm.

To install:

8. Fit the control arm over the end of the strut rod. Install the arm in the crossmember but do not fully tighten the nut.

9. Install the ball joint in the control arm. Tighten the nut to 44 ft. lbs. Install a new cotter pin.

10. Install the bushing, washer and bolt for the strut rod. tighten the bolt to 70 ft. lbs.

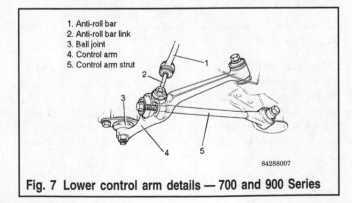

1. Anti-roll bar
2. Anti-roll bar link
3. Ball joint
4. Control arm
5. Control arm strut

84288007

Fig. 7 Lower control arm details — 700 and 900 Series

11. Attach the stabilizer link to the control arm and tighten it to 63 ft. lbs.

12. Install the wheel on the hub assembly, while aligning the marking made earlier. Alternately tighten the nuts to specifications.

13. Lower the vehicle. Jounce the front of the vehicle up and down. This 'normalizes' the front suspension and allows the control arm to seek its final position.

14. Tighten the control arm-to-crossmember bolt to 63 ft. lbs. Tighten the wheel lugs evenly to 63 ft. lbs.

Front Wheel Bearings

INSPECTION

Checking 'Wheel Bearing Play': Raise the vehicle and support it safely. Rock the wheel at 12 and 6 o'clock position. If there is play, wheel bearing should be serviced.

Checking 'Wheel Bearing Noise': Spin the wheel by hand and let the wheel rotate freely after spinning. Check for wheel bearing noise. If the wheel bearing remains noisy after proper adjustment, replace the wheel bearing.

➡**A wheel bearing which is not properly adjusted can cause noise.**

REPLACEMENT

▶ See Figures 8, 9 and 10

✳✳CAUTION

This procedure requires removal of the brakes. Brake pads and shoes contain asbestos, which has been determined to a cancer causing agent. Never clean the brake surfaces with compressed air! Avoid inhaling and dust from brake surfaces! When cleaning brakes, use commercially available brake cleaning fluids.

✳✳WARNING

The use of the correct special tools or their equivalent is REQUIRED for this procedure.

1. Raise and support the vehicle safely.

2. Mark the position of the wheel stud nearest to the valve.

3. Wheel is marked to facilitate installation and to avoid the need for rebalancing.

4. Loosen the retaining bolts and remove the brake caliper. Hang the caliper out of the way with a piece of stiff wire.

5. Pry off the grease cap. Remove the cotter pin and castle nut.

6. Remove the hub and brake disc assembly (integrated hub). Use a bearing puller (2722 or equivalent) to remove the inner bearing from the spindle, if it is difficult to remove.

➡**If the vehicle is equipped with separate brake disc and hub, the guide pin and brake disc must be removed from the hub prior to bearing replacement.**

7. Use a brass drift and carefully tap out the grease seal and inner bearing race.

8. Remove the outer bearing race, using a suitable handle and drift (2725 or equivalent).

To install:

9. Press in a new inner bearing race, using a suitable handle and drift (5005 or equivalent).

10. Press in a new outer bearing race, using a suitable handle and drift (2724 or equivalent).

11. Pack the wheel bearing between the cage and inner race with as much grease as possible. Also smear grease on the outer side of the bearing and bearing races inside the hub. Fill the space in the hub with grease to a diameter of the smallest ball races.

12. On hub with integrated brake disc: Position the inner bearing seal in the hub and press the seal in, using a suitable handle and drift (5005 or equivalent), so that the edge lies in the same plane as the hub.

13. On hub with separate hub and brake disc:

   a. Press the sealing ring onto the spindle, making sure that the seal ring is square. The sealing ring lip should face outwards.

   b. Install the inner bearing in the hub. Press in the sealing washer, using a suitable handle and drift.

14. Install the hub, outer race and castle nut.

➡**On vehicles with separate hub and brake disc, install the brake disc and guide pin.**

15. Install the brake caliper, using new mounting bolts. Torque to 74 ft. lbs. (100 Nm).

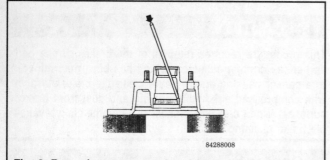

Fig. 8 Removing grease seal and inner bearing race — brake disc with integrated hub

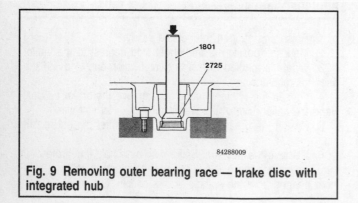

Fig. 9 Removing outer bearing race — brake disc with integrated hub

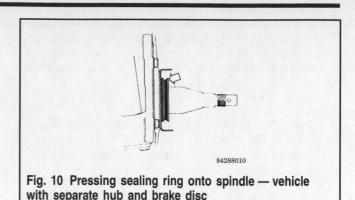

Fig. 10 Pressing sealing ring onto spindle — vehicle with separate hub and brake disc

16. Adjust the front wheel bearings (Refer to Front Wheel Bearing 'ADJUSTMENT' in this Section.

17. Install the protective cap. Install the wheel on the hub assembly, while aligning the marking made earlier. Alternately tighten the nuts to specifications.

18. Lower the vehicle.

ADJUSTMENTS

Except 900 Series

Adjust the front wheel bearings by spinning the hub and simultaneously tightening the center nut to 42 ft. lbs. (57 Nm). Loosen the nut 1/2 turn; then tighten nut by hand, approximately 1 ft. lb. (1.5 Nm). Install the cotter pin. If the pin hole in the spindle does not align with the pin hole in the nut, unscrew nut slightly to nearest pin hole.

940 and 960 Series

A maintenance free type of front hub is used on all 900 Series. The hub functions as the outer bearing race and is mounted on a double row, grooved ball bearing. Torque the stub axle locknut to 74 ft. lbs. (100 Nm) PLUS an additional 45 degrees.

➡**The stub axle locknut must not be reused.**

Front End Alignment

Alignment of the front wheels is essential for your vehicle to have good steering ability and minimum tire wears.

CASTER

▶ **See Figure 11**

Caster angel (B) is the angle between the vertical (A) and a line which passes through the center of the lower ball joint and the upper mount. Caster ensures that the wheels return to a straight-ahead position, making steering easier.Caster angle is non-adjustable. If caster reading is incorrect, replacement of bent components is required.

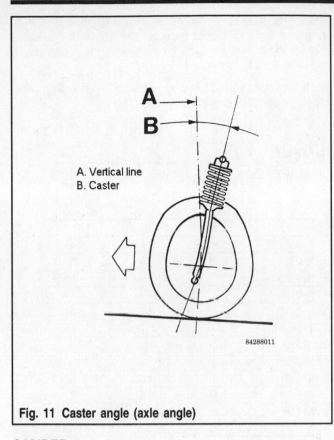

Fig. 11 Caster angle (axle angle)

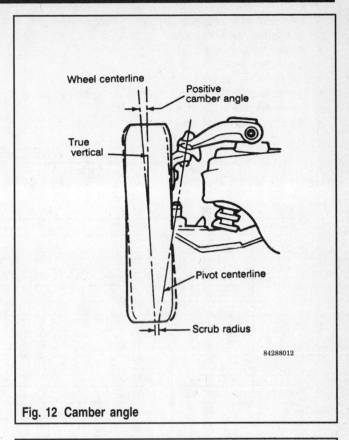

Fig. 12 Camber angle

CAMBER

▶ See Figure 12

Camber is the tilting of the wheels from the vertical (leaning in or out) when viewed from the front of the vehicle. When the wheels tilt outward at the top, the camber is said to be positive. When the wheels tilt inward at the top the camber is said to be negative. The amount of tilt is measured in degrees from the vertical. This measurement is called camber angle.

Camber affects the position of the tire on the road surface during vertical suspension movement and cornering. Changes in camber affect the handling and ride qualities of the vehicle as well as tire wear. Many tire wear patterns indicate camber related problems from misalignment, overloading or poor driving habits.

TOE

▶ See Figure 13

Toe is the turning in or out (parallelism) of the wheels. The actual amount of toe setting is normally only a fraction of an inch. The purpose of toe-in (or out) specification is to ensure parallel rolling of the wheels. Toe-in also serves to offset the small deflections of the steering support system which occur when the vehicle is rolling forward.

Changing the toe setting will radically affect the overall 'feel' of the steering, the behavior of the vehicle under braking, tire

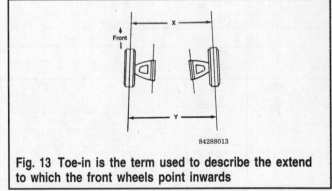

Fig. 13 Toe-in is the term used to describe the extend to which the front wheels point inwards

wear and even fuel economy. Excessive toe (in or out) causes excessive drag or scrubbing on the tires.

Toe is adjustable on all Volvos. It is generally measured in decimal inches or degrees. It is adjusted by loosening the locknut on each tie rod end and turning the rod until the correct reading is achieved. The rods left and right must remain equal in length during all adjustments.

BEFORE ALIGNMENT CHECKS:

If bizarre handling and/or poor road manners are experienced, the first place to look is the tires. Although the tires may wear as a result of an alignment problem, worn or poorly inflated tires can make you chase alignment problems which don't exist. Before checking or performing front wheel alignment, check the following items:

- Uneven tire pressure
- Uneven tire wear
- Excessive play in front wheel bearings
- Excessive play in ball joints, tie rods or linkage
- Broken springs or damage steering gear
- Damage upper shock observe mount

Once you have eliminated all other causes, unload everything from the trunk except the spare tire, set the tire pressures to the correct level and take the vehicle to a reputable alignment facility.

➡**Alignment can be altered by collision, overloading, poor repair or bent components.**

WHEEL ALIGNMENT

Year	Model	Caster Range (deg.)	Caster Preferred Setting (deg.)	Camber① Range (deg.)	Camber Preferred Setting (deg.)	Toe-in (in.)	Steering Axis Inclination (deg.)
1990	240DL	3P–4P	3.5P	0.25P–0.75P	0.5P	1/8	12
	240DL	3P–4P	3.5P	0.25P–0.75P	0.5P	1/8	12
	740	4.5P–5.5P	5P	0.2N–0.8P	0.3P	1/32	NA
	740GL	4.5P–5.5P	5P	0.2N–0.8P	0.3P	1/32	NA
	740GLE	4.5P–5.5P	5P	0.2N–0.8P	0.3P	1/32	NA
	740 Turbo	4.5P–5.5P	5P	0.2N–0.8P	0.3P	1/32	NA
	760GLE	4.5P–5.5P	5P	0.2N–0.8P	0.3P	9/64	NA
	760 Turbo	4.5P–5.5P	5P	0.2N–0.8P	0.3P	9/64	NA
	780	4.5P–5.5P	5P	0.2N–0.8P	0.3P	9/64	NA
	780 Turbo	4.5P–5.5P	5P	0.2N–0.8P	0.3P	9/64	NA
1991	240	3P–4P	3.5P	0.25P–0.75P	0.5P	1/8	12
	740	4.5P–5.5P	5P	0.2N–0.8P	0.3P	1/32	NA
	740GL	4.5P–5.5P	5P	0.2N–0.8P	0.3P	1/32	NA
	740 Turbo	4.5P–5.5P	5P	0.2N–0.8P	0.3P	1/32	NA
	940GLE	4.5P–5.5P	5P	0.2N–0.8P	0.3P	1/32	NA
	940SE	4.5P–5.5P	5P	0.2N–0.8P	0.3P	1/32	NA
	940 Turbo	4.5P–5.5P	5P	0.2N–0.8P	0.3P	1/32	NA
	Coupe	4.5P–5.5P	5P	0.2N–0.8P	0.3P	9/64	NA
1992	240	3P–4P	3.5P	0.25P–0.75P	0.5P	1/8	12
	240GL	3P–4P	3.5P	0.25P–0.75P	0.5P	1/8	12
	740	4.5P–5.5P	5P	0.2N–0.8P	0.3P	1/32	NA
	740 Turbo	4.5P–5.5P	5P	0.2N–0.8P	0.3P	1/32	NA
	940GL	4.5P–5.5P	5P	0.2N–0.8P	0.3P	1/32	NA
	940 Turbo	4.5P–5.5P	5P	0.2N–0.8P	0.3P	1/32	NA
	960	4.5P–5.5P	5P	0.2N–0.8P	0.3P	1/32	NA
1993	240	3P–4P	3.5P	0.25P–0.75P	0.5P	1/8	12
	940	4.5P–5.5P	5P	0.2N–0.8P	0.3P	1/32	NA
	940 Turbo	4.5P–5.5P	5P	0.2N–0.8P	0.3P	1/32	NA
	960	4.5P–5.5P	5P	0.2N–0.8P	0.3P	1/32	NA

NOTE: Camber must always be adjusted before Toe-in. All measurements to be carried out on an empty vehicle.
NA—Not available
N—Negative
P—Positive
① Difference between left and right-hand locks must not exceed 0.7 degrees

84288030

REAR SUSPENSION

► **See Figures 14, 15, 16 and 17**

All 240 Series and some 700 Series use a solid type rear suspension. The solid rear axle is suspended from the rigid frame member by a pair of support arms and damped by a pair of double-acting telescopic shock absorbers. A pair of torque rods control rear axle wind-up and a track rod limits the lateral movement of the rear axle in relation to the vehicle. A rear stabilizer bar, attached to both rear support (trailing) arms, is installed on certain models.

Some variant of the 700 Series and 900's are equipped with Volvo's Multi-Link suspension system. This independently suspends each rear wheel, allowing improved ride and road handling as well as allowing each rear wheel to be aligned separately. The rear suspension is two-way adjustable, allowing setting of camber and toe at the rear wheels. Caster is fixed

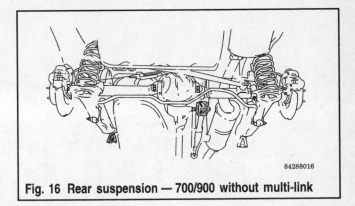

84288016

Fig. 16 Rear suspension — 700/900 without multi-link

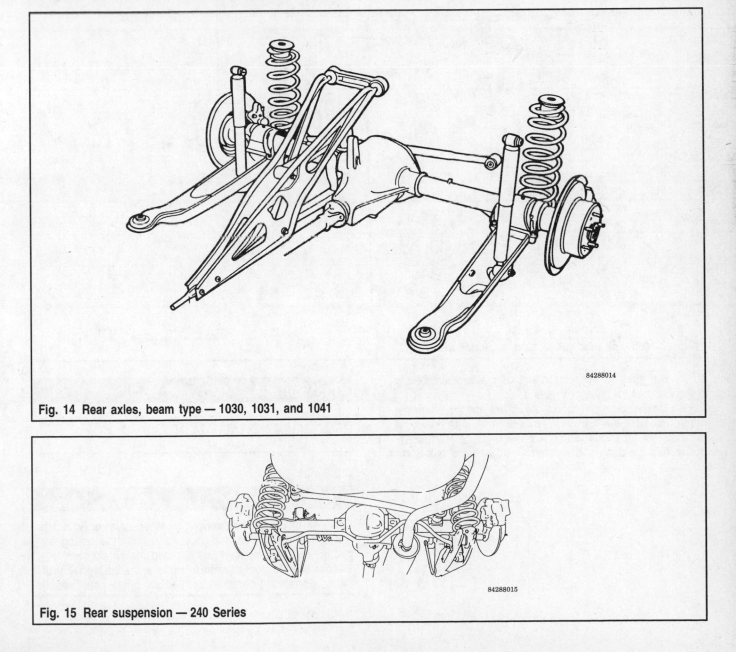

84288014

Fig. 14 Rear axles, beam type — 1030, 1031, and 1041

84288015

Fig. 15 Rear suspension — 240 Series

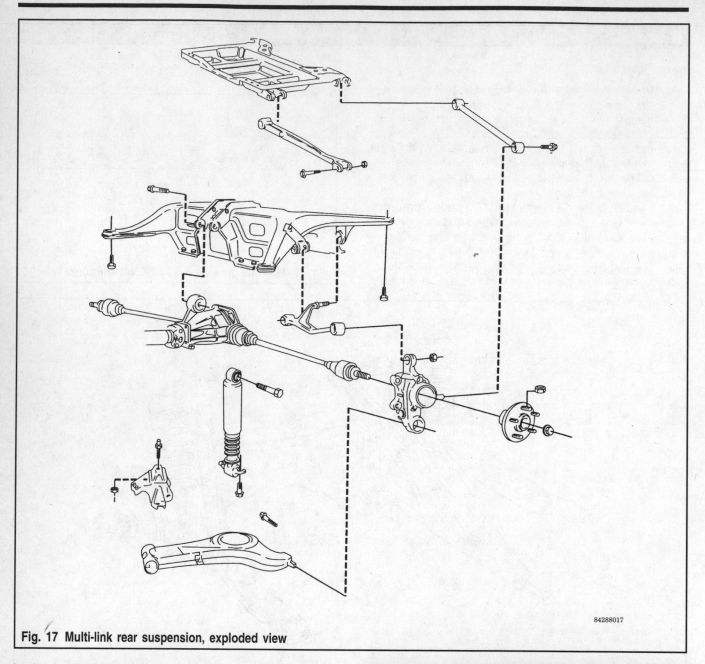

84288017

Fig. 17 Multi-link rear suspension, exploded view

by the design of the suspension and cannot be altered except by replacement of damaged parts.

Multi-Link suspensions require alignment any time the suspension components are disassembled. Position of components is critical as are torque values when retightening bolts. Multi-link repairs are discussed separately at the end of this Section.

Coil Springs

REMOVAL & INSTALLATION

240 Series

> ❊❊**WARNING**
>
> The use of the correct special tools or their equivalent is REQUIRED for this procedure. To remove the spring, a coil spring compressor must be used. Under no circumstances should you attempt to remove the spring without the proper spring compressor. Serious injury could result.

1. Loosen the rear wheel lug nuts a few turns. Blocks the front wheels, jack up the rear of the vehicle and place jack-

stands in front of the rear jacking points. Remove the rear wheels.

2. Place a hydraulic jack beneath the rear axle housing and raise the housing sufficiently to compress the spring. Install the spring compressor and tighten it to hold the spring in its compressed position. Make sure there are at least 3 coils of spring between the attachment points of the compressor. Loosen the nuts for the upper and lower spring attachments.

✳✳CAUTION

The spring is compressed under several hundred pounds of pressure! When it is freed from its lower attachment, it will attempt to suddenly return to its extended position. It is therefore imperative that the axle housing be lowered with extreme care until the spring is extended. As an added safety measure, a chain may be attached to the lower spring coil and secured to the axle housing.

3. Disconnect the shock absorber at its upper attachment. Carefully lower the jack and axle housing until the spring is extended. Remove the spring.

To install:

4. Position the retaining bolt and inner washer for the upper attachment inside the spring. While holding the outer washer and rubber spacer to the upper body attachment, install the spring and inner washer to the upper attachment (sandwiching the rubber spacer). Tighten the retaining bolt.

5. Raise the jack and secure the bottom of the spring to its lower attachment with the washer and retaining bolt. Slowly remove the spring compressor.

6. Connect the shock absorber to its upper attachment. Install the wheel and torque to specifications.

7. Lower the vehicle.

700 Series, Except Multi-Link Suspension

1. Loosen the rear wheel lug nuts a few turns. Blocks the front wheels. Jack up the rear of the vehicle and place jackstands in front of the rear jacking points.

2. Remove the rear wheels. Remove the rear caliper and support it out of the way with a piece of wire. Do not allow it to hang by its hose.

3. Place a jack under the rear axle and raise the axle just enough to take the tension off the lower shock absorber mount.

4. As a safety precaution, install a spring compressor on the spring and tighten it enough to hold it in a partially compressed position. Loosen and remove the lower shock absorbers bolt.

5. Lower the rear axle to unload the spring. Remove the upper bolt, washers and rubber spacer. Remove the spring.

To install:

6. Fit the rubber spacer and washer to the new spring. Make sure that the recess in the spacer is properly seated.

7. Press and secure the lower washer to the rubber spacer.

8. Attach the spring to the upper mount. Tighten the nut to 35 ft. lbs. Position the spring in the lower (trailing) arm.

9. Raise the rear axle with the jack and install the lower shock absorber bolt. Tighten it to 63 ft. lbs.

10. Use new mounting bolts and install the rear brake caliper. Tighten the mounting bolts to 43 ft. lbs. Install the wheel

and lower the vehicle to the ground. Final tighten the lugs to 63 ft. lbs.

Shock Absorbers

REMOVAL & INSTALLATION

The damping effect of the shock absorber may be tested by securing the lower attachment in a vise and extending and compressing it. A properly operating shock absorber should offer about 3 times as much resistance to extending the unit as to compressing it.

Replace the shock absorber if any impaired function is found. Also replace it if any leakage is present or if the rubber bushings are damaged.

240 Series

1. Remove the hub cap and loosen the lug nuts a few turns. Place blocks in front of the front wheels. Jack up the rear of the vehicle and place jackstands in front of the rear jacking points. Remove the wheel.

2. Remove the nuts and bolts which retain the shock absorber to its upper and lower attachments and remove the shock absorber. Make sure that the spacing sleeve (inside the axle support arm for the lower attachment) is not misplaced.

To install:

3. Position the shock absorber to its upper and lower attachments. Make sure that the spacing sleeve is installed inside the axle support (trailing) arm and is aligned with the lower attachment bolt hole.

4. Install the retaining nuts and bolts and tighten to 63 ft. lbs.

5. Install the wheel and tire assembly. Remove the jackstands and lower the vehicle. Tighten the lug nuts to 85-90 ft. lbs., and install the hub cap.

700 Series except Multi-Link suspension.

1. Loosen the lug nuts a few turns. Place blocks in front of the front wheels. Jack up the rear of the vehicle and place jackstands in front of the rear jacking points.

2. Remove the wheel. (While not absolutely necessary, access is improved.)

3. Place a jack under the rear axle and elevate the axle just enough to take the tension off the lower shock absorber mount.

4. Remove the lower shock absorber bolt.

5. In the spare tire well, locate and remove the rubber plug which covers the access hole to the upper shock mount.

✳✳WARNING

Remember the vehicle is on jackstands. Do not climb into the trunk or the vehicle may become imbalanced and fall off the stands. Work from the side of the vehicle and reach into the trunk.

6. Remove the upper bolt and remove the shock absorber.

To install:

7. Install the new unit by first tightening the upper bolt and then the lower one. Tighten both bolts to 63 ft. lbs. Replace the rubber plug in the spare tire well.

8. Lower the rear axle and remove the jack.

9. Install the wheel and lower the vehicle. Tighten the wheel lugs to 63 ft. lbs.

Trailing Arms

REMOVAL & INSTALLATION

In all cases (except Multi-Link suspension), replacing the trailing arm requires removal of the axle assembly. The reader is referred to 'Rear Axle (Axle Housing) Removal & Installation' in Section 7. When the axle assembly is removed, the trailing arm is simply unbolted and removed. Check the arm carefully for any deformation or rusting. Also check all the bushings for any sign of wear or elongation.

Sway Bar

The sway bar, also called the anti-roll bar or stabilizer bar, serves to control the sideways roll of the body during cornering. While the bar itself rarely fails, the links and bushings around it are prone to wear. If the bar is not rigidly mounted to the vehicle, it cannot do its job properly.

REMOVAL & INSTALLATION

Except Multi-Link Suspension

1. Raise the vehicle and support it safely. Place the stands at the rear jacking points. If required, remove the wheels.

2. Use a floor jack to raise the rear axle just enough to unload the lower shock absorber mount. Remove the lower shock retaining bolt.

3. Remove the nut holding the sway bar to the bracket.

4. On the other side of the vehicle, remove the shock retaining bolt and the nut holding the sway bar to the bracket. Remove the sway bar.

To install:

5. When installing the new bar, install both the bracket nut and the lower shock retaining bolt hand tight on one side. Then install the nut and bolt hand tight on the other side.

6. Once all four mounting points are snug, tighten the bracket nuts to 35 ft. lbs. (48 Nm) and the shock absorber bolts to 63 ft. lbs. (86 Nm)

7. Remove the jack from the axle. Install the wheels, if removed. Lower the vehicle to the ground. Tighten the wheel lugs to specifications.

Multi-Link Rear Suspension

➡**Multi-Link suspensions require alignment any time the suspension components are disassembled. Position of components is critical as are torque values when retightening bolts.**

COMPONENT REMOVAL & INSTALLATION

▶ **See Figures 18, 19 and 20**

Spring, Shock Absorber and Support arm

➡**It is important that the vehicle be parked in a straight-ahead position with no side loadings in the suspension. After the vehicle is in the work area, roll it forward and backwards 6-8 ft. and make sure the front and rear wheels point straight.**

1. Raise and support the vehicle safely. Make sure the front supports are placed as far forward as possible. Check that the rear supports will not interfere with the support arm.

2. Remove the wheels. Loosen and remove the bolts holding the protective cover (guard) to the arm and remove the guard.

3. At the front of the arm, remove the two retaining bolts which hold the bracket (for the support arm) to the frame. Don't attempt to remove the through bolt (eye bolt).

4. Remove the retaining bolt at the rear of the support arm.

5. Separate the rear end of the support arm from the wheel bearing housing.

6. Using either Volvo tool 5972 or two floor jacks, support the arm at the front and rear ends. Raise the jacks just enough to relieve the tension on the shock absorber.

7. Remove the retaining bolt at the top of the shock absorber.

8. Lower the jacks slowly; the arm will come free with the spring and shock attached.

9. Remove the spring and the upper and lower rubber seats. Unbolt the shock absorber from the arm. If the support arm is to be replaced, unbolt and remove the bracket at the front of the arm. Take note of the relationship between the bracket and the arm; the bracket correctly mounts one way only.

To install:

10. When installing, install the support arm bracket in the correct position and tighten the nut to 91 ft. lbs. PLUS 120 degrees of rotation.

11. Install the shock absorber on the arm and tighten the bottom mount to 41 ft. lbs.

12. Install the bottom spring seat on the support arm. Take care to properly locate the grooves in the seat.

13. Install the spring and the top rubber seat. Place the assembled support arm on the jacks and raise into position.

14. Gently raise the jacks and compress the spring until the shock absorber is in the correct position. The shock may be held in place temporarily with a drift or screwdriver in the hole. Insert the bolt and tighten it to 62 ft. lbs.

15. Reinstall the mounting bolts at the front of the support arm bracket. Tighten the bolts to 35 ft. lbs. and the large nut to 51 ft. lbs.

16. At the rear of the support arm, tap the arm into place on the wheel bearing housing. Tighten the bolt to 44 ft. lbs. PLUS 90 degrees of rotation. Do not overtighten this fitting.

17. Reinstall the protective cover on the control arm. Install the wheel.

18. Lower the vehicle to the ground and final tighten the lugs to 62 ft. lbs.

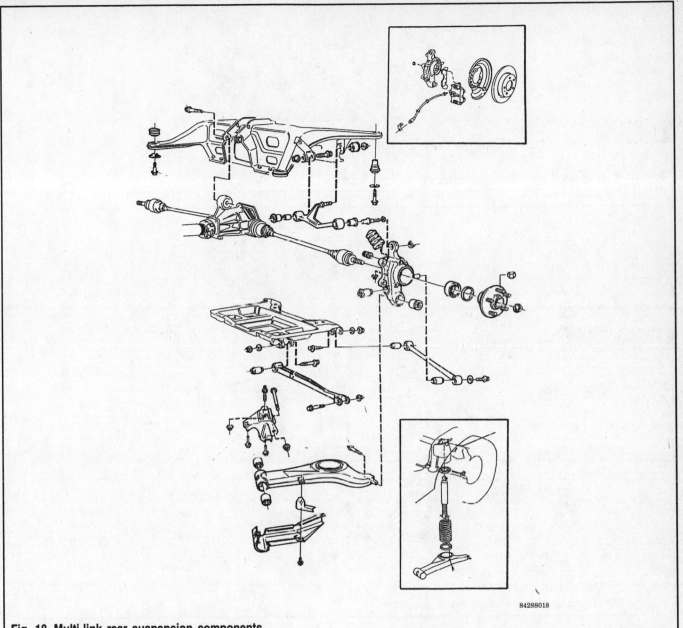

Fig. 18 Multi-link rear suspension components

84288018

19. Have the rear alignment checked and adjusted if necessary.

Upper Control Arm

> **✳✳CAUTION**
>
> The following procedure requires removal of the brakes. Brake pads and shoes contain asbestos, which has been determined to a cancer causing agent. Never clean the brake surfaces with compressed air! Avoid inhaling and dust from brake surfaces! When cleaning brakes, use commercially available brake cleaning fluids.

1. Raise and support the vehicle safely. Make sure the front supports are placed as far forward as possible. Check that the rear supports will not interfere with the support arm.

2. Remove the wheels. Remove the brake caliper and tie it with wire out of the way. Do not allow it to hang by its hose.

3. Remove the bolt holding the lower support arm to the wheel bearing housing and tap the support arm loose.

4. Remove the nut and bolt holding the lower control arm (intermediate arm) to the wheel bearing housing.

5. Remove the bolt attaching the track rod to the wheel bearing housing. Use a small bearing puller and a long 12mm bolt to disconnect the track rod.

6. Remove the nut which holds the upper control arm to the wheel bearing housing. Collect and note the location of the spacers between the upper control arm and the bearing housing. They are alignment shims and must be reinstalled properly.

7. At the rear of the upper control arm, remove the nut holding it to the rear axle member (support).

8. At the front of the upper control arm, remove the nut and bolt which holds it to the rear axle member.

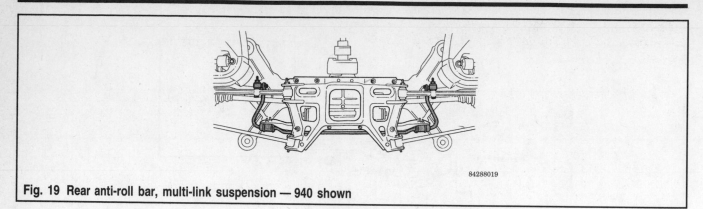

Fig. 19 Rear anti-roll bar, multi-link suspension — 940 shown

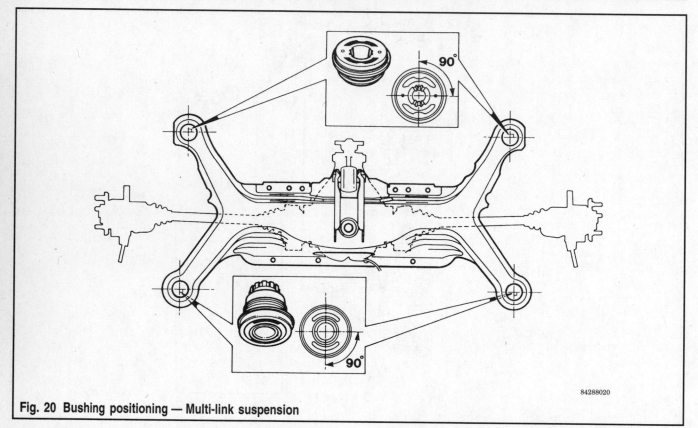

Fig. 20 Bushing positioning — Multi-link suspension

9. Use a pair of adjustable pliers to remove the control arm from the vehicle.

To install:

10. Install the new arm and install the nuts and bolts holding it to the rear axle member. Install both the front and rear mounts.

11. Install the spacers at the wheel bearing housing, position the arm and install the nut holding the arm to the housing.

12. Inboard, (at the rear axle support) tighten the rear-most nut to 62 ft. lbs. Tighten the front nut and bolt to 51 ft. lbs. PLUS 60 degrees of rotation.

13. Pull the top of the wheel bearing housing outwards (away from the center of the vehicle). This is essential for correct wheel alignment.

14. Tighten the upper control arm nut (at the bearing housing) to 84 ft. lbs.

15. Pull the wheel bearing housing outward and install the lower control arm with its bolt and nut, but do not tighten it.

16. Pull the wheel bearing housing inwards (towards the center of the vehicle). This is essential for correct wheel alignment.

17. Tighten the control arm nut to 37 ft. lbs. PLUS 90 degrees of rotation.

18. Reinstall the support arm; tighten its mount to 44 ft. lbs. PLUS 90 degrees of rotation.

19. Install the track rod and tighten to 62 ft. lbs.

20. Install the brake caliper, tightening its mounting bolts to 44 ft. lbs.

21. Install the wheel. Lower the vehicle to the ground and tighten the wheel lugs to 62 ft. lbs.

22. Have the rear alignment checked and adjusted if necessary.

Rear Wheel Alignment

▶ **See Figures 21 and 22**

The tracking of the rear wheels is as important as the tracking of the front. Any misalignment at the rear will give the vehicle a loose or 'slippery' feel under cornering. All the handling and tire wear conditions discussed under front end alignment apply equally to the rear; at the rear they are often harder to diagnose and cure.

On all but the Multi-Link rear suspensions, the position of the rear wheels is fixed in all three dimensions by the correct location of the components. Any tire or handling problems not traced to other causes will require replacement of suspension parts. The alignment dimensions — caster, camber and toe — can be measured on an alignment rack but are not adjustable.

It should be noted that any time the rear wheel alignment is checked, the front must also be checked and set. Ideally this is done on a four wheel alignment machine which will provide data on the comparative front and rear track as well as each front and each rear wheel.

The Multi-Link suspension is adjusted for camber and toe through the use of eccentric bolts in the suspension links. The camber adjuster is located on the inboard end of the lower link. The toe adjuster is located at the inboard end of the track rod. Neither should be adjusted by anyone who is not using a four wheel alignment machine and the specifications book.

An additional adjustment controls toe variation. Although the toe setting can be numerically correct with the vehicle at rest, it can change as a function of load and suspension motion. This very minor change can greatly upset the handling of the vehicle. By inserting precisely sized shims between the upper control arm and the wheel bearing housing, this minor variation can be further controlled. This is particularly handy if the vehicle constantly has a load in the trunk or constantly carries several people. The rear suspension can be fine-tuned for the best road manners under given load conditions.

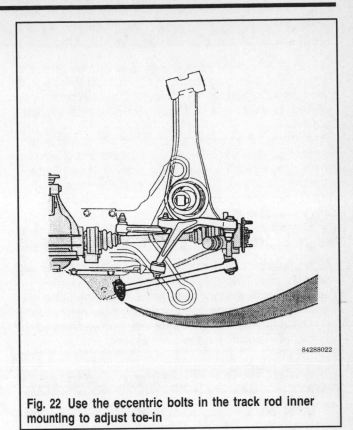

84288022

Fig. 22 Use the eccentric bolts in the track rod inner mounting to adjust toe-in

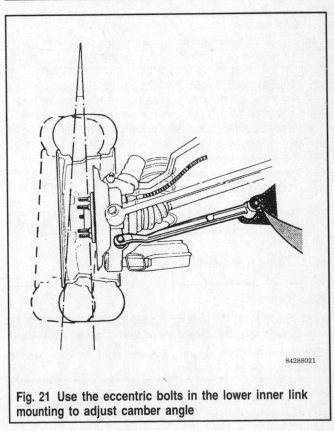

84288021

Fig. 21 Use the eccentric bolts in the lower inner link mounting to adjust camber angle

STEERING

All 90-93 Volvo's are equipped with a servo operated steering system. The steering gear is of the rack and pinion type. A vane-type servo pump is belt-driven from the crankshaft. Wheel deflection is limited by a stop in the steering gear and cannot be adjusted.

In addition, these vehicles are equipped with Supplemental Restraint System (SRS). The SRS system consists of an inflatable bag located in the center of the steering wheel. The bag is normally folded up, but is instantly inflated in the event of certain types of collision. The SRS system provides extra safety, in addition to the seat belts.

✳✳WARNING

All work which includes removing or replacing the air bag assembly must be carried out with the battery disconnected and with the ignition turned OFF for the duration of work. This is to ensure that the air bag does not accidentally inflate during service repairs and that no faults codes will register, requiring subsequent cancellation.

Safety Precautions

- Before beginning work which could affect the SRS system, always turn the ignition OFF, disconnect the negative battery lead AND TAPE the end of the lead.
- When working around the instrument panel or steering column, take special care to ensure that the SRS wirings are not pinched, chafed or penetrated by bolts/screws etc. This is most likely to happen when installing the sound insulation, knee bolsters, ignition lock or steering column cover.
- Never service the steering shaft or steering gear without first locking the contact reel and removing the steering wheel.
- When fault tracing the SRS system with the air bag assembly in place, install the special tool 998 8695 or equivalent. This tool has the same resistance as the air bag assembly. The use of this tool prevent accidental air bag inflation and fault code registration during work.

Air Bag

REMOVAL & INSTALLATION

▶ See Figure 23

✳✳WARNING

Before working the steering system, read the SRS service precautions in this Section.

1. Place the front wheels in straight-ahead position.
2. Disconnect the negative battery lead AND TAPE the lead end.
3. Turn the ignition key to position I so that the steering lock is OFF.
4. Remove the sound insulation knee guard and the side panel from the center console.

5. Remove the air bag assembly. Turn the steering wheel slightly in order to reach the 2 Torx bolts in back of the steering wheel. Disconnect the connector and remove the air bag.

➡**Do not turn the ignition switch ON while the air bag assembly is removed, as this will register a fault code.**

To install:

6. Rest the bottom of the air bag assembly on the steering wheel and reconnect the connector. Place the bag in position being careful not to get the leads caught. Install and tighten the retaining bolts to 4.4 ft. lbs. (6 Nm).

➡**When tightening the air bag assembly retaining bolts, tighten the right side bolt first.**

Steering Wheel

REMOVAL & INSTALLATION

✳✳WARNING

Before working the steering system, read the SRS service precautions in this Section.

240 Series

▶ See Figure 24

1. Drive the vehicle forward on a level surface so that the wheels are straight.
2. Disconnect the negative battery lead AND TAPE the lead end.
3. Turn the ignition key to position I so that the steering lock is OFF.
4. Remove the sound insulation knee guard and the side panel from the center console.
5. Remove the air bag assembly. Turn the steering wheel slightly in order to reach the 2 Torx bolts in back of the steering wheel. Disconnect the connector and remove the air bag.

➡**Do not turn the ignition switch ON while the air bag assembly is removed, as this will register a fault code.**

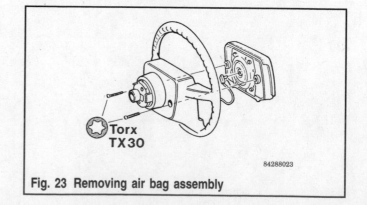

Torx
TX30

84288023

Fig. 23 Removing air bag assembly

6. Remove the steering wheel mounting bolt.

7. Lock the contact real: Release the locking screw in the end of the plastic strip from its 'parking hole' in the steering wheel. Screw must always remain in plastic strip. Attach the locking screw to the contact reel pin. The contact reel is now locked in the zero position.

✳✳WARNING

Do not turn the steering, as this will cause the pin to snap, requiring replacement of the contact reel!8.

Remove the steering wheel and pull the lead and plastic strip with screw through the hole in the middle.
To install:

8. Install the steering wheel. Set the steering wheel so that the contact reel pin is in the center of the steering wheel hole. Install the steering wheel nut finger-tight. Remove the screw in the contact reel plastic strip and install in its parking hole in steering wheel. Tighten the steering wheel nut 42 ft. lbs. (60 Nm).

9. Connect the air bag tester (8695 or equivalent) to the system. Connect the negative battery cable. Check the SRS lamp operation and that no fault codes have been registered.

10. Disconnect the negative battery cable again and remove the air bag tester.

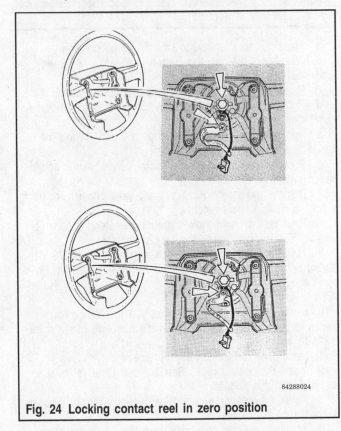

84288024

Fig. 24 Locking contact reel in zero position

11. Install the air bag assembly and reconnect the negative battery cable. Check the vehicle operation and SRS system for fault codes.

Contact Reel

REMOVAL & INSTALLATION

✳✳WARNING

Before working the steering system, read the SRS service precautions in this Section.

240 Series
▶ **See Figure 25**

1. Place the front wheels in straight-ahead position.

2. Disconnect the negative battery lead AND TAPE the lead end.

3. Remove the air bag assembly. See 'Air Bag' removal & installation in this Section.

➡**Do not turn the ignition switch ON while the air bag assembly is removed, as this will register a fault code.**

4. Remove the steering wheel. See 'Steering Wheel' removal & installation in this Section.

5. Disconnect the connector and remove the contact reel.
To install:

6. Set contact reel to zero position: If contact reel must be zero, turn the reel to the far right end and then back 3 revolution to the left. Lock the contact reel with screw in plastic strip.

7. Install the steering wheel. See 'Steering Wheel' rremoval & installation in this Section.

8. Install the air bag assembly. See 'Air Bag' removal & installation in this Section.

9. Reconnect the negative battery cable. Check the vehicle operation and SRS system for fault codes.

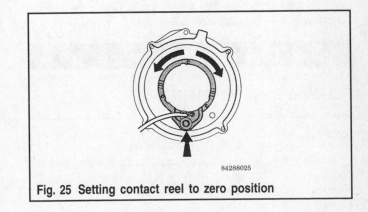

84288025

Fig. 25 Setting contact reel to zero position

Combination Switch

REMOVAL & INSTALLATION

❋❋CAUTION

This procedure requires removal of the steering wheel. Refer to the air bag safety precautions in this Section. DO NOT remove the wheel until these precautions have been followed.

1. Disconnect the negative battery lead AND TAPE the lead end.

2. Remove the air bag assembly. See 'Air Bag' removal & installation in this Section.

➡**Do not turn the ignition switch ON while the air bag assembly is removed, as this will register a fault code.**

3. Remove the steering wheel. See 'Steering Wheel' removal & installation in this Section.

4. Remove the contact reel. See 'Contact Reel' removal & installation in this Section.

5. Remove the upper and lower steering column covers.

6. Disconnect the connector for the wiper control. Remove the retaining bolts for the combination switch control holder. Lift the holder over the steering shaft and remove. Note the position of the indicator switch lead and remove.

To install:

7. Install the holder for the combination switch control and connect the leads. Connect the ground lead to 1 of the retaining bolts.

8. Install the upper and lower steering column covers.

9. Install the contact reel. See 'Contact Reel' removal & installation in this Section.

10. Install the steering wheel. See 'Steering Wheel' removal & installation in this Section.

11. Install the air bag assembly. See 'Air Bag' removal & installation in this Section.

12. Reconnect the negative battery cable. Check the vehicle operation and SRS system for fault codes.

Ignition Lock Cylinder

REMOVAL & INSTALLATION

240 Series

The ignition lock cylinder is mounted on the steering column and incorporates a steering wheel lock to deter vehicle theft. Removal of the lock assembly requires the removal of the steering column assembly.

1. Disconnect the negative battery lead AND TAPE the lead end.

2. Remove the steering column assembly. See 'Steering Column' removal & installation in this Section.

3. Mount the steering column in a vice.

4. Break off the washers from the rear end edge of the shearing bolts, then using a pair of channel locks, remove the shearing bolts.

5. Press the ignition lock assembly from the steering column, using a suitable drift and counterhold tool (5295 or equivalent). Install the key in lock and turn.

To install:

6. Install the key in lock and turn. Press the new ignition lock assembly onto the steering column, using a suitable drift and counterhold tool (5295 or equivalent). The lock assembly, when installed, should be positioned as follows: Measure the distance from the top of the lock assembly to the end of the steering column, above splined area. The distance should be 5.98 inches (152mm).

7. Remove the key form the lock. Turn the steering shaft and check that the lock barrel locks it.

8. Install the steering column assembly. See 'Steering Column' removal & installation in this Section.

9. Reconnect the negative battery cable. Check the vehicle operation and SRS system for fault codes.

Except 240 Series

❋❋WARNING

Before working the steering system, read the SRS service precautions in this Section.

1. Place the front wheels in straight-ahead position.

2. Disconnect the negative battery lead AND TAPE the lead end.

3. Raise the front of the vehicle and support it safely.

4. Remove the air bag assembly. See 'Air Bag' removal & installation in this Section.

5. Remove the steering wheel. See 'Steering Wheel' removal & installation in this Section.

6. Remove the contact reel assembly. Remove the combination switch.

7. Remove the steering column rake adjustment lever using a 0.12 in. (3mm) hex wrench.

8. Remove the parking plate around the steering tube (4 screws). Disconnect the ignition lock connector.

9. Turn the ignition switch to position I. Take a 0.079 inch (2mm) drift and press down the tumblers in the cylinder. Remove the lock assembly.

To install:

10. Install the steering lock assembly. Turn the ignition switch to position I and press down the tumblers with a suitable drift. Install the lock assembly.

11. Install the combination switch assembly.

12. Install the contact reel. See 'Contact Reel' removal & installation in this Section.

13. Install the steering wheel. See 'Steering Wheel' removal & installation in this Section.

14. Install the air bag assembly. See 'Air Bag' removal & installation in this Section.

15. Reconnect the negative battery cable. Check the vehicle operation and SRS system for fault codes.

Steering Column

REMOVAL & INSTALLATION

❋❋WARNING

Before working the steering system, read the SRS service precautions in this Section.

240 Series

▶ **See Figures 26, 27, 28 and 29**

1. Place the front wheels in straight-ahead position.

2. Disconnect the negative battery lead AND TAPE the lead end.

3. Remove the air bag assembly. See 'Air Bag' removal & installation in this Section.

4. Remove the steering wheel. See 'Steering Wheel' rremoval & installation in this Section.

5. Disconnect the connector and remove the contact reel.

6. Pull up the cover from the lower steering shaft joint, if required.

7. Loosen the upper bolts in the upper and lower joints. Pull down the lower steering shaft so that the upper joint is freed from the upper steering shaft.

8. Remove the upper and lower steering column covers.

9. Disconnect the connector for the wiper control. Remove the retaining bolts for the wiper and indicator controls holder. Lift the holder over the steering shaft and remove. Note the position of the indicator switch lead and remove.

10. Remove the connector from the starter switch, if required.

11. Remove the steering column's lower retaining bracket, seal in bulkhead and defroster hose from heater unit.

12. Tap the shearing bolts so that the bolts and plastic washers slide out of their slots in member. Carefully remove the steering column with steering lock. Avoid getting the steering column caught while passing through the bulkhead.

To install:

13. Before installing, check that the upper steering shaft's collapsible coupling is intact. Its upper end (A) should not be able to move axially in relation to its lower end (B). Also, check the total length. Should be 27.78±0.4 inches (705.5±1mm). If measurement is incorrect, replace the complete steering column.

14. Install the plastic guides in the column support. Turn the guides so that the washers faces downwards. Install the steering column into position, but do not tighten the shearing bolts completely. Pull the steering column towards the rear as far as possible; tighten the bolts further, but do not shear them yet.

15. Install the rubber grommets. Install the lower retaining bracket and tighten the bolts lightly.

16. Coat the bulkhead rubber seals with vaseline. Install the seal on the steering column (cone turn inwards) from the engine compartment side.

17. Tighten the upper bolts, but do not shear them yet.

18. Tighten the lower retaining bolts. Torque to 11-17 ft. lbs. (15-25 Nm).

19. Attach the defroster hose and reconnect the ignition lock connector.

20. Attach the universal joint to the upper steering column shafts. First tighten the upper bolt, then the lower. Install the locking pins.

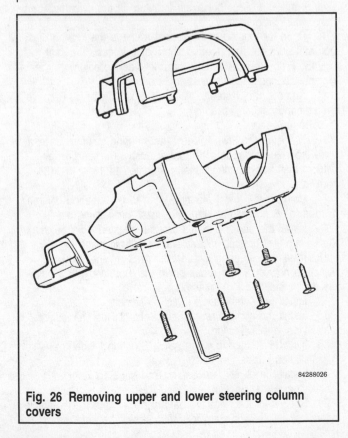

Fig. 26 Removing upper and lower steering column covers

84288026

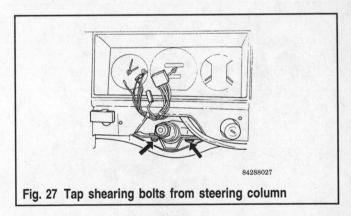

84288027

Fig. 27 Tap shearing bolts from steering column

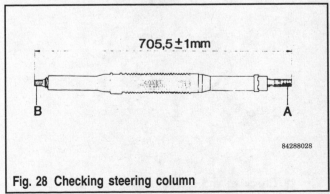

705,5±1mm

B   A

84288028

Fig. 28 Checking steering column

21. Checking and adjusting steering shaft:

a. When checking, the distance (A) between the upper steering shaft joint and shoulder on the lower steering shaft should be 0.39-0.75 inch (10-19mm).

b. If incorrect, loosen the upper bolted at (B) the lower joint. Loosen the lower bolt (C) of the upper shaft universal joint. Adjust the distance (A), by moving the shaft up or down. Tighten the bolts (B and C) to 14-20 ft. lbs. (18-28 Nm).

➡ **Make sure the position of the upper steering shaft does not change, as this can affect the distance between the steering wheel and the steering column cover.**

22. Install the holder for the combination switch control and connect the leads. Connect the ground lead to 1 of the retaining bolts.

23. Install the upper and lower steering column covers.

24. Set contact reel to zero position: If contact reel must be zero, turn the reel to the far right end and then back 3 revolution to the left. Lock the contact reel with screw in plastic strip.

25. Ensure the front wheels are perfectly in straight-ahead position. Install the contact reel bracket and contact reel. Reconnect and properly position the lead.

✳✳WARNING

Do not turn the steering, as this will cause the pin to snap, requiring replacement of the contact reel!

26. Install the steering wheel. Set the steering wheel so that the contact reel pin is in the center of the steering wheel hole. Install the steering wheel nut finger-tight. Remove the screw in the contact reel plastic strip and install in its parking hole in

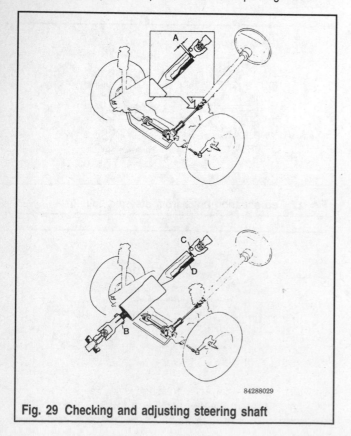

84288029

Fig. 29 Checking and adjusting steering shaft

steering wheel. Tighten the steering wheel nut 42 ft. lbs. (60 Nm).

27. Connect the air bag tester (8695 or equivalent) to the system. Connect the negative battery cable. Check the SRS lamp operation and that no fault codes have been registered.

28. Disconnect the negative battery cable again and remove the air bag tester.

29. Install the air bag assembly and reconnect the negative battery cable. Check the vehicle operation and SRS system for fault codes.

Except 240 Series

✳✳WARNING

Before working the steering system, read the SRS service precautions in this Section.

1. Place the front wheels in straight-ahead position.

2. Disconnect the negative battery lead AND TAPE the lead end.

3. Raise the front of the vehicle and support it safely.

4. Remove the air bag assembly. See 'Air Bag' removal & installation in this Section.

5. Remove the steering wheel. See 'Steering Wheel' rremoval & installation in this Section.

6. Remove the contact reel assembly. Remove the combination switch.

7. Remove the steering column rake adjustment lever using a 0.12 inch (3mm) hex wrench.

8. Remove the parking plate around the steering tube (4 screws). Disconnect the ignition lock connector.

9. Turn the ignition switch to position I. Take a 0.079 inch (2mm) drift and press down the tumblers in the cylinder. Remove the lock assembly.

10. From the engine compartment, remove the locking pins, bolt and nut from the steering shaft joint. Loosen the joint slightly. Free the lower shaft from the steering column by moving the steering shaft towards the steering gear.

11. Remove the 4 steering column mounting bolts. Remove the steering column assembly.

To install:

12. Lubricate the lower part of the steering column. Careful slide the column through the rubber bushing in the firewall.

13. Install the retaining bolts and tighten to 18 ft. lbs. (24 Nm).

14. Connect the lower steering shaft to the steering column. Torque to 18 ft. lbs. (24 Nm) and install the locking pins.

15. Install the packing plates around the steering tube, making certain that the rubber seals are tightly in place.

16. Install the steering lock assembly. Turn the ignition switch to position I and press down the tumblers with a suitable drift. Install the lock assembly.

17. Install the combination switch assembly.

18. Install the contact reel. See 'Contact Reel' removal & installation in this Section.

19. Install the steering wheel. See 'Steering Wheel' rremoval & installation in this Section.

20. Install the air bag assembly. See 'Air Bag' removal & installation in this Section.

21. Reconnect the negative battery cable. Check the vehicle operation and SRS system for fault codes.

Steering Linkage

All models are equipped with rack and pinion steering (manual or power). Rack and pinion systems save space and weight, improve steering response and eliminate most of the rods and linkage under the vehicle.

TIE-RODS

Inspection

CHECKING STEERING ROD PLAY

1. Raise the vehicle and support it safely.
2. Place the front wheels in straight-ahead position.
3. Jiggle the wheel at 9 and 3 o'clock positions. Maximum radial play permitted: 0.02 inches (0.5mm).

CHECKING STEERING RODS ENDS

1. Check the rubber seals for damage.
2. Check the steering rod for damage. Jiggle with a pairs of pliers and check that the joints does not have any wear. Squeeze the joints with a pair of pliers to check for axial play.
3. If rubber seal or rods are damaged or if joints are worn, replace immediately.
4. Maximum allowable axial play for joints are 0.12 inches (3mm).

Removal & Installation

1. Disconnect the negative battery cable.
2. Raise the vehicle and support it safely.
3. Mark the position of the wheel stud nearest to the valve. Wheel is marked to facilitate installation and to avoid the need for rebalancing. Remove the wheel and tire assembly.
4. Remove the cotter pin, if equipped, and locknut. Separate the tie-rod from the steering knuckle.
5. Loosen the locknut and unscrew the tie-rod. Count every full turn needed to remove the tie rod end.

To install:

6. Install the new tie rod-end the exact number of turns noted during removal. Tighten the locknut.
7. Attach the tie-rod end at the steering knuckle. Install the locknut and cotter pin, if equipped.
8. Install the wheel and tire assembly. Install the wheel on the hub assembly, while aligning the marking made earlier. Alternately tighten the nuts to specifications.
9. Check the front-end alignment checked and reset if necessary. If close attention was paid to the exact number of turns of each tie rod end, the alignment should not be far off specification.

Manual Steering Gear

REMOVAL & INSTALLATION

240 Series

1. Remove the lock bolt and nut from the column flange. Bend apart the flange slightly with a screwdriver.

2. Raise and support the vehicle safely. Remove the front wheels.
3. Disconnect the tie rod ends, using a ball joint puller.
4. Remove the splash guard.
5. Disconnect the steering gear from the front axle member (beam).
6. Disconnect the steering gear at the steering shaft flange. Remove the steering gear. Save the dowel pins.

To install:

7. Install rubber spacers and plates for the steering gear attachment points.
8. Position the steering gear and guide the pinion shaft into the steering shaft. The recess on the pinion shaft should be aligned towards the lock bolt opening in the shaft.
9. Attach the steering gear to the front axle member. Check that the U-bolts are aligned in the plate slots. Install flat washers and nuts. Tighten the nuts to 10-18 ft. lbs.
10. Install the splash guard.
11. Connect the steering rods to the steering arms. Tighten the nuts to 44 ft. lbs.
12. Install the front wheels and lower the vehicle.
13. Install the lock bolt for the steering shaft flange. Tighten the bolt to 18 ft. lbs.
14. Have the alignment checked and reset if needed.

Power Steering Gear

INSPECTION

Checking Steering Gear

240 SERIES

Check the steering gear rubber bellows for damage. Also, check that the steering gear is firmly attached by trying to move it by hand.

Turn the steering wheel fully to the right and left positions. Check the steering effort and steering gear for play. Also, check the steering lock function.

REMOVAL & INSTALLATION

240 Series

1. Disconnect the steering column shaft flange at the steering gearbox. Remove the clamp screw and pry the flange open.
2. Raise the vehicle and support it safely. Remove the front wheels.
3. Use a ball joint separator and disconnect the tie rods at the outer ends.
4. Remove the splash guard.
5. Disconnect the hydraulic hoses at the steering gear. Install protective plugs in the hose connections.
6. Remove the bolts holding the steering gear. Remove the steering gear from its mounts and save the spacers.
7. Remove the steering gear from the vehicle by pulling it down until it is free from the steering shaft flange. Then remove the unit through the left side of the vehicle. Save the dowel pins.

To install:

8. When reinstalling, position the steering gear and attach the pinion shaft to the steering shaft flange. Take care to align the recess for the lock bolt.

9. Install right side U-bolt and bracket, but do NOT tighten the nuts.

10. Install left side retaining bolts, and tighten. Tighten the U-bolts.

11. Connect the steering rods to the steering arms.

12. Install the lock bolt on the steering column flange.

13. Connect the return and pressure hoses to the steering gear.

14. Fill the reservoir with Type A automatic transmission fluid and bleed the system as outlined under Power Steering System Bleeding.

Except 240 Series

1. Disconnect the negative battery cable. Raise and support the vehicle safely.

2. Remove the splash guard and the small jacking panel on the front crossmember.

3. Disconnect the lower steering shaft from the steering gear.

4. At the lower universal joint, remove the snaprings and loosen the upper clamp bolt. Then remove the lower clamp bolt and slide the joint up on the shaft.

5. Use a ball joint separator and disconnect the tie rods at the outer ends.

6. Disconnect the fluid lines from the steering gear. Catch the spilled fluid in a pan and install plugs in the lines.

7. Remove the sway bar mounting brackets from the side members and move them out of the way. Remove the steering gear retaining bolts and lower the assembly out of the vehicle.

To install:

8. When reinstalling, position the rack in position and install the retaining bolts. Tighten them to 32 ft. lbs.

9. Install the sway bar mounting brackets.

10. Use new copper washers and connect the fluid lines to the assembly.

11. Connect the tie rods and tighten their nuts to 44 ft. lbs.

12. Slide the lower universal joint down the shaft and into position. Tighten the lower clamp bolt first, then the upper. Both bolts are tightened to 15 ft. lbs. Install the snaprings.

13. Reinstall the jacking plate and the splash guard.

14. Lower the vehicle to the ground. Fill the reservoir with ATF. Start the engine and smoothly turn the steering wheel from lock to lock 3 or 4 times; recheck the fluid level in the reservoir.

Power Steering Pump

REMOVAL & INSTALLATION

240 Series

1. Remove all dirt and grease from around the line connections at the pump.

2. Using a container to catch any power steering fluid that might run out, disconnect the lines, and plug them to prevent dirt from entering the system.

3. Remove the tensioner locking screws on both sides of the pump and remove the drive belt.

4. Turn the pump up and remove the three bolts holding the bracket to the engine block. Remove the pump and bracket.

5. If the pump is being replaced with a new one, remove the nut and pulley from the old pump and transfer it to the new one. Separate the bracket and tensioner from the pump and install them loosely on the new pump.

To install:

6. Place the pump in position on the engine and install the retaining bolts and spacer.

7. Install the drive belt and install the tensioner lock.

8. Adjust the belt tension and then tighten the nuts of the long bolts.

9. Use new copper washers and reconnect the fluid lines to the pump.

10. Fill the reservoir with Type A or Dexron®II automatic transmission fluid and bleed the system as outlined under Power Steering System Bleeding.

Except 240 Series

1. Remove the splash guard from under the engine.

2. Loosen the belt tensioner. Remove the mounting bracket and bolt.

3. Disconnect the lines at or near the pump. Depending on the type of pump, it may be necessary to disconnect the rubber hose(s) from the metal pipes instead of removing the lines at the pump body. Use a catch pan under the vehicle for spillage and plug the lines and fittings immediately to avoid contamination.

4. Remove the large retaining bolt and remove the drive belt from the pump.

5. Lower the pump slightly and disconnect the filler hose from the pump. Remove the pump from the vehicle.

6. If the pump is to be replaced with a new one, transfer the pulley, the mounting bracket and the washers to the new pump. Install the mounting bracket on the new pump; make sure the thick washer is between the bracket and the pump body. Install the pulley; remember that the conical face of the washer must be to the outside.

To install:

7. Reconnect the filler hose to the pump.

8. Position the pump and install the retaining bolts loosely.

9. Install the mounting bracket and belt. Adjust the belt tension.

10. Tighten the lower retaining bolts.

11. Reconnect the fluid hoses to the pump. Use new washers and/or hose clamps. Tighten the banjo fittings (if any) to 31 ft. lbs.

12. Fill the fluid reservoir and start the engine. Slowly turn the wheel lock to lock once or twice and check for leaks. Top the fluid to the proper level.

13. Reinstall the splash guard. The power steering system is self-bleeding; no external bleeding is required.

POWER STEERING SYSTEM BLEEDING

Bleeding removes any air which become trapped within the fluid system. The system should be bled every time any hose or component has been loosened or removed. The system should also be bled if it has run low on fluid during operation.

1. Fill the reservoir with the proper type of fluid. Raise and support the vehicle safely. Place the transmission in **N** and apply the parking brake.

2. Start the engine and fill the reservoir as the level drops.

3. When the reservoir level has stopped dropping, slowly turn the steering wheel from lock to lock several times. Fill the reservoir if necessary.

4. Continue to turn the steering wheel slowly until the fluid in the reservoir is free of air bubbles.

5. Stop the engine and observe the oil level in the reservoir. If the oil level rises more than ¼ in. (6mm) past the level mark, air still remains in the system. Continue bleeding until the level rise is correct.

6. Lower the vehicle.

240 FRONT SUSPENSION—TORQUE SPECIFICATIONS

Component	U.S.	Metric
Control arm bushing, rear nut:	41 ft. lbs.	55 Nm
Control arm bushing, rear bracket:	30 ft. lbs.	40 Nm
Control arm bushing, front bolt:	55 ft. lbs.	75 Nm
Ball joint-to-control arm:	85 ft. lbs.	115 Nm
Ball joint-to-attachment or spring strut:	44 ft. lbs.	60 Nm
Ball joint attachment to spring strut:	17 ft. lbs.	23 Nm
Steering rod-to-steering arm:	44 ft. lbs.	60 Nm
Upper bearing, nut:	15 ft. lbs.	20 Nm
Steering wheel nut:	44 ft. lbs.	60 Nm
Shock absorber, upper bearing (front):	15 ft. lbs.	20 Nm
Spring, upper anchorage (rear):	33 ft. lbs.	45 Nm
Spring, lower anchorage (rear):	14 ft. lbs.	19 Nm
Wheel nuts:	85 ft. lbs.	115 Nm

84288031

700/900 FRONT SUSPENSION—TORQUE SPECIFICATIONS

Component	U.S.	Metric
Front axle member (body):	70 ft. lbs.	95 Nm
Control arm, front axle member:	66 ft. lbs.	90 Nm
Control arm, ball joint:	52 ft. lbs.	70 Nm
Control arm stay, control arm:	74 ft. lbs.	100 Nm
Control arm stay, body:	89 ft. lbs.	120 Nm
Anti-roll bar link, control arm:	66 ft. lbs.	90 Nm
Ball joint, spring strut (*):	22 + 90 degrees	30 + 90 degrees
Steering rod, steering arm:	44 ft. lbs.	60 Nm
Upper bearing, body:	37 ft. lbs.	50 Nm
Upper bearing, shock absorber:	52 ft. lbs.	70 Nm
Front wheel hub, stub axle (*):	74 + 45 degrees	100 + 45 degrees
Support arm cap:	37 ft. lbs.	50 Nm
Rear spring, upper anchorage:	37 ft. lbs.	50 Nm
Wheel:	66 ft. lbs.	90 Nm

* = angle-tighten

84288032

240/700/900 STEERING—TORQUE SPECIFICATIONS

Component	U.S.	Metric
Steering wheel nut:	44 ft. lbs.	60 Nm
Steering column (front bolt) 240:	15 ft. lbs.	20 Nm
Steering shaft rubber coupling, bolt 240:	15 ft. lbs.	20 Nm
Steering shaft connection flange, bolt 240:	17 ft. lbs.	23 Nm
Steering shaft, steering column 700/900:	18 ft. lbs.	24 Nm
Steering shaft knuckle, bolt 700/900:	17 ft. lbs.	23 Nm
Steering gear, front axle member (bolts/nuts) 240:	15 ft. lbs.	20 Nm
700/900 (*):	30 + 180 degrees	35 + 120 degrees
Steering rod, outer ball joint (nut) 240:	52 ft. lbs.	70 Nm
700/900:	52 ft. lbs.	70 Nm
Steering arm, outer ball joint (nut) 240:	44 ft. lbs.	60 Nm
700/900:	44 ft. lbs.	60 Nm
SRS module 240 (In steering wheel hub):	4.4 ft. lbs.	6 Nm
700/900:	4.4 ft. lbs.	6 Nm
ZF pinion nut:	18 ft. lbs.	24 Nm

* = Angle-tighten

84288033

REAR AXLE TORQUE SPECIFICATIONS

Component	U.S.	Metric
Inspection cover bolts:	15–22 ft. lbs.	20–30 Nm
Pinion without compression sleeve:	147–184 ft. lbs.	200–250 Nm
Driveshaft pressure plate bolts:	30 ft. lbs.	40 Nm
Rear brake caliper bolts:	44 ft. lbs.	60 Nm
Rear axle-support arm clamp bolt:	33 ft. lbs.	45 Nm
Support arm bracket-body bolt:	35 ft. lbs.	48 Nm
Support arm bracket-nut:	63 ft. lbs.	85 Nm
Damper support arm mounting nut:	63 ft. lbs.	85 Nm
Panhard rod rear axle bolt:	63 ft. lbs.	85 Nm
Torque arm rear axle nut:	103 ft. lbs.	140 Nm
Limited slip differential (differential housing halves bolt:	44–52 ft. lbs.	60–70 Nm
Differential lock (differential housing end-plate bolt:	6–8 ft. lbs.	8–10 Nm

84288034

MULTI-LINK REAR SUSPENSION TORQUE SPECIFICATIONS

Component	U.S.	Metric
Wheel nuts:	62 ft. lbs.	85 Nm
Body studs bolt:	51 ft. lbs.	70 Nm
Support arm/body mounting bolt:	35 ft. lbs.	48 Nm
Upper control arm/wheel bearing housing nut:	84 ft. lbs.	115 Nm
Upper control arm/rear axle member, rear nut:	62 ft. lbs.	85 Nm
Track rod/wheel bearing housing bolt:	62 ft. lbs.	85 Nm
Track rod/rear axle member nut:	51 ft. lbs.	70 Nm
Differential (front)/rear axle member bolt:	116 ft. lbs.	160 Nm
Differential (rear)/rear axle member bolt:	116 ft. lbs.	160 Nm
Damper/support arm nut:	41 ft. lbs.	56 Nm
Damper/body bolt:	62 ft. lbs.	85 Nm
Brake caliper/wheel bearing housing bolt:	44 ft. lbs.	60 Nm
Universal joint, rear nut:	37 ft. lbs.	50 Nm
Lower control arm/wheel bearing housing nut:	37 ft. lbs. (3)	50 Nm (3)
Lower control arm/rear axle member nut:	37 ft. lbs. (3)	50 Nm (3)
Support arm/body nut:	51 ft. lbs. (3)	70 Nm (3)
Support arm/support arm bracket nut:	91 ft. lbs. (4)	125 Nm (4)
Support arm/wheel bearing housing bolt:	44 ft. lbs. (3)	60 Nm (3)
Upper control arm/rear axle member front nut:	51 ft. lbs. (2)	70 Nm (2)
Rear axle member front/body bolt:	51 ft. lbs. (2)	70 Nm (2)
Rear axle member rear/body bolt:	51 ft. lbs. (2)	70 Nm (2)
Hub nut:	102 ft. lbs. (2)	140 Nm (2)
Rear axle member upper/rear axle member, lower bolt:	51 ft. lbs. (2)	70 Nm (1)

1 = Torque + angle-tightened joints 30 degrees
2 = Torque + angle-tightened joints 60 degrees
3 = Torque + angle-tightened joints 90 degrees
4 = Torque + angle-tightened joints 120 degrees

84288035

9

BRAKES

BRAKE OPERATING SYSTEM

Basic Operating Principles

All Volvos are equipped with a four wheel power-assisted disc brake system. Disc brakes offer better stopping, ease of repair and simplified construction.

Instead of the traditional expanding brakes that press outward against a circular drum, disc brake systems utilize a disc (rotor) with brake pads positioned on either side of it. Some models may be equipped with a solid type disc, while other models are equipped with a vented-type disc. Vented-type disc enables air to circulate between the braking surfaces making them less sensitive to heat buildup and more resistant to fade. The braking action, on disc brake system, is not affected by dirt and water since contaminants are thrown off by the centrifugal action of the rotor or scraped off by the pads. Also, the equal clamping action of the two brake pads tends to ensure uniform, straight line stops. The brake pad on the inside of the brake rotor is moved in contact with the rotor by hydraulic pressure. The caliper, which is not held in a fixed position, moves slightly, bringing the outside brake pad into contact with the disc rotor.

The calipers are manufactured either by Girling or ATE, so when ordering disc pads or caliper rebuilding kits, you must identify which you have. The name of the manufacturer is cast into the metal of the caliper. All 1991 700/900 series, with ABS, are equipped with Girling single piston caliper assembly on the front brakes.

Understanding the Brake Hydraulic System

Hydraulic systems are used to actuate the brakes of all modern automobiles. The system transports the power required to force the frictional surfaces of the braking system together from the pedal to the individual brake units at each wheel. A hydraulic system is used for two reasons. First, fluid under pressure can be carried to all parts of an automobile by small hoses, some of which are flexible, without taking up a significant amount of room or posing routing problems. Second, a great mechanical advantage can be given to the brake pedal end of the system, and the foot pressure required to actuate the brakes can be reduced by making surface area of the master cylinder pistons smaller than that of any of the pistons in the calipers.

The master cylinder consists of a double reservoir and piston assembly as well as other springs, fittings etc. Double (dual) master cylinders are designed to separate the front and rear hydraulic system from each other.

Steel lines carry the brake fluid to a point on the vehicle's frame near each wheel. A flexible hose usually carries the fluid to the disc caliper or wheel cylinder. The flexible line allows for suspension and steering movements.

The front disc brake calipers contain two pistons each, which push inwards toward the brake disc. The rear disc brake calipers contain one piston each. From model year 1991, all 700/900 series, with ABS, are equipped with Girling single piston caliper assembly on the front brakes.

The hydraulic system operates as follows: When at rest, the entire system, from the piston(s) in the master cylinder to those in the calipers, is full of brake fluid. Upon application of the brake pedal, fluid trapped in front of the master cylinder piston(s) is forced through the lines to the brake calipers piston(s). Here, it forces the pistons inward toward the disc.

Upon release of the brake pedal, a spring located inside the master cylinder immediately return the master cylinder pistons to the normal position. The pistons contain check valves and the master cylinder has compensating ports drilled in it. These are uncovered as the pistons reach their normal position. The piston check valves allow fluid to flow toward the calipers as the pistons withdraw. Then, as the brake pads are force away from the brake disc, the excess fluid reservoir through the compensating ports. It is during the time the pedal is in the released position that any fluid that has leaked out of the system will be replaced from the reservoirs through the compensating ports.

The brake system uses a switch to warn the driver when only one section of the hydraulic system is operational. This switch is located at the brake pedal. A hydraulic piston receives pressure from both circuits, each circuit's pressure being applied to one end of the piston. When the pressures are in balance, the piston remains stationary. When one circuit has a leak, however, the greater pressure in the circuit during application of the brakes will push the piston to one side, closing the switch and activating the brake warning light.

The hydraulic system may be checked for leaks by applying pressure to the pedal gradually and steadily. If the pedal sinks very slowly to the floor, the system has a leak. This is not to be confused with a springy or spongy feel due to the compression of air within the lines. If the system leaks, there will be a gradual change in the position of the pedal with a constant pressure.

Check for leaks along all lines and at wheel cylinders or calipers. If no external leaks are apparent, the problem is inside the master cylinder.

Brake Fluid

Only top grade brake fluids that satisfy the requirements of the DOT 4 standard should be used in the brake system. Unspecified brake fluids or those of a grade other than the specified one should never be used. Using inferior brake fluids may result in premature failure of the hydraulic components or in impaired braking function. Fluids not meeting specifications may not withstand the great temperatures generated at the disc and caliper during braking. If the fluid boils within the lines, the pedal will feel spongy and give little response at the wheels.

Brake fluid should normally be changed at least once every two years or every 30,000 miles (48,000 km). If the vehicle's brake system is subjected to particularly hard wear, such as driving in mountainous regions, it should be changed at least once a year or every 15,000 miles (24,000 km).

Contaminated brake fluid is often darker or of a different color than new fluid, and is relatively odorless and watery. Brake fluid normally deteriorate after a long period of use, due to absorption of moisture and other impurities.

Whenever adding to or replacing the brake fluid, the greatest cleanliness should be observed to prevent dirt entering the system. Only clean, new brake fluid should be used. Brake fluid collected from the system during bleeding, should never be returned to the system. Avoid mixing brake fluids from different manufacturers.

Cleaning of Parts

The components of the hydraulic brake system should only be cleaned with fresh brake fluid or denatured alcohol that does not contain benzol.

Petrol/gasoline, washing naptha, trichloroethylene or spirits containing benzol may NOT be used for cleaning purposes, because benzol or the slightest trace of mineral oil will penetrate the rubber seals and cause them to swell. Therefore, it is necessary that all traces of cleaning agent be removed from the system before filling up with brake fluid. Traces of alcohol in the brake system will lower its boiling point, can cause the formation of vapor and lead to malfunctions.

Brake fluid is an excellent cleaning agent. The brake fluid recovered during bleeding can be used for cleaning components during disassembly, but don't introduce any into the brake fluid system.

Adjustments

Disc brakes are inherently self-adjusting. The only adjustment needed will be for the parking brakes, which are small brake shoes located the drum of the rear disc brake rotors.

Brake Light Switch

The switch controlling the brake lights is located at the brake pedal. As the pedal moves from its rest position, the switch engages and turns on the brake lights.

REMOVAL & INSTALLATION

1. Remove the soundproofing.
2. Disconnect the connectors at the switch, unscrew the locknut and remove the switch.
3. Place the new switch into position. Install the locknut and electrical connectors.
4. After installing the new switch, it must be adjusted so that the brake lights comes ON when the brake pedal is depressed approximately ⅜-½ inches (8-14mm) of pedal travel.

Brake Pedal

REMOVAL & INSTALLATION

1. Disconnect the negative battery cable.
2. Remove the soundproofing on the left-hand side of the central console.

3. Disconnect the pedal from the pressure rod, by removing the lock spring and bolt.
4. Unhook the spring from the pedal and remove the bolt and pedal. Remove the old bushings from the pedal.

To install:

5. Lubricate the bearing sleeve and spring. Install new bushings to the pedal.
6. Install the spring on the pedal and tighten it.
7. Install the pressure rod. Install the bolt and lock spring.
8. Install the soundproofing.
9. Reconnect the negative battery cable.

Master Cylinder

REMOVAL & INSTALLATION

▸ See Figure 1

1. To prevent brake fluid from spilling onto and damaging the paint, place a protective cover over the fender apron, and rags beneath the master cylinder.
2. Label and disconnect the brake lines from the master cylinder and plug them immediately. If the vehicle has a hydraulic clutch, disconnect its line from the fluid reservoir. Plug it and secure the line out of the way.
3. Remove the two nuts which retain the master cylinder and reservoir assembly to the vacuum booster, and lift the assembly forward, being careful not to spill any fluid on the fender. Empty out and discard the brake fluid.

❋❋WARNING

Do not depress the brake pedal while the master cylinder is removed!

4. To install, place a new sealing rim (if equipped) onto the sealing flange of the master cylinder. Position the master cylinder and reservoir assembly onto the booster studs, and install the washer and nuts. Tighten the nuts to 8.6-10.8 ft. lbs.
5. Remove the plugs and loosely connect the brake lines. Have a helper depress the brake pedal to remove air from the cylinder. Tighten the nuts for the lines when the brake fluid (free of air bubbles) is forced out. Reconnect the lines for the hydraulic clutch if so equipped.
6. On vehicles equipped with hydraulic clutch, connect the clutch hose to the reservoir.

84289001

Fig. 1 Master cylinder and brake booster assembly — 740/940/960

7. Bleed the entire brake system and, where applicable, the clutch system. See 'Bleeding The System' in this section.

OVERHAUL

▶ **See Figure 2**

1. Remove the master cylinder from the booster as outlined previously.
2. Drain the reservoir of fluid.
3. Firmly fasten the flange of the master cylinder in a vise.
4. Position both hands beneath the reservoir and pull it free of its rubber seals. Remove the filler cap and strainer from the reservoir, as well as the rubber seals and nuts (if so equipped) from the cylinder.
5. Remove the circlip and withdraw the pistons and return spring.
6. **Cleaning and Inspection:**
    a. Polish the inner surface of the master cylinder with a honing tool (cylinder grinding tool).
    b. Clean the master cylinder and all parts that are not to be replaced, using methylated spirits. Use compressed air to blow clean the equalizer and overflow holes.
    c. Examine the master cylinder bore carefully. If it is scored or scratched, replace it. Replace both pistons, with connecting sleeve and seals, as a unit.
    d. Apply brake fluid to the master cylinder and lubricate the piston seals with special grease. Assemble the pistons, spring seat and spring.
    e. Install the master cylinder over the pistons and spring; then install the piston circlip.
7. Install new reservoir seals into the master cylinder. Fit the reservoir to the master cylinder.
8. Install the master cylinder assembly as outlined.
9. Bleed the brake system and, where applicable, the clutch system.

Power Brake Booster

CHECKING POWER BRAKE FUNCTION

▶ **See Figure 3**

Remove the vacuum by depressing the brake pedal approximately 5 times. Depress the brake pedal and start the engine. The pedal position should drop slightly if the power brake is functioning properly.

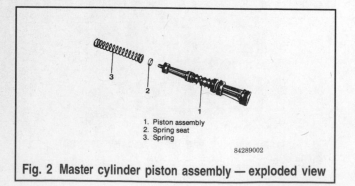

1. Piston assembly
2. Spring seat
3. Spring

84289002

Fig. 2 Master cylinder piston assembly — exploded view

PRESSURE TESTING THE SYSTEM

Apply moderate pressure on the brake pedal for approximately 20 seconds. Then, repeat with high pedal pressure for 5 seconds. The pedal position must not drop. A drop indicates brake fluid leakage or booster vacuum leak.

REMOVAL & INSTALLATION

1. Disconnect the negative battery cable.
2. Remove the master cylinder to power booster retaining bolts and position the master cylinder aside. Be careful not to damage the brake lines.
3. Disconnect the vacuum hose and check valve from the booster.
4. If required, disconnect the fuel filter and vacuum pump. Position them aside.
5. From inside the vehicle, remove the soundproofing and disconnect the brake pedal rod.
6. Remove the power booster retaining bolts. Remove the power booster from the vehicle.
To install:
7. Before installing the booster, check the valve seal. Replace it if necessary. When installing the new check valve seal, ensure that the flange of the seal is in the correct position.
8. On the 2 x 8 inch booster, install the sealing washer and seal onto the booster.
9. Install the booster to the vehicle.
10. Reconnect the brake pedal to the booster rod. Refit the soundproofing.
11. Install the master cylinder, check valve and vacuum hose.
12. Connect the negative battery cable.

Pressure Differential Warning Valve

Each of the brake circuits has a proportioning (relief) valve located inline between the rear wheels. The purpose of this valve is to ensure that brake pressure on all four wheels compensates for the change in weight distribution under varied braking conditions.

The harder the brakes are applied, the more weight there is on the front wheels. The valve regulates the hydraulic pressure to the rear wheels so that under hard braking conditions they

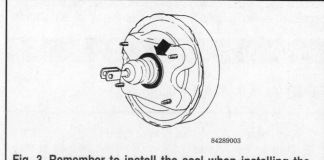

84289003

Fig. 3 Remember to install the seal when installing the power brake booster

receive a smaller percentage of the total braking effort. This prevents premature rear wheel lockup and possible skidding or loss of control.

VALVE RESETTING

1. Disconnect the plug contact and screw out the warning switch so the pistons inside the valve may return to their normal position.
2. Repair and bleed the faulty hydraulic circuit.
3. Screw in the warning switch and tighten it to a torque of 10-14 ft. lbs. (14-19 Nm). Connect the plug contact.

REMOVAL & INSTALLATION

1. Placing a rag under the valve to catch the brake fluid.
2. Disconnect the electrical connector from the switch and slacken the brake pipe connections.
3. Remove the bolt(s) which retain the valve to the underbody and unscrew the brake pipe connections. Remove the differential warning valve.

To install:

4. Place a new seal on it and screw the valve onto the rear brake hose and hand tighten. Secure the valve to the underbody with the retaining bolt(s).
5. Connect the brake pipe and tighten both connections, making sure there is no tension on the flexible rear hose.
6. Bleed the brake system.

Brake Hoses and Pipes

INSPECTION

HOSES

- Check the brake hoses for leaks.
- Check that the hoses are correctly installed and that the connections are tight.
- Check that the brake hoses are not chafed and are free from sharp edges or other objects that could cause wear.

PIPES

- Check that all brake lines are correctly installed and secured.
- Check that they are free from damage and do not rub against sharp edges.
- Check for leakage.

➡ **Pay particular attention to ABS brake lines.**

REMOVAL & INSTALLATION

➡ **Any time the lines are removed or disconnected, extreme cleanliness must be observed. The slightest bit of dirt in the system can plug a fluid port and render the brakes defective. Clean all joints and connections before disassembly (use a stiff brush and clean brake fluid) and plug the lines as soon as they are disconnected. New lines and hoses should be blown or flushed clean before installation to remove any contamination.**

1. Clean the surrounding area on the joints to be disconnected.
2. To reduce fluid spillage during the repair, either plug the vent hole in the reservoir cap or substitute another cap without a vent hole.
3. Disconnect the hose or line to be replaced. If disconnecting rubber hoses at the brake caliper, label or identify each hose so that they may be replaced in the same location. Plug the line ends as soon as the joint is disconnected.
4. Install the new line paying close attention to the proper routing and installation of any retaining clips. Make sure the new line will not rub against any other parts. Brake lines must be at least 3/8 inch away from the steering column.

➡ **If the new line requires bending, do so gently using a pipe bending tool. Do not attempt to bend the tubing by hand; it will kink the pipe and render it useless.**

5. Remove the line plugs and tighten the line connections at both ends.
6. Bleed the brake system beginning with the wheel closest to the replaced line or hose.

➡ **All brake tubing should be flared properly to provide a good leakproof connection. Clean the brake tubing by flushing it with clean brake fluid before installation. When connecting a tube to a hose, tube connector or brake cylinder, tighten the tube fitting nut to specifications with a suitable torque wrench.**

Brake System Bleeding

▶ **See Figures 4 and 5**

Whenever a spongy brake pedal indicates that there is air in the system, or when any part of the hydraulic system has been removed for service, the system must be bled. In addition, if the level in the master cylinder reservoir is allowed to drop below the minimum mark for too long a period of time, air may enter the system, necessitating bleeding.

If only one caliper is removed for servicing, it is usually necessary to bleed only that unit. If, however, the master cylinder, warning valve, or any of the main system lines are removed, the entire system must be bled.

Be careful not to spill any brake fluid onto the brake surfaces or the paint. When bleeding the entire system, the rear of the car should be raised higher than the front. Only use brake fluid bearing the designation DOT 4.

➡ **The following procedure is acceptable for use on vehicles with and without ABS.**

1. Check to make sure that floor mats are not obstructing pedal travel. Full pedal travel should be 6 inches (150 mm).
2. Clean the cap and top of the master cylinder reservoir, and make sure that the vent hole in the cap is open. Fill the reservoir to the maximum mark.

➡ **Never allow the level to drop below the minimum mark during bleeding.**

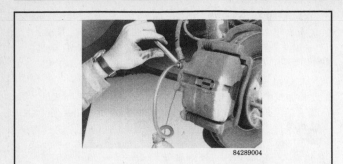

Fig. 4 Bleeding the front hydraulic brake system — 940 shown

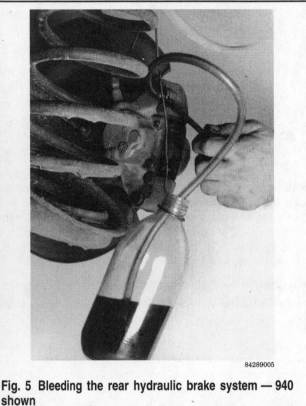

Fig. 5 Bleeding the rear hydraulic brake system — 940 shown

3. If only one brake caliper or line was removed, it will usually suffice to bleed only that wheel. Otherwise, prepare to bleed the entire system beginning at the rear right-hand wheel.

4. Raise the vehicle and support it safely. Remove the protective cap for the bleeder and fit a suitable line wrench on the nipple.

➡**The calipers, on some models, are equipped with 2 bleeder screws. Attach one hose to each screw and submerge in brake fluid.**

5. Install a tight plastic hose onto the nipple and insert the other end of the hose into a glass bottle containing clean brake fluid. The hose must hang down below the surface of the fluid, or air will be sucked into the system when the brake pedal is released.

6. Open the bleeder nipple and pump the brake pedal 5 times. Keep the brake pedal depressed and close the nipple. Release the brake pedal and check the brake fluid. This should be repeated until the fluid flowing into the bottle is completely free of air bubbles. Continue to bleed the system in the following manner.
   — rear left wheel
   — front right wheel
   — front left wheel

➡**During this procedure, check the master cylinder reservoir frequently.**

7. When completed, press the pedal to the bottom of its stroke and tighten the bleeder screw. Install the protective cap. If the pedal still feels spongy after bleeding the entire system, repeat the bleeding sequence.

8. Fill the reservoir to the maximum line. Turn the ignition **ON** but do not start the engine. Apply moderate force to the brake pedal. The pedal must travel no more than 2.4 inches (61 mm) without ABS; 2.17 inches (55 mm) with ABS. The brake warning light (and ABS warning light) must not be on.

➡**After bleeding the brake system, pressure test the brake system, by depressing the brake pedal with a force corresponding to an abrupt halt, almost sufficient to lock the wheels, for 30 seconds. Then check whether there has been any leakage of brake fluid from the master cylinder.**

9. Lower the vehicle.

FRONT DISC BRAKES

✳✳CAUTION

Brake linings contain asbestos, which has been determined to be a cancer causing agent. DO NOT attempt to clean the brake surfaces using compressed air! Avoid inhaling any dust from any brake surface! When cleaning brake surfaces, use a commercially available brake cleaning fluid.

Brake Pads

▶ See Figure 6

CHECKING BRAKE PADS THICKNESS

200 SERIES

If necessary, remove the wheels. Using a mirror and wire gauge, insert the wire gauge in the center groove of the pad. If the wire gauge cannot be inserted, the pads are considered worn. If the wire gauge fits, but a little clearance is left, the

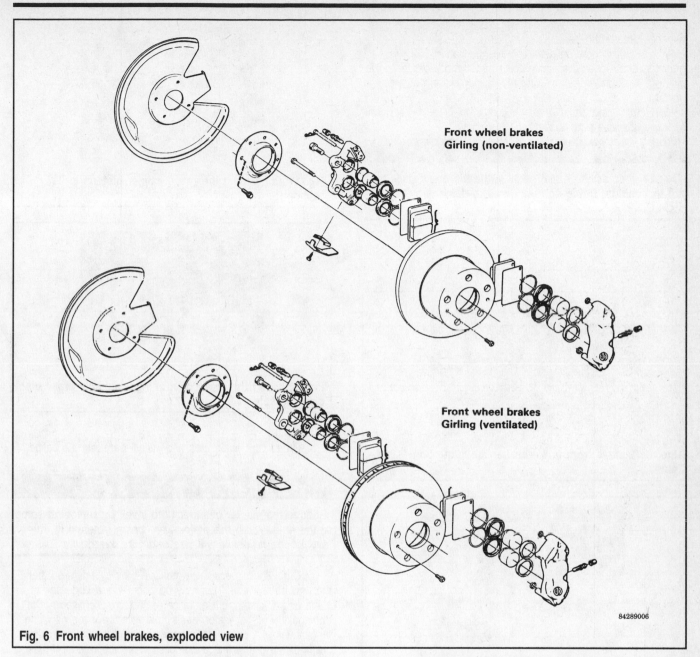

Front wheel brakes
Girling (non-ventilated)

Front wheel brakes
Girling (ventilated)

84289006

Fig. 6 Front wheel brakes, exploded view

pads will have to be replaced within less than 15,000 miles (18,000 km). Minimum brake pad thickness is 0.12 inch (3mm).

700/900 SERIES

▶ See Figure 7

Use a caliper to measure the distance between points A and B. With normally used brake pads, distance must not exceed 1.37 inch (35mm). If the pad thickness is close to be considered worn, replace with a new set. Minimum brake pad thickness is 0.12 inch (3mm).

REMOVAL & INSTALLATION

▶ See Figures 8, 9, 10, 11 and 12

1. Raise the vehicle and support safely.

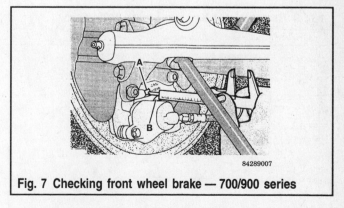

84289007

Fig. 7 Checking front wheel brake — 700/900 series

2. Mark the position of the wheels on the hubs and remove the front wheels.

3. On ATE type calipers, remove the retaining pins using a punch. Remove the retaining spring.

4. On Girling type calipers, remove the bolt in the lower guidepin and loosen the upper bolt a few turns. Hold the guide pin with a 17mm wrench. Swing the caliper piston housing upward.

5. Remove the pads. A special tool 2917 or equivalent can be used, if brake pads are difficult to remove.

❋❋WARNING

Do not depress the brake pedal while the brake pads are not in position. Doing so may result in damage to the piston.

Fig. 8 Remove front brake caliper mounting bolt — 940 shown

Fig. 9 Remove front brake caliper — 940 shown

Fig. 10 Remove brake pads — 940 shown

Fig. 11 Depressing the brake caliper pistons in its cylinders

Fig. 12 Clean the brake disc using a suitable brake disc cleaning solvent

To install:

6. Grease the guide pins and install them into the caliper holder.

❋❋WARNING

Reduce the master cylinder fluid level, by removing some of the fluid. When the pistons are being pressed in, the level of the reservoir will rise and may overflow.

7. Carefully depress the pistons in their cylinders so that the new pads will fit. This may be done with a large pair of pliers or a C-clamp, but extra care must be exercised not to damage the rubber piston seals, the pistons, or the new pads themselves. A piston depressing tool (Volvo 2809) is available from the dealer that accomplishes the job without danger to the caliper components.

8. If necessary, clean the brake disc using a suitable brake disc cleaning solvent. Install the new pads into position and secure the caliper. Check to ensure the springs on the pads are correctly positioned.

➡Always use new caliper mounting bolts. Torque the mounting bolts to the specified value.

9. Check the master cylinder fluid level. Depress the pedal repeatedly.

10. Align the marks made previously and install the wheels. Torque the lug nuts to specifications.

11. Lower the vehicle and connect the negative battery cable.

12. Check the brake pedal operation prior to driving the vehicle.

INSPECTION

Before replacing the pads:

1. Check the rubber dust caps for the brake pistons, replace if defective. If dirt has penetrated into the cylinders, due to a defective dust cap, recondition the caliper.

2. Check the friction surface of the disc, if required, replace or machine it in a lathe.

3. Check the rubber seals on the guide pins, replace them if they are defective.

Brake Caliper

REMOVAL & INSTALLATION

1. Raise and support the vehicle safely. Remove the wheels.

2. Place a suitable container under the brake pipes. Label and disconnect the brake lines at the caliper. Plug the lines to prevent the entry of dirt.

3. Remove the 2 caliper attaching bolts and remove the caliper.

To install:

4. Check the mating surfaces of the caliper and retainer to ensure they are clean. Always use new retaining bolts.

5. Install the brake pads making sure that the caliper is parallel to the disc and that the disc can rotate freely. Position the caliper to its retainer over the disc and install the 2 retaining bolts. Tighten and torque the bolts to specifications.

6. Connect the brake lines to the caliper. Unplug the reservoir cap vent hole.

7. Bleed the brake system. Install the wheels and lower the vehicle.

8. Check the brake pedal operation prior to driving the vehicle.

OVERHAUL

▶ **See Figures 13 and 14**

➡️The following procedure applies to front and rear calipers of both Girling and ATE design.

1. Remove the brake caliper and pads from the car as outlined previously.

2. Remove the retaining rings and the rubber dust covers. Place a wooden block (1) between the pistons. Using compressed air applied through the brake line port, force the pistons toward the wooden block. Remove the pistons from their bores, taking care not to burr or scratch them.

➡️**Compressed air is the only reliable way to force out the pistons. Do not attempt to lever or pry out the pistons. The metal will become gouged and function will be impaired. If one piston has been removed and the other is difficult to remove, use a press tool 2809 or equivalent, and a rubber washer to provide a counterforce in place of the removed piston.**

3. Remove the sealing rings with a blunt plastic tool. Be careful not to damage the edges of the grooves. Screw out the bleeder nipple(s), and on front calipers, remove the external connecting line if still attached.

✳️✳️WARNING

Do not attempt to separate the caliper halves. Assembling the halves requires special pressure testing equipment. Overhaul can be completed without splitting the caliper.

4. Clean all reusable metal parts in clean brake fluid or methylated spirit. Be especially careful to clean the fluid passages. Dry all parts with compressed air or allow to air dry. Make sure that all of the passages are clear. If any of the cylinders are scored or scratched, the entire housing must be replaced. Minor scratching may be removed from the pistons by fine polishing. Replace any piston that is damaged or worn.

5. Coat the mating surfaces of the pistons and cylinder with fresh brake fluid.

6. Install new sealing rings in the cylinders.

7. On Girling brakes and ATE front brakes, press the pistons into their bores with the large end facing inward. Make sure that the pistons are installed straight and are not scratched in the process.

8. On ATE rear brakes, make sure that the pistons are in the proper positions to prevent brake squeal. The piston notches should incline 20° in relation to the lower guide area on the caliper. Check the location of the piston with a template such as Volvo tool 2919. When the template is placed against the one recess, the distance (A) to the other recess may be no greater then 0.039 inch (1mm). If the location of the piston needs adjusting, use Volvo tool 2918 or similar and press it against the piston. Force out the shoes by screwing in the handle. Turn the piston in the required direction, release the tool and remeasure with the template. Repeat this operation for the other piston.

9. Lubricate the pistons working surfaces, cylinders and seals with clean brake fluid. Install the seals into the cylinders, making certain they are properly positioned. Place the new dust caps over the lower edges of the pistons and pull out the dust caps. Install the new retaining rings.

10. Screw in the bleeder nipples(s).

11. Install the assembled caliper, then install the brake pads. Connect the brake line(s).

12. Add brake fluid to the reservoir to replace that lost during removal. Bleed the brake system.

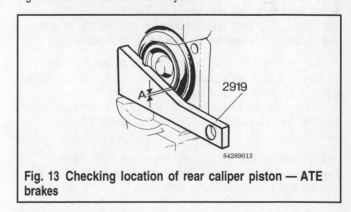

84289013

Fig. 13 Checking location of rear caliper piston — ATE brakes

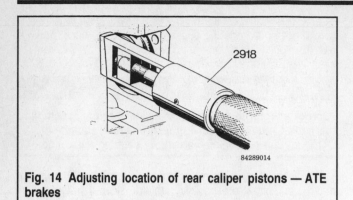

Fig. 14 Adjusting location of rear caliper pistons — ATE brakes

Brake Disc (Rotor)

REMOVAL & INSTALLATION

240 Series

1. Raise and support the vehicle safely. Remove the wheels.

2. Remove the brake caliper but do not disconnect the brake hose. Hang the caliper out of the way.

3. Loosen and remove the small retaining screws on the face of the disc. Remove the disc.

To install:

4. Ensure that the disc is sitting squarely on the mount and install the retaining screws.

5. Install the caliper and pads. Check that the disc can turn freely and that the caliper is seated.

6. Install the wheel and lower the vehicle.

✳✳CAUTION

Check the brake pedal operation prior to driving the vehicle.

Except 240 Series

1. Raise and support the vehicle safely. Remove the wheels.

2. Remove the caliper and pads. Do not disconnect the brake hose, hang it out of the way.

➡**Vehicles equipped with Multi-Link Suspension have a small stud threaded into the disc. While helping to locate the wheel, this stud also retains the disc to the hub. Do not loosen the large center hub to remove the disc.**

3. Use a 10 mm Allen wrench to disconnect the caliper bracket. Remove the center grease cap, the cotter pin and the castle nut. Remove the outer wheel bearing.

4. Remove the brake disc and the inner wheel bearing. It may be necessary to use a bearing puller, tool 2722, or equivalent.

➡**Vehicles equipped with ABS have the pulse wheel mounted within the disc. This toothed wheel must be removed and transferred to a new rotor if one is being in-** stalled. Use a universal gear puller and carefully lift off the pulse wheel. Use a bearing installation tool and a press to install the pulse wheel on the new disc.

To install:

5. Reassemble the wheel bearings and pack with grease. Install the inner bearing in the hub. Using a seal installation tool, install the new grease seal. Ensure that the face of the seal is even with the hub.

6. Install the brake disc, the outer wheel bearing and the castle nut. Rotate the disc while tightening the nut to 41 ft. lbs. (55 Nm). Loosen the nut ½ turn.

7. Install the brake caliper. Use new attaching bolts and tighten them to specifications. Install the brake pads.

8. Install the wheel and lower the vehicle.

9. Check the brake pedal operation prior to driving the vehicle.

INSPECTION

Front and Rear Discs
▶ **See Figure 15**

The brake disc may be inspected without removal, however viewing the back (inner) face of the disc is difficult. Ideally, the caliper should be removed allowing full access to both faces of the disc. Run-out measurements must be taken with the disc mounted on the vehicle and the wheel bearings properly adjusted.

The friction surface on both sides of the disc should be examined for surface deviations such as scoring or corrosion. Minor radial scratches and small rust spots may be removed by resurfacing or fine polishing the disc. The lateral run-out of the disc must not exceed 0.004 inch (0.1mm) for the front, and 0.060 inch (0.15mm) for the rear, measured at the outer edge of the disc. Do not mistake a faulty wheel bearing adjustment, or an improperly mounted disc for lateral runout.

Actual disc thickness, which varies from model to model; however, no individual disc should vary more than 0.0012 inch (0.03mm) when taken at several points on the disc. If the disc is worn at any point to less than the minimum permissible thickness (see specifications), it must be replaced. A brake disc which is too thin cannot handle the heat generated by braking. If the disc cracks under braking, the wheel can lock instantly, causing loss of control and a possible collision.

After the disc has been resurfaced, measure the thickness to insure it is still above the minimum specification. A resurfaced disc should be washed in solvent inside and out to remove

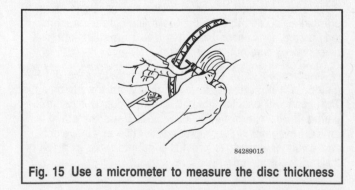

Fig. 15 Use a micrometer to measure the disc thickness

any metal filings which could get caught in the wheel bearings. Dry the disc thoroughly and repack the wheel bearings and

inner hub. A new set of brake pads is highly recommended when installing a new or reconditioned disc.

REAR DISC BRAKES

❋❋CAUTION

Brake linings contain asbestos, which has been determined to be a cancer causing agent. DO NOT attempt to clean the brake surfaces using compressed air! Avoid inhaling any dust from any brake surface! When cleaning brake surfaces, use a commercially available brake cleaning fluid.

Brake Pads

▶ **See Figure 16**

CHECKING BRAKE PADS THICKNESS

▶ **See Figure 17**

1. Raise the vehicle and support safely.
2. Mark the position of the wheels on the axle and remove the wheels.
3. Replace if the lining is less that 0.078 inch (2mm) thick.
4. On models with Multi-Link suspension with Girling brake calipers, pad thickness can be measured without removing the wheels.
5. Check the measurement from shoulder C. It must not exceed 1 inch (25mm).

REMOVAL & INSTALLATION

740 SERIES

▶ **See Figures 13 and 14**

1. Raise the vehicle and support safely.
2. Mark the position of the wheels on the axle and remove the wheels.
3. Using a 0.12 inch (3mm) punch, remove the lock pins.
4. Remove the spring clip and brake pads.

➡**If the brake pads are difficult to remove, use tool 2917 or equivalent. Do not depress the brake pedal while the brake pads are not in position. Doing so may result in damage to the piston.**

To install:
5. Bottom the piston in the cylinder, using a pair of pliers.

❋❋WARNING

Reduce the master cylinder fluid level, by removing some of the fluid. When the pistons are being pressed in, the level of the reservoir will rise and may overflow.

6. Check to ensure the piston is in the proper positions to prevent brake squeal. Rotate the piston until the shoulder in-

clines 20°±2° in relation to the brake caliper lower surface. Use tool 2919 or equivalent. When the template is pressed against one shoulder, the distance to the other 'A' should be a maximum of 0.04 inch (1mm). If the location of the piston needs adjusting, use Volvo tool 2918 or similar and press it against the piston. Force out the shoes by screwing in the handle. Turn the piston in the required direction, release the tool and remeasure with the template. Repeat this operation for the other piston.

7. Install the brake pads. Install the lock pins and new spring clips.
8. Check the master cylinder fluid level. Depress the pedal repeatedly.
9. Align the marks made previously and install the wheels. Torque the lug nuts to specifications.
10. Lower the vehicle.
11. Check the brake pedal operation prior to driving the vehicle.

EXCEPT 740 SERIES

1. Raise the vehicle and support safely.
2. Mark the position of the wheels on the axle and remove the wheels.
3. Insert a screwdriver through the recess between the outer pad and caliper.

❋❋WARNING

Reduce the master cylinder fluid level, by removing some of the fluid. When the pistons are being pressed in, the level of the reservoir will rise and may overflow.

4. Remove the lower guide bolt and loosen the upper bolt a few turns. Hold the guide pin with a 15mm wrench.
5. Support the caliper with a piece of wire.
6. Remove the brake pads.

❋❋WARNING

Do not depress the brake pedal while the brake pads are not in position. Doing so may result in damage to the piston.

To install:
7. Lubricate and install the guide bolts.
8. Install the new pads into position and install the piston housing. Install new mounting bolts and torque to specifications.

➡**Always use new caliper mounting bolts.**

9. Check the master cylinder fluid level. Depress the pedal repeatedly.
10. Align the marks made previously and install the wheels. Torque the lug nuts to specifications.
11. Lower the vehicle.
12. Check the brake pedal operation prior to driving the vehicle.

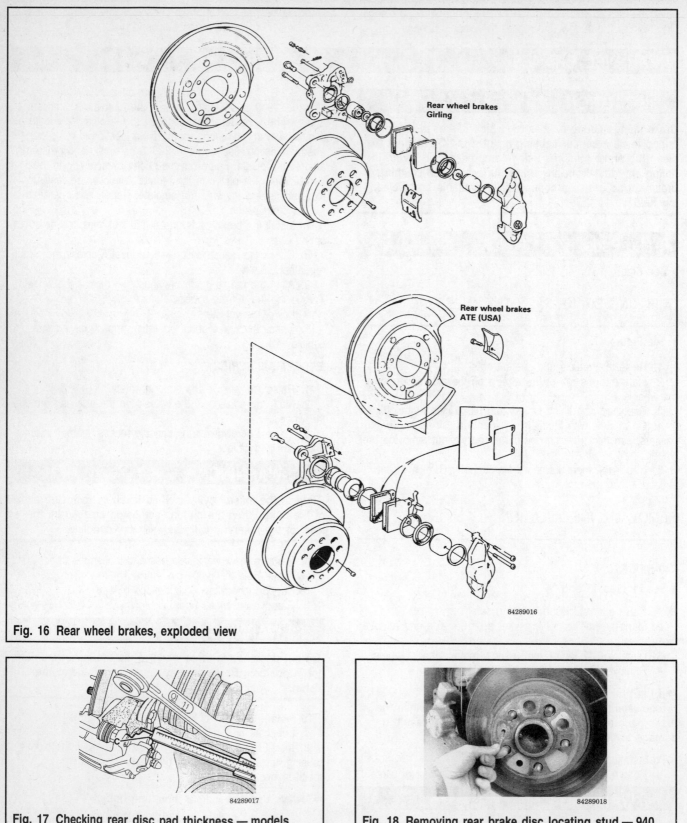

Rear wheel brakes
Girling

Rear wheel brakes
ATE (USA)

84289016

Fig. 16 Rear wheel brakes, exploded view

84289017

Fig. 17 Checking rear disc pad thickness — models with Multi-Link suspension

84289018

Fig. 18 Removing rear brake disc locating stud — 940 shown

INSPECTION

Before replacing the pads:

1. Check the dust caps for the brake pistons, replace if defective. If dirt has penetrated into the cylinders, due to a defective dust cap, recondition the caliper.

2. Check the friction surface of the disc, if required, replace or machine it in a lathe.

3. Check the rubber seals on the guide bolts, replace them if they are defective.

Brake Calipers

REMOVAL & INSTALLATION

1. Raise and support the vehicle safely. Remove the rear wheels.

2. Clean the caliper from debris. Place a suitable container under the brake pipes. Disconnect the brake lines at the caliper. Plug the lines to prevent the entry of dirt.

3. Remove the 2 caliper attaching bolts and remove the caliper.

To install:

4. Place the caliper assembly into position and install the mounting bolts. Torque the bolts to specifications.

5. Connect the brake lines to the caliper.

6. Bleed the brake system. Install the wheels and lower the vehicle.

7. Check the brake pedal operation prior to driving the vehicle.

OVERHAUL

1. Remove the brake caliper as outlined previously.

2. Secure the caliper assembly in a vice. Loosen the guide bolts and remove the caliper from the retainer.

3. Place a wooden block (1) between the pistons. Using compressed air applied through the brake line port, force the pistons toward the wooden block. Remove the pistons from their bores, taking care not to burr or scratch them.

➡**Compressed air is the only reliable way to force out the pistons. Do not attempt to lever or pry out the pistons. The metal will become gouged and function will be impaired.**

✳✳CAUTION

Be careful when pressing the piston from the caliper, as damage to your finger can occur.

4. Remove the dust cap and seal from the caliper, using a blunt tool. Be careful not to damage the edges of the grooves.

5. Clean all reusable metal parts in clean brake fluid or methylated spirit. Be especially careful to clean the fluid passages. Dry all parts with compressed air or allow to air dry. Make sure that all of the passages are clear.   If the cylinder

is scored or scratched, the entire housing must be replaced. Minor scratching may be removed from the pistons by fine polishing. Replace any piston that is damaged or worn.

6. Lubricate the mating surfaces of the pistons, cylinder and seal with fresh brake fluid.

7. Install new seal in the cylinders, making certain it is properly positioned. Place the new dust caps over the lower edges of the pistons and pull out the dust caps. Attach the dust cap to the piston housing.

8. Carefully press the piston into position, making certain the dust cap seats in the piston groove. Screw in the bleeder nipple and torque to specifications.

9. Secure the caliper to the retainer. Install the brake pads and caliper assembly, using new mounting bolts. Connect the brake line.

10. Refill the master cylinder. Bleed the brake system.

11. Check the brake pedal operation prior to driving the vehicle.

Brake Disc (Rotor)

REMOVAL & INSTALLATION

240 Series

1. Raise and support the vehicle safely. Remove the wheels.

2. Remove the brake caliper but do not disconnect the brake hose. Hang the caliper out of the way.

3. Loosen and remove the small retaining screws on the face of the disc. Remove the disc.

To install:

4. Ensure that the disc is sitting squarely on the mount and install the retaining screws.

5. Install the caliper and pads. Check that the disc can turn freely and that the caliper is seated.

6. Install the wheel and lower the vehicle.

✳✳CAUTION

Check the brake pedal operation prior to driving the vehicle.

Except 240 Series

◗ **See Figures 18 and 19**

1. Raise and support the vehicle safely. Remove the wheels.

2. Remove the caliper and pads. Do not disconnect the brake hose, hang it out of the way.

➡**Late vehicle vehicles equipped with Multi-Link Suspension have a small stud threaded into the disc. While helping to locate the wheel, this stud also retains the disc to the hub. Do not loosen the large center hub to remove the disc.**

3. Use a 10mm Allen wrench to disconnect the caliper bracket. Remove the center grease cap, the cotter pin and the castle nut. Remove the outer wheel bearing.

4. Remove the brake disc and the inner wheel bearing. It may be necessary to use a bearing puller, tool 2722, or equivalent.

➡**Vehicles equipped with ABS have the pulse wheel mounted within the disc. This toothed wheel must be removed and transferred to a new rotor if one is being installed. Use a universal gear puller and carefully lift off the pulse wheel. Use a bearing installation tool and a press to install the pulse wheel on the new disc.**

To install:

5. Reassemble the wheel bearings and pack with grease. Install the inner bearing in the hub. Using a seal installation tool, install the new grease seal. Ensure that the face of the seal is even with the hub.

6. Install the brake disc, the outer wheel bearing and the castle nut. Rotate the disc while tightening the nut to 41 ft. lbs. (55 Nm). Loosen the nut ½ turn.

7. Install the brake caliper. Use new attaching bolts and tighten them to 72 ft. lbs. (97 Nm). Install the brake pads.

8. Install the wheel and lower the vehicle.

84289019

Fig. 19 Removing rear brake disc assembly — 940 shown

9. Check the brake pedal operation prior to driving the vehicle.

INSPECTION

Refer to the brake disc rotor inspection under 'Front Disc Brakes' in this Section.

PARKING BRAKE

▶ **See Figure 20**

The cable operated emergency brake is a complete separate brake system acting only on the rear wheels. When the lever in the vehicle is pulled up, cables running to the rear of the vehicle actuate 2 sets of brake shoes. These shoes expand against the machined surface inside the rear brake disc. The system must, however, remain in proper repair and adjustment so that it will hold the vehicle when parked and be available for emergency use if needed.

Cables

REMOVAL & INSTALLATION

240 Series

1. Apply the parking brake. Remove the hub caps for the rear wheels and loosen the lug nuts a few turns.

2. Raise and safely support the vehicle. Remove the wheel and tire assembly. Release the parking brake.

3. Remove the bolt and the wheel from the pulley.

4. Remove the rubber cover for the front attachment of the cable sleeve and nut, as well as the attachment for the rubber suspension ring on the frame. Remove the cable from the other side of the attachment in the same manner.

5. Hold the return spring in position. Pry up the lock and remove the lock pin so the cable releases form the lever.

6. Remove the return spring with washers. Loosen the nut for the rear attachment of the cable sleeve. Lift the cable forward after loosening both side of the attachments and remove it.

To install:

7. Adjust the rear brake shoes of the parking brake by removing the rear ashtray between the front seat backs

8. Tighten the parking brake cable adjusting screw so the brake is fully applied when pulled up 2-3 notches.

9. If one cable is stretched more than the other, they can be individually adjusted by removing the parking brake cover (2 screws) and turning the individual cable adjusting nut at the front of each yoke pivot.

10. Install the ashtray and parking brake cover, if equipped.

11. Install new rubber cable guides for the cable suspension. Place the cable in position in the rear attachment and tighten the nut. Install the washers and return spring. Oil the lock pin and install it, together with the cable, on the lever. Install the attachment and rubber cable guide on the frame.

12. Install the cable in the same manner on the side of the vehicle.

13. Place the cable sleeve in position in the front attachments and install the rubber covers.

14. Lubricate and install the pulley on the pull rod. Adjust the pulley so the parking brake is fully engaged with the lever at the 3rd or 4th notch.

15. Install the wheel and tire assemblies. Lower the vehicle. Tighten the lug nut to 70-100 ft. lbs. (95-135 Nm) and install the hub caps.

Except 240 Series

SHORT CABLE — RIGHT SIDE

1. Raise and safely support the vehicle.

2. Remove the right brake caliper rear wheel. Remove the right brake caliper and hang it from the coil spring with a wire. Remove the brake disc. Unhook the rear return spring and remove the brake shoes.

3. Push out the pin holding the cable to the brake lever. Remove the rubber bellows (boot) from the backing plate and remove the bellows from the cable.

4. Remove the spring clip, pin and cable from the back of the differential housing. Remove the cable guide on the differ-

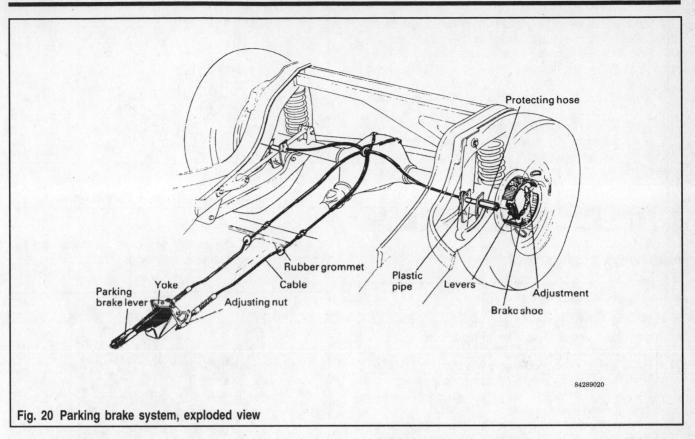

Fig. 20 Parking brake system, exploded view

ential by removing the top bolt from the housing cover. Remove the cable.

To install:

5. Install the cable guide on the new cable. Check the rubber bellows for wear or damage and replace if necessary. Install the bellows and position it through the hole in the backing plate. Make sure the bellows sits correctly on the backing plate.

6. Smear the contact surfaces of the brake levers with a thin layer of heat resistant graphite grease. Connect the cable to the lever and install the pin.

➡The arrow stamped on the lever should point upward and outwards.

7. Push the cable through and place the lever in position behind the rear axle flange.

8. Install the cable guide on the axle. Connect the cable to the equalizer using the pin and spring clip.

9. Install the brake shoes and rear return spring. Install the brake disc and caliper. Use new bolts. and torque to 43 ft. lbs. (58 Nm). Make sure the disc rotates freely. Adjust the parking brake. Install the wheel and lower the vehicle.

LONG CABLE — LEFT SIDE

1. Remove the center console.

2. Slacken the parking brake adjusting screw. Remove the cable lock ring and remove the cable. Pull out the cable from the spring sleeve.

3. Raise and safely support the vehicle. Remove the left rear wheel.

4. Remove the left rear brake caliper and hang it from the coil spring with a piece of wire. Remove the brake disc and rear return spring. Remove the brake shoes.

5. Push out the pin holding the cable to the lever. Remove the rubber bellows from the backing plate and remove the bellows from the cable.

6. Pull out the cable from the backing plate and the equalizer on top of the rear axle.

7. Remove the cable clamp on the sub-frame, above the driveshaft, and the cable.

To install:

8. Install the new cable through the grommet in the floor; check that the grommet sits correctly. Clamp the cable to the sub-frame.

9. Smear the contact surfaces of the brake levers with a thin layer of heat resistant graphite grease. Connect the cable to the lever and install the pin.

➡The arrow stamped on the lever should point upward and outwards.

10. Push the cable through and place the lever in position behind the rear axle flange.

11. Install the cable guide on the axle. Connect the cable to the equalizer using the pin and spring clip.

12. Install the brake shoes and rear return spring. Install the brake disc and caliper. Use new bolts. and torque to 43 ft. lbs. (58 Nm). Make sure the disc rotates freely. Adjust the parking brake. Install the wheel and lower the vehicle.

ADJUSTMENT

◆ **See Figures 21 and 22**

1. Apply the parking brake. Adjust if it is not fully applied after pulling 10-11 notches.

2. After adjustment, adequate braking power should be obtained after pulling 3 — 7 (200 series) or 3 — 5 (700 and 900 series) notches, with a pulling force of approximately 65 lbs. Adjust through the rear brake console.

3. Check that the catch is operating correctly.

4. Check that the indicator light on the instrument panel goes ON. Release the lever and check that the light is out when the lever is in bottom position.

5. Yoke should be at right angles to the parking brake lever. If yoke is out of alignment, use nuts at cable ends to adjust. There should always be at least 0.1 inch (2mm) thread protruding.

Parking Brake Shoes

REMOVAL & INSTALLATION

▶ **See Figures 23, 24, 25, 26 and 27**

1. Using the appropriate procedure under, Brake Cable — Adjustment, gain access to the adjuster and loosen it so that the tension is removed from the cable.

2. Raise and safely support the vehicle safely

3. Remove the brake line-to-axle clamp, as required.

4. Remove the caliper and hang it out of the way. Be careful not to crimp hoses or lines.

5. Remove the disc. Don't attempt to remove the hub.

6. Using brake spring pliers, remove one retaining spring from the shoe assembly. Remove the shoes from the vehicle, taking note of the location and placement of the adjuster.

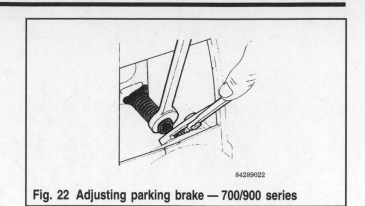

Fig. 22 Adjusting parking brake — 700/900 series

To install:

7. Assemble the shoes with one spring and install onto the vehicle. Install the other retaining spring.

Fig. 23 Parking brake shoes — 940 shown

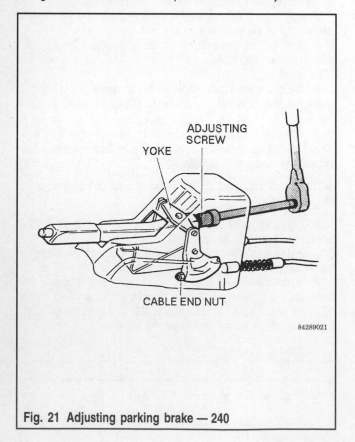

Fig. 21 Adjusting parking brake — 240

Fig. 24 Remove parking brake shoes retaining springs

Fig. 25 Parking brake components

Fig. 26 Clean the brake disc using a suitable brake disc cleaning solvent

Fig. 27 Assembling parking brake shoes

8. Install the brake disc. Check that the disc turns freely without binding on the shoes.

9. Reinstall the brake caliper. Always use new retaining bolts and tighten them to 42 ft. lbs.

10. Reinstall the brake line-to-axle clamp, as required.

11. Adjust the brake shoes (except 700 Series) and then the cables, as described in Brake Cables — Adjustment.

12. Reinstall the wheels and lower the vehicle. Check the emergency brake for proper holding and adjust the cables as necessary. Full braking effect must be possible within 3-5 notches, after adjustment.

VOLVO ANTI-LOCK BRAKE SYSTEM

General Description

The Anti-lock Braking System, designated ABS, prevents wheel lock-up. The ABS provides the shortest possible braking distance while maintaining full directional stability. The ABS controls the front wheels individually and the rear wheels together. The rear piston in the master cylinder operates the front brakes and the front piston operates the rear axle brakes.

SYSTEM COMPONENTS

Wheel Speed Sensors
▶ See Figure 28

The speed signal for each front wheel and the rear axle is sent to the control unit via a sensor and pulse wheel assembly. Each front wheel has its own assembly. Rear wheel speed is measured by one sensor and pulse wheel assembly.

As the teeth of the pulse generator pass the tip of the sensor, the changes from peak to valley to peak generate a small AC voltage in the sensor. The frequency of the voltage — which increases with wheel speed — is used by the CU

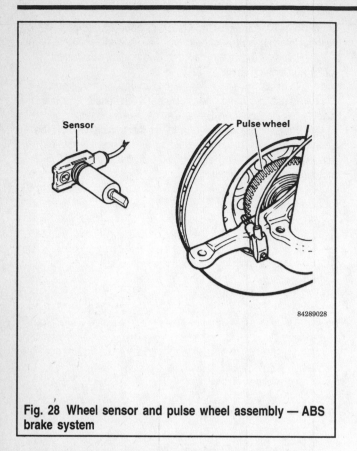

Fig. 28 Wheel sensor and pulse wheel assembly — ABS brake system

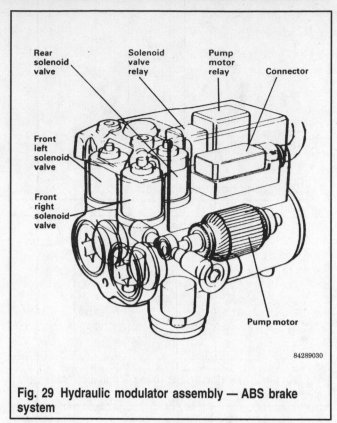

Fig. 29 Hydraulic modulator assembly — ABS brake system

to determine wheel speed. By comparing wheel speed during braking, the control unit determines impending wheel lock.

Electronic Control Unit (CU)

The CU is located below the left dashboard, above the left kick panel. It is located on the right front wheel housing 760's w/B280 engine. The unit is a microprocessor that receives and processes signals according to predetermined logic, and supplies control signal to the solenoid valves located on the hydraulic modulator.

The control unit contains the safety or monitor circuitry which will disable the ABS system if any electrical fault is detected. The safety circuit also monitors battery voltage and will disable the system if voltage becomes too high or too low.

The electronic control unit cannot be repaired or serviced; if an internal fault is detected, the unit must be replaced.

Hydraulic Modulator

▶ **See Figure 29**

Usually located at the right front of the engine compartment, the hydraulic modulator contains the solenoid valves, the system recirculation pump, the solenoid control relay and the pump control relay. Certain engine and body combinations will locate the hydraulic modulator on the left wheel arch.

The 3 internal solenoids are electrically operated valves. When no current is applied, the valves are in the normal or open position, allowing brake fluid pressure to be controlled by the brake pedal. Engagement of ABS causes the solenoid to move through part of its travel, blocking the brake fluid passage. This puts the valve in the hold position, maintaining existing brake line pressure. If the CU still senses a wheel locking or about to lock, the solenoid is moved to the full

extent of its travel, opening the pressure relief passage. Brake fluid in the circuit is allowed to escape, reducing line pressure and releasing the brake. The released fluid is momentarily held in a pressure accumulator which serves to reduce the pedal pounding sensation to the operator. Once released from the accumulator, the fluid is pumped back into the system for reuse.

With the exception of the two relays mounted on the unit, the hydraulic unit has no serviceable parts and cannot be repaired. If an internal fault is found, the unit must be replaced.

Brake Lamp

The red dashboard BRAKE warning lamp functions in a manner identical to non-ABS vehicles. If the fluid level should drop below an acceptable level, the lamp will light as a warning to the operator. If the BRAKE lamp is lit, braking function on the vehicle may be impaired; do not operate the vehicle until the status and reliability of the braking system is determined.

Anti-lock Lamp

The ANTI-LOCK warning lamp is coupled to the ABS CU. The lamp will light briefly during engine start-up as the CU performs an initial check of the system. If no faults are found, the CU will extinguish the lamp within a few seconds. After this initial test, the lamp should not come on during vehicle operation.

If the ANTI-LOCK lamp does come on during operation, the CU has detected a fault and disabled the system. If only the ANTI-LOCK warning lamp is lit, the vehicle retains normal braking characteristics and may be safely driven. If both warning lamps are lit, the braking capacity of the vehicle may be impaired.

System Operation

Under normal conditions, the ABS system functions in the same manner as a standard brake system and is transparent to the operator. The system is a combination of electrical and hydraulic components, working together to control the flow of brake fluid to the wheels when necessary.

The electronic Control Unit (CU) is the electronic brain of the system, receiving and interpreting signals from the wheel speed sensors. The unit will enter anti-lock mode when it senses impending wheel lock at any wheel and immediately control the brake line pressures to the affected wheel(s) by issuing output signals to the hydraulic modulator.

The hydraulic modulator contains solenoids which react to the signals from the CU. When not activated, the solenoids allow brake line pressure to be modulated by the brake pedal in the normal fashion. At the direction of the control unit, the solenoids move to positions either isolating the brake line from pedal pressure (pressure hold) or isolating the line and opening a passage to relieve line pressure (pressure release). In this manner, brake application is controlled or actually lessened, dependent on the locking tendency of each wheel.

The decisions regarding these functions are made very rapidly and each solenoid can be cycled several times per second. Volvo employs a 3-channel control system. The front wheels are controlled separately; the rears are watched by a single sensor and the common feed line to the rear brakes is controlled by one output on the hydraulic modulator.

The operator may feel a slight pulsing in the brake pedal and/or hear popping or clicking noises when the system engages. These sensations are due to the valves cycling and the pressures being changed rapidly within the brake system. While completely normal and not a sign of system failure, these sensations can be disconcerting to an operator unfamiliar with the system.

Although the ABS system prevents wheel lock-up under hard braking, as brake pressure increases, wheel slip is allowed to increase as well. This slip will result in some tire chirp during ABS operation. The sound should not be interpreted as lock-up but rather as an indication of the system holding the wheel(s) just outside the locking point. Additionally, the final few feet of an ABS-engaged stop may be completed with the wheels locked; the system is inoperative below 3 mph.

When the ignition is ON and vehicle speed is over 3 mph (5 kph), the CU monitors the function of the system. Should a fault be noted, such a loss of signal from a sensor, the ABS system is immediately disabled by the CU. The ANTI-LOCK dashboard warning lamp is illuminated to inform the operator. When the ABS system is disabled, the vehicle retains normal braking capacity without the benefits of anti-lock.

Diagnosis and Testing

SYSTEM PRECAUTIONS

- If the vehicle is equipped with an air bag system, always properly disable the system before commencing work on the ABS system.
- Certain components within the ABS system are not intended to be serviced or repaired individually. Only those components with removal and installation procedures should be serviced.
- Do not use rubber hoses or other parts not specifically specified for the ABS system. When using repair kits, replace all parts included in the kit. Partial or incorrect repair may lead to functional problems and require the replacement of other components.
- Lubricate rubber parts with clean, fresh brake fluid to ease assembly. Do not use lubricated shop air to clean parts; damage to rubber components may result.
- Use only brake fluid from an unopened container. Use of suspect or contaminated brake fluid can reduce system performance and/or durability.
- A clean repair area is essential. Perform repairs after components have been thoroughly cleaned. Do not allow ABS components to come into contact with any substance containing mineral oil; this includes used shop rags.
- The control unit is a microprocessor similar to other computer units in the vehicle. Insure that the ignition switch is **OFF** before removing or installing controller harnesses. Avoid static electricity discharge at or near the controller.
- Never disconnect any electrical connection with the ignition switch **ON** unless instructed to do so in a test.
- Avoid touching connector pins with fingers.
- Leave new components and modules in the shipping package until ready to install them.
- To avoid static discharge, always touch a vehicle ground after sliding across a vehicle seat or walking across carpeted or vinyl floors.
- If any arc welding is to be done on the vehicle, the ABS control unit should be disconnected before welding operations begin.
- Never allow welding cables to lie on, near or across any vehicle electrical wiring.
- If the vehicle is to be baked after paint repairs, disconnect and remove the control unit from the vehicle.

INITIAL CHECKS

Visual Inspection

Before diagnosing an apparent ABS problem, make absolutely certain that the normal braking system is in correct working order. Many common brake problems (dragging parking brake, seepage, etc.) will affect the ABS system. A visual check of specific system components may reveal problems creating an apparent ABS malfunction. Performing this inspection may reveal a simple failure, thus eliminating extended diagnostic time.

1. Inspect the tire pressures; they must be approximately equal for the system to operate correctly.

2. Inspect the brake fluid level in the reservoir.

3. Inspect brake lines, hoses, master cylinder assembly and brake calipers for leakage.

4. Visually check brake lines and hoses for excessive wear, heat damage, punctures, contact with other parts, missing clips or holders, blockage or crimping.

5. Check the calipers for rust or corrosion. Check for proper sliding action if applicable.

6. Check the calipers for freedom of motion during application and release.

7. Inspect the wheel speed sensors for proper mounting and connections.

8. Inspect the sensor wheels for broken teeth or poor mounting.

9. Inspect the wheels and tires on the vehicle. They must be of the same size and type to generate accurate speed signals.

10. Confirm the fault occurrence with the operator. Certain driver induced faults, such as not releasing the parking brake fully, spinning the wheels under acceleration, sliding due to excessive cornering speed or driving on extremely rough surfaces may fool the system and trigger the dash warning light. These induced faults are not system failures but examples of vehicle performance outside the parameters of the control unit.

11. Many system shut-downs are due to loss of sensor signals to or from the controller. The most common cause is not a failed sensor but a loose, corroded or dirty connector. Check harness and component connectors carefully.

SYSTEM DIAGNOSIS

If the ANTI-LOCK warning lamp is on during vehicle operation, the control unit has detected a fault and disabled the system. The Control Unit does not store diagnostic codes; therefore diagnosis must be made in a progressive and logical order. Use great care when probing terminals and connectors so as not to damage or displace a terminal pin.

FAULT TRACING

▶ **See Figures 30, 31, 32, 33 and 34**

The control unit contains a monitoring circuit to detect any internal faults within the control unit as well as electrical faults in the sensors, solenoids, modulator unit, etc.

If the monitoring circuit detects a fault, the control unit will disable the ABS system and light the warning lamp on the dash. If the light comes on during vehicle operation, perform the following checks. All tests must be performed, in order.

1. Remove the soundproofing under left dash. Inspect the 10 amp fuse on the transient surge protector located adjacent to the ABS CU.

2. Check all connectors, wires and ground connections for the ABS system. Inspect connectors at each component.

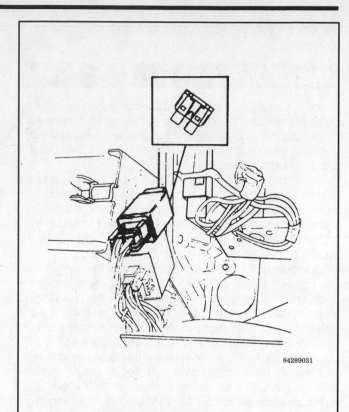

Fig. 30 Transient surge protector fuse

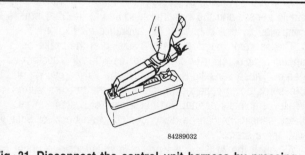

Fig. 31 Disconnect the control unit harness by pressing the lock spring and swinging the connector out of the mount

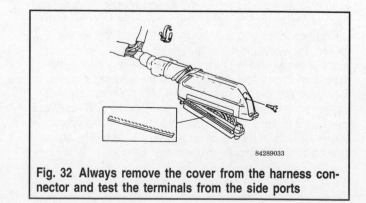

Fig. 32 Always remove the cover from the harness connector and test the terminals from the side ports

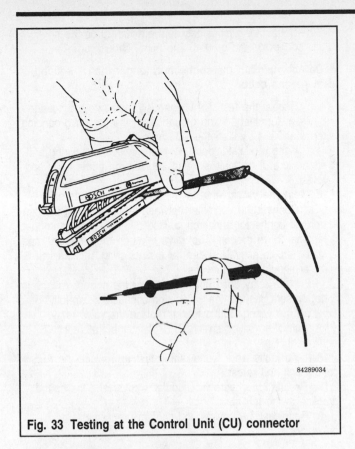

Fig. 33 Testing at the Control Unit (CU) connector

3. Insure ignition is switched **OFF**.

a. At the Control Unit under the dash, depress the lock spring and swing out the connector, disconnecting it from the CU.

b. Remove the cover from the connector. Remove the white protective moldings from the sides of the connector.

c. Use an ohmmeter to check ground circuits. terminal numbers are stamped into the side of the connector. The ABS wiring grounds at the left A-pillar. Test between ground and terminals 10, 20, 32 and 34.

➡**Never check connectors from the front or terminal side; damage may be caused. Always check through the holes in the side of the connector without using excess force to make contact.**

d. Resistance should be 0 ohms in all cases. If any other reading is encountered, check for damaged wiring or improper connections. Wires are grounded on the left A-post.

e. If a fault is found at terminal 32, replace the solenoid relay on the hydraulic modulator and retest.

4. **Check transient surge protector:**

a. Turn the ignition switch **ON**.

b. Connect a voltmeter between ground and terminal 1 on the control unit connector; 12 volts should be present.

c. If no voltage is present, measure voltage directly at the transient surge protector connector. terminals 1, 2 and 4 should be energized and terminal 3 should be grounded.

d. If only terminal 1 and 4 are energized when terminal 3 is grounded, the transient surge protector has failed and must be replaced.

5. **Check power supply to the control unit connector:**

a. Connect the voltmeter to a known good ground. Depress the brake pedal and at the same time to terminals 25, 27, 28 and 29.

b. The voltmeter should read 12 volts at all terminals, except terminal 29.

c. Voltage should read 0.5 — 1.0 volts at terminal 29.

6. Start the engine. Voltmeter should read 12 volts at terminal 15.

7. If no voltage or incorrect voltage is found in the above tests, proceed as follows. For problem at:

a. terminal 25: Check brake lamp switch and replace if needed. Inspect brake light bulbs and replace as needed.

b. terminal 27: Replace defective solenoid relay.

c. terminal 28: Replace defective pump relay.

d. terminal 29: If reading at 27 is correct, voltage at 29 should be 0.5-1.0 volts. If not, replace solenoid relay.

8. Turn the ignition switch **OFF**.

9. **Check voltage to the hydraulic modulator:**

a. Remove the cover from the hydraulic modulator. Disconnect the connector from the hydraulic modulator.

b. Switch the ignition **ON**.

c. Connect the voltmeter to a know good ground and between terminals 6, 7, 10 and 12. Voltage in all cases should be 12 volts.

10. If there is no voltage or improper voltage to any terminal, proceed as follows. For problem at:

a. terminal 6: Inspect wiring for shorts and/or poor connections.

b. terminal 7: Connect connector to hydraulic modulator with ignition **OFF**. Turn ignition **ON** when connected; the ABS warning lamp on the dash should come on. If not, replace the warning lamp bulb.

c. terminal 10: Transient surge protector failed.

d. terminal 12: Inspect wiring for shorts and/or poor connections.

11. Turn the ignition **OFF**; reconnect the connector to the hydraulic modulator.

12. At the Control Unit connector, use an ohmmeter to measure resistance of each wheel speed sensor.

a. Test the left front sensor between terminals 4 and 6. Test the right front sensor between terminals 11 and 21.

b. Resistance for the front sensors must be 900-2200 ohms (0.9-2.2 kilo-ohms). If the resistance is not within specifications, disconnect the harness connectors in the engine compartment and measure resistance directly at the sensor. If readings still differ, inspect wiring and/or replace the sen-

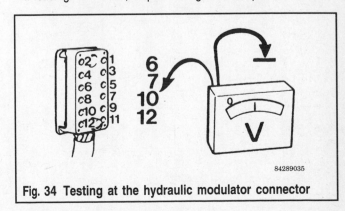

Fig. 34 Testing at the hydraulic modulator connector

sor.   Also, check the pulse wheels for defects or damage; maximum radial run-out is 0.006 inch (0.15mm).

c. Measure resistance of the rear speed sensor by testing at terminals 7 and 9. Resistance should be 600-1600 ohms (0.6-1.6 kilo-ohms).

d. If resistance is not correct, disconnect the sensor connector on the fuel filler pipe in the trunk. It will be necessary to break the connector seal; do so without damaging the wiring.   If readings are still not within specification, inspect wiring and/or replace the sensor.

13. Check the wiring to each sensor.

a. Raise and safely support the vehicle.

b. Connect an ohmmeter to the pairs of terminals use in Step 11.

c. As each pair is tested, have an assistant turn the correct wheel on the vehicle including the rear. Rotate the wheel(s) about 1 revolution per second; the resistance should vary as the wheel spins.

14. **Test the hydraulic modulator solenoid valves**: Connect one ohmmeter lead to terminal 32 on the control unit connector. Connect the other test lead to terminal 2 (LF solenoid), then 35 (RF) and then 18 (Rear); Resistance should be 0.7-1.7 ohms.

15. **Test the pump relay in the hydraulic modulator**:

a. Turn the ignition **ON**.

b. Connect a jumper between terminal 28 on the control unit connector and ground. The pump should run.

➡**Do not maintain the connection longer than 2 seconds; damage can occur.**

c. Repeat the test. Simultaneously, measure the voltage between terminal 14 and ground. With the jumper grounding terminal 28, 12 volts should be present.

d. If the modulator does not start, inspect the wiring and connectors. If no fault is found, replace the pump relay and retest.

16. **Test the valve relay in the hydraulic modulator**:

a. Connect the voltmeter between terminal 32 on the control unit connector and ground. Use a jumper wire to connect terminal 27 to ground. The valve relay on the hydraulic modulator should activate (listen for distinct click) and the voltmeter should show 12 volts.

b. If the relay does not energize, or the correct voltage is not present, inspect the wiring and connectors carefully.

c. If no wiring fault is found, replace the valve relay.

17. Turn the ignition switch **OFF**. Disconnect all test equipment.

18. If no faults were found during testing, replace the ABS control unit and retest.

19. Reinstall the hydraulic modulator cover and the sound-proofing at the left dash.

20. Road test the vehicle and confirm proper system operation.

ABS WIRING SCHEMATIC - 740

2	Ignition switch	E	Pump motor relay
3	4-pole connector at instrument panel	F	Connector for hydraulic modulator
10	Alternator with built-in regulator	G	Solenoid, left front
11	Fuse box	H	Solenoid, right front
22	Brake lights	I	Solenoid, rear
29	Positive terminal	J	Connector, left suspension tower
66	Brake light switch	K	Connector, left A-post
85	Speedometer	L	Connector, boot
100	Brake failure warning light	M	Pump motor
105	Battery charge indicator lamp	N	Connector, right suspension tower
107	ABS warning light	P	Connector, left suspension tower
180	Sensor, speedometer and ABS	Q	Connector, left A-post
252	Control unit, ABS	V	Ground point, left front wing
253	Hydraulic modulator		
254	Transient surge protector		
256	Sensor, ABS, left front		
257	Sensor, ABS, right front		
258	Motor, hydraulic modulator,		
378	Ground point, A-post		
384	Brake level fluid sensor		
B	6-pole connector, left A-post		
C	Ground point, right front wing		
D	Solenoid relay		

Colour code

= no voltage
= ground connection
= system voltage
= less than system voltage
= shielded wire

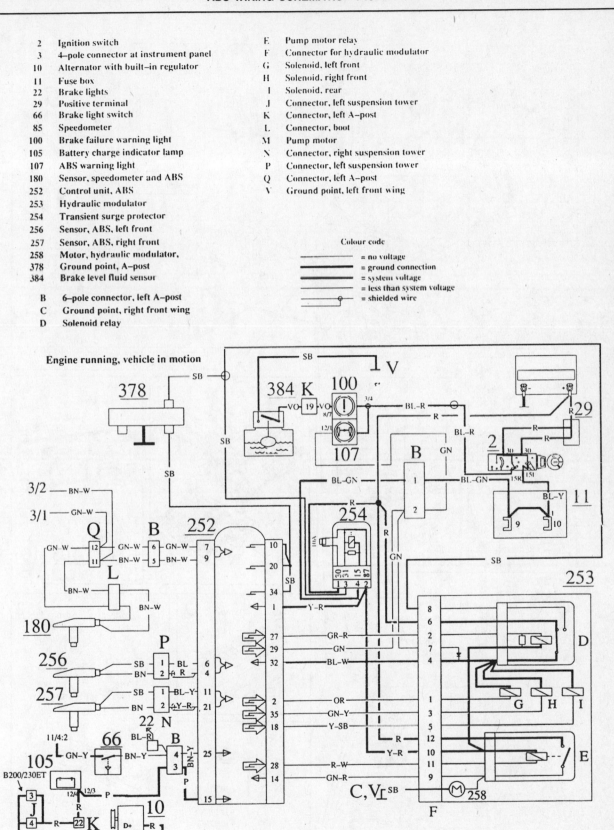

Engine running, vehicle in motion

84289037

ABS WIRING SCHEMATIC - 740, CONT.

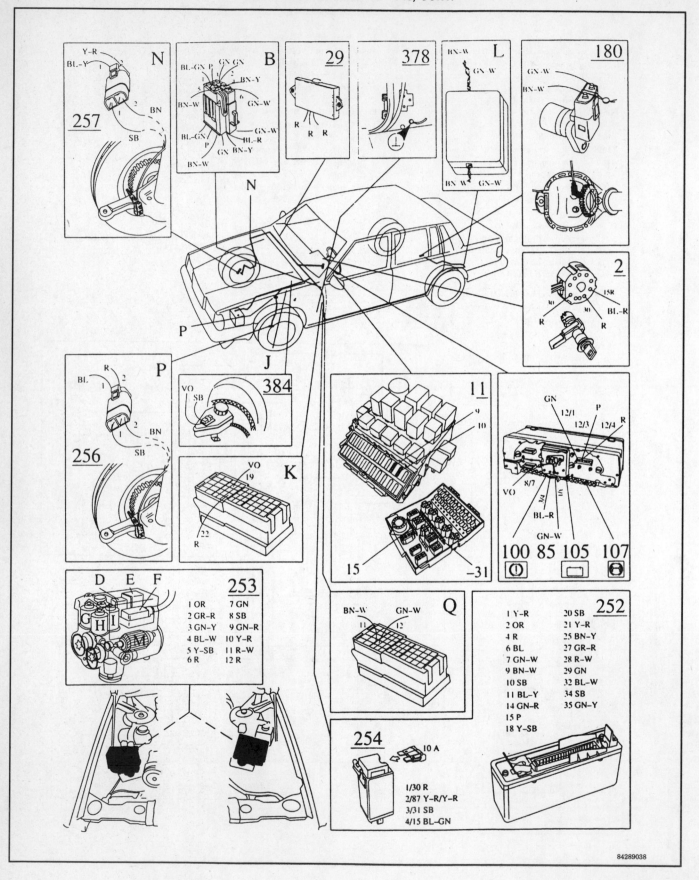

84289038

ABS WIRING SCHEMATIC - 760 AND 940

1/1	Battery
2/8	Transient surge protector ABS
3/1	Ignition switch
3/9	Brake light switch
4/16	Control unit ABS
5/1	Combined instrument panel
6/26	Alternator
7/4	Brake fluid level sensor
7/31	ABS sensor, front left
7/32	ABS sensor, front right
7/33	Sensor, ABS and speedometer
8/15	Hydraulic unit ABS
10/82	Indicator lamp, ABS
10/84	Indicator lamp, brake failure
11/1–35	Fuses
15/1	Positive terminal
31/1	Ground connection, right wing
31/2	Ground connection, left wing
31/6	Ground connection, left A-post

A	Connector, left A-post
B	Connector, inside boot
C	Connector, right suspension tower
D	Relay for solenoids
E	Relay for pump motor
F	Connector, hydraulic unit
G	Solenoid, left front
H	Solenoid, right front
I	Solenoid, rear
J	Connector, left suspension tower
K	Connector, left suspension tower
L	Connector, left A-post

Colour code

= no voltage
= ground connection
= system voltage
= less than system voltage
= shielded wire

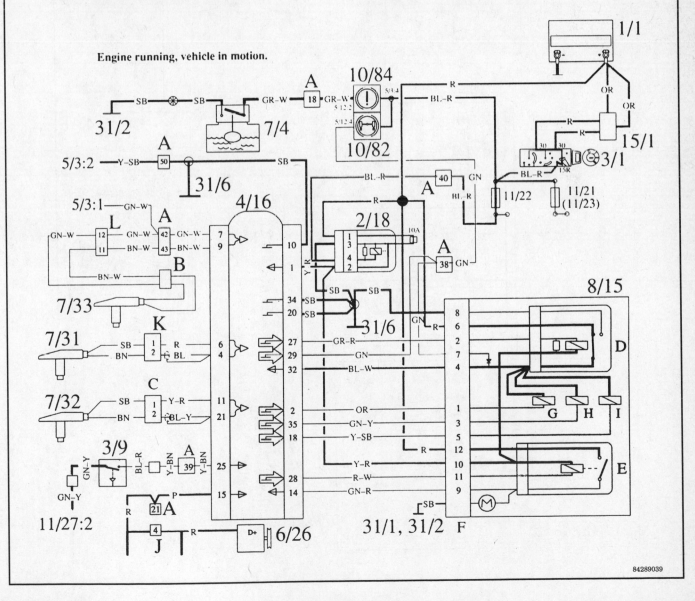

Engine running, vehicle in motion.

84289039

ABS WIRING SCHEMATIC - 760 AND 940, CONT.

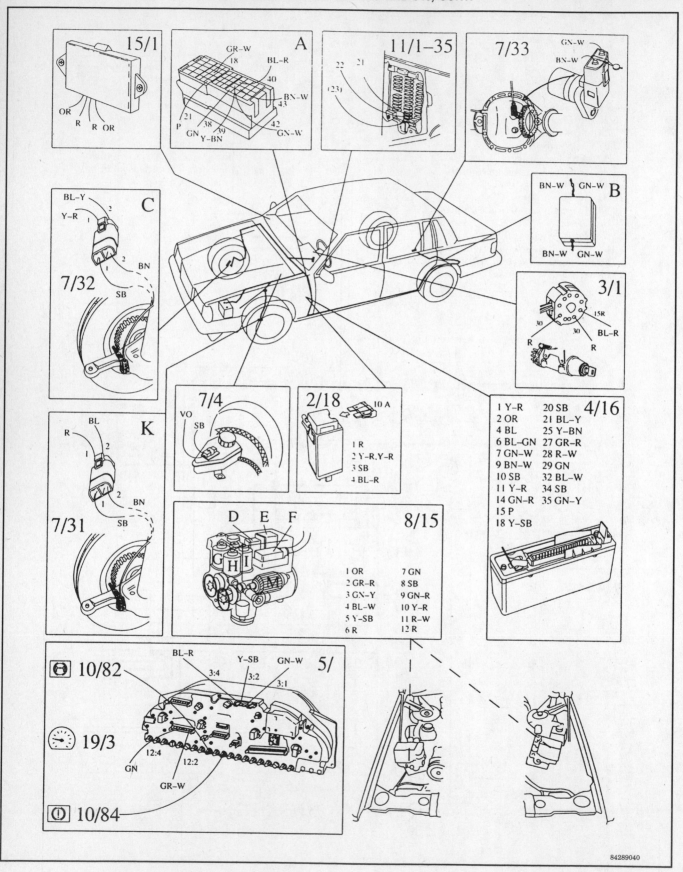

84289040

ABS WIRING SCHEMATIC - 780 AND COUPE

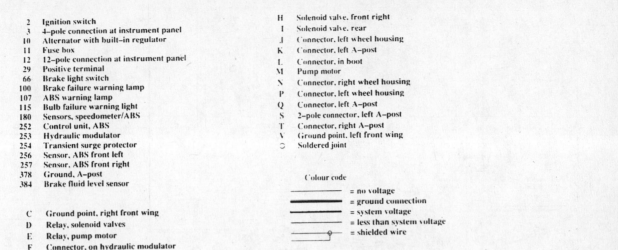

2	Ignition switch	H	Solenoid valve, front right
3	4–pole connection at instrument panel	I	Solenoid valve, rear
10	Alternator with built–in regulator	J	Connector, left wheel housing
11	Fuse box	K	Connector, left A–post
12	12–pole connection at instrument panel	L	Connector, in boot
29	Positive terminal	M	Pump motor
66	Brake light switch	N	Connector, right wheel housing
100	Brake failure warning lamp	P	Connector, left wheel housing
107	ABS warning lamp	Q	Connector, left A–post
115	Bulb failure warning light	S	2–pole connector, left A–post
180	Sensors, speedometer/ABS	T	Connector, right A–post
252	Control unit, ABS	V	Ground point, left front wing
253	Hydraulic modulator	○	Soldered joint
254	Transient surge protector		
256	Sensor, ABS front left		
257	Sensor, ABS front right		
378	Ground, A–post		
384	Brake fluid level sensor		

C	Ground point, right front wing
D	Relay, solenoid valves
E	Relay, pump motor
F	Connector, on hydraulic modulator
G	Solenoid valve, front left

Colour code

= no voltage
= ground connection
= system voltage
= less than system voltage
= shielded wire

Engine running, vehicle in motion

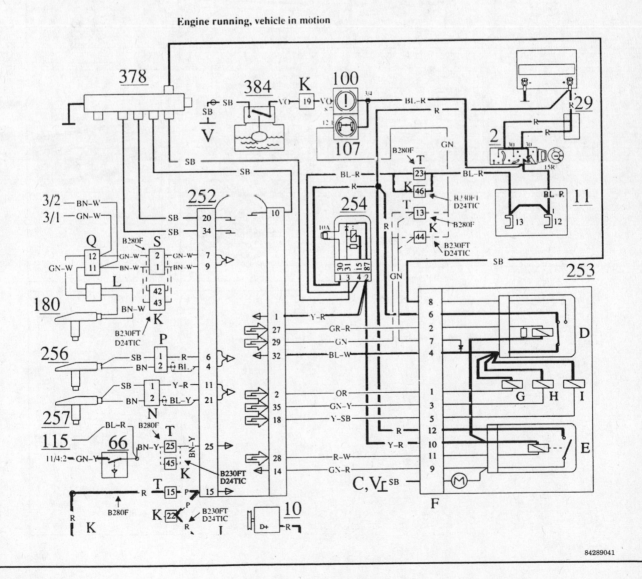

84289041

ABS WIRING SCHEMATIC - 780 AND COUPE, CONT.

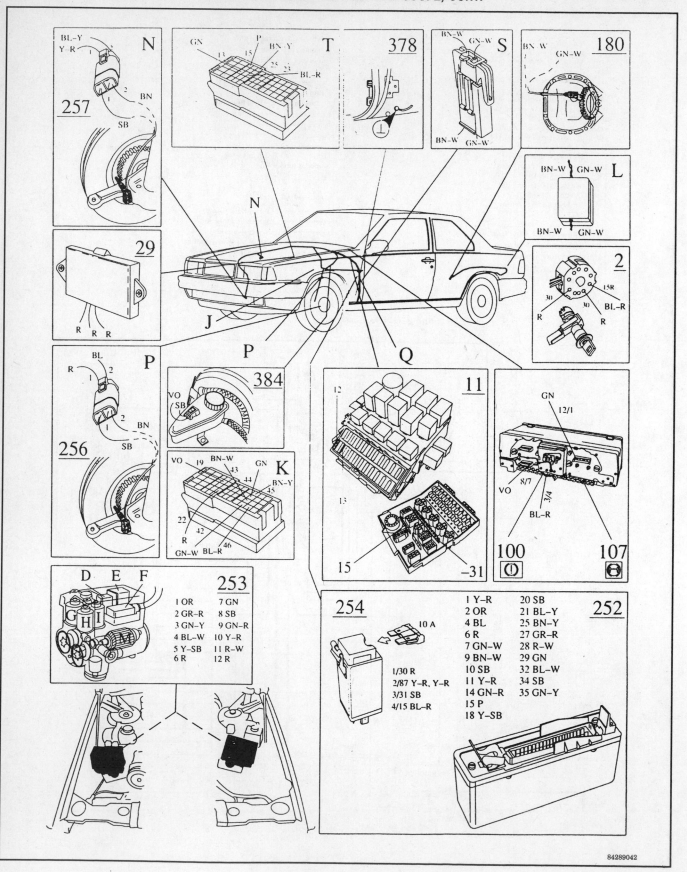

253

1 OR	7 GN
2 GR-R	8 SB
3 GN-Y	9 GN-R
4 BL-W	10 Y-R
5 Y-SB	11 R-W
6 R	12 R

254

10 A

1/30 R
2/87 Y-R, Y-R
3/31 SB
4/15 BL-R

252

1 Y-R	20 SB
2 OR	21 BL-Y
4 BL	25 BN-Y
6 R	27 GR-R
7 GN-W	28 R-W
9 BN-W	29 GN
10 SB	32 BL-W
11 Y-R	34 SB
14 GN-R	35 GN-Y
15 P	
18 Y-SB	

84289042

Component Replacement

FILLING THE SYSTEM

The reservoir on the master cylinder assembly is filled in the usual manner with no special procedures being necessary. Always wipe the cap and surrounding area clean of dirt and debris before opening the reservoir; the smallest bit of dirt may impair the operation of the system. When adding fluid, fill the reservoir only to the MAX line on the reservoir; do not overfill.

Only DOT 4 brake fluid must be used; silicone or DOT 5 fluid is specifically prohibited. Do not use any fluid which contains a petroleum base; these fluids will cause swelling and distortion of the rubber parts within the system. Do not use old or contaminated brake fluid. Do not reuse fluid which has been bled from the system.

BLEEDING THE SYSTEM

Bleeding is performed using the 2-person manual method. Bleeding may be performed with the wheels in place. Always begin with the reservoir filled to the MAX line. Begin bleeding at a rear wheel.

For vehicles without multi-link rear suspension, connect hoses to both bleed nipples and immerse the other ends in a container of clean brake fluid. On vehicles with multi-link, connect the hose only to the top nipple. Open the nipples. Have an assistant pump the brake pedal 5 times; on the 5th stroke, hold the pedal depressed and close the bleed port(s). Release the pedal and check the brake fluid level in the reservoir.

Repeat the procedure for the opposite rear wheel and then at each front wheel.

HYDRAULIC MODULATOR

Removal & Installation
▶ **See Figure 35**

1. Disconnect the negative battery cable.
2. Remove the cover from the hydraulic modulator.
3. Remove both relays from the top of the unit; disconnect the wiring connector at the unit.
4. Disconnect the ground strap from the hydraulic modulator.
5. Place rags or towels around the unit to absorb brake fluid which will be spilled.
6. Clean the line connections thoroughly. Label each line using the letters marked on the hydraulic modulator (V, H, L, R, H).
7. Remove the brake lines from the modulator. Remove the bolt from the modulator support and push the support to the right. Remove the hydraulic modulator.
   To install:
8. If a new modulator is being installed, remove the hexagonal plugs from the old unit and install on the new unit. Check that the rubber pads are not damaged; install the rubber pads onto the hexagonal plugs.

9. Install the modulator and tighten the support. If installing a new unit, remove the plugs from the brake line ports.
10. Reconnect the brake lines according to the labels made at removal. The lines must be in their exact original positions.
11. Remove the rags from the work area and dispose of them properly.
12. Install the relays on the hydraulic modulator.
13. Connect the wiring harness and the ground strap.
14. Install the cover on the unit.
15. Bleed the brake system. Vehicles with hydraulic clutches may require bleeding of the clutch system as well.
16. When bleeding is complete, test the brake system by having an assistant press hard on the brake pedal; keep it depressed for 30 seconds. During the 30 second period, check that no leakage occurs at the brake line connections on the hydraulic modulator.
17. Connect the negative battery cable. Test drive the vehicle, confirming system function.

CONTROL UNIT

Removal & Installation

1. Disconnect the negative battery cable.
2. Remove the soundproofing under the left dashboard.
3. Loosen or remove the clips and retainers holding the control unit. Lift the unit out.
4. Remove the electrical harness from the unit.
5. Reinstall in reverse order. Connect the negative battery cable.

WHEEL SPEED SENSORS

Removal & Installation
FRONT

1. Raise and safely support the front of the vehicle.
2. Remove the tire and wheel.
3. With the ignition switch **OFF**, disconnect the wheel speed sensor lead from the ABS harness. Remove any retaining bolts or clips holding the harness in place.

➡**Clips and retainers must be reinstalled in their exact original location. Take careful note of the position of each retainer and of the correct harness routing during removal.**

4. Remove the single bolt holding the speed sensor.
5. Carefully remove the sensor straight out of its mount. Do not subject the sensor to shock or vibration; protect the tip of the sensor at all times.
   To install:
6. Fit the sensor into position. Make certain the sensor sits flush against the mounting surface; it must not be crooked.
7. Install the retaining bolt.
8. Route the sensor cable correctly and install the harness clips and retainers. The cable must be in its original position and completely clear of moving components.
9. Connect the sensor cable to the ABS harness.
10. Install the wheel and tire.
11. Lower the vehicle to the ground.

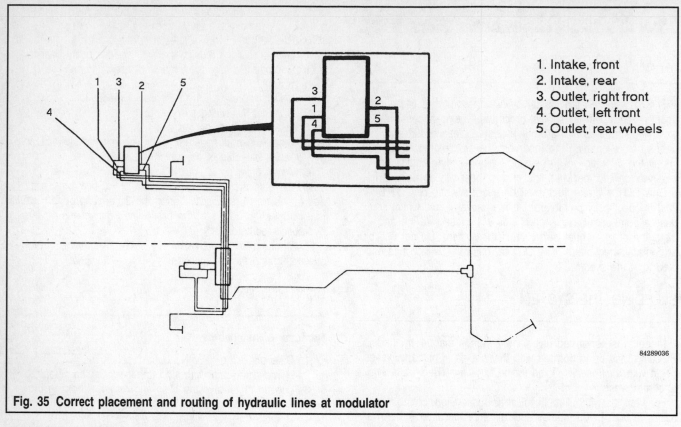

1. Intake, front
2. Intake, rear
3. Outlet, right front
4. Outlet, left front
5. Outlet, rear wheels

84289036

Fig. 35 Correct placement and routing of hydraulic lines at modulator

REAR WITHOUT MULTI-LINK SUSPENSION

1. Raise and safely support the vehicle.
2. Disconnect the sensor connector from the harness.
3. Remove the clips and retainers holding the sensor wire to the axle. Take note of the routing of the sensor wire; exact reinstallation is required.
4. Remove the retaining bolt holding the sensor to the differential housing.
5. Remove the sensor straight out of the housing; protect the tip from impact.
6. Reinstall in reverse order.

REAR WITH MULTI-LINK SUSPENSION

1. Remove the spare tire and fold back the trunk carpet to expose the fuel filler pipe. Remove the cover(s) from the filler pipe.
2. Break the seal on the speed sensor harness connector and disconnect the sensor from the ABS harness.
3. Press the rubber grommet free of the bodywork and feed the sensor harness to the outside of the vehicle.
4. Raise and safely support the vehicle.
5. Install a jack with support fixture 5972 or its equivalent under the rear axle.
6. Remove the 2 bolts on each side of the rear axle assembly which hold the member to the body. Lower the rear axle slightly, but do not allow the drive shaft to press against the fuel tank.

7. Disconnect the right brake wire from its attachment.
8. Remove the sensor cable from the retaining clips and clamps. Take note of the routing of the cable; it must be reinstalled in its exact original position.
9. Clean the sensor area; remove the retaining bolts and remove the sensor. Protect the tip from damage or impact.
   To install:
10. Apply a light coat of oil to the O-ring on the new sensor. Fit the sensor into place without damaging the tip. Tighten the retaining bolts to 7.5 ft. lbs. (10 Nm).
11. Install the sensor harness into the cable retainers, making certain it is routed correctly and out of the way of all moving parts.
12. Feed the cable through the body and secure the grommet.
13. Connect the right brake wire.
14. Raise the rear axle assembly and install the 4 bolts. Tighten each bolt to 52 ft. lbs. (70 Nm), then angle tighten each an additional 60 degrees.
15. Lower the vehicle to the ground.
16. Connect the sensor wiring harness to the ABS harness in the trunk and reseal the connector. Clamp the cable to the filler pipe.
17. Install the filler covers, reposition the carpet and install the spare tire.
18. Test drive the vehicle, confirming correct function of the ABS system and the dashboard warning lamp.

BRAKE SPECIFICATIONS

All measurements in inches unless noted.

Year	Model	Master Cylinder Bore	Front Brake Disc			Rear Brake Disc			Minimum Lining Thickness	
			Original Thickness	Minimum Thickness	Maximum Runout	Original Thickness	Minimum Thickness	Maximum Runout	Front	Rear
1990	240	①	0.870	0.790	0.0024	0.393	0.314	0.003	0.120	0.078
	240DL	①	0.870	0.790	0.0024	0.393	0.314	0.003	0.120	0.078
	740	NA②	0.870	0.790	0.0024	0.378	0.330	0.004	0.120	0.078
	740GL	NA②	0.870	0.790	0.0024	0.378	0.330	0.004	0.120	0.078
	740GLE	NA	0.870	0.790	0.0024	0.378	0.330	0.004	0.120	0.078
	740 Turbo	NA	0.870	0.790	0.0024	0.378	0.330	0.004	0.120	0.078
	760GLE	NA	0.870	0.790	0.0024	0.393	0.314	0.003	0.120	0.078
	760 Turbo	NA	0.870	0.790	0.0024	③	④	⑤	0.120	0.078
	780 Coupe	NA	0.870	0.790	0.0024	0.393	0.314	0.003	0.120	0.078
	780 Turbo	NA	0.870	0.790	0.0024	0.393	0.314	0.003	0.120	0.078
1991	240	NA	0.870	0.790	0.0024	0.393	0.314	0.003	0.120	0.078
	740	NA	1.020	0.910	0.0024	0.378	0.330	0.004	0.120	0.078
	740GL	NA②	0.870	0.790	0.0024	0.378	0.330	0.004	0.120	0.078
	740 Turbo	NA	0.870	0.790	0.0024	0.378	0.330	0.004	0.120	0.078
	940GLE	NA	1.020	0.910	0.0024	0.378	0.330	0.004	0.120	0.078
	940SE	NA	1.020	0.910	0.0024	③	④	⑤	0.120	0.078
	940 Turbo	NA	1.020	0.910	0.0024	0.378	0.330	0.004	0.120	0.078
	940 Coupe	NA	1.020	0.910	0.0024	0.378	0.330	0.004	0.120	0.078
1992	240	①	0.870	0.790	0.0024	0.393	0.314	0.003	0.120	0.078
	240GL	①	0.870	0.790	0.0024	0.393	0.314	0.003	0.120	0.078
	740	NA	1.020	0.910	0.0024	0.378	0.330	0.004	0.120	0.078
	740 Turbo	NA	1.020	0.910	0.0024	0.378	0.330	0.004	0.120	0.078
	940GL	NA	1.020	0.910	0.0024	0.378	0.330	0.004	0.120	0.078
	940 Turbo	NA	1.020	0.910	0.0024	0.378	0.330	0.004	0.120	0.078
	960	NA	1.020	0.910	0.0024	③	④	⑤	0.120	0.078
1993	240	①	0.870	0.790	0.0024	0.393	0.314	0.003	0.120	0.078
	940	NA	1.020	0.910	0.0024	0.378	0.330	0.004	0.120	0.078
	940 Turbo	NA	1.020	0.910	0.0024	0.378	0.330	0.004	0.120	0.078
	960	NA	1.020	0.910	0.0024	③	④	⑤	0.120	0.078

NA—Not available
① Stepped bore—0.620/0.878
② Stepped bore
③ 4-door—0.393
   5-door—0.378
④ 4-door—0.314
   5-door—0.330
⑤ 4-door—0.003
   5-door—0.004

84289043

TORQUE SPECIFICATIONS

Component	U.S.	Metric
Caliper mounting bolts		
240 Series		
Front:	74 ft. lbs.	100 Nm
Rear:	43 ft. lbs.	58 Nm
700/900 Series		
Front:	77 ft. lbs.	105 Nm
Rear:	44 ft. lbs.	60 Nm
Shield attaching bolts		
240 Series		
Front:	18 ft. lbs.	24 Nm
Rear:	30 ft. lbs.	40 Nm
700/900 Series		
Front:	18 ft. lbs.	25 Nm
Rear:	18 ft. lbs.	25 Nm
Caliper slide pin		
240 Series:	25 ft. lbs.	34 Nm
700/900 Series:	22 ft. lbs.	30 Nm
Wheel nuts		
240 Series:	85 ft. lbs.	115 Nm
700/900 Series:	66 ft. lbs.	90 Nm
Master cylinder retaining nuts:	22 ft. lbs.	30 Nm
Tie bolt:	37 ft. lbs.	50 Nm
Sensors (ABS):	6–9 ft. lbs.	8–12 Nm

84289044

10

BODY AND TRIM

EXTERIOR

✳✳WARNING

To avoid damage to the Electronic Control Module (ECM) and/or other electronic components, always disconnect the negative battery cable before using any electric welding equipment on the vehicle.

Doors

REMOVAL & INSTALLATION

➡The door(s) are heavy! Provide proper support for the door when removing. Do not allow the door to sag while partially attached and do not subject the door to impact or twisting movements.

1. Disconnect the negative battery cable.
2. Disconnect any wiring harnesses running into the door. This may be done either inside the door (remove the door liner) or under the dash inside the pillar. Make sure the wiring harness will not catch or bind as the door is removed from the vehicle.
3. Scribe marks around the hinges to facilitate door installation.
4. Support the door with a jack. Place a piece of wood on the jack to protect the paintwork.
5. Have a helper support the door; loosen and remove the hinge mounting bolts and remove the door from the vehicle.
6. When reinstalling, have your helper position the door and install the hinge bolts. Do not fully tighten the hinge mounting bolts at this time.
7. Check the door for proper alignment. If required, loosen the mounting bolts just enough to allow the door to be moved into position. Tighten all the hinge bolts and check the final fit.
8. If the door stop bracket was removed, reinstall it.
9. Connect the wiring harness and check the function of electrical components in the door.

ADJUSTMENT

◆ See Figures 1, 2 and 3

The primary door adjustments are carried out at the hinge bolts at the forward end of each door. Further adjustment for closed position and for smoothness of latching may be made at the latch plate or striker. This piece is located at the rear edge of the door and is attached to the bodywork of the vehicle; it is the piece the door engages when closed.

Although the striker or latchplate is different on various models, the procedure for adjusting is the same:

1. Adjust the position of the door by moving the striker plate sideways.

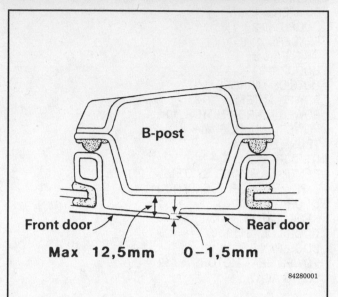

Fig. 1 Make sure that the clearance between the B-post and the outside of the front door does not exceed 0.492 inch (12.5mm). Rear doors should be 0.413 inch (10.5mm) further than the front doors — 700 Series shown, others similar

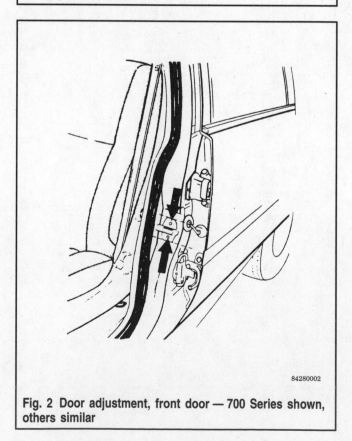

Fig. 2 Door adjustment, front door — 700 Series shown, others similar

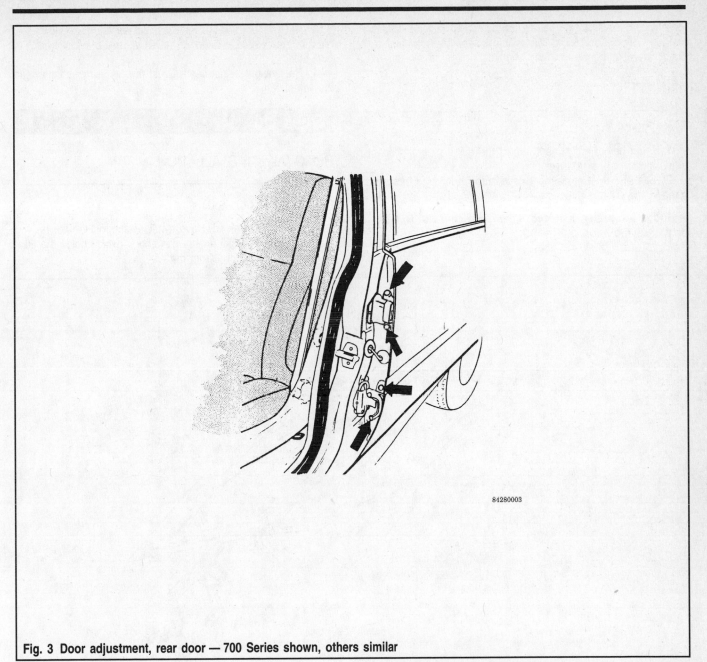

Fig. 3 Door adjustment, rear door — 700 Series shown, others similar

2. If further adjustments are necessary, first slacken the upper door hinge bolts then if necessary, the lower 2 bolts. Push the door toward the body.

➡**Never loosen more than 3 bolts at a time or the door may drop. — Do not attempt to correct height variations (sag) by adjusting the striker.**

3. After the striker bolts have been tightened, open and close the door several times. Observe the motion of the door as it engages the striker; it should continue its straight-in motion and not deflect up or down as it hits the striker.

4. Check the feel of the latch during opening and closing. It must be smooth and linear, without any trace of grinding or binding during engagement and release.

➡**It may be necessary to repeat the striker adjustment procedure several times (and possibly adjust the hinges) before the proper door-to-body alignment is corrected.**

Hood

REMOVAL & INSTALLATION

1. Raise the hood. Disconnect any electrical or fluid lines between the hood and the body.

2. Scribe marks around the hinges to facilitate hood installation. Have a helper support the hood so it doesn't damage the body during removal. Remove the hinge-to-hood bolts on each side and lift the hood clear of the vehicle.

➡**Hood can be easily damaged; take great care not to bend or dimple the hood. Store it on pads and cover it to protect it while off the vehicle.**

3. When reinstalling, position the hood and install the bolts just tight enough to hold it in position. Lower the hood and check the alignment — the gap should be even all around.

ALIGNMENT

▶ **See Figure 4**

1. Front height adjustment: adjust the guide pins or rubber bump stops on the front panel.

2. Left and right adjustment: loosen the hood and move the hood in the desired direction.

➡**Hoods are easily damaged; take great care not to bend or dimple the hood.**

3. Hood length: loosen the hood hinges and move the hood in the desired direction. The hinges are provided with oval holes.

4. Rear height adjustment: Adjust the hinge mountings near the wheelarch.

Trunk Lid

REMOVAL & INSTALLATION

2-Door and 4-Door models

1. Open the trunk lid. Have a helper support the lid; re-move the retaining clip for the gas shock (which holds the lid open) and disconnect it from the lid.

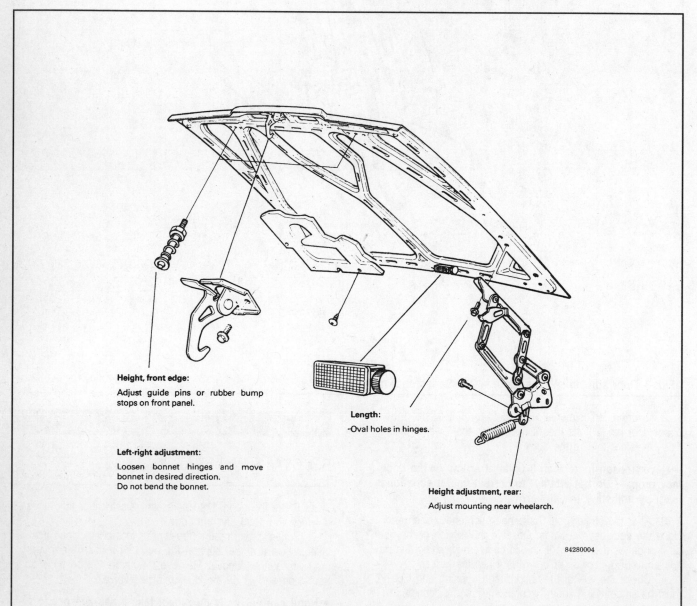

Height, front edge:
Adjust guide pins or rubber bump stops on front panel.

Left-right adjustment:
Loosen bonnet hinges and move bonnet in desired direction.
Do not bend the bonnet.

Length:
-Oval holes in hinges.

Height adjustment, rear:
Adjust mounting near wheelarch.

84280004

Fig. 4 Hood, adjustment

2. Disconnect any wiring to the trunk lid at the nearest connector. Make sure the wiring will not bind when the lid is removed.

3. Scribe marks around the hinges to facilitate door installation.

4. Remove the bolts which hold the hinges to the trunk lid and lift the lid clear of the vehicle.

➡️**Trunk lid can be easily damaged; take great care not to bend or dimple the trunk lid. Store it on pads and cover it to protect it while off the vehicle.**

5. When reinstalling, the lid is placed in position and the bolts tightened only snug. Check the lid-to-body match and adjust the trunk lid as necessary.

6. Reconnect the gas shock to the trunk lid and reconnect the wiring, if any.

Wagon (5-door)

> ❋❋**CAUTION**
>
> Because of the size and weight of the door, this procedure requires 2 people during removal & installation.

1. Disconnect the negative battery cable.

2. Remove the inner cover panel on the door. Disconnect any electrical connectors within the door. Tag or identify the connectors for ease of reassembly.

3. Pull the harness through the hole in the top of the door.

4. Have your helper support the door; disconnect the gas shock(s) from the door.

5. With the door well supported, remove the door-to-hinge bolts on each side at the top. On the 740, one of the bolts is beneath a rubber plug which must be removed. Remove the door from the vehicle and store on pads.

To install:

6. When reinstalling, install the bolts snug but not tight; check the alignment of the door in relation to the body and adjust the door as necessary. When the alignment is correct, tighten the hinge bolts. Left-right alignment is critical. Take your time and work for an even fit.

7. Connect the gas shock(s) to the door.

8. Feed the wire harness through the hole at the top of the door and into position. Connect the wires to the proper points.

ALIGNMENT

All Models

Both trunk lids and wagon doors are adjustable on their hinges due to slotted holes. The trunk lids are also adjustable by loosening the hinge-to-body bolts and repositioning the hinge vertically.

Wagon cargo doors have additional adjustors on the sides of the door. Loosen their screws a few turns and close the door. The adjustor should seek the correct position for smooth operation. Because of the curve of the body and roofline, the wagon door needs to be checked carefully for alignment to the

body. Seams should be straight and even and panels should be flush with no obvious high or low points.

Final adjustments are made at the latch (on the lid) and the striker (on the body). Each can be loosened and moved on its mounts to control tightness and ease of operation. It is recommended to start by loosening the striker only; close the lid and let the striker seek its position. Continue adjusting until the latch has no bind in its operation, the key turns freely and the weatherstrip is evenly compressed around the door.

Bumpers

REMOVAL & INSTALLATION

▶ **See Figures 5 and 6**

1. Loosen the sides of the bumper cover by either removing the nuts or releasing the plastic clip. The nuts will be found inside the trunk or on the inside of the front fender. On certain models, the front air dam (spoiler) must be removed before removing the front bumper.

2. Under the vehicle, identify the bolts which hold the bumper assembly to the shock absorbers. Loosen them a few turns and wiggle the bumper outwards, checking that it will come free without damage.

3. Remove the bolts on one side. Support the bumper until the other side is free.

4. Remove the bolts on the other side and remove the bumper. Take note of any spacers which may have been placed for alignment.

5. With the bumper removed, the shocks may be unbolted and replaced if needed.

> ❋❋**CAUTION**
>
> **Gas filled shocks must not be discarded in the trash. Take them to your dealer or a reputable body shop so that they may be properly drilled and vented before disposal. Do not attempt to drill the shocks yourself — injury can result.**

6. When reinstalling, make sure the bumper lines up straight to the body work. Install the retaining bolts and tighten them.

7. Secure the side mounts of the bumper cover with the proper nuts or clips. Reinstall the air dam if it was removed.

Grille

REMOVAL & INSTALLATION

The plastic grilles on these vehicles are retained by a variety of plastic clips and screws. With the hood raised, remove all the retaining hardware and lift the grille clear of the vehicle. Be careful of any wires and/or tubing running between the grille and the radiator. Do not force the grille into position or it will crack; work carefully and make sure everything lines up before tightening the mounting hardware.

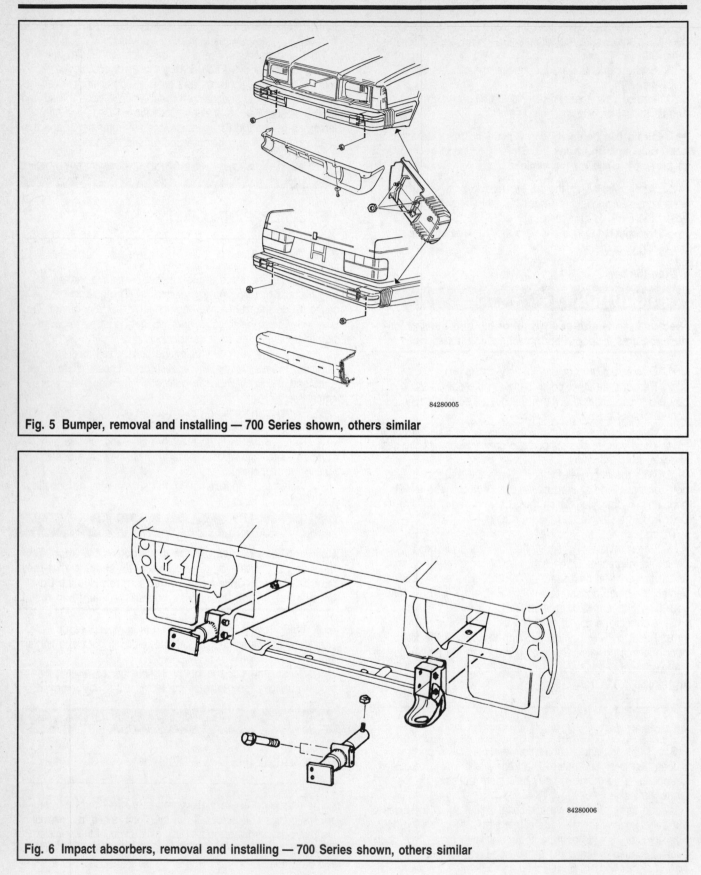

84280005

Fig. 5 Bumper, removal and installing — 700 Series shown, others similar

84280006

Fig. 6 Impact absorbers, removal and installing — 700 Series shown, others similar

Outside Mirrors

REMOVAL & INSTALLATION

▶ **See Figures 7 and 8**

1. Remove the door trim panel. See 'Door Panel' removal and installation in this section.
2. Remove the panel and rubber cover. Remove the screws and clips.
3. Remove the mirror assembly.
4. Installation is the reverse of the removal procedure.

MIRROR GLASS

▶ **See Figure 9**

1. Press on the lower edge of the mirror so that the gear is revealed in the slit in bottom of mirror.
2. Move the cogs to the right with a small screwdriver and remove the mirror glass.
3. To install, align the assembly lugs on the rear of the mirror glass.
4. Depress the lower edge of the glass and move the cogs to the left. Check to ensure the new glass is firmly installed.

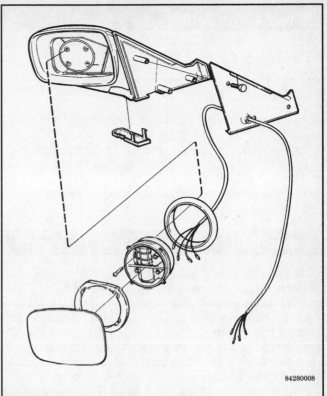

84280008

Fig. 8 Power door mirror construction

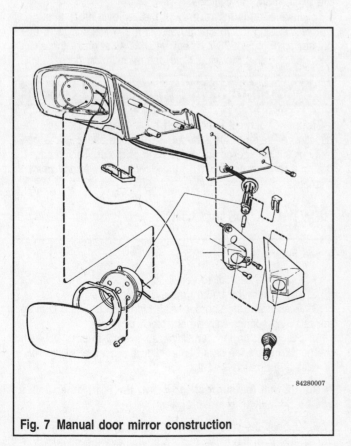

84280007

Fig. 7 Manual door mirror construction

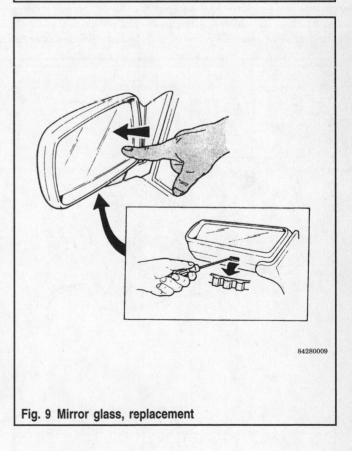

84280009

Fig. 9 Mirror glass, replacement

Power Mirror Motor

REMOVAL & INSTALLATION

▶ **See Figure 10**

1. Remove the mirror glass. See 'MIRROR GLASS' in this section.
2. Remove the retaining screws and lift out the motor.
3. Disconnect the electrical connector and remove the motor from the vehicle.
4. To install: Reconnect the wires and install the motor.
5. Install the mirror glass.

Power Antenna

The power antenna extends when the radio is turned ON. The mast will retract when the radio is turned **OFF**. The 700 and 900 Series vehicles have a switch that allows the antenna to be retracted with the radio **ON**. The switch will also prevent the mast from extending when the radio is first turned **ON**. There are 3 leads to the power antenna unit. There is a ground lead that is electrically connected to the chassis and a green or green and red power lead connected to the fusebox to provide operating voltage. The third lead is connected to the radio (through a switch for the 700 and 900 Series vehicles) to provide the signal for antenna operation. When there is power on this lead the antenna extends and when the power is removed, by turning **OFF** the radio or turning **OFF** the antenna switch on the 700 and 900 Series vehicles, the antenna retracts.

REMOVAL & INSTALLATION

1. Disconnect the battery ground cable.
2. Remove trim panel covering the antenna assembly.
3. Disconnect the electrical leads and ground strap, if used.
4. Unbolt the antenna assembly securing fasteners. Unscrew upper antenna retaining nut. Remove antenna assembly.
5. Installation is the reverse of removal. Tighten the upper antenna retaining nut then the lower securing fasteners.

Fenders

REMOVAL & INSTALLATION

Front

1. Remove the wipers and seals from wiper spindles.
2. Remove the air inlet grille bolts and air inlet grille.
3. Remove the bumper end-piece, headlight and directional indicator cluster.
4. Remove the fender retaining bolts and carefully remove the fender from the vehicle.
5. Installation is the reverse of the removal procedure. Before installing the retaining bolts at the wheelarch joint, apply sealer (P/N 591278-7 or equivalent). Also, press the air inlet grille against the windshield before installing bolts.

Power Sunroof

The power sunroof is controlled by a switch that selects the direction of travel of the sunroof. The switch changes the polarity of the voltage going to the sunroof motor. This changes the rotation of the motor, thus the direction of sunroof travel changes.

REMOVAL & INSTALLATION

▶ **See Figure 11**

1. Open the sunroof to ventilation position.
2. Disconnect the battery ground cable.
3. Push down the sunroof headlining with a finger. Unhook the retaining springs with a bent piece of wire.
4. Pull down on the headlining sufficiently to pass beneath the gutter rail. At the same time, slide the sunroof to the rear to release the catches at the front.

➡ **Do not pull the sunroof too far to the rear; otherwise, it will be difficult to remove again.**

5. Unhook the spring retaining brackets. Remove the retaining screws from the sides and front. Remove the sunroof.
6. To install: Fit the sunroof into position and install the retaining screws. Install the spring mounting bracket.

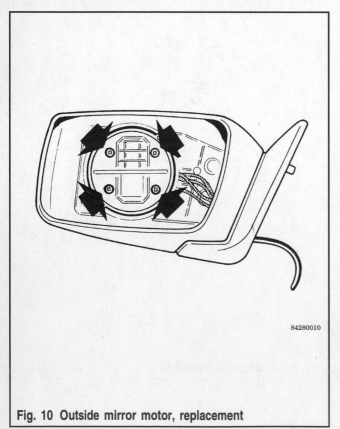

84280010

Fig. 10 Outside mirror motor, replacement

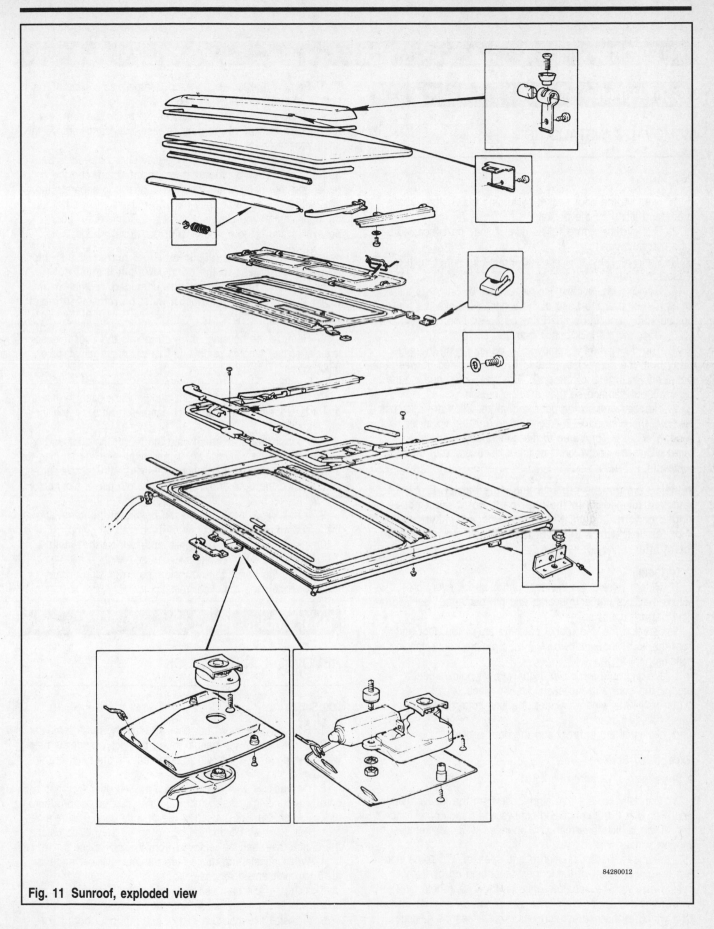

Fig. 11 Sunroof, exploded view

84280012

INTERIOR

Door Panels

REMOVAL & INSTALLATION

200 Series

1. Remove the door pocket by turning the 3 studs 90 degrees and lifting off the pocket.
2. Remove the armrest. The screws may be concealed behind plastic covers.
3. Remove the plastic housing around the inner latch release (door handle).
4. Remove the window winder. Do this by lifting up the small trim strip at the base of the winder. Remove the concealed screw and the winder may be pulled free.
5. Unscrew the lock button from the shaft.
6. The door panel is removed by gently prying the edge away from the door. Use a broad flat tool inserted between the panel and the metal of the door. The idea is to separate the clips without damage so they may be reused.
7. Proceed around the door until all the clips are released. Remove the door panel by lifting up to free the lip at the window edge. Be prepared to disconnect any wiring encountered within the door (courtesy lights, speakers, etc) during removal.

➡️**Inside the door is a plastic moisture barrier. It may be removed for access to the door parts but it must not be ripped or torn. Should it become damaged, either replace it or repair it with waterproof tape. It must be reinstalled intact after any door repairs**

To install

8. Before reinstalling the door panel, check every clip to insure that it is properly located and not damaged. Replace any that are unusable.
9. Position the door panel onto the top of the door and seat the lip at the window rail. It may require gentle tapping to seat properly.
10. Making sure each clip aligns with its hole, proceed around the door and tap each clip into place.
11. Install the window winder, the lock button and the release handle housing.
12. Reinstall the armrest and the door pocket.

Except 200 Series

▶ **See Figures 12 and 13**

1. Carefully pry the trim strip loose from the face of handgrip. Remove the 2 concealed screws and remove the handgrip. If the vehicle has manually operated windows, remove the window winder.
2. Remove the speaker grille and speaker. On some models, the grille is part of the longer panel held on by 2 concealed screws. The separate grille on the 780 is held by 2 screws located under the plastic trim at the lower end. Disconnect wiring at the nearest connectors as access is gained.

3. Remove the lock button and 2 large plastic clips at the bottom of the door panel, as required.
4. Remove the 2 screws located just below the arm rest (just behind the line of the door release lever) and remove the knob from the release lever.
5. Remove the door panel by gently prying the edge away from the door. Use a broad flat tool inserted between the panel and the metal of the door. The idea is to separate the clips without damage so they may be reused. Proceed around the door until all the clips are released. Remove the door panel by lifting up to free the lip at the window edge.

➡️**Inside the door is a plastic moisture barrier. It may be removed for access to the door parts but it must not be ripped or torn. Should it become damaged, replace it or repair it with waterproof tape. It must be reinstalled intact after any door repairs**

6. Remove the housing which surrounds the door release lever after the panel is removed. This will make reinstallation much easier.

To install:

7. Before reinstalling the door panel, check each to insure that it is properly located and not damaged. Replace any that are unusable.
8. Position the door panel onto the top of the door and seat the lip at the window rail. It may require gentle tapping to seat properly. Making sure each clip aligns with its hole, proceed around the door and tap each clip into place. Connect the wiring harnesses as the components move into place.
9. Install the 2 large clips at the bottom of the panel and the 2 screws under the armrest, if equipped.
10. Install the speaker and grille and connect the wiring.
11. Install the door release housing and knob.
12. Install the handgrip and install the cover strip. If the window winder was removed, reinstall it.

Door Locks

REMOVAL & INSTALLATION

200 Series

1. Remove the inner door liner and the moisture barrier.
2. For vehicles with manual locks, the lock cylinder is held within the door by a clip which slides across the back of the cylinder.
3. On vehicles with electric locks, the left door lock has a collar surrounding it. This electrical fitting causes all the doors to lock when the key is used in the driver's door. The retainer on this switch may be opened by prying up the plastic catch; the switch may then be removed from the lock cylinder.
4. When reinstalling, make sure the lock cylinder engages the latch mechanism properly.
5. If the vehicle has electric locks, make sure the switch collar is in its correct position and the clip is secure.
6. Reinstall the moisture barrier and the inner door panel.

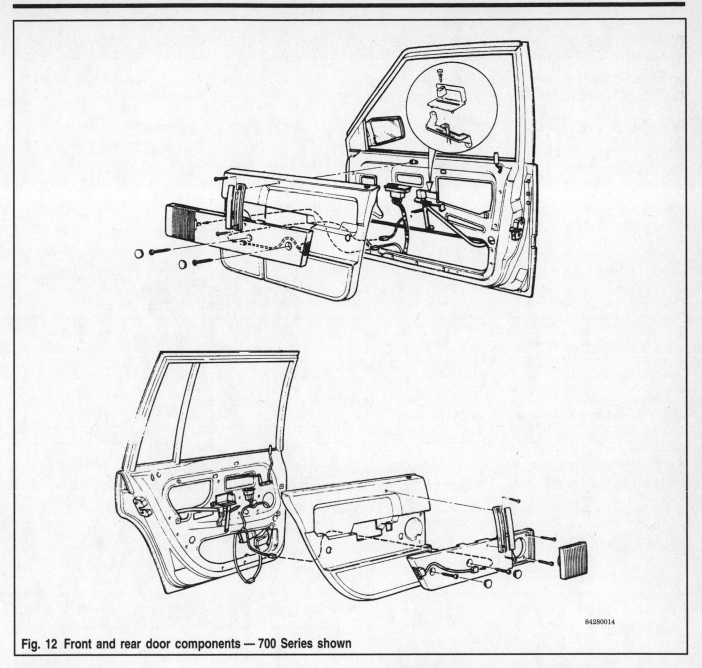

Fig. 12 Front and rear door components — 700 Series shown

84280014

Except 200 Series

▶ **See Figures 14 and 15**

1. Remove the door trim pad and the moisture barrier.

2. The back of the lock cylinder has a rod connected to it. Disconnect the rod by swinging the clip away from the shaft and then separating the shaft from the lock. Don't break or deform the clip during removal.

3. If removing the left door lock, loosen the electrical switch around the lock by releasing the plastic catch on the collar. Remove the switch from the lock.

4. Remove the 2 screws holding the lock retaining bracket. Remove the bracket and remove the lock from the door.

5. When reassembling, make sure the rod is properly attached and secure. Install the retaining bracket and retaining screws.

6. Reinstall the switch on the left door lock and make sure it is properly positioned and secure.

7. Check the operation of the keylock and the power locks.

8. Install the moisture barrier and the door panel.

Central Locking System (Power Door Locks)

The central locking system will lock or unlock the doors and the trunk or tailgate locks. The system is activated by either the key in the drivers door lock cylinder or the locking knob on the door. The locking or unlocking signal is sent to a controller that sends voltage to the lock actuators. When the reverse signal is sent, the controller reverses the polarity of the voltage to the lock actuators.

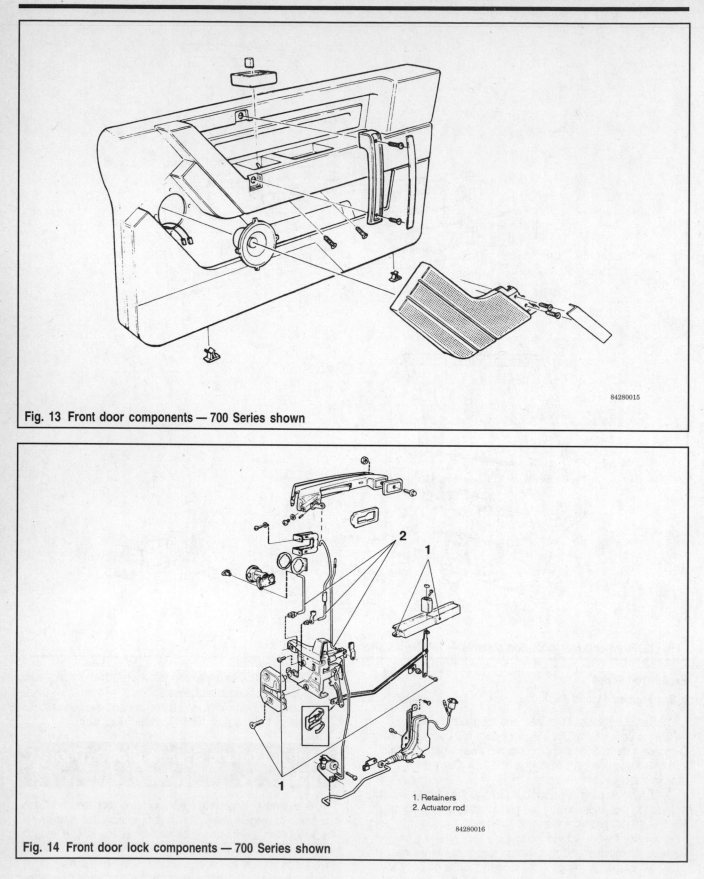

84280015

Fig. 13 Front door components — 700 Series shown

1. Retainers
2. Actuator rod

84280016

Fig. 14 Front door lock components — 700 Series shown

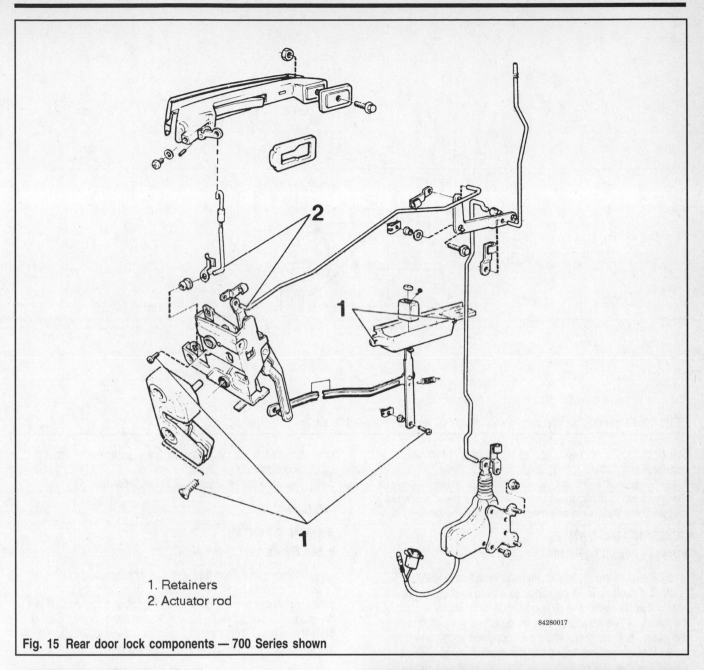

1. Retainers
2. Actuator rod

84280017

Fig. 15 Rear door lock components — 700 Series shown

REMOVAL & INSTALLATION

Lock Actuator

1. Disconnect the battery ground cable.
2. Remove the door panel or trunk trim to gain access to the lock actuator.
3. Remove the actuator mounting screws and disconnect the actuator rod.
4. Pull the actuator out of cavity and disconnect the electrical leads. Remove unit completely.
5. Installation is reverse of removal. Check operation of lock mechanism before reinstalling the door panel or trunk trim.

Door Glass and Regulator

REMOVAL & INSTALLATION

200 Series

MANUAL WINDOWS

▶ **See Figure 16**

1. Remove the door pad and the moisture barrier.
2. If the glass is to be replaced or removed, remove the safety catches from the pins on the 2 lower arms and lift out the glass.   The regulator can be removed without removing the glass, but the glass must be supported within the door.
3. To remove the regulator (lift mechanism), remove the safety clips from the pins on the 2 lower arms. Remove the

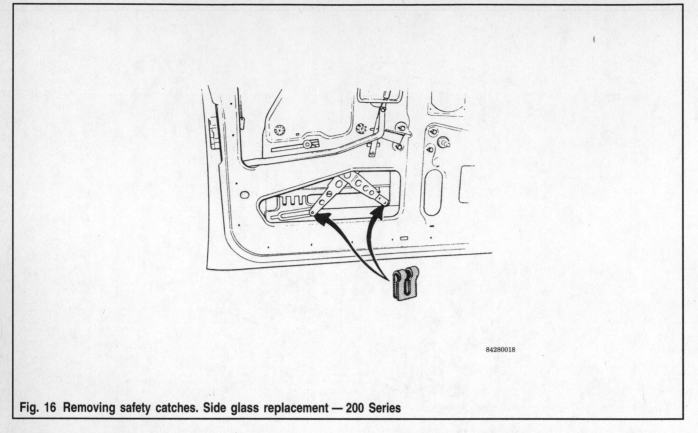

84280018

Fig. 16 Removing safety catches. Side glass replacement — 200 Series

five bolts holding the regulator to the door and remove the regulator.

4. When reassembling, be careful not to scratch or knock the glass while fitting the new regulator into the door. Make certain the safety clips are firmly seated on the pins.

ELECTRIC WINDOWS

▶ **See Figures 17 and 18**

1. Remove the door pad and the moisture barrier.

2. If the glass is to be replaced or removed, remove the safety catches from the pins on the 2 lower arms and lift out the glass. The regulator can be removed without removing the glass, but the glass must be supported within the door.

3. Disconnect the wiring for the motor.

4. Remove the bolts holding the regulator and remove regulator from the door.

   To install:

5. When reinstalling, tighten the mounting screws just enough to hold position and no more. Attach the glass to the regulator with the safety clips and make sure they are properly seated.

6. Hook up the electrical connections and check the operation of the motor. Run the window up and down, checking for ease of motion and smoothness of operation. The 4 frontmost mounting bolts can be loosened to eliminate binding. Loosen the screws and operate the window up and down. As the regulator seeks its best position, tighten the bolts to hold it in place. It should take 5 seconds for the window to open fully.

7. Raise the window to its stopped position. Loosen the stop (at the forward edge of the regulator) and raise the window as far as it will go. Readjust the stop to mesh with the gears and tighten it in place.

8. Reinstall the moisture barrier and the door pad.

700 Series

MANUAL WINDOWS

▶ **See Figure 19**

1. Remove the door pad and the moisture barrier.

2. If the glass is to be replaced or removed, remove the safety catches from the pins on the 2 lower arms and lift out the glass. It may be necessary to remove the lower channel from the glass. The regulator can be removed without removing the glass, but the glass must be supported within the door.

➡**If replacing the glass in a rear door, the front window track must be removed. Loosen the retaining bolts in the edge of the door and the track will come free.**

3. To remove the regulator (lift mechanism), remove the safety clips from the pins on the 2 lower arms. Remove the five bolts holding the regulator to the door and remove the regulator.

4. When reassembling, be careful not to scratch or knock the glass while fitting the new regulator into the door. Make certain the safety clips are firmly seated on the pins.

5. If installing new glass, a new piece of cushioning tape must be placed in the lower channel.

6. After reinstallation, check the travel of the glass and eliminate and binding or stiffness. Loosen the upper stop bolt (located just forward of the spring for the door release) and wind the window to its full up position. Press the bolt rearwards and retighten it.

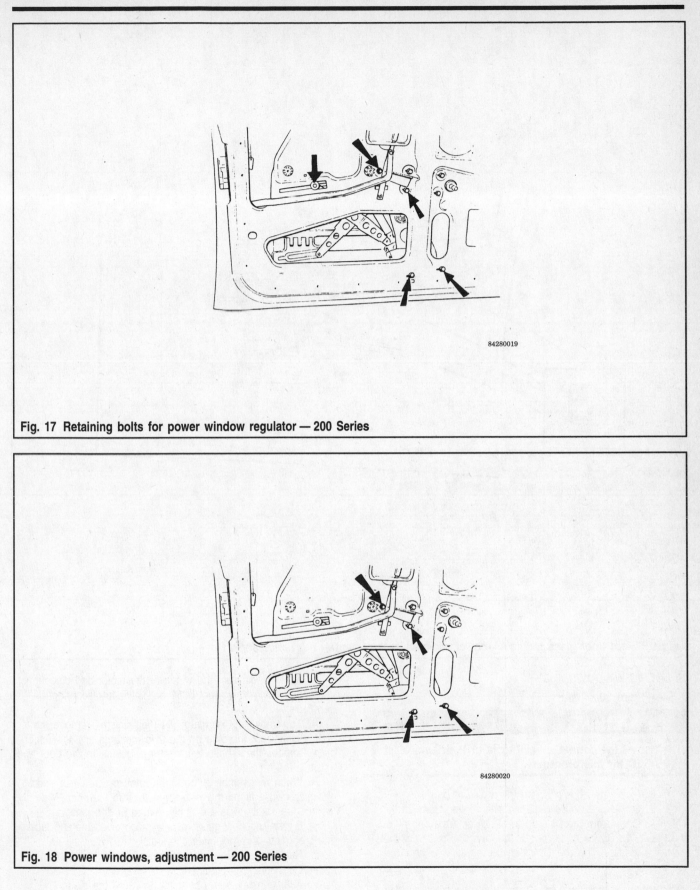

84280019

Fig. 17 Retaining bolts for power window regulator — 200 Series

84280020

Fig. 18 Power windows, adjustment — 200 Series

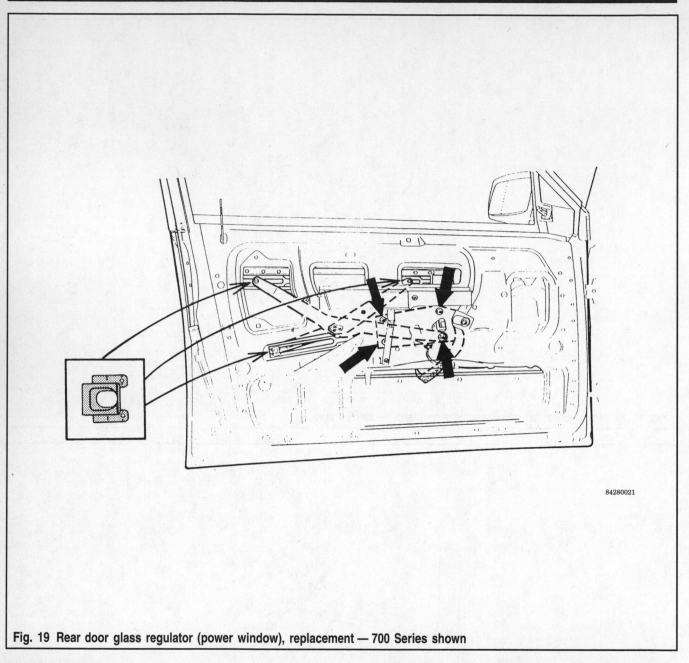

84280021

Fig. 19 Rear door glass regulator (power window), replacement — 700 Series shown

ELECTRIC WINDOWS

▶ See Figure 20

✳✳WARNING

The use of the correct special tools or their equivalent is REQUIRED for this procedure.

1. Remove the door pad and the moisture barrier.
2. If the glass is to be replaced or removed, remove the safety catches from the pins on the 2 lower arms and lift out the glass. It may be necessary to remove the lower channel from the glass.   The regulator can be removed without removing the glass, but the glass must be supported within the door.

➡If replacing the glass in a rear door, the front window track must be removed. Loosen the 2 bolts in the edge of the door and the track will come free.

3. Label or diagram the wiring at the motor and disconnect the wiring using Volvo tool 6351 or similar to disconnect the terminals.
4. To remove the regulator (lift mechanism), remove the safety clips from the pins on the 2 lower arms and the upper arm. Remove the 4 bolts holding the regulator to the door and remove the regulator.
5. When reassembling, be careful not to scratch or knock the glass while fitting the new regulator into the door. Make certain the safety clips are firmly seated on the pins.
6. If installing new glass, a new piece of cushioning tape must be placed in the lower channel.
7. Reconnect the wiring to the motor making certain that correct positioning is obtained.
8. After reinstallation, check the travel of the glass and eliminate and binding or stiffness. Loosen the upper stop bolt (located just forward of the spring for the door release) and

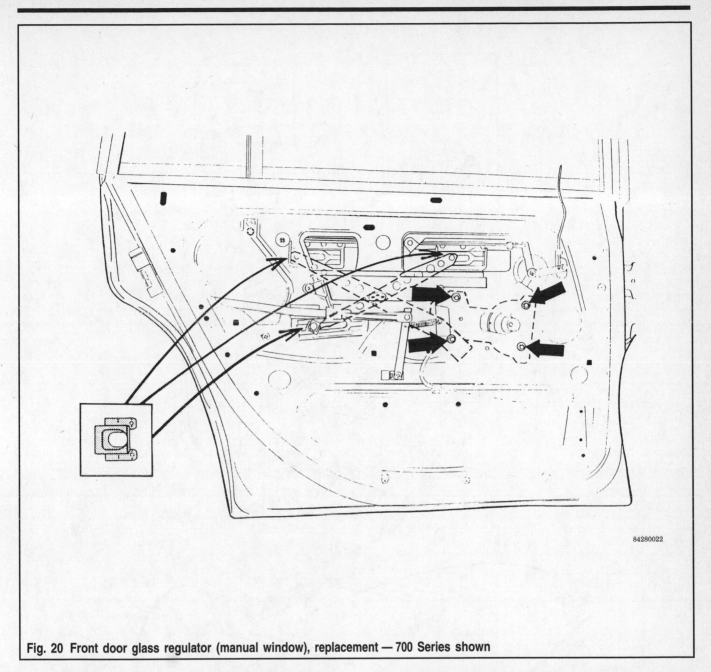

84280022

Fig. 20 Front door glass regulator (manual window), replacement — 700 Series shown

press it forward. Wind the window to its full up position. Press the bolt rearwards and retighten it.

Seats

REMOVAL & INSTALLATION

Manual Seats

▶ See Figures 21 and 22

The front seat and its rails may be unbolted from the floor of the vehicle. Many vehicles have heated seats; it will be necessary to disconnect the wiring harness for this system before removing the seat.

It is necessary to remove the seat belt anchor from the side of the seat. Remove the screw in the rear of the side pocket, lift the pocket out of the way and remove the seat belt bolt.

After all the retaining bolts are removed, the front seat is removed by sliding the seat to the rear of its track and lifting upwards to free the seat from the catches.

The rear seat cushion is removed by pressing down directly over the retaining clips (freeing the hook from the loop) and lifting the cushion clear. The rear seat backrest is held by catches which hold the upper bar in place. These catches can be released with a screwdriver; don't bend them anymore than needed or reassembly will be very difficult.

When reassembling the rear seat, always install the backrest first. Make sure that every clip engages properly and is firmly closed.

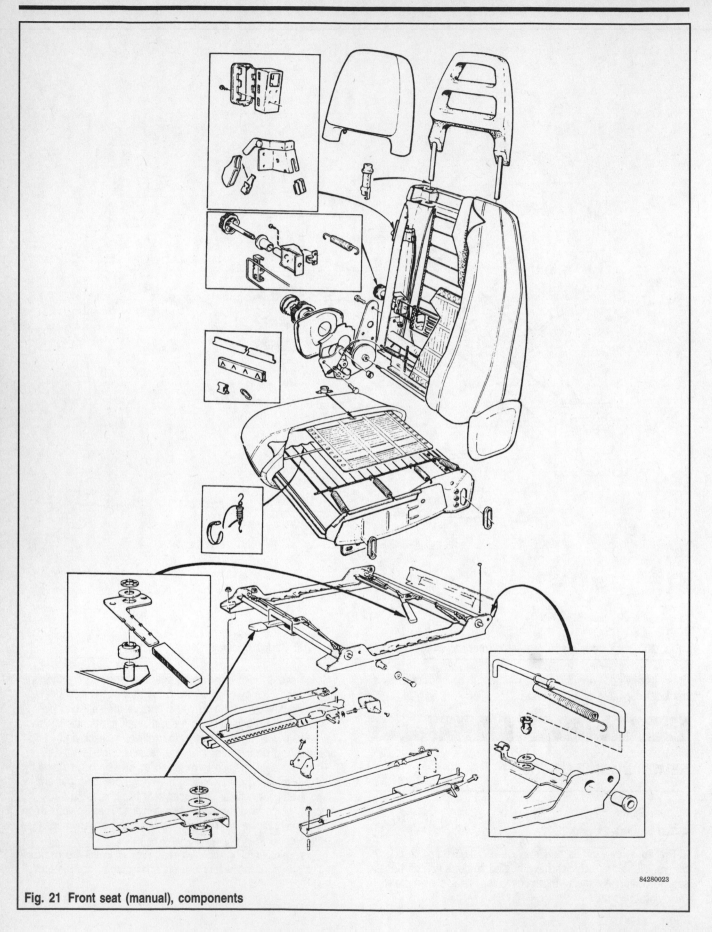

Fig. 21 Front seat (manual), components

84280023

Power Seats

1. Disconnect the negative battery cable.

2. Remove the plastic rail covers as necessary and remove the front bolts holding the seat tracks to the vehicle. Loosen but do not remove the bolts at the rear of the tracks.

3. Gently elevate the front of the seat; identify and label the wiring running to the seat components. Disconnect the seat wiring connectors.

✳✳WARNING

Do not disconnect any wiring for other components. Many other units may be found under the seat — leave them connected at all times.

4. Remove the rear mounting bolts and lift the seat clear of the vehicle. It will be heavy — a helper inside the vehicle can ease removal.

5. Either support the seat on crates or a clean workbench or place the seat on a clean blanket to protect it.

Power Seat Motors

REMOVAL & INSTALLATION

▶ **See Figure 23**

1. Disconnect the negative battery cable.

2. Remove the seat from the vehicle following the procedure outlined previously.

3. Turn the seat upside down and remove the 4 screws holding the motor to its bracket.

4. Lift out the motor and remove the drive cable from the motor. Use care not to kink or crease the cable.

5. Disconnect the wiring to the motor. Remove the pins from the connector case, if required. To remove the fore-and-aft motor, remove the middle connector from the control unit. Open the connector and remove the wiring at the terminals.

6. When reinstalling, make sure the wiring is properly located and secure in its connector. Fit the cable into the motor and install the retainer if any.

7. Install the motor and final check the wiring. Make sure it is out of the way of any moving parts.

8. Reinstall the seat in the vehicle, connect the wiring harnesses and connect the negative battery cable. Check the operation of the seat.

➡**The motor controlling the seatback tilt is within the seatback. Access to this motor involves removal of the seatback and disassembly of upholstery pieces. If trouble is experienced with this motor, repair by trained personnel is recommended.**

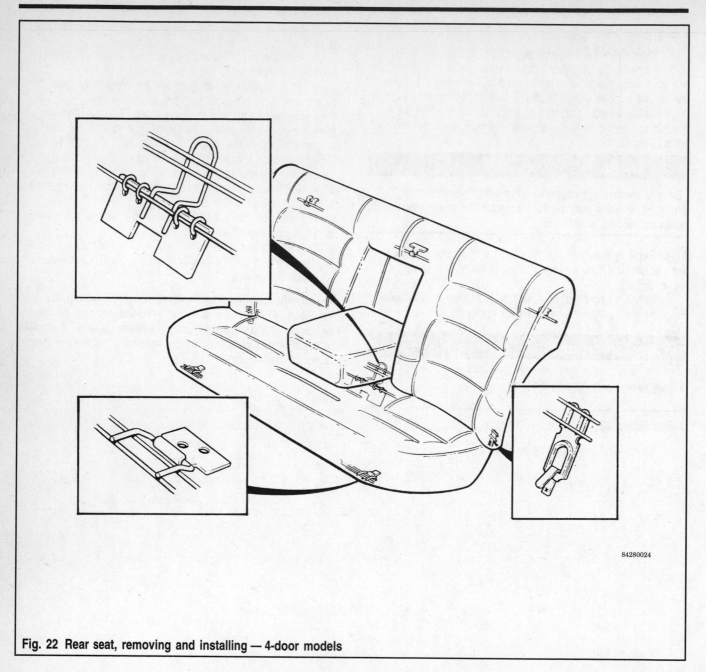

84280024

Fig. 22 Rear seat, removing and installing — 4-door models

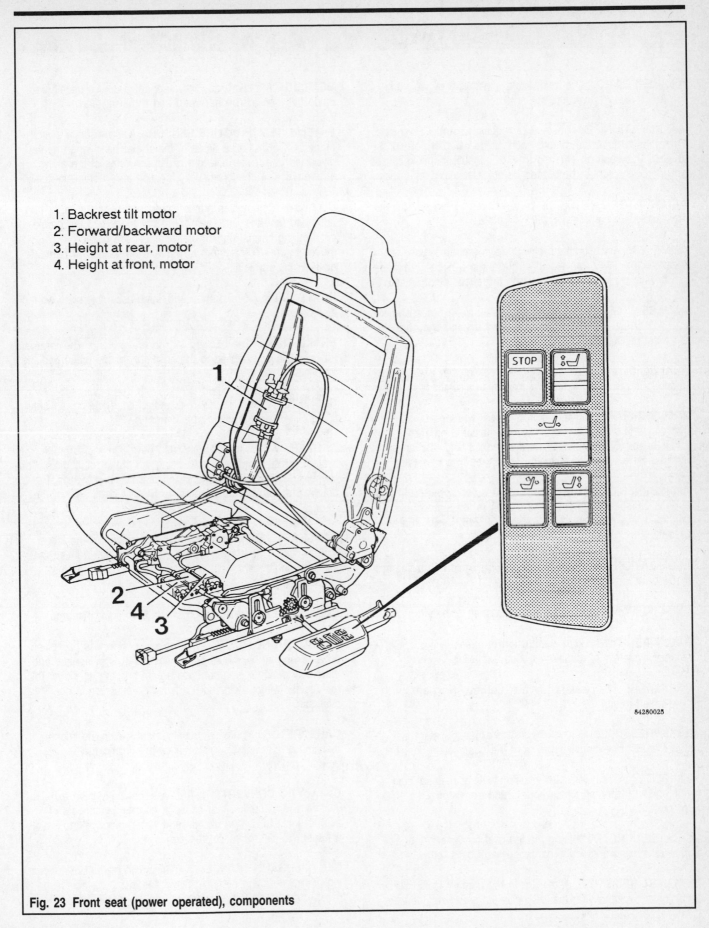

1. Backrest tilt motor
2. Forward/backward motor
3. Height at rear, motor
4. Height at front, motor

84280025

Fig. 23 Front seat (power operated), components

GLOSSARY

AIR/FUEL RATIO: The ratio of air to gasoline by weight in the fuel mixture drawn into the engine.

AIR INJECTION: One method of reducing harmful exhaust emissions by injecting air into each of the exhaust ports of an engine. The fresh air entering the hot exhaust manifold causes any remaining fuel to be burned before it can exit the tailpipe.

ALTERNATOR: A device used for converting mechanical energy into electrical energy.

AMMETER: An instrument, calibrated in amperes, used to measure the flow of an electrical current in a circuit. Ammeters are always connected in series with the circuit being tested.

AMPERE: The rate of flow of electrical current present when one volt of electrical pressure is applied against one ohm of electrical resistance.

ANALOG COMPUTER: Any microprocessor that uses similar (analogous) electrical signals to make its calculations.

ARMATURE: A laminated, soft iron core wrapped by a wire that converts electrical energy to mechanical energy as in a motor or relay. When rotated in a magnetic field, it changes mechanical energy into electrical energy as in a generator.

ATMOSPHERIC PRESSURE: The pressure on the Earth's surface caused by the weight of the air in the atmosphere. At sea level, this pressure is 14.7 psi at 32{248}F (101 kPa at 0{248}C).

ATOMIZATION: The breaking down of a liquid into a fine mist that can be suspended in air.

AXIAL PLAY: Movement parallel to a shaft or bearing bore.

BACKFIRE: The sudden combustion of gases in the intake or exhaust system that results in a loud explosion.

BACKLASH: The clearance or play between two parts, such as meshed gears.

BACKPRESSURE: Restrictions in the exhaust system that slow the exit of exhaust gases from the combustion chamber.

BAKELITE: A heat resistant, plastic insulator material commonly used in printed circuit boards and transistorized components.

BALL BEARING: A bearing made up of hardened inner and outer races between which hardened steel balls roll.

BALLAST RESISTOR: A resistor in the primary ignition circuit that lowers voltage after the engine is started to reduce wear on ignition components.

BEARING: A friction reducing, supportive device usually located between a stationary part and a moving part.

BIMETAL TEMPERATURE SENSOR: Any sensor or switch made of two dissimilar types of metal that bend when heated or cooled due to the different expansion rates of the alloys. These types of sensors usually function as an on/off switch.

BLOWBY: Combustion gases, composed of water vapor and unburned fuel, that leak past the piston rings into the crankcase during normal engine operation. These gases are removed by the PCV system to prevent the buildup of harmful acids in the crankcase.

BRAKE PAD: A brake shoe and lining assembly used with disc brakes.

BRAKE SHOE: The backing for the brake lining. The term is, however, usually applied to the assembly of the brake backing and lining.

BUSHING: A liner, usually removable, for a bearing; an anti-friction liner used in place of a bearing.

CALIPER: A hydraulically activated device in a disc brake system, which is mounted straddling the brake rotor (disc). The caliper contains at least one piston and two brake pads. Hydraulic pressure on the piston(s) forces the pads against the rotor.

CAMSHAFT: A shaft in the engine on which are the lobes (cams) which operate the valves. The camshaft is driven by the crankshaft, via a belt, chain or gears, at one half the crankshaft speed.

CAPACITOR: A device which stores an electrical charge.

CARBON MONOXIDE (CO): A colorless, odorless gas given off as a normal byproduct of combustion. It is poisonous and extremely dangerous in confined areas, building up slowly to toxic levels without warning if adequate ventilation is not available.

CARBURETOR: A device, usually mounted on the intake manifold of an engine, which mixes the air and fuel in the proper proportion to allow even combustion.

CATALYTIC CONVERTER: A device installed in the exhaust system, like a muffler, that converts harmful byproducts of combustion into carbon dioxide and water vapor by means of a heat-producing chemical reaction.

CENTRIFUGAL ADVANCE: A mechanical method of advancing the spark timing by using flyweights in the distributor that react to centrifugal force generated by the distributor shaft rotation.

CHECK VALVE: Any one-way valve installed to permit the flow of air, fuel or vacuum in one direction only.

CHOKE: A device, usually a moveable valve, placed in the intake path of a carburetor to restrict the flow of air.

CIRCUIT: Any unbroken path through which an electrical current can flow. Also used to describe fuel flow in some instances.

CIRCUIT BREAKER: A switch which protects an electrical circuit from overload by opening the circuit when the current flow exceeds a predetermined level. Some circuit breakers must be reset manually, while most reset automatically

COIL (IGNITION): A transformer in the ignition circuit which steps up the voltage provided to the spark plugs.

COMBINATION MANIFOLD: An assembly which includes both the intake and exhaust manifolds in one casting.

COMBINATION VALVE: A device used in some fuel systems that routes fuel vapors to a charcoal storage canister instead of venting them into the atmosphere. The valve relieves fuel tank pressure and allows fresh air into the tank as the fuel level drops to prevent a vapor lock situation.

COMPRESSION RATIO: The comparison of the total volume of the cylinder and combustion chamber with the piston at BDC and the piston at TDC.

CONDENSER: 1. An electrical device which acts to store an electrical charge, preventing voltage surges.
2. A radiator-like device in the air conditioning system in which refrigerant gas condenses into a liquid, giving off heat.

CONDUCTOR: Any material through which an electrical current can be transmitted easily.

CONTINUITY: Continuous or complete circuit. Can be checked with an ohmmeter.

COUNTERSHAFT: An intermediate shaft which is rotated by a mainshaft and transmits, in turn, that rotation to a working part.

CRANKCASE: The lower part of an engine in which the crankshaft and related parts operate.

CRANKSHAFT: The main driving shaft of an engine which receives reciprocating motion from the pistons and converts it to rotary motion.

CYLINDER: In an engine, the round hole in the engine block in which the piston(s) ride.

CYLINDER BLOCK: The main structural member of an engine in which is found the cylinders, crankshaft and other principal parts.

CYLINDER HEAD: The detachable portion of the engine, fastened, usually, to the top of the cylinder block, containing all or most of the combustion chambers. On overhead valve engines, it contains the valves and their operating parts. On overhead cam engines, it contains the camshaft as well.

DEAD CENTER: The extreme top or bottom of the piston stroke.

DETONATION: An unwanted explosion of the air/fuel mixture in the combustion chamber caused by excess heat and compression, advanced timing, or an overly lean mixture. Also referred to as "ping".

DIAPHRAGM: A thin, flexible wall separating two cavities, such as in a vacuum advance unit.

DIESELING: A condition in which hot spots in the combustion chamber cause the engine to run on after the key is turned off.

DIFFERENTIAL: A geared assembly which allows the transmission of motion between drive axles, giving one axle the ability to turn faster than the other.

DIODE: An electrical device that will allow current to flow in one direction only.

DISC BRAKE: A hydraulic braking assembly consisting of a brake disc, or rotor, mounted on an axle, and a caliper assembly containing, usually two brake pads which are activated by hydraulic pressure. The pads are forced against the sides of the disc, creating friction which slows the vehicle.

DISTRIBUTOR: A mechanically driven device on an engine which is responsible for electrically firing the spark plug at a predetermined point of the piston stroke.

DOWEL PIN: A pin, inserted in mating holes in two different parts allowing those parts to maintain a fixed relationship.

DRUM BRAKE: A braking system which consists of two brake shoes and one or two wheel cylinders, mounted on a fixed backing plate, and a brake drum, mounted on an axle, which revolves around the assembly.

DWELL: The rate, measured in degrees of shaft rotation, at which an electrical circuit cycles on and off.

ELECTRONIC CONTROL UNIT (ECU): Ignition module, module, amplifier or igniter. See Module for definition.

ELECTRONIC IGNITION: A system in which the timing and firing of the spark plugs is controlled by an electronic control unit, usually called a module. These systems have no points or condenser.

ENDPLAY: The measured amount of axial movement in a shaft.

ENGINE: A device that converts heat into mechanical energy.

EXHAUST MANIFOLD: A set of cast passages or pipes which conduct exhaust gases from the engine.

FEELER GAUGE: A blade, usually metal, of precisely predetermined thickness, used to measure the clearance between two parts.

FIRING ORDER: The order in which combustion occurs in the cylinders of an engine. Also the order in which spark is distributed to the plugs by the distributor.

FLOODING: The presence of too much fuel in the intake manifold and combustion chamber which prevents the air/fuel mixture from firing, thereby causing a no-start situation.

FLYWHEEL: A disc shaped part bolted to the rear end of the crankshaft. Around the outer perimeter is affixed the ring gear. The starter drive engages the ring gear, turning the flywheel, which rotates the crankshaft, imparting the initial starting motion to the engine.

FOOT POUND (ft.lb. or sometimes, ft. lbs.): The amount of energy or work needed to raise an item weighing one pound, a distance of one foot.

FUSE: A protective device in a circuit which prevents circuit overload by breaking the circuit when a specific amperage is present. The device is constructed around a strip or wire of a lower amperage rating than the circuit it is designed to protect. When an amperage higher than that stamped on the fuse is present in the circuit, the strip or wire melts, opening the circuit.

GEAR RATIO: The ratio between the number of teeth on meshing gears.

GENERATOR: A device which converts mechanical energy into electrical energy.

HEAT RANGE: The measure of a spark plug's ability to dissipate heat from its firing end. The higher the heat range, the hotter the plug fires.

HUB: The center part of a wheel or gear.

HYDROCARBON (HC): Any chemical compound made up of hydrogen and carbon. A major pollutant formed by the engine as a byproduct of combustion.

HYDROMETER: An instrument used to measure the specific gravity of a solution.

INCH POUND (in.lb. or sometimes, in. lbs.): One twelfth of a foot pound.

INDUCTION: A means of transferring electrical energy in the form of a magnetic field. Principle used in the ignition coil to increase voltage.

INJECTOR: A device which receives metered fuel under relatively low pressure and is activated to inject the fuel into the engine under relatively high pressure at a predetermined time.

INPUT SHAFT: The shaft to which torque is applied, usually carrying the driving gear or gears.

INTAKE MANIFOLD: A casting of passages or pipes used to conduct air or a fuel/air mixture to the cylinders.

JOURNAL: The bearing surface within which a shaft operates.

KEY: A small block usually fitted in a notch between a shaft and a hub to prevent slippage of the two parts.

MANIFOLD: A casting of passages or set of pipes which connect the cylinders to an inlet or outlet source.

MANIFOLD VACUUM: Low pressure in an engine intake manifold formed just below the throttle plates. Manifold vacuum is highest at idle and drops under acceleration.

MASTER CYLINDER: The primary fluid pressurizing device in a hydraulic system. In automotive use, it is found in brake and hydraulic clutch systems and is pedal activated, either directly or, in a power brake system, through the power booster.

MODULE: Electronic control unit, amplifier or igniter of solid state or integrated design which controls the current flow in the ignition primary circuit based on input from the pick-up coil. When the module opens the primary circuit, the high secondary voltage is induced in the coil.

NEEDLE BEARING: A bearing which consists of a number (usually a large number) of long, thin rollers.

OHM:(Ω) The unit used to measure the resistance of conductor to electrical flow. One ohm is the amount of resistance that limits current flow to one ampere in a circuit with one volt of pressure.

OHMMETER: An instrument used for measuring the resistance, in ohms, in an electrical circuit.

OUTPUT SHAFT: The shaft which transmits torque from a device, such as a transmission.

OVERDRIVE: A gear assembly which produces more shaft revolutions than that transmitted to it.

OVERHEAD CAMSHAFT (OHC): An engine configuration in which the camshaft is mounted on top of the cylinder head and operates the valve either directly or by means of rocker arms.

OVERHEAD VALVE (OHV): An engine configuration in which all of the valves are located in the cylinder head and the camshaft is located in the cylinder block. The camshaft operates the valves via lifters and pushrods.

OXIDES OF NITROGEN (NOx): Chemical compounds of nitrogen produced as a byproduct of combustion. They combine with hydrocarbons to produce smog.

OXYGEN SENSOR: Used with the feedback system to sense the presence of oxygen in the exhaust gas and signal the computer which can reference the voltage signal to an air/fuel ratio.

PINION: The smaller of two meshing gears.

PISTON RING: An open ended ring which fits into a groove on the outer diameter of the piston. Its chief function is to form a seal between the piston and cylinder wall. Most automotive pistons have three rings: two for compression sealing; one for oil sealing.

PRELOAD: A predetermined load placed on a bearing during assembly or by adjustment.

PRIMARY CIRCUIT: Is the low voltage side of the ignition system which consists of the ignition switch, ballast resistor or resistance wire, bypass, coil, electronic control unit and pick-up coil as well as the connecting wires and harnesses.

PRESS FIT: The mating of two parts under pressure, due to the inner diameter of one being smaller than the outer diameter of the other, or vice versa; an interference fit.

RACE: The surface on the inner or outer ring of a bearing on which the balls, needles or rollers move.

REGULATOR: A device which maintains the amperage and/or voltage levels of a circuit at predetermined values.

RELAY: A switch which automatically opens and/or closes a circuit.

RESISTANCE: The opposition to the flow of current through a circuit or electrical device, and is measured in ohms. Resistance is equal to the voltage divided by the amperage.

RESISTOR: A device, usually made of wire, which offers a preset amount of resistance in an electrical circuit.

RING GEAR: The name given to a ring-shaped gear attached to a differential case, or affixed to a flywheel or as part a planetary gear set.

ROLLER BEARING: A bearing made up of hardened inner and outer races between which hardened steel rollers move.

ROTOR: 1. The disc-shaped part of a disc brake assembly, upon which the brake pads bear; also called, brake disc.
2. The device mounted atop the distributor shaft, which passes current to the distributor cap tower contacts.

SECONDARY CIRCUIT: The high voltage side of the ignition system, usually above 20,000 volts. The secondary includes the ignition coil, coil wire, distributor cap and rotor, spark plug wires and spark plugs.

SENDING UNIT: A mechanical, electrical, hydraulic or electromagnetic device which transmits information to a gauge.

SENSOR: Any device designed to measure engine operating conditions or ambient pressures and temperatures. Usually electronic in nature and designed to send a voltage signal to an on-board computer, some sensors may operate as a simple on/off switch or they may provide a variable voltage signal (like a potentiometer) as conditions or measured parameters change.

SHIM: Spacers of precise, predetermined thickness used between parts to establish a proper working relationship.

SLAVE CYLINDER: In automotive use, a device in the hydraulic clutch system which is activated by hydraulic force, disengaging the clutch.

SOLENOID: A coil used to produce a magnetic field, the effect of which is produce work.

SPARK PLUG: A device screwed into the combustion chamber of a spark ignition engine. The basic construction is a conductive core inside of a ceramic insulator, mounted in an outer conductive base. An electrical charge from the spark plug wire travels along the conductive core and jumps a preset air gap to a grounding point or points at the end of the conductive base. The resultant spark ignites the fuel/air mixture in the combustion chamber.

SPLINES: Ridges machined or cast onto the outer diameter of a shaft or inner diameter of a bore to enable parts to mate without rotation.

TACHOMETER: A device used to measure the rotary speed of an engine, shaft, gear, etc., usually in rotations per minute.

THERMOSTAT: A valve, located in the cooling system of an engine, which is closed when cold and opens gradually in response to engine heating, controlling the temperature of the coolant and rate of coolant flow.

TOP DEAD CENTER (TDC): The point at which the piston reaches the top of its travel on the compression stroke.

TORQUE: The twisting force applied to an object.

TORQUE CONVERTER: A turbine used to transmit power from a driving member to a driven member via hydraulic action, providing changes in drive ratio and torque. In automotive use, it links the driveplate at the rear of the engine to the automatic transmission.

TRANSDUCER: A device used to change a force into an electrical signal.

TRANSISTOR: A semi-conductor component which can be actuated by a small voltage to perform an electrical switching function.

TUNE-UP: A regular maintenance function, usually associated with the replacement and adjustment of parts and components in the electrical and fuel systems of a vehicle for the purpose of attaining optimum performance.

TURBOCHARGER: An exhaust driven pump which compresses intake air and forces it into the combustion chambers at higher than atmospheric pressures. The increased air pressure allows more fuel to be burned and results in increased horsepower being produced.

VACUUM ADVANCE: A device which advances the ignition timing in response to increased engine vacuum.

VACUUM GAUGE: An instrument used to measure the presence of vacuum in a chamber.

VALVE: A device which control the pressure, direction of flow or rate of flow of a liquid or gas.

VALVE CLEARANCE: The measured gap between the end of the valve stem and the rocker arm, cam lobe or follower that activates the valve.

VISCOSITY: The rating of a liquid's internal resistance to flow.

VOLTMETER: An instrument used for measuring electrical force in units called volts. Voltmeters are always connected parallel with the circuit being tested.

WHEEL CYLINDER: Found in the automotive drum brake assembly, it is a device, actuated by hydraulic pressure, which, through internal pistons, pushes the brake shoes outward against the drums.

MASTER

INDEX